CLYMER®

HONDA

100-350cc OHC SINGLES • 1969-1982

The world's finest publisher of mechanical how-to manuals

PRIMEDIA
Business Magazines & Media
P.O. Box 12901, Overland Park, Kansas 66282-2901

FIRST EDITION
First Printing September, 1972

SECOND EDITION
Revised to include 1973-1974 models
First Printing November, 1974

THIRD EDITION
Revised to include 1975-1976 models
First Printing August, 1976

FOURTH EDITION
Revised to include 1977 models
First Printing August, 1977

FIFTH EDITION
Revised by Mike Bishop to include 1978 models
First Printing January, 1979

SIXTH EDITION
Revised by Ed Scott to include 1979-1982 models
First Printing September, 1983
Second Printing November, 1984
Third Printing January, 1986
Fourth Printing September, 1987
Fifth Printing September, 1988
Sixth Printing September, 1989
Seventh Printing September, 1990
Eighth Printing April, 1992
Ninth Printing June, 1993
Tenth Printing July, 1994
Eleventh Printing January, 1996
Twelfth Printing August, 1997
Thirteenth Printing January, 1999
Fourteenth Printing September, 2000
Fifteenth Printing July, 2002

Printed in U.S.A.

CLYMER and colophon are registered trademarks of PRIMEDIA Business Magazines & Media Inc.

ISBN: 0-89287-184-9

TECHNICAL ILLUSTRATIONS: Mitzi McCarthy.

COVER: Photographed by Michael Brown Photographic Productions, Los Angeles, California. Motorcycle courtesy of Tony Vine.

TOOLS AND EQUIPMENT: K & L Supply Co. at www.klsupply.com.

Chapter One
General Information 1

Chapter Two
Troubleshooting 2

Chapter Three
Lubrication, Maintenance and Tune-up 3

Chapter Four
100 and 125cc Engines 4

Chapter Five
175, 250 and 350cc Engines 5

Chapter Six
Clutch and Transmission 6

Chapter Seven
Fuel and Exhaust Systems 7

Chapter Eight
Electrical System 8

Chapter Nine
Front Suspension and Steering 9

Chapter Ten
Rear Suspension 10

Chapter Eleven
Brakes 11

Index 12

Wiring Diagrams 13

CLYMER PUBLICATIONS

PRIMEDIA Business Magazines & Media

Chief Executive Officer Timothy M. Andrews
President Ron Wall

EDITORIAL

Editor
James Grooms

Technical Writers
Ron Wright
Ed Scott
George Parise
Mark Rolling
Michael Morlan
Jay Bogart

Production Supervisor
Dylan Goodwin

Lead Editorial Production Coordinator
Shirley Renicker

Editorial Production Coordinators
Greg Araujo
Shara Pierceall

Editorial Production Assistants
Susan Hartington
Holly Messinger
Darin Watson

Technical Illustrators
Steve Amos
Robert Caldwell
Mitzi McCarthy
Bob Meyer
Mike Rose

MARKETING/SALES AND ADMINISTRATION

Vice President,
PRIMEDIA Business Directories & Books
Rich Hathaway

Marketing Manager
Elda Starke

Advertising & Promotions Coordinator
Melissa Abbott

Associate Art Directors
Chris Paxton
Tony Barmann

Sales Manager/Marine
Dutch Sadler

Sales Manager/Motorcycles
Matt Tusken

Operations Manager
Patricia Kowalczewski

Sales Manager/Manuals
Ted Metzger

Customer Service Manager
Terri Cannon

Customer Service Supervisor
Ed McCarty

Customer Service Representatives
Susan Kohlmeyer
April LeBlond
Courtney Hollars
Jennifer Lassiter
Ernesto Suarez

Warehouse & Inventory Manager
Leah Hicks

The following books and guides are published by PRIMEDIA Business Directories & Books.

More information available at *primediabooks.com*

CONTENTS

CHAPTER ONE
GENERAL INFORMATION **1**

Manual organization
Service hints
Torque specifications
Safety first
Special tips
Parts replacement
Expendable supplies
Serial numbers
Tune-up and troubleshooting tools

CHAPTER TWO
TROUBLESHOOTING **9**

Operating requirements
Troubleshooting instruments
Emergency troubleshooting
Engine starting
Engine performance
Excessive vibration
Front suspension and steering
Brake problems

CHAPTER THREE
LUBRICATION, MAINTENANCE AND TUNE-UP **13**

Routine checks
Service intervals
Tires and wheels
Crankcase breather hose
Battery
Periodic lubrication
Periodic maintenance
Engine tune-up

CHAPTER FOUR
100 AND 125 CC ENGINES **53**

Engine principles
Engine cooling
Servicing engine in frame
Engine removal/installation
Camshaft
Cylinder head
Cylinder head cover and camshaft
Camshaft chain
Valves and valve components
Cylinder
Piston, piston pin and piston rings
Oil pump
Crankcase and crankshaft
Camshaft chain and tensioner
Kickstarter
Break-in procedure

CHAPTER FIVE
175, 250 AND 350 CC ENGINES **103**

Engine principles
Engine cooling
Servicing in frame
Engine removal/installation
Cylinder head cover and camshaft
Camshaft chain
Cylinder head
Valves and valve components
Cylinder
Piston, piston pin and piston rings
Oil pump
Crankcase and crankshaft
Camshaft chain and tensioner
Kickstarter
Break-in procedure

CHAPTER SIX
CLUTCH AND TRANSMISSION **147**

Clutch operation
Clutch
Clutch inspection
Clutch cable
External shift mechanism
Drive sprocket
Transmission and internal shift mechanism
5-speed transmission and
internal shift mechanism

CHAPTER SEVEN
FUEL AND EXHAUST SYSTEMS **190**

Air cleaner
Carburetor operation
Carburetor service
Carburetor adjustments
Throttle cable
Fuel tank
Fuel filter
Crankcase breather system
Exhaust system

CHAPTER EIGHT
ELECTRICAL SYSTEM **223**

Charging system
Rectifier
Voltage regulator/rectifier
Alternator
Breaker point ignition
Capacitor discharge ignition
Ignition coil
Ignition pulse generator
Ignition advance mechanism
Lighting system
Switches

CHAPTER NINE
FRONT SUSPENSION AND STEERING **253**

Front wheel
Front hub
Wheels
Tire changing
Tire repairs
Handlebar
Steering head
Front fork

CHAPTER TEN
REAR SUSPENSION **298**

Rear wheel
Rear hub and driven sprocket
Drive chain
Drive chain case
Swing arm

CHAPTER ELEVEN
BRAKES **323**

Drum brakes
Front brake cable
Front disc brake
Brake pad replacement
Brake caliper body

INDEX **335**

WIRING DIAGRAMS .... **end of book**

QUICK REFERENCE DATA

TUNE-UP SPECIFICATIONS

Valve clearance	
Intake	0.05 mm (0.002 in.)
Exhaust	
100 and 125 cc	0.05 mm (0.002 in.)
175, 250 and 350 cc	0.08 mm (0.003 in.)
Compression pressure	
100, 125 and 175 cc	10.8-13.2 kg/cm² (153-187 psi)
TL250	11.0 kg/cm² (156 psi)
XL250 and XL350	12.6-15.5 kg/cm² (180-220 psi)
Spark plug type	
100, 125 and 175 cc (through 1976)	ND X24ES or NGK D8ES-L
1977-1982 CB125S	ND X24ES-U or NGK D8EA
1977-on 175 cc	ND W22ES or NGK B7ES
TL250	ND X22ES or NGK D7ES
XL250 and XL350	ND X24ES or NGK D8ES-L
Spark plug gap	0.6-0.7 mm (0.024-0.028 in.)
Ignition timing*	
CB100, CL100, SL100, XL100, 1973-1978 CB125, SL125, XL175, XL250, XL350	1,200 ±100 rpm
1978-on CB125S, CT125, XL125, TL125	1,300 ±100 rpm
TL250	1,000 ±100 rpm
Idle speed	
CB100, CL100, SL100, XL100, 1973-1978 CB125, SL125, XL175, XL250, XL350	1,200 ±100 rpm
1978-on CB125S, CT125, XL125, TL125	1,300 ±100 rpm
TL250	1,00 ±100 rpm
Contact breaker point gap	0.3-0.4 mm (0.012-0.016 in.)

* "F" mark aligns with pointer at specified rpm.

ENGINE OIL CAPACITY

Engine size	Liter	U.S. qt.	Imp. qt.
100-125 cc	1.0	1.0	0.9
175 cc	1.5	1.6	1.5
250-350 cc			
1972-1975	1.8	1.9	1.6
1976-1978	1.9	2.0	1.7

FRONT FORK OIL CAPACITY*

Model	Drain		Reassembly	
	cc	fl. oz.	cc	fl. oz.
CB100, CL100	120-130	4.1-4.4	130-140	4.4-4.7
SL100, SL100 K1	170-180	5.8-6.1	180-190	6.1-6.4
SL100 K2-K3, XL100, XL100 K1	135-145	4.6-4.9	145-155	4.9-5.3
1976 XL100	115-118	3.9-4.0	145-155	4.9-5.3
1977-1978 XL100	145	4.9	155-160	5.3-5.6
CB125 S, CB125 S1-S2, CT125	120-130	4.1-4.4	130-140	4.4-4.7
1976-1978 CB125	90-95	3.1-3.2	105-110	3.6-3.7
1979-on CB125	N.A.	N.A.	80-85	2.7-2.9
SL125	165-175	5.6-5.9	180-190	6.1-6.4
SL125 K1-K2	130-140	4.4-4.7	145-155	4.9-5.3
TL125	N.A.	N.A.	130-140	4.4-4.7
XL125	140-145	4.7-4.9	155-160	5.3-5.6
XL175, XL175 K1-K2	130	4.5	143-147	4.9-5.0
1976-1978 XL175	140-150	4.7-5.1	160	5.4
XL250, XL250 K1	145	4.9	160	5.4
XL250 K2, 1976 XL250	150	5.1	160	5.4
XL350, XL350 K1	150	5.1	170	5.8
1976-1978 XL350	145	4.9	165	5.6

* Capacity for each fork leg. Honda does not provide information for all models. "N.A." indicates that the information is not available.

DRIVE CHAIN REPLACEMENT NUMBERS

Model	Standard	Optional
CB100	RK428-102L	DK428-102L
CL100	DK428-104L	DK428-103L
SL100	DK428-104L	
SL100 K1	DK428-104L	DID428-108L
SL100 K2-K3, XL100, XL100 K1	DK428-110L	
1976 XL100	DK 428H-110L	
1977-1978 XL100	N.A.	
CB125 S, CB125 S1-S2	RK428D-102L	DID428D-102L
1976-on CB125 S	DID428D-100L	
SL125	DK428-110L	
CT125	DID428H-102L	DID428-118L
TL125, TL125 K1-K2	DID428H-120L	
1976 TL125	N.A.-102L	
XL125	N.A.	
XL175	N.A.	
TL250	Diado-102L	Diado-122L
XL250, XL250 K1	N.A.-100L	N.A.-98L
1976 XL250 K2, XL250	N.A.-102L	
XL350	DID500DS-100L	

N.A. = Honda does not provide information for all models.

CHAPTER ONE

GENERAL INFORMATION

This detailed, comprehensive manual covers Honda overhead cam (OHC) singles manufactured from 1969-1982. **Table 1**, at the end of this chapter, lists the specific models and years covered. The expert text gives complete information on maintenance, tune-up, repair and overhaul. Hundreds of photos and drawings guide you through every step. The book includes all you need to keep your Honda running right and performing in top condition.

A shop manual is a reference. You want to be able to find information fast. As in all Clymer books, this one is designed with you in mind. All chapters are thumb tabbed. Important items are extensively indexed at the rear of the book. All procedures, tables, photos, etc., in this manual assume that the reader may be working on the bike or using this manual for the first time. All the most frequently used specifications and capacities are summarized on the *Quick Reference Data* pages at the front of the book.

Keep the book handy in your tool box. It will help you to better understand how the vehicle runs, lower repair and maintenance costs and generally improve your satisfaction with the bike.

MANUAL ORGANIZATION

All dimensions and capacities are expressed in English and metric units.

This chapter provides general information and discusses equipment and tools useful both for preventive maintenance and troubleshooting.

Chapter Two provides methods and suggestions for quick and accurate diagnosis and repair of problems. Troubleshooting procedures discuss typical symptoms and logical methods to pinpoint the trouble.

Chapter Three explains all periodic lubrication and routine maintenance necessary to keep the Honda running well. Chapter Three also includes recommended tune-up procedures, eliminating the need to constantly consult chapters on the various assemblies.

Subsequent chapters describe specific systems such as the engine, clutch, transmission, fuel, exhaust, suspension and brakes. Each chapter provides disassembly, repair and assembly procedures in simple step-by-step form. If a repair is impractical for a home mechanic, it is so indicated. It is usually faster and less expensive to take such repairs to a dealer or competent repair shop. Specifications concerning a particular system are included at the end of the appropriate chapter.

Some of the procedures in this manual specify special tools. In most cases, the tool is illustrated either in actual use or alone. Well-equipped mechanics may find they can substitute similar tools already on hand or can fabricate their own.

The terms NOTE, CAUTION and WARNING have a specific meaning in this manual. A NOTE provides additional information to make a step or procedure easier or clearer. Disregarding a NOTE could cause inconvenience, but would not cause equipment damage or personal injury.

A CAUTION emphasizes areas where equipment damage could result. Disregarding a

CAUTION could cause permanent mechanical damage; however, personal injury is unlikely.

A WARNING emphasizes areas where personal injury or even death could result from negligence. Mechanical damage may also occur. WARNINGS *are to be taken seriously*. In some cases, serious injury or death has resulted from disregarding similar warnings.

Remember the following points when using this manual. "Front" refers to the front of the bike. The front of any component, such as the engine, is the end which faces toward the front of the bike. The "left-" and "right-hand" side refers to the position of the parts as viewed by a rider sitting on the seat facing forward. For example, the throttle control is on the right-hand side and the clutch lever is on the left-hand side. These rules are simple, but even experienced mechanics occasionally become disoriented.

SERVICE HINTS

Most of the service procedures covered are straightforward and can be performed by anyone reasonably handy with tools. It is suggested, however, that you consider your own capabilities carefully before attempting any operation involving major disassembly of the engine.

Some operations, for example, require the use of a press. It would be wiser to have these performed by a shop equipped for such work, rather than to try to do the job yourself with makeshift equipment. Other procedures require precise measurements. Unless you have the skills and equipment required, it would be better to have a qualified repair shop make the measurements for you.

There are many items available that can be used on your hands before and after working on your bike. A little preparation prior to getting "all greased up" will help when cleaning up later.

Before starting out, work Vaseline, soap or a product such as Pro Tek (**Figure 1**) onto your forearms, into your hands and under your fingernails and cuticles. This will make cleanup a lot easier.

For cleanup, use a waterless hand soap, such as Sta-Lube, and then finish up with powdered Boraxo and a fingernail brush.

Repairs go much faster and easier if the bike is clean before you begin work. There are special cleaners, such as Gunk or Bel-Ray Degreaser, for washing the engine and related parts. Just spray or brush on the cleaning solution, let it stand, then rinse it away with a garden hose.

Clean all oily or greasy parts with cleaning solvent as you remove them. A number of solvents can be used to remove old dirt, grease and oil. Kerosene is readily available and comparatively inexpensive. Another inexpensive solvent similar to kerosene is ordinary diesel fuel. Both of these solvents have a very high temperature flash point (they have to be very hot in order to ignite and catch fire) and can be used safely in any adequately ventilated area away from open flames (this includes pilot lights on home water heaters and clothes driers that are sometimes located in the garage).

WARNING

***Never use gasoline**. Gasoline is extremely volatile and contains tremendously destructive potential energy. The slightest spark from metal parts accidently hitting, or a tool slipping, could cause a fatal explosion.*

Special tools are required for some repair procedures. These may be purchased at a dealer, rented from a tool rental dealer or fabricated by a mechanic or machinist (often at a considerable savings).

Much of the labor charged for repairs made by dealers is for the removal and disassembly of other parts to reach the defective unit. You can often save money by removing the defective part yourself and then taking it to a dealer for repair.

Once you have decided to tackle the job yourself, read the entire section in this manual which

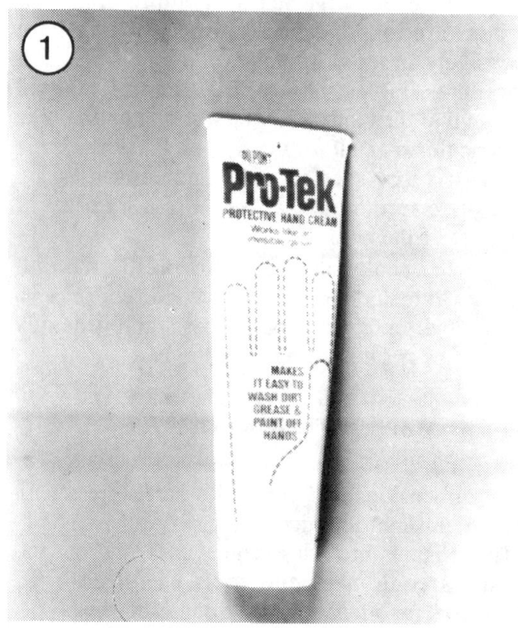

pertains to it, making sure you have identified the proper one. Study the illustrations and text until you have a good idea of what is involved in completing the job satisfactorily. If special tools are required, make arrangements to get them before you start. It is frustrating and time-consuming to get partly into a job and then be unable to complete it.

Simple wiring checks can be easily made at home, but knowledge of electronics is almost a necessity for performing tests with complicated electronic testing gear.

During disassembly of parts, keep a few general cautions in mind. Force is rarely needed to get things apart. If parts are a tight fit, such as a bearing in a case, there is usually a tool designed to separate them. Never use a screwdriver to pry apart parts with machined surfaces such as crankcase halves. You will mar the surfaces and end up with leaks.

Make diagrams (or take a Polaroid picture) wherever similar-appearing parts are found. For instance, crankcase bolts are often not the same length. You may think you can remember where everything came from, but mistakes are costly. There is also the possibility you may be sidetracked and not return to work for days or even weeks, in which interval carefully laid out parts may have become disturbed.

Tag all similar internal parts for location and mark all mating parts for position. Record number and thickness of any shims as they are removed. Small parts such as bolts can be identified by placing them in plastic sandwich bags. Seal and label them with masking tape.

Wiring should be tagged with masking tape and marked as each wire is removed. Again, do not rely on memory alone.

Protect finished surfaces from physical damage or corrosion. Keep gasoline and hydraulic brake fluid off painted surfaces.

Frozen or very tight bolts and screws can often be loosened by soaking with penetrating oil, such as WD-40 or Liquid Wrench, then sharply striking the bolt head a few times with a hammer and punch (or screwdriver for screws). Avoid heat unless absolutely necessary, since it may melt, warp or remove the temper from many parts.

No parts, except those assembled with a press fit, require unusual force during assembly. If a part is hard to remove or install, find out why before proceeding.

Cover all openings after removing parts to keep dirt, small tools, etc., from falling in.

When assembling 2 parts, start all fasteners, then tighten evenly.

Wiring connections and brake components should be kept clean and free of grease and oil.

When assembling parts, be sure all shims and washers are placed exactly as they came out.

Whenever a rotating part butts against a stationary part, look for a shim or washer.

Use new gaskets if there is any doubt about the condition of the old ones. A thin coat of oil on gaskets may help them seal effectively.

Heavy grease can be used to hold small parts in place if they tend to fall out during assembly. However, keep grease and oil away from electrical and brake components.

High spots may be sanded off a piston with sandpaper, but fine emery cloth and oil will do a much more professional job.

Carbon can be removed from the head, the piston crowns and the exhaust ports with a dull screwdriver. *Do not* scratch either surface. Wipe off the surface with a clean cloth when finished.

The carburetor is best cleaned by disassembling it and soaking the parts in a commercial carburetor cleaner. Never soak gaskets and rubber parts in these cleaners. Never use wire to clean out jets and air passages; they are easily damaged. Use compressed air to blow out the carburetor only if the float has been removed first.

A baby bottle makes a good measuring device for adding oil to the front forks. Get one that is graduated in fluid ounces and cubic centimeters. After it has been used for this purpose, do not let a small child drink out of it, as there will always be an oil residue in it.

Take your time and do the job right. Do not forget that a newly rebuilt engine must be broken in the same as a new one. Keep the rpm within the limits given in your owner's manual when you get back in the dirt or sand.

TORQUE SPECIFICATIONS

Torque specifications throughout this manual are given in Newton meters (N•m) and foot-pounds (ft.-lb.). Newton meters have been adopted in place of meter kilograms (mkg) in accordance with the International Modernized Metric System. Tool manufacturers offer torque wrenches calibrated in Newton meters and Sears has a Craftsman line calibrated in both values.

Existing torque wrenches, calibrated in meter kilograms, can be used by performing a simple conversion. All you have to do is move the decimal point one place to the right; e.g. 4.7 mkg =

47 N•m. This conversion is sufficient for use on the bike even though the exact mathematical conversion is 3.5 mkg = 34.3 N•m.

SAFETY FIRST

Professional mechanics can work for years and never sustain a serious injury. If you observe a few rules of common sense and safety, you can enjoy many hours servicing your own machine. If you ignore these rules you can hurt yourself or damage the bike.

1. Never use gasoline as a cleaning solvent.
2. Never smoke or use a torch in the vicinity of flammable liquids such as cleaning solvent in open containers.
3. If welding or brazing is required on the bike, remove the fuel tank to a safe distance, at least 50 feet away.
4. Use the proper sized wrenches to avoid damage to nuts and injury to yourself.
5. When loosening a tight or stuck nut, be guided by what would happen if the wrench should slip. Be careful; protect yourself accordingly.
6. Keep your work area clean and uncluttered.
7. Wear safety goggles during all operations involving drilling, grinding or the use of a cold chisel.
8. Never use worn tools.
9. Keep a fire extinguisher handy and be sure it is rated for gasoline and electrical fires.

SPECIAL TIPS

Because of the extreme demands placed on a bike several points should be kept in mind when performing service and repair. The following items are general suggestions that may improve the overall life of the machine and help avoid costly failures.

1. Use a locking compound such as Loctite Lock N' Seal No. 2114 (blue Loctite) on all bolts and nuts, even if they are secured with lockwashers. This type of Loctite does not harden completely and allows easy removal of the bolt or nut. A screw or bolt lost from an engine cover or bearing retainer could easily cause serious and expensive damage before its loss is noticed.

When applying Loctite, use a small amount. If too much is used, it can work its way down the threads and stick parts together not meant to be stuck.

Keep a tube of Loctite in your tool box; when used properly it is cheap insurance.

2. Use a hammer driven impact driver tool to remove and install all bolts, particularly engine cover screws. These tools help prevent the rounding off of bolt heads and ensure a tight installation.
3. When straightening out the fold-over type lockwasher, if possible, use a wide-blade tool such as an old and dull wood chisel. Such a tool provides a better purchase on the folded tab, making straightening out easier.
4. When installing the fold-over type lockwasher, always use a new washer if possible. If a new washer is not available, always fold over a part of the washer that has not been previously folded. Reusing the same fold may cause the washer to break, resulting in the loss of its locking ability and also resulting in a loose piece of metal adrift in the engine.

When folding the washer over, start the fold with a screwdriver and finish it with a pair of pliers. If a punch is used to make the fold, the fold may be too sharp, thereby increasing the chances of the washer breaking under stress.

These washers are relatively inexpensive and it is suggested that you keep several of each size in your tool box for field repairs.

5. When replacing missing or broken fasteners (bolts, nuts and screws), especially on the engine or frame components, always use Honda replacement parts. They are specially hardened for each application. The wrong 75-cent bolt could easily cause many dollars' worth of serious damage, not to mention rider injury.
6. When installing gaskets in the engine, always use Honda replacement gaskets *without* sealer, unless designated. These gaskets are designed to swell when they come in contact with oil. Gasket sealer will prevent the gaskets from swelling as intended, which can result in oil leaks. These Honda gaskets are also cut from material of the

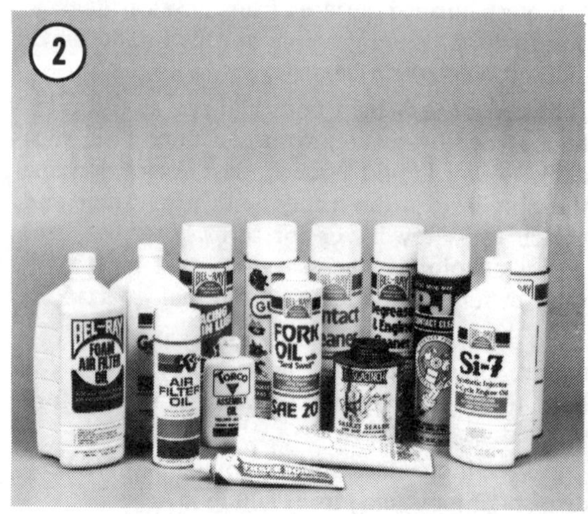

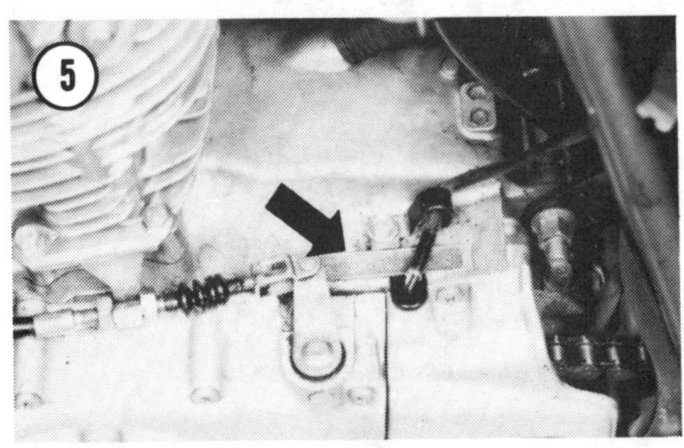

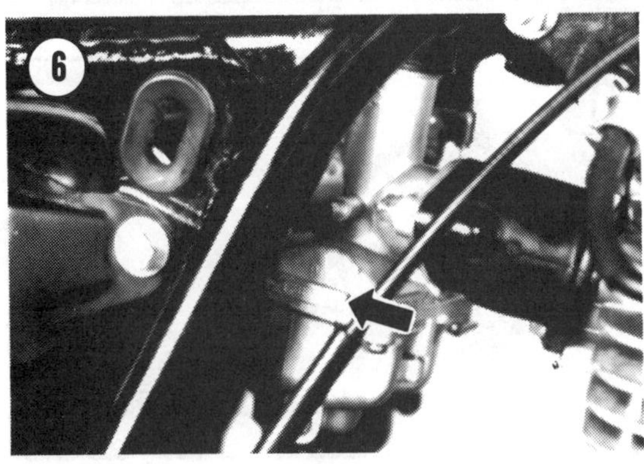

precise thickness needed. Installation of a too thick or too thin gasket in a critical area could cause engine damage.

PARTS REPLACEMENT

Honda makes frequent changes during a model year—some minor, some relatively major. When you order parts from the dealer or other parts distributor, always order by engine and frame number. Write the numbers down and carry them with you. Compare new parts to old before purchasing them. If they are not alike, have the parts manager explain the difference to you.

EXPENDABLE SUPPLIES

Certain expendable supplies are also required. These include grease, oil, gasket cement, wiping rags and cleaning solvent. Ask your dealer for the special locking compounds, silicone lubricants and lube products (**Figure 2**) which make vehicle maintenance simpler and easier. Cleaning solvent or kerosene is available at some service stations.

SERIAL NUMBERS

You must know the model serial number and VIN number (on later models) for registration purposes and when ordering replacement parts.

The frame serial number is stamped on the side of the steering head (**Figure 3**). The vehicle identification number (VIN) is on the left-hand side of the steering head (on later models). The engine serial number is located on the lower left-hand side of the crankcase (**Figure 4**) on 100 and 125 cc engines. On 250 and 350 cc engines, the serial number is located on the top left-hand side of the crankcase above the clutch (**Figure 5**). The carburetor identification number is located on the side of the carburetor body above the float bowl as shown in **Figure 6**.

TUNE-UP AND TROUBLESHOOTING TOOLS

Multimeter or VOM

This instrument (**Figure 7**) is invaluable for electrical system troubleshooting and service. A few of its functions may be duplicated by homemade test equipment, but for the serious mechanic it is a must. Its uses are described in the applicable sections of the book.

Strobe Timing Light

This instrument is necessary for tuning. By flashing a light at the precise instant the spark plug fires, the position of the timing mark can be seen. Marks on the alternator flywheel are lined up with the stationary mark on the crankcase while the engine is running.

Suitable lights range from inexpensive neon bulb types to powerful xenon strobe lights (**Figure 8**). Neon timing lights are difficult to see and must be used in dimly lit areas. Xenon strobe timing lights can be used outside in bright sunlight. Both types work on the bike; use according to the manufacturer's instructions.

Portable Tachometer

A portable tachometer (**Figure 9**) is necessary for tuning. Ignition timing and carburetor adjustments must be performed at the specified idle speed. The best instrument for this purpose is one with a low range of 0-1,000 or 0-2,000 rpm and a high range of 0-4,000 rpm. Extended range (0-6,000 or 0-8,000 rpm) instruments lack accuracy at lower speeds. The instrument should be capable of detecting changes of 25 rpm on the low range.

Compression Gauge

A compression gauge measures the engine compression. The one shown in **Figure 10** is the type needed for the Honda singles covered in this manual.

7

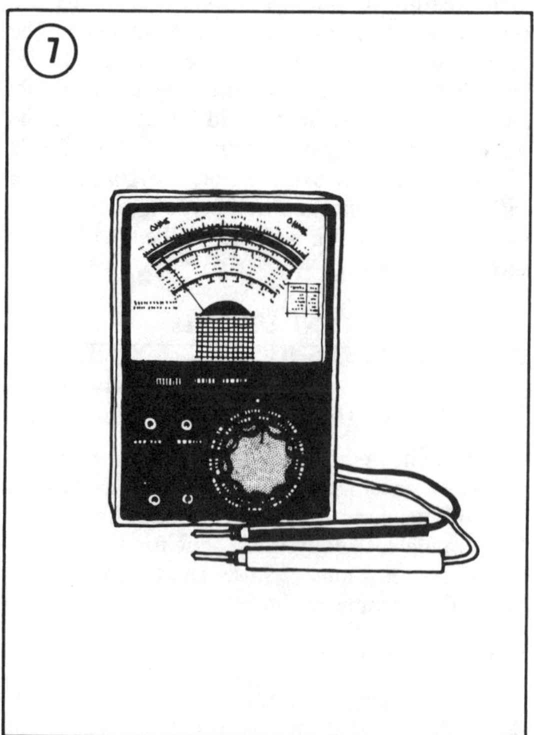

8

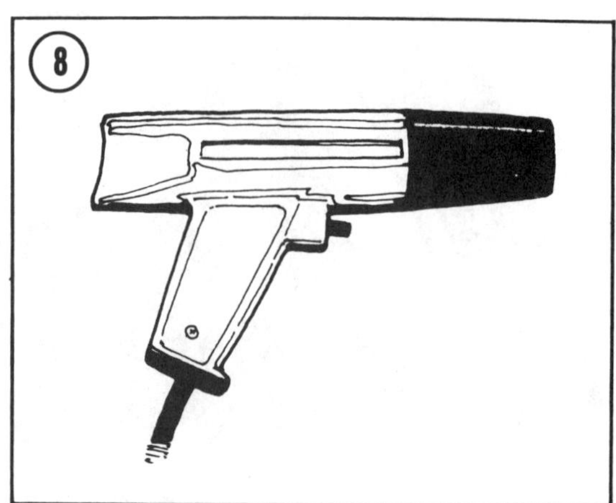

9

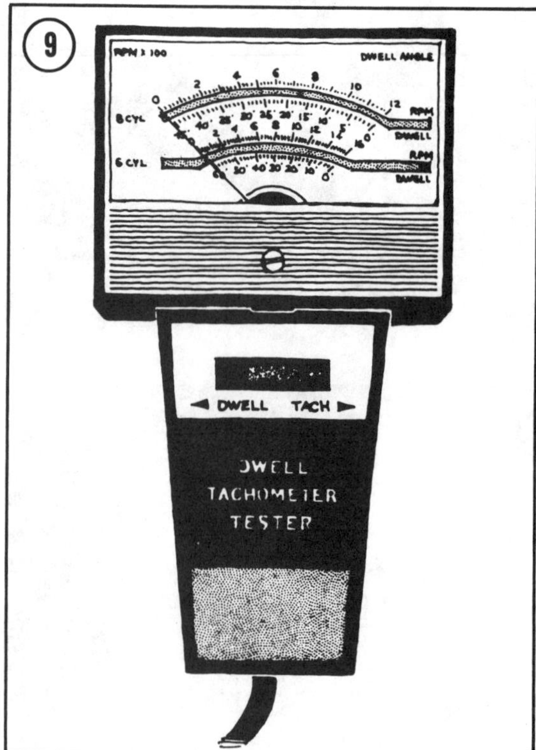

10

Table 1 MODEL IDENTIFICATION

Model	Year	Frame Beginning Serial Number
CB100	1970	100001-on
CB100 K1	1971	200000-on
CB100 K2	1972	1200001-on
CL100	1970	CL100-1000001-on
CL100 K1	1971	CL100 K1-2000001-on
CL100 K2	1972	CL100 K2-1200001-on
CL100 S	1971	CL100 S-1000001-on
CL100 SK2	1972	CL100 SK2-1200001-on
CL100 S3	1973	CL100 S3-1300001-on
SL100	1969	SL100-100001-on
SL100 K1	1970	SL100-200000-on
SL100 K2	1971	SL100-120001-on
SL100 K3	1972	SL100-120000-on
XL100	1974	XL100-1000001-on
XL100 K1	1975	XL100-1100001-on
XL100 76	1976	XL100 76-1200001-on
XL100 77	1977	XL100 77-1300023-on
XL100 78	1978	XL100 78-1400001-on
CB125 S	1973	CB125S-1021992-on
CB125 S1	1974	CB125S-1100001-on
CB125 S2	1975	CB125S-1200001-on
CB125S 76	1976	CB125S-1300001-on
No 1977 model		
CB125S 78	1978	CB125S-150000-on
CB125S 79	1979	CB125S-500001-on
CB125S 80	1980	JC04-5100011-on
CB125S 81	1981	JC040-BK700005-on
CB125S 82	1982	JC040-CK800002-on
SL125	1971	1000001-on
SL125 K1	1972	1100001-on
SL125 K2	1973	1200001-on
TL125	1973	TL125-1000003-on
TL125 K1	1974	TL125-1100001-on
TL125 K2	1975	TL125-1200001-on
TL125S 76	1976	TL125S-100417-on
XL125	1974	XL125-10000001-on
XL125 K1	1975	XL125-11000001-on
CT125	1977	1010051-on
XL175	1973	XL175-1000001-on
XL175 K1	1974	XL175-2000001-on
XL175 K2	1975	XL175-3000001-on
XL175 76	1976	XL175-4000001-on
XL175 77	1977	XL175-4100001-on
XL175 78	1978	XL175-4200004-on
.TL250	1975	TL250-1000001-on
TL250	1976	TL250-2000001-on

(continued)

Table 1 MODEL IDENTIFICATION (continued)

Model	Year	Frame Beginning Serial Number
XL250	1972	XL250-1000001-on
No 1973 model		
XL250 K1	1974	XL250-2000001-on
XL250 K2	1975	XL250-3000001-on
XL250 76	1976	XL250-4000001-on
XL350	1974	XL350-1000001-on
XL350 K1	1975	XL350-2000001-on
XL350 76	1976	XL350-3000001-on
XL350 77	1977	XL350-3100001-on
XL350 78	1978	XL350-3200001-on

CHAPTER TWO

TROUBLESHOOTING

Diagnosing mechanical problems is relatively simple if you use orderly procedures and keep a few basic principles in mind.

The troubleshooting procedures in this chapter analyze typical symptoms and show logical methods of isolating causes. These are not the only methods. There may be several ways to solve a problem, but only a systematic, methodical approach can guarantee success.

Never assume anything. Do not overlook the obvious. If you are riding along and the engine suddenly quits, check the easiest, most accessible problems first. Is there gasoline in the tank? Is the fuel shutoff valve in the ON position? Has the spark plug wire fallen off?

If nothing obvious turns up in a quick check, look a little further. Learning to recognize and describe symptoms will make repairs easier for you or a mechanic at the shop. Describe problems accurately and fully. Saying that "it won't run" isn't the same as saying "it quit climbing a hill and won't start" or that it "sat in my garage for 3 months and then wouldn't start."

Gather as many symptoms together as possible to aid in diagnosis. Note whether the engine lost power gradually or all at once. Remember that the more complicated a machine is, the easier it is to troubleshoot because symptoms point to specific problems.

After the symptoms are defined, areas which could cause the problems are tested and analyzed. Guessing at the cause of a problem may provide the solution, but it can easily lead to frustration, wasted time and a series of expensive, unnecessary parts replacements.

You do not need fancy equipment or complicated test gear to determine whether repairs can be attempted at home. A few simple checks could save a large repair bill and time lost while the bike sits in a dealer's service department. On the other hand, be realistic and don't attempt repairs beyond your abilities. Service departments tend to charge a lot for putting together a disassembled engine that may have been abused. Some dealers won't even take on such a job—so use common sense and don't get in over your head.

OPERATING REQUIREMENTS

An engine needs 3 basics to run properly: correct fuel-air mixture, compression and a spark at the correct time. If one or more are missing, the engine just won't run. The electrical system is the weakest link of the 3 basics. More problems result from electrical breakdowns than from any other source. Keep that in mind before you begin tampering with carburetor adjustments and the like.

If the bike has been sitting for any length of time and refuses to start, check and clean the spark plugs and then look to the gasoline delivery system. This includes the fuel tank, fuel shutoff valve and the fuel line to the carburetor. Gasoline deposits may have formed and gummed up the carburetor jets and air passages. Gasoline tends to lose its potency after standing for long periods. Condensation may contaminate the fuel with water. Drain the old fuel and try starting with a fresh tankful.

TROUBLESHOOTING INSTRUMENTS

Chapter One lists the instruments needed and detailed instructions on their use.

EMERGENCY TROUBLESHOOTING

When the bike is difficult to start or won't start at all, it does not help to wear out your leg on the kickstarter. Check for obvious problems even before getting out your tools. Go down the following list step by step. Do each one; you may be embarrassed to find your kill switch is stuck in the OFF position, but it's better than wearing out your leg. If it still will not start, refer to the appropriate troubleshooting procedure which follows in this chapter.

1. Is there fuel in the tank? Open the fuel filler cap (A, **Figure 1**) and rock the bike. Listen for fuel sloshing around. Make sure the vent line (B, **Figure 1**) is not obstructed or kinked.

WARNING
Do not use an open flame to check in the tank. A serious explosion is certain to result.

2. Is the fuel shutoff valve in the ON position? Turn the valve to the RESERVE position to be sure you get the last remaining gas.
3. Make sure the kill switch (**Figure 2**) is not stuck in the OFF position.
4. Is the spark plug wire on tight (**Figure 3**)? Push the wire on and slightly rotate it to clean the electrical connection between the plug and the connector.
5. Is the choke in the right position? The lever or knob should be moved *up* for a cold engine and *down* for a warm engine.

ENGINE STARTING

An engine that refuses to start or is difficult to start is very frustrating. More often than not, the problem is very minor and can be found with a simple and logical troubleshooting approach.

The following items show a beginning point from which to isolate engine starting problems.

Engine Fails to Start

Perform the following spark test to determine if the ignition system is operating properly.

1. Remove the spark plug from the cylinder.

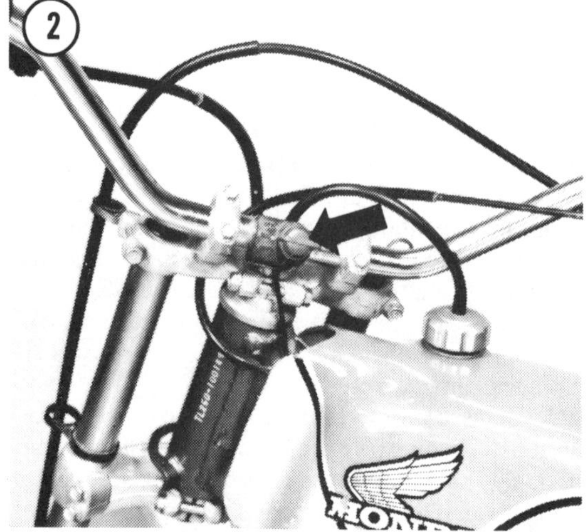

2. Connect the spark plug wire and connector to the spark plug and touch the spark plug's base to a good ground like the engine cylinder head. Position the spark plug so you can see the electrode.
3. Crank the engine over with the kickstarter. A fat blue spark should be evident across the spark plug electrodes.

WARNING
On 1981-on CB125S models, if it is necessary to hold the high voltage lead, do so with an insulated pair of pliers. The high voltage generated by the CDI could produce serious or fatal shocks.

4. If the spark is good, check for one or more of the following possible malfunctions:
   a. Obstructed fuel line.
   b. Leaking head gasket.
   c. Low compression.
5. If spark is not good, check for one or more of the following:
   a. Weak ignition coil.
   b. Faulty contact breaker points.
   c. Weak CDI pulse generator (1981-on CB125S).
   d. Broken or shorted high tension lead to the spark plug.
   e. Loose electrical connections.
   f. Ignition coil ground wire—it may be loose or broken.

Engine Is Difficult to Start

Check for one or more of the following possible malfunctions:

a. Fouled spark plug.
b. Improperly adjusted choke.
c. Contaminated fuel system.
d. Improperly adjusted carburetor.
e. Weak ignition coil.
f. Faulty contact breaker points.
g. Weak CDI pulse generator (1981-on CB125S).
h. Incorrect type ignition coil.
i. Poor compression.

Engine Will Not Crank

Check for one or more of the following possible malfunctions:

a. Seized piston.
b. Seized crankshaft bearings.
c. Broken connecting rod.
d. Locked up transmission or clutch assembly.
e. Broken kickstarter.

ENGINE PERFORMANCE

In the following check list, it is assumed that the engine runs, but is not operating at peak performance. This will serve as a starting point from which to isolate a performance malfunction.

The possible causes for each malfunction are listed in a logical sequence and in order of probability.

Engine Will Not Idle

a. Carburetor incorrectly adjusted.
b. Fouled or improperly gapped spark plug.
c. Leaking head gasket.
d. Ignition timing incorrect.
e. Incorrect contact braker point gap.
f. Weak or faulty pulse generator (1981-on CB125S).
g. Valve clearance incorrect.
h. Obstructed fuel line or fuel shutoff valve.

Engine Misses at High Speed

a. Fouled or improperly gapped spark plug.
b. Improper ignition timing.
c. Improper valve clearance.
d. Improper carburetor main jet selection.
e. Clogged jets in the carburetor.
f. Weak ignition coil.
g. Incorrect contact breaker point gap.
h. Weak or faulty pulse generator (1981-on CB125S).
i. Obstructed fuel line or fuel shutoff valve.

Engine Overheating

a. Obstructed cooling fins on cylinder head and cylinder.
b. Improper ignition timing.
c. Improper spark plug heat range.

Smoky Exhaust and Engine Runs Roughly

a. Carburetor adjustment incorrect (mixture too rich).
b. Choke not operating correctly.
c. Water or other contaminants in fuel.
d. Clogged fuel line.
e. Clogged air filter element.

Engine Loses Power

a. Carburetor incorrectly adjusted.
b. Engine overheating.
c. Improper ignition timing.

d. Incorrectly gapped spark plug.
e. Weak ignition coil.
f. Faulty contact breaker points.
g. Weak CDI pulse generator (1981-on CB125S).
h. Obstructed muffler.
i. Dragging brake(s).

Engine Lacks Acceleration

a. Carburetor mixture too lean.
b. Clogged fuel line.
c. Improper ignition timing.
d. Improper valve clearance.
e. Dragging brake(s).

ENGINE NOISES

1. *Knocking or pinging during acceleration*—Caused by using a lower octane fuel than recommended. May also be caused by poor fuel. Pinging can also be caused by a spark plug of the wrong heat range. Refer to *Correct Spark Plug Heat Range* in Chapter Three.
2. *Slapping or rattling noises at low speed or during acceleration*—May be caused by piston slap, i.e., excessive piston to cylinder wall clearance.
3. *Knocking or rapping while decelerating*—Usually caused by excessive rod bearing clearance.
4. *Persistent knocking and vibration*—Usually caused by excessive main bearing clearance.
5. *Rapid on-off squeal*—Compression leak around cylinder head gasket or spark plug.

EXCESSIVE VIBRATION

This can be difficult to find without disassembling the engine. Usually this is caused by loose engine mounting hardware.

FRONT SUSPENSION AND STEERING

Poor handling may be caused by improper front tire pressure or uneven rear tire pressure, a damaged or bent frame or front steering components, a worn front fork assembly, worn wheel bearings or dragging brakes.

BRAKE PROBLEMS

A sticking drum brake may be caused by worn or weak return springs, dry pivot and cam bushings or improper adjustment. Grabbing brakes may be caused by greasy linings which must be replaced. Brake grab may also be due to an out-of-round drum. Glazed linings will cause loss of stopping power.

Table 1 HOME WORKSHOP TOOLS

Tool	Size or Specification
Screwdrivers	
Slot	5/16 x 8 in. blade
Slot	3/8 x 12 in. blade
Phillips	Size 2 tip, 6 in. blade
Pliers	
Gas pliers	6 in. overall
Vise grips	10 in. overall
Needlenose	6 in. overall
Channel lock	12 in. overall
Snap ring	—
Wrenches	
Box-end set	10-17, 20, 32 mm
Open-end set	10-17, 20, 32 mm
Crescent (adjustable)	6 and 12 in. overall
Socket set	1/2 in. drive ratchet with 10-17, 20, 32 mm sockets
Allen set	2-10 mm
Cone wrenches	—
Spoke wrench	—
Other special tools	
Impact driver	1/2 in. drive with assorted tips
Torque wrench	1/2 in. drive—0-100 ft.-lb., 0-150 N•m
Tire levers	for motorcycle tires

CHAPTER THREE

3

LUBRICATION, MAINTENANCE AND TUNE-UP

A motorcycle, even in normal use, is subjected to tremendous heat, stress and vibration. When neglected, any bike becomes unreliable and actually dangerous to ride. To keep the bike properly maintained, look into the tune-up tools and parts and check out the different lubricants, motor oil, fork oil, locking compounds and greases. Also check engine degreasers, such as Gunk or Bel-Ray Degreaser, for cleaning your engine prior to working on it.

The more you get involved in your Honda the more you will want to work on it. Start out by doing simple tune-up, lubrication and maintenance. Tackle the more involved jobs as you become more acquainted with the bike.

The Honda singles covered in this book are some of the most reliable bikes available but to gain the utmost in safety, performance and useful life from them, it is necessary to make periodic inspections and adjustments. It frequently happens that minor problems are found during such inspections that are simple and inexpensive to correct at the time, but which could lead to major problems if not corrected.

This chapter explains lubrication, maintenance and tune-up procedures. **Table 1** shows a recommended maintenance schedule. **Tables 2-8** list maintenance and tune-up specifications. **Tables 1-8** are at the end of the chapter.

ROUTINE CHECKS

The following simple checks should be performed at each stop at a service station for gas or whenever the fuel tank is refilled.

Engine Oil Level

Refer to *Engine Oil Level Check* under *Periodic Lubrication* in this chapter.

General Inspection

1. Quickly inspect the engine for signs of oil or fuel leakage.
2. Check the tires for embedded stones. Pry them out with your ignition key.
3. Make sure all lights work, especially the brake light. It can burn out anytime. Motorists cannot stop as quickly as you and need all the warning you can give.

Tire Pressure

Tire pressure must be checked with the tires cold. Correct tire pressure depends on the load you are carrying. See **Table 2**.

Battery

Remove the left-hand side cover and check the battery electrolyte level. The level must be between the upper and lower level marks on the case (**Figure 1**).

For complete details see *Battery Removal/Installation and Electrolyte Level Check* in this chapter.

Check the level more frequently in hot weather, when evaporation increases.

Lights, Horn and Kill Switch

With the engine running, check the following.

1. On models equipped with a front brake lever switch, pull the front brake lever on and check that the brake light comes on.
2. Push the rear brake pedal down and check that the brake light comes on soon after you have begun depressing the pedal.
3. Move the headlight dimmer switch up and down between the HI and LO positions and check that both headlight elements are working.
4. On models equipped with turn signals, turn the switch to the left and right positions and check that all turn signals are working.
5. On models so equipped, push the horn button and make sure that the horn blows loudly.
6. Make sure that the engine kill switch works properly.
7. If during these tests the rear brake pedal traveled too far before the brake light came on, adjust the rear brake light switch as described in Chapter Eight. If the switches, horn or any of the lights failed to operate properly, refer to Chapter Eight.

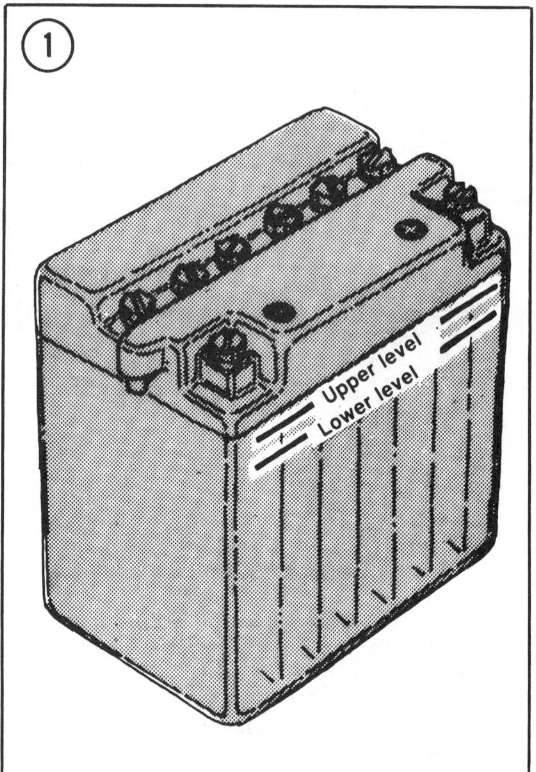

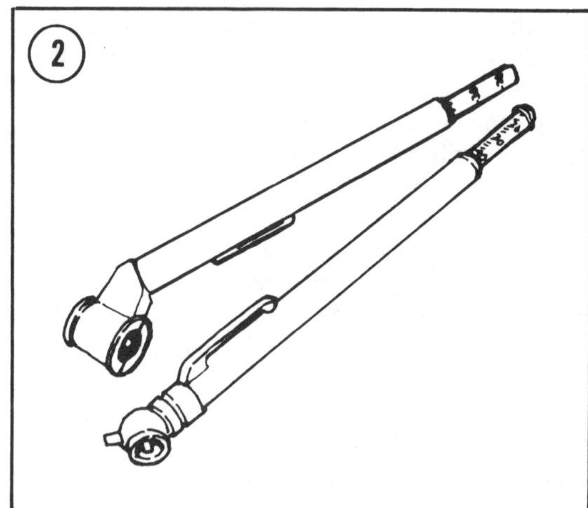

SERVICE INTERVALS

The services and intervals shown in **Table 1** are recommended by the factory. Strict adherence to these recommendations will ensure long service from your Honda. However, if the bike is run in an area of high humidity the lubrication services must be done more frequently to prevent possible rust damage.

For convenience when maintaining your motorcycle, most of the services shown in the table are described in this chapter. However, some procedures which require more than minor disassembly or adjustment are covered elsewhere in the appropriate chapter.

TIRES AND WHEELS

Tire Pressure

Tire pressure should be checked and adjusted to maintain the smoothness of the tire, good traction and handling and to get the maximum life out of the tire. A simple, accurate gauge (**Figure 2**) can be purchased for a few dollars and should be carried in your motorcycle tool kit. The appropriate tire pressures are shown in **Table 2**.

Tire Inspection

The tires take a lot of punishment so inspect them periodically for excessive wear, cuts, abrasions, etc. If you find a nail or other object in the tire, mark its location with a light crayon prior to removing it. This will help locate the hole for repair. Refer to Chapter Nine for tire changing and repair information.

Wheel Spoke Tension

Tap each spoke with a wrench. The higher the pitch of sound it makes, the tighter the spoke. The

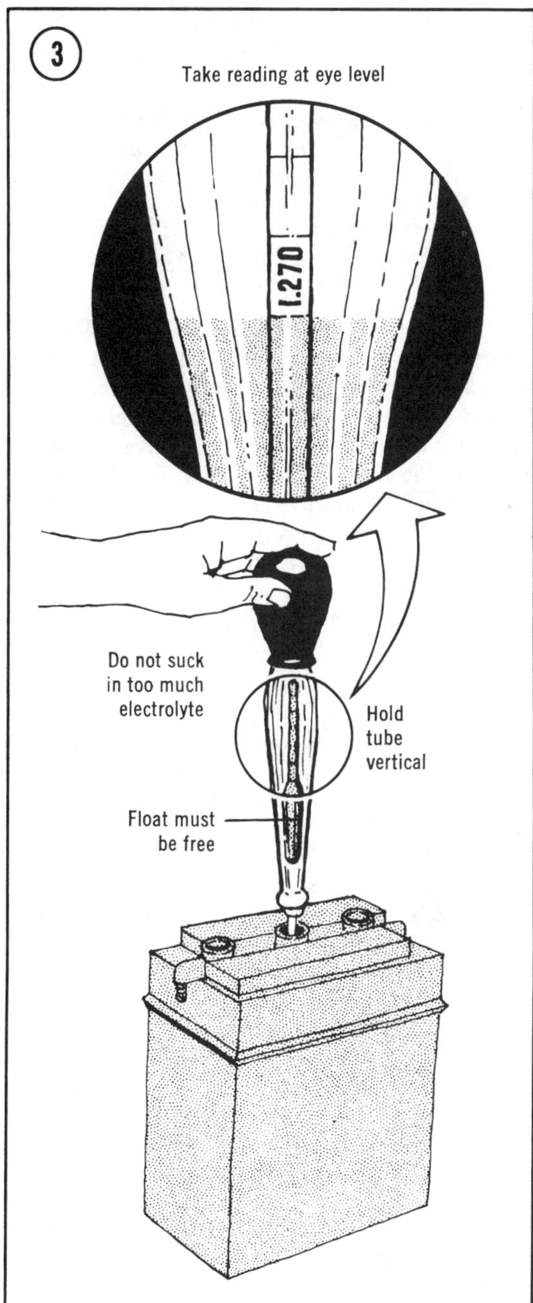

lower the sound frequency, the looser the spoke. A "ping" is good, a "klunk" says the spoke is too loose.

If one or more spokes are loose, tighten them as described under *Wheels* in Chapter Nine.

Rim Inspection

Frequently inspect the wheel rims. If a rim has been damaged, it might have been enough to knock it out of alignment. Improper wheel alignment can cause severe vibration and result in an unsafe riding condition. See Chapter Nine.

CRANKCASE BREATHER HOSE (1979-ON U.S. MODELS ONLY)

On models so equipped, inspect the breather hoses for cracks and deterioration and make sure that the hose clamps are tight.

BATTERY

Battery Removal/Installation and Electrolyte Level Check

The battery is the heart of the electrical system. It should be checked and serviced as indicated in **Table 1**. The majority of electrical system troubles can be attributed to neglect of this vital component.

The electrolyte level may be checked with the battery installed by removing the left-hand side panel. The electrolyte level should be maintained between the 2 marks on the battery case (**Figure 1**). If the electrolyte level is low, it's a good idea to remove the battery from the bike so it can be thoroughly serviced and checked.

1. Remove the left-hand side cover.
2. Disconnect the battery negative (-) and positive (+) leads from the battery terminals.
3. Remove the battery holder or strap.
4. Disconnect the battery vent tube from the battery; leave it routed through the bike's frame.
5. Slide the battery out of the frame.
6. Wipe off any of the highly corrosive residue that may have dripped from the battery during removal.

CAUTION
Be careful not to spill battery electrolyte on painted or polished surfaces. The liquid is highly corrosive and will damage the finish. If it is spilled, wash it off immediately with soapy water and thoroughly rinse with clean water.

7. Remove the caps from the battery cells and add distilled water to correct the fluid level. Gently shake the battery for several minutes to mix the existing electrolyte with the new water. Never add electrolyte (acid) to correct the level.
8. After the fluid level has been corrected and the battery has been allowed to stand a few minutes, check the specific gravity of the electrolyte in each cell with a hydrometer (**Figure 3**) as described under *Testing* in this chapter.

9. After the battery has been refilled, recharged or replaced, install it by reversing these removal steps.

CAUTION
If the breather tube was moved during battery removal, be sure to route it so that any residue will not drain onto any part of the bike's frame. The tube must be free of bends or twists as any restriction may pressurize the battery and damage it.

Testing

Hydrometer testing is the best way to check battery condition. Use a hydrometer with numbered graduations from 1.100 to 1.300 rather than one with color-coded bands. To use the hydrometer, squeeze the rubber ball, insert the tip into the cell and release the pressure on the ball. Draw enough electrolyte to float the weighted float inside the hydrometer. Note the number in line with the surface of the electrolyte; this is the specific gravity for this cell. Squeeze the rubber ball again and return the electrolyte to the cell from which it came.

The specific gravity of the electrolyte in each battery cell is an excellent indication of that cell's condition. A fully charged cell will read 1.260-1.280, a cell in good condition reads from 1.230-1.250 and anything below 1.160 is discharged.

Specific gravity varies with temperature. For each 10° the electrolyte temperature exceeds 80° F (27° C), add 0.004 to readings indicated on the hydrometer. Subtract 0.004 for each 10° below 80° F (27° C).

If the cells test in the poor range, the battery requires recharging. The hydrometer is useful for checking the progress of the charging operation. **Table 3** shows approximate state of charge.

Charging

WARNING
During the charging process, highly explosive hydrogen gas is released from the battery. The battery should be charged only in a well-ventilated area and away from any open flames (including pilot lights on home gas appliances). Do not allow any smoking in the area. Never check the charge of the battery by arcing across the electrical connections; the resulting spark can ignite the hydrogen gas.

CAUTION
Always remove the battery from the bike before connecting the battery charger. Never recharge a battery in the bike's frame due to the corrosive mist that is emitted during the charging process. If this mist settles on the bike's frame, it will corrode the surface.

1. Connect the positive (+) charger lead to the positive (+) battery lead and the negative (-) charger lead to the negative (-) battery lead.
2. Remove all vent caps from the battery, set the charger at 6 volts and switch the charger on. If the output of the charger is variable, it is best to select a low setting, somewhere between 1/2 and 2 amps.

CAUTION
The electrolyte level must be maintained at the upper level during the charging cycle; check and refill as necessary.

3. After the battery has been charged for about 8 hours, turn the charger off, disconnect the leads and check the specific gravity. It should be within the limits specified in **Table 3**. If it is, and remains stable for 1 hour, the battery is considered charged.
4. Clean the battery case and battery compartment in the bike's frame and reinstall the battery in the bike, reversing the removal steps.

CAUTION
Route the breather tube so that it does not drain onto any part of the bike's frame. The tube must be free of bends or twists as any restriction may pressurize the battery and damage it.

New Battery Installation

When replacing the old battery with a new one, be sure to charge it completely (specific gravity 1.260-1.280) before installing it in the bike. Failure to do so, or using the battery with a low electrolyte level, will permanently damage the new battery.

PERIODIC LUBRICATION

Engine Oil Level Check

Engine oil level is checked with the dipstick/oil filler cap, located on the right-hand side of the engine adjacent to the clutch mechanism cover (A, **Figure 4**).

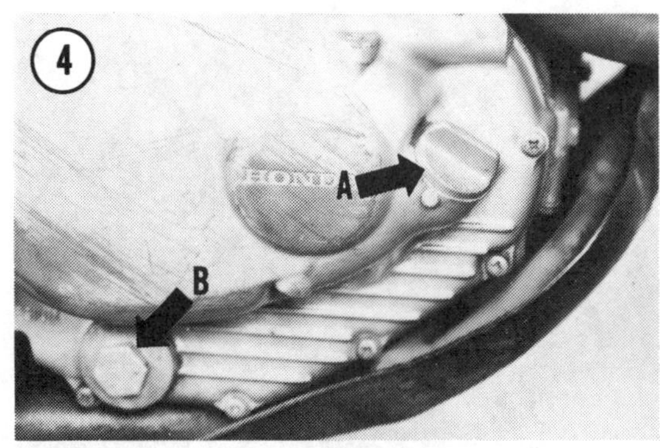

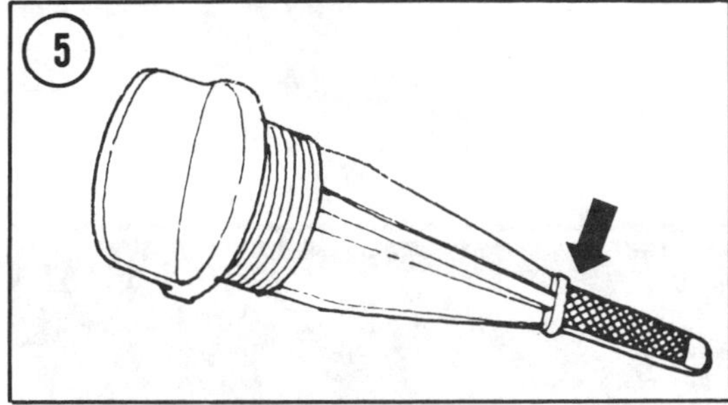

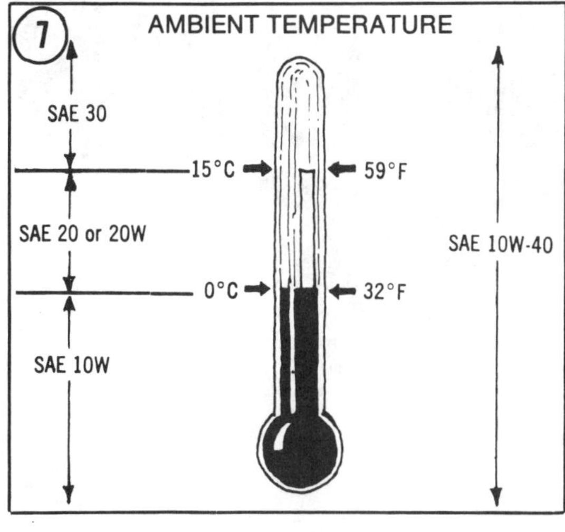

1. Start the engine and let it warm up approximately 2-3 minutes. Shut off the engine and let the oil settle.
2. Place the bike on a level surface and place a block of wood under the side stand to maintain the bike in an upright position. Be careful that the bike does not fall over from this position.
3. Unscrew the dipstick/oil filler cap and wipe it clean. Reinsert it onto the threads in the hole; do not screw it in. Remove it and check the oil level. The bike must be level for a correct reading.
4. The level should be between the 2 lines and not above the upper one (**Figure 5**). If necessary, add the recommended type oil to correct the level. Install the dipstick/oil filler cap and tighten it securely.

Engine Oil Change and Oil Filter Screen Cleaning

Regular oil changes will contribute more to engine longevity than any other maintenance operation performed. The factory recommended oil change and oil filter screen cleaning interval is listed in **Table 1**.

This interval assumes that the bike is operated in moderate climates. If it is operated under dusty conditions, the oil will get dirty more quickly and should be changed more frequently than recommended.

Use only a high quality detergent motor oil with an API rating of SE or SF. The rating is stamped or printed on top of the can (**Figure 6**). Try to use the same brand of oil at each oil change. Refer to **Figure 7** for correct oil viscosity to use under anticipated ambient temperatures (not engine oil temperature).

NOTE

*Never dispose of motor oil in the trash, on the ground, or down a storm drain. Many service stations accept used motor oil and waste haulers provide curbside used motor oil collection. Do not combine other fluids with motor oil to be recycled. To locate a recycler, contact the American Petroleum Institute (API) at **www.recycleoil.org**.*

To change the engine oil and filter you will need the following:

a. Drain pan.
b. Funnel.
c. Can opener or pour spout.

3

d. 1-2 quarts of oil (refer to **Table 4** for correct oil capacity for each model).

There are a number of ways to discard the old oil safely. Some service stations and oil retailers will accept your used oil for recycling; some may even give you money for it. Never drain the oil onto the ground.

1. Place the bike on the side stand.
2. Start the engine and let it reach operating temperature.
3. Shut the engine off and place a drain pan under the engine drain plug.
4. Remove the drain plug (**Figure 8**).

NOTE
*On 175 cc engines, don't lose the spring and filter screen that will come out with the drain plug (**Figure 9**).*

5. Remove the dipstick/oil filler cap; this will speed up the flow of oil.
6. Let it drain for at least 15-20 minutes. During this time, turn the engine over a couple of times with the kickstarter to drain any remaining oil.

CAUTION
Do not let the engine start and run without oil in the crankcase. Make sure the ignition switch is in the OFF position.

7. On 100, 125, 250 and 350 cc engines, remove the oil pump filter screen drain plug (B, **Figure 4**) located on either the right- or left-hand crankcase cover. Remove the spring and filter screen.
8. Clean the drain plug screen on 175 cc engines, the oil pump filter screen, the springs and the drain plugs in solvent and thoroughly dry with compressed air. Inspect the filter screen for holes or defects; replace as necessary. Thoroughly clean out the drain plug area in the crankcase with a shop rag and solvent.
9. Inspect the O-ring seals on the drain plug (**Figure 10**) and the oil filter screen plug. Replace the O-ring if its condition is in doubt.

10A. On 175 cc engines, install the filter screen, the spring and the drain plug. Tighten the drain plug securely.

10B. On all other models, install the drain plug and tighten securely.

11. On 100, 125, 250 and 350 cc engines, install the spring, filter and oil pump filter drain plug. Tighten the drain plug securely.

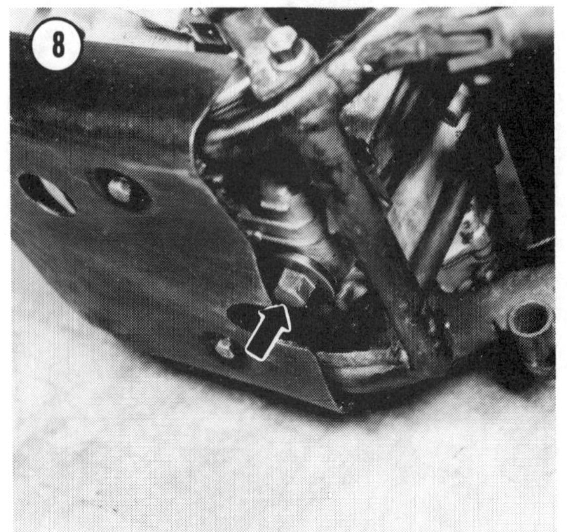

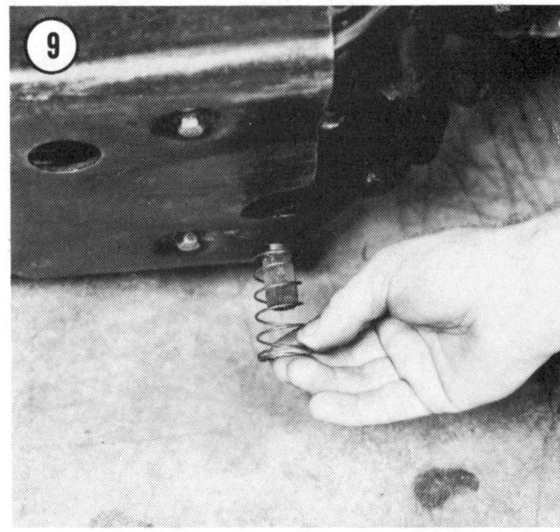

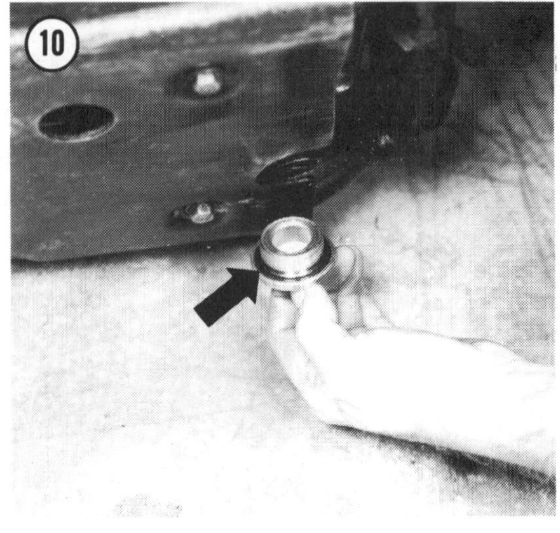

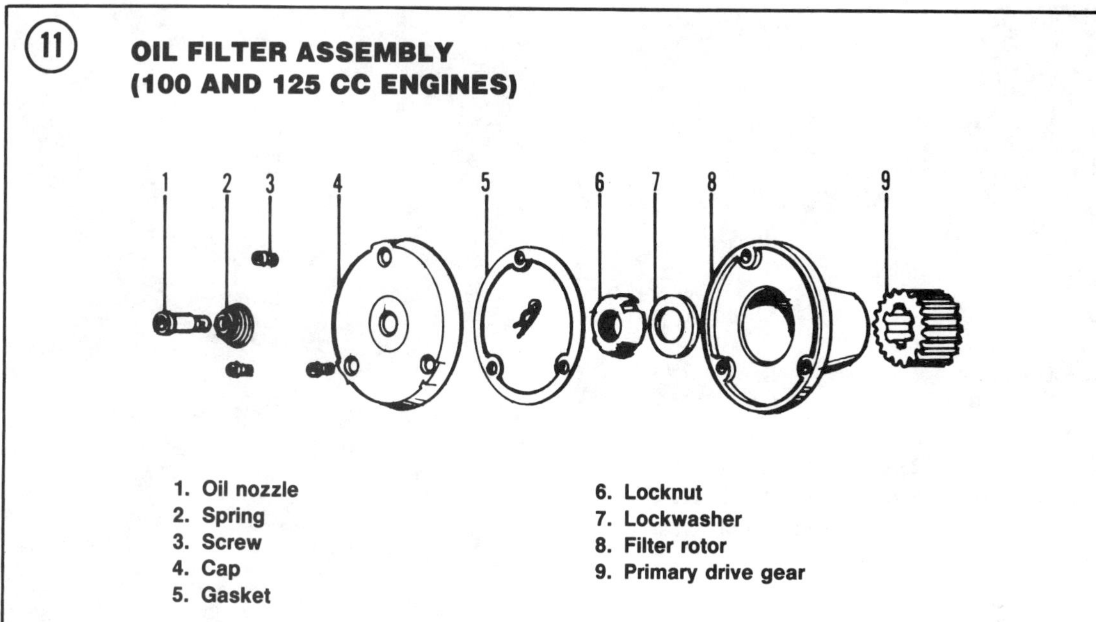

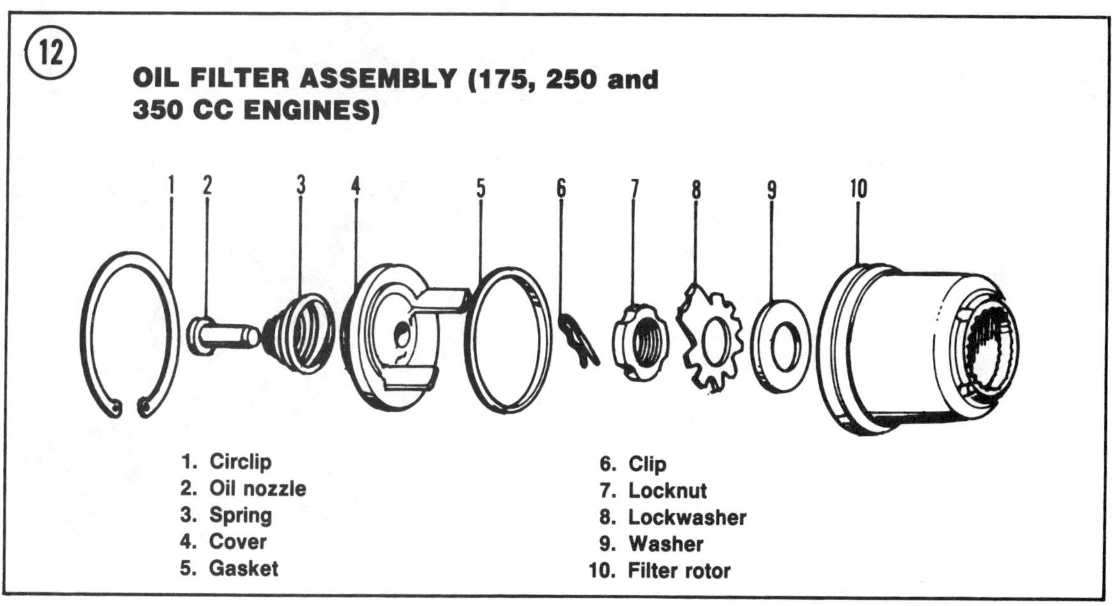

12. Clean the oil filter rotor as described in this chapter before refilling the crankcase with new engine oil.
13. Insert a funnel into the oil fill hole and fill the engine with the correct viscosity and quantity of oil. Refer to **Table 4**.
14. Screw in the dipstick/oil filler cap securely.
15. Start the engine, let it run at moderate speed and check for leaks.
16. Turn the engine off and check for correct oil level; adjust as necessary.

Oil Filter Rotor Cleaning

The factory recommended interval for cleaning the oil filter rotor is listed in **Table 1**.

This interval assumes that the bike is operated in moderate climates. If it is operated under dusty conditions, the oil will get dirty more quickly and cleaning should be done more frequently than recommended.

Refer to **Figure 11** for 100 and 125 cc engines or **Figure 12** for 175, 250 and 350 cc engines.

1. Drain the engine oil as described in this chapter.

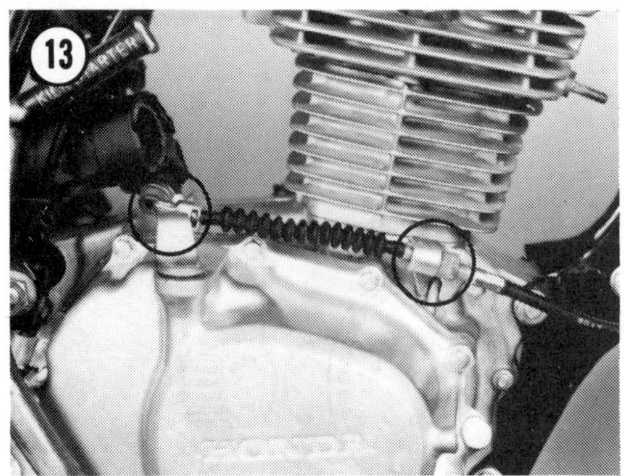

2. On 100 and 125 cc engines, slacken the clutch cable at the hand lever. Disconnect the clutch cable (**Figure 13**) from the right-hand crankcase cover and actuating lever.

NOTE
On all other models, the clutch cable is on the left-hand crankcase cover and does not require removal.

3. Remove the rear brake pedal as described in Chapter Eleven.
4. Remove the bolt securing the kickstarter lever and remove the kickstarter lever.
5. Move an oil drain pan under the right-hand crankcase cover as residual oil will drain out when this cover is removed. Remove the bolts securing the right-hand crankcase cover (**Figure 14**) and remove the cover, gasket and 2 locating dowels.
6A. On 100 and 125 cc engines, remove the screws (**Figure 15**) securing the oil filter rotor cover and remove the cover.
6B. On all other models, remove the circlip (**Figure 16**) securing the oil filter rotor cover and remove the cover.
7. Clean the inside of the rotor in solvent and, if necessary, scrape out any oil sludge with a broad-tipped dull screwdriver.
8A. On 100 and 125 cc engines, install the oil filter rotor cover and install the screws (**Figure 15**). Tighten the screws securely.
8B. On all other models, inspect the O-ring seal (A, **Figure 17**) on the cover and replace if necesssary. Align one of the tabs on the cover with the groove in the filter rotor (B, **Figure 17**) and install the cover. Install the circlip.
9. Install the crankcase cover dowel pins and the gasket.
10. On 100 and 125 cc engines, which have the clutch actuating lever mounted on the top surface of the crankcase cover, hold the clutch actuating

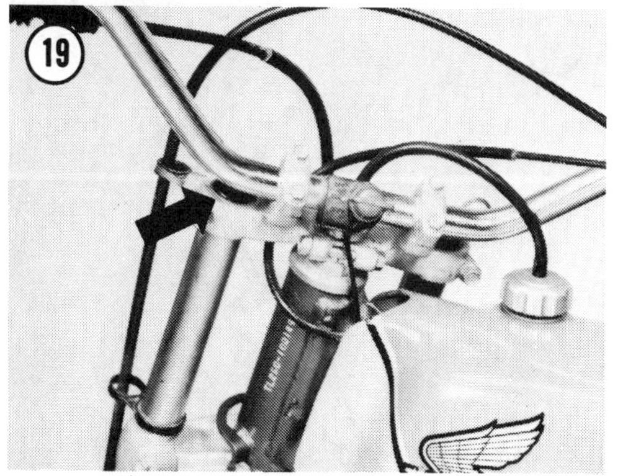

lever in the released position so the recess in the actuator (**Figure 18**) will mesh properly with the clutch lifter.

11. Install the right-hand crankcase cover. Push it all the way into place. Install the screws and tighten in a crisscross pattern until they are secure.

CAUTION
Do not install any of the crankcase cover screws until the crankcase cover is snug up against the crankcase surface. Do not try to force the cover into place with screw pressure. If the cover will not fit up against the crankcase, remove the crankcase cover and repeat Step 10 and Step 11.

12. Install the kickstarter lever and tighten the bolt securely.
13. On 100 and 125 cc engines, connect the clutch cable to the actuating lever on the crankcase cover.
14. Install the rear brake pedal as described in Chapter Eleven.
15. Refill the engine with the recommended type and quantity of oil as described in this chapter.
16. On 100 and 125 cc engines, adjust the clutch as described in this chapter.

Front Fork Oil Change

Change the fork oil at the interval indicated in **Table 1** or when it becomes contaminated.

1. Place a wood block(s) under the engine to support the bike securely.
2A. On TL250 models, remove the trim cap (**Figure 19**), the circlip and the fork cap. Remove the top cap carefully, as it is under spring pressure from the fork spring.
2B. On all other models, unscrew the fork cap bolt (**Figure 20**) slowly, as it is under spring pressure from the fork spring.
3. Place a drain pan under the drain screw (**Figure 21**) and remove the drain screw. Allow the oil to drain for at least 5 minutes. *Never reuse the oil.*

CAUTION
Do not allow the fork oil to come in contact with any of the brake components.

4. Inspect the gasket on the drain screw; replace it if necessary. Install the drain screw.
5. Repeat for the other fork.

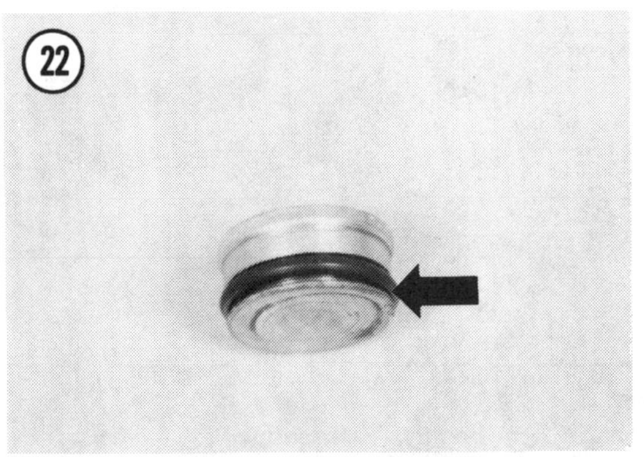

6. Refill each fork leg with the specified quantity of Dexron automatic transmission fluid (ATF) or fork oil. Refer to **Table 5** for specified quantity.

NOTE
To measure the correct amount of fluid, use a plastic baby bottle. These have measurements in fluid ounces (oz.) and cubic centimeters (cc) on the side.

7. After filling each fork tube, slowly pump the fork tubes several times to expel air from the upper and lower fork chambers and to distribute the oil.
8A. On TL250 models, inspect the O-ring seal on the fork top cap (**Figure 22**) and replace if necessary. Install the fork top cap while pushing down on the spring. Install the circlip and make sure it seats correctly in the groove in the fork tube. Install the trim cap.
8B. On all other models, inspect the O-ring seal on the fork cap bolt (**Figure 23**); replace if necessary. Install the fork cap bolt while pushing down on the spring. Start the bolt slowly—don't cross thread it. Tighten the bolt to approximately 15-25 N•m (11-18 ft.-lb.).
9. Road test the bike and check for leaks.

Drive Chain Lubrication

Oil the drive chain at the interval indicated in **Table 1** or sooner if it becomes dry. A properly maintained chain will provide maximum service life and reliability.

1. Place a wood block(s) under the engine to support the bike securely.
2. Shift the transmission to NEUTRAL.
3. Oil the bottom run of the chain with a commercial chain lubricant. Concentrate on getting the lubricant down between the side plates, pins, bushings and rollers of each chain link.
4. Rotate the wheel to bring the unoiled portion of the chain within reach. Continue until all of the chain is lubricated.

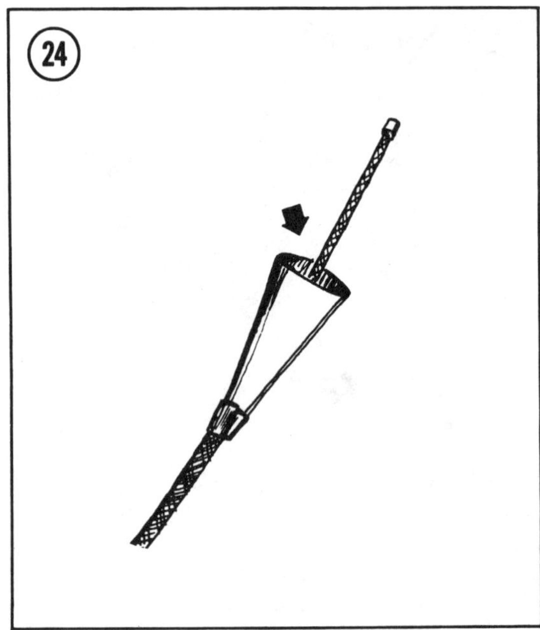

Control Cables

The control cables should be lubricated at the interval indicated in **Table 1**.

They should be also inspected at this time for fraying and the cable sheath should be checked for chafing. The cables are relatively inexpensive and should be replaced when found to be faulty.

The control cables can be lubricated either with oil or with any of the popular cable lubricants and a cable lubricator. The first method requires more time and the complete lubrication of the entire cable is less certain.

Examine the exposed end of the inner cable. If it is dirty or if the cable feels gritty when moved up and down in its housing, first spray it with a lubricant/solvent such as LPS-25 or WD-40. Let this solvent drain out, then proceed with the following steps.

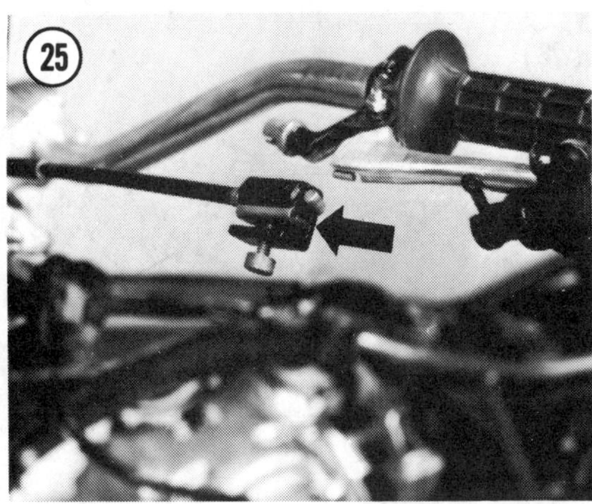

Oil method

1. Disconnect the cables from the front brake lever, the clutch lever and the throttle grip assembly.

> NOTE
> *On the throttle cable, it is necessary to remove the screws that clamp the housing together to gain access to the cable end.*

2. Make a cone of stiff paper and tape it to the end of the cable sheath (**Figure 24**).
3. Hold the cable upright and pour a small amount of light oil (SAE 10W/30) into the cone. Work the cable in and out of the sheath for several minutes to help the oil work its way down to the end of the cable.

> NOTE
> *To avoid a mess, place a shop cloth at the end of the cable to catch the oil as it runs out.*

4. Remove the cone, reconnect the cable(s) and adjust the cable(s) as described in this chapter.

Lubricator method

1. Disconnect the cables from the front brake lever, the clutch lever and the throttle grip assembly.

> NOTE
> *On the throttle cable, it is necessary to remove the screws that clamp the housing together to gain access to the cable end.*

2. Attach a lubricator (**Figure 25**) following the manufacturer's instructions.
3. Insert the nozzle of the lubricant can in the lubricator, press the button on the can and hold it down until the lubricant begins to flow out of the other end of the cable.

> NOTE
> *Place a shop cloth at the end of the cable(s) to catch all excess lubricant that will flow out.*

4. Remove the lubricator, reconnect the cable(s) and adjust the cable(s) as described in this chapter.

3

Swing Arm Bushing Lubrication

On models equipped with a grease fitting, lubricate the swing arm bushings as indicated in **Table 1**. Apply with a small hand-held grease gun. Use a good grade multipurpose grease.

On models not equipped with a grease fitting, the swing arm bushings should be greased whenever the swing arm is disassembled.

1. Wipe the grease fitting clean of all road dirt and grease residue. Force the grease into the fitting until the grease runs out of both ends of the swing arm.
2. Clean off excess grease.
3. If the grease will not run out of the ends of the swing arm, unscrew the grease fitting from the swing arm. Clean it out with solvent; make sure the check valve is free. Reinstall the fitting or replace with a new one.
4. Apply the grease gun again. If grease still does not run out of both ends of the swing arm, remove the swing arm as described in Chapter Ten. Disassemble the swing arm and thoroughly clean and regrease.

Brake Cam Lubrication

Lubricate the front and rear brake cams as indicated in **Table 1** or whenever the wheel is removed.

1. Remove the wheel as described in Chapter Nine or Chapter Ten.
2. Remove the brake panel assembly from the wheel hub.
3. Remove the brake shoes from the backing plate by pulling upon the center of each shoe (**Figure 26**).

> NOTE
> *Place a clean shop rag on the linings to protect them from oil and grease during removal.*

4. Wipe away old grease from the camshaft and pivot pins on the backing plate. Also clean the pivot hole and camshaft contact area of each shoe. Be careful not to get any grease on the linings.

5. Sparingly apply a high-temperature grease to all pivot and rubbing surfaces of the backing plate and the camshaft (**Figure 27**), the brake shoe pivot points (**Figure 28**) and to the spring ends.
6. Reassemble the brake assembly.
7. Reinstall the brake panel assembly into the wheel hub and reinstall the wheel.
8. On rear wheels, adjust the drive chain and rear brake as described in this chapter.

Meter Cable Lubrication

Lubricate the cable as indicated in **Table 1** or whenever needle operation is erratic.

1. Unscrew the retaining collar and remove the cable from the instrument (**Figure 29**).
2. Pull the cable from the cable sheath.
3. If the grease on the cable is contaminated, thoroughly clean off all old grease.
4. Thoroughly coat the cable with a good grade multipurpose grease and reinstall into the sheath.
5. Make sure the cable is correctly seated into the drive unit.

Miscellaneous Lubrication Points

Lubricate the clutch lever, front brake lever, side stand pivot point and foot peg pivot points. Use 10W/30 motor oil.

PERIODIC MAINTENANCE

Drive Chain Adjustment (Except TL125 and TL250)

The drive chain should be checked and adjusted as indicated in **Table 1**.

The correct amount of chain free play, when pushed up midway between the sprockets on the lower chain run, is approximately 20 mm (3/4 in.). See **Figure 30**. If adjustment is necessary, perform the following.

1. Place a wood block(s) under the engine to support the bike securely with the rear wheel off of the ground.
2. Shift the transmission into NEUTRAL.
3. Remove the cotter pin and loosen the axle nut (A, **Figure 31**).
4. Turn the axle adjuster nuts (B, **Figure 31**) in or out as required, in equal amounts. Be sure that the mark (**Figure 32**) on each adjuster aligns with the same mark on each side of the swing arm.
5. Rotate the rear wheel to move the chain to another position and recheck the adjustment; chains rarely wear or stretch evenly and, as a result, the free play will not remain constant over the entire chain. If the chain cannot be adjusted within

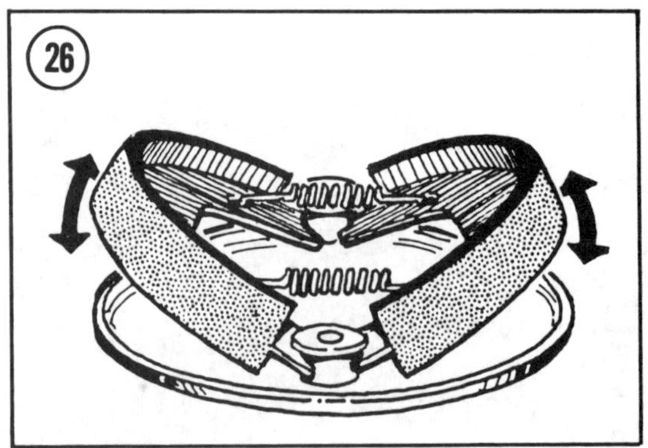

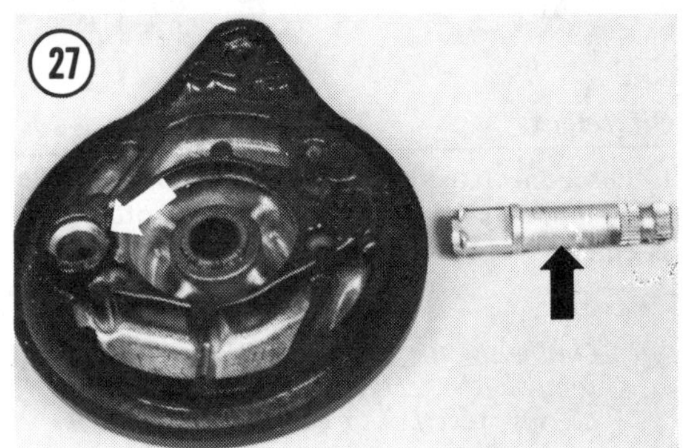

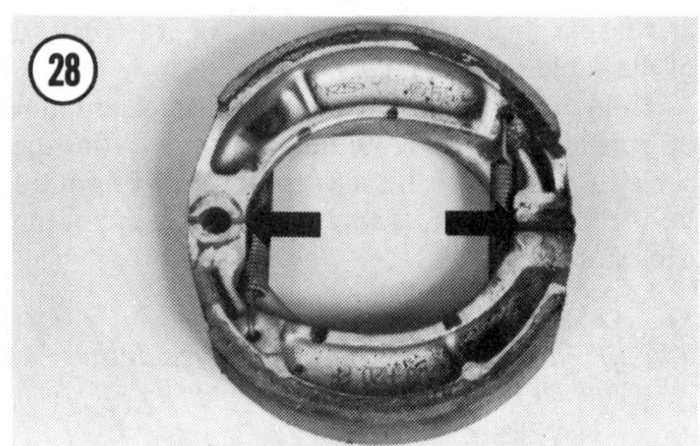

30

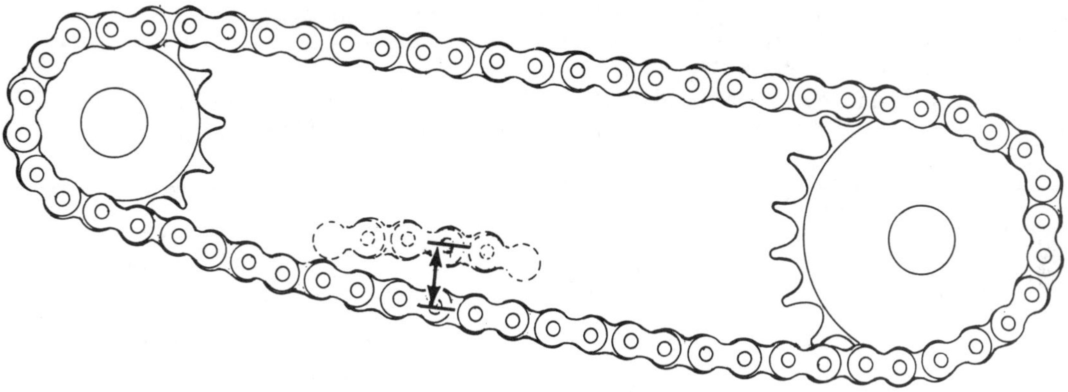

these limits, it is excessively worn and stretched and should be replaced. Always replace both sprockets when replacing the drive chain; never install a new chain over worn sprockets. Refer to **Table 6** for drive chain replacement numbers.

WARNING
Excess free play can result in chain breakage which could cause a serious accident.

6. Sight along the top of the drive chain from the rear sprocket to see that it is correctly aligned. It should leave the top of the rear sprocket in a straight line (A, **Figure 33**). If it is cocked to one side or the other (B and C, **Figure 33**), the wheel is incorrectly aligned and must be corrected. Refer to Step 4.

7. Tighten the rear axle nut to the torque specifications listed in **Table 7**. Install a new cotter pin and bend the ends over completely.

NOTE
Always install a new cotter pin; never reuse an old one.

8. After the drive chain has been adjusted, the rear brake pedal free play must be adjusted as described in this chapter.

Drive Chain Adjustment (TL125 and TL250)

The drive chain should be checked and adjusted as indicated in **Table 1**.

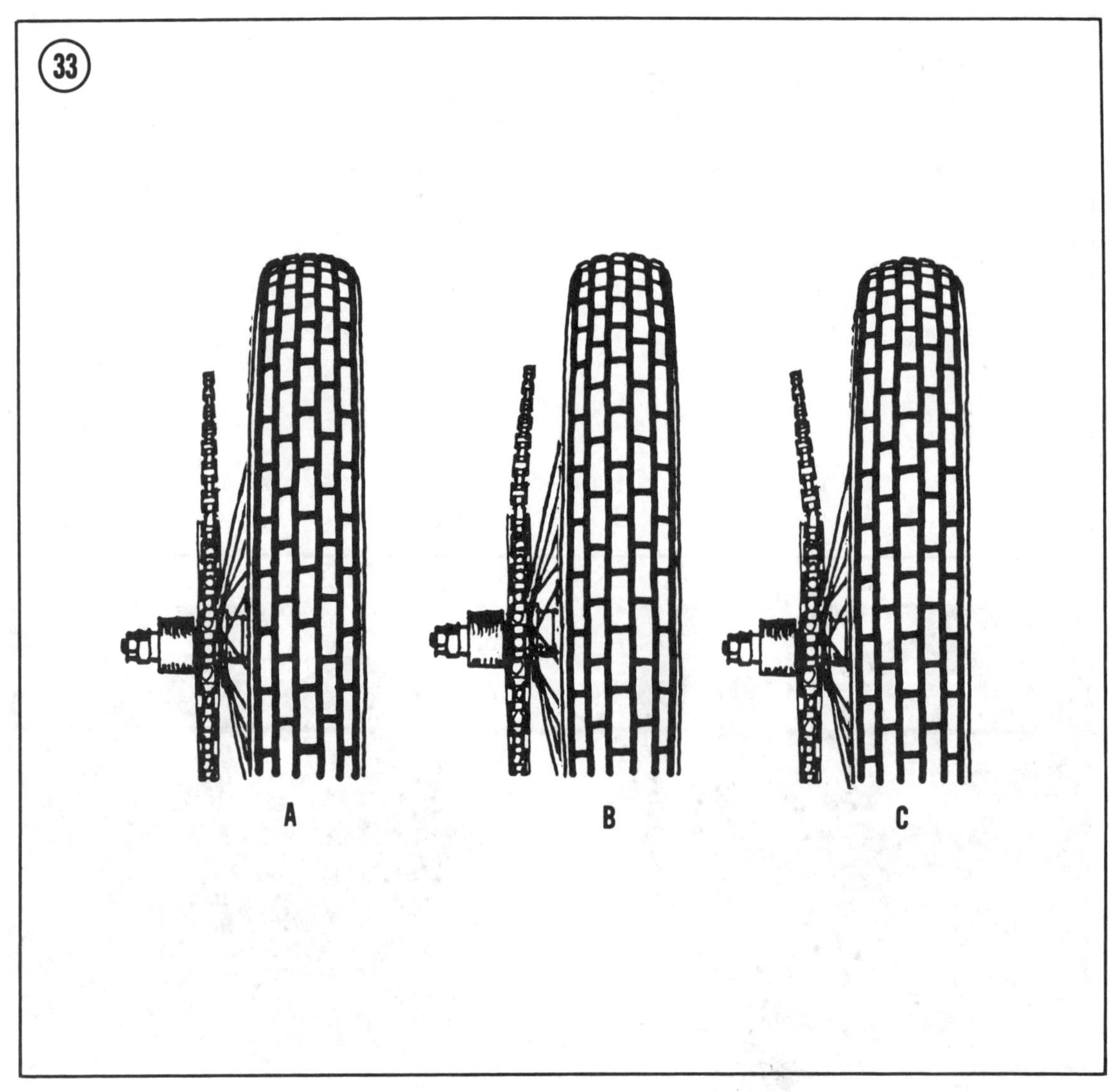

To check the amount of free play, push the drive chain tensioner (**Figure 34**) down until it does not contact the drive chain. Push the chain up midway between the sprockets on the upper chain run; the correct amount of chain free play is 20 mm (3/4 in.). See **Figure 35**. If adjustment is necessary, perform the following.

1. Place a wood block(s) under the engine to support the bike securely with the rear wheel off of the ground.
2. Shift the transmission into NEUTRAL.
3. Remove the cotter key or clip and loosen the axle nut (**Figure 36**).
4. Turn both axle snail adjusters (**Figure 37**) in equal amounts to either increase or decrease chain tension. After adjustment is complete, make sure

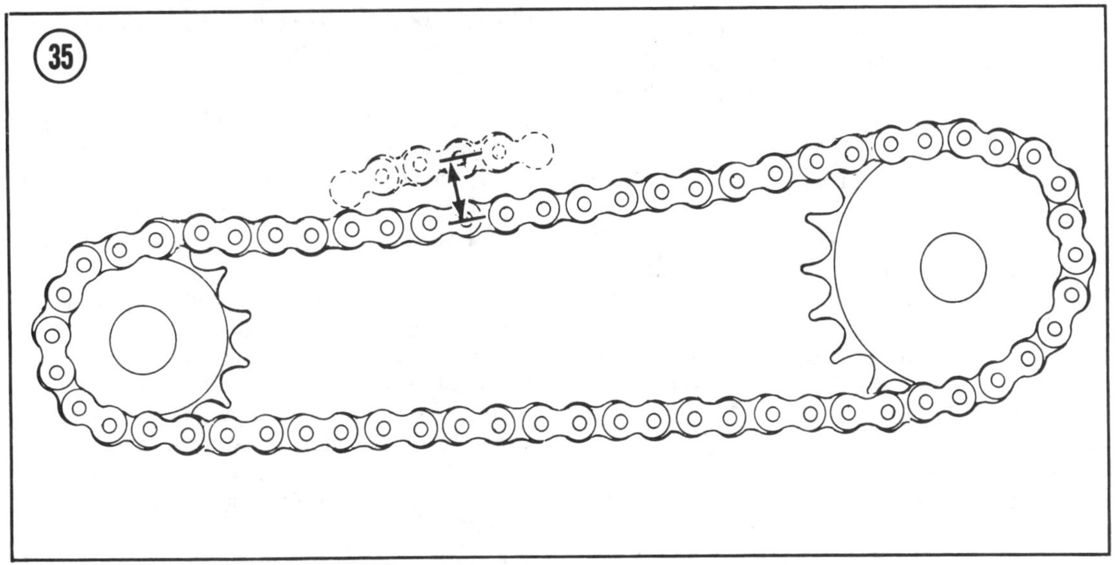

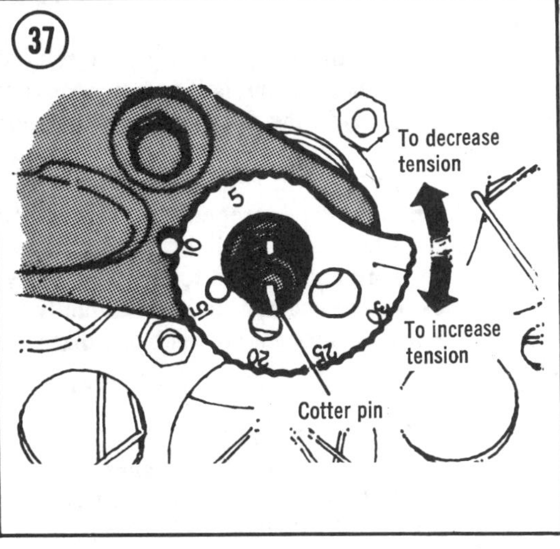

that the same mark on the snail adjuster aligns with the stopper pin (**Figure 38**) on each side of the swing arm.

5. Rotate the rear wheel to move the chain to another position and recheck the adjustment; chains rarely wear or stretch evenly and, as a result, the free play will not remain constant over the entire chain. If the chain cannot be adjusted within these limits, it is excessively worn and stretched and should be replaced. Always replace both sprockets when replacing the drive chain; never install a new chain over worn sprockets. Refer to **Table 6** for drive chain replacement numbers.

WARNING
Excess free play can result in chain breakage which could cause a serious accident.

6. Sight along the top of the drive chain from the rear sprocket to see that it is correctly aligned. It should leave the top of the rear sprocket in a straight line (A, **Figure 33**). If it is cocked to one side or the other (B and C, **Figure 33**) the wheel is incorrectly aligned and must be corrected. Refer to Step 4.

7. Tighten the rear axle nut to 60-80 N•m (43-58 ft.-lb.). Install a new cotter pin and bend the ends over completely or install a clip into the hole in the axle.

8. After the drive chain has been adjusted, the rear brake pedal free play must be adjusted as described in this chapter.

Drive Chain Cleaning, Inspection and Lubrication

Remove, thoroughly clean and lubricate the chain at the interval indicated in **Table 1**.

1. Remove the drive chain as described in Chapter Ten.

2. Immerse the chain in a pan of cleaning solvent and allow it to soak for about half an hour. Move it around and flex it during this period so that dirt between the pins and rollers may work its way out.

3. Scrub the rollers and side plates with a stiff brush and rinse away loosened grit. Rinse it a couple of times to make sure all dirt is washed out. Hang up the chain and allow it to thoroughly dry.

4. After cleaning the chain, examine it carefully for wear or damage. If any signs are visible, replace the chain.

CAUTION
*Always check both sprockets (**Figure 39**) every time the drive chain is removed. If any wear is visible on the teeth, replace*

the sprocket. Never install a new chain over worn sprockets or a worn chain over new sprockets.

5. Check the inner faces of the inner plates (**Figure 40**). They should be lightly polished on both sides. If they show considerable wear on both sides, the sprockets are not aligned. Adjust alignment as described in Step 4 of *Drive Chain Adjustment* in this chapter.

6. After cleaning the drive chain, lay the drive chain alongside a ruler (**Figure 41**). Compress the links together then stretch them apart. If more than 1/4 in. of movement is possible, replace the drive chain; it is too worn to be used again. Refer to **Table 6** for drive chain replacement numbers.

7. Lubricate the chain with a good grade of chain lubricant carefully following the manufacturer's instructions.

8. Reinstall the chain as described in Chapter Ten.

9. Adjust chain free play as described in this chapter.

Drive Chain Tensioners (TL250, XL350, SL350 K1)

The slider or roller is located on the left-hand side of the swing arm (**Figure 42**). There is no wear limit line on the slider or the roller. On the TL250 slider, if a groove is worn 3/4 of the way through the top surface of the slider it should be replaced. On the XL350 and SL350 K1 roller, when the roller is worn to within 1/4 in. of the collar the roller should be replaced.

Replacement (TL250)

Remove the screws and washers securing the slider to the tensioner arm. Replace with a new slider and tighten the screws securely.

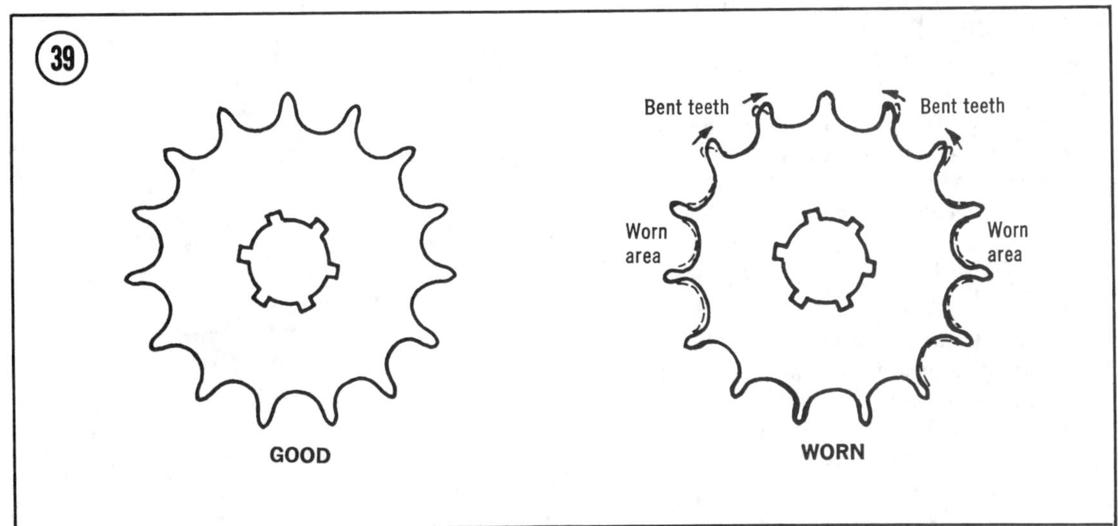
39
Bent teeth
Bent teeth
Worn area
Worn area
GOOD
WORN

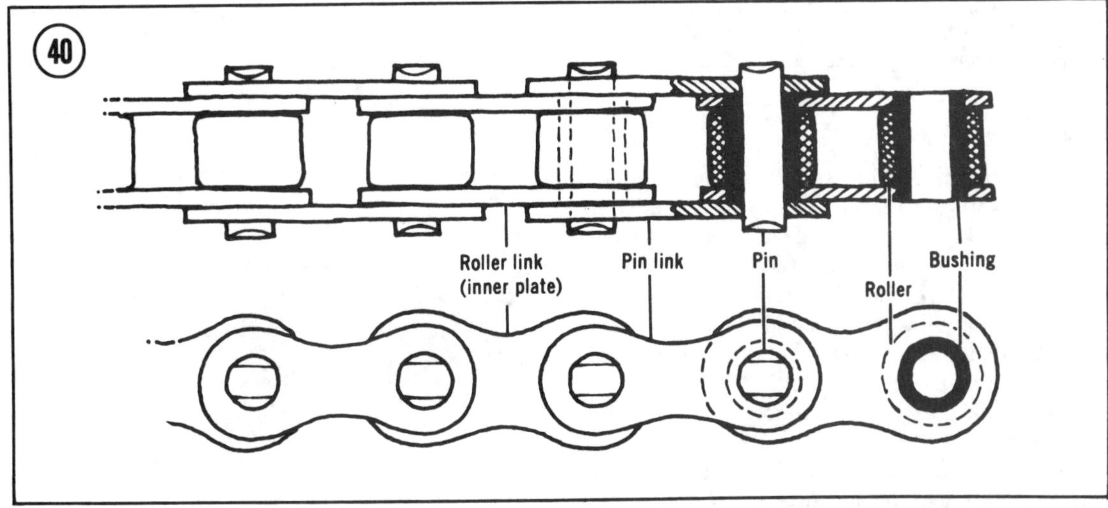
40
Roller link (inner plate)
Pin link
Pin
Bushing
Roller

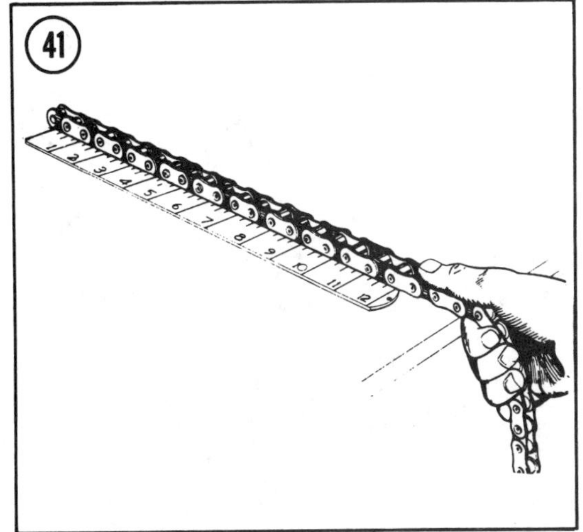
41

42

Replacement (XL350, SL350 K1)

Remove the long screw, nut, lockwasher and washer. Remove the roller, washers and collar from the tensioner arm. Replace the roller and the collar (if necessary). Be sure to install a washer on each side of the collar and roller during installation. Tighten the screw and nut securely.

Brake Lining Inspection

Inspect the brake lining wear indicators as indicated in **Table 1**. Apply the brake fully; if the wear indicator arrow on the brake arm aligns with the raised triangle reference mark on the brake panel (**Figure 43**), the brake shoes must be replaced. Refer to Chapter Eleven.

NOTE
Figure 43 *is shown with the brake panel assembly removed from the wheel for clarity. It is not necessary to remove the brake panel to see the wear indicators.*

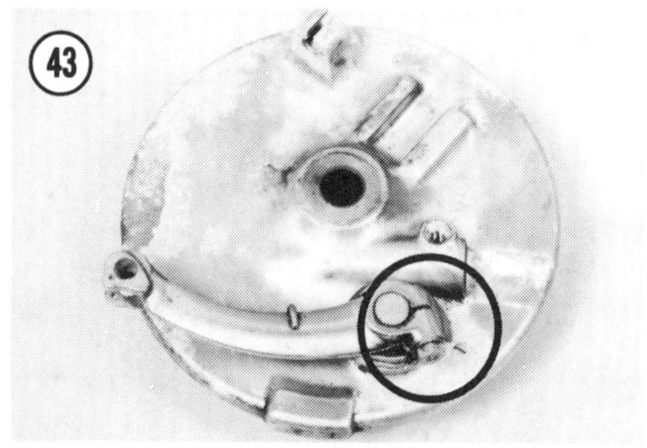
43

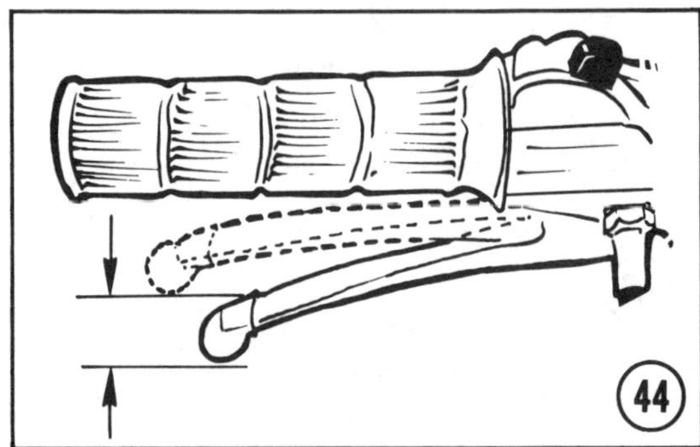
44

Front Brake Lever Adjustment

The front brake cable should be adjusted so there is 20-30 mm (3/4-1 1/4 in.) of brake lever movement (**Figure 44**) required to actuate the brake, but it must not be adjusted so closely that the brake shoes contact the drum with the lever relaxed. Minor adjustments should be made at the brake lever and major adjustments should be made at the brake panel on the wheel.

1. Slide back the rubber protective boot at the brake lever.
2. Loosen the locknut and turn the adjusting barrel (**Figure 45**) to achieve the correct amount of free play. Tighten the locknut.
3. Because of normal brake wear, this adjustment will eventually be "used up." It is then necessary to loosen the locknut and screw the adjusting barrel all the way toward the hand grip. Tighten the locknut.
4. At the brake panel, loosen the locknut and turn the adjuster nut (**Figure 46**) until the brake lever can be used once again for the minor adjustment. Tighten the locknut.
5. At the hand lever, loosen the locknut and turn the adjusting barrel (**Figure 45**) to achieve the correct amount of free play. Tighten the locknut.
6. Slide the rubber protective boot back into place.

NOTE
If the correct lever free play cannot be obtained, replace the cable.

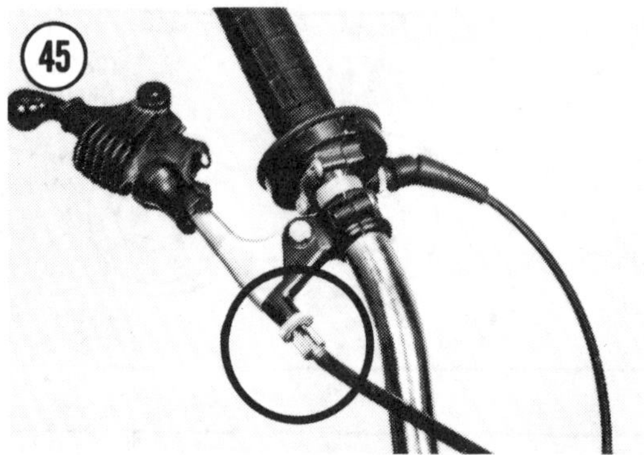
45

46

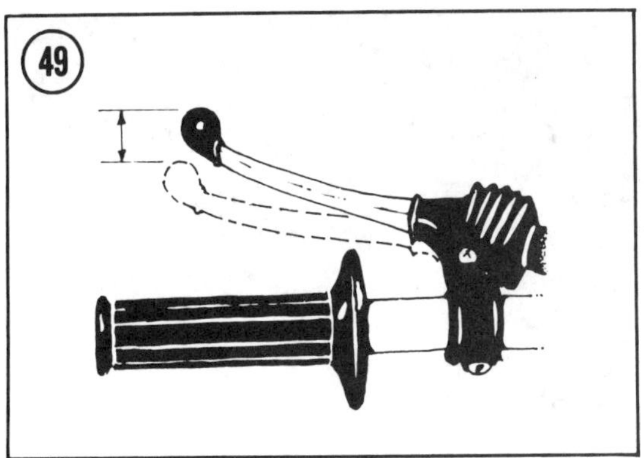

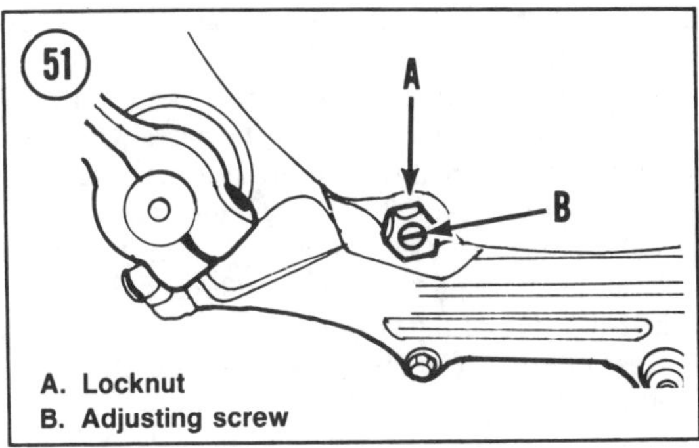

A. Locknut
B. Adjusting screw

Rear Brake Pedal Adjustment

Free play is the distance the pedal travels from the at-rest position to the applied position (**Figure 47**) when the pedal is lightly depressed by hand.

Turn the adjustment nut on the end of the brake rod (**Figure 48**) until the pedal has 20-30 mm (3/4-1 1/4 in.) of free play.

Rotate the rear wheel and check for brake drag. Also operate the pedal several times to make sure it returns to the at-rest position immediately after release.

Clutch Adjustment

The clutch free play adjustment should be checked at the interval listed in **Table 1**. Free play is the distance that the tip of the lever travels from the at-rest to the applied position (**Figure 49**). This distance should be 10-20 mm (3/8-3/4 in.) on all models. The cable adjustment takes up slack caused by cable stretching. On some models, the clutch mechanism can also be adjusted.

If the proper amount of free play cannot be achieved by using this adjustment procedure, the cable has stretched and needs to be replaced. Refer to Chapter Six.

CB100, CL100, SL100, XL100, 1973-1978 CB125S, SL125 and TL125 models

1. Slide back the rubber protective boot at the hand lever.
2. Loosen the locknut and turn the adjuster barrel (**Figure 50**) all the way in toward the hand lever. Tighten the locknut.
3. On the right-hand side of the engine, loosen the locknut and turn the adjuster screw (**Figure 51**) clockwise until a slight drag can be felt. Stop and turn the adjuster screw counterclockwise 1/8-1/4 turn. Tighten the locknut.
4. At the clutch actuating lever on the engine, loosen the locknut and turn the adjust nut until the

correct amount of free play is obtained at the hand lever. Tighten the locknut.

5. For fine adjustment, loosen the locknut on the hand lever and screw the adjuster barrel (**Figure 50**) until the correct amount of free play is obtained at the tip of the lever. Tighten the locknut.

6. After adjustment is completed, check that the locknuts are tight on both the hand lever and at the right-hand side of the engine.

7. Test ride the bike and make sure the clutch is operating correctly.

XL175 models

1. On the left-hand side of the engine, loosen the lock bolt and turn the adjuster (**Figure 52**) clockwise to decrease free play or counterclockwise to increase lever free play. Tighten the lock bolt when free play is correct.

2. For additional adjustment there is an adjuster at each end of the clutch cable.
   a. At the hand lever, slide back the rubber protective boot and loosen the locknut. Screw the adjuster barrel (**Figure 50**) until the correct amount of free play is obtained at the tip of the lever. Tighten the locknut.
   b. At the clutch actuating end of the cable, slide up the rubber protective boot, loosen the locknut and turn the adjusting nut (**Figure 53**) until the correct amount of lever free play is obtained at the hand lever. Tighten the locknut.

3. After adjustment is complete, check that the locknuts are tight on both ends of the cable and the lock bolt is tight on the left-hand side of the engine.

4. Test ride the bike and make sure the clutch is operating correctly.

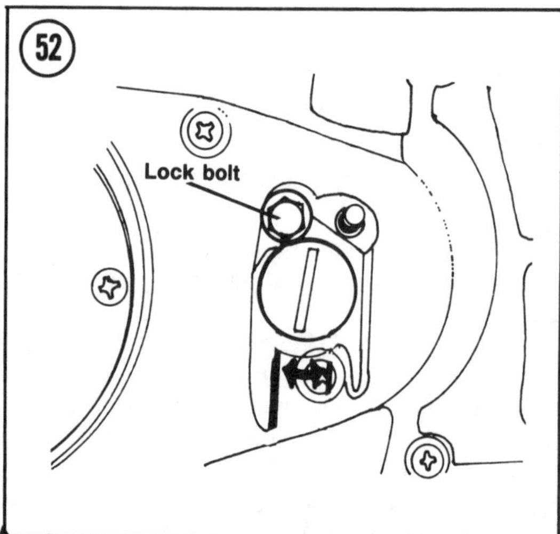

TL250 models

1. Slide back the rubber protective boot at the hand lever.

2. Loosen the locknut (**Figure 50**) and turn the adjuster barrel all the way in toward the hand lever. Tighten the locknut.

3. On the left-hand side of the engine, loosen the locknut and turn the adjusting nut (**Figure 54**) on the lower end of the cable all the way toward the cable sheath. Tighten the locknut.

4. On the left-hand side of the engine, remove the rubber cap (**Figure 55**). Loosen the locknut and

turn the adjusting bolt clockwise until it stops. Turn the adjusting bolt counterclockwise 1/2-1 full turn and tighten the locknut.

NOTE

*A special Honda tool (**Figure 56**) was made for this adjustment. One may still be available from a Honda dealer. A small crescent wrench or open-end ignition wrench may be substituted.*

5. Install the rubber cap; align its arrow with the index mark on the left-hand crankcase cover (**Figure 57**).
6. For additional adjustment there is an adjuster at each end of the clutch cable.
   a. At the hand lever, slide back the rubber protective boot and loosen the locknut. Screw the adjuster barrel (**Figure 50**) until the correct amount of free play is obtained at the tip of the lever. Tighten the locknut.
   b. At the clutch actuating lever, loosen the locknut and turn the adjusting nut (**Figure 54**) until the correct amount of free play is obtained at the hand lever. Tighten the locknut.
7. After adjustment is complete, check that the locknuts are tight on both the hand lever and at the right-hand side of the engine.
8. Test ride the bike and make sure the clutch is operating correctly.

XL125, CT125, 1979-on CB125S, XL250 and XL350 models

1. Slide back the rubber protective boot at the hand lever.
2. Loosen the locknut and screw in the adjuster barrel (**Figure 50**) until the correct amount of free play is obtained at the tip of the lever. Tighten the locknut.

NOTE

If the proper amount of free play cannot be achieved at the hand lever, additional adjustment can be made close to the clutch actuating lever on the right-hand side of the engine.

3. At the hand lever, loosen the locknut and turn the adjuster barrel all the way in toward the hand lever. Tighten the locknut.
4. On the left-hand side of the engine, loosen the locknut and turn the adjuster barrel (**Figure 58**) until the correct amount of lever free play is obtained. Tighten the locknut.
5. If necessary, repeat Step 1 for fine adjustment.

3

6. After adjustment is complete, check that the locknuts are tight on both the hand lever and at the right-hand side of the engine.
7. Test ride the bike and make sure the clutch is operating correctly.

Throttle Adjustment and Operation

The throttle grip should have 10-15° of rotational free play. If adjustment is necessary, slide back the rubber boot if used, loosen the locknut (**Figure 59**) and turn the adjuster in or out to achieve proper free play rotation. Tighten the locknut.

If the proper amount of free play cannot be accomplished at the throttle grip there is an additional adjustment point at the carburetor. Remove the seat and remove the fuel tank as described in Chapter Seven. Loosen the locknut and turn the adjuster to achieve the proper amount of free play. Tighten the locknut.

Check the throttle cable(s) from grip to carburetor. Make sure it is not kinked or chafed. Replace as necessary.

Make sure the throttle grip rotates freely from a fully closed to fully open position. Check with the handlebar at center, at full right and at full left. If necessary, remove the throttle grip and apply a lithium base grease to it.

Air Filter Element Cleaning

The air filter element should be removed and cleaned at the interval shown in **Table 1**.

The air filter removes dust and abrasive particles before the air enters the carburetor and engine. Without the air filter, very fine particles could enter into the engine and cause rapid wear of the piston rings, cylinder and bearings. They also might clog small passages in the carburetor. Never run the bike without the element installed.

Proper air filter servicing can ensure long service from your engine.

The following procedure is a typical for all models covered in this book. All air filters are located on the right-hand side of the bike.

1. Place the bike on the side stand.
2. Remove the right-hand side cover.
3. Remove the screws (or nuts) securing the air filter cover (**Figure 60**) and remove the cover.
4. On models so equipped, also remove the clamping band (**Figure 61**) and remove the air filter inlet from the carburetor.
5. On models so equipped, remove the element spring holder (**Figure 62**) and remove the element from the air box.

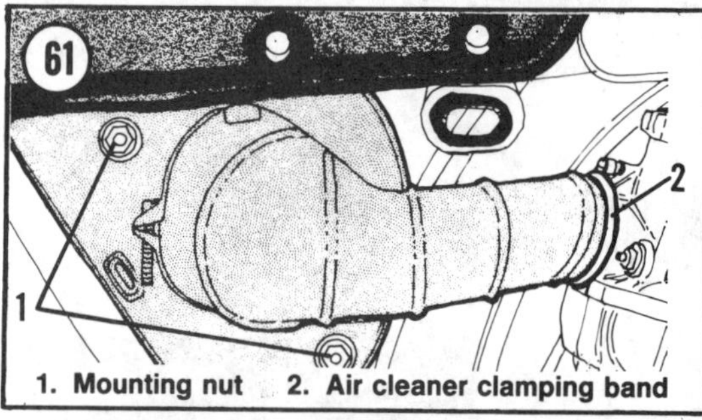

1. Mounting nut 2. Air cleaner clamping band

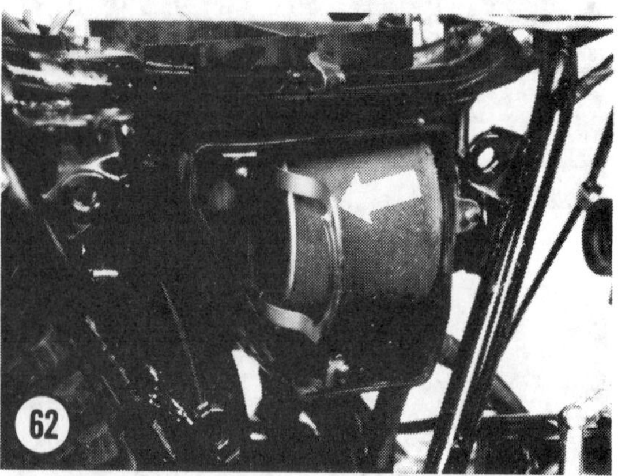

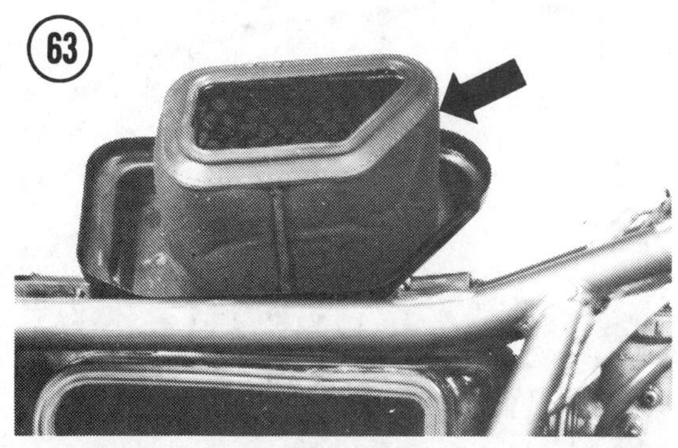

(63)

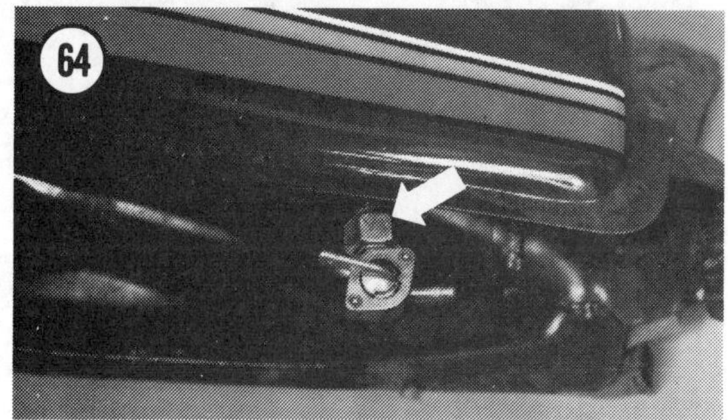

(64)

6. Remove the air filter element from the holder (**Figure 63**).
7. Wipe out the interior of the air box with a shop rag and cleaning solvent. Remove any foreign matter that may have passed through a broken element.
8. Clean the element gently in cleaning solvent until all dirt is removed. Thoroughly dry in a clean shop cloth until all solvent residue is removed. Let it dry for about one hour.

NOTE
Inspect the element; if it is torn or broken in any area it should be replaced. Do not run with a damaged element as it may allow dirt to enter the engine.

9. Pour a small amount of SAE 80 or 90 gear oil or special foam air filter oil onto the element and work it into the porous foam material. Do not oversaturate the element as too much oil will restrict air flow. The element will be discolored by the oil and should have an even color indicating that the oil is distributed evenly.

CAUTION
If foam air filter oil is used, let the element dry for another hour prior to installation. If installed too soon, the chemical carrier in the oil will be drawn into the engine and may cause damage.

10. Install the element onto the element holder.
11. Apply a light coat of multipurpose grease to the inside sealing edge of the element where it seats against the air box.
12. Install the element and holder into the air box. Make sure that the element is properly seated against the air box.

CAUTION
An improperly seated element will allow dirt and grit to enter the carburetor and engine, causing expensive engine damage.

13. On models so equipped, inspect the sealing gasket on the air box or side cover. Replace if damaged. Apply a light coat of multipurpose grease to the sealing edge of the gasket. This will provide a good airtight seal between the element and the side cover.
14. Install the air cleaner cover and tighten the screws (or nuts) securely.
15. On models so equipped, install the air cleaner inlet and clamping band (**Figure 61**) onto the carburetor.
16. Install the right-hand side cover.

Fuel Shutoff Valve and Filter Cleaning (1979-on CB125S and 1977-1978 XL350)

The integral fuel filter in the fuel shutoff valve removes particles in the fuel which might otherwise enter the carburetor. Such particles could cause the float needle to stay in the open position or clog one of the jets.

1. Turn the fuel shutoff valve to the OFF position and remove the fuel line from the valve.

NOTE
The fuel tank can either be removed or left in place; drain all fuel from it in either case.

2. Install a longer piece of clean fuel line to the valve and place the loose end into a clean, sealable metal container. If the fuel is kept clean, it can be reused.
3. Turn the fuel shutoff valve to the RES position and open the fuel filler cap. This will speed up the flow of fuel. Drain the tank completely.
4. Unscrew the locknut (**Figure 64**) securing the fuel shutoff valve to the fuel tank and remove the valve.
5. After removing the valve, insert a corner of a clean shop rag into the opening in the tank to stop the dribbling of fuel onto the engine and frame.

6. Remove the fuel filter from the shutoff valve. Clean it with a medium soft toothbrush and blow out with compressed air. Replace if it is defective.
7. Install by reversing these removal steps. Do not forget to install the gasket between the valve and the tank. Check for fuel leakage after installation is completed.

Fuel Shutoff Valve and Filter Cleaning (All Other Models)

1. Turn the fuel shutoff valve to the S position.
2. Unscrew the fuel filter bowl or cap (**Figure 65**) from the base of the fuel shutoff valve.
3. Remove the fuel filter from the filter bowl.
4. Clean the filter with a medium soft toothbrush and blow out with compressed air. Replace if it is defective.
5. Inspect the O-ring seal for damage or deterioration; replace if necessary.
6. Install the O-ring seal and the fuel filter onto the filter bowl. Insert this assembly into the fuel shutoff valve and tighten securely.
7. Turn the fuel shutoff valve to the ON position and check for fuel leakage. If fuel is leaking, tighten the bowl or replace the O-ring seal.

Fuel Line Inspection

Inspect the fuel line from the fuel tank to the carburetor. If it is cracked or starting to deteriorate it must be replaced. Make sure the small hose clamps are in place and holding securely.

WARNING
A damaged or deteriorated fuel line presents a very dangerous fire hazard to both the rider and the bike if fuel should spill onto a hot engine or exhaust pipe.

Crankcase Breather (1979-on U.S. Models Only)

To clean out the breather system, remove the drain plug and drain out all residue from the hose line at the interval indicated in **Table 1**. This operation should be performed more often if a considerable amount of riding is done at full throttle or in the rain.

Install the drain plug; make sure the clamp is tight.

Refer to Chapter Seven for complete details on the breather system.

Wheel Bearings

There is no factory recommended mileage interval for cleaning and repacking the wheel

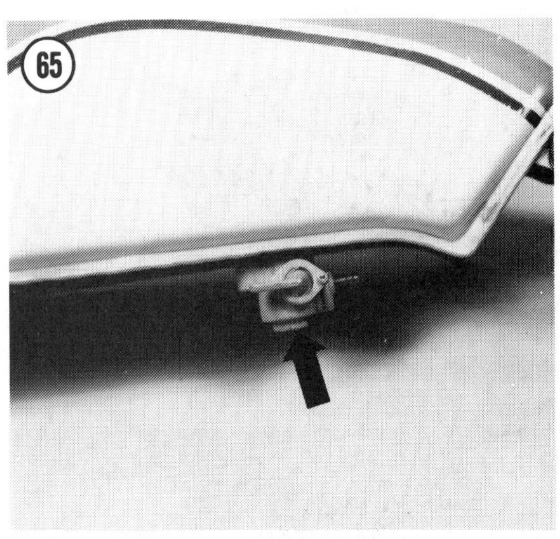

bearings. They should be serviced whenever they are removed from the wheel hub or whenever there is the likelihood of water contamination. The correct service procedures are covered in Chapter Nine and Chapter Ten.

Steering Head Adjustment Check

The steering head is fitted with loose ball bearings. It should be checked at the interval indicated in **Table 1**.

Place a milk crate or wood block(s) so that the front wheel is off the ground. Hold onto the front fork tubes and gently rock the fork assembly back and forth. If you can feel looseness, refer to Chapter Nine.

Wheel Hubs, Rims and Spokes

Check wheel hubs and rims for bends and other signs of damage. Check both wheels for broken or bent spokes. Replace damaged or broken spokes as described in Chapter Nine.

Pluck each spoke with your finger like a guitar string or tap each one lightly with a small hammer. All spokes should emit the same sound. A spoke that is too tight will have a higher pitch than the others; one that is too loose will have a lower pitch. If only one or two spokes are slightly out of adjustment, adjust them with a spoke wrench made for this purpose. If more are affected, the wheel should be removed and trued. Refer in Chapter Nine.

Front Suspension Check

1. Apply the front brake and pump the forks up and down as vigorously as possible. Check for smooth operation and check for any oil leaks.

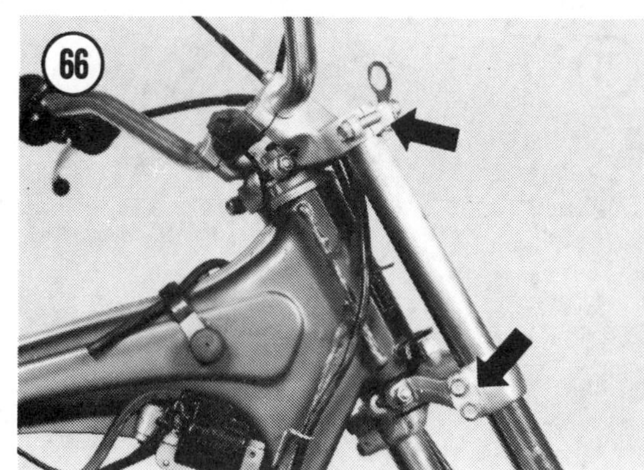

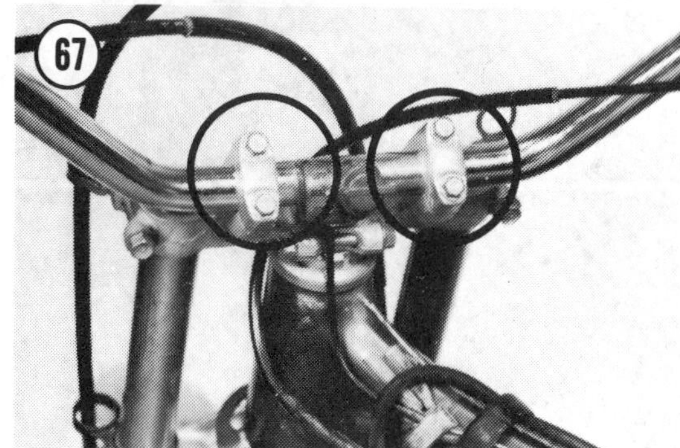

2. Make sure the upper and lower fork bridge bolts (**Figure 66**) are tight.
3. Check the tightness of the handlebar holder bolts (**Figure 67**).
4A. On models so equipped, check that the 4 nuts securing the front axle holder are tight.
4B. On all other models, make sure the front axle nut (**Figure 68**) is tight and that the cotter pin is in place.

CAUTION
If any of the previously mentioned bolts and nuts are loose, refer to Chapter Nine for correct procedures and torque specifications.

Rear Suspension Check

1. Place a wood block(s) under the engine to support it securely with the rear wheel off of the ground.
2. Push hard on the rear wheel (sideways) to check for side play in the swing arm bushings.
3. Check the tightness of the upper and lower shock absorber mounting bolts and nuts (**Figure 69**).
4. Make sure the rear axle nut is tight and the cotter pin is in place (A, **Figure 70**).
5. Check the tightness of the rear brake torque arm bolts (B, **Figure 70**). Make sure the cotter pin is in place.

CAUTION
If any of the previously mentioned bolts and nuts are loose, refer to Chapter Ten for correct procedures and torque specifications.

Nuts, Bolts and Other Fasteners

Constant vibration can loosen many of the fasteners on the motorcycle. Check the tightness of all fasteners, especially those on:

a. Engine mounting hardware.
b. Engine crankcase covers.
c. Handlebar and front forks.
d. Gearshift lever.
e. Kickstarter lever.
f. Brake pedal and lever.
g. Exhaust system.

Side Stand Rubber

On models so equipped, the rubber tip on the side stand kicks the side stand up if you should forget. If it wears down to the molded line, it will no longer be effective and must be replaced. Remove the bolt and replace the rubber tip with a new one.

ENGINE TUNE-UP

A tune-up is general adjustment and maintenance to ensure peak engine performance. A complete tune-up should be performed at the interval listed in **Table 1**. More frequent tune-ups may be required if the bike is ridden primarily in stop-and-go traffic.

Table 8 summarizes tune-up specifications.

The spark plug should be routinely replaced at every other tune-up or if the electrodes show signs of erosion. Have new parts on hand before you begin.

Because different systems in an engine interact, the procedures should be done in the following order:

a. Clean or replace the air filter element.
b. Adjust camshaft chain tension.
c. Adjust valve clearance.
d. Run a compression test.
e. Check or replace the spark plug.
f. Check and adjust the ignition timing.
g. Adjust the carburetor idle speed.

To perform a tune-up on your Honda, you will need the following tools and equipment:

a. Spark plug wrench.
b. Socket wrench and assorted sockets.
c. Flat feeler gauge.
d. Spark plug wire feeler gauge and gapper tool.
e. Compression gauge.
f. Ignition timing light.
g. Portable tachometer.

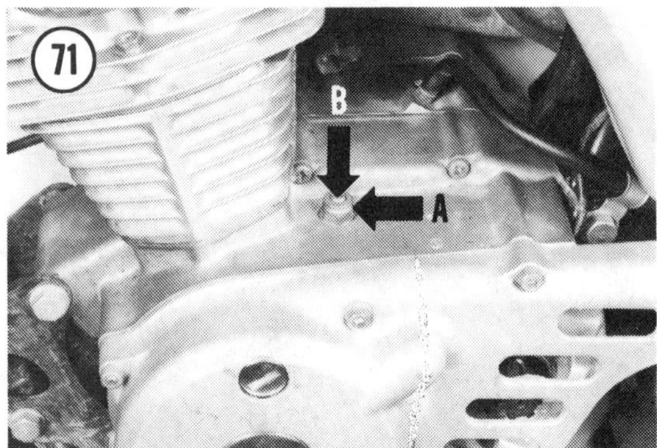

Air Filter Element

The element should be cleaned or replaced as described in this chapter prior to doing other tune-up procedures.

Camshaft Chain Tensioner Adjustment

In time, the camshaft chain and guide will wear and develop slack. This will cause engine noise and, if neglected too long, will cause engine damage. The chain tension should be adjusted as indicated in **Table 1** or whenever it becomes noisy.

CB100, CL100, SL100, 1969-1975 CB125S and 1969-1975 TL125

1. Place the bike on the side stand.
2. Loosen the locknut (A, **Figure 71**). It is located on the upper left-hand side of the crankcase just behind the cylinder.
3. Turn the adjusting screw (B, **Figure 71**) counterclockwise 1-2 full turns.
4. Turn the adjusting screw clockwise until resistance is felt.
5. Tighten the locknut.

(73)

(74)

XL100, XL125 and CT125

1. Place the bike on the side stand.
2. Start the engine and let it reach normal operating temperature. Shut off the engine.
3. Connect a portable tachometer following the manufacturer's instructions.
4. Restart the engine and let it idle at 1,300 ±100 rpm.
5. Loosen the locknut (A, **Figure 71**). It is located on the upper left-hand side of the crankcase just behind the cylinder.
6. Turn the adjusting screw (B, **Figure 71**) counterclockwise if the cam chain is noisy (too loose) or clockwise if the cam chain is whining (too tight). Turn the adjuster in either direction until the cam chain is operating quietly.
7. Tighten the locknut.
8. Turn the engine off and disconnect the portable tachometer.

1976-on CB125S, 1976 TL125

1. Place the bike on the side stand.
2. Start the engine and let it reach normal operating temperature. Shut off the engine.
3. Connect a portable tachometer following the manufacturer's instructions.
4. Remove the rubber cap covering the adjuster bolt assembly. It is located on the upper left-hand side of the crankcase just behind the cylinder.
5. Restart the engine and let it idle at 1,300 ±100 rpm.
6. Loosen the lower adjuster bolt (**Figure 72**). Retighten the adjuster bolt to 15-22 N•m (11-16 ft.-lb.).

NOTE
Do not loosen the upper 6 mm bolt as engine oil will spurt out.

7. Turn the engine off and disconnect the portable tachometer.
8. Install the rubber boot.

XL175, TL250, XL250 and XL350

1. Place the bike on the side stand.
2. Start the engine and let it reach normal operating temperature. Shut off the engine.
3. Remove the alternator inspection cover and the valve adjustment covers.
4. On models so equipped, remove the rubber cover on the cam chain tensioner assembly.
5. Remove the spark plug (this will make it easier to rotate the engine).
6. Rotate the crankshaft with the nut on the alternator rotor. Turn it *counterclockwise* until the piston is at top dead center (TDC) on the compression stroke.

NOTE
A cylinder at TDC of its compression stroke will have free play in both of its rocker arms, indicating that both the intake and exhaust valves are closed.

7. Make sure the "T" mark on the alternator rotor aligns with the fixed notch in the crankcase (**Figure 73**).
8. If both rocker arms are not loose with the engine timing mark on the "T," rotate the engine an additional 180° until both valves have free play.
9. Have an assisant hold the alternator rotor on the "T" mark.
10. Loosen the cam chain adjuster locknut and then loosen the cam chain adjuster bolt (**Figure 74**). The tensioner will automatically adjust. Tighten the locknut.
11. Leave the spark plug, the alternator inspection cover and the valve adjustment covers off if you are continuing with a tune-up. Otherwise, install these parts.

3

12. On models so equipped, install the rubber cover on the cam chain tensioner assembly.

Valve Clearance Adjustment

Valve clearance adjustment must be made with the engine cool, at room temperature—below 35° C (95° F). For correct intake and exhaust valve clearance for all models refer to **Table 8.**

The exhaust valve is located at the front of the engine (near the exhaust pipe) and the intake valve is at the rear of the engine (near the carburetor).

NOTE
In the following procedure, 3 engines are shown. Some are shown removed from the frame for clarity.

1. Place the bike on the side stand.
2. Remove the seat and remove the fuel tank as described in Chapter Seven.
3. Remove both valve adjustment covers (**Figure 75**).
4. Disconnect the spark plug lead and remove the spark plug. This will make it easier to rotate the engine.
5. Remove the alternator inspection cover and gasket (**Figure 76**).
6. Rotate the crankshaft with the nut or bolt on the alternator rotor. Turn it *counterclockwise* until the piston is at top dead center (TDC) on the compression stroke.

NOTE
A cylinder at TDC of its compression stroke will have free play in both of its rocker arms, indicating that both the intake and exhaust valves are closed.

7. Make sure the "T" mark on the alternator rotor aligns with the fixed notch in the crankcase (**Figure 77**).
8. If both rocker arms are not loose with the engine timing mark on the "T," rotate the engine an additional 180° until all valves have free play.
9. Check the clearance of both the intake and exhaust valves by inserting a flat feeler gauge between the rocker arm pad and the camshaft lobe. When the clearance is correct, there will be a slight resistance on the feeler gauge when it is inserted and withdrawn.
10. To correct the clearance, use the valve adjusting wrench or a small open-end wrench (**Figure 78**) and back off the locknut. Screw the adjuster in or out until there is a slight resistance felt on the feeler gauge. Hold the adjuster to prevent it from turning further and tighten the locknut securely. Then recheck the clearance to make sure the adjuster did not slip when the locknut was tightened. Readjust if necessary.

NOTE
On 250 and 350 cc engines, adjust all 4 valves to the correct clearance.

11. Rotate the engine 360° and repeat Step No. 10 to make sure the adjustment is correct. If the clearance is still not correct, repeat Step No. 10.
12. Inspect the rubber gasket on each valve adjusting cover. Replace if they are starting to deteriorate or harden. Replace as a set even if only one is bad. Install both covers and tighten securely.
13. Leave the spark plug and alternator inspection cover off if you are continuing with a tune-up. Otherwise, install them.

Compression Test

A compression test should be run at the interval listed in **Table 1**. This test requires a compression gauge as described in Chapter One.

Record the results and compare them with the test readings at the next test interval. A running record will show trends in deterioration so that corrective action can be taken before complete failure occurs to a given set of parts.

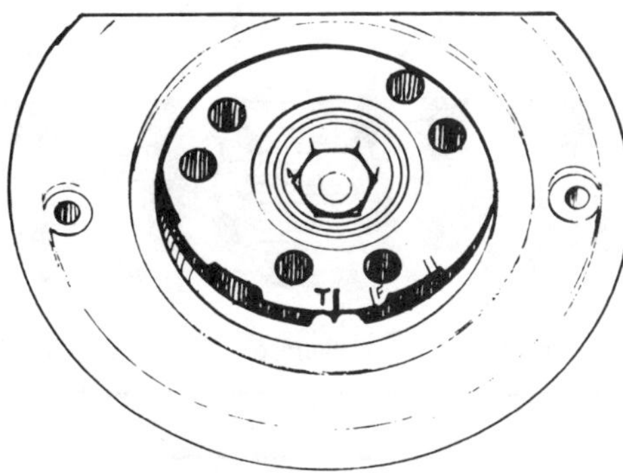

CB100, CL100, SL100,
1973-1980 CB125S,
SL125, XL100, XL175

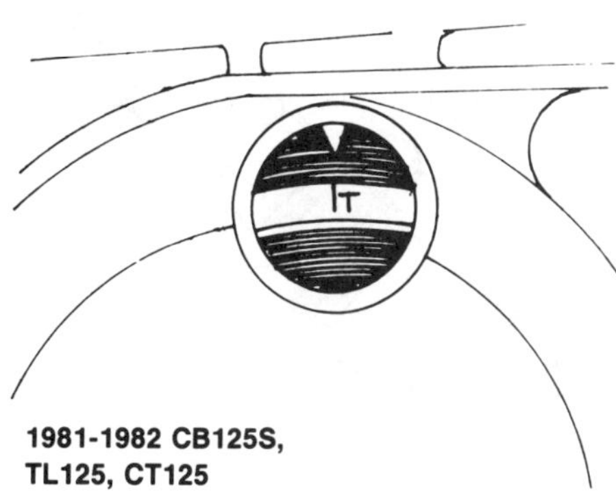

1981-1982 CB125S,
TL125, CT125

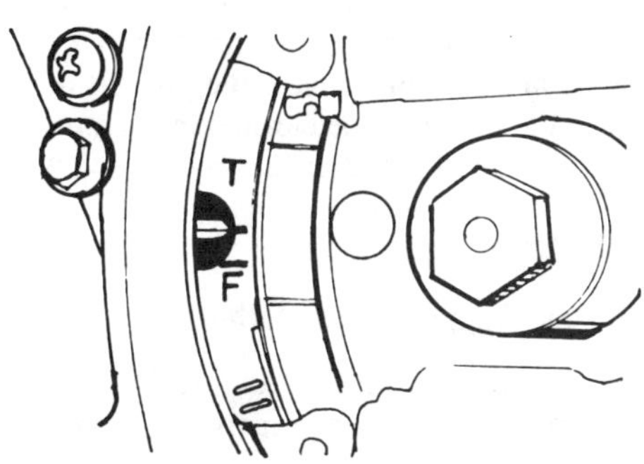

TL250, XL250, XL350

The results, when properly interpreted, can indicate general cylinder, piston ring and valve condition.

1. Place the bike on the side stand.
2. Start the engine and let it reach normal operating temperature. Shut the engine off.
3. Fully open the throttle lever and move the choke lever or knob all the way to the completely open position.
4. Disconnect the spark plug wire and remove the spark plug.
5. Connect a compression gauge to the cylinder following the manufacturer's instructions.
6. Operate the kickstarter several times and check the readings.

CAUTION

On 1981-on CB125S models, do not turn the engine over more than absolutely necessary. When the spark plug lead is disconnected the electronic ignition will produce the highest voltage possible and the ignition coil may overheat and be damaged.

7. Remove the compression gauge and record the reading. Standard compression pressures are listed in **Table 8**.

If the reading is higher than normal, there may be a buildup of carbon deposits in the combustion chamber or on the piston crown.

If a low reading (10% or more) is obtained it can be caused by one or more of the following items:

a. A leaking cylinder head gasket.
b. Incorrect valve clearance.
c. Valve leakage (burned valve face).
d. Worn or broken piston ring(s).

If the head gasket is okay, determine which other component is faulty by performing a "wet" test. To do this, pour about one teaspoon of engine oil through the spark plug hole onto the top of the piston.

Turn the engine over once to distribute the oil, then take another compression reading. If the compression increases significantly, the valves are good but the piston rings are defective. If compression does not increase, the valves require servicing. A valve could be hanging open but not burned or a piece of carbon could be on a valve seat.

Leave a spark plug out if you are continuing with a tune-up. Otherwise, install it.

Correct Spark Plug Heat Range

Spark plugs are available in various heat ranges, hotter or colder than the plugs originally installed at the factory.

Select a plug of the heat range designed for the loads and conditions under which the bike will be run. The use of an incorrect heat range spark plug can cause a seized piston, scored cylinder wall or damaged piston crown.

In general, use a hot plug for low speeds and low temperatures. Use a cold plug for high speeds, high engine loads and high temperatures. The plug should operate hot enough to burn off unwanted deposits, but not so hot that it is damaged or causes preignition. A spark plug of the correct heat range will show a light tan color on the portion of the insulator within the cylinder after the plug has been in service.

The reach (length) of a plug is also important. A longer than normal plug could interfere with the piston, causing permanent and severe damage; refer to **Figure 79**. Refer to **Table 8** for recommended spark plug heat ranges.

Spark Plug Removal/Cleaning

1. Grasp the spark plug lead as near the plug as possible and pull it off the plug. If it is stuck to the plug, twist it slightly to break it loose.
2. Blow away any dirt that has accumulated in the spark plug well.

CAUTION
The dirt could fall into the cylinder when the plug is removed, causing serious engine damage.

3. Remove the spark plug with a spark plug wrench.

NOTE
If the plug is difficult to remove, apply penetrating oil, such as WD-40 or Liquid Wrench around the base of the plug and let it soak in about 10-20 minutes.

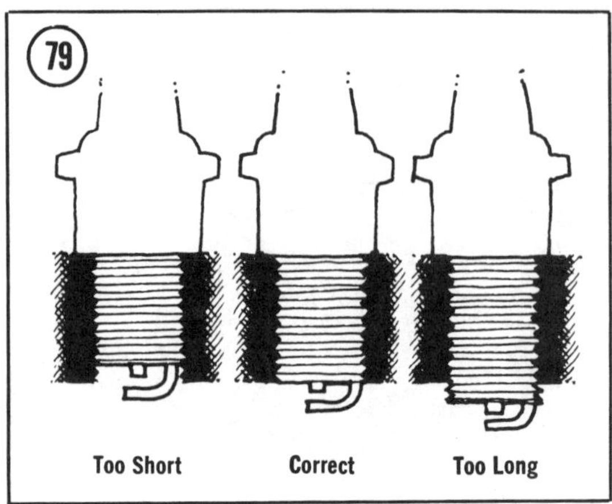

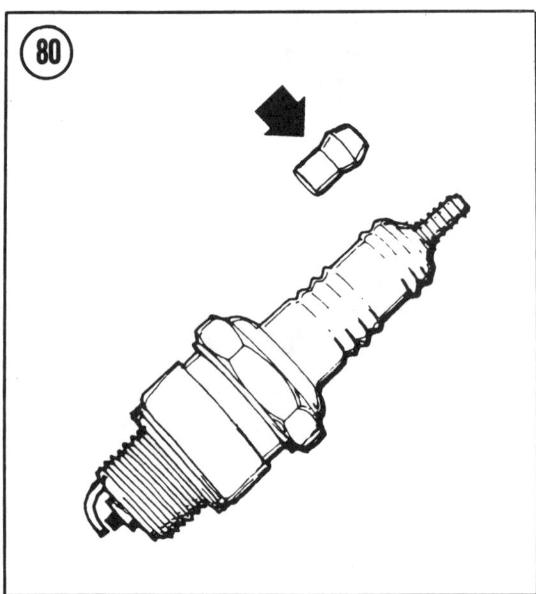

4. Inspect the plug carefully. Look for a broken center porcelain, excessively eroded electrodes and excessive carbon or oil fouling. If any of these problems are present, replace the plug. If deposits are light, the plug may be cleaned in solvent with a wire brush or cleaned in a special spark plug sandblast cleaner. Regap the plug as explained in this chapter.

Spark Plug Gapping/ Installation

A spark plug should be carefully gapped to ensure a reliable, consistent spark. You must use a special spark plug gapping tool and a wire feeler gauge.

1. Remove the new spark plug from its box. *Do not* screw on the small piece that is loose in the box **(Figure 80)**; it is not used.

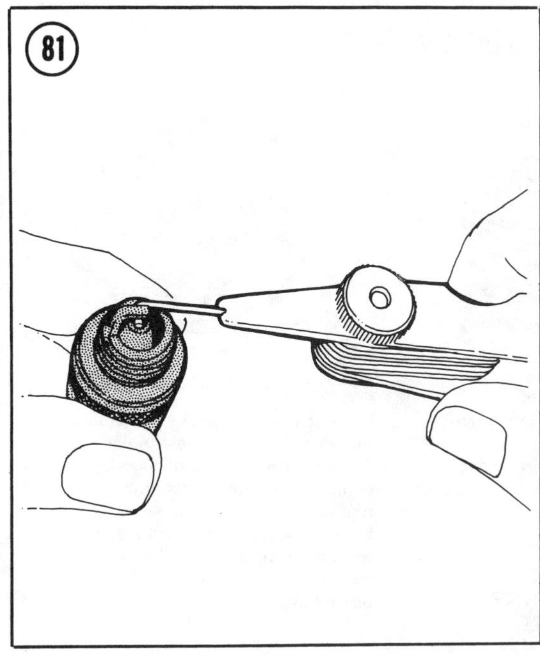

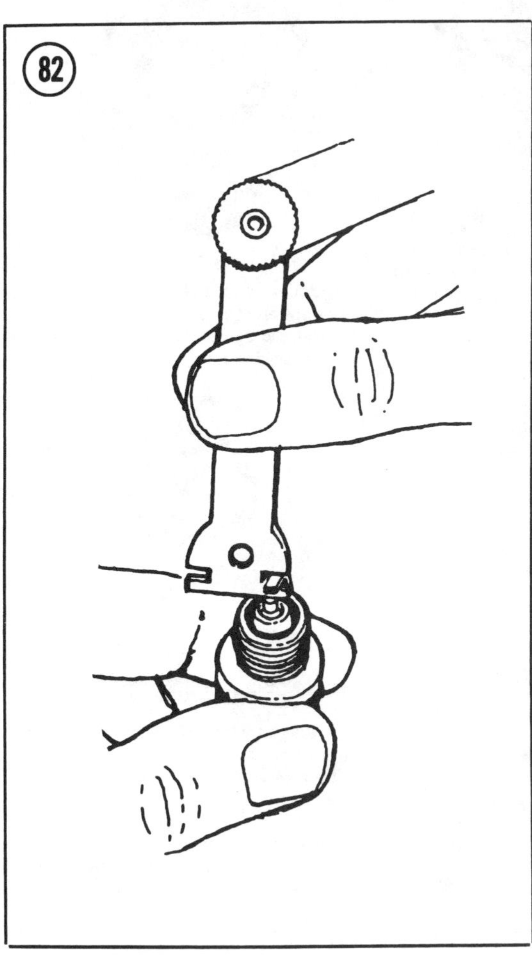

2. Insert a wire feeler gauge between the center and side electrode of the plug (**Figure 81**). The correct gap is listed in **Table 8**. If the gap is correct, you will feel a slight drag as you pull the wire through. If there is no drag, or the gauge won't pass through, bend the side electrode with a gapping tool (**Figure 82**) to set the proper gap.
3. Put a small drop of oil on the threads of the spark plug.
4. Screw the spark plug in by hand until it seats. Very little effort is required. If force is necessary, you have the plug cross threaded; unscrew it and try again.
5. Use a spark plug wrench and tighten the plug an additional 1/4 to 1/2 turn after the gasket has made contact with the head. If you are installing an old, regapped plug and reusing the old gasket, only tighten an additional 1/4 turn.

NOTE
Do not overtighten. This will only squash the gasket and destroy its sealing ability.

6. Install the spark plug lead; make sure it is on tight.

Reading Spark Plugs

Much information about engine and spark plug performance can be determined by careful examination of the spark plug. This information is more valid after performing the following steps.
1. Ride the bike a short distance at full throttle in any gear.
2. Turn the ignition switch to the OFF position before closing the throttle and simultaneously shift to NEUTRAL; coast and brake to a stop.
3. Remove the spark plug and examine it. Compare it to **Figure 83** as follows:
   a. If the insulator is white or burned, the plug is too hot and should be replaced with a colder one.
   b. A too-cold plug will have sooty or oily deposits ranging in color from dark brown to black. Replace with a hotter plug and check for too-rich carburetion or evidence of oil blow-by at the piston rings.
   c. If the plug has a light tan or gray colored deposit and no abnormal gap wear or electrode erosion is evident, the plug and the engine are running properly.
   d. If the plug exhibits a black insulator tip, a damp and oily film over the firing end and a carbon layer over the entire nose, it is oil

3

SPARK PLUG CONDITION

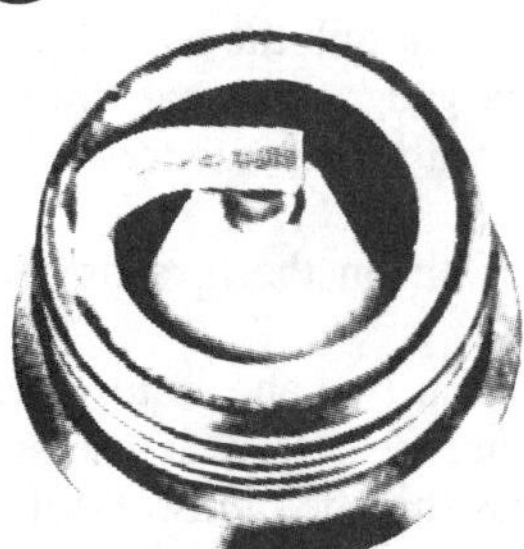

NORMAL

- Identified by light tan or gray deposits on the firing tip.
- Can be cleaned.

GAP BRIDGED

- Identified by deposit buildup closing gap between electrodes.
- Caused by oil or carbon fouling. If deposits are not excessive, the plug can be cleaned.

OIL FOULED

- Identified by wet black deposits on the insulator shell bore and electrodes.
- Caused by excessive oil entering combustion chamber through worn rings and pistons, excessive clearance between valve guides and stems, or worn or loose bearings. Can be cleaned. If engine is not repaired, use a hotter plug.

CARBON FOULED

- Identified by black, dry fluffy carbon deposits on insulator tips, exposed shell surfaces and electrodes.
- Caused by too cold a plug, weak ignition, dirty air cleaner, too rich a fuel mixture, or excessive idling. Can be cleaned.

LEAD FOULED

- Identified by dark gray, black, yellow, or tan deposits or a fused glazed coating on the insulator tip.
- Caused by highly leaded gasoline. Can be cleaned.

WORN

- Identified by severely eroded or worn electrodes.
- Caused by normal wear. Should be replaced.

FUSED SPOT DEPOSIT

- Identified by melted or spotty deposits resembling bubbles or blisters.
- Caused by sudden acceleration. Can be cleaned.

OVERHEATING

- Identified by a white or light gray insulator with small black or gray brown spots and with bluish-burnt appearance of electrodes.
- Caused by engine overheating, wrong type of fuel, loose spark plugs, too hot a plug, or incorrect ignition timing. Replace the plug.

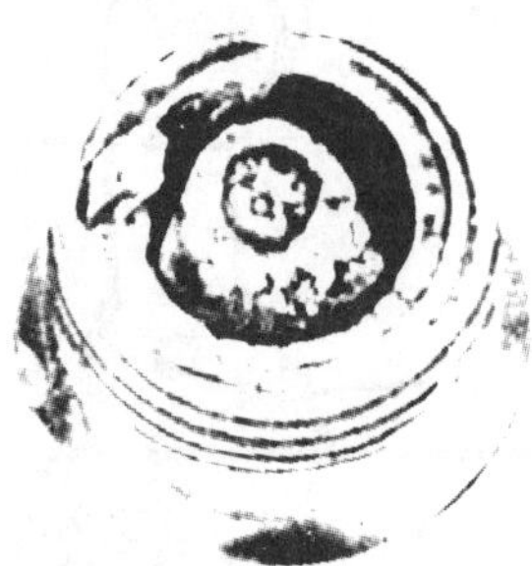

PREIGNITION

- Identified by melted electrodes and possibly blistered insulator. Metallic deposits on insulator indicate engine damage.
- Caused by wrong type of fuel, incorrect ignition timing or advance, too hot a plug, burned valves, or engine overheating. Replace the plug.

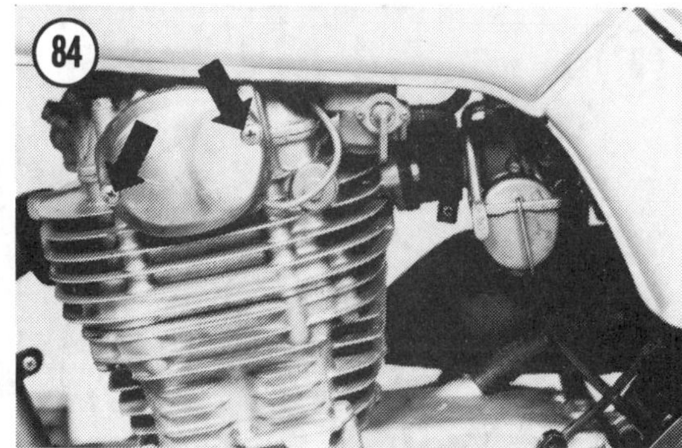

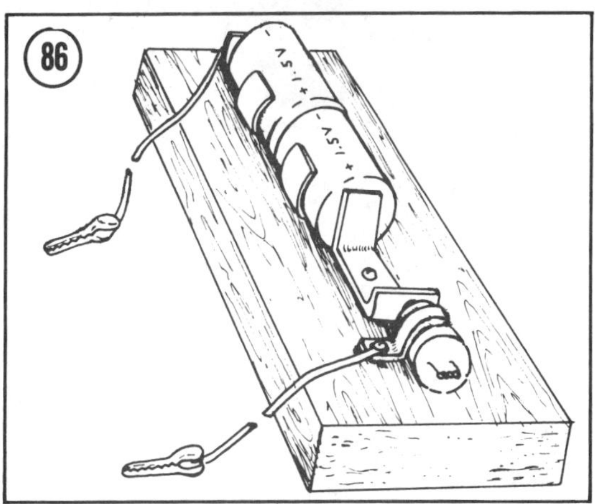

fouled. An oil fouled plug can be cleaned, but it is better to replace it.

Contact Breaker Point Adjustment

NOTE
Contact breaker point ignition is used on all models except the 1981-on CB125S. The electronic ignition system on that model is covered separately in this chapter.

The contact breaker point assembly is attached to the left-hand end of the camshaft in the cylinder head.

1. Place the bike on the side stand.
2. Shift the transmission into NEUTRAL.
3. Remove the spark plug. This will make it easier to rotate the engine.
4. Remove the screws (**Figure 84**) securing the contact breaker point cover and remove the cover and the gasket.
5. Remove the alternator inspection cover.
6. Rotate the crankshaft with the nut (or bolt) on the alternator *counterclockwise* until the point gap is at the maximum opening.
7. Insert a flat feeler gauge and measure the gap. Compare to **Table 8**.
8. If the gap is not within limits, loosen the contact breaker point attachment screws (A, **Figure 85**). Insert a screwdriver into the pry point (B, **Figure 85**) and move the point assembly until the gap is correct. Tighten the screws securely.

NOTE
Make sure the point assembly does not move while tightening the screw(s).

9. After tightening the screw(s), repeat Step 7 to make sure the gap is correct. Readjust if necessary.
10. Adjust the ignition timing as described in this chapter.

NOTE
*Ignition timing **must** be adjusted after the contact breaker point gap has been changed.*

Contact Breaker Point Replacement

Refer to Chapter Eight.

Static Ignition Timing Adjustment (Contact Breaker Point Ignition)

Static ignition timing is acceptable but if you have a stroboscopic timing light, dynamic timing (as described in this chapter) is more accurate. This procedure requires a test light unit. It can be a homemade unit (**Figure 86**) that consists of 2 "C" or "D" size flashlight batteries and a light bulb, all mounted on a piece of wood, some light gauge electrical wire and alligator clips. These items can be purchased from any hardware store.

The following procedure is based on the test light unit shown in **Figure 86**. If another type is used, follow the manufacturer's instructions.

1. Adjust the contact breaker point gap as described in this chapter.

NOTE
Prior to attaching the test light unit, check the condition of the batteries by touching the test leads together. The light should go on. If not, replace the batteries and/or the light bulb and check all electrcial connections on the tester. The test light unit must be operating correctly prior to using it.

2. Connect one lead of the test light unit to a good ground, such as one of the cooling fins on the cylinder, and the other to the contact breaker point electrical terminal (C, **Figure 85**). The test light should be on. If a commercial tester is used, follow the manufacturer's instructions.
3. Rotate the crankshaft with the nut (or bolt) on the alternator rotor *counterclockwise* until the "F" mark on the rotor aligns with the fixed pointer (**Figure 87**). At this exact moment the contact breaker points should just begin to open. If they open at this moment, the test light will dim indicating that the ignition timing is correct. If the timing is correct, proceed to Step 6.
4. To adjust the timing, loosen the contact breaker point base plate attachment screws (A, **Figure 85**). Insert a screwdriver into the pry point (B, **Figure 85**) on the outer perimeter of the base plate and slightly move the base plate assembly until the breaker points just begin to open. The light will dim when the points open; tighten the screws securely. Make sure the base plate assembly does not move while tightening the screws.

NOTE
*Rotating the base plate clockwise will **advance** the timing. Rotating the base plate counterclockwise will **retard** the timing.*

5. Repeat Step 3.
6. After the timing is correct, recheck the maximum point gap. Rotate the crankshaft with the nut (or bolt) on the alternator rotor *counterclockwise* until the point gap is at its maximum. Insert a flat feeler gauge and measure the gap. The gap should be within specifications (**Table 8**). If the minimum gap cannot be maintained when the ignition timing is correct the contact breaker point assembly is worn and must be replaced. Refer to Chapter Eight.

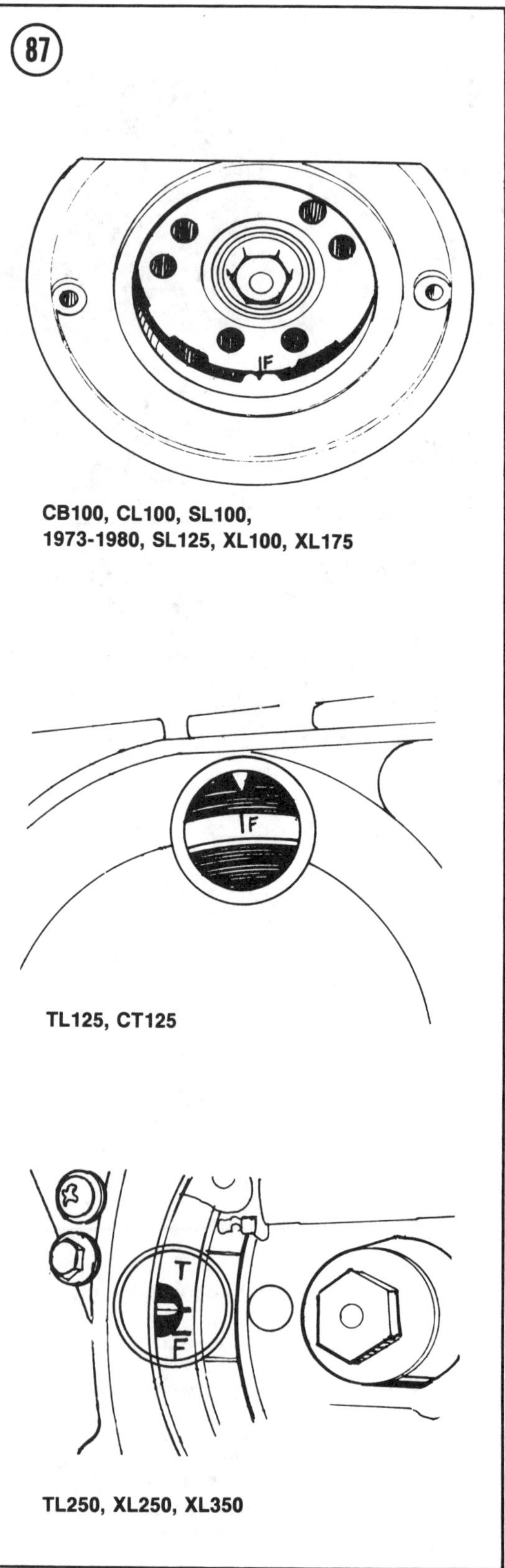

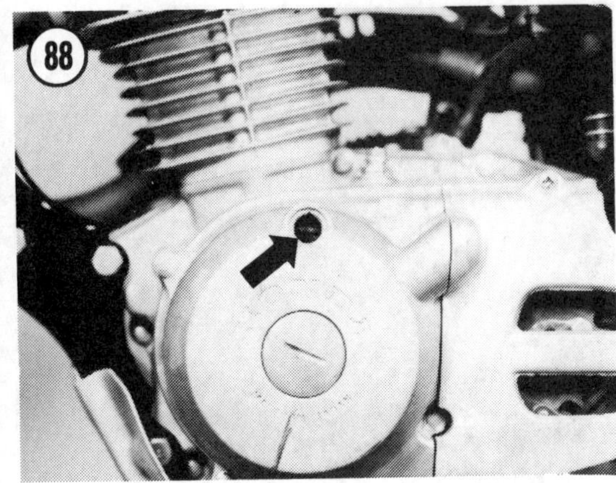

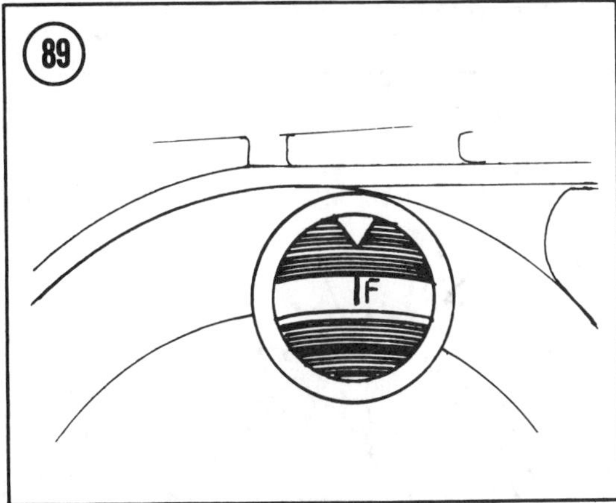

7. Disconnect the test light and install the contact breaker point cover and gasket. Install the alternator cover.
8. Install the spark plug and spark plug lead.

Dynamic Ignition Timing Adjustment (Contact Breaker Point Ignition)

Dynamic timing requires a stroboscopic timing light as described in Chapter One.

1. Perform *Contact Breaker Point Adjustment* as described in this chapter.
2. Start the engine and let it reach normal operating temperature. Turn the engine off.
3. Connect a portable tachometer and stroboscopic timing light following the manufacturer's instructions.
4. Restart the engine and let it idle at the rpm indicated in **Table 8**.
5. Adjust the idle speed, if necessary, as described in this chapter.
6. Shine the timing light at the alternator rotor and pull the trigger. The timing is correct if the "F" mark aligns with the fixed index mark (**Figure 87**).
7. If timing is incorrect, stop the engine and continue with this procedure.
8. To adjust the timing, loosen the contact breaker point attachment screw (A, **Figure 85**). Insert a screwdriver into the pry point (B, **Figure 85**) and slightly move the point assembly. Rotating the base plate clockwise will *advance* the timing. Rotating the base plate counterclockwise will *retard* the timing. Tighten the screw securely. Make sure the point assembly does not move while tightening the screw.
9. Repeat Step 6 and readjust, if necessary, until timing is correct.
10. Disconnect the timing light and portable tachometer.
11. Install all items removed.

Dynamic Ignition Timing (Electronic Ignition)

The 1981-on CB125S is equipped with a capacitor discharge ignition system (CDI). This system uses no breaker points, but timing does have to be checked as the base plate may move and alter timing. Faulty ignition system components can also affect timing. This system's timing can only be checked dynamically—there is no static method. Dynamic timing requires a stroboscopic timing light as described in Chapter One.

Incorrect ignition timing can cause a drastic loss of engine performance and efficiency. It may also cause overheating.

Before starting on this procedure, check all electrical connections related to the ignition system. Make sure all connections are tight and free from corrosion and that all ground connections are clean and tight.

1. Place the bike on the side stand.
2. Start the engine and let it reach normal operating temperature. Turn the engine off.
3. Remove the timing mark hole cap to expose the timing window (**Figure 88**).
4. Connect a portable tachometer following the manufacturer's instructions.
5. Connect a timing light following the manufacturer's instructions.
6. Restart the engine and let it idle at 1,300 ± 100 rpm.
7. Adjust the idle speed, if necessary, as described in this chapter.
8. Shine the timing light at the timing window and pull the trigger. The timing is correct if the "F" mark aligns with the fixed index mark (**Figure 89**).
9. If timing is correct, proceed to Step 13.
10. If timing is incorrect, stop the engine and align the timing marks (**Figure 89**).

3

11. Remove the pulse generator cover and gasket (**Figure 90**).

12. Loosen the screws securing the base plate (**Figure 91**). Rotate the base plate to align the index mark on the pulse generator with the index mark on the pulse rotor (**Figure 92**). Repeat Steps 6-8 and check if timing is now correct. If not, loosen the screws securing the base plate and rotate the base plate *clockwise* to advance the timing or *counterclockwise* to retard the timing. Tighten the screws, restart the engine and recheck the timing. Repeat this step until timing is corrrect. Be sure to tighten the screws securely.

NOTE
If correct timing cannot be achieved, inspect and test all ignition components as described in Chapter Eight.

13. Disconnect the timing light and portable tachometer.

14. Install the pulse generator cover and gasket and the timing mark hole cap.

Idle Mixture Adjustment

The idle mixture (pilot screw) is preset at the factory and *is not to be reset*. Do not adjust the pilot screw unless the carburetor has been overhauled. Refer to Chapter Seven.

Idle Speed Adjustment

Before making this adjustment, the air filter must be clean and the engine must have adequate compression. Otherwise, this procedure cannot be done properly.

1. Place the bike on the side stand.
2. Connect a portable tachometer following the manufacturer's instructions.
3. Start the engine and let it reach normal operating temperature.

91

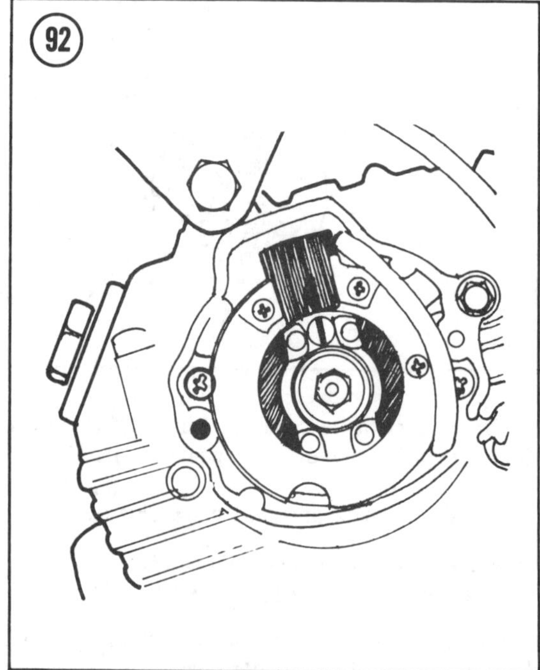

92

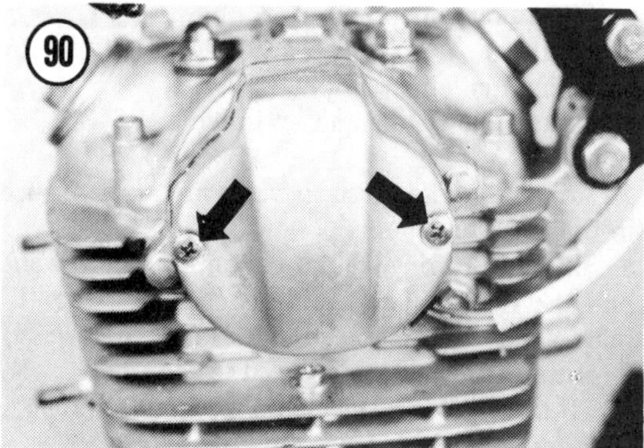

90

93

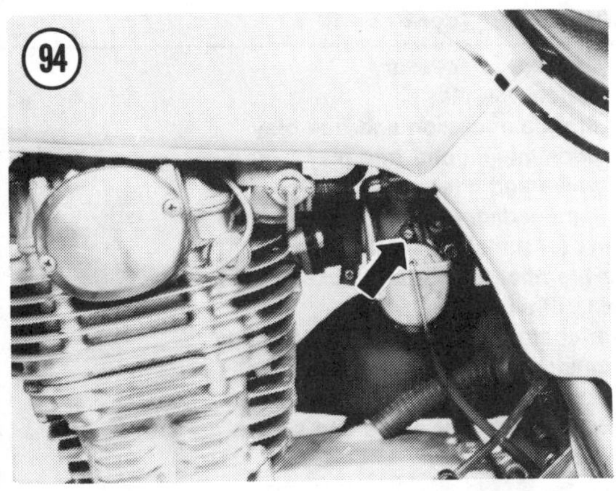
94

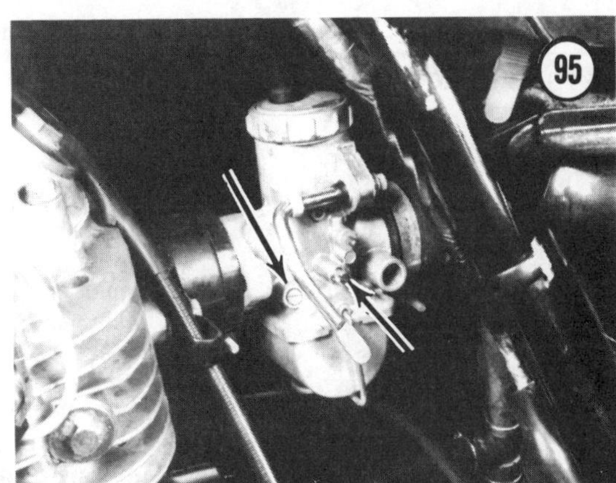
95

3

4. Set the idle speed by turning the idle speed adjust screw (**Figures 93-95**).

5. The correct idle speed is listed in **Table 8**.

6. Open and close the throttle a couple of times; check for variations in idle speed. Readjust if necessary.

WARNING
With the engine idling, move the handlebar from side to side. If idle speed increases during this movement, the throttle cable needs adjusting or may be incorrectly routed through the frame. Correct this problem immediately. Do not ride the bike in this unsafe condition.

7. Turn the engine off and disconnect the portable tachometer.

Table 1 MAINTENANCE SCHEDULE*

Every 300 miles (500 km) or when dry	
	• Lubricate and adjust the drive chain
Every 600 miles (1,000 km) or 6 months	
	• Check engine oil level
	• Check battery specific gravity and electrolyte level
	• Lubricate rear brake pedal and shift lever
	• Lubricate side stand pivot point
	• Inspect front steering for looseness
	• Check wheel bearings for smooth operation
	• Check wheel spoke condition
	• Check wheel runout
	• Check and adjust clutch lever free play
Every 1,500 miles (2,500 km)	
	• Change engine oil
	• Clean and inspect air cleaner element
Every 3,000 miles (5,000 km)	
	• Check and adjust valve clearance
	• Check and adjust contact breaker points
	• Adjust the cam chain tension
	• Check and adjust ignition timing
	• Check and adjust the carburetor

(continued)

Table 1 MAINTENANCE SCHEDULE* (continued)

Every 3,000 miles (5,000 km)	• Inspect spark plug, regap if necessary • Check and adjust clutch free play • Check and adjust throttle operation and free play • Adjust rear brake pedal height and free play • Clean fuel shutoff valve and filter • Check and adjust the headlight aim • Inspect brake shoes (or pads) for wear • Inspect crankcase breather hoses for cracks or loose hose clamps, drain out all residue • Inspect fuel line for chafed, cracked or swollen ends • Check engine mounting bolts for tightness • Check all suspension components • Inspect all drive chain, roller tensioners and sliders • Lubricate control cables
Every 6,000 miles (10,000 km)	• Remove and clean centrifugal oil filter rotor • Remove and clean oil screen on drain plug • Adjust steering head bearings • Change front fork oil • Inspect wheel bearings • Dismantle and clean the carburetor • Replace the spark plug • Run a compression test • Inspect and repack the steering head bearings • Lubricate the speedometer and tachometer drive cables

* This Honda factory maintenance schedule should be considered as a guide to general maintenance and lubrication intervals. Harder than normal use and exposure to mud, water, sand, high humidity, etc., will naturally dictate more frequent attention to most maintenance items.

Table 2 TIRE INFLATION PRESSURE*

Model	Front		Rear	
	psi	kg/cm²	psi	kg/cm²
CB100, CL100, SL100, CB125, SL125	26	1.8	28	2.0
XL100	28	2.0	21	1.5
CT125	25	1.8	32	2.5
XL125, TL125, XL175, XL250, XL350	21	1.5	21	1.5
TL250	5.7	0.4	4.3	0.3

*Original equipment tires.

Table 3 BATTERY STATE OF CHARGE

Specific Gravity	State of Charge
1.110-1.130	Discharged
1.140-1.160	Almost discharged
1.170-1.190	One-quarter charged
1.200-1.220	One-half charged
1.230-1.250	Three-quarter charged
1.260-1.280	Fully charged

Table 4 ENGINE OIL CAPACITY

Engine size	Liter	U.S. qt.	Imp. qt.
100-125 cc	1.0	1.0	0.9
175 cc	1.5	1.6	1.5
250-350 cc			
1972-1975	1.8	1.9	1.6
1976-1978	1.9	2.0	1.7

Table 5 FRONT FORK OIL CAPACITY*

Model	Drain		Reassembly	
	cc	fl. oz.	cc	fl. oz.
CB100, CL100	120-130	4.1-4.4	130-140	4.4-4.7
SL100, SL100 K1	170-180	5.8-6.1	180-190	6.1-6.4
SL100 K2-K3, XL100, XL100 K1	135-145	4.6-4.9	145-155	4.9-5.3
1976 XL100	115-118	3.9-4.0	145-155	4.9-5.3
1977-1978 XL100	145	4.9	155-160	5.3-5.6
CB125 S, CB125 S1-S2, CT125	120-130	4.1-4.4	130-140	4.4-4.7
1976-1978 CB125	90-95	3.1-3.2	105-110	3.6-3.7
1979-on CB125	N.A.	N.A.	80-85	2.7-2.9
SL125	165-175	5.6-5.9	180-190	6.1-6.4
SL125 K1-K2	130-140	4.4-4.7	145-155	4.9-5.3
TL125	N.A.	N.A.	130-140	4.4-4.7
XL125	140-145	4.7-4.9	155-160	5.3-5.6
XL175, XL175 K1-K2	130	4.5	143-147	4.9-5.0
1976-1978 XL175	140-150	4.7-5.1	160	5.4
XL250, XL250 K1	145	4.9	160	5.4
XL250 K2, 1976 XL250	150	5.1	160	5.4
XL350, XL350 K1	150	5.1	170	5.8
1976-1978 XL350	145	4.9	165	5.6

* Capacity for each fork leg. Honda does not provide information for all models. "N.A." indicates that the information is not available.

Table 6 DRIVE CHAIN REPLACEMENT NUMBERS

Model	Standard	Optional
CB100	RK428-102L	DK428-102L
CL100	DK428-104L	DK428-103L
SL100	DK428-104L	
SL100 K1	DK428-104L	DID428-108L
SL100 K2-K3, XL100, XL100 K1	DK428-110L	
1976 XL100	DK 428H-110L	
1977-1978 XL100	N.A.	
CB125 S, CB125 S1-S2	RK428D-102L	DID428D-102L
1976-on CB125 S	DID428D-100L	
SL125	DK428-110L	
CT125	DID428H-102L	DID428-118L

(continued)

Table 6 DRIVE CHAIN REPLACEMENT NUMBERS (continued)

Model	Standard	Optional
TL125, TL125 K1-K2	DID428H-120L	
1976 TL125	N.A.-102L	
XL125	N.A.	
XL175	N.A.	
TL250	Diado-102L	Diado-122L
XL250, XL250 K1	N.A.-100L	N.A.-98L
1976 XL250 K2, XL250	N.A.-102L	
XL350	DID500DS-100L	

N.A. = Honda does not provide information for all models.

Table 7 REAR AXLE NUT TORQUE SPECIFICATION

Model	N•m	ft.-lb.
CB100, CL100, SL100, CB125S, SL125, TL125	40-50	29-36
XL100, XL125 CT125	40-60	29-43
XL175, TL250	60-80	43-58
XL250, XL350	80-100	58-72

Table 8 TUNE-UP SPECIFICATIONS

Valve clearance	
Intake	0.05 mm (0.002 in.)
Exhaust	
100 and 125 cc	0.05 mm (0.002 in.)
175, 250 and 350 cc	0.08 mm (0.003 in.)
Compression pressure	
100, 125 and 175 cc	10.8-13.2 kg/cm² (153-187 psi)
TL250	11.0 kg/cm² (156 psi)
XL250 and XL350	12.6-15.5 kg/cm² (180-220 psi)
Spark plug type	
100, 125 and 175 cc (through 1976)	ND X24ES or NGK D8ES-L
1977-1982 CB125S	ND X24ES-U or NGK D8EA
1977-on 175 cc	ND W22ES or NGK B7ES
TL250	ND X22ES or NGK D7ES
XL250 and XL350	ND X24ES or NGK D8ES-L
Spark plug gap	0.6-0.7 mm (0.024-0.028 in.)
Ignition timing*	
CB100, CL100, SL100, XL100, 1973-1978 CB125, SL125, XL175, XL250, XL350	1,200 ±100 rpm
1978-on CB125S, CT125, XL125, TL125	1,300 ±100 rpm
TL250	1,000 ±100 rpm
Idle speed	
CB100, CL100, SL100, XL100, 1973-1978 CB125, SL125, XL175, XL250, XL350	1,200 ±100 rpm
1978-on CB125S, CT125, XL125, TL125	1,300 ±100 rpm
TL250	1,000 ±100 rpm
Contact breaker point gap	0.3-0.4 mm (0.012-0.016 in.)

* "F" mark aligns with pointer at specified rpm.

CHAPTER FOUR

4

100 AND 125 CC ENGINES

All 100 and 125 cc models covered in this book are equipped with an air-cooled, 4-stroke, single cylinder engine with a single overhead camshaft. The crankshaft is supported by 2 main ball bearings. The camshaft is chain-driven from the timing sprocket on the left-hand side of the crankshaft and operates rocker arms that are individually adjustable.

Engine lubrication is by wet sump with the oil pump located on the right-hand side of the engine next to the clutch. The oil pump delivers oil under pressure throughout the engine and is gear-driven off of the crankshaft.

The difference between the 100 cc and the 125 cc engines is a larger bore dimension to achieve a larger displacement. The stroke remains the same on all models. Engines prior to 1976 have a different cylinder head design. Cylinder head and camshaft removal and installation are covered in separate procedures, depending on model year (pre-1976 or 1976-on).

This chapter contains information for removal, inspection, service and reassembly of the engine. Although the clutch and transmission are located within the engine, they are covered in Chapter Six to simplify this material. Ignition system and alternator components are covered in Chapter Eight.

Before beginning work, re-read Chapter One of this book. You will do a better job with this information fresh in your mind.

Engine specifications and tightening torques are in **Table 1** and **Table 2** at the end of this chapter.

ENGINE PRINCIPLES

Figure 1 explains how the engine works. This will be helpful when troubleshooting or repairing the engine.

ENGINE COOLING

Cooling is provided by air passing over the cooling fins on the engine cylinder head and cylinder. It is very important to keep these fins free from buildup of dirt, oil, grease and other foreign matter. Brush out the fins with a whisk broom or small stiff paint brush.

CAUTION

Remember, these fins are thin in order to dissipate heat and may be damaged if struck too hard.

SERVICING ENGINE IN FRAME

The engine must be removed from the frame to remove the cylinder head, cylinder and piston.

The following components can be serviced while the engine is mounted in the frame (the bike's frame is a great holding fixture for breaking loose stubborn bolts and nuts):

a. Carburetor.
b. Alternator.
c. Clutch assembly.
d. External shift mechanism.

ENGINE REMOVAL/INSTALLATION

1. Drain the engine oil as described in Chapter Three.

1

4-STROKE OPERATING PRINCIPLES

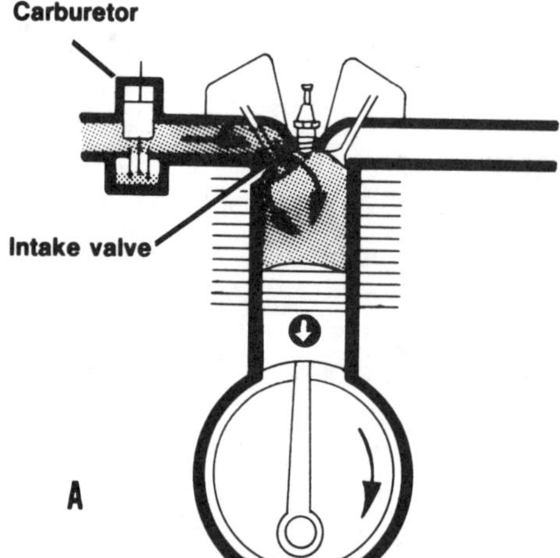

As the piston travels downward, the exhaust valve is closed and the intake valve opens, allowing the new air-fuel mixture from the carburetor to be drawn into the cylinder. When the piston reaches the bottom of its travel (BDC), the intake valve closes and remains closed for the next 1 1/2 revolutions of the crankshaft.

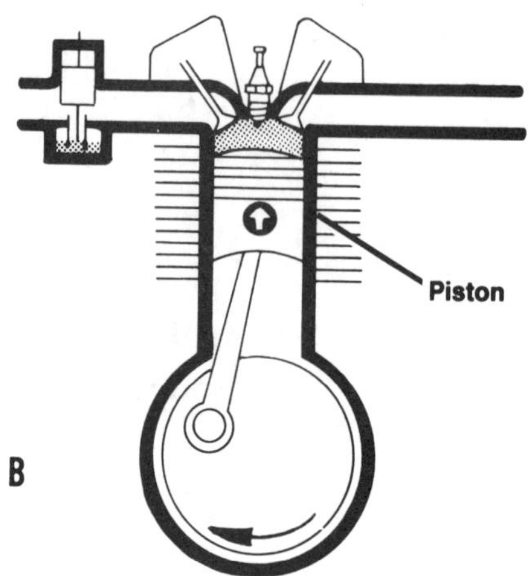

While the crankshaft continues to rotate, the piston moves upward, compressing the air-fuel mixture.

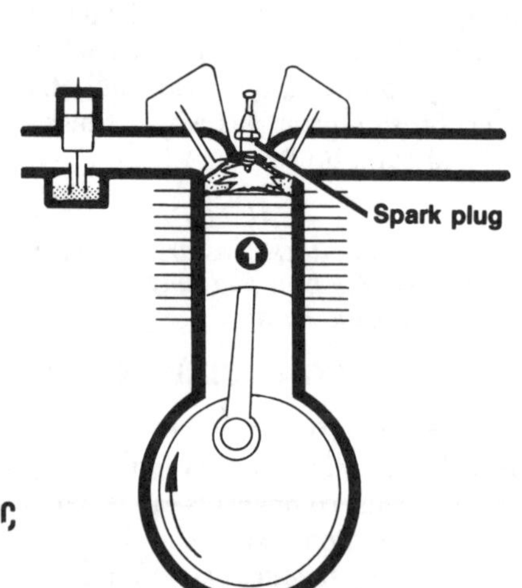

As the piston almost reaches the top of its travel, the spark plug fires, igniting the compressed air-fuel mixture. The piston continues to top dead center (TDC) and is pushed downward by the expanding gases.

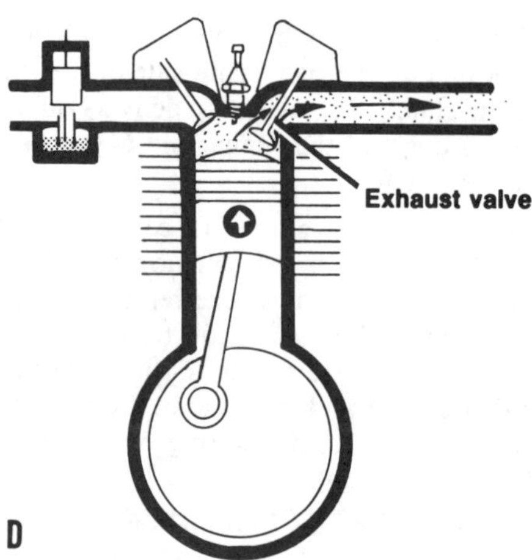

When the piston almost reaches BDC, the exhaust valve opens and remains open until the piston is near TDC. The upward travel of the piston forces the exhaust gases out of the cylinder. After the piston has reached TDC, the exhaust valve closes and the cycle starts all over again.

2. Remove the side covers and the seat.
3. Remove the fuel tank as described in Chapter Seven.
4. Remove the exhaust system as described in Chapter Seven.
5. Remove the carburetor as described in Chapter Seven.
6. On models so equipped, remove the bolts securing the skid plate and remove the skid plate.
7. Disconnect the spark plug lead and tie it up out of the way. Disconnect the engine breather hose from the crankcase.
8. Remove the alternator as described in Chapter Eight.
9. Remove the drive chain master link and remove the bolts securing the drive sprocket. Remove the drive sprocket.
10. Remove the clutch assembly as described in Chapter Six.
11. On models so equipped, disconnect the tachometer cable from the engine.
12. Take a final look all over the engine to make sure everything has been disconnected.
13. Remove the upper engine hanger bolts and nuts and remove the hanger plates.
14. Place a suitable size hydraulic jack, with a piece of wood to protect the crankcase, under the engine. Apply a *small amount* of jack pressure up on the engine.
15. Remove the bolts and nuts securing the front engine hanger bolts and remove the engine hanger.
16. Remove the upper and lower rear through bolts from the left-hand side. Don't lose any spacers on the bolts.

CAUTION
The following steps require the aid of a helper to safely remove the engine assembly from the frame.

17. Pull the engine up and slightly forward. Remove the engine from either side. Take it to a workbench for further disassembly.
18. Install by reversing these removal steps, noting the following.
19. Be sure to install any spacers on the mounting bolts.
20. Tighten all bolts to the torque specifications listed in **Table 2**.
21. Fill the engine with the recommended type and quantity of oil; refer to Chapter Three.
22. Adjust the clutch, drive chain and rear brake pedal as described in Chapter Three.
23. Start the engine and check for leaks.

4

CAMSHAFT (1969-1975)

Removal

1. Place a wood block(s) under the engine to support the bike securely.
2. Remove the side covers and the seat.
3. Remove the fuel tank as described in Chapter Seven.
4. Remove the screws securing the contact breaker assembly cover and remove the cover and the gasket.
5. Disconnect the electrical connector for the contact breaker point assembly from the wiring harness.

NOTE
Prior to removing the contact breaker point base plate, make a mark on the base plate that aligns with the centerline of one of the mounting screws. That way the ignition timing will be correct upon installation (providing the timing was correct before removal).

6. Remove the screws securing the contact breaker point base plate and remove the base plate assembly.
7. Remove the bolt securing the ignition advance mechanism to the camshaft. Remove the ignition advance mechanism.
8. Loosen the cam chain tensioner locknut and turn the adjuster bolt (**Figure 2**) clockwise until there is slack in the cam chain.
9. Remove both valve adjuster covers.
10. Rotate the crankshaft until the piston is at top dead center (TDC) on the compression stroke.

Align the "O" mark on the cam sprocket (A, **Figure 3**) with the punch mark on the cylinder head.

NOTE
A piston at TDC will have play in both of the rocker arms, indicating that both the intake and exhaust valves are closed.

11. Loosen both valve adjusters so there will be no pressure on the camshaft.
12. Remove the cam sprocket mounting bolts (B, **Figure 3**). Be careful the bolts do not fall down the cam chain cavity as they will end up in the crankcase.
13. Pull the cam sprocket off of the shoulder on the camshaft.
14. Remove the cam chain from the cam sprocket and tie a piece of wire onto the cam chain. Tie the other end of the wire to an external part of the engine.
15. Remove the cam sprocket from the camshaft.
16. Align the cam lobes with the opening in the cylinder head and withdraw the camshaft from the cylinder head.

Inspection

NOTE
*Honda does not provide service limit specifications for all models. **Table 2** lists all service limit specifications that are available.*

1. Check the cam bearing journals for wear and scoring.
2. Measure both the left- and right-hand bearing journals with a micrometer (**Figure 4**). Compare to dimensions given in **Table 2**. If worn to the service limit the cam must be replaced.

NOTE
The left-hand bearing journal is the larger of the two.

3. Check the cam lobes for wear (**Figure 5**). The lobes should show no signs of scoring and the edges should be square. Slight damage may be removed with a silicone carbide oilstone. Use No. 100-120 grit stone initially, then polish with a No. 280-320 grit stone.

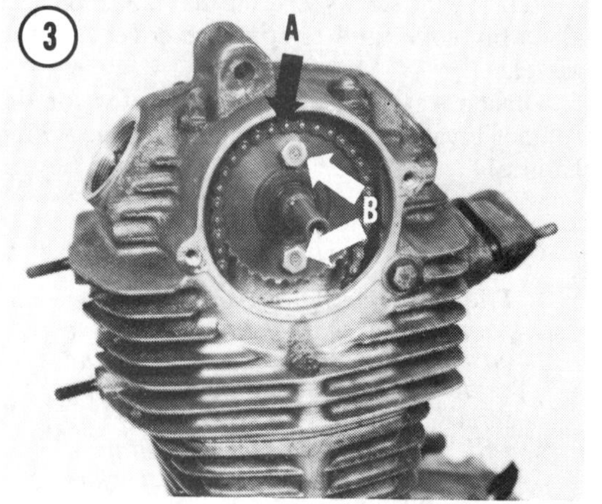

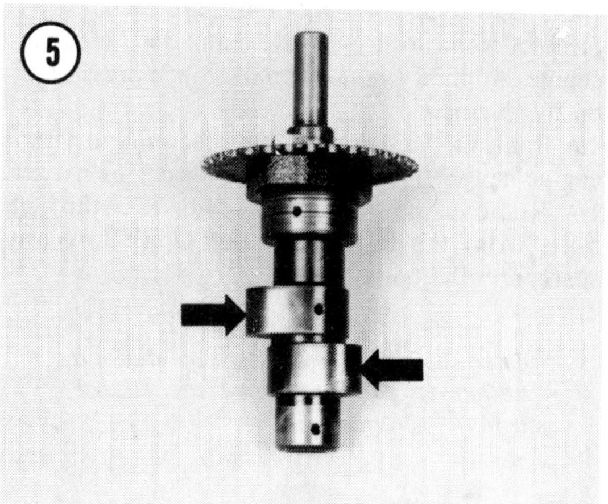

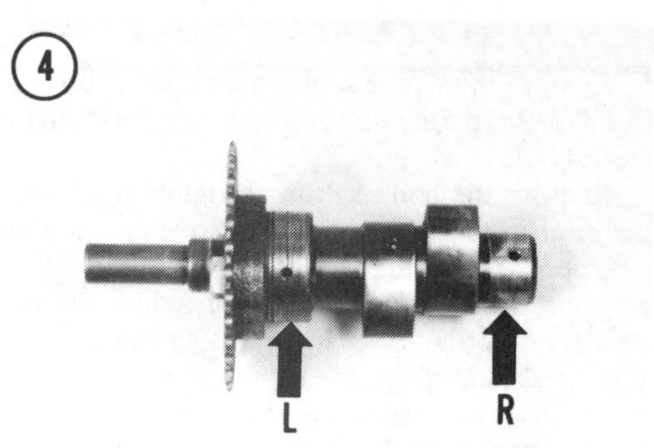

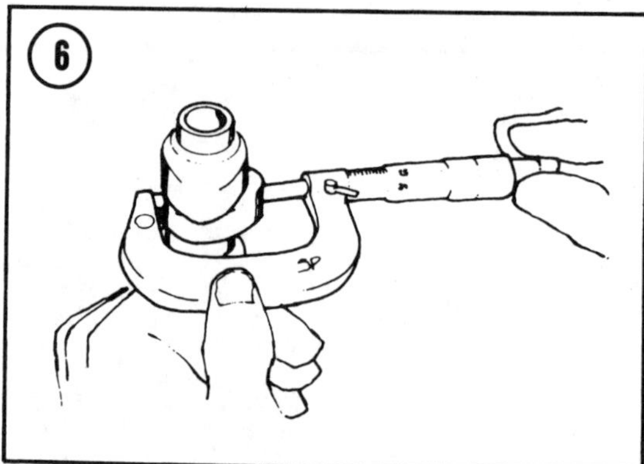

4. Even the cam lobe surface appears to be satisfactory, with no visible signs of wear, the cam lobes must be measured with a micrometer as shown in **Figure 6**. Compare to dimensions given in **Table 2**.

NOTE
The right-hand cam lobe is the exhaust and the left-hand is the intake.

5. Check the cam bearing surface within the cylinder head (**Figure 7**). It should not be scored or excessively worn. The cylinder head must be replaced if the bearing surface is worn or damaged.
6. Inspect the cam sprocket (**Figure 8**) for wear; replace if necessary.

4

Installation

1. Lubricate all cam lobes and bearing journals with molybdenum disulfide grease. Also coat the cam bearing surfaces in the cylinder head.
2. Loosen all valve adjusters fully. This is to relieve strain on the rocker arms and allow room for the cam to be inserted into the cylinder head.

CAUTION
When rotating the crankshaft in the following steps, keep the cam chain taut and engaged with the sprocket on the crankshaft.

3. Hold the cam chain up and taut while rotating the crankshaft to avoid damage to the chain and/or the crankcase. Rotate the crankshaft *counterclockwise* until the "T" timing mark aligns with the stationary pointer (**Figure 9**). Use the bolt on the alternator rotor to turn the crankshaft.
4. Align the cam lobes with the cutouts in the cylinder head. Install the cam through the cam chain and into position in the cylinder head (**Figure 10**).
5. Install and position the cam sprocket onto the cam with the alignment mark "O" at the 12 o'clock position and aligned with the index mark on the cylinder head.
6. Make sure the cam chain is meshed properly with the drive sprocket on the crankshaft.
7. Pull the cam chain up and onto the cam sprocket. Check that the alignment mark "O" is still at the top. Pull the cam chain and sprocket up and into place on the shoulder of the camshaft.

CAUTION
Very expensive damage could result from improper camshaft alignment. Recheck your work several times to be sure alignment is correct.

8. When alignment is correct, install the cam sprocket bolts and tighten to the torque specification listed in **Table 2**.
9. Make one final check to make sure alignment is correct. The "T" timing mark must be aligned with the stationary pointer (A, **Figure 11**) and the "O" alignment mark on the sprocket must align with the index mark on the cylinder head (B, **Figure 11**).
10. Align the dowel pin on the camshaft with the notch in the ignition advance unit (**Figure 12**) and install the ignition advance unit.
11. Install the bolt securing the ignition advance unit and tighten to the torque specification listed in **Table 2.**
12. Install the contact breaker point base plate assembly. Align the mark made during removal to ensure correct ignition timing (providing it was correct prior to removal).
13. Install the contact breaker point cover and gasket. Tighten the screws securely. Connect the electrical connector from the contact breaker point assembly to the wiring harness.
14. Adjust the cam chain tensioner, the valves and the ignition timing as described in Chapter Three.

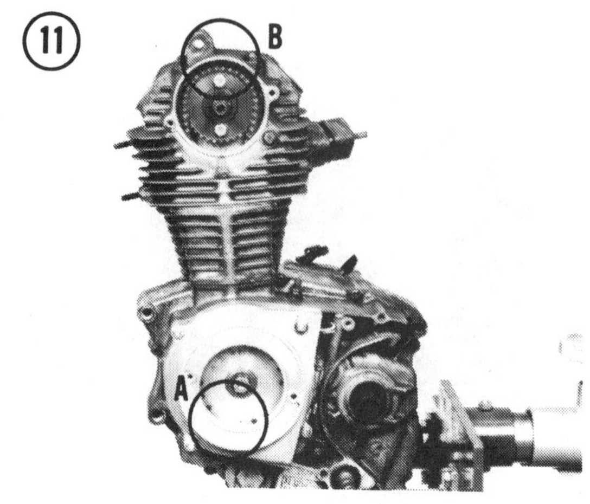

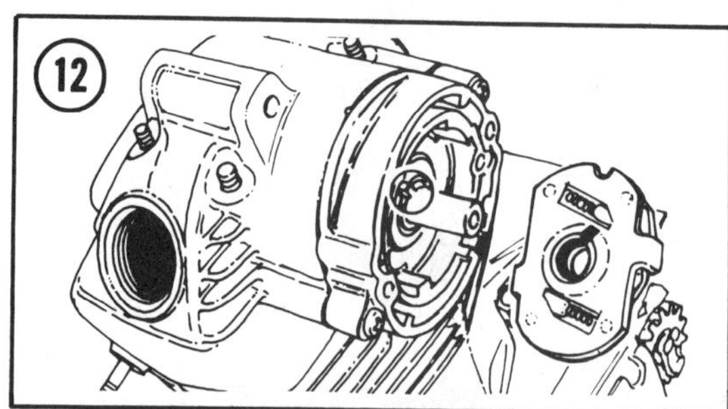

CYLINDER HEAD

(1969-1975)

Removal/Installation

CAUTION
To prevent any warpage and damage, remove the cylinder head only when the engine is at room temperature.

1. Remove the engine as described in this chapter.
2. Remove the cam chain tensioner pivot bolt (**Figure 13**) in the cylinder head. Move the tensioner forward and away from the attachment area in the cylinder head.
3. Remove the camshaft as described in this chapter.
4. Remove the bolt (A, **Figure 14**) on the left-hand side of the cylinder head in line with the camshaft.
5. Loosen the 8 mm acorn nuts and washers (B, **Figure 14**) securing the cylinder head in a crisscross pattern. Remove the nuts and the washers.
6. Loosen the cylinder head by tapping around the perimeter with a rubber or soft-faced mallet. If necessary, *gently* pry the head loose with a broad-tipped screwdriver.

CAUTION
Remember, the cooling fins are fragile and may be damaged if tapped or pried on too hard. Never use a metal hammer.

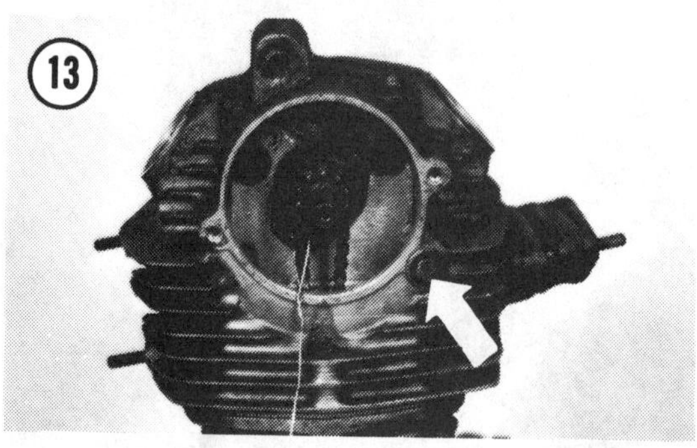

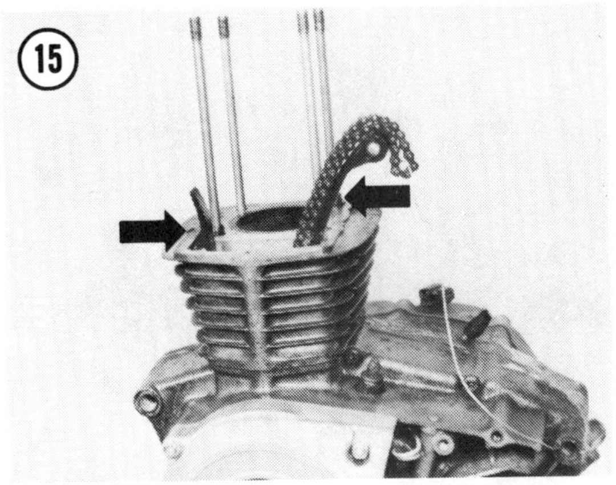

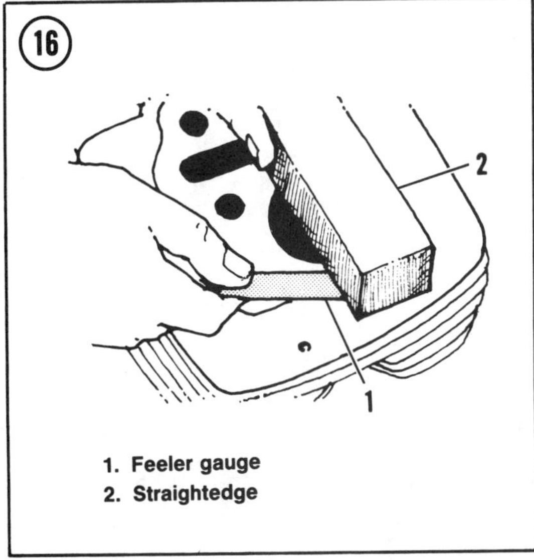

1. Feeler gauge
2. Straightedge

7. Untie the wire securing the cam chain.
8. Pull the cylinder head straight up and off the crankcase studs and cylinder. Pull the cam chain through the opening in the cylinder head and retie the wire to the engine.
9. Remove the cylinder head gasket and discard it.

NOTE
Don't lose the locating dowels. Discard the small O-ring on one of the dowels.

10. Place a clean shop cloth into the cam chain cavity in the cylinder to prevent the entry of foreign matter.
11. Install by reversing these removal steps, noting the following.
12. Clean the mating surfaces of the head and the cylinder of any gasket material.
13. Install the locating dowels and the O-ring seal (**Figure 15**).
14. Install a new head gasket.
15. Install the cylinder head. Install the washers and the acorn nuts. Tighten the nuts in a crisscross pattern in 2-3 steps to the final torque listed in **Table 2.**
16. Install the bolt on the left-hand side of the cylinder head and tighten the bolt securely.
17. Correctly position the upper end of the cam chain tensioner and install the bolt and washer (**Figure 13**). Tighten the bolt securely.
18. Install the engine as described in this chapter.
19. Adjust the valves and the cam chain tensioner as described in Chapter Three.

4

Inspection

1. Remove all traces of gasket material from the cylinder head mating surfaces.
2. *Without removing the valves*, remove all carbon deposits from the combustion chambers and valve ports with a wire brush. A blunt screwdriver or chisel may be used if care is taken not to damage the head, valves and spark plug threads.
3. After the carbon is removed from the combustion chambers and the valve intake and exhaust ports, clean the entire head in cleaning solvent. Blow dry with compressed air.
4. Clean away all carbon from the piston crown. Do not remove the carbon ridge at the top of the cylinder bore.
5. Check for cracks in the combustion chamber and exhaust ports. A cracked head must be replaced.
6. After the head has been thoroughly cleaned, place a straightedge across the cylinder head gasket surface (**Figure 16**) at several points. Measure the warp by inserting a flat feeler gauge between the straightedge and the cylinder head at each location. There should be no warpage; if a small amount is present, it can be resurfaced by a dealer or qualified machine shop.
7. Check the condition of the valves and valve guides as described under *Valves and Valve Components* in this chapter.

Rocker Arm Removal/Inspection/Installation

It is recommended that one rocker arm assembly be disassembled, inspected and then assembled to avoid the interchanging of parts. This is especially true on a well run-in engine (high mileage) as the different sets of parts have developed wear patterns.

1. Remove the screw securing the rocker arm shaft set plate and remove the set plate.

2. Screw a 6 mm bolt (**Figure 17**) into the end of the rocker arm shaft and withdraw the rocker arm shaft.
3. Remove the rocker arm.
4. Wash all parts in cleaning solvent and thoroughly dry.
5. Inspect the rocker arm pad (**Figure 18**) where it rides on the cam lobe and where the adjuster rides on the valve stem. If the pad is scratched or unevenly worn, inspect the cam lobe for scoring, chipping or flat spots. Replace the rocker arm or camshaft if defective.
6. Measure the inside diameter of the rocker arm bore (A, **Figure 19**) with an inside micrometer and note this dimension.
7. Inspect the rocker arm shaft for signs of wear or scoring. Measure the outside diameter (B, **Figure 19**) with a micrometer and note this dimension. Subtract the dimension of the rocker arm shaft from the rocker arm bore dimension to determine the clearance between the 2 parts. The clearance service limit is listed in **Table 1**. Replace worn part(s).
8. Inspect the cam bearing surface for excessive wear. If worn excessively, the cylinder head must be replaced.
9. Coat the rocker arm shaft and rocker arm bore with assembly oil.
10. Install the rocker arm into the cylinder head (**Figure 20**) with the rocker arm pad end in first. Install the rocker arm shaft with the threaded hole and locating notch (**Figure 21**) facing out. Insert the rocker arm shaft into the cylinder head and into the rocker arm. Push the rocker arm in until it seats.
11. Make sure the locking relief on the end of the rocker arm shaft is vertical (**Figure 22**) and facing toward the camshaft to accept the set plate.
13. Repeat Steps 2-12 for the other rocker arm assembly.
14. Install the set plate and tighten the bolt securely.

CYLINDER HEAD COVER AND CAMSHAFT (1976-0N)

The cylinder head cover carries the rocker arm assemblies. The camshaft is held in place between the cylinder head cover and the cylinder head and is driven through a chain from the sprocket on the crankshaft. The cam can be removed with the engine in the frame, but it is easier to do with the engine removed.

17

18

19

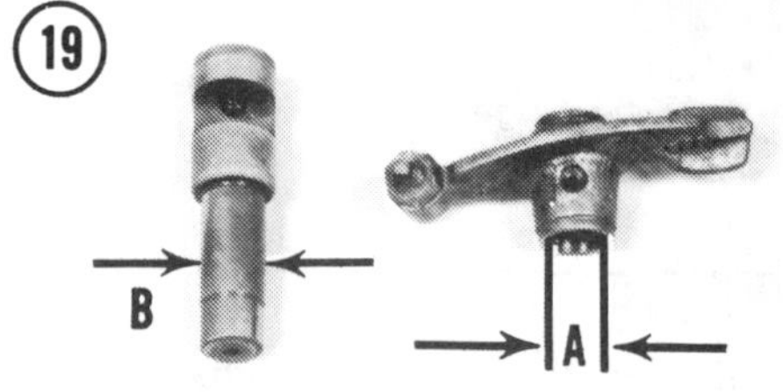

20

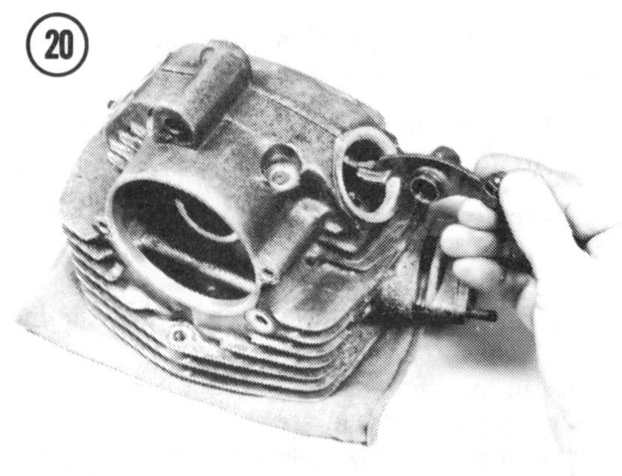

Removal

CAUTION
To prevent any warpage and damage, remove the cylinder head cover and cam only when the engine is at room temperature.

1. Place a wood block(s) under the engine to support the bike securely.
2. Remove the side covers and the seat.
3. Remove the fuel tank as described in Chapter Seven.

NOTE
Prior to removing the contact breaker point base plate on models so equipped, make a mark on the base plate that aligns with the centerline of one of the mounting screws. That way the ignition timing will be correct upon installation (providing the timing was correct before removal).

4A. On models with contact breaker point ignition, perform the following:
   a. Remove the screws securing the contact breaker assembly cover and remove the cover and the gasket.
   b. Disconnect the electrical connection from the contact breaker point assembly to the wiring harness.
   c. Remove the screws (A, **Figure 23**) securing the contact breaker point base plate. Remove the rubber grommet (B, **Figure 23**) from the cylinder head and remove the base plate assembly.
   d. Remove the bolt securing the ignition advance mechanism to the camshaft. Remove the ignition advance mechanism.

4B. On models with electronic ignition (CDI), perform the following:
   a. Remove the ignition pulse generator as described in Chapter Eight.
   b. Remove the ignition advance mechanism as described in Chapter Eight.
   c. Remove the dowel pin (A, **Figure 24**) on the camshaft.
   d. Remove the bolts (B, **Figure 24**) securing the pulse base and remove the pulse base.

5. Remove the spark plug as this will make it easier to rotate the engine.
6. Shift the transmission into NEUTRAL.
7. Remove the engine as described in this chapter.
8. Temporarily install the alternator rotor and rotate the engine until the "O" mark on the

camshaft sprocket aligns with the V-notch index mark on the cylinder head (**Figure 25**).

9. Loosen both cam sprocket bolts (**Figure 26**).

10. Remove the 6 mm Allen bolts and 8 mm cap nuts (**Figure 27**) securing the cylinder head cover. Remove the cylinder head cover and gasket. Don't lose the locating dowels.

11. Remove the cam sprocket bolts (**Figure 28**).

12. Pull the cam chain and cam sprocket off of the shoulder on the cam and let them rest on the extended portion of the cam.

13. Remove the cam sprocket from the cam chain. Rest the cam chain on the cam (A, **Figure 29**).

14. Tie a piece of wire to the cam chain and tie it to an external part of the engine or insert a long drift or similar tool in the chain loop and rest this tool on the cylinder head. This will prevent the chain from falling into the crankcase. Remove the cam (B, **Figure 29**) from the cylinder head. Don't lose the large thrust washer on the cam.

CAUTION

If the crankshaft must be rotated when the camshaft is removed, pull up on the cam chain and keep it taut while rotating the crankshaft. Make certain that the chain is positioned onto the crankshaft sprocket. If this is not done, the chain may become kinked and may damage both the chain and the sprocket on the crankshaft.

Camshaft Inspection

1. Check the cam bearing journals for wear and scoring.

2. Measure both the left- and right-hand bearing journals with a micrometer (**Figure 30**). Compare

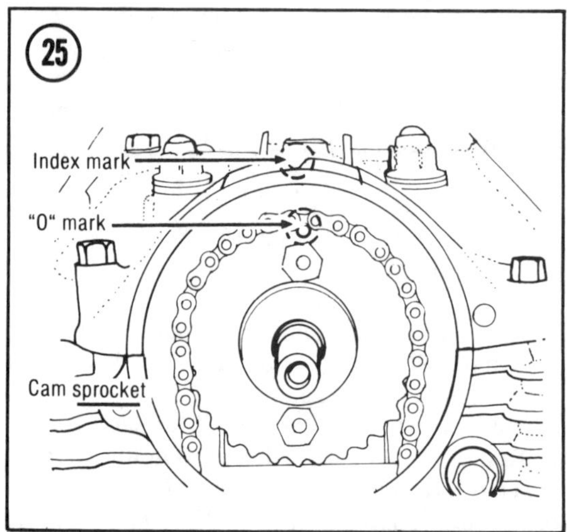

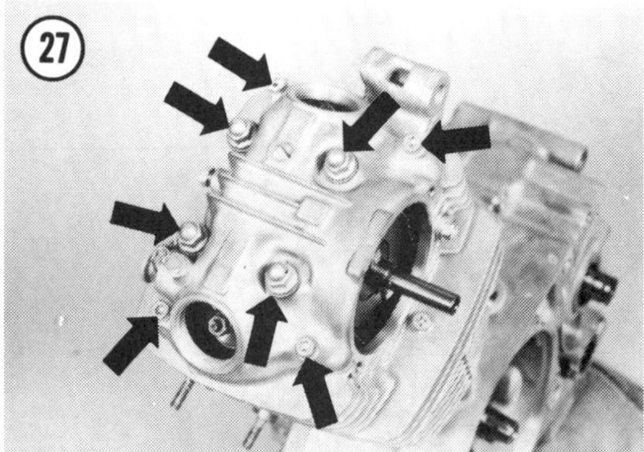

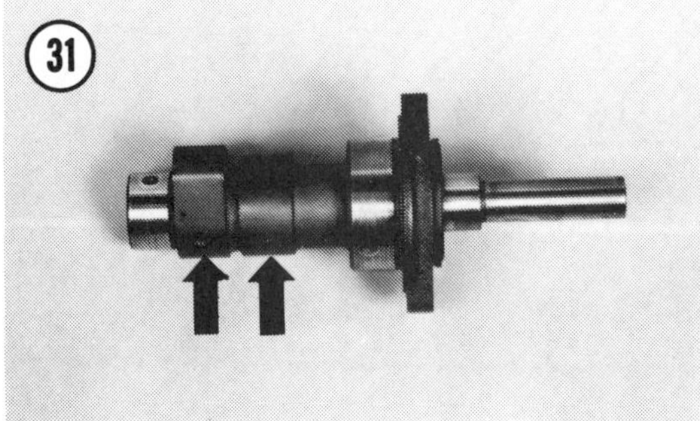

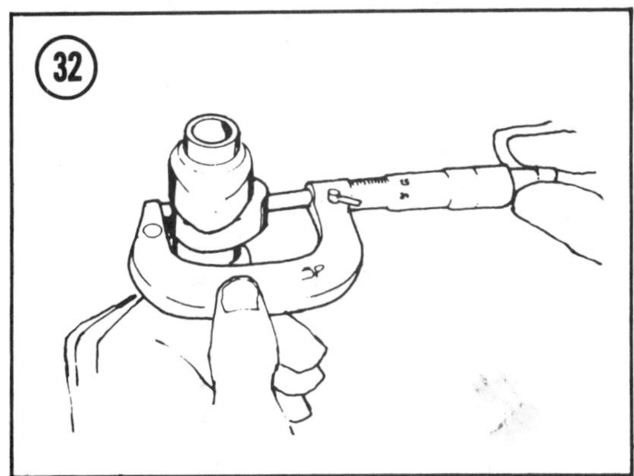

to dimensions given in **Table 1**. If worn to the service limit the cam must be replaced.

NOTE
The left-hand bearing journal is the larger of the two.

3. Check the cam lobes for wear (**Figure 31**). The lobes should show no signs of scoring and the edges should be square. Slight damage may be removed with a silicone carbide oilstone. Use No. 100-120 grit stone initially, then polish with a No. 280-320 grit stone.
4. Even though the cam lobe surface appears to be satisfactory, with no visible signs of wear, the cam lobes must be measured with a micrometer as shown in **Figure 32**. Compare to dimensions given in **Table 1**.

NOTE
The right-hand cam lobe is the exhaust and the left-hand is the intake.

5. Check the cam bearing surfaces in the cylinder head cover (**Figure 33**) and cylinder head (**Figure 34**). They should not be scored or excessively worn. Replace either part if wear is evident.
6. Inspect the cam sprocket for wear; replace if necessary.

Cylinder Head Cover Disassembly/Inspection/Assembly

It is recommended that one rocker arm assembly be disassembled, inspected and then assembled to avoid the interchanging of parts. This is especially true on a well run-in engine (high mileage) as the different sets of parts have developed wear patterns.

NOTE
Both rocker arms look the same but they are different and have different part numbers. If you remove both

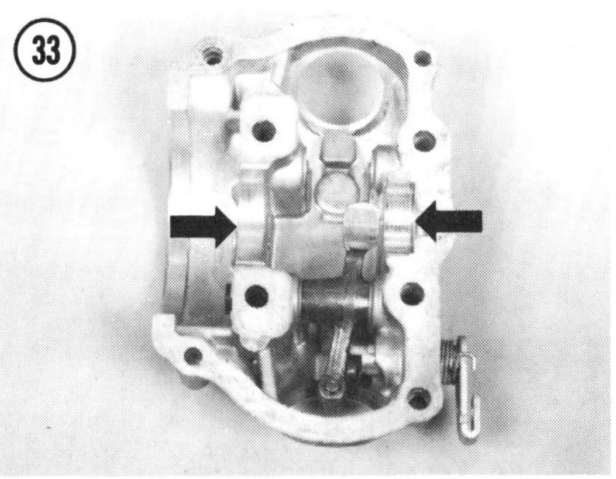

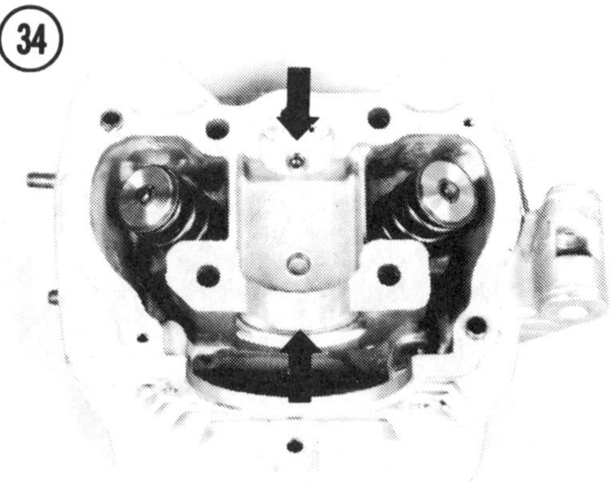

rocker arm assemblies at the same time, mark them with "I" (intake—to the rear) or "E" (exhaust—to the front) so they will be reinstalled in the correct location in the cylinder head cover.

1. Remove the screw securing the rocker arm shaft set plate (**Figure 35**) and remove the set plate.
2. Screw in a 6 mm bolt (**Figure 36**) and withdraw the rocker arm shaft.
3. Remove the rocker arm.
4. Wash all parts in cleaning solvent and thoroughly dry.
5. Inspect the rocker arm pad (**Figure 37**) where it rides on the cam lobe and where the adjuster rides on the valve stem. If the pad is scratched or unevenly worn, inspect the cam lobe for scoring, chipping or flat spots. Replace the rocker arm or camshaft if defective.
6. Measure the inside diameter of the rocker arm bore (A, **Figure 38**) with an inside micrometer and note this dimension.
7. Inspect the rocker arm shaft for signs of wear or scoring. Measure the outside diameter (B, **Figure 38**) with a micrometer and note this dimension. Subtract the dimension of the rocker arm shaft from the rocker arm bore dimension to determine the clearance between the 2 parts. The clearance service limit is listed in **Table 1**. Replace worn part(s).
8. Inspect the cam bearing surface for excessive wear. If worn excessively, the cylinder head cover must be replaced.
9. Coat the rocker arm shaft and rocker arm bore with assembly oil.
10. Install the rocker arm shaft with the threaded hole facing out. Partially insert the rocker arm shaft into the cover (**Figure 39**) and position the rocker arm into the cylinder head cover.
11. Make sure the locking relief in the rocker arm shaft (**Figure 40**) is aligned with the hole in the

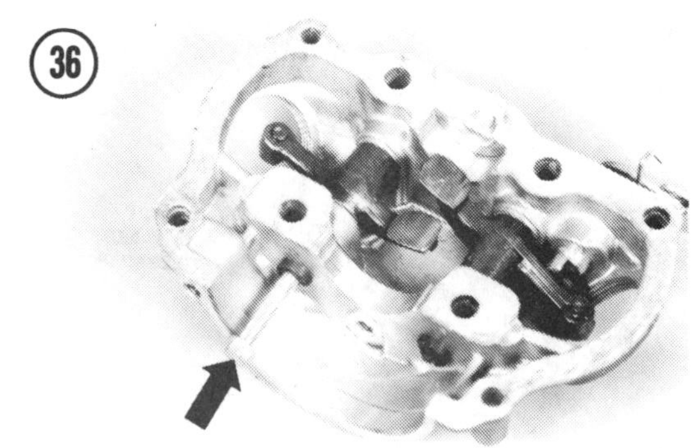

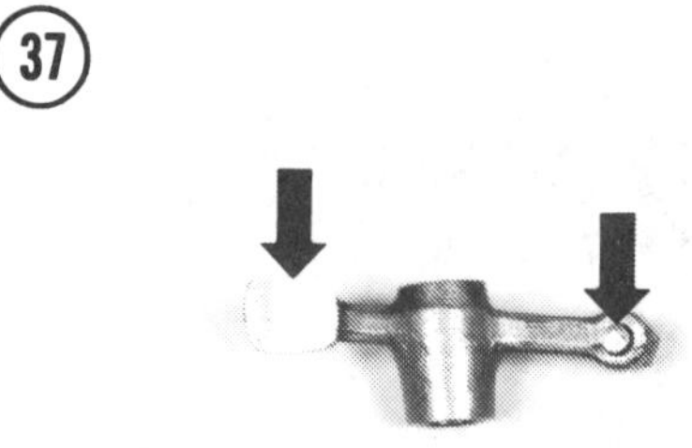

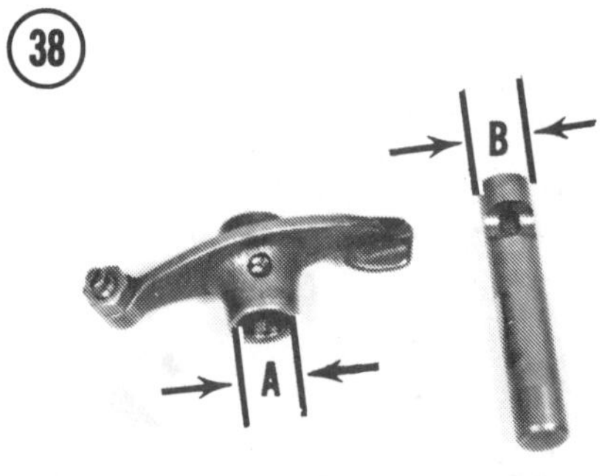

40

41

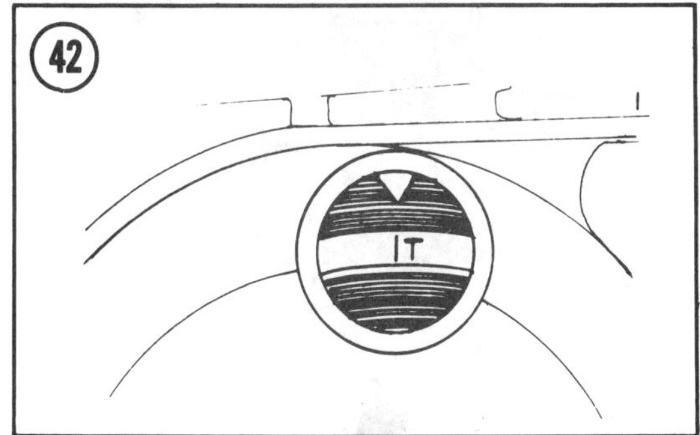

42

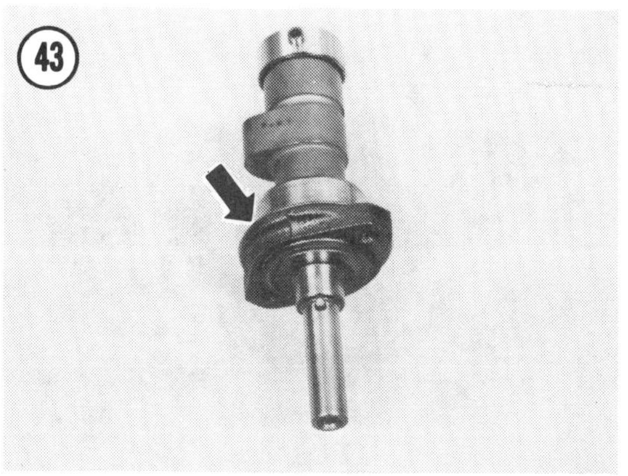
43

cylinder head to allow the crankcase stud to pass by it upon installation.

12. The notch on the end of the rocker arm (**Figure 41**) must be facing toward the inside to accept the set plate.

13. Repeat Steps for the other rocker arm assembly.

Installation

1. Lubricate all cam lobes and bearing journals with molybdenum disulfide grease. Also coat the bearing surfaces in the cylinder head and cylinder head cover.

CAUTION
When rotating the crankshaft in the following steps, keep the cam chain taut and engaged with the sprocket on the crankshaft.

2. Hold the cam chain up and taut while rotating the crankshaft to avoid damage to the chain and/or the crankcase. Temporarily install the alternator rotor (if removed) and rotate the crankshaft *counterclockwise* until the "T" timing mark is pointing straight up at the cam. Temporarily install the alternator cover. On 1976-1980 models, leave off the inspection cover; on 1981-on models, remove the timing hole cap. Make sure the "T" mark aligns with the stationary pointer (**Figure 42**).

3. Make sure the large thrust washer (**Figure 43**) is installed on the cam's large bearing journal, up against the sprocket mounting flange.

4. Install the cam through the cam chain (A, **Figure 44**) and into position in the cylinder head (B, **Figure 44**).

5. Fill the oil pocket with fresh engine oil so the cam lobes will be covered for the initial engine start-up.

6. On the cylinder head, loosen the cam chain tensioner bolt. On the crankcase, remove the

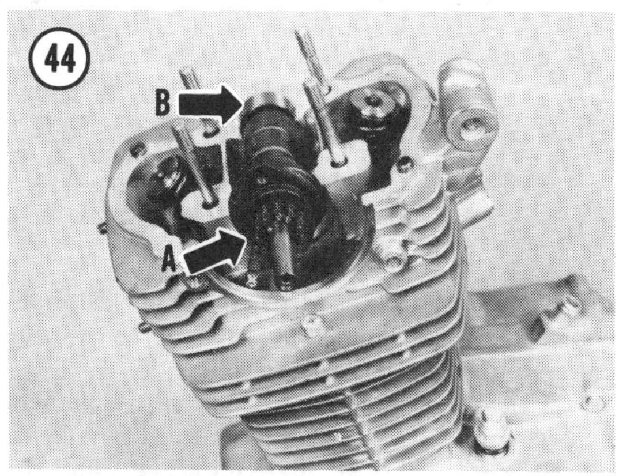

44

4

adjusting bolt and washer (A, **Figure 45**) on the cam chain tensioner. Loosen the lower bolt (B, **Figure 45**). To gain the maximum amount of chain slack, insert a narrow punch into the hole in the tensioner and push down on the tensioner assembly, then tighten the adjusting bolt and reinstall the bolt and washer. Tighten the cam chain tensioner bolt.

7. Install and position the cam sprocket onto the cam with the alignment mark "O" at the 12 o'clock position.

8. Make sure the cam chain is meshed properly with the drive sprocket on the crankshaft.

9. Pull the cam chain up and onto the cam sprocket. Check that the alignment mark "O" is still at the top (**Figure 46**). Pull the cam chain and sprocket up and into place onto the shoulder of the camshaft.

10. Make sure the locating dowels (**Figure 47**) are in place in the cylinder head.

11. Loosen all valve adjusters fully. This is to relieve strain on the rocker arms and cylinder head cover during installation.

12. Apply a light coat of gasket sealer to the sealing surface of the cylinder head cover. Cover only the flat sealing surface. Do not apply the sealer too close to the edge of the right-hand bearing surface, as it will restrict oil flow.

NOTE

Use Gasgacinch Gasket Sealer, 4-Three Bond or equivalent. When selecting an equivalent, avoid thick or hard setting materials.

13. Install the Allen bolts and cap nuts and tighten in the torque pattern shown in **Figure 48**. Tighten to the torque specifications listed in **Table 2**.

14. Check the alignment of the cam sprocket. Make sure that the alignment mark "O" is straight up and is aligned with the V-notch index mark on the cylinder head cover (**Figure 49**). If alignment is not correct, reposition the cam chain on the sprocket so alignment is correct.

CAUTION

Very expensive damage could result from improper cam and chain alignment. Recheck your work several times to be sure alignment is correct.

15. When alignment is correct install the camshaft sprocket bolts and tighten to the torque specification listed in **Table 2**.

16. Make one final check to make sure alignment is correct. The "T" timing mark must be aligned with the stationary pointer (**Figure 42**) and the

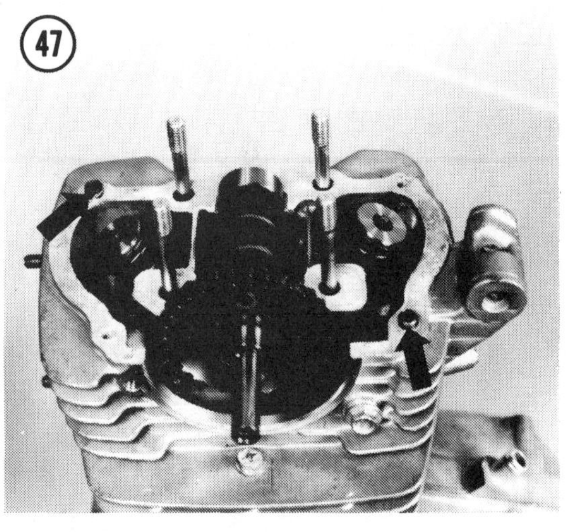

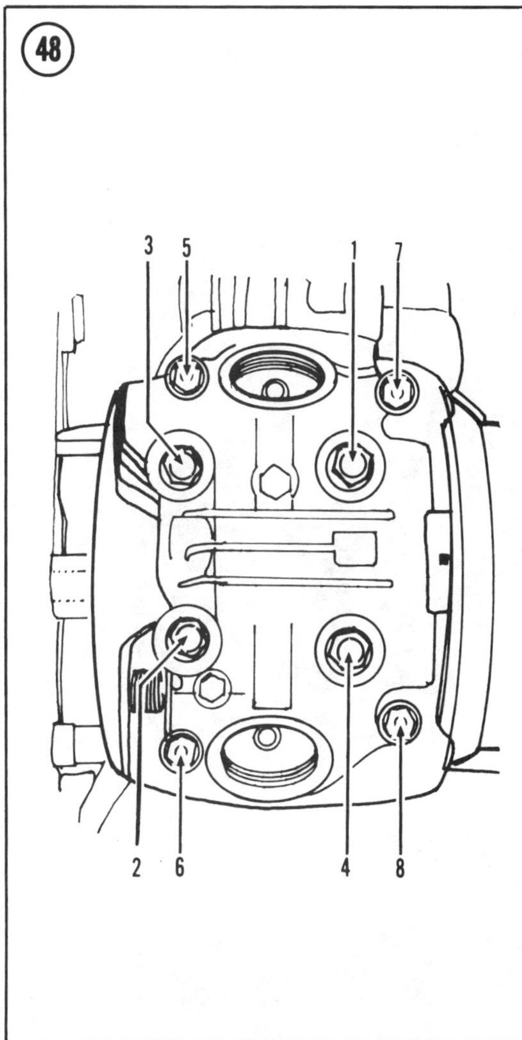

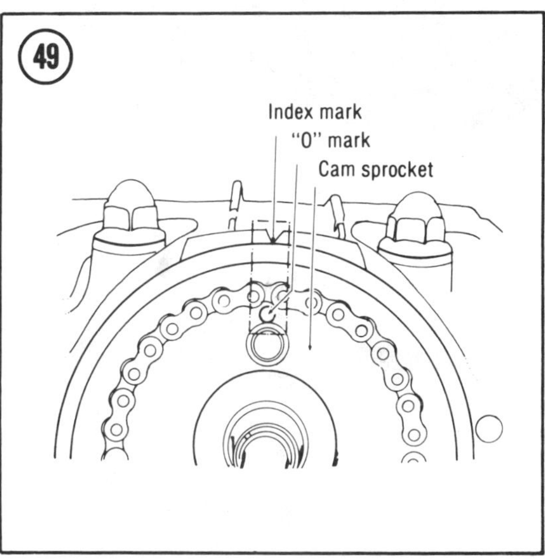

alignment mark on the sprocket must align with the V-notch in the cylinder head cover (**Figure 49**).
17. After the engine has been reinstalled in the frame, adjust the valves and cam chain tension as described in Chapter Three.

CAMSHAFT CHAIN (ALL MODELS)

Removal/Installation

1. Remove the cylinder head as described in this chapter.
2. Remove the alternator as described in Chapter Eight.
3. On models so equipped, remove the bolt securing the locating tab (**Figure 50**) on the camshaft chain. Remove the tab.
4. Remove the chain from the drive sprocket on the crankshaft and remove the camshaft chain out through the opening in the cylinder.
5. Install by reversing these removal steps.

Inspection

Refer to *Camshaft Chain and Tensioner Inspection* in this chapter.

Camshaft Chain Tensioner Adjustment

After the cam chain has been replaced, adjust the chain as described under *Camshaft Chain Tensioner Adjustment* in Chapter Three.

Camshaft Chain Sprocket

Inspect the condition of the cam chain sprocket. Replace if it shows signs of wear or has any teeth missing.

4

CYLINDER HEAD (1976-ON)

Removal/Installation

CAUTION
To prevent any warpage and damage, remove the cylinder head only when the engine is at room temperature.

1. Remove the engine as described in this chapter.
2. Remove the cylinder head cover and camshaft as described in this chapter.
3. Remove the cylinder head bolts and washers, one on each side of the head in line with the camshaft (A, **Figure 51**).
4. Remove the bolt (B, **Figure 51**) securing the cam chain tensioner to the cylinder head.
5. Loosen the head by tapping around the perimeter with a rubber or plastic mallet. If necessary, *gently* pry the head loose with a broad-tipped screwdriver.

CAUTION
Remember the cooling fins are fragile and may be damaged if tapped or pried on too hard. Never use a metal hammer.

6. Untie the wire securing the cam chain and retie it to the cylinder head.
7. Remove the cylinder head by pulling it straight up and off the crankcase studs and cylinder. Pull the cam chain and wire through the opening in the cylinder head and retie the cam chain to the engine.
8. Remove the cylinder head gasket and discard it.

NOTE
Don't lose the 3 locating dowels. Discard the small O-ring.

9. Place a clean shop cloth into the cam chain opening in the cylinder to prevent the entry of foreign matter.
10. Install by reversing these removal steps, noting the following.
11. Clean the mating surfaces of the head and cylinder of any gasket material.
12. Install 2 locating dowels (A, **Figure 52**) on the left-hand crankcase studs. On the right-hand rear stud, install a locating dowel and new O-ring seal (B, **Figure 52**).
13. Install a new head gasket (**Figure 53**).

NOTE
***Figure 52** and **Figure 53** are shown with the cam chain tensioner removed for*

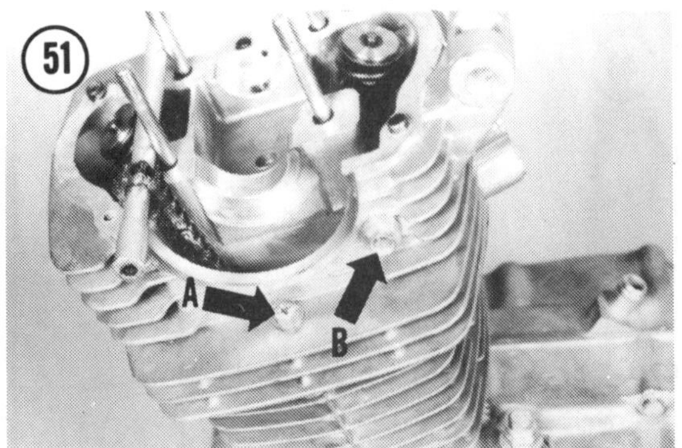

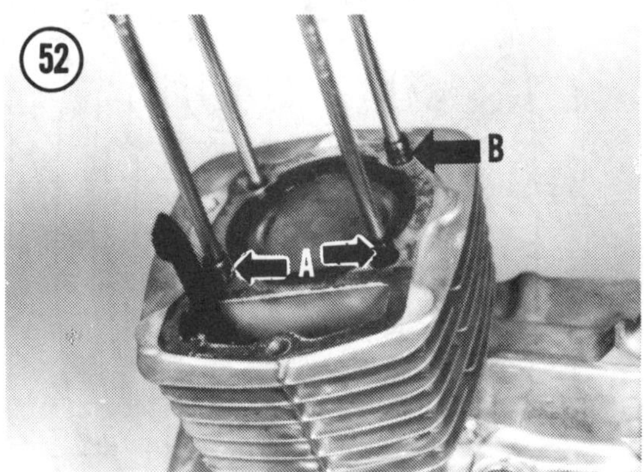

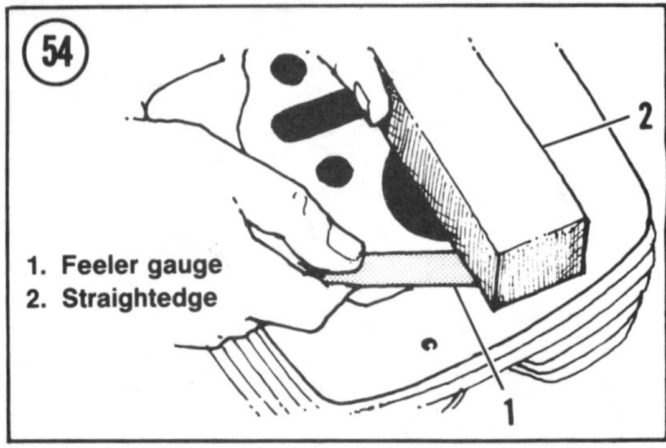

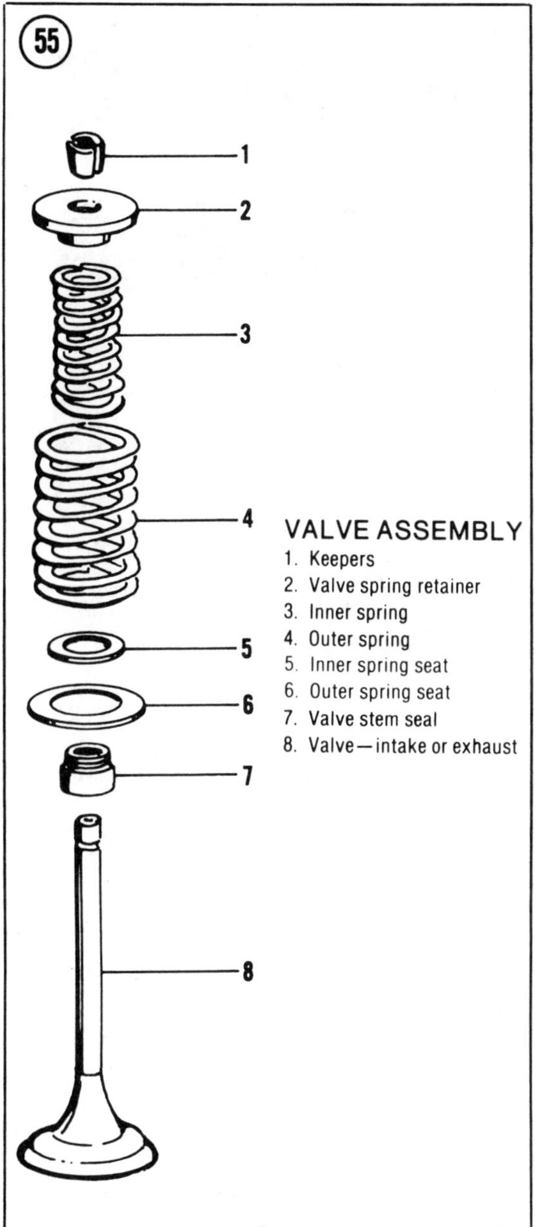

clarity. It should be installed during this operation.

14. Install the cylinder head and secure it with the bolts and washers. Tighten the bolts securely.
15. Correctly position the upper end of the cam chain tensioner and install the bolt and washer. Tighten the bolt securely.

Inspection

1. Remove all traces of gasket material from the cylinder head mating surfaces.

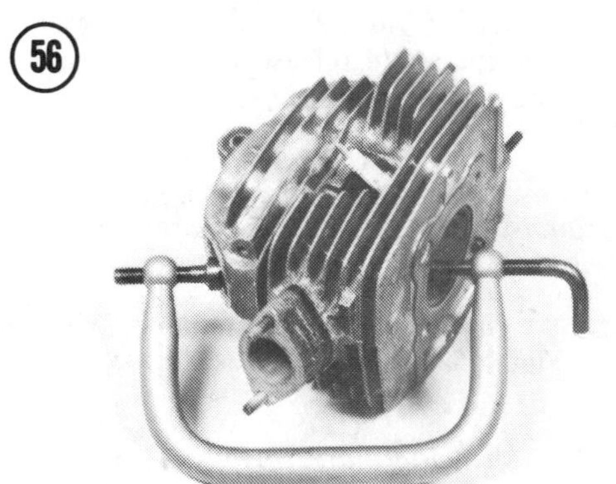

2. *Without removing the valves,* remove all carbon deposits from the combustion chamber and valve ports with a wire brush. A blunt screwdriver or chisel may be used if care is taken not to damage the head, valves and spark plug threads.
3. After the carbon is removed from the combustion chamber and the valve intake and exhaust ports, clean the entire head in cleaning solvent. Blow dry with compressed air.
4. Clean away all carbon from the piston crown. Do not remove the carbon ridge at the top of the cylinder bore.
5. Check for cracks in the combustion chamber and exhaust ports. A cracked head must be replaced.
6. After the head has been thoroughly cleaned, place a straightedge across the cylinder head/cylinder gasket surface (**Figure 54**) at several points. Measure the warp by inserting a flat feeler gauge between the straightedge and the cylinder head at each location. There should be no warpage; if a small amount is present, it can be resurfaced by a dealer or qualified machine shop.
7. Check the cylinder head cover mating surface using the procedure in Step 6. There should be no warpage.
8. Check the condition of the valves and valve guides as described under *Valves and Valve Components* in this chapter.

VALVES AND VALVE COMPONENTS

Removal

Refer to **Figure 55** for this procedure.

1. Remove the cylinder head as described in this chapter.
2. Compress the valve springs with a valve compressor tool. Refer to **Figure 56** for 1969-1975

models or **Figure 57** for 1976-on models. Remove the valve keepers and release the compression. Remove the valve compressor tool.

CAUTION
To avoid loss of spring tension, do not compress the springs any more than necessary to remove the keepers.

3. Remove the valve spring retainer and valve springs (**Figure 58**).

NOTE
The inner and outer valve seats and valve stem seal will stay in the cylinder head.

4. Prior to removing the valve, remove any burrs from the valve stem (**Figure 59**). Otherwise the valve guide will be damaged.
5. Mark all parts as they are disassembled so that they will be installed in their same location.

Inspection

1. Clean valves with a wire brush and solvent.
2. Inspect the contact surface of each valve for burning or pitting (**Figure 60**). Unevenness of the contact surface is an indication that the valve is not serviceable. The valve contact surface can be ground.
3. Measure the valve stem for wear (**Figure 61**). Compare with specifications given in **Table 1**.
4. Remove all carbon and varnish from the valve guide with a stiff spiral wire brush.
5. Insert each valve in its guide. Hold the valve with the head just slightly off the valve seat and rock it sideways. Measure the play along both the "X" and "Y" axes (**Figure 62**). If it rocks more than slightly, the guide is probably worn and should be replaced. As a final check, take the cylinder head to a dealer and have the valve guides measured.

57

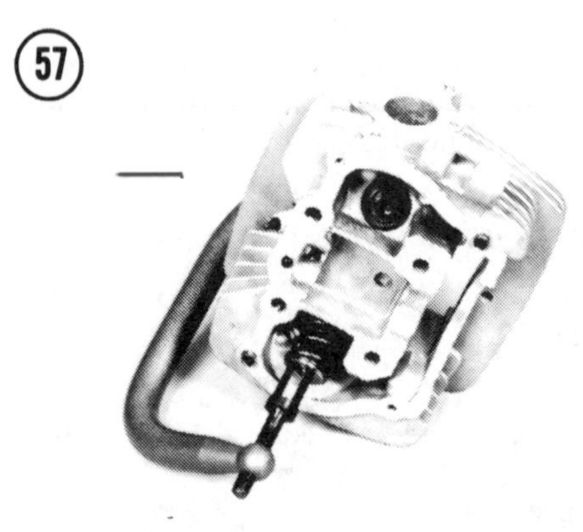

58

59

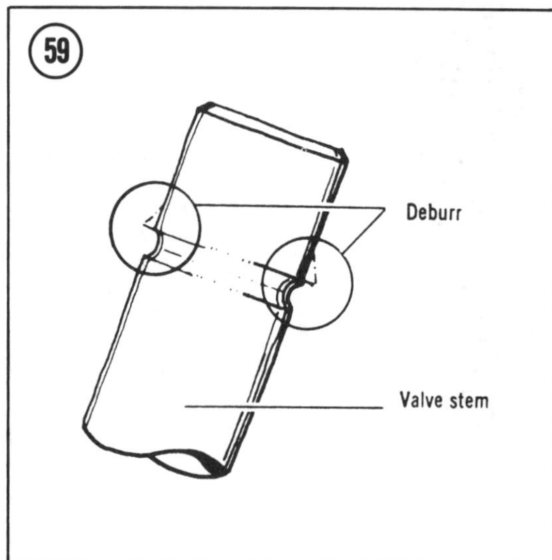

60

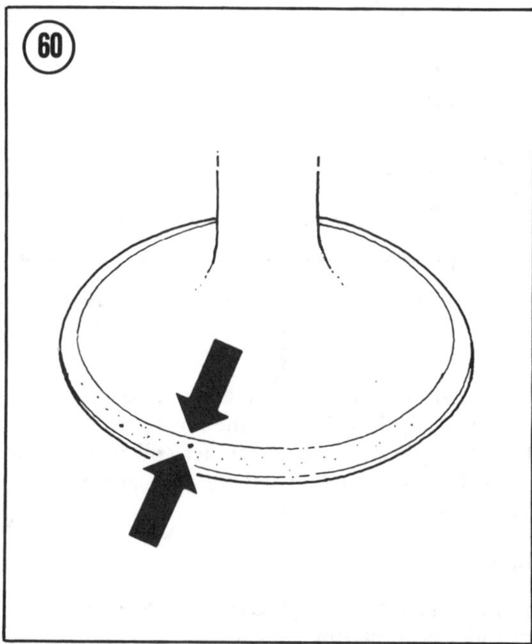

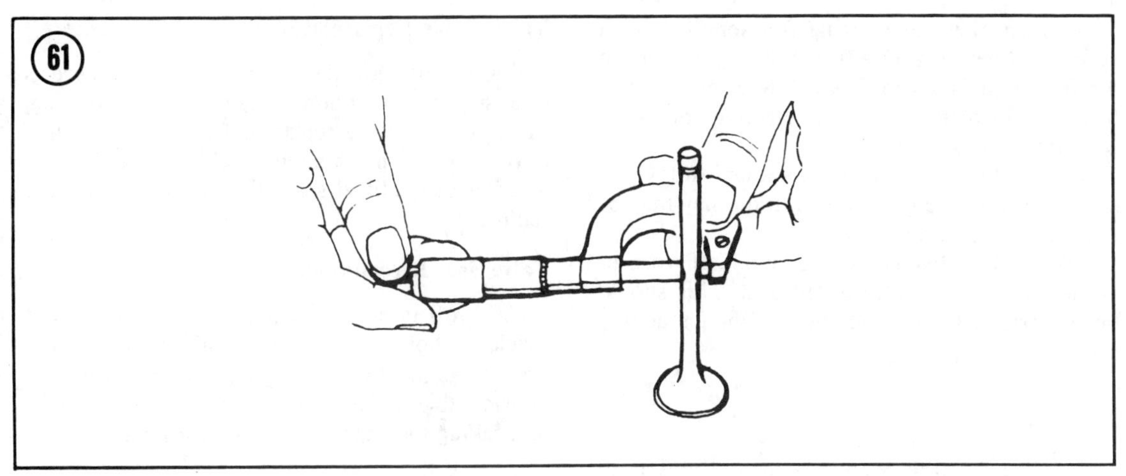

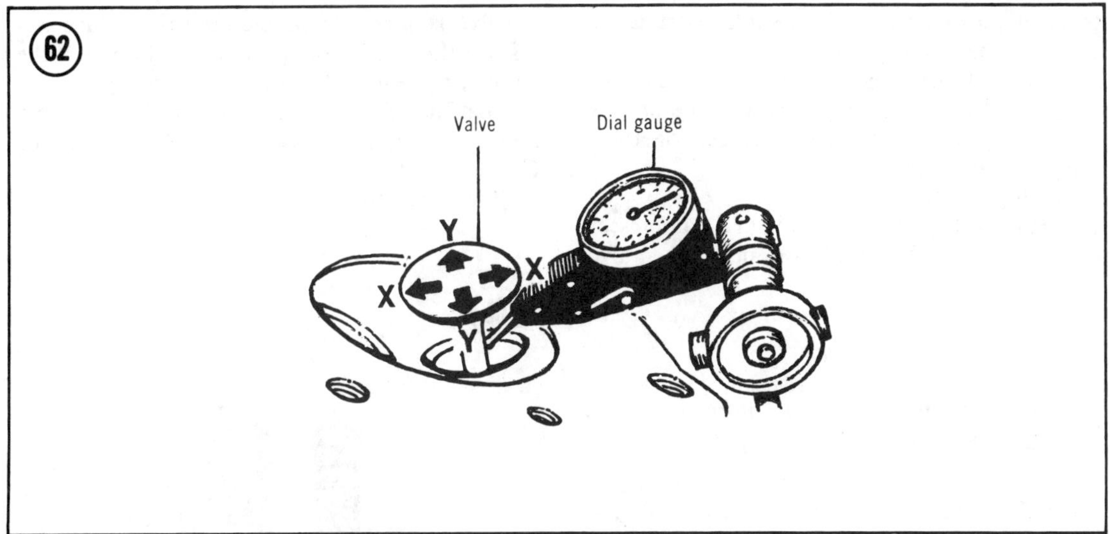

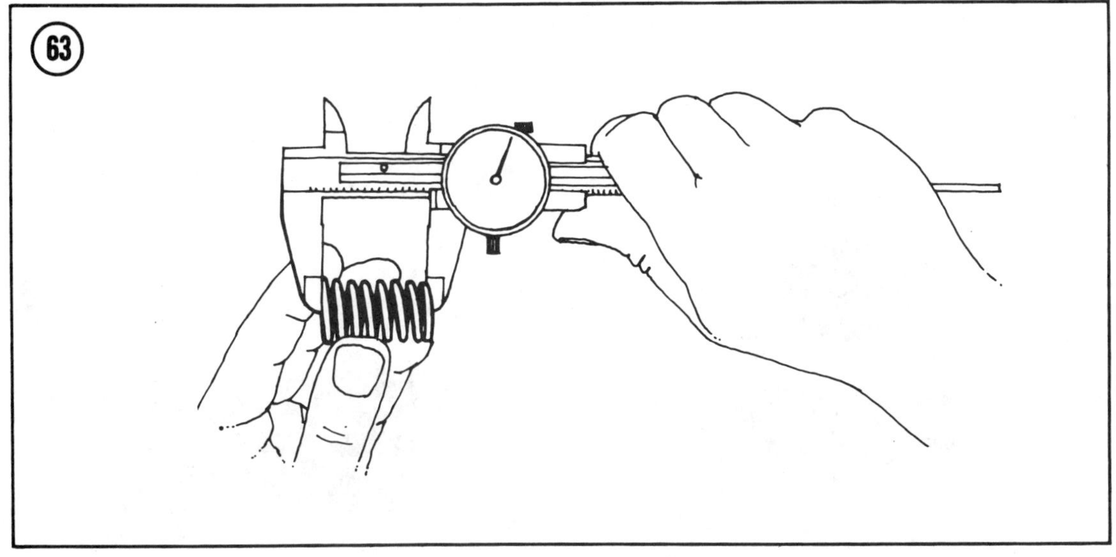

4

6. Measure the valve spring free length with a vernier caliper (**Figure 63**). All should be within the length specified in **Table 1** with no signs of bends or distortion. Replace defective springs in pairs (inner and outer).
7. Check the valve spring retainer and valve keepers. If they are in good condition they may be reused; replace as necesary.
8. Inspect the valve seats (**Figure 64**). If worn or burned, they must be reconditioned. This should be performed by a dealer or qualified machine shop.

Installation

1. Coat the valve stems with molybdenum disulfide grease. To avoid damage to the valve stem seal, turn the valve slowly while inserting the valve into the cylinder head.
2. On models with progressively wound valve springs, install the valve springs with the narrow pitch end (end with the coils closest together) facing the head (**Figure 65**).
3. Install the valve spring retainer.
4. Compress the valve springs with a compressor tool (**Figure 57** or **Figure 58**) and install the valve keepers.

CAUTION
To avoid loss of spring tension, do not compress the springs any more than necessary to install the keepers.

5. After all springs have been installed, gently tap the end of the valve stem with a soft aluminum or brass drift and hammer (**Figure 66**). This will ensure that the keepers are properly seated.

64

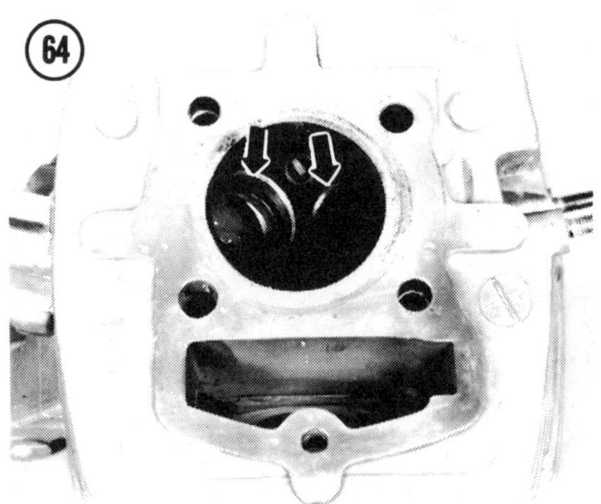

Valve Guide Replacement

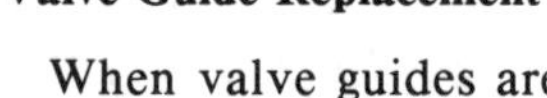

When valve guides are worn so that there is excessive stem-to-guide clearance or valve tipping, the guides must be replaced. Replace all, even if only one is worn. This job should only be done by a dealer or qualified specialist as special tools are required.

Valve Seat Reconditioning

This job is best left to a dealer or qualified machine shop. They have special equipment and knowledge for this exacting job. You can still save considerable money by removing the cylinder head and taking the head to the shop for repairs.

Valve Lapping

Valve lapping is a simple operation which can restore the valve seal without machining if the amount of wear or distortion is not too great.
1. Coat the valve seating area in the head with a lapping compound such as Carborundum or Clover Brand.
2. Insert the valve in the cylinder head.

65

66

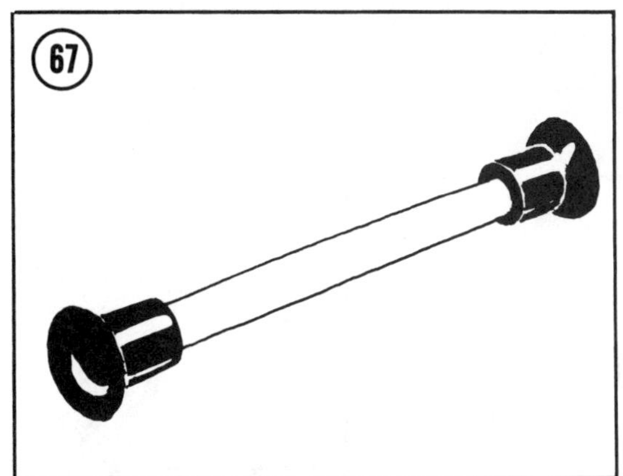

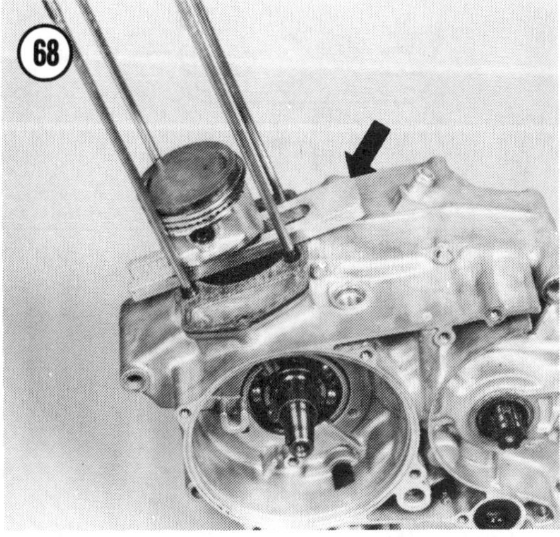

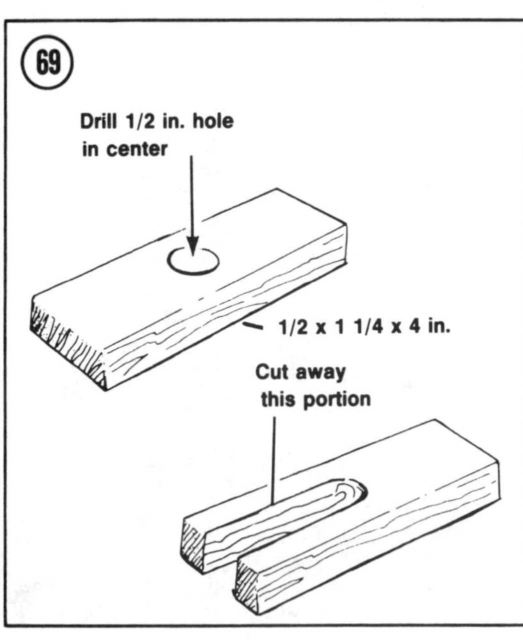

3. Wet the suction cup of the lapping stick (**Figure 67**) and stick it to the valve head.
4. Lap the valve to the seat by rotating the lapping stick in both directions. Every 5 to 10 seconds, rotate the valve 180° in the seat; continue lapping until the contact surfaces of the valve and the valve seat are a uniform grey. Stop as soon as they are, to avoid removing too much material.
5. Thoroughly clean the valves and the cylinder head in solvent to remove all grinding compound. Any compound left in the head or on the valves will end up in the oil supply and cause damage to the engine.
6. After the valve lapping is completed and the valves are reinstalled in the cylinder head, the valve seal should be tested. Check the seal of each valve by pouring solvent into the intake and exhaust ports. There should be no leakage past the valve seat. If fluid leaks past either seat, disassemble the valve assembly and repeat the lapping procedure until there is no leakage.

If there is still a leak either the valve or the valve seat must be ground or replaced.

CYLINDER

Removal

1. Remove the cylinder head as described in this chapter.
2. Loosen the cylinder by tapping around the perimeter with a rubber or plastic mallet. If necessary, *gently* pry the cylinder loose with a broad-tipped screwdriver.
3. Pull the cylinder straight up and off of the crankcase studs. Work the cam chain wire thorugh the opening in the cylinder.
4. Remove the cylinder base gasket and discard it. Remove the 2 dowel pins from the crankcase studs.
5. Install a piston holding fixture under the piston (**Figure 68**) to protect the piston skirt from damage. This fixture may be purchased or may be a homemade unit of wood. See **Figure 69** for dimensions.

Inspection

The following procedure requires the use of highly specialized and expensive measuring instruments. If such equipment is not readily available, have the measurements performed by a dealer or qualified machine shop.

1. Soak with solvent any old cylinder head gasket material on the cylinder. Use a broad-tipped *dull* chisel and gently scrape off all gasket residue. Do not gouge the sealing surface as oil and air leaks will result.

4

2. Measure the cylinder bore with a cylinder gauge or inside micrometer at the points shown in **Figure 70**. Measure in 2 axes—in line with the piston pin and at 90° to the pin. If the taper or out-of-round is 0.10 mm (0.004 in.) or greater, the cylinder must be rebored to the next oversize and a new piston installed.

NOTE
The new piston should be obtained before the cylinder is rebored so that the piston can be measured; slight manufacturing tolerances must be taken into account to determine the actual size and working clearance.

3. Check the cylinder wall (**Figure 71**) for scratches; if evident, the cylinder should be rebored. The maximum wear limit on the cylinder is listed in **Table 1**. If the cylinder is worn to this limit, it must be replaced. Never rebore a cylinder if the finished rebore diameter will be this dimension or greater.

Installation

1. Check that the top surface of the crankcase and the bottom surface of the cylinder are clean prior to installing a new base gasket.
2. Install a new cylinder base gasket (A, **Figure 72**).
3. Install the 2 dowel pins (B, **Figure 72**) on the left-hand crankcase studs.
4. Install a piston holding fixture under piston (C, **Figure 72**).
5. Make sure the end gaps of the piston rings are *not* lined up with each other—they must be staggered. Lightly oil the piston rings and the inside of the cylinder bore with assembly oil.
6. Untie the cam chain wire and tie it to the cylinder.
7. Install the cylinder and slide it down onto the crankcase studs.
8. Carefully feed the cam chain and wire up through the opening in the cylinder and tie it to the engine.
9. Start the cylinder down over the piston (**Figure 73**). Compress each piston ring as it enters the cylinder either with your fingers or by using aircraft type hose clamps (**Figure 74**) of the appropriate size.
10. Slide the cylinder down until it bottoms on the piston holding fixture.
11. Remove the piston holding fixture and slide the cylinder down into place on the crankcase.
12. Install the cylinder head as described in this chapter.

70

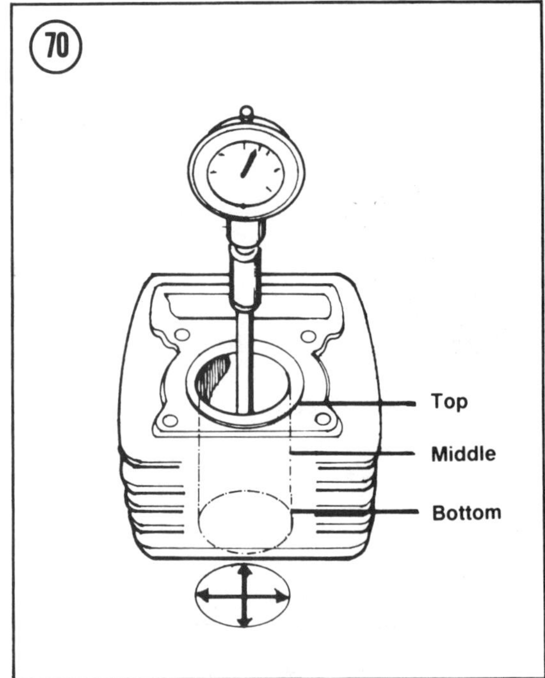

71

72

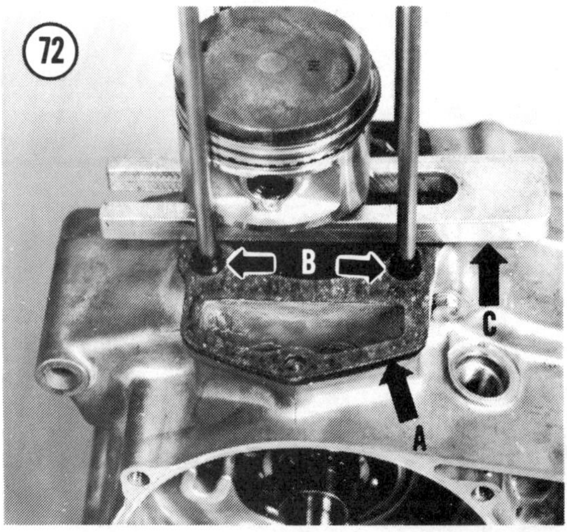

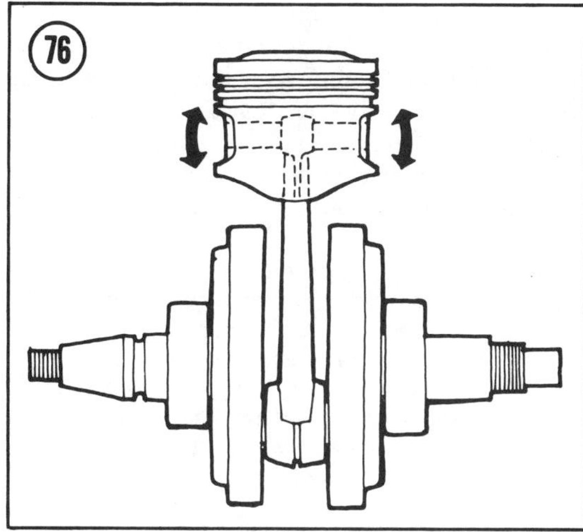

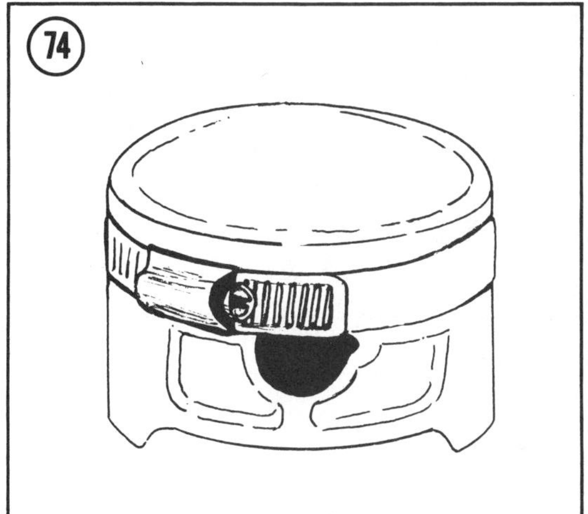

75

13. Adjust the valves, cam chain tensioner and ignition timing as described in Chapter Three.
14. Follow the *Break-in Procedure* in this chapter if the cylinder was rebored or honed or a new piston or piston rings were installed.

PISTON, PISTON PIN AND PISTON RINGS

The piston is made of an aluminum alloy. The piston pin is made of steel and is a precision fit. The piston pin is held in place by a clip at each end.

Piston Removal

1. Remove the cylinder head and cylinder as described in this chapter.

WARNING
The edges of all piston rings are very sharp. Be careful when handling them to avoid cut fingers.

2. Remove the top ring with a ring expander tool or by spreading the ends with your thumbs just enough to slide the ring up over the piston (**Figure 75**). Repeat for the remaining rings.
3. Before removing the piston, hold the rod tightly and rock the piston as shown in **Figure 76**. Any rocking motion (do not confuse with the normal sliding motion) indicates wear on the piston pin, piston pin bore or connecting rod bore (more likely a combination of all).

NOTE
Wrap a clean shop cloth under the piston so that the piston pin clip will not fall into the crankcase.

4. Remove the clips from each side of the piston pin bore (**Figure** 77) with a small screwdriver or scribe. Hold your thumb over one edge of the clip when removing it to prevent the clip from springing out.
5. Use a proper size wooden dowel or socket extension and push out the piston pin.

CAUTION
Be careful when removing the pin to avoid damaging the connecting rod. If it is necessary to gently tap the pin to remove it, be sure that the piston is properly supported so that lateral shock is not transmitted to the lower connecting rod bearing.

6. If the piston pin is difficult to remove, heat the piston and pin with a butane torch. The pin will probably push right out. Heat the piston to only about 60° C (140° F), i.e., until it is too warm to touch, but not excessively hot. If the pin is still difficult to push out, use a homemade tool as shown in **Figure 78**.

NOTE
A special tool, the universal piston pin extractor, is available from British Marketing, P.O. Box 219, San Juan Capistrano, CA 92693.

7. Lift the piston off the connecting rod.
8. If the piston is going to be left off for some time, place a piece of foam insulation tube over the end of the rod to protect it.

Inspection

1. Carefully clean the carbon from the piston crown with a chemical remover or with a soft scraper (**Figure 79**). Do not remove or damage the carbon ridge around the circumference of the piston above the top ring (**Figure 80**). If the piston, rings and cylinder are found to be dimensionally correct and can be reused, removal of the carbon ring from the top of the piston or the carbon ridge from the top of the cylinder will promote excessive oil consumption.

CAUTION
Do not wire brush the piston skirts.

2. Examine each ring groove for burrs, dented edges and wide wear. Pay particular attention to the top compression ring groove as it usually wears more than the others.
3. Measure piston-to-cylinder clearance as described in this chapter.

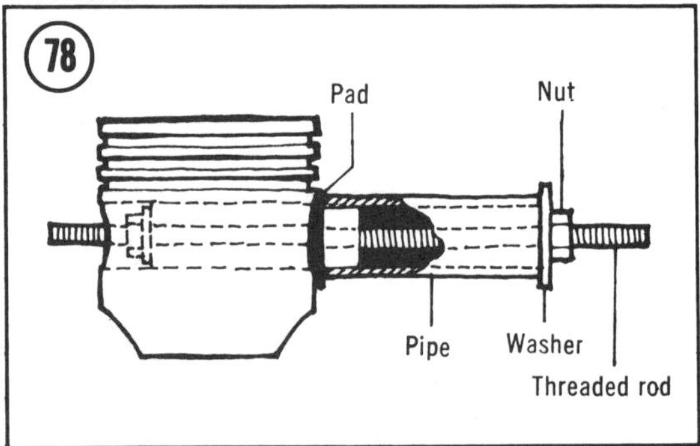

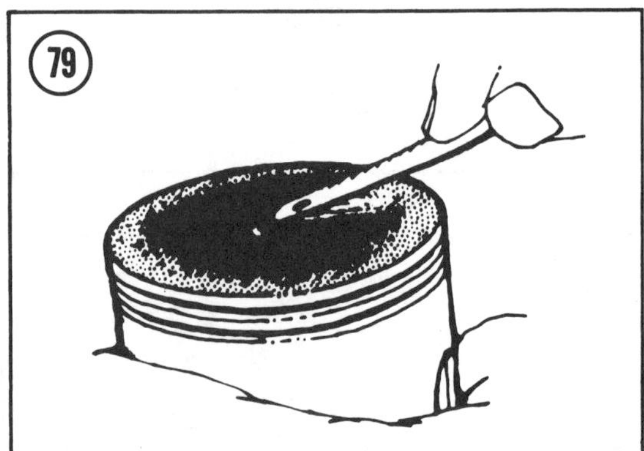

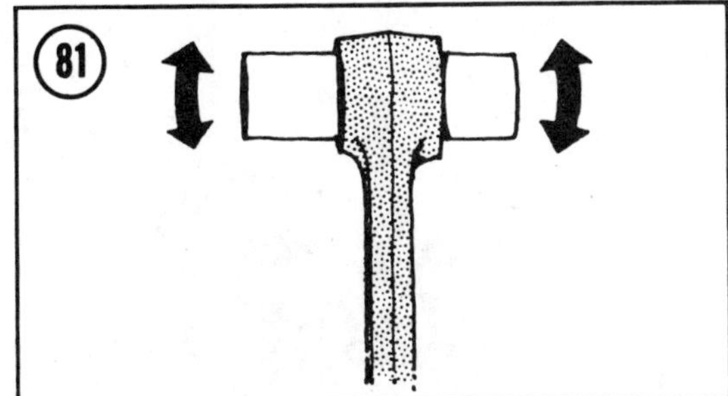

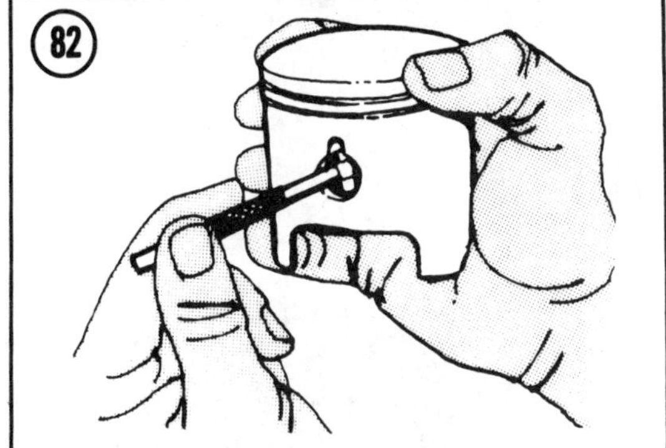

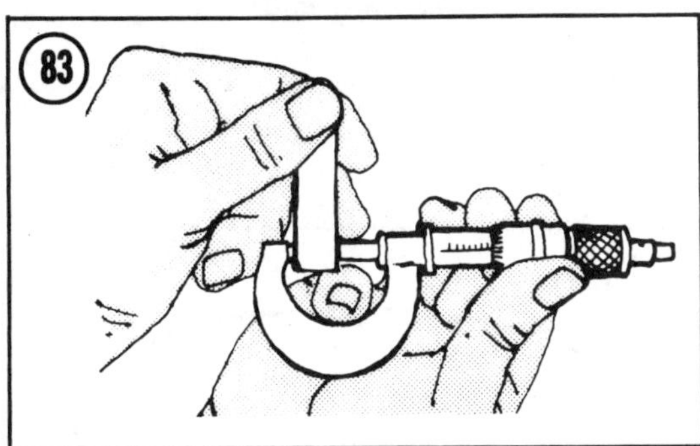

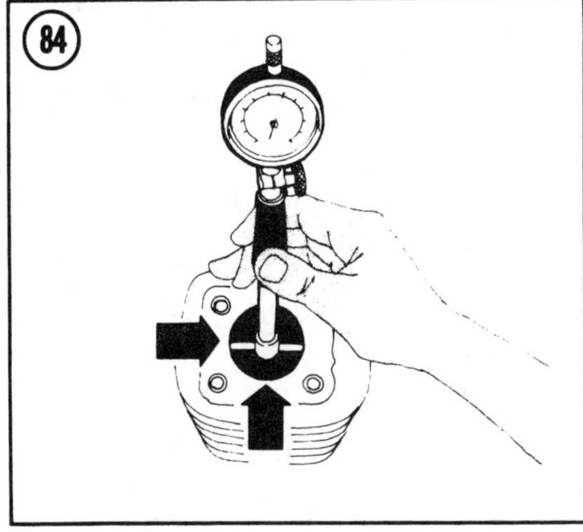

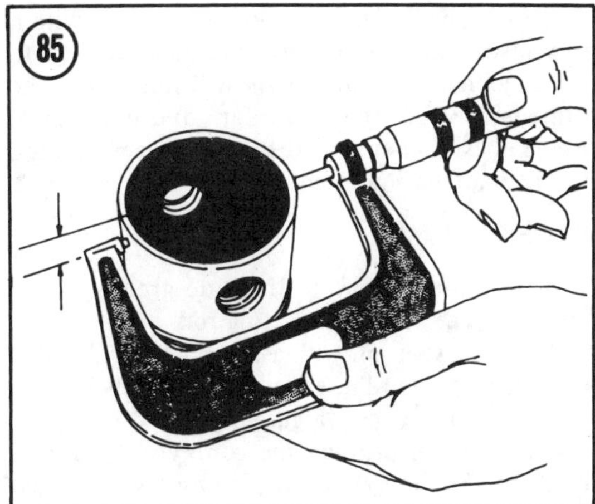

4. If damage or wear indicates piston replacement, select a new piston as described under *Piston Clearance* in this chapter.
5. Oil the piston pin and install it in the connecting rod. Slowly rotate the piston pin and check for radial and axial play (**Figure 81**). If any play exists, the piston pin should be replaced, providing the rod bore is in good condition. Measure the inside diameter of the piston pin bore with a snap gauge (**Figure 82**) and measure the outside diameter of the piston pin with a micrometer (**Figure 83**). Compare with dimensions given in **Table 1**. Replace the piston and piston pin as a set if either or both are worn.
6. Check the piston skirt for galling and abrasion which may have been caused by piston seizure. If light galling is present, smooth the affected area with No. 400 emery paper and oil or a fine oilstone. If galling is severe or if the piston is deeply scored, replace it.

Piston Clearance

1. Make sure the piston and cylinder walls are clean and dry.
2. Measure the inside diameter of the cylinder bore at a point 13 mm (1/2 in.) from the upper edge with a bore gauge (**Figure 84**).
3. Measure the outside diameter of the piston across the skirt at right angles to the piston pin. Measure at a distance 10 mm (0.40 in.) up from the bottom of the piston skirt (**Figure 85**).
4. Piston clearance is the difference between the maximum piston diameter and the minimum cylinder diameter. Subtract the dimension of the piston from the cylinder dimension. If the clearance exceeds 0.10 mm (0.004 in.), the cylinder should be rebored to the next oversize and a new piston installed.

5. To establish a final overbore dimension with a new piston, add the piston skirt measurement to the specified clearance. This will determine the dimension for the cylinder overbore size. Remember, do not exceed the cylinder maximum inside diameter indicated in **Table 1**.

Piston Installation

1. Apply molybdenum disulfide grease to the inside surface of the connecting rod.
2. Oil the piston pin with assembly oil and install it in the piston until its end extends slightly beyond the inside of the boss (**Figure 86**).
3. Place the piston over the connecting rod with the "IN" (**Figure 87**) on the piston crown directed rearward toward the intake port.
4. Line up the piston pin with the hole in the connecting rod. Push the piston pin through the connecting rod and into the other side of the piston until it is even with the piston pin clip grooves.

CAUTION
If it is necessary to tap the piston pin into the connecting rod, do so gently with a block of wood or a soft-faced hammer. Make sure you support the piston to prevent the lateral shock from being transmitted to connecting rod bearing.

NOTE
*In the next step, install the clips with the gap away from the cutout in the piston (**Figure 88**).*

5. Install new piston pin clips in both ends of the piston pin bore. Make sure they are seated in the grooves in the piston.
6. Check the installation by rocking the piston back and forth around the pin axis and from side to side along the axis. It should rotate freely back and forth but not slide from side to side.
7. Install the piston rings as described in this chapter.
8. Install the cylinder and cylinder head as described in this chapter.

Piston Ring Replacement

WARNING
The edges of all piston rings are very sharp. Be careful when handling them to avoid cut fingers.

1. Remove the top ring by spreading the ends with your thumbs just enough to slide the ring up over the piston. Repeat for the remaining rings.

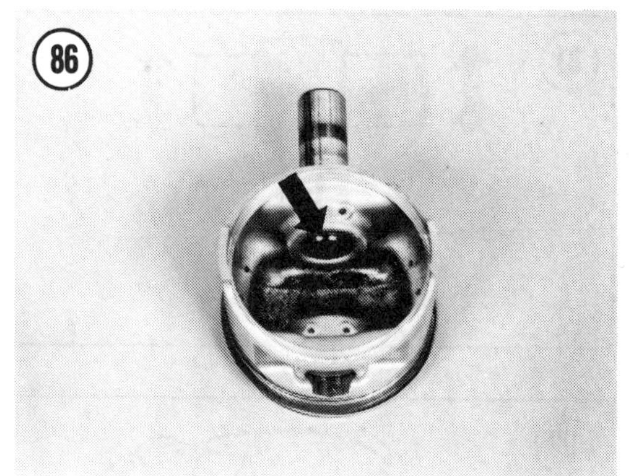

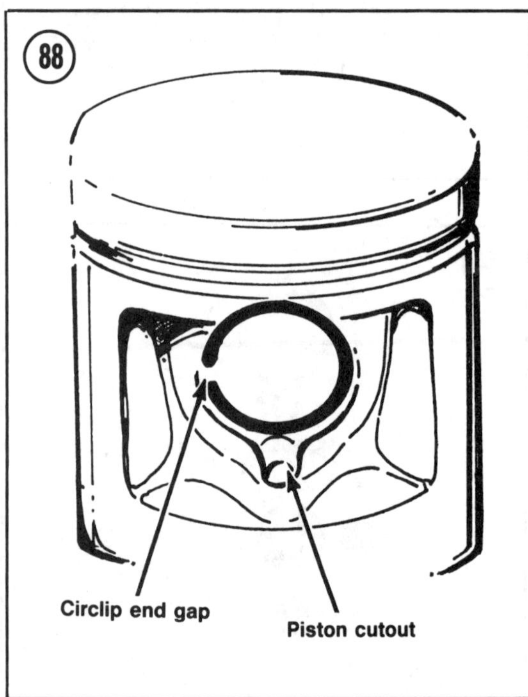

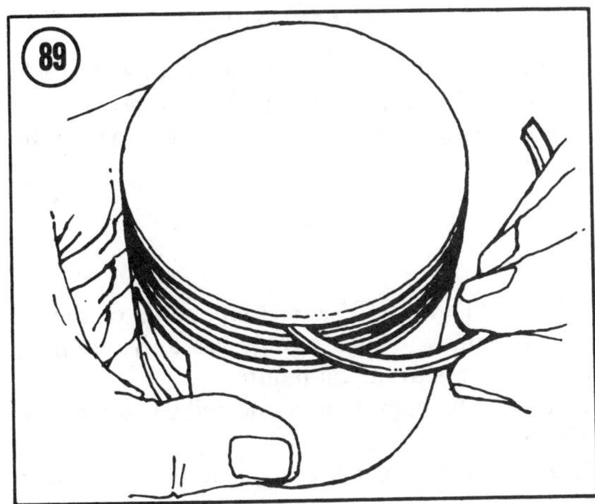

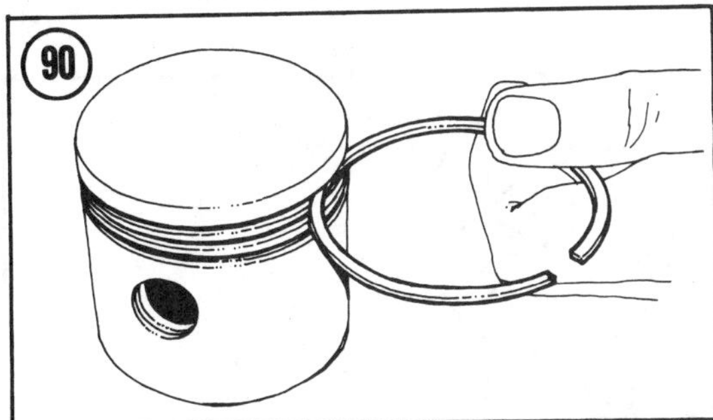

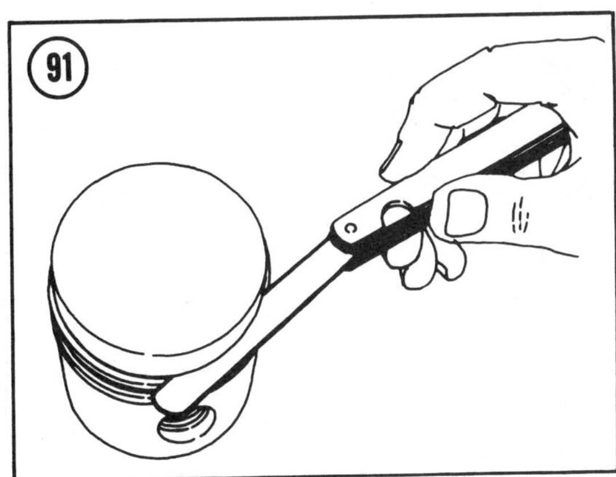

2. Carefully remove all carbon buildup from the ring grooves with a broken piston ring (**Figure 89**). Inspect the grooves carefully for burrs, nicks or broken and cracked lands. Recondition or replace the piston if necessary.
3. Roll each ring around its piston groove as shown in **Figure 90** to check for binding. Minor binding may be cleaned up with a fine-cut file.
4. Measure the side clearance of each ring in its groove with a flat feeler gauge (**Figure 91**) and compare to dimensions given in **Table 1**. If the clearance is greater than specified, the rings must be replaced. If the clearance is still excessive with the new rings, the piston must also be replaced.

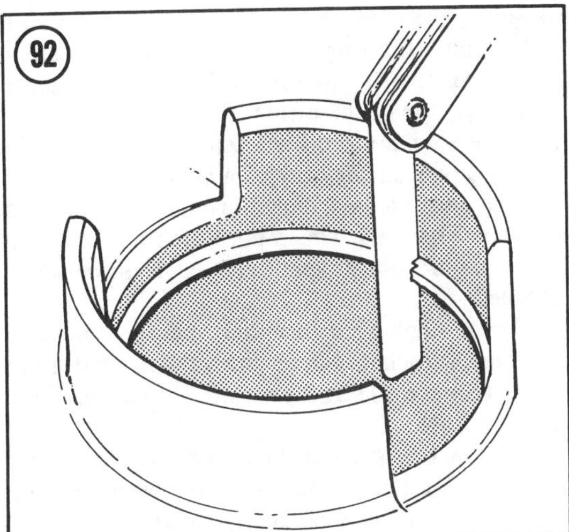

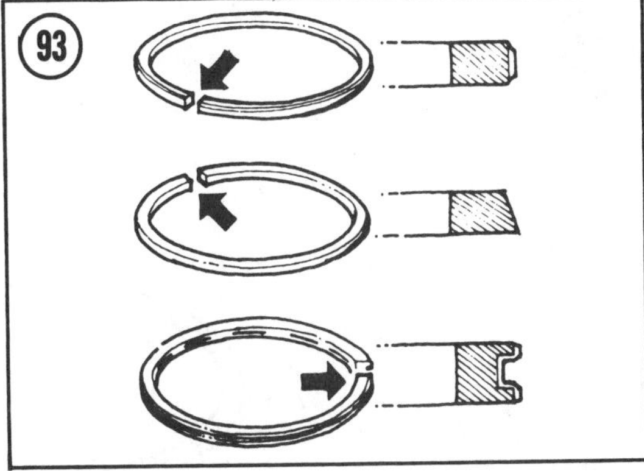

5. Measure each ring for wear as shown in **Figure 92**. Place each ring, one at a time, into the cylinder and push it in about 20 mm (3/4 in.) with the crown of the piston to ensure that the ring is square in the cylinder bore. Measure the gap with a flat feeler gauge and compare to dimensions in **Table 1**. If the gap is greater than specified, the rings should be replaced. When installing new rings, measure their end gap in the same manner as for old ones. If the gap is less than specified, carefully file the ends with a fine-cut file until the gap is correct.
6. Install the piston rings in the order shown in **Figure 93**.

NOTE
Install all rings with the marking facing up.

7. Install the piston rings—first the bottom one, then the middle one, then the top—by carefully

4

spreading the ends of the ring with your thumbs and slipping the ring over the top of the piston. Remember that the marks on the piston rings are toward the top of the piston.
8. Make sure the rings are seated completely in their grooves all the way around the piston and that the ends are distributed around the piston as shown in **Figure 94**. The important thing is that the ring gaps are not aligned with each other when installed.
9. If new rings were installed, measure the side clearance of each ring in its groove with a flat feeler gauge (**Figure 91**) and compare to dimensions given in **Table 1**.
10. Follow the *Break-in Procedure* in this chapter if a new piston or piston rings have been installed or the cylinder was rebored or honed.

OIL PUMP

The oil pump is located on the right-hand side of the engine forward of the clutch assembly. The oil pump can be removed with the engine in the frame.

Removal

Refer to **Figure 95** for components of the oil filter assembly. This assembly has to be removed to gain access to the oil pump.
1. Drain the engine oil as described in Chapter Three.
2. Remove the rear brake pedal as described in Chapter Eleven.
3. Slacken the clutch cable at the hand lever.

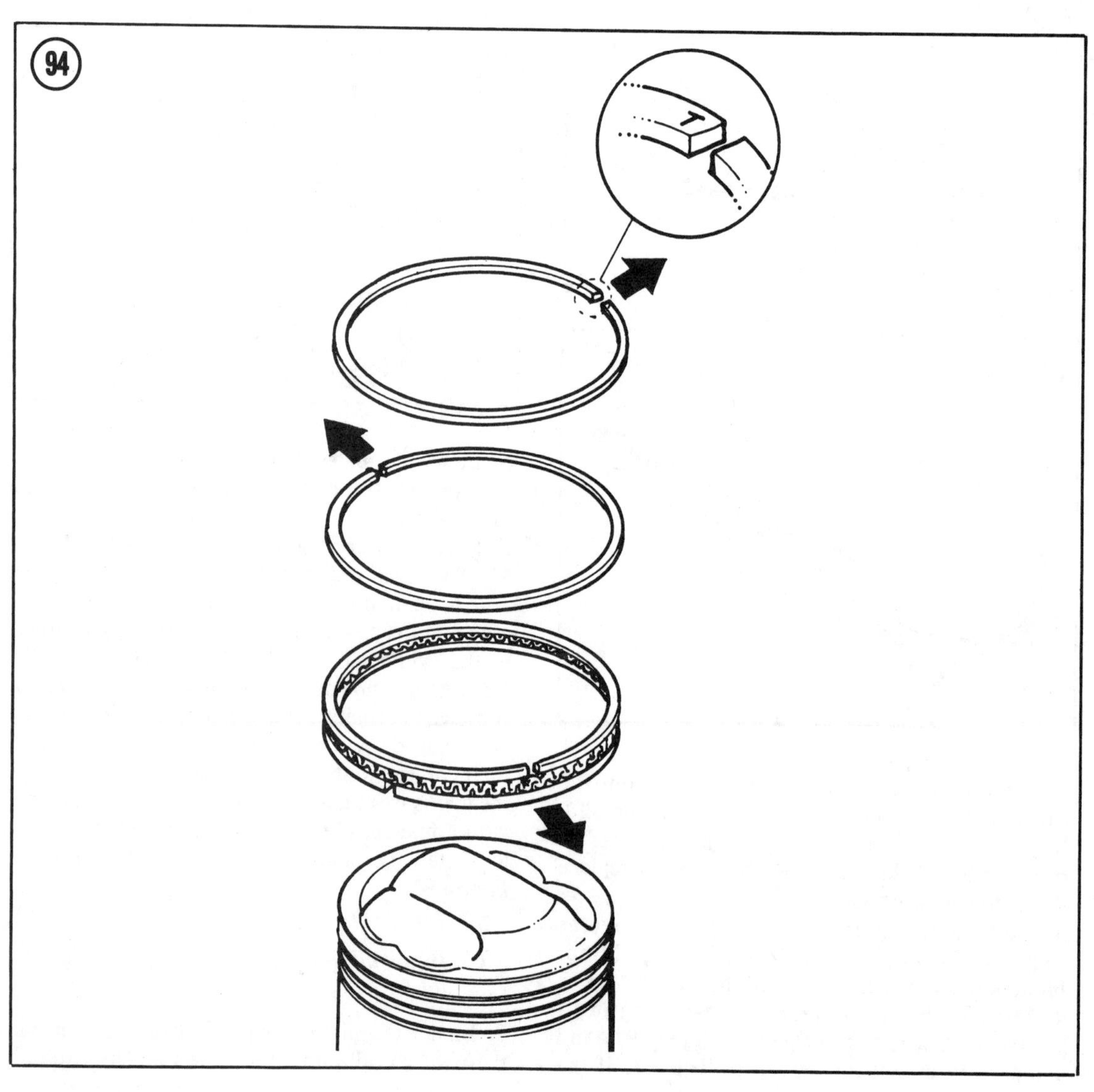

4. Disconnect the clutch cable at the crankcase cover.
5. Remove the bolt securing the kickstarter and remove the kickstarter lever.
6. Remove the bolts securing the right-hand crankcase cover (**Figure 96**) and remove the cover, gasket and 2 locating dowels.
7. Remove the screws (**Figure 97**) securing the oil filter rotor cover and remove the cover.
8. Place a copper washer (or copper penny) into mesh with the primary drive gear behind the oil filter rotor and the clutch outer housing. This will keep the oil rotor from turning during the next step.

OIL FILTER ASSEMBLY (100 AND 125 CC ENGINES)

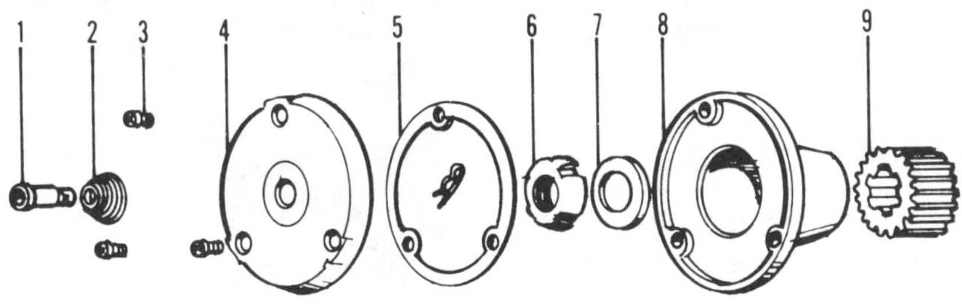

1. Oil nozzle
2. Spring
3. Screw
4. Cap
5. Gasket
6. Locknut
7. Lockwasher
8. Filter rotor
9. Primary drive gear

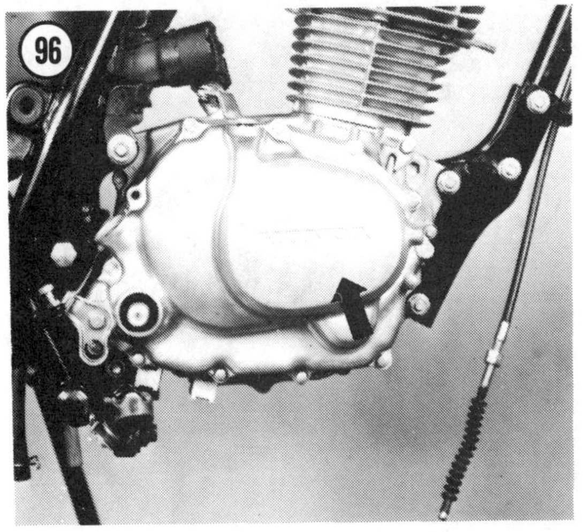

9. Remove the nut and lockwasher (**Figure 98**) securing the oil rotor housing in place. Remove the housing.

NOTE
Oil rotor nut removal requires a special tool available from a Honda dealer (Locknut Wrench 20×24, part No. 07716-0020100).

10. Remove the bolts (**Figure 99**) securing the oil pump gear cover and remove the cover.
11. Remove the oil pump driven gear (**Figure 100**).
12. Remove the screws (**Figure 101**) securing the oil pump body assembly and remove the assembly.
13. Don't lose the O-ring seals (**Figure 102**) in the crankcase recesses.

Disassembly/Inspection/Assembly

Refer to **Figure 103** for XL125 models or **Figure 104** for all other models during this procedure.

1. Inspect the pump body for cracks.
2. Remove the gear shaft (**Figure 105**).
3. Remove the Phillips screws (**Figure 106**) securing the pump cover to the body and remove the cover.
4. Remove the inner and outer rotors. Inspect both parts for scratches and abrasions. Replace both parts if evidence of this is found.
5. If damaged, remove the gasket (**Figure 107**).
6. Clean all parts in solvent and thoroughly dry. Coat all parts with fresh engine oil prior to assembly.
7. Inspect the teeth on the drive gear. Replace the drive gear if the teeth are damaged or any are missing.
8. Install the inner and outer rotors into the pump body.
9. Measure the clearance between the inner rotor tip and the outer rotor as shown in **Figure 108**. If the clearance is greater than specified in **Table 1**, replace the worn part.
10. Measure the clearance between the outer rotor and the oil pump body with a flat feeler gauge (**Figure 109**). If the clearance is greater than specified in **Table 1**, replace the worn part.
11. Install a new gasket if the old one was removed.
12. Install the cover and screws and tighten the screws securely.
13. Install the oil pump gear shaft.

Installation

1. Install the O-ring seals (**Figure 102**) into the crankcase recesses.
2. Install the oil pump body assembly (**Figure 101**) and tighten the bolts securely.
3. Install the oil pump driven gear (**Figure 100**).
4. Install the oil pump gear cover and screws (**Figure 99**).
5. Install the oil rotor housing. Install the lockwasher with the marking "OUTSIDE" facing toward the outside (**Figure 110**).

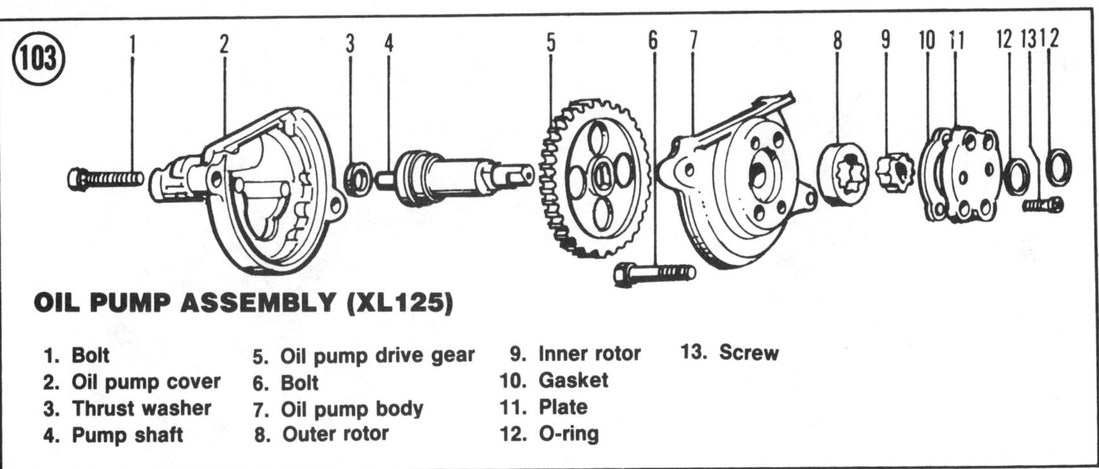

OIL PUMP ASSEMBLY (XL125)

1. Bolt
2. Oil pump cover
3. Thrust washer
4. Pump shaft
5. Oil pump drive gear
6. Bolt
7. Oil pump body
8. Outer rotor
9. Inner rotor
10. Gasket
11. Plate
12. O-ring
13. Screw

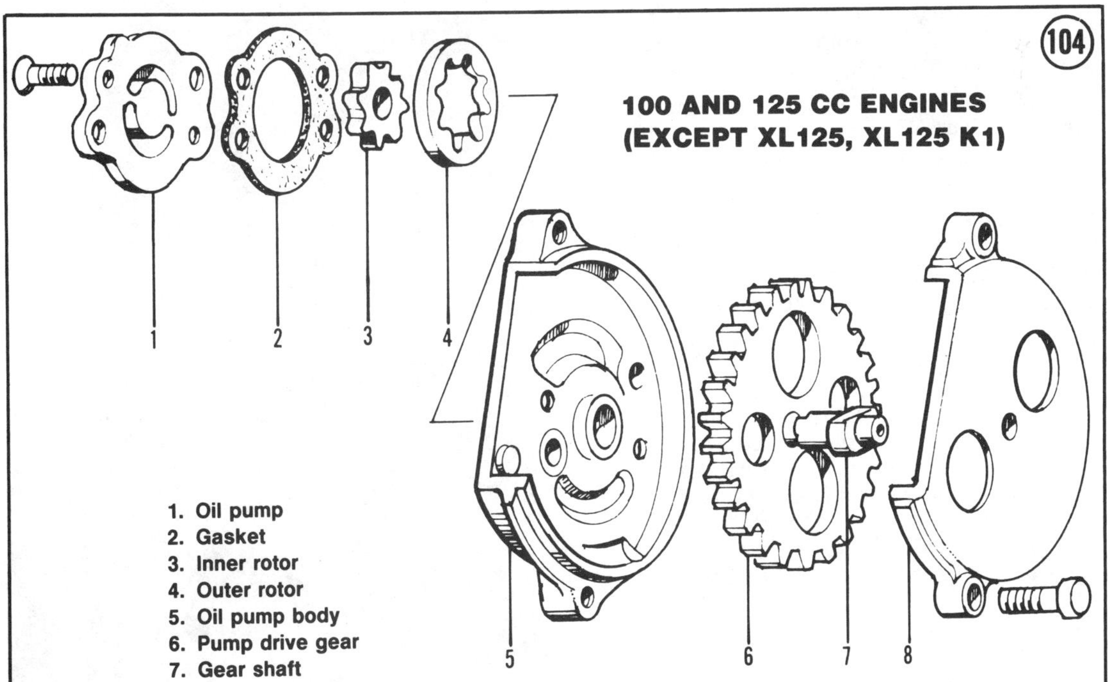

104

100 AND 125 CC ENGINES (EXCEPT XL125, XL125 K1)

1. Oil pump
2. Gasket
3. Inner rotor
4. Outer rotor
5. Oil pump body
6. Pump drive gear
7. Gear shaft
8. Gear cover

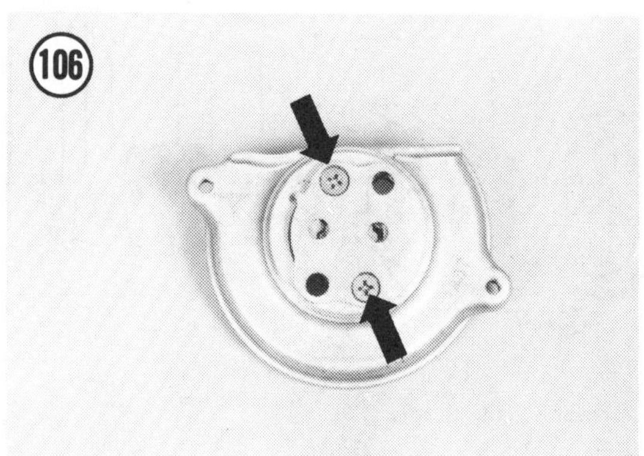

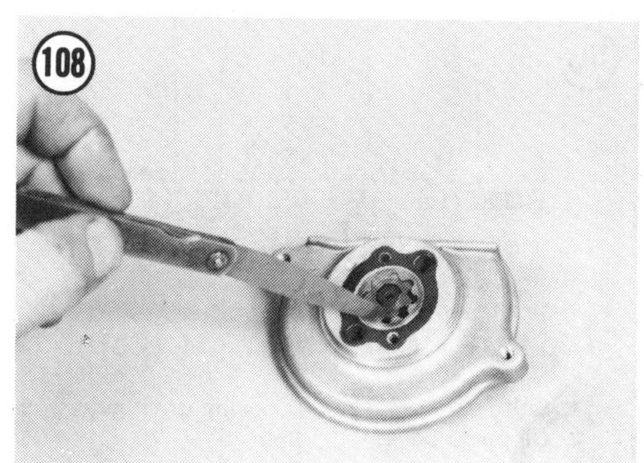

6. Install the locknut (**Figure 98**) and tighten to the torque specification listed in **Table 2**. Use the same tool setup as used in *Removal* Step 8 and Step 9.
7. Install the oil filter rotor cover and install the screws (**Figure 97**). Tighten the screws securely.
8. Install the dowel pins (A, **Figure 111**) and the gasket (B, **Figure 111**).
9. Pull the clutch actutator lever on the crankcase cover so the recess in the actuator (**Figure 112**) will mesh properly with the clutch lifter.
10. Install the right-hand crankcase cover. Push it all the way into place. Install the screws and tighten in a crisscross pattern until they are secure.

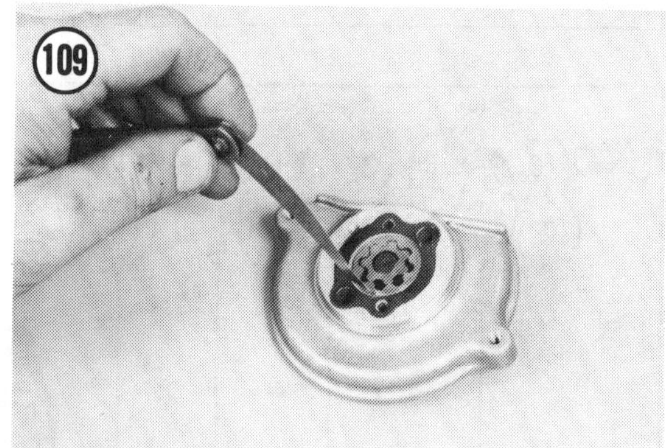

CAUTION
Do not install any of the crankcase cover screws until the crankcase cover is snug up against the crankcase surface. Do not try to force the cover into place with screw pressure. If the cover will not fit up against the crankcase, remove the crankcase cover and repeat Step 9 and Step 10.

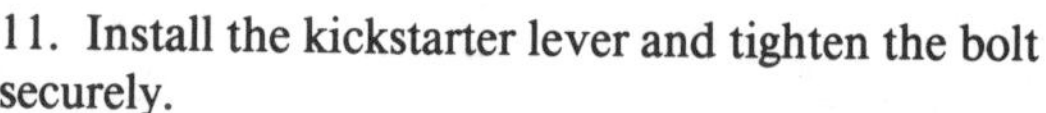
11. Install the kickstarter lever and tighten the bolt securely.

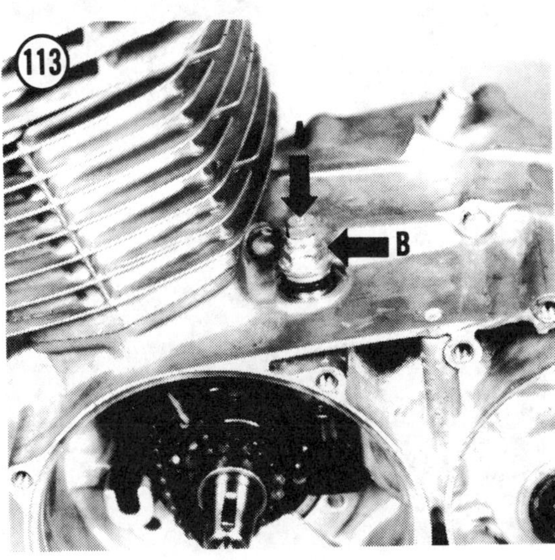

12. Connect the clutch cable to the lever on the crankcase cover.
13. Install the rear brake pedal as described in Chapter Eleven.
14. Refill the engine with the recommended type and quantity of oil; refer to Chapter Three.
15. Adjust the clutch as described in Chapter Three.

CRANKCASE AND CRANKSHAFT

Disassembly of the crankcase (splitting the cases) and removal of the crankshaft assembly require that the engine be removed from the frame.

The crankcase is made in 2 halves of precision diecast aluminum alloy and is of the "thin-walled" type. To avoid damage, do not hammer or pry on any of the interior or exterior projected walls. The crankcase is assembled with a gasket between the 2 halves and dowel pins align the halves when they are bolted together. These areas are easily damaged.

The crankshaft assembly is made up of 2 full-circle flywheels pressed together on a hollow crankpin. The connecting rod big-end bearing on the crankpin is a needle bearing assembly. The crankshaft assembly is supported by 2 ball bearings in the crankcase. Service to the crankshaft assembly is limited to removal and replacement.

The procedure which follows is presented as a complete, step-by-step, major lower end rebuild that should be followed if an engine is to be completely reconditioned. However, if you're replacing a part that you know is defective, the disassembly should be carried out only until the failed part is accessible; there is no need to disassemble the engine beyond that point so long as you know the remaining components are in good condition and that they were not affected by the failed part.

Crankcase Disassembly

1. Remove the engine as described in this chapter.
2. Remove the cam chain adjusting bolt and washer (A, **Figure 113**) and the bolt assembly (B, **Figure 113**).
3. Remove all exterior engine assemblies as described in this chapter and other related chapters:
   a. Cylinder head cover (1976-on models).
   b. Cylinder head.
   c. Cylinder.
   d. Piston.
   e. Alternator.

f. Clutch.
g. External shift mechanism.

4A. On 1968-1975 models, remove the cam chain tensioner set plate (A, **Figure 114**). Remove the cam chain tensioner hinge (B, **Figure 114**).

4B. On 1976-on models, remove the bolt (A, **Figure 115**) securing the cam chain tensioner arm and remove the tensioner arm and spring (B, **Figure 115**).

5. Remove the cam chain tensioner assembly.

6. On 1976-on models, turn the crankcase assembly over and catch the tensioner assembly lock collars located within the adjusting bolt assembly cavity.

7. Remove the cam chain.

8. On the left-hand crankcase side, remove the bolts securing the crankcase halves together (**Figure 116**). To prevent warpage, loosen them in a crisscross pattern.

NOTE

Set the engine on wood blocks or fabricate a holding fixture of 2 X 4 inch wood.

9. Turn the crankcase over and remove the only bolt (**Figure 117**) on the right-hand side. Don't lose the clip located under the bolt.

CAUTION

Perform the next step directly over and close to the workbench as the crankcase halves may easily separate. ***Do not*** *hammer on the crankcase halves or they will be damaged.*

10. Hold onto the right-hand crankcase and studs and tap on the right-hand end of the crankshaft and transmission shafts with a plastic or rubber mallet until the crankshaft and crankcase separate.

11. If the crankcase and crankshaft will not separate using this method check to make sure that all screws are removed. If you still have a problem, take the crankcase assembly to a dealer and have it separated.

NOTE

Never pry between case halves. Doing so may result in oil leaks, requiring replacement of the case halves.

12. Don't lose the 2 locating dowels if they came out of the case. They do not have to be removed from the case if they are secure.

13. Lift up and carefully remove the transmission, shift drum and shift fork shaft assemblies.

14. Carefully remove the crankshaft assembly from the crankcase half.

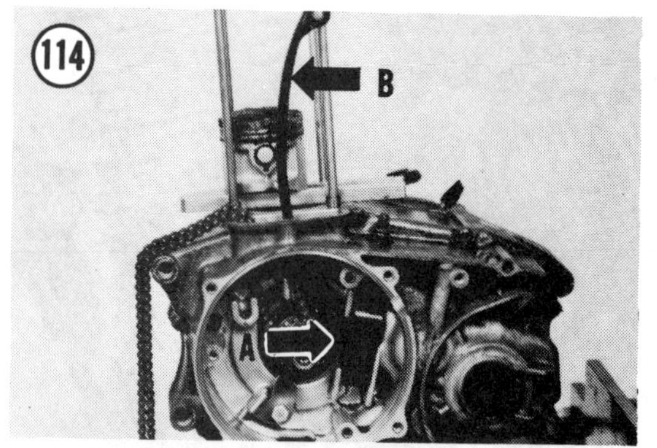

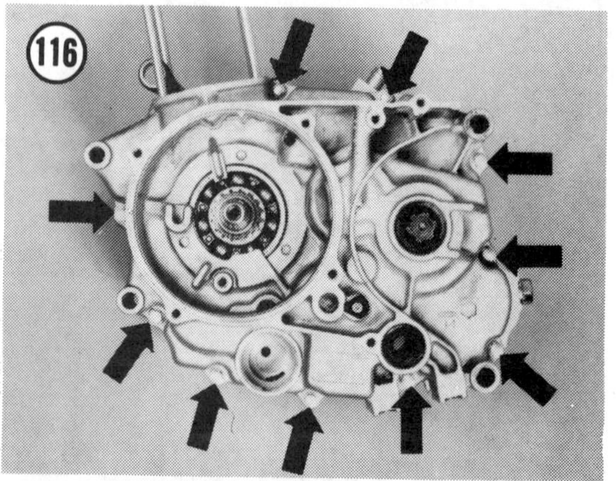

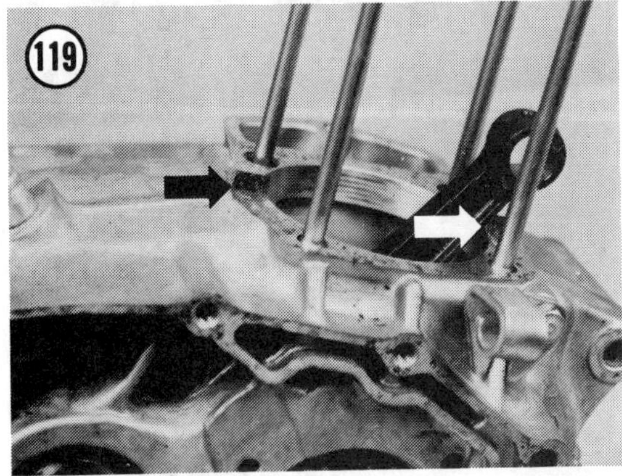

15. Inspect the crankcase halves and crankshaft as described in this chapter.

Crankcase Assembly

1. Apply assembly oil to the inner race of all bearings in both crankcase halves.

NOTE
Set the crankcase half assembly on wood blocks or the wood holding fixture shown in the disassembly procedure.

2. Install the transmission assemblies, shift shafts and shift drum in the left-hand crankcase half and lightly oil all shaft ends. Refer to Chapter Six for the correct procedure.
3. Install the crankshaft.

NOTE
Make sure the mating surfaces are clean and free of all old gasket material. Make sure you get a leak-free seal.

4. Install the 2 locating dowels (A, **Figure 118**) if they were removed.
5. Install a new crankcase gasket (B, **Figure 118**).
6. Set the upper crankcase half over the one on the blocks. Push it down squarely into place until it reaches the crankshaft bearing. There is usually about 1/2 inch left to go.
7. Lightly tap the case halves together with a plastic or rubber mallet until they seat.

CAUTION
Crankcase halves should fit together without force. If the crankcase halves do not fit together completely, do not attempt to pull them together with the crankcase screws. Separate the crankcase halves and investigate the cause of the interference. If the transmission shafts were disassembled, recheck to make sure that a gear is not installed backwards. Do not risk damage by trying to force the cases together.

4

8. Into the left-hand crankcase, install all of the 50 mm crankcase screws (**Figure 116**) and tighten only finger-tight.
9. Securely tighten the screws in 2 stages in a crisscross pattern.
10. Turn the crankcase over and install the one 55 mm crankcase screw and clip on the right-hand side (**Figure 117**). Tighten this screw securely.
11. After the crankcase halves are completely assembled, rotate the crankshaft and transmission shafts to make sure there is no binding. If any is present, disassemble the crankcase and correct the problem.

NOTE
*After a new crankcase gasket is installed, it must be trimmed. Carefully trim off all excess crankcase gasket material where the cylinder base gasket comes in contact with the crankcase (**Figure 119**). If it is not trimmed the cylinder base gasket will not seal properly.*

12. Feed the cam chain down through the top of the chain opening in the crankcase and install the cam chain onto the crankshaft sprocket. Make sure it is correctly engaged with the sprocket.
13A. On 1968-1975 models, install the cam chain tensioner hinge (B, **Figure 114**). Install the cam chain set plate (A, **Figure 114**) and bolt. Tighten the bolt securely.
13B. On 1976-on models, install the parts in the following order:

a. Install the cam chain tensioner setting bar assembly (**Figure 120**).
b. Install the spring as shown in **Figure 121**.
c. Install the cam chain tensioner arm and start the bolt (A, **Figure 122**). Position the spring up onto the arm (B, **Figure 122**). Push the arm into place under the setting bar and tighten the bolt securely.
d. Install the cam chain tensioner lock collars. Install one with the flat end in first then install one with the angled end in first.

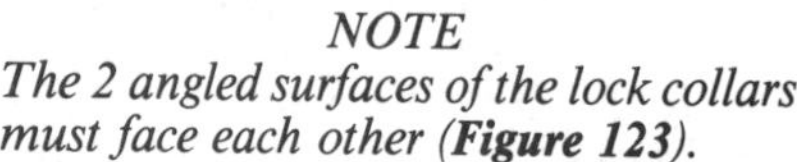

NOTE
*The 2 angled surfaces of the lock collars must face each other (**Figure 123**).*

14. Install the cam chain adjusting bolt assembly. Don't forget to install the O-ring seal on the adjusting bolt.
15. Install all exterior engine assemblies as described in this chapter and other related chapters:
    a. External shift mechanism.
    b. Clutch.
    c. Alternator.
    d. Piston.
    e. Cylinder.
    f. Cylinder head.
    g. Cylinder head cover (1976-on models).

Crankcase and Crankshaft Inspection

1. Clean both crankcase halves inside and out with cleaning solvent. Thoroughly dry with compressed air and wipe off with a clean shop cloth. Be sure to remove all traces of old gasket material from all mating surfaces.
2. Check the transmission and shift drum bearings (**Figure 124** and **Figure 125**) for roughness, pitting, galling and play by rotating them slowly by hand. If any roughness or play can be felt in the bearing it must be replaced.
3. Carefully inspect the cases for cracks and fractures, especially in the lower areas; they are vulnerable to rock damage. Also check the areas around the stiffening ribs, around bearing bosses and threaded holes. If any damage is found, have them repaired by a shop specializing in the repair of precision aluminum castings or replace them.
4. Make sure the oil control orifice (A, **Figure 126**) in the right-hand case half is clean and free of dirt. Clean it out with a small piece of wire, if necessary, and blow out with compressed air.
5. Make sure the crankcase studs (B, **Figure 126**) are tight in each case half. Retighten if necessary.

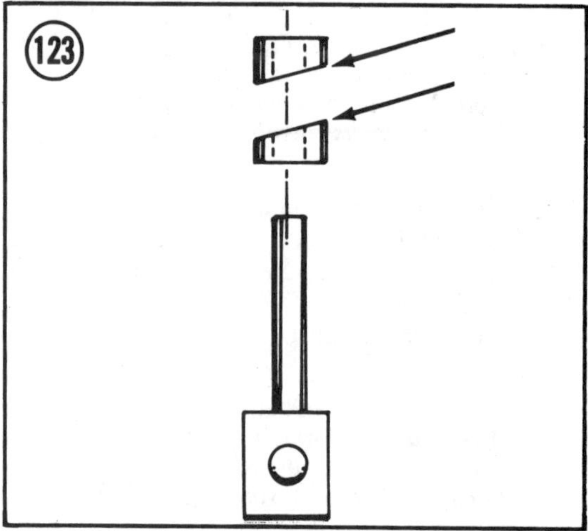

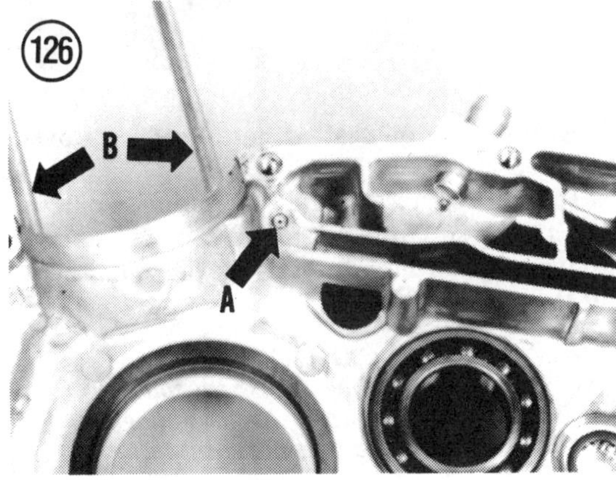

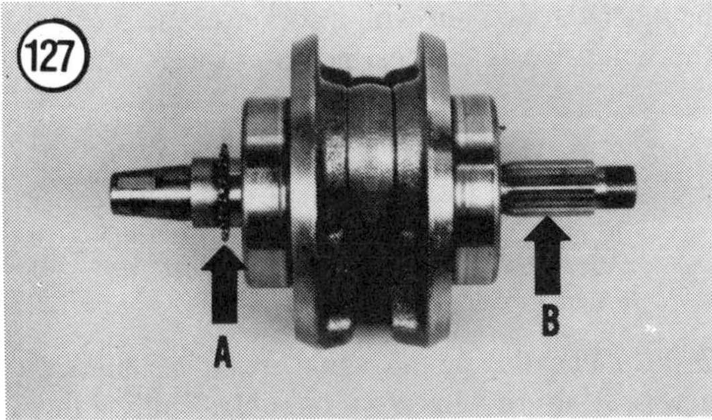

6. Inspect the cam chain sprocket (A, **Figure 127**) and the primary drive gear spline (B, **Figure 127**) for wear, missing teeth or spline damage. If either is damaged, replacement should be entrusted to a dealer.

7. Check the crankshaft main bearings (**Figure 128**) for roughness, pitting, galling and play by rotating them slowly by hand. If any roughness or play can be felt in the bearing, it must be replaced. This must be entrusted to a dealer as special tools are required. The cam chain sprocket and oil pump drive gear must also be removed and realigned properly upon installation.

8. Inspect the connecting rod small end (**Figure 129**). If worn or damaged the crankshaft assembly must be replaced.

9. Check the connecting rod big-end bearing by grasping the rod in one hand and lifting up on it. With the heel of your other hand, rap sharply on the top of the rod. A sharp metallic sound, such as a click, is an indication that the bearing or crankpin or both are worn and the crankshaft assembly should be replaced.

4

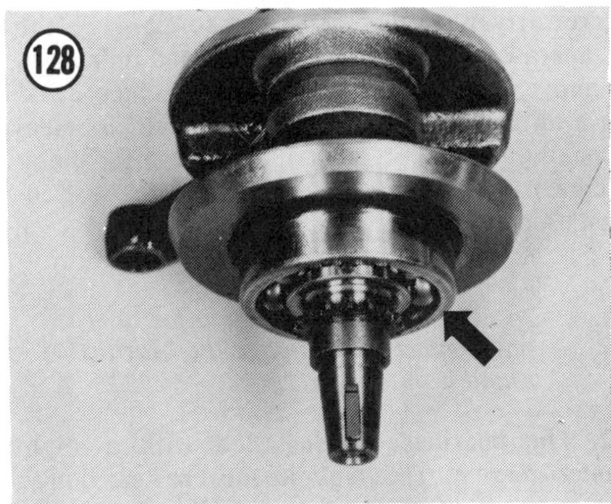

10. Check the connecting rod to crankshaft side clearance with a flat feeler gauge (**Figure 130**). Compare to dimensions listed in **Table 1**. If the clearance is greater than specified the crankshaft assembly must be replaced.
11. Other inspections of the crankshaft assembly involve accurate measuring equipment and should be entrusted to a dealer or competent machine shop. The crankshaft assembly operates under severe stress and dimensional tolerances are critical. These dimensions are listed in **Table 1**. If any are off by the slightest amount it may cause a considerable amount of damage or destruction of the engine. The crankshaft assembly must be replaced as a unit, as it cannot be serviced without the aid of a 10-12 ton (9,000-11,000 kilogram) capacity press, holding fixtures and crankshaft jig.
12. Inspect the condition of the oil seals. They should be replaced every other time the crankcase is disassembled. Refer to *Bearing and Oil Seal Replacement* in this chapter.

Bearing and Oil Seal Replacement

1. Pry out the oil seals (**Figure 131**) with a small screwdriver, taking care not to damage the crankcase bore. If the seals are old and difficult to remove, heat the cases as described in Step 2 and use an awl to punch a small hole in the steel backing of the seal. Install a small sheet metal screw part way into the seal and pull the seal out with a pair of pliers.

CAUTION
Do not install the screw too far or it may contact and damage the bearing behind it.

2. The bearings are installed with a slight interference fit. The crankcase must be heated in an oven to a temperature of about 100° C (212° F). An easy way to check the proper temperature is to drop tiny drops of water on the case; if they sizzle and evaporate immediately, the temperature is correct. Heat only one case at a time.

CAUTION
Do not heat the cases with a torch (propane or acetylene); never bring a flame into contact with the bearing or case. The direct heat will destroy the case hardening of the bearing and will likely cause warpage of the case.

3. Remove the case from the oven and hold onto the 2 crankcase studs with a kitchen pot holder, heavy gloves or heavy shop cloths—*it is hot.*
4. Remove the oil seals if not already removed (see Step 1).
5. Hold the crankcase with the bearing side down and tap it squarely on a piece of soft wood. Continue to tap until the bearing(s) fall out. Repeat for the other half.

CAUTION
Be sure to tap the crankcase squarely on the piece of wood. Avoid damaging the sealing surface of the crankcase.

6. If the bearings are difficult to remove, they can be gently tapped out with a socket or piece of pipe the same size as the bearing outer race.

NOTE
If the bearings or seals are difficult to remove or install, don't take a chance on expensive damage. Have the work performed by a dealer or competent machine shop.

7. While heating up the crankcase halves, place the new bearings in a freezer if possible. Chilling them

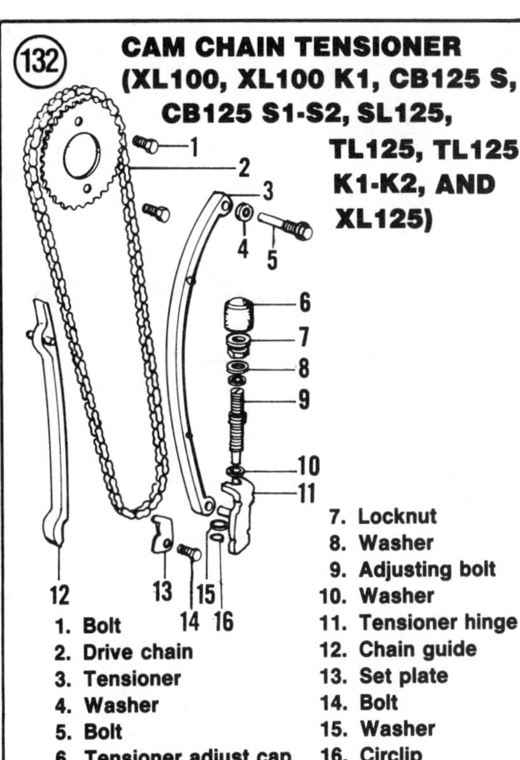

will slightly reduce their overall diameter while the hot crankcase is slightly larger due to heat expansion. This will make bearing installation much easier.

8. While the crankcase is still hot, press each new bearing(s) into place in the crankcase by hand until it seats completely. Do not hammer it in. If the bearing will not seat, remove it and cool it again. Reheat the crankcase and install the bearing again.

9. Oil seals are best installed with a special tool available at a dealer or motorcycle supply store. However, a proper size socket or piece of pipe can be substituted. Make sure that the bearings and seals are not cocked in the crankcase hole and that they are seated properly.

CAMSHAFT CHAIN AND TENSIONER

The cam chain tensioner shown in **Figure 132** is used on the following models:

a. XL100 and XL100 K1.
b. CB125 S and CB125 S1-S2.
c. All SL125.
d. TL125 and TL125 K1-K2.
e. All XL125.

The cam chain tensioner shown in **Figure 133** is used on the following models:

133

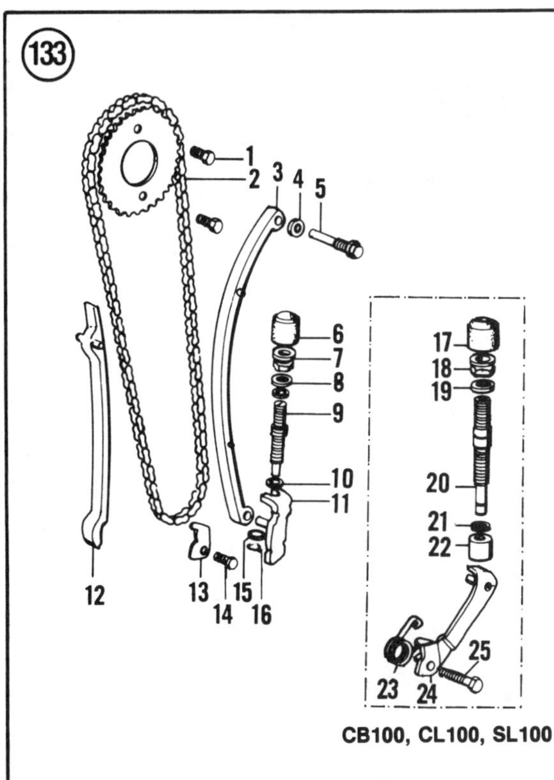

CAM CHAIN TENSIONER (CB100, CL100, SL100)

1. Bolt
2. Drive chain
3. Tensioner
4. Washer
5. Bolt
6. Tensioner adjust cap
7. Locknut
8. Washer
9. Adjusting bolt
10. Washer
11. Tensioner hinge
12. Chain guide
13. Set plate
14. Bolt
15. Washer
16. Circlip
17. Tensioner adjust cap
18. Locknut
19. Washer
20. Adjusting bolt
21. Washer
22. Tensioner arm push rubber
23. Spring
24. Tensioner arm
25. Bolt

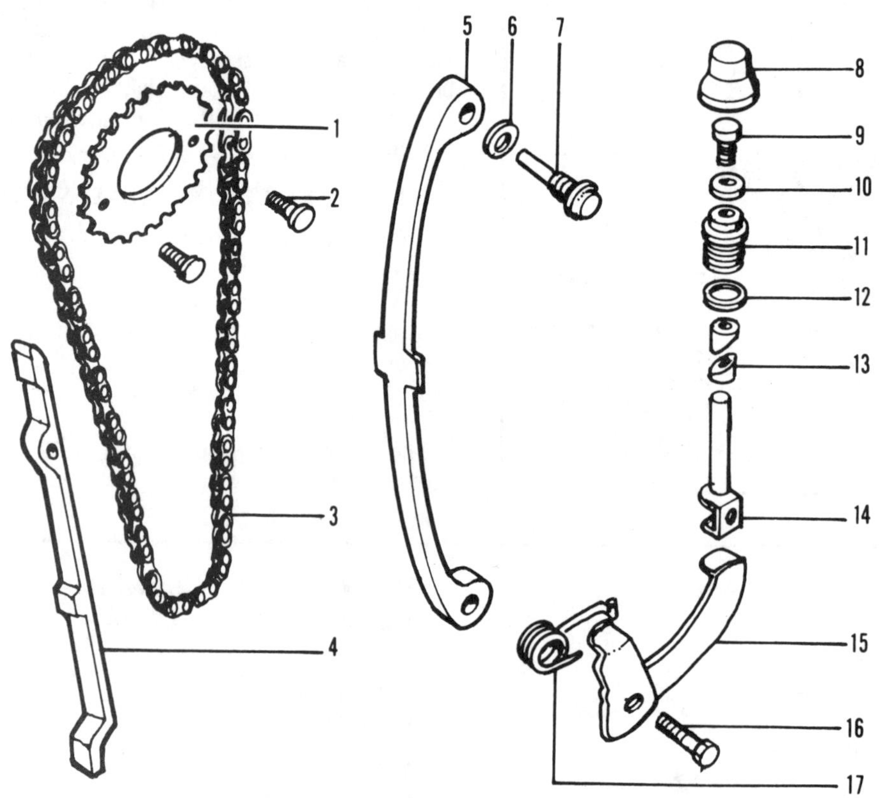

CAM CHAIN TENSIONER (1976-1978 XL100, 1976-ON CB125S, 1976 TL125, 1976 TL125)

1. Sprocket
2. Bolt
3. Cam chain
4. Cam chain guide
5. Cam chain tensioner
6. Washer
7. Pivot bolt
8. Rubber cap
9. Bolt
10. Sealing washer
11. Adjusting bolt
12. O-ring seal
13. Locking collar
14. Tensioner setting bar
15. Tensioner arm
16. Bolt
17. Tensioner arm spring

a. All CB100.
b. All CL100.
c. All SL100.

The cam chain tensioner shown in **Figure 134** is used on the following models:

a. 1976-1978 XL100.
b. 1976-on CB125.
c. 1976 TL125.
d. All CT125.

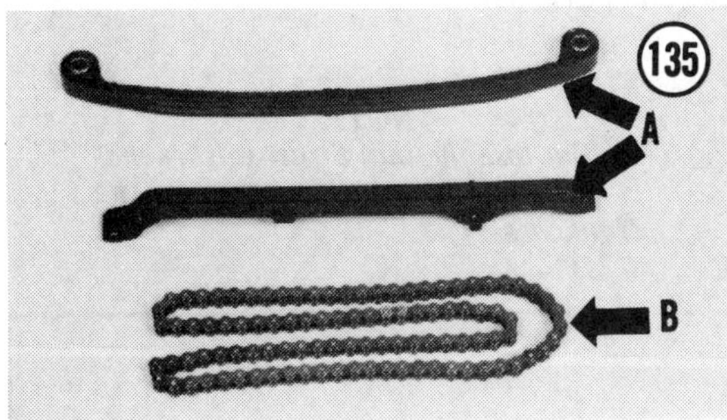

Inspection

Inspect the surface of the chain guide and chain tensioner (A, **Figure 135**). If either is worn or disintegrating, it must be replaced. This may indicate a worn cam chain or improper chain adjustment.

Check all the components of the tensioner assembly; if any part is defective, replace the assembly.

Inspect the cam chain (B, **Figure 135**) for wear and damage. If the chain needs replacing, also check the drive sprocket on the crankshaft and cam sprocket. They also may be worn or damaged.

KICKSTARTER

The Type I kickstarter (**Figure 136**) is used on the following models:

136

KICKSTARTER ASSEMBLY (CB100, CL100, SL100, XL100, XL100 K1, XL100 1976, CB125S, CB125 S1-S2, SL125, TL125, XL125, XL125 K1)

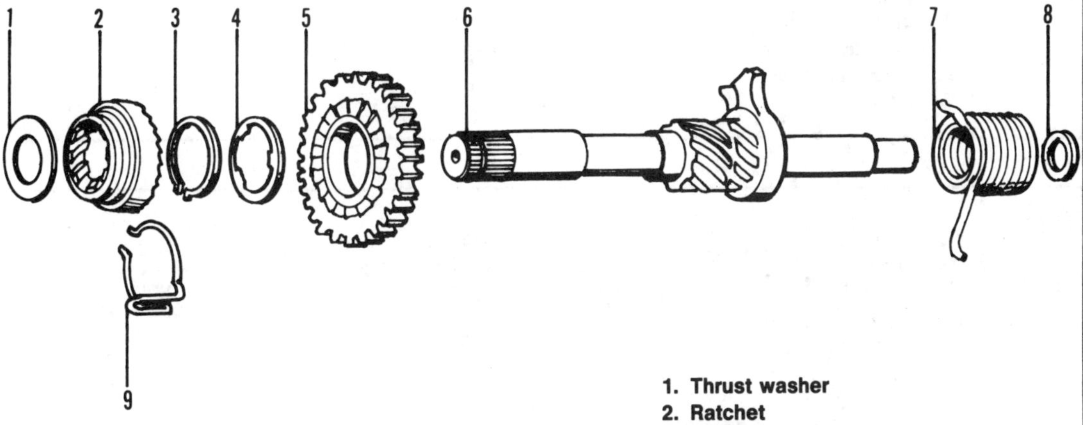

1. Thrust washer
2. Ratchet
3. Circlip
4. Thrust washer
5. Kickstarter gear
6. Kickstarter shaft
7. Return spring
8. Washer
9. Friction spring

a. All CB100.
b. All CL100.
c. All SL100.
d. XL100, XL100 K1 and 1976 XL100.
e. CB125 S and CB125 S1-S2.
f. All SL125.
g. All TL125.
h. All XL125.

The Type II kickstarter (**Figure 137**) is used on the following models:

a. 1976-1978 XL100.
b. 1976-on CB125.
c. 1976 TL125.
d. All CT125.

The Type III kickstarter (**Figure 138**) is used on the 1981-1982 CB125S.

Removal
(Type I)

1. Remove the engine from the frame as described in this chapter.
2. Perform Steps 1-12 of *Crankcase Disassembly* in this chapter.
3. Use Vise Grip pliers to remove the return spring from the recess in the crankcase.
4. Withdraw the kickstarter shaft assembly from the crankcase half.

NOTE
Do not lose the thin thrust washer that is against the inside surface of the crankcase.

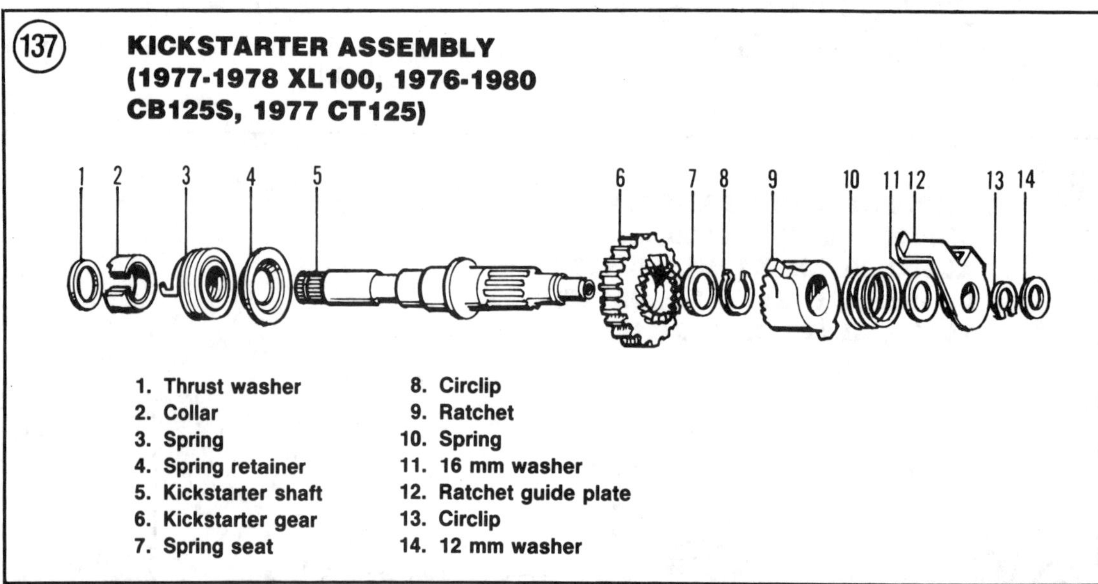

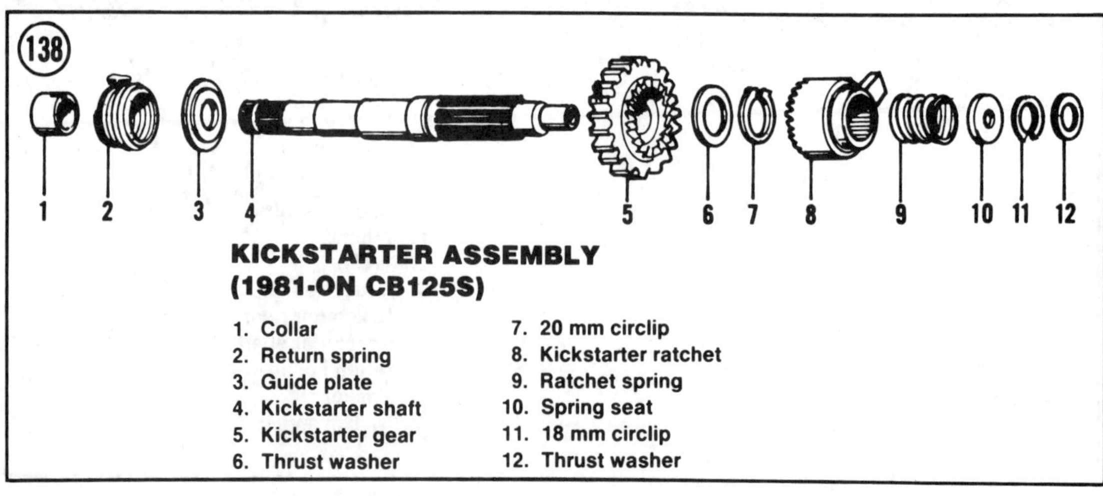

Disassembly/Inspection/Assembly (Type I)

1. Clean the assembled shaft in solvent and dry with compressed air.
2. Remove the thrust washer and the return spring.
3. From the other end of the shaft, remove the thrust washer, ratchet, ratchet spring, the 25 mm circlip, the thrust washer and the kickstarter gear.
4. Check for chipped, broken or missing teeth on the gears. Replace as necessary.
5. Make sure the ratchet gear operates smoothly on the shaft.
6. Check all parts for uneven wear; replace any that show signs of wear.
7. Apply assembly oil to all sliding surfaces of all parts prior to assembly.
8. Install the kickstarter gear onto the shaft.
9. Install the thrust washer and 25 mm circlip.
10. Install the ratchet, the ratchet spring and the thrust washer.
11. Onto the other end of the shaft, slide on the return spring and the thrust washer.

Installation (Type I)

1. Apply a light coat of grease to the thrust washer to hold it against the ratchet.

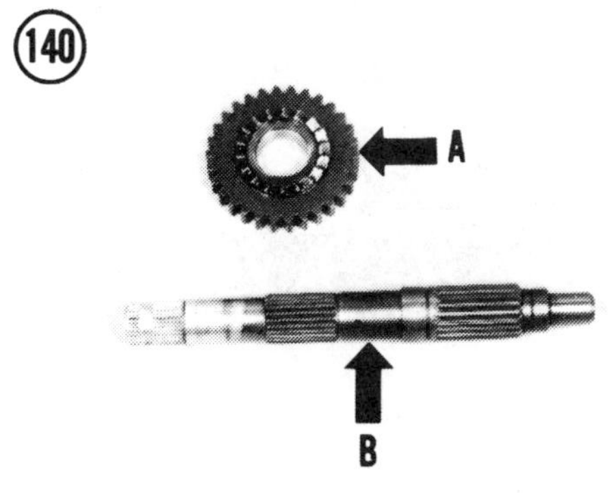

2. Install the assembled shaft into the crankcase. Insert the end of the ratchet spring into the hole in the crankcase.
3. Hook the return spring into the recess in the crankcase.
4. Assemble the crankcase as described in this chapter.

Removal (Type II and Type III)

1. Remove the engine from the frame as described in this chapter.
2. Perform Steps 1-12 of *Crankcase Disassembly* in this chapter.
3A. On Type II models, remove the 12 mm thrust washer, the circlip and the ratchet guide plate from the kickstarter shaft.
3B. On Type III models, loosen the stopper bolt (**Figure 139**).
4. Use a screwdriver to unhook the return spring from the rib on the crankcase. Withdraw the kickstarter shaft assembly from the crankcase half.

NOTE
Do not lose the thin thrust washer that is against the inside surface of the crankcase.

Disassembly/Inspection/Assembly (Type II and Type III)

1. Clean the assembled shaft in solvent and dry with compressed air.
2. Remove the collar, the return spring and the guide plate.
3A. On Type II models, from the other end of the shaft, remove the 16 mm thrust washer, ratchet spring and kickstarter ratchet.
3B. On Type III models, from the other end of the shaft, remove the thrust washer, the circlip, the spring seat and the starter ratchet.
4. Remove the 20 mm circlip, the thrust washer and the kickstarter gear.
5. Check for chipped, broken or missing teeth on the gears (A, **Figure 140**). Replace as necessary.
6. Make sure the ratchet gear operates smoothly on the shaft (B, **Figure 140**).
7. Check all parts for uneven wear; replace any that show signs of wear.
8. Apply assembly oil to all sliding surfaces of all parts prior to assembly.
9A. On Type II models install the parts in the following order:
   a. Install the kickstarter gear, thurst washer and the 20 mm circlip.

b. Install the kickstarter ratchet onto the shaft. The punch marks on both parts must align.
c. Install the ratchet spring and the 16 mm thrust washer.

9B. On Type III models install the parts in the following order:

a. Install the kickstarter ratchet onto the shaft. The punch marks on both parts must align (**Figure 141**).
b. Install the ratchet spring, spring seat, 18 mm circlip and thurst washer (**Figure 142**).
c. Compress the starter ratchet onto the ratchet spring and install the 20 mm circlip (A, **Figure 143**) from the other side.
d. Install the thrust washer (B, **Figure 143**).
e. Onto the other end of the shaft, slide on the kickstarter gear (A, **Figure 144**).
f. Install the guide plate with the inner raised section on first toward the kickstarter gear (B, **Figure 144**).
g. Install the return spring and place the hook into the hole in the shaft (A, **Figure 145**). Slide on the collar (B, **Figure 145**).
h. Push the collar into place within the return spring (**Figure 146**).

NOTE

*Prior to installing the assembled shaft into the crankcase, check with **Figure 147** for correct placement of all components.*

Installation
(Type II and Type III)

1. Apply a light coat of grease to the shim and install the shim onto the raised surface of the crankcase (**Figure 148**).
2. Install the assembled shaft into the crankcase.
3. Hook the return spring over the rib on the crankcase (**Figure 149**).

4A. On Type II models, rotate the starter ratchet 90° clockwise and hook the arm onto the boss on the crankcase.

4B. On Type III models, rotate the kickstarter shaft assembly until the starter ratchet boss aligns with the flat on the screw boss in the crankcase (**Figure 150**).

5A. On Type III models, tighten the stopper bolt securely.

5B. On Type II models, install the ratchet guide plate, circlip and the 12 mm thrust washer.

6. Assemble the crankcase as described in this chapter.
7. Install the spring and kickstarter cam. Align the punch marks on both parts (**Figure 151**).

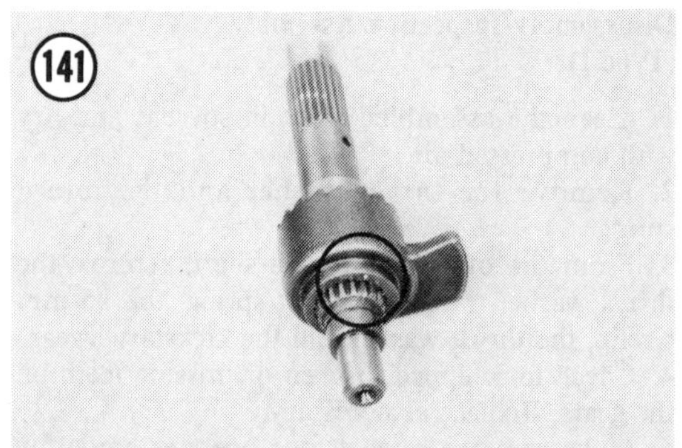

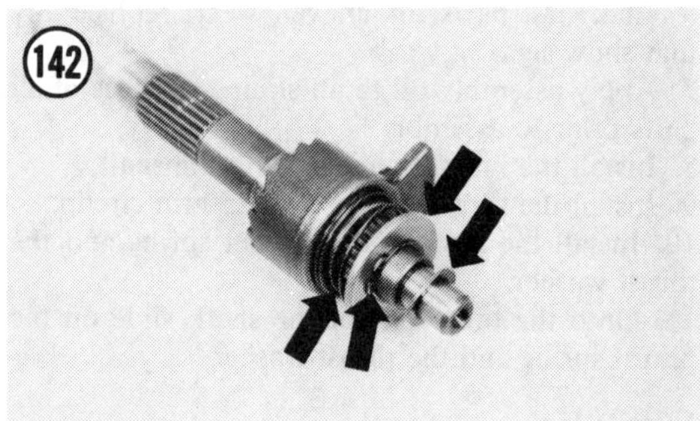

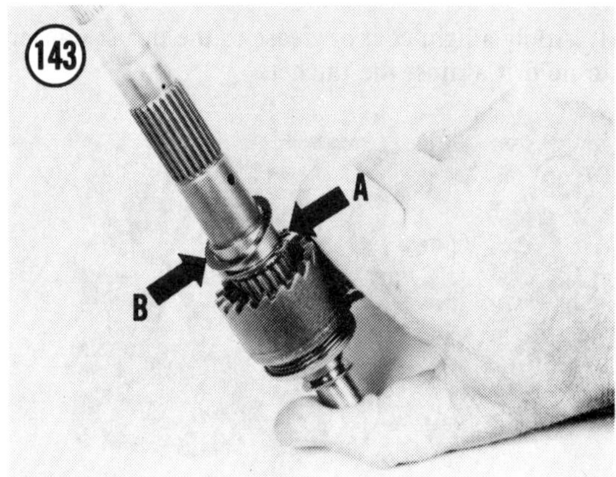

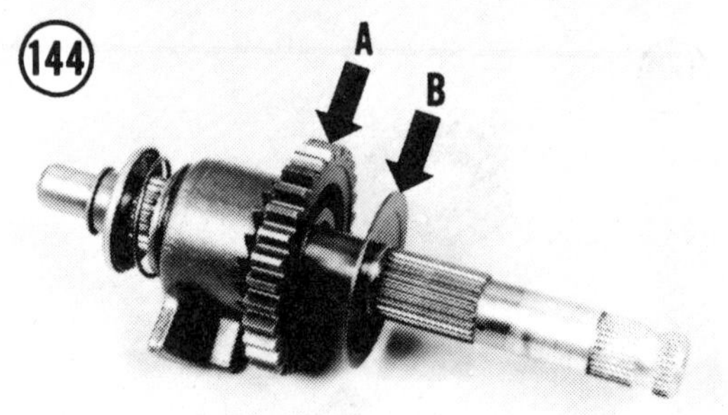

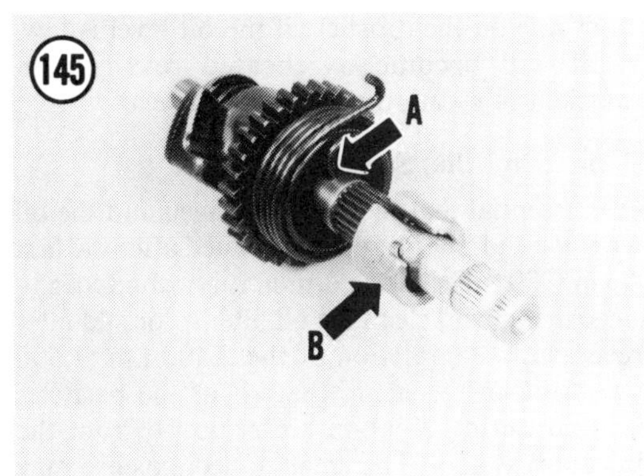

BREAK-IN PROCEDURE

If the rings were replaced, a new piston installed, the cylinder rebored or honed or major lower end work performed, the engine should be broken in just as though it were new. The performance and service life of the engine depends greatly on a careful and sensible break-in.

For the first 800 km (100 miles) , no more than one-third throttle should be used and speed should be varied as much as possible within the one-third throttle limit. Prolonged steady running at one speed, no matter how moderate, is to be avoided as well as hard acceleration.

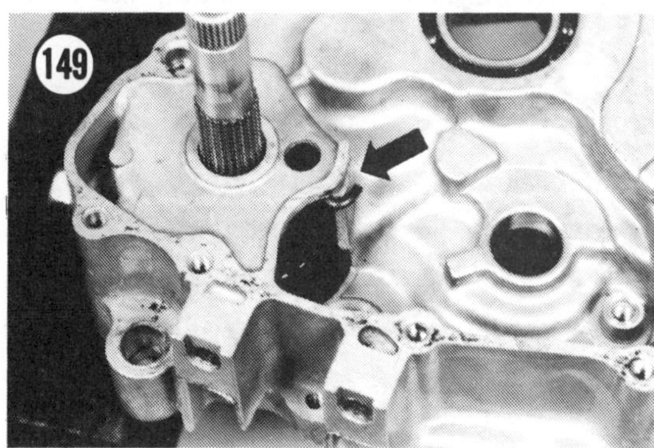

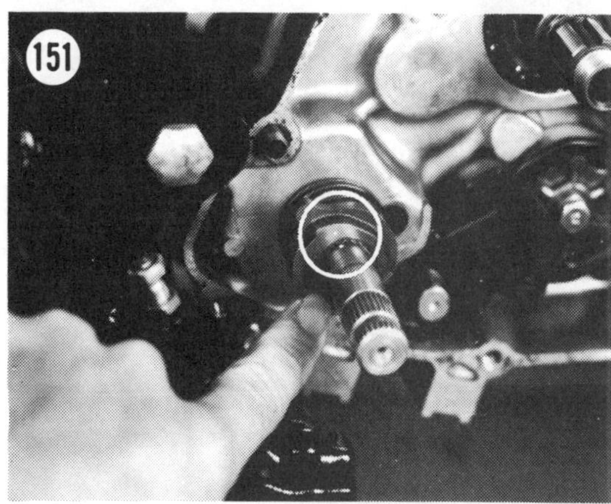

Following the *800 km (500 Mile) Service* described in this chapter more throttle should not be used until the motorcycle has covered at least 1,601 km (1,000 miles) and then it should be limited to short bursts of speed until 2,400 km (1,500 miles) have been logged.

The mono-grade oils recommended for break-in and normal use provide a better bedding pattern for rings and cylinder than do multi-grade oils. As a result, piston ring and cylinder bore life are greatly increased. During this period, oil consumption will be higher than normal. It is therefore important to frequently check and correct oil level. At no time, during the break-in or later, should the oil level be allowed to drop below the bottom line on the dipstick; if the oil level is low, the oil will become overheated resulting in insufficient lubrication and increased wear.

800 km (500 Mile) Service

It is essential that the oil be changed and the oil filter rotor and filter screen be cleaned after the first 800 km (500 miles). In addition, it is a good idea to change the oil and clean the oil filter rotor and filter screen at the completion of the 2,400 km (1,500 mile) break-in to ensure that all of the particles produced during break-in are removed from the lubrication system. The small added expense may be considered a smart investment that will pay off in increased engine life.

Table 1 ENGINE SPECIFICATIONS*

Item	Specification	Wear Limit
General		
Type	4-stroke, air-cooled, SOHC	
Number of cylinders	1	
Bore and stroke		
100 cc	50.5 x 49.5 mm (1.99 x 1.94 in.)	
125 cc	56.0 x 49.5 mm (2.21 x 1.95 in.)	
Displacement		
100 cc	99 cc (6.04 cu. in.)	
125 cc	122 cc (7.44 cu. in.)	
Compression ratio	9.5 to 1	
Compression pressure	10.8-13.2 kg/cm² (156-187 psi)	
Lubrication	Wet sump	
Cylinder		
Bore		
100 cc	50.50-50.51 mm	50.6 mm (1.992 in.)
125 cc	(1.9881-1.9885 in.)	
1971-1975	56.00-56.01 mm (2.2047-2.2051 in.)	56.1 mm (2.209 in.)
1976-on	56.50-56.51 mm (2.2047-2.2051 in.)	56.6 mm (2.228 in.)
Out of round	—	0.10 mm (0.004 in.)
Piston/cylinder clearance	0.010-0.050 mm (0.0004-0.0020 in.)	0.1 mm (0.004 in.)
Piston		
Diameter		
100 cc	50.47-50.49 mm (1.987-1.988 in.)	50.3 mm (1.980 in.)
CB125S, SL125, TL125		
1971-1975	55.97-55.99 mm (2.2035-2.2043 in.)	55.8 mm (2.197 in.)
1976-1982	56.46-56.48 mm	56.35 mm (2.218 in.)
XL125, CT125	(2.2228-2.2236 in.)	
	55.74-55.76 mm (2.1945-2.1953 in.)	55.65 mm (2.181 in.)
Clearance in bore	N.A.	0.10 mm (0.004 in.)
Piston pin bore		
CB100, CL100, SL100	N.A.	N.A.
XL100	14.002-14.008 mm (0.5513-0.5515 in.)	14.04 mm (0.553 in.)
CB125S, SL125, TL125	N.A.	N.A.
XL125, CT125	15.002-15.008 mm (0.5906-0.5909 in.)	15.04 mm (0.592 in.)
Piston pin outer diameter		
CB100, CL100, SL100	N.A.	N.A.
XL100	13.994-14.000 mm (0.5509-0.5512 in.)	13.96 mm (0.5496 in.)
CB125S, SL125, TL125	N.A.	N.A.
XL125, CT125	14.994-15.000 mm (0.5903-0.5906 in.)	14.96 mm (0.589 in.)
Piston to pin clearance	N.A.	N.A.

(continued)

Table 1 ENGINE SPECIFICATIONS* (continued)

Item	Specification	Wear Limit
Piston rings		
Number of rings		
Compression	2	
Oil control	1	
Ring end gap		
Top and second	0.15-0.35 mm (0.006-0.014 in.)	0.5 mm (0.02 in.)
Oil (side rail)	0.3-0.9 mm (0.0118-0.0354 in.)	N.A.
Ring side clearance		
Top and second ring		
CB100, CL100, SL100, CB125S, SL125, TL125	0.025-0.030 mm (0.0008-0.0011 in.)	0.7 mm (0.027 in.)
XL100	0.15-0.35 mm (0.0059-0.0138 in.)	0.5 mm (0.0197 in.)
Top ring		
XL125, CT125	0.025-0.055 mm (0.0010-0.0022 in.)	0.09 mm (0.0035 in.)
Second ring		
XL125, CT125	0.015-0.045 mm (0.0006-0.0018 in.)	0.09 mm (0.0035 in.)
Connecting rod		
Small end inner diameter	N.A.	N.A.
Crankshaft		
Runout	N.A.	0.05 mm (0.002 in.)
Connecting rod big end side clearance	0.05-0.30 mm (0.002-0.0118 in.)	0.80 mm (0.032 in.)
Camshaft		
Cam lobe height		
XL100		
Intake	31.903-32.063 mm (1.2560-1.2623 in.)	31.85 mm (1.254 in.)
Exhaust	31.039-31.199 mm (1.2220-1.2273 in.)	30.98 mm (1.220 in.)
XL125, CT125		
Intake	31.906 mm (1.2561 in.)	31.776 mm (1.251 in.)
Exhaust	31.496 mm (1.2400 in.)	31.366 mm (1.235 in.)
All other models	N.A.	N.A.
Cam journal OD		
CB100, CL100, SL100, CB125S, SL125, TL125		
Left-hand end	19.927-19.937 mm (0.7849-0.7845 in.)	19.88 mm (0.7827 in.)
Right-hand end	29.917-29.930 mm (1.1779-1.1784 in.)	29.87 mm (1.176 in.)
All other models	N.A.	N.A.
Cam bearing surface in cylinder head		
CB100, CL100, SL100, CB125S, SL125, TL125		
Left-hand side	20.000-20.021 mm (0.7874-0.7882 in.)	20.079 mm (0.788 in.)
Right-hand side	30.000-30.021 mm (1.1811-1.1819 in.)	30.079 mm (1.182 in.)
All other models	N.A.	N.A.

(continued)

Table 1 ENGINE SPECIFICATIONS* (continued)

Item	Specification	Wear Limit
Valves		
Valve stem outer diameter		
XL100, XL125, CT125		
Intake	5.450-5.465 mm (0.2146-0.2175 in.)	5.41 mm (0.213 in.)
Exhaust	5.430-5.445 mm (0.2138-0.2167 in.)	5.39 mm (0.2122 in.)
All other models		
Intake	5.450-5.465 mm (0.2146-0.2150 in.)	5.42 mm (0.213 in.)
Exhaust	5.430-5.445 mm (0.2138-0.2146 in.)	5.40 mm (0.2126 in.)
Valve guide inner diameter	N.A.	N.A.
Stem to guide clearance		
XL100, XL125, CT125		
Intake	0.010-0.035 mm (0.0004-0.0014 in.)	0.12 mm (0.0047 in.)
Exhaust	0.030-0.055 mm (0.0012-0.0022 in.)	0.14 mm (0.0055 in.)
All other models	N.A.	N.A.
Valve seat width		
XL125, CT125	1.0-1.5 mm (0.0394-0.0591 in.)	1.5 mm (0.059 in.)
All other models	0.75 mm (0.0295 in.)	1.5 mm (0.059 in.)
Valve face width	N.A.	N.A.
Valve springs free length		
CB100, CL100, SL100		
Inner	35.7 mm (1.406 in.)	34.5 mm (1.358 in.)
Outer	40.4 mm (1.591 in.)	39.0 mm (1.535 in.)
1973-1975 CB125S, SL125		
Inner	33.5 mm (1.318 in.)	32.0 mm (1.259 in.)
Outer	40.9 mm (1.610 in.)	39.5 mm (1.555 in.)
1976-on CB125S		
Inner	39.2 mm (1.543 in.)	35.2 mm (1.386 in.)
Outer	44.9 mm (1.766 in.)	40.5 mm (1.595 in.)
Rocker arm assembly		
Rocker arm to shaft clearance		
XL100, XL125, CT125	0.016-0.052 mm (0.0006-0.0021 in.)	0.08 mm (0.0032 in.)
All other models	N.A.	N.A.
Oil pump		
XL100, XL125, CT125		
Inner to outer rotor tip clearance	0.15 mm (0.0059 in.)	0.20 mm (0.008 in.)
Outer rotor to body clearance	0.15-0.20 mm (0.0059-0.0079 in.)	0.20 mm (0.008 in.)
All other models	N.A.	N.A.

*Honda does not provide service information for all items nor all models. All available information is included in this table. "N.A." indicates that information is not available.

4

Table 2 ENGINE TORQUE SPECIFICATIONS

Item	N•m	ft.-lb.
Cylinder head cap nuts		
Through 1975	18-20	13-14
1976-on	28-30	20-22
Cylinder head socket bolts	18-20	13-14
Cylinder mounting bolt	12-18	9-13
Cam sprocket bolts	8-12	6-9
Ignition advance bolt	8-12	6-9
Pulse rotor bolt	8-12	6-9
Oil filter rotor nut	40-50	29-36
Alternator rotor bolt		
Through 1980	26-32	19-23
1981-on	40-50	29-36

CHAPTER FIVE

175, 250 AND 350 CC ENGINES

5

All 175, 250 and 350 cc models covered in this manual are equipped with an air-cooled, 4-stroke, single cylinder engine with a single overhead camshaft. The crankshaft is supported by 2 main ball bearings. The camshaft is chain-driven from the sprocket on the left-hand side of the crankshaft and operates rocker arms that are individually adjustable.

Engine lubrication is by wet sump with the oil pump located on the right-hand side of the engine adjacent to the clutch. The oil pump delivers oil under pressure throughout the engine and is gear-driven off of the crankshaft.

The main difference among the engines is the number of valves in the cylinder head. The 175 cc engine has 2 valves, while the 250 and 350 cc engines have 4 valves (2 intake, 2 exhaust).

This chapter contains information for removal, inspection, service and reassembly of the engine. Although the clutch and transmission are located within the engine they are covered in Chapter Six to simplify this material. Ignition system and alternator components are covered in Chapter Eight.

Before beginning work, re-read Chapter One of this book. You will do a better job with this information fresh in your mind.

Engine specifications and tightening torques are in **Table 1** and **Table 2** at the end of this chapter.

ENGINE PRINCIPLES

Figure 1 explains how the engine works. This will be helpful when troubleshooting or repairing the engine.

ENGINE COOLING

Cooling is provided by air passing over the cooling fins on the engine cylinder head and cylinder. It is very important to keep these fins free from buildup of dirt, oil, grease and other foreign matter. Brush out the fins with a whisk broom or small stiff paint brush.

CAUTION
Remember, these fins are thin in order to dissipate heat and may be damaged if struck too hard.

SERVICING ENGINE IN FRAME

The engine must be removed from the frame to remove the cylinder head, cylinder and piston.

The following components can be serviced while the engine is mounted in the frame (the bike's frame is a great holding fixture for breaking loose stubborn bolts and nuts):

a. Carburetor.
b. Alternator.
c. Clutch assembly.
d. External shift mechanism.

ENGINE REMOVAL/INSTALLATION

1. Drain the engine oil as described in Chapter Three.
2. Remove the side covers and the seat.
3. Remove the fuel tank as described in Chapter Seven.
4. Remove the exhaust system as described in Chapter Seven.

(1)

4-STROKE OPERATING PRINCIPLES

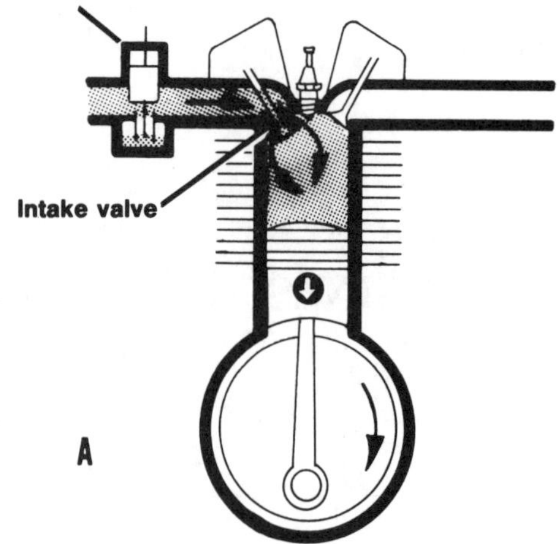

As the piston travels downward, the exhaust valve is closed and the intake valve opens, allowing the new air-fuel mixture from the carburetor to be drawn into the cylinder. When the piston reaches the bottom of its travel (BDC), the intake valve closes and remains closed for the next 1 1/2 revolutions of the crankshaft.

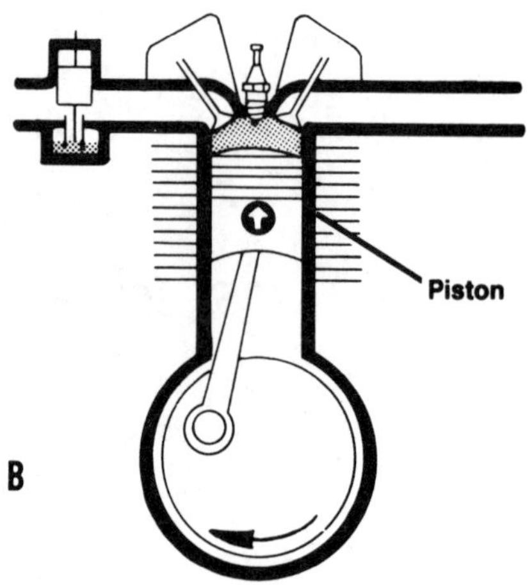

While the crankshaft continues to rotate, the piston moves upward, compressing the air-fuel mixture.

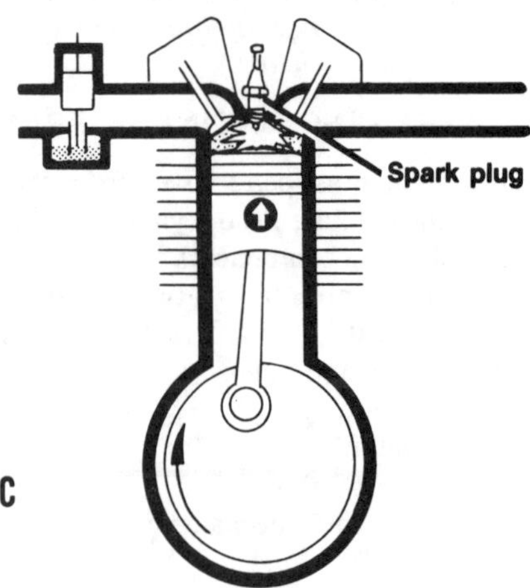

As the piston almost reaches the top of its travel, the spark plug fires, igniting the compressed air-fuel mixture. The piston continues to top dead center (TDC) and is pushed downward by the expanding gases.

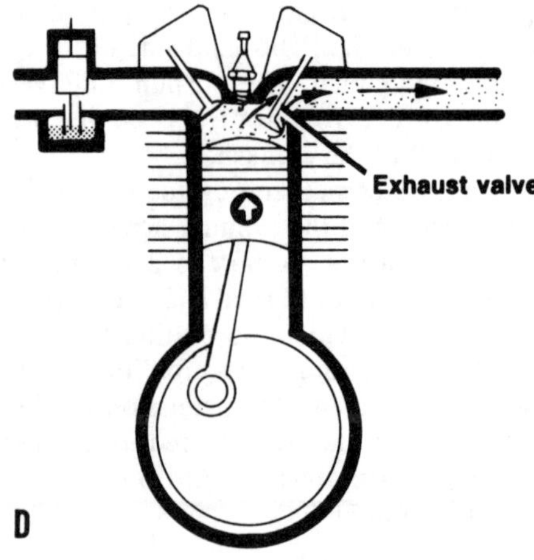

When the piston almost reaches BDC, the exhaust valve opens and remains open until the piston is near TDC. The upward travel of the piston forces the exhaust gases out of the cylinder. After the piston has reached TDC, the exhaust valve closes and the cycle starts all over again.

5. Remove the carburetor as described under *Carburetor Removal/Installation* in Chapter Seven.
6. On models so equipped, remove the bolts (**Figure 2**) securing the skid plate and remove the skid plate.
7. Disconnect the spark plug lead and tie it up out of the way. Disconnect the engine breather hose from the crankcase.
8. Remove the alternator as described in Chapter Eight.
9. Remove the drive chain master link and remove the bolts securing the drive sprocket. Remove the drive sprocket.
10. Remove the clutch assembly as described in Chapter Six.
11. On models so equipped, disconnect the tachometer cable from the engine.
12. Take a final look all over the engine to make sure everything has been disconnected.
13. On models so equipped, remove the engine upper hanger bolt and nut and remove the upper hanger plates (**Figure 3**).
14. Place a suitable size hydraulic jack, with a piece of wood to protect the crankcase, under the engine. Apply a *small amount* of jack pressure up on the engine.
15. Remove the bolts and nuts securing the front engine hanger bolts and remove the engine hanger plates (A, **Figure 4**).
16. Remove the upper and lower rear through bolts (B, **Figure 4**). Don't lose any spacers on the bolts. On some models the foot pegs (C, **Figure 4**) are also attached to the lower rear through bolt.

CAUTION
The following steps require the aid of a helper to safely remove the engine assembly from the frame.

17. Pull the engine up and slightly forward. Remove the engine from either side. Take it to a workbench for further disassembly.
18. Install by reversing these removal steps, noting the following.
19. Be sure to install any spacers on the mounting bolts.
20. Tighten all bolts to the torque specifications listed in **Table 2**.
21. Fill the engine with the recommended type and quantity of oil; refer to Chapter Three.
22. Adjust the clutch, drive chain and rear brake pedal as described in Chapter Three.
23. Start the engine and check for leaks.

CYLINDER HEAD COVER AND CAMSHAFT

The cylinder head cover carries the rocker arm assemblies. The cam is held in place between the cylinder head cover and the cylinder head and is driven through a chain from the sprocket on the crankshaft. The cam can be removed with the engine in the frame, but it is easier to do with the engine removed.

This procedure is shown with the engine removed from the frame for clarity.

Removal

CAUTION
To prevent any warpage and damage, remove the cylinder head cover and cam only when the engine is at room temperature.

1. Place a wood block(s) under the engine to support the bike securely.
2. Remove the side covers and the seat.
3. Remove the fuel tank as described in Chapter Seven.

NOTE
Prior to removing the contact breaker point base plate, make a mark on the base plate that aligns with the centerline of one of the mounting screws. That way the ignition timing will be correct upon installation (providing the timing was correct before removal).

4. Remove the screws securing the contact breaker assembly cover and remove the cover and the gasket.
5. Disconnect the electrical connection from the contact breaker point assembly to the wiring harness.
6. Remove the screws (**Figure 5**) securing the contact breaker point base plate and remove the base plate assembly.
7. Remove the bolt (**Figure 6**) securing the ignition advance mechanism to the camshaft. Remove the ignition advance mechanism.
8. Remove the spark plug as this will make it easier to rotate the engine.
9. Shift the transmission into NEUTRAL.
10. Remove the engine as described in this chapter.
11. Loosen the cam chain adjuster locknut and loosen the adjuster bolt (**Figure 7**). This will allow maximum chain slack and aid in cam sprocket removal.

8

9

10

11

12. Remove both valve adjuster covers. Loosen the locknuts on all valve adjusters. Loosen all valve adjusters so there is no tension on the rocker arms.
13. Using a crisscross pattern, remove the cylinder head cover bolts. Refer to **Figure 8** for 175 cc engines or **Figure 9** for 250 and 350 cc engines.
14. Remove the cylinder head cover and gasket. Don't lose the locating dowels.
15. Temporarily install the alternator rotor and rotate the engine until one of the camshaft sprocket bolts is exposed. Remove that bolt (**Figure 10**).
16. Rotate the crankshaft 180° and remove the other camshaft sprocket bolt.
17. Pull the cam chain and cam sprocket off of the shoulder on the cam and let it rest on the extended portion of the cam.
18. Remove the cam chain from the cam sprocket. Rest the cam chain on the cam and remove the cam sprocket.
19. Tie a piece of wire to the cam chain and tie the other end to an external part of the engine. This will prevent the chain from falling into the crankcase.
20. Remove the cam from the cylinder head.

CAUTION
If the crankshaft must be rotated when the camshaft is removed, pull up on the cam chain and keep it taut while rotating the crankshaft. Make certain that the chain is positioned onto the crankshaft sprocket. If this is not done, the chain may become kinked and may damage both the chain and the sprocket on the crankshaft.

Camshaft Inspection

1. Check the cam bearing journals for wear and scoring.
2. Measure both the left- and right-hand bearing journals with a micrometer (**Figure 11**). Measure the left-hand journal at 2 places, one on each side of the sprocket mounting flange. Compare to dimensions listed in **Table 1**. If worn to the service limit, the cam must be replaced.

NOTE
The left-hand bearing journal is the larger one of the two.

3. Check the cam lobes for wear (A, **Figure 12**). The lobes should show no signs of scoring and the edges should be square. Slight damage may be removed with a silicone carbide oilstone. Use No. 100-120 grit stone initially, then polish with a No. 280-320 grit stone.

4. Even if the cam lobe surface appears to be satisfactory, with no visible signs of wear, the cam lobes must be measured with a micrometer as shown in **Figure 13**. Compare to dimensions listed in **Table 1**.

NOTE
The right-hand cam lobe is the exhaust and the left-hand is the intake.

5. Inspect the cam sprocket (B, **Figure 12**) for wear; replace if necessary.
6. Check the cam bearing surfaces in the cylinder head cover and cylinder head. Refer to **Figure 14** for 175 cc engines or **Figure 15** for 250 and 350 cc engines. They should not be scored or excessively worn. Replace either part if wear is evident.

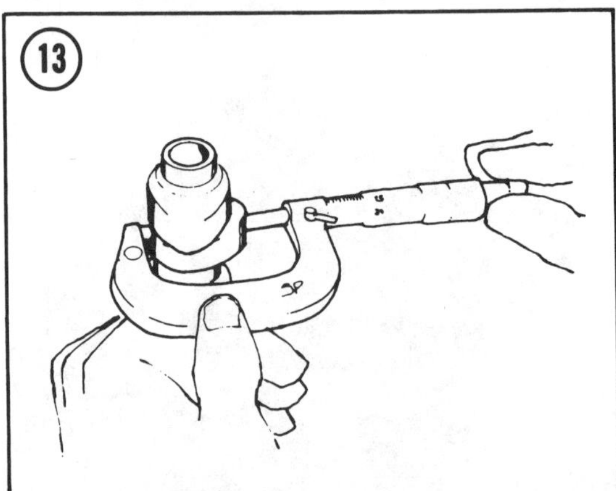

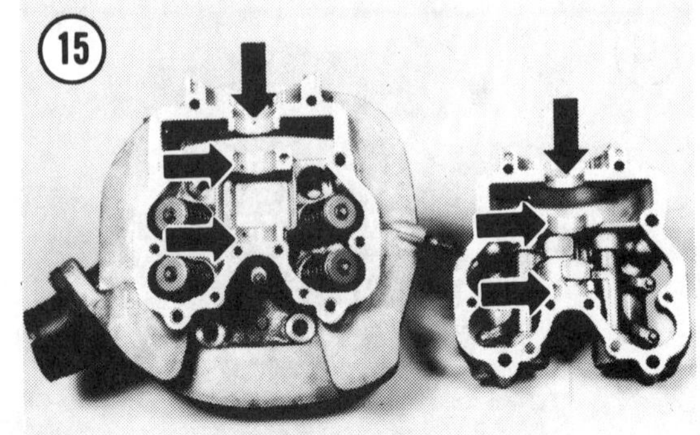

Cylinder Head Cover Disassembly/Inspection/Assembly

It is recommended that one rocker arm assembly be disassembled, inspected and then assembled to avoid the interchanging of parts. This is especially true on a well run-in engine (high mileage) as the different sets of parts have developed wear patterns.

NOTE
On 175 cc engines, both rocker arms are identical (same Honda part no.). If you remove both rocker arm assemblies at the same time, mark them "I" (intake—to the rear) or "E" (exhaust—to the front) so they will be reinstalled in the correct location in the cylinder head cover.

1. Remove the locking pin (A, **Figure 16**) holding the rocker arm shaft into place.
2. With a pair of gas pliers, twist back and forth slightly and pull the rocker arm shaft plug (B, **Figure 16**) from the cylinder head cover.
3. Tap on the opposite end of the cylinder head cover with a plastic mallet. This will help move the rocker arm shaft out of the receptacle in the cylinder head cover. Withdraw the rocker arm shaft.
4. Remove the rocker arm.
5. Wash all parts in cleaning solvent and thoroughly dry.
6. Inspect the rocker arm pad where it rides on the cam lobe and where the adjuster rides on the valve stem(s). Refer to **Figure 17** for 175 cc engines or **Figure 18** for 250 and 350 cc engines. If the pad is scratched or unevenly worn, inspect the cam lobe for scoring, chipping or flat spots. Replace the rocker arm if defective.

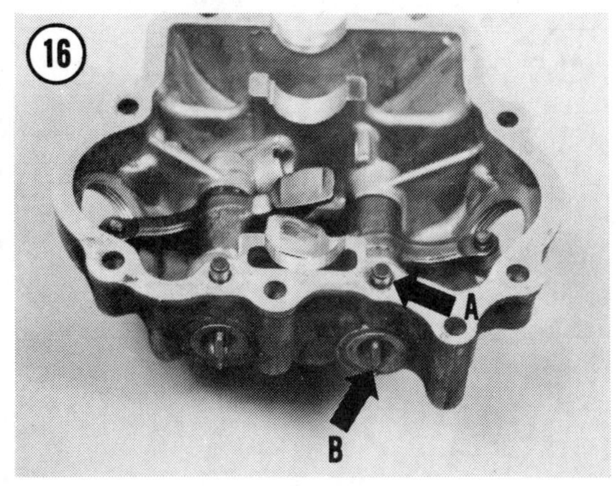

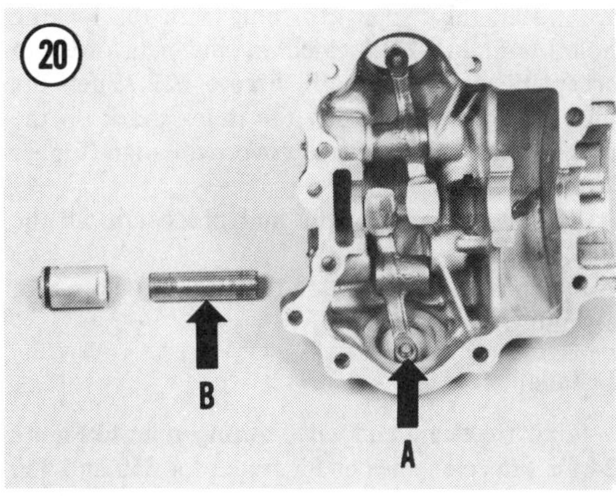

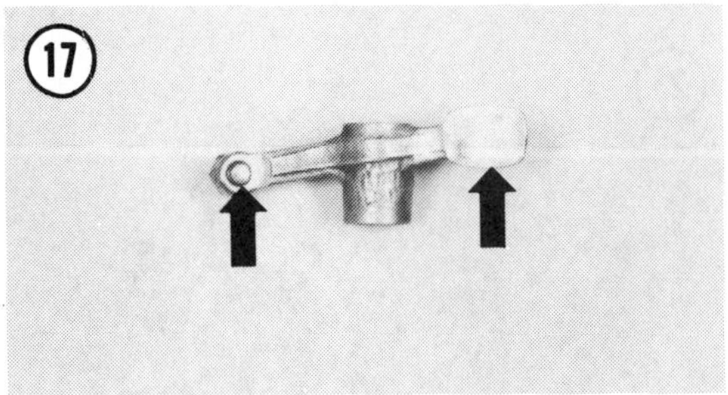

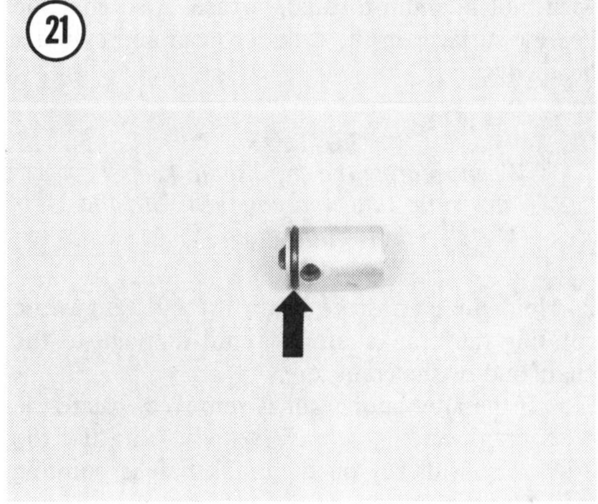

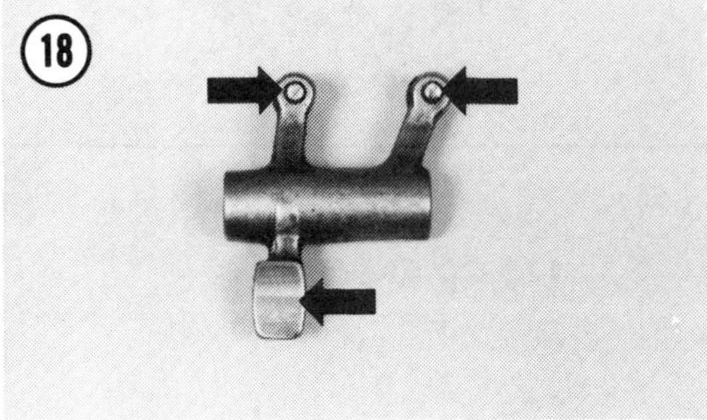

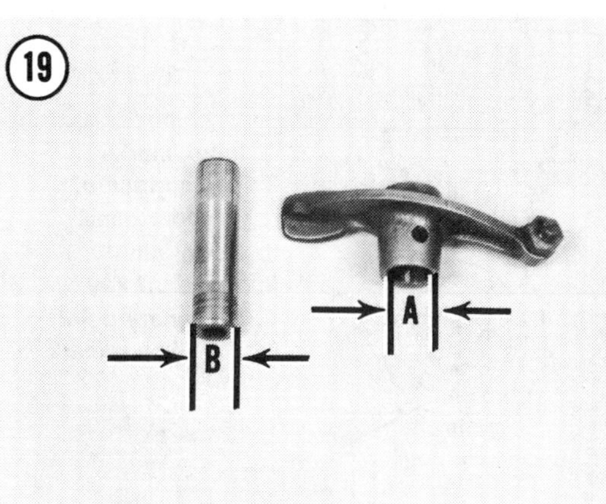

7. Measure the inside diameter of the rocker arm bore (A, **Figure 19**) with an inside micrometer and note this dimension.
8. Inspect the rocker arm shaft for signs of wear or scoring. Measure the outside diameter (B, **Figure 19**) with a micrometer and note this dimension. Subtract the dimension of the rocker arm shaft from the rocker arm bore dimension to determine the clearance between the 2 parts. The clearance service limit is listed in **Table 1**. Replace worn part(s).
9. Inspect the cam bearing surface for excessive wear. If worn excessively, the cylinder head and cylinder head cover must be replaced.
10. Coat the rocker arm shaft and rocker arm bore with assembly oil.
11. Position the rocker arm into the cylinder head cover (A, **Figure 20**). Insert the rocker arm shaft (B, **Figure 20**) into the cylinder head cover and through the rocker arm.
12. Inspect the O-ring seal (**Figure 21**) on the rocker arm plug. Replace if necessary.

5

13. Install the rocker arm plug with the locking hole (A, **Figure 22**) located as shown in order to accept the locking pin (B, **Figure 22**). When the plug is installed correctly the index mark on the plug and the cylinder head cover will align (**Figure 23**).
14. Install the locking pin and press it in all the way.
15. Repeat Step 1-14 for the other rocker arm assembly.

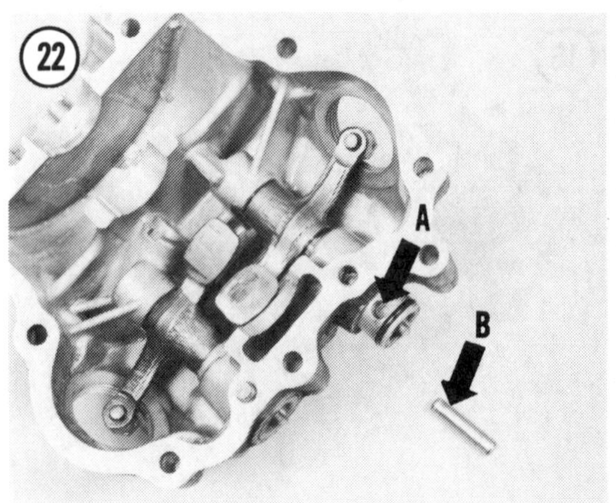

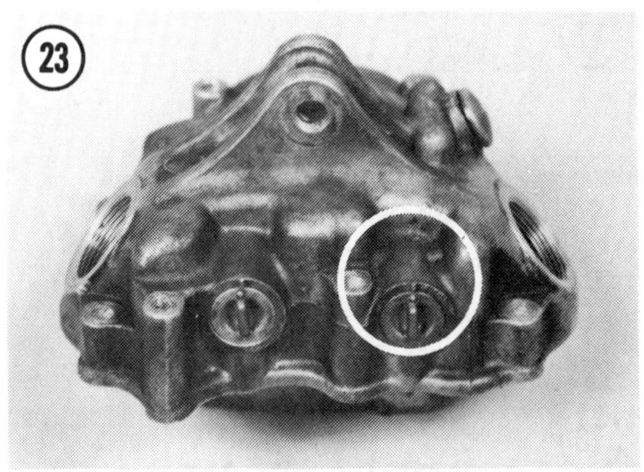

Installation

For correct cam and valve timing, refer to **Figure 24** for 175 cc engines or **Figure 25** for 250 and 350 cc engines.

1. Lubricate all cam lobes and bearing journals with molybdenum disulfide grease. Also coat the bearing surfaces in the cylinder head and cylinder head cover.

CAUTION
When rotating the crankshaft, keep the cam chain taut and engaged with the sprocket on the crankshaft.

2. Hold the cam drive chain up and taut while rotating the crankshaft to avoid damage to the chain and/or the crankcase.
   a. If the alternator rotor is removed, rotate the crankshaft *counterclockwise* until the Woodruff key on the crankshaft is pointing directly up toward the cam.
   b. If the alternator rotor is installed, rotate the crankshaft *counterclockwise* until the "T" timing mark is aligned with the stationary pointer on the crankcase cover (**Figure 26**).
3. Install the cam sprocket (with the index marks facing toward the outside) onto the cam.
4. Install the cam through the cam chain and into position in the cylinder head (A, **Figure 27**).
5. Fill the oil pocket (B, **Figure 27**) in the cylinder head with fresh engine oil so the cam lobes will be covered for the initial engine start-up.
6. Align the index marks on the cam sprocket with the top surface of the cylinder head.
7. Make sure the cam chain is meshed properly with the drive sprocket on the crankshaft.
8. Pull the cam chain up onto the cam sprocket (A, **Figure 28**). Make sure the oil seal (B, **Figure 28**) is in place on the cam.
9. Pull the cam chain and sprocket up onto the shoulder of the cam. Make sure that the timing mark "T" is still aligned with the crankcase and that the index marks on the cam sprocket are still aligned with the top surface of the cylinder head. If

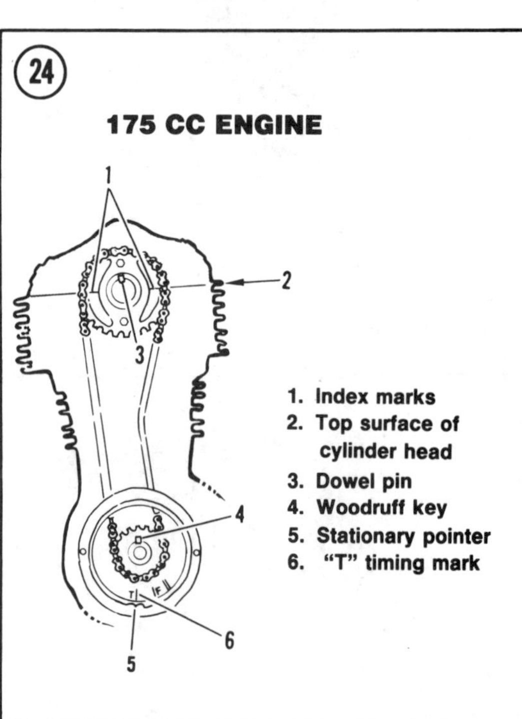

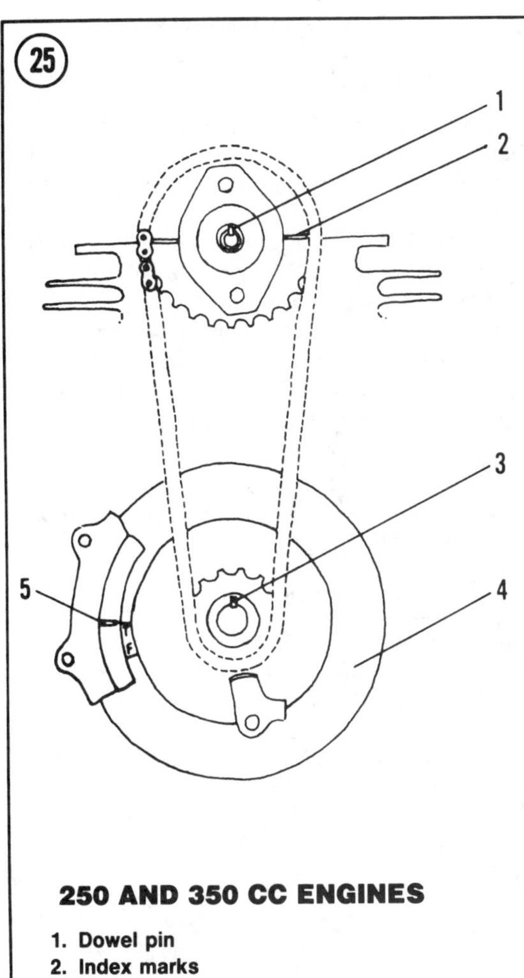

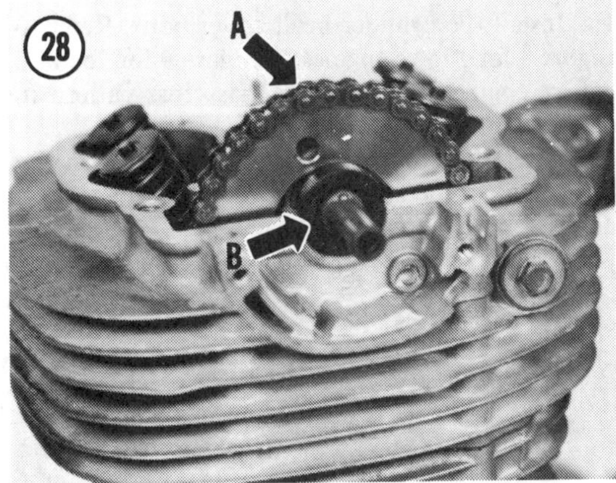

necessary, readjust the cam chain on the cam sprocket.

10. Align the holes in the cam with the holes in the cam sprocket and install the exposed bolt finger-tight. Rotate the engine 180° and install the other cam sprocket bolt. Tighten this bolt to the torque specification listed in **Table 2**.

11. Rotate the engine 180° and tighten the other cam sprocket bolt to the torque specification listed in **Table 2**.

12. Check the alignment of the cam sprocket. Make sure that the index marks (**Figure 29**) align with the top surface of the cylinder head with the alternator rotor timing mark "T" aligned with the stationary pointer. Refer to **Figure 24** for 175 cc engines or **Figure 25** for 250 and 350 cc engines. If alignment is not correct, repeat Steps 9-11 until alignment is correct.

CAUTION

Very expensive damage could result from improper cam and chain alignment. Recheck your work several times to be sure alignment is correct.

13. Make sure the locating dowels are in place in the cylinder head.
14. If necessary, rotate the crankshaft until the lobes on the cam are facing down. This is to relieve strain on the rocker arms and cylinder head cover during installation.
15. Apply a light coat of gasket sealer to the sealing surface of the cylinder head cover. Cover all of the flat sealing surface. Do not apply the sealer too close to the edge of the right-hand bearing surface as it will restrict oil flow.

NOTE
Use Gasgacinch Gasket Sealer, 4-Three Bond or equivalent. When selecting an equivalent, avoid thick or hard setting materials.

16. Install the cylinder head cover bolts. Refer to **Figure 8** for 175 cc engines or **Figure 9** for 250 and 350 cc engines. Tighten in a crisscross pattern in 2-3 steps to the final torque listed in **Table 2**.
17. After the engine has been reinstalled in the frame, adjust the valves and cam chain tension as described in Chapter Three.

CAMSHAFT CHAIN

Removal/Installation

1. Remove the cylinder head as described in this chapter.
2. Remove the alternator as described in Chapter Eight.
3. On models so equipped, remove the bolt (A, **Figure 30**) securing the chain set plate on the camshaft chain adjacent to the crankshaft.
4. Remove the chain from the drive sprocket on the crankshaft and remove the camshaft chain (B, **Figure 30**) out through the opening in the cylinder.
5. Install by reversing these removal steps.

Inspection

Refer to *Camshaft Chain and Tensioner Inspection* in this chapter.

Camshaft Chain Tensioner Adjustment

After the cam chain has been replaced, adjust the chain as described under *Camshaft Chain Tensioner Adjustment* in Chapter Three.

Camshaft Chain Sprocket

Inspect the condition of the teeth on the cam chain sprocket (**Figure 31**). Replace if it shows signs of wear or has any teeth missing.

CYLINDER HEAD

Removal/Installation

CAUTION
To prevent any warpage and damage, remove the cylinder head only when the engine is at room temperature.

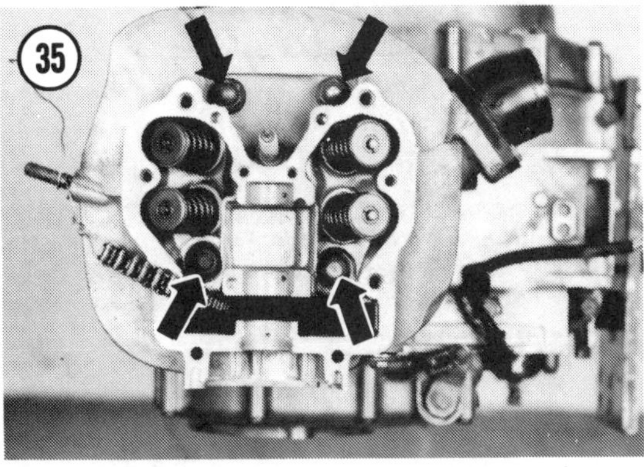

1. Remove the engine as described in this chapter.
2. Remove the cylinder head cover (A, **Figure 32**) and camshaft as described in this chapter.

3A. On 175 cc engines, remove the bolt (B, **Figure 32**) adjacent to the spark plug.

3B. On 250 cc engines, remove the internal sealing plug (**Figure 33**) to expose the cylinder head nut below.

4. Loosen the cylinder head nuts in a crisscross pattern. Refer to **Figure 34** for 175 cc engines or **Figure 35** for 250 and 350 cc engines. Remove the cylinder head nuts and washers. Note the location of sealing washers and different type nuts. They must be reinstalled in the same location.
5. On 250 cc engines, there are additional nuts under the left-hand side of the cylinder head. Remove the front left-hand nuts (**Figure 36**) and the rear left-hand nuts (**Figure 37**) securing the cylinder head to the cylinder.

6. Remove the bolt (**Figure 38**) securing the cam chain tensioner to the cylinder head.
7. Loosen the head by tapping around the perimeter with a rubber or plastic mallet. If necessary, *gently* pry the head loose with a broad-tipped screwdriver.

CAUTION
Remember the cooling fins are fragile and may be damaged if tapped or pried on too hard. Never use a metal hammer.

8. Untie the wire securing the cam chain and retie it to the cylinder head.
9. Remove the cylinder head by pulling it straight up and off the crankcase studs and cylinder. Pull the cam chain and wire through the opening in the cylinder head and retie the cam chain to the engine.
10. Remove the cylinder head gasket and discard it.

NOTE
Don't lose the locating dowels and, on 175 cc engines, the oil control orifice and O-ring seal.

11. Place a clean shop cloth into the cam chain opening in the cylinder to prevent the entry of foreign matter.
12. Install by reversing these removal steps, noting the following.
13. Clean the mating surfaces of the head and cylinder of any gasket material.
14A. On 175 cc engines, install a new head gasket (A, **Figure 39**), the locating dowels (B, **Figure 39**) and the oil control orifice (**Figure 40**).
14B. On 250 and 350 cc engines, install the locating dowels (A, **Figure 41**) and a new O-ring seal (B, **Figure 41**) on the right-hand rear dowel. Install a new head gasket.
15. Install the cylinder head and secure it with the nuts and washers. Install the sealing washers and nuts in the correct location as noted during removal. Tighten the nuts to the torque specification listed in **Table 2**.
16. On 250 cc engines, inspect the O-ring seal on the internal sealing plug; replace if necessary. Install the sealing plug (**Figure 33**) into the cylinder head. Make sure it is seated correctly or an oil leak will result.
17. Correctly position the upper end of the cam chain tensioner. Inspect the O-ring seal (**Figure 42**) on the bolt; replace if necessary. Install the bolt and tighten securely.

38

39

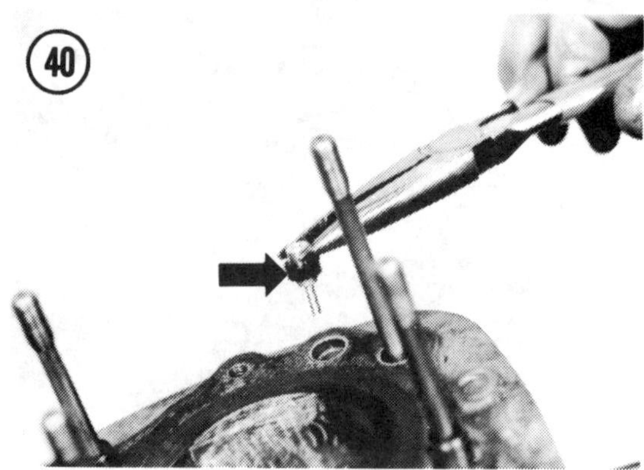
40

41

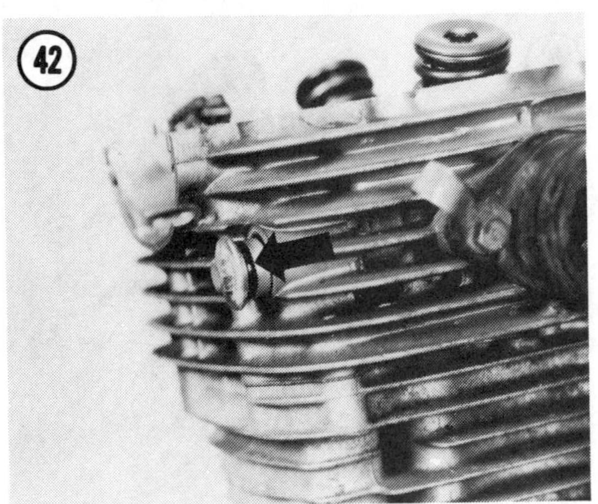

42

43

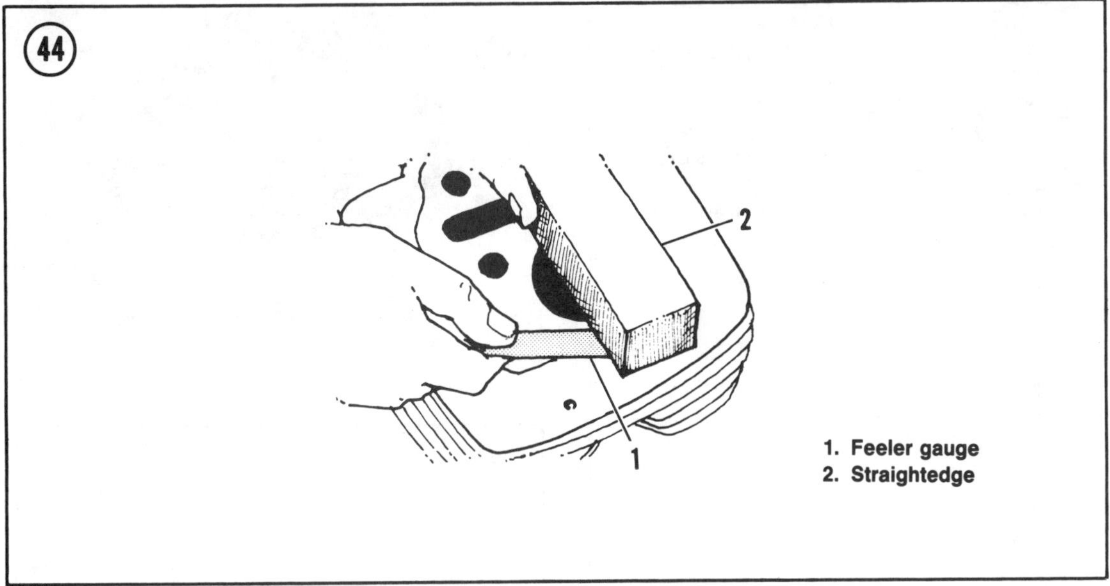

44

Inspection

1. Remove all traces of gasket material from the cylinder head mating surfaces.
2. *Without removing the valves*, remove all carbon deposits from the combustion chamber and valve ports (**Figure 43**) with a wire brush. A blunt screwdriver or chisel may be used if care is taken not to damage the head, valves and spark plug threads.
3. After the carbon is removed from the combustion chamber and the valve intake and exhaust ports, clean the entire head in cleaning solvent. Blow dry with compressed air.
4. Clean away all carbon from the the piston crown. Do not remove the carbon ridge at the top of the cylinder bore.
5. Check for cracks in the combustion chamber and exhaust ports. A cracked head must be replaced.
6. After the head has been thoroughly cleaned, place a straightedge across the cylinder head/cylinder gasket surface (**Figure 44**) at several points. Measure the warp by inserting a flat feeler gauge between the straightedge and the cylinder head at each location. There should be no warpage; if a small amount is present, it can be resurfaced by a dealer or qualified machine shop.
7. Check the cylinder head cover mating surface using the procedure in Step 6. There should be no warpage.
8. Check the condition of the valves and valve guides as described under *Valves and Valve Components* in this chapter.

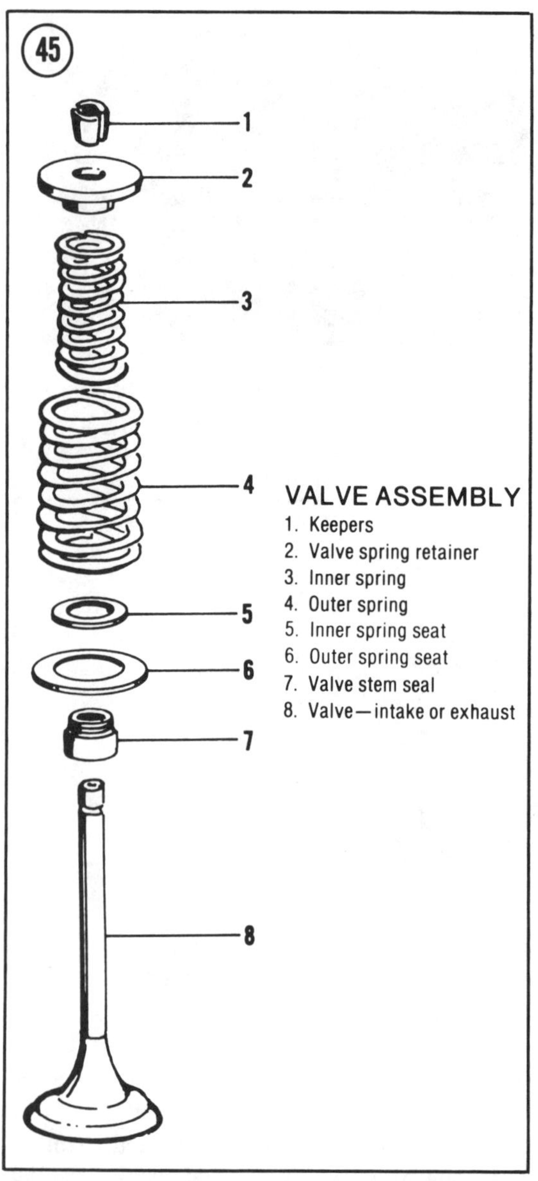

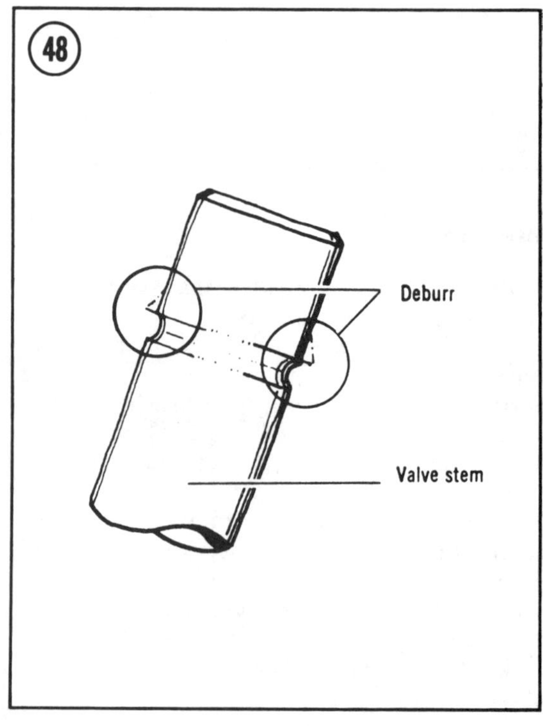

VALVES AND VALVE COMPONENTS

Removal

Refer to **Figure 45** for this procedure.

1. Remove the cylinder head as described in this chapter.
2. Compress the valve springs with a valve compressor tool (**Figure 46**). Remove the valve keepers and release the compression. Remove the valve compressor tool.

CAUTION
To avoid loss of spring tension, do not compress the springs any more than necessary to remove the keepers.

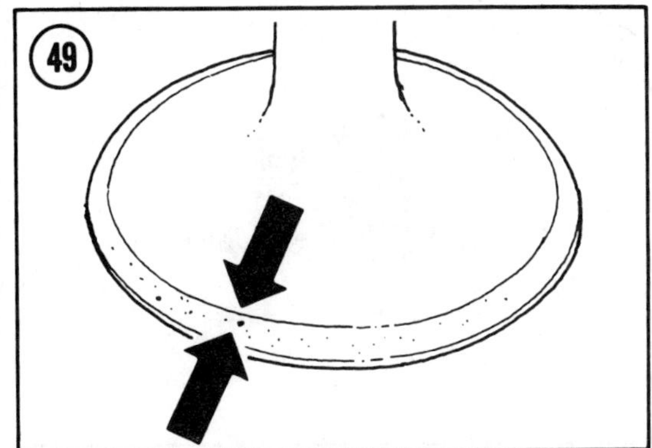

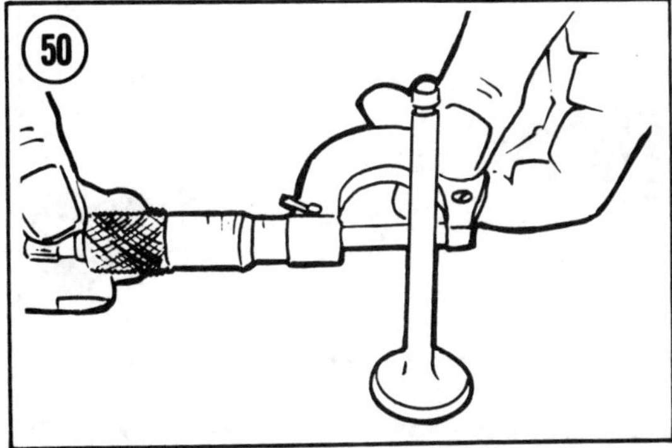

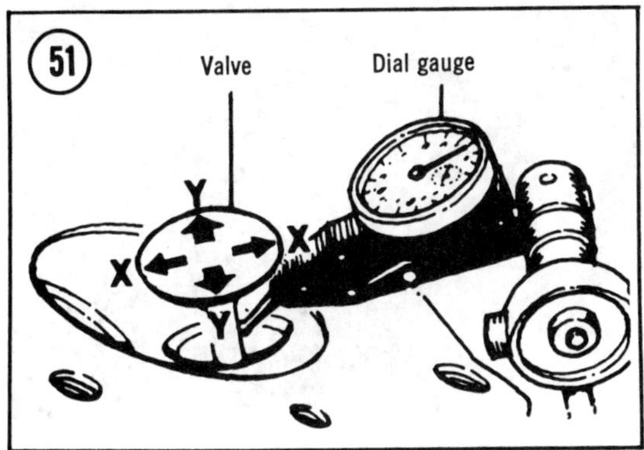

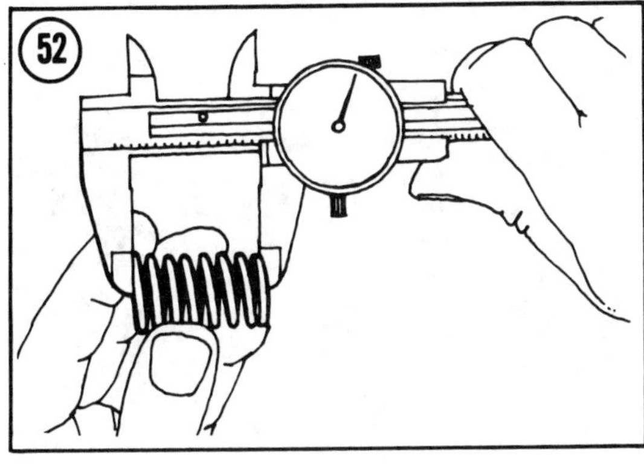

3. Remove the valve spring retainer and valve springs (**Figure 47**).

> NOTE
> *The inner and outer valve seats and valve stem seal will stay in the cylinder head.*

4. Prior to removing the valve, remove any burrs from the valve stem (**Figure 48**). Otherwise the valve guide will be damaged.
5. Mark all parts as they are disassembled so that they can be installed in their original location.

Inspection

1. Clean valves with a wire brush and solvent.
2. Inspect the contact surface of each valve for burning or pitting (**Figure 49**). Unevenness of the contact surface is an indication that the valve is not serviceable. The valve contact surface can be ground.
3. Measure the valve stem for wear (**Figure 50**). Compare with specifications given in **Table 1**.
4. Remove all carbon and varnish from the valve guide with a stiff spiral wire brush.
5. Insert each valve in its guide. Hold the valve with the head just slightly off the valve seat and rock it sideways. Measure the play along both the "X" and "Y" axes (**Figure 51**). If it rocks more than slightly, the guide is probably worn and should be replaced. As a final check, take the cylinder head to a dealer and have the valve guides measured.
6. Measure the valve spring free length with a vernier caliper (**Figure 52**). All should be within the length specified in **Table 1** with no signs of bends or distortion. Replace defective springs in pairs (inner and outer).
7. Check the valve spring retainer and valve keepers. If they are in good condition they may be reused; replace as necessary.
8. Inspect the valve seats (**Figure 53**). If worn or burned, they must be reconditioned. This should

be performed by a dealer or qualified machine shop.

Installation

1. Coat the valve stems with molybdenum disulfide grease. To avoid damage to the valve stem seal, turn the valve slowly while inserting the valve into the cylinder head.
2. Install the valve springs with the narrow pitch end (end with the coils closest together) facing the head (**Figure 54**).
3. Install the valve spring retainer.
4. Compress the valve springs with a compressor tool (**Figure 46**) and install the valve keepers.

CAUTION
To avoid loss of spring tension, do not compress the springs any more than necessary to install the keepers.

5. After all springs have been installed, gently tap the end of the valve stem with a soft aluminum or brass drift and hammer. This will ensure that the keepers are properly seated.

Valve Guide Replacement

When valve guides are worn so that there is excessive stem-to-guide clearance or valve tipping, the guides must be replaced. Replace all, even if only one is worn. This job should only be done by a dealer as special tools are required.

Valve Seat Reconditioning

This job is best left to a dealer or qualified machine shop. They have special equipment and knowledge for this exacting job. You can still save considerable money by removing the cylinder head and taking the head to the shop for repairs.

Valve Lapping

Valve lapping is a simple operation which can restore the valve seal without machining if the amount of wear or distortion is not too great.
1. Coat the valve seating area in the head with a lapping compound such as Carborundum or Clover Brand.
2. Insert the valve in the cylinder head.
3. Wet the suction cup of the lapping stick (**Figure 55**) and stick it to the valve head.
4. Lap the valve to the seat by rotating the lapping stick in both directions. Every 5 to 10 seconds, rotate the valve 180° in the seat; continue lapping until the contact surfaces of the valve and the valve seat are a uniform grey. Stop as soon as they are, to avoid removing too much material.

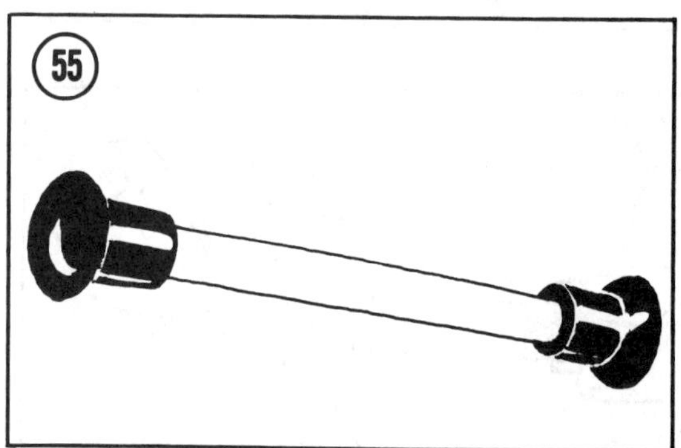

5. Thoroughly clean the valves and the cylinder head in solvent to remove all grinding compound. Any compound left in the head or on the valves will end up in the oil supply and cause damage to the engine.
6. After the valve lapping is completed and the valves are reinstalled in the cylinder head, the valve seal should be tested. Check the seal of each valve by pouring solvent into the intake and exhaust ports. There should be no leakage past the valve seat. If fluid leaks past either seat, disassemble the valve assembly and repeat the lapping procedure until there is no leakage.

If there is still a leak either the valve or the valve seat must be ground or replaced.

CYLINDER

Removal

1. Remove the cylinder head as described in this chapter.
2. Remove the bolts securing the cylinder on the left-hand side. Refer to **Figure 56** for 175 cc engines or **Figure 57** for 250 and 350 cc engines.
3. Remove the cam chain front guide and tensioner.
4. Loosen the cylinder by tapping around the perimeter with a rubber or plastic mallet. If necessary, *gently* pry the cylinder loose with a broad-tipped screwdriver.
5. Pull the cylinder straight up and off of the crankcase studs. Work the cam chain wire through the opening in the cylinder and retie the chain to an external engine part.
6. Remove the cylinder base gasket and discard it. Remove the 2 dowel pins from the crankcase studs.
7. Install a piston holding fixture under the piston (**Figure 58**) to protect the piston skirt from damage. This fixture may be purchased or may be a homemade unit of wood. See **Figure 59** for dimensions.

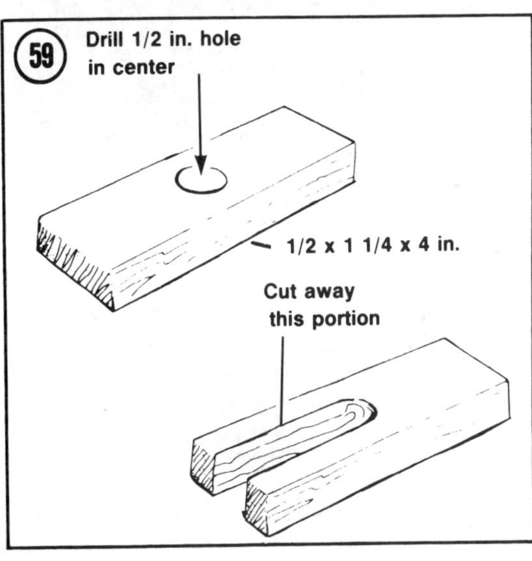

Inspection

The following procedure requires the use of highly specialized and expensive measuring instruments. If such equipment is not readily available, have the measurements performed by a dealer or qualified machine shop.

1. Soak with solvent any old cylinder head gasket material on the cylinder. Use a broad-tipped *dull* chisel and gently scrape off all gasket residue. Do not gouge the sealing surface as oil and air leaks will result.
2. Measure the cylinder bore with a cylinder gauge or inside micrometer at the points shown in **Figure 60**. Measure in 2 axes—in line with the piston pin

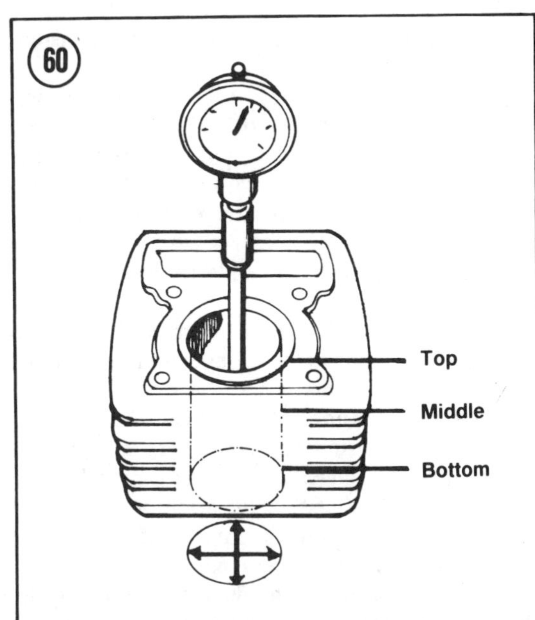

5

and at 90° to the pin. If the taper or out-of-round is 0.10 mm (0.004 in.) or greater, the cylinder must be rebored to the next oversize and a new piston installed.

NOTE
The new piston should be obtained before the cylinder is rebored so that the piston can be measured; slight manufacturing tolerances must be taken into account to determine the actual size and working clearance. Piston-to-cylinder wear limit is specified in ***Table 1***.

3. Check the cylinder wall (**Figure 61**) for scratches; if evident, the cylinder should be rebored. The maximum wear limit on the cylinder is listed in **Table 1**. If the cylinder is worn to this limit, it must be replaced. Never rebore a cylinder if the finished rebore diameter will be this dimension or greater.

Installation

1. Check that the top surface of the crankcase and the bottom surface of the cylinder are clean prior to installing a new base gasket.
2. Install a new cylinder base gasket (A, **Figure 62**).
3. Install the 2 dowel pins (B, **Figure 62**), one on the front right-hand stud and one on the rear left-hand stud.

NOTE
Figure 62 *is shown with the piston removed for clarity.*

4. Install a piston holding fixture under the piston (**Figure 63**).
5. Make sure the end gaps of the piston rings are *not* lined up with each other—they must be staggered. Lightly oil the piston rings and the inside of the cylinder bore with assembly oil.
6. Untie the cam chain wire and tie it to the cylinder.
7. Install the cylinder and slide it down onto the crankcase studs.
8. Carefully feed the cam chain and wire up through the opening in the cylinder and tie it to the engine.
9. Start the cylinder down over the piston. Compress each piston ring as it enters the cylinder either with your fingers or by using aircraft type hose clamps (**Figure 64**) of the appropriate size.
10. Slide the cylinder down until it bottoms on the piston holding fixture (**Figure 65**).
11. Remove the piston holding fixture and slide the cylinder down into place on the crankcase.

61

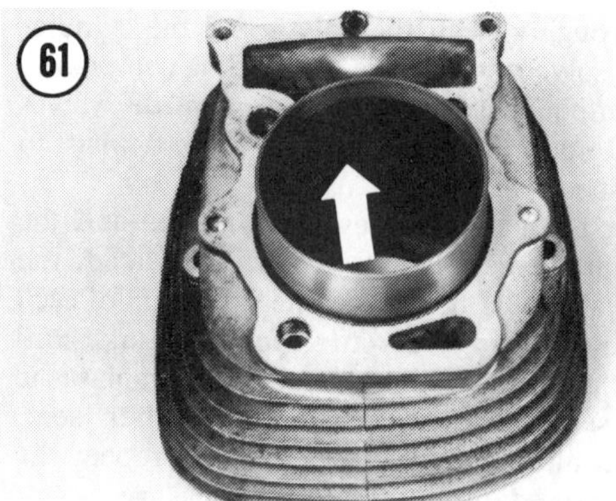

62

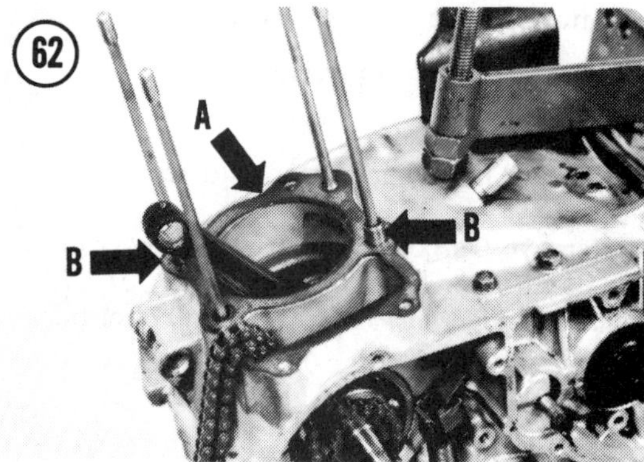

63

64

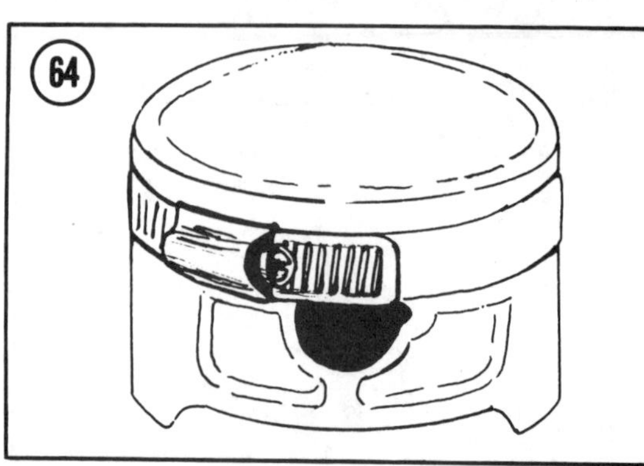

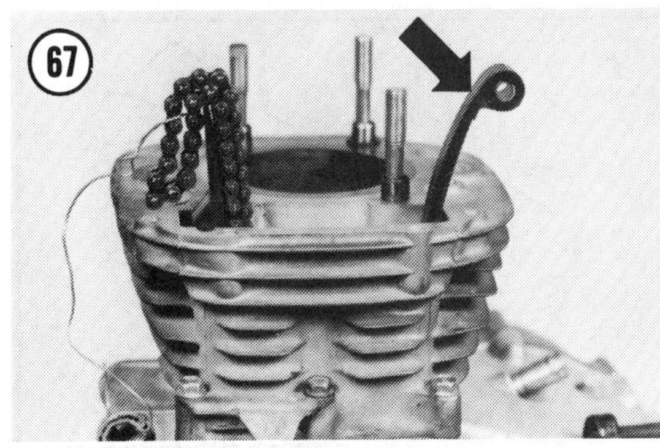

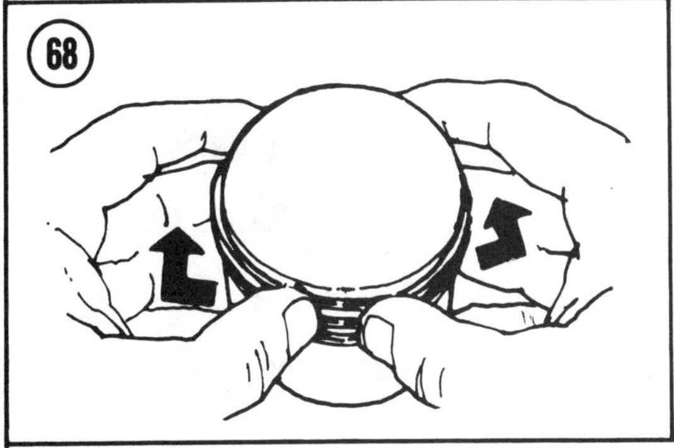

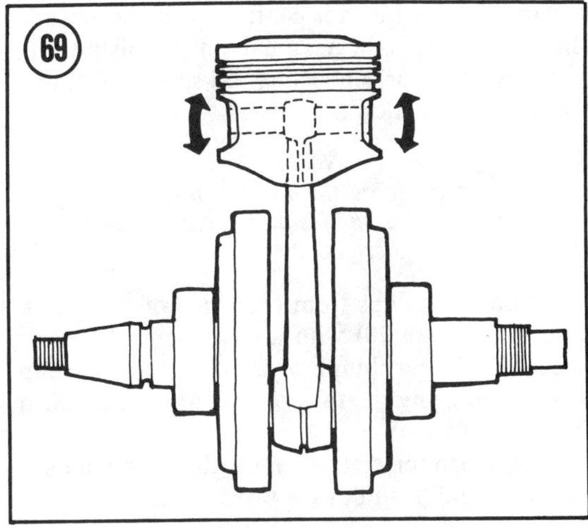

5

12. Install the cam chain guide with the offset (**Figure 66**) down toward the crankcase.
13. Install the tensioner (**Figure 67**). Make sure the lower end is inserted into the receptacle in the tensioner set bar.
14. Install the bolts securing the cylinder on the left-hand side. Tighten the bolts to the torque specification listed in **Table 2**.
15. Install the cylinder head as described in this chapter.
16. Adjust the valves, cam chain tensioner and ignition timing as described in Chapter Three.
17. Follow the *Break-in Procedure* in this chapter if the cylinder was rebored or honed or a new piston or piston rings were installed.

PISTON, PISTON PIN AND PISTON RINGS

The piston is made of an aluminum alloy. The piston pin is made of steel and is a precision fit. The piston pin is held in place by a clip at each end.

Piston Removal

1. Remove the cylinder head and cylinder as described in this chapter.

WARNING
The edges of all piston rings are very sharp. Be careful when handling them to avoid cut fingers.

2. Remove the top ring with a ring expander tool or by spreading the ends with your thumbs just enough to slide the ring up over the piston (**Figure 68**). Repeat for the remaining rings.
3. Before removing the piston, hold the rod tightly and rock the piston as shown in **Figure 69**. Any

rocking motion (do not confuse with the normal sliding motion) indicates wear on the piston pin, piston pin bore or connecting rod small end (more likely a combination of all).

NOTE
Wrap a clean shop cloth under the piston so that the piston pin clip will not fall into the crankcase.

4. Remove the clips from each side of the piston pin bore (**Figure 70**) with a small screwdriver or scribe. Hold your thumb over one edge of the clip when removing it to prevent the clip from springing out.
5. Use a proper size wooden dowel or socket extension and push out the piston pin.

CAUTION
Be careful when removing the pin to avoid damaging the connecting rod. If it is necessary to gently tap the pin to remove it, be sure that the piston is properly supported so that lateral shock is not transmitted to the lower connecting rod bearing.

6. If the piston pin is difficult to remove, heat the piston and pin with a butane torch. The pin will probably push right out. Heat the piston to only about 60° C (140° F), i.e., until it is too warm to touch, but not excessively hot. If the pin is still difficult to push out, use a homemade tool as shown in **Figure 71**.

NOTE
A special tool, the universal piston pin extractor, is available from British Marketing, P.O. Box 219, San Juan Capistrano, CA 92693.

7. Lift the piston off the connecting rod.
8. If the piston is going to be left off for some time, place a piece of foam insulation tube over the end of the rod to protect it.

Inspection

1. Carefully clean the carbon from the piston crown with a chemical remover or with a soft scraper (**Figure 72**). Do not remove or damage the carbon ridge around the circumference of the piston above the top ring (**Figure 73**). If the piston, rings and cylinder are found to be dimensionally correct and can be reused, removal of the carbon ring from the top of the piston or the carbon ridge from the top of the cylinder will promote excessive oil consumption.

CAUTION
Do not wire brush the piston skirts.

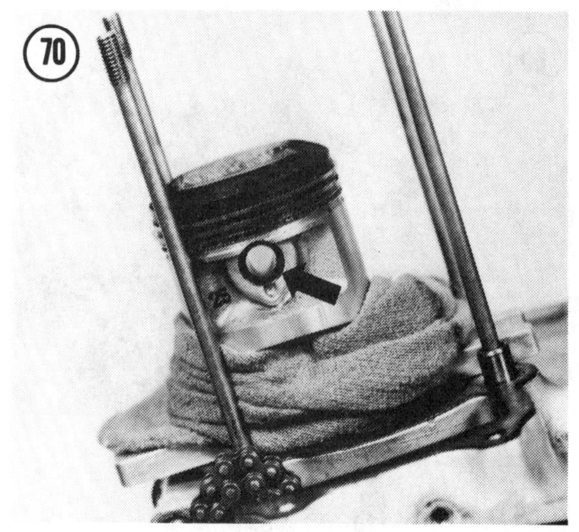

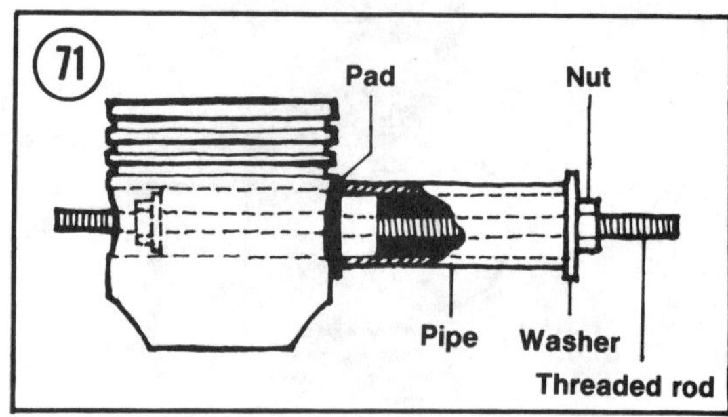

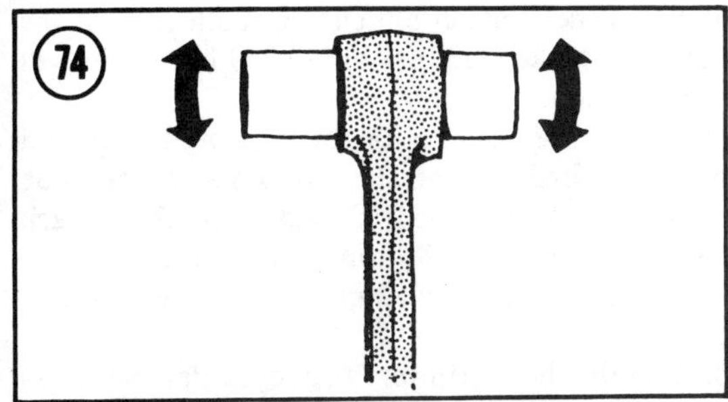

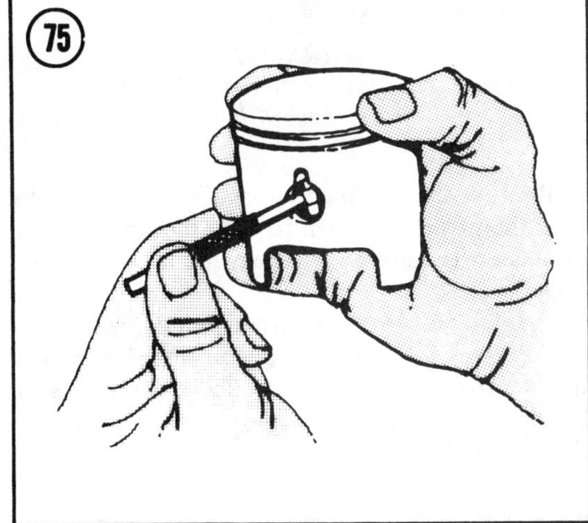

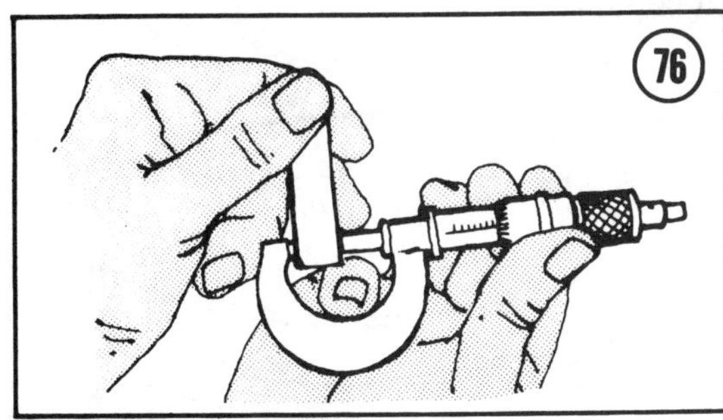

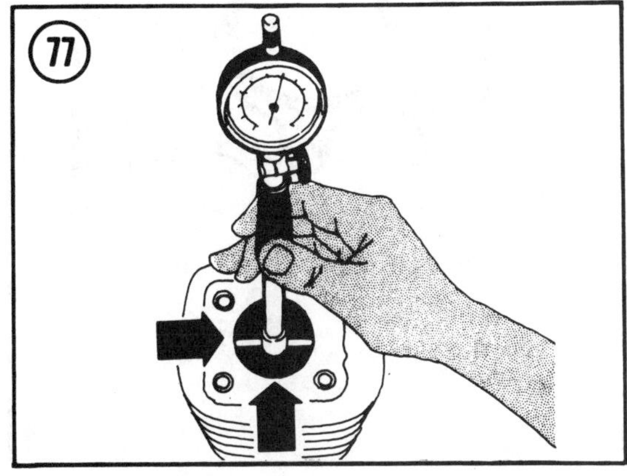

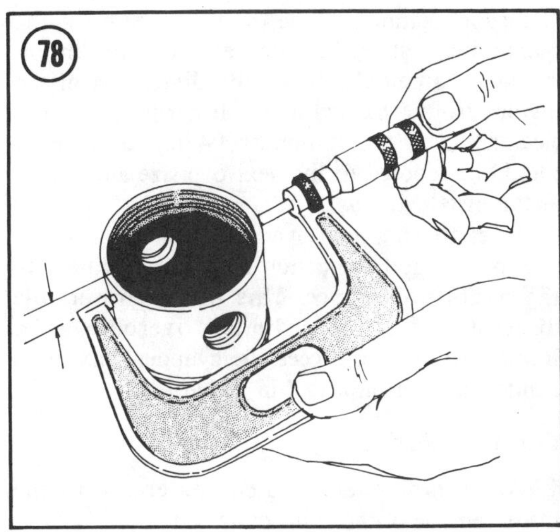

2. Examine each ring groove for burrs, dented edges and wide wear. Pay particular attention to the top compression ring groove as it usually wears more than the others.
3. Measure piston-to-cylinder clearance as described in this chapter.
4. If damage or wear indicates piston replacement, select a new piston as described under *Piston Clearance* in this chapter.
5. Oil the piston pin and install it in the connecting rod. Slowly rotate the piston pin and check for radial and axial play (**Figure 74**). If any play exists, the piston pin should be replaced, providing the rod bore is in good condition. Measure the inside diameter of the piston pin bore with a snap gauge (**Figure 75**) and measure the outside diameter of the piston pin with a micrometer (**Figure 76**). Compare with dimensions given in **Table 1**. Replace the piston and piston pin as a set if either or both are worn.
6. Check the piston skirt for galling and abrasion which may have been caused by piston seizure. If light galling is present, smooth the affected area with No. 400 emery paper and oil or a fine oilstone. However, if galling is severe or if the piston is deeply scored, replace it.

Piston Clearance

1. Make sure the piston and cylinder walls are clean and dry.
2. Measure the inside diameter of the cylinder bore at a point 13 mm (1/2 in.) from the upper edge with a bore gauge (**Figure** 77).
3. Measure the outside diameter of the piston across the skirt at right angles to the piston pin. Measure at a distance 10 mm (0.40 in.) up from the bottom of the piston skirt (**Figure 78**).

4. Piston clearance is the difference between the maximum piston diameter and the minimum cylinder diameter. Subtract the dimension of the piston from the cylinder dimension. If the clearance exceeds 0.10 mm (0.004 in.), the cylinder should be rebored to the next oversize and a new piston installed.
5. To establish a final overbore dimension with a new piston, add the piston skirt measurement to the specified clearance. This will determine the dimension for the cylinder overbore size. Remember, do not exceed the cylinder maximum inside diameter indicated in **Table 1**.

Piston Installation

1. Apply molybdenum disulfide grease to the inside surface of the connecting rod.
2. Oil the piston pin with assembly oil and install it in the piston until its end extends slightly beyond the inside of the boss (**Figure 79**).
3. Place the piston over the connecting rod with the "IN" on the piston crown directed rearward toward the intake port.
4. Line up the piston pin with the hole in the connecting rod. Push the piston pin through the connecting rod and into the other side of the piston until it is even with the piston pin clip grooves.

CAUTION
If it is necessary to tap the piston pin into the connecting rod, do so gently with a block of wood or a soft-faced hammer. Make sure you support the piston to prevent the lateral shock from being transmitted to connecting rod bearing.

NOTE
*In the next step, install the clips with the gap away from the cutout in the piston (**Figure 80**).*

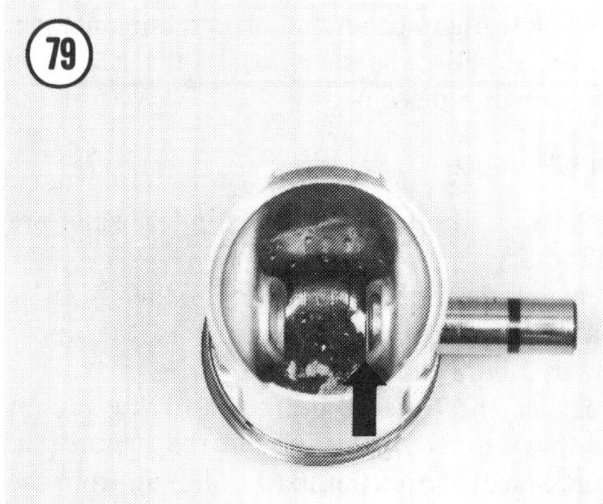

5. Install new piston pin clips in both ends of the pin boss. Make sure they are seated in the grooves in the piston.
6. Check the installation by rocking the piston back and forth around the pin axis and from side to side along the axis. It should rotate freely back and forth but not slide from side to side.
7. Install the piston rings as described in this chapter.
8. Install the cylinder and cylinder head as described in this chapter.

Piston Ring Replacement

WARNING
The edges of all piston rings are very sharp. Be careful when handling them to avoid cut fingers.

1. Remove the top ring by spreading the ends with your thumbs just enough to slide the ring up over the piston (**Figure 68**). Repeat for the remaining rings.
2. Carefully remove all carbon buildup from the ring grooves with a broken piston ring (**Figure 81**). Inspect the grooves carefully for burrs, nicks or broken and cracked lands. Recondition or replace the piston if necessary.

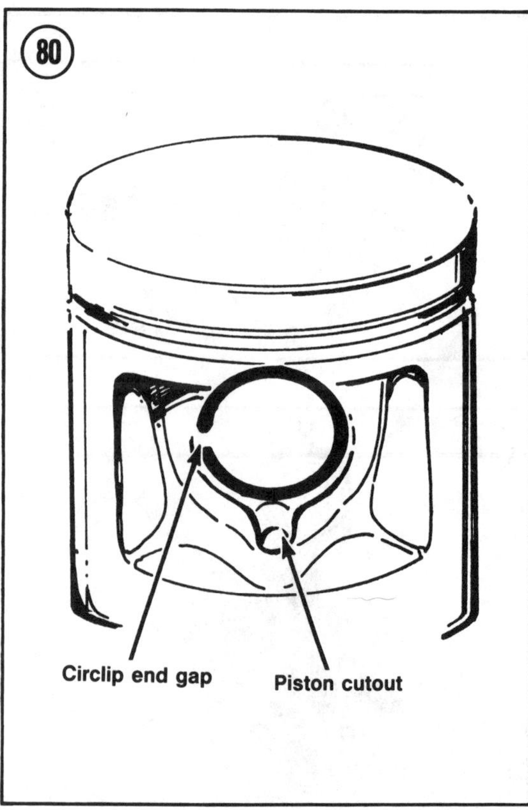

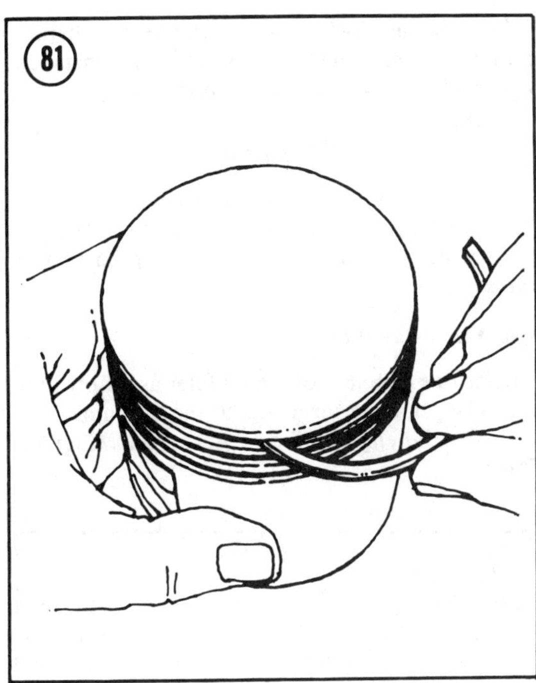

3. Roll each ring around its piston groove as shown in **Figure 82** to check for binding. Minor binding may be cleaned up with a fine-cut file.
4. Measure the side clearance of each ring in its groove with a flat feeler gauge (**Figure 83**) and compare to dimensions given in **Table 1**. If the clearance is greater than specified, the rings must be replaced. If the clearance is still excessive with the new rings, the piston must also be replaced.
5. Measure each ring for wear as shown in **Figure 84**. Place each ring, one at a time, into the cylinder and push it in about 20 mm (3/4 in.) with the crown of the piston to ensure that the ring is square in the cylinder bore. Measure the gap with a flat feeler gauge and compare to dimensions in **Table 1**. If the gap is greater than specified, the rings should be replaced. When installing new rings, measure their end gap in the same manner as for old ones. If the gap is less than specified, carefully file the ends with a fine-cut file until the gap is correct.
6. Install the piston rings in the order shown in **Figure 85**. Install all rings with their marking facing up.

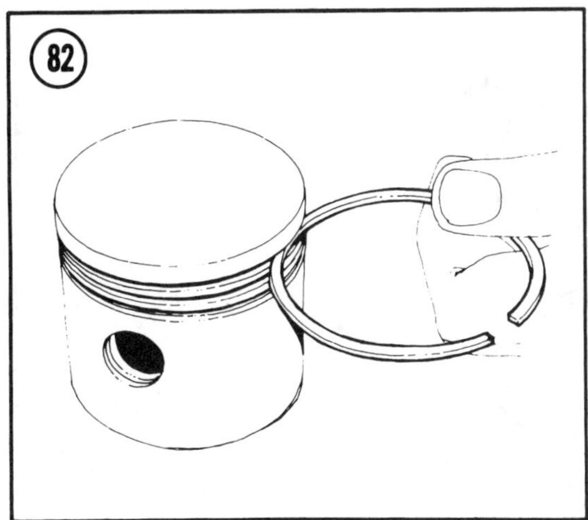

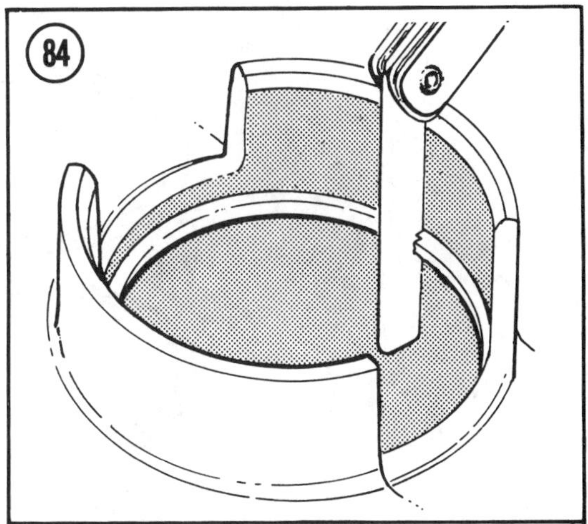

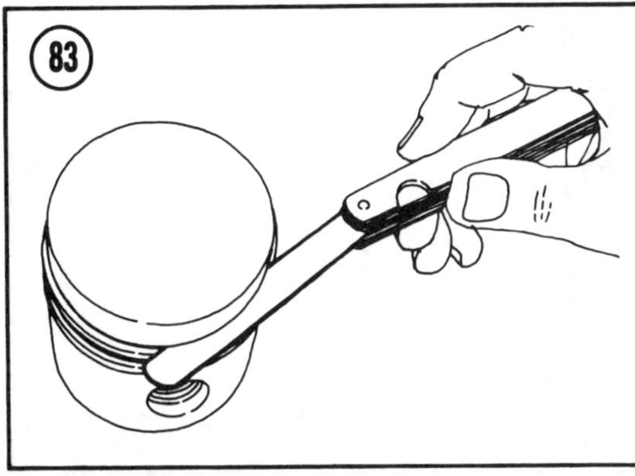

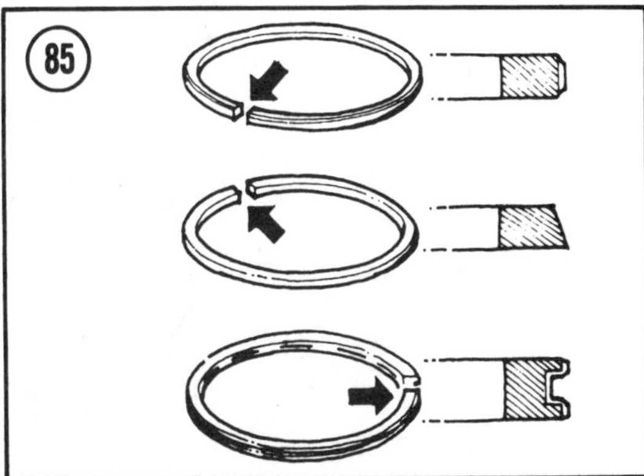

7. Install the piston rings—first the bottom one, then the middle one, then the top—by carefully spreading the ends of the ring with your thumbs and slipping the ring over the top of the piston. Remember that the marks on the piston rings are toward the top of the piston.
8. Make sure the rings are seated completely in their grooves all the way around the piston and that the ends are distributed around the piston as shown in **Figure 86**. The important thing is that the ring gaps are not aligned with each other when installed.
9. If new rings were installed, measure the side clearance of each ring in its groove with a flat feeler gauge (**Figure 83**) and compare to dimensions given in **Table 1**.
10. Follow the *Break-in Procedure* in this chapter if a new piston or piston rings have been installed or the cylinder was rebored or honed.

OIL PUMP

The oil pump is located on the right-hand side of the engine behind the clutch assembly. The oil pump can be removed with the engine in the frame.

Removal/Installation

Refer to **Figure 87** for the oil filter assembly that has to be removed for access to the oil pump.
1. Drain the engine oil as described in Chapter Three.

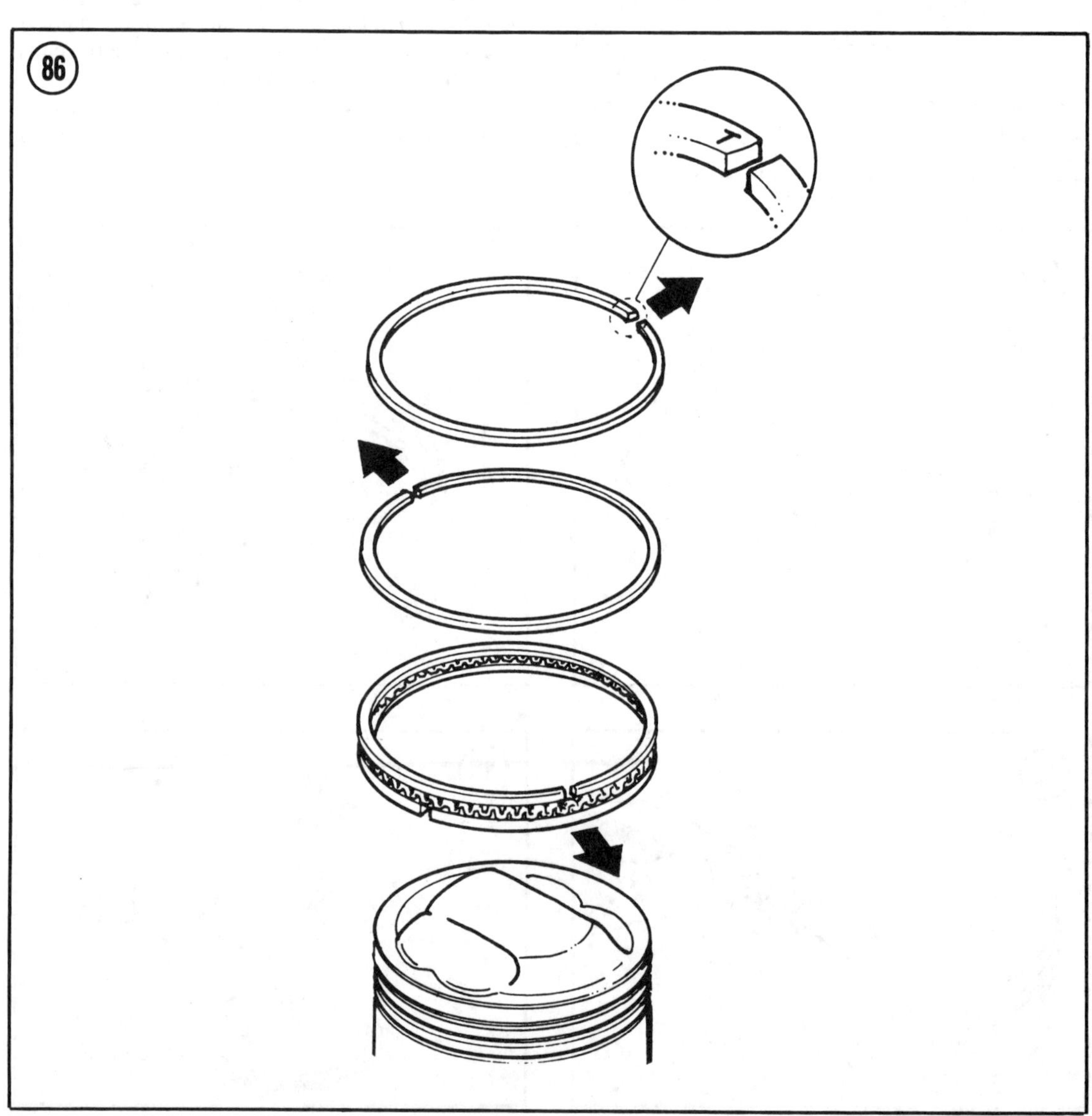

2. Remove the clutch as described under *Clutch Removal/Disassembly* in Chapter Six.
3. Remove the kickstarter as described in this chapter.
4A. On the 175 cc engine, remove the screws (**Figure 88**) securing the oil pump assembly to the crankcase. Remove the oil pump assembly.

NOTE

Figure 88 *is shown with the engine removed and partially disassembled for clarity.*

4B. On 250 and 350 cc engines, remove the screws and bolt (**Figure 89**) securing the oil pump assembly to the crankcase. Remove the oil pump assembly.
5. Don't lose the O-ring seals in the crankcase recesses. Refer to **Figure 90** for 175 cc engines or **Figure 91** for 250 and 350 cc engines.
6. Install by reversing these removal steps.

Disassembly/Inspection/Assembly (175 cc Engine)

Refer to **Figure 92** for for this procedure.
1. Remove the screw (A, **Figure 93**) securing the gear retainer plate (B, **Figure 93**) to the assembly. Remove the plate.
2. Inspect the pump body for cracks.
3. Remove the gear assembly (C, **Figure 93**).
4. Separate the cover from the pump body.
5. Remove the inner and outer rotors. Inspect

87

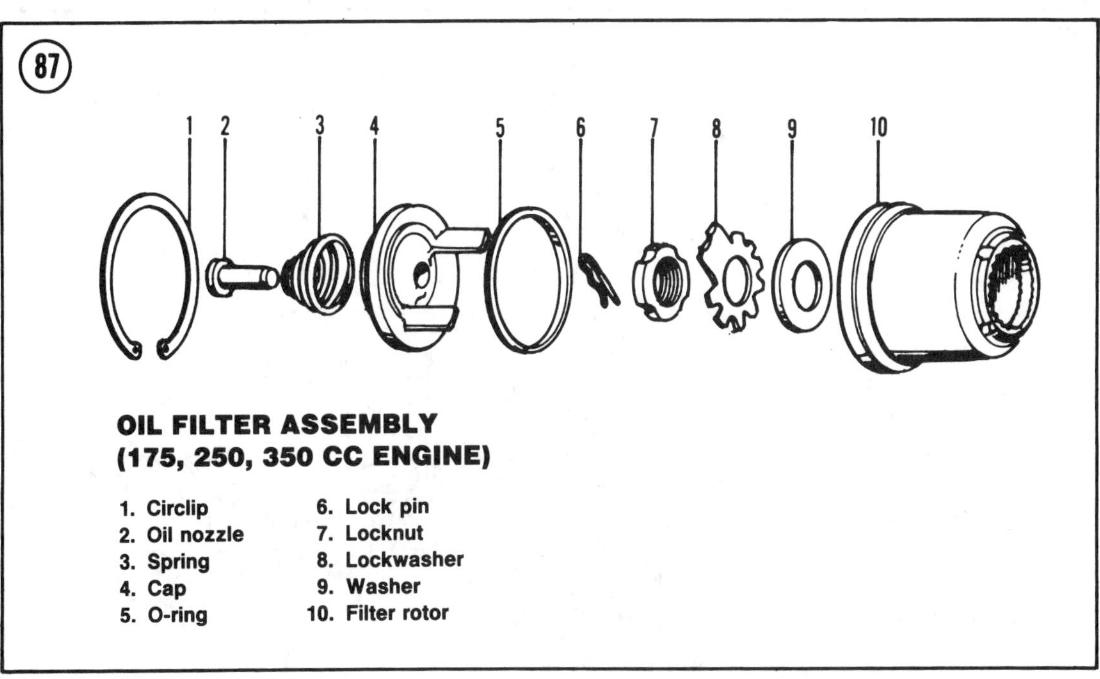

OIL FILTER ASSEMBLY (175, 250, 350 CC ENGINE)

1. Circlip
2. Oil nozzle
3. Spring
4. Cap
5. O-ring
6. Lock pin
7. Locknut
8. Lockwasher
9. Washer
10. Filter rotor

88

89

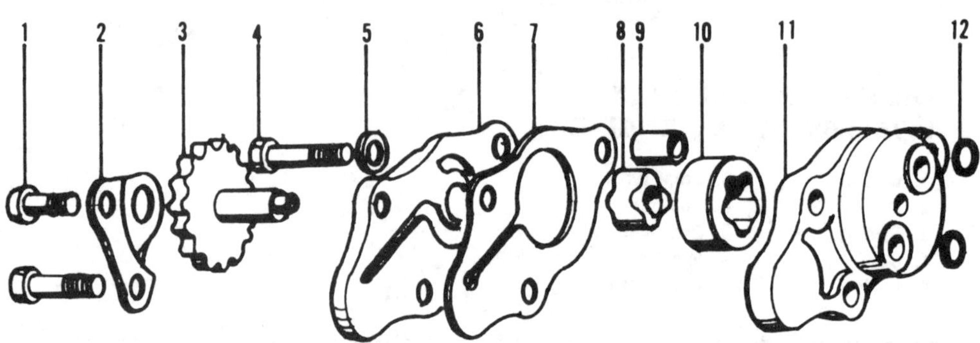

OIL PUMP ASSEMBLY (175 CC ENGINE)

1. Screw
2. Plate
3. Gear assembly
4. Bolt
5. Washer
6. Cover
7. Gasket
8. Inner rotor
9. Dowel pin
10. Outer rotor
11. Body
12. O-ring

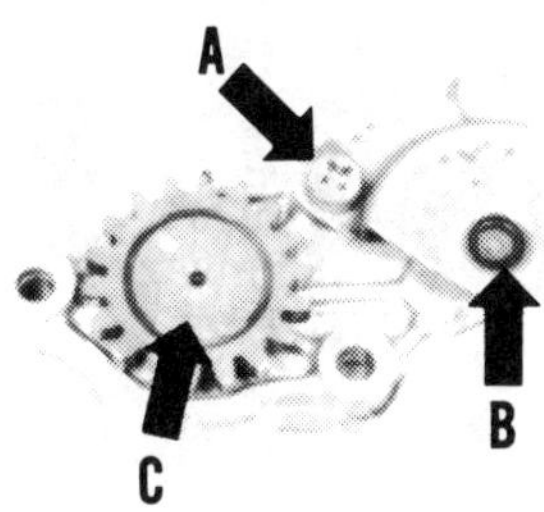

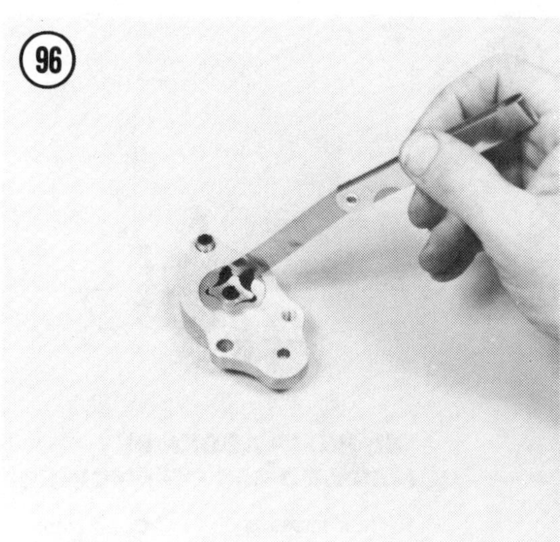

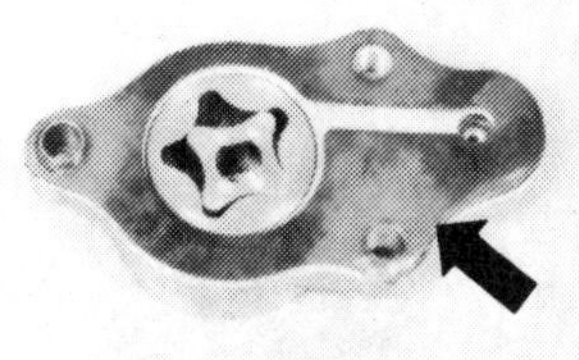

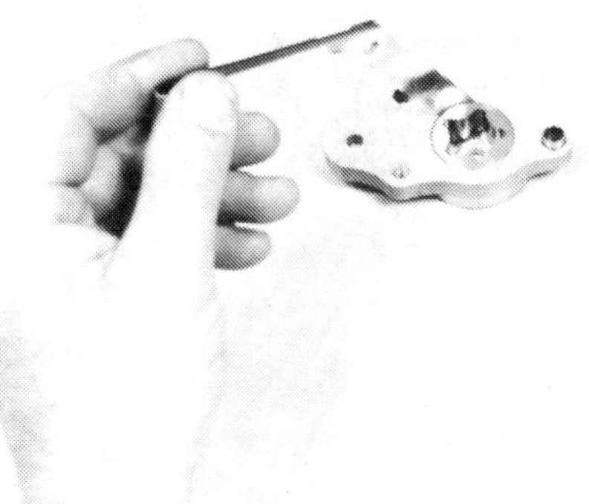

both parts for scratches and abrasions. Replace both parts if evidence of this is found.

6. If damaged, remove the gasket (**Figure 94**).
7. Clean all parts in solvent and thoroughly dry. Coat all parts with fresh engine oil prior to assembly.
8. Inspect the teeth on the drive gear. Replace the drive gear if the teeth are damaged or any are missing.
9. Install the outer rotor into the pump body.
10. Measure the clearance between the outer rotor and the oil pump body with a flat feeler gauge (**Figure 95**). If the clearance is greater than listed in **Table 1**, replace the worn part.
11. Install the inner rotor into the pump body.
12. Measure the clearance between the inner rotor tip and the outer rotor as shown in **Figure 96**. If the clearance is greater than listed in **Table 1**, replace the worn part.
13. Install a new gasket if the old one was removed and install the cover.
14. Install the drive gear and the plate.
15. Install the screw and tighten only finger-tight.

Disassembly/Inspection/Assembly (250 and 350 cc Engines)

Refer to **Figure 97** for for this procedure.

1. Remove the screws (**Figure 98**) securing the gear retainer plate to the assembly. Remove the plate.
2. Inspect the pump body for cracks.
3. Remove the gear assembly (**Figure 99**).
4. Separate the cover from the pump body.
5. Remove the inner and outer rotors. Inspect both parts for scratches and abrasions. Replace both parts if evidence of this is found.

5

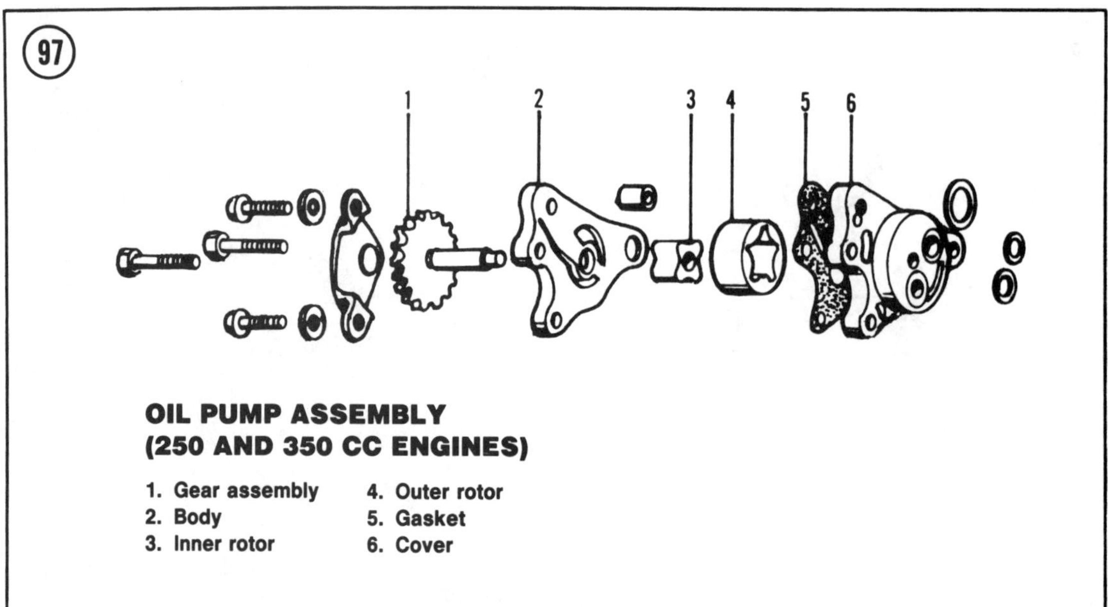

OIL PUMP ASSEMBLY (250 AND 350 CC ENGINES)

1. Gear assembly
2. Body
3. Inner rotor
4. Outer rotor
5. Gasket
6. Cover

6. If damaged, remove the gasket (**Figure 100**).
7. Clean all parts in solvent and thoroughly dry. Coat all parts with fresh engine oil prior to assembly.
8. Inspect the teeth on the drive gear. Replace the drive gear if the teeth are damaged or any are missing.
9. Install the outer rotor into the pump body.
10. Measure the clearance between the outer rotor and the oil pump body with a flat feeler gauge (**Figure 101**). If the clearance is greater than listed in **Table 1**, replace the worn part.
11. Install the inner rotor into the pump body.
12. Measure the clearance between the inner rotor tip and the outer rotor as shown in **Figure 102**. If the clearance is greater than the service limit specification listed in **Table 1** replace the worn part.

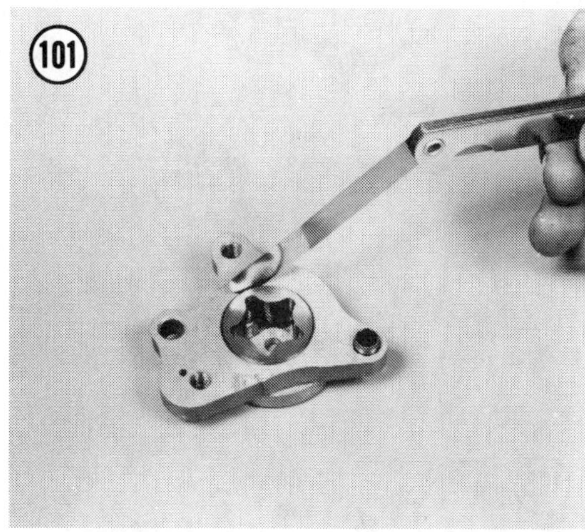

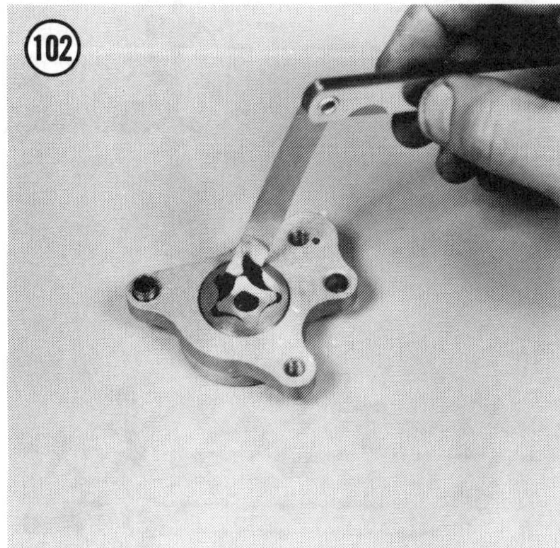

13. Install a new gasket if the old one was removed and install the cover.
14. Install the drive gear and the plate.
15. Install the screws and tighten securely.

Oil Pressure Test (250 and 350 cc Engines)

NOTE
Honda does not provide a test procedure for 175 cc engines.

The oil temperature must be at 20° C (68° F) and the oil level must be correct for this test to be accurate.

1. Remove the right-hand rear acorn nut and washer (**Figure 103**) securing the cylinder head cover.
2. Start the engine and let it idle at 1,000 rpm.
3. Oil should come out of the stud hole where the acorn nut was removed within 12 seconds of starting the engine.

NOTE
In colder weather it will take a little longer for the oil to flow to this inspection point.

4. If oil does not flow out of the opening, one of the following may be the problem:
   a. Oil pump.
   b. Clogged oil line(s).
   c. Low oil level.
5. Correct the problem.
6. Install the acorn nut and washer. Tighten the nut to the torque specification listed in **Table 2**.

CRANKCASE AND CRANKSHAFT

Disassembly of the crankcase (splitting the cases) and removal of the crankshaft assembly require that the engine be removed from the frame.

The crankcase is made in 2 halves of precision diecast aluminum alloy and is of the "thin-walled" type. To avoid damage, do not hammer or pry on any of the interior or exterior projected walls. These areas are easily damaged. The crankcase is assembled without a gasket between the 2 halves. Instead, gasket sealer is used. Dowel pins align the crankcase halves when they are bolted together.

The crankshaft assembly is made up of 2 full-circle flywheels pressed together on a hollow crankpin. The connecting rod big-end bearing on the crankpin is a needle bearing assembly. The crankshaft assembly is supported by 2 ball bearings in the crankcase. Service to the crankshaft assembly is limited to removal and replacement.

5

The procedure which follows is presented as a complete, step-by-step, major lower end rebuild that should be followed if an engine is to be completely reconditioned. However, if you're replacing a part that you know is defective, the disassembly should be carried out only until the failed part is accessible; there is no need to disassemble the engine beyond that point so long as you know the remaining components are in good condition and that they were not affected by the failed part.

Crankcase Disassembly

1. Remove the engine as described in this chapter.
2. Remove all exterior engine assemblies as described in this chapter and other related chapters:
   a. Cylinder head cover.
   b. Cylinder head.
   c. Cylinder.
   d. Piston.
   e. Alternator.
   f. Clutch.
   g. External shift mechanism.
3. Remove the bolt securing the cam chain set plate and remove the set plate and the cam chain.
4A. On 175 cc engines, remove the upper crankcase bolts (**Figure 104**). To prevent warpage, loosen them in a crisscross pattern.
4B. On 250 and 350 cc engines, remove the upper crankcase bolts (**Figure 105**). To prevent warpage, loosen them in a crisscross pattern.
5. On the TL250 engine, there is one additional bolt. Its location is indicated by A, **Figure 105**. The bolt cannot be seen in this figure, only its location is indicated.
6. In the following steps, set the crankcase assembly either on its side or on wood block(s) to prevent damage to the crankcase studs.
7A. On 175 cc engines, remove the lower crankcase bolts (**Figure 106**). To prevent warpage, loosen them in a crisscross pattern.
7B. On 250 and 350 cc engines, remove the lower crankcase bolts (**Figure 107**). To prevent warpage, loosen them in a crisscross pattern.

CAUTION
Perform the next step directly over and close to the workbench as the crankcase halves may easily separate. ***Do not*** *hammer on the crankcase halves or they will be damaged.*

8. Hold onto the crankcase studs and tap on each end of the crankshaft and transmission shafts with

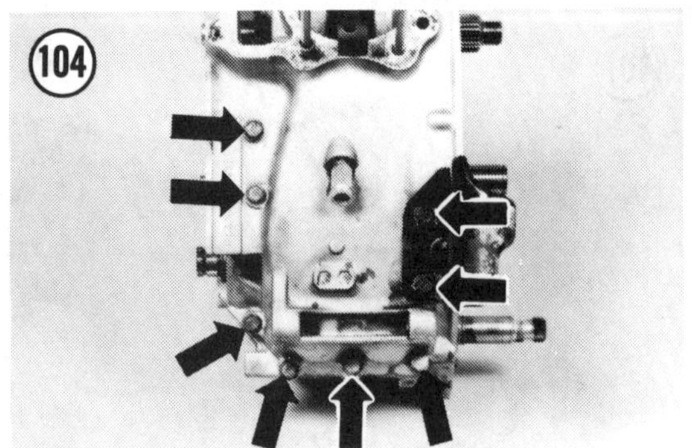

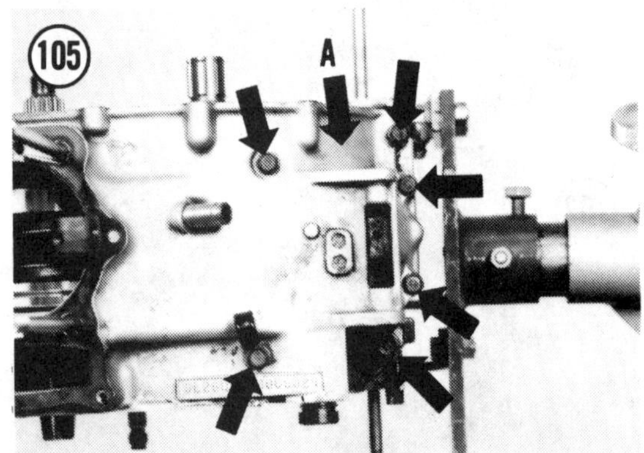

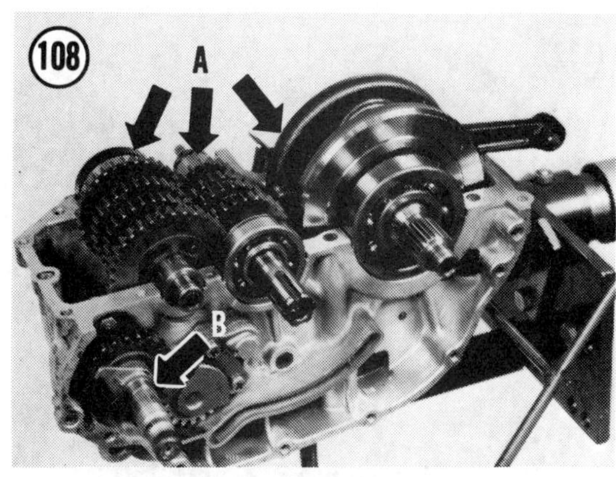

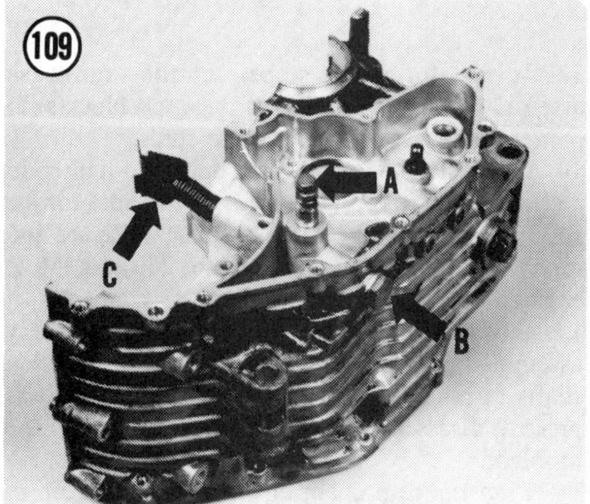

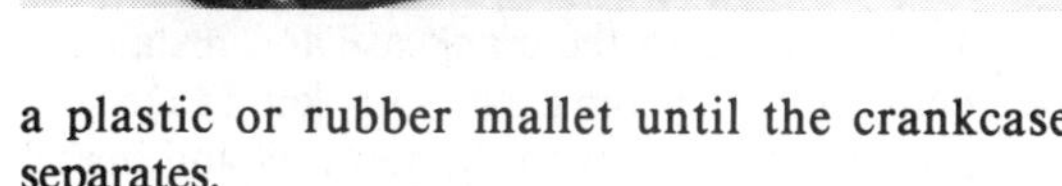

a plastic or rubber mallet until the crankcase separates.

9. If the crankcase will not separate using this method check to make sure that all bolts are removed. If you still have a problem, take the crankcase assembly to a dealer and have it separated .

NOTE
Never pry between case halves. Doing so may result in oil leaks, requiring replacement of the case halves.

10. Don't lose the 2 locating dowels if they came out of the case. They do not have to be removed from the case if they are secure.

11. Lift up and carefully remove the crankshaft assembly and the transmission assemblies (A, **Figure 108**).

12. Remove the oil pump and the kickstarter assembly (B, **Figure 108**) as described in this chapter.

13. Remove the internal shift mechanism as described in Chapter Six.

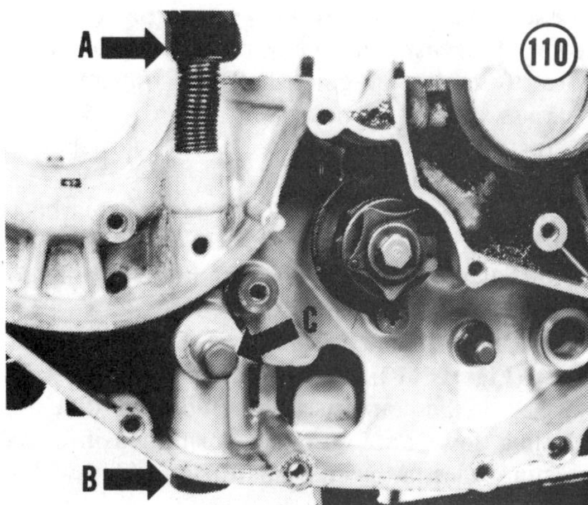

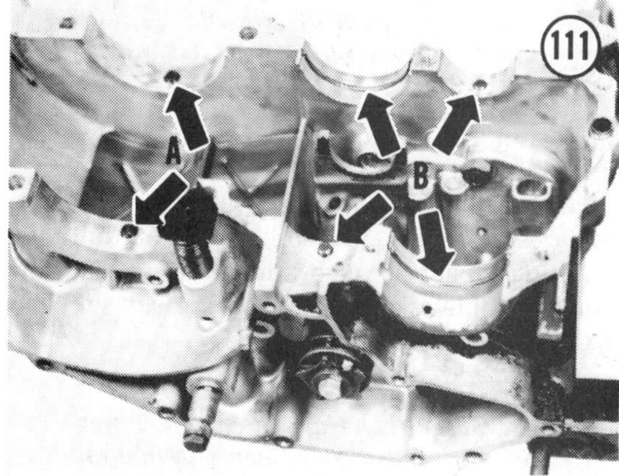

14. Don't lose the 2 locating dowels and transmission bearing 1/2 set rings in the lower crankcase half. They do not have to be removed from the case if they are secure.

15. Loosen the locknut and the adjusting bolt (A, **Figure 109**) on the cam chain tensioner assembly. Remove the drain bolt (B, **Figure 109**) and remove the cam chain tensioner assembly (C, **Figure 109**) from the crankcase.

16. Inspect the crankcase halves and crankshaft as described in this chapter.

Crankcase Assembly

1. Apply assembly oil to the inner race of all bearings in both crankcase halves.

2. Install the cam chain tensioner assembly (A, **Figure 110**) and install the drain bolt and sealing washer (B, **Figure 110**). Install the adjusting bolt and locknut (C, **Figure 110**).

3. Make sure the locating dowels (A, **Figure 111**) for the crankshaft bearings are in place. Also check that the transmission locating dowels and bearing

1/2 set rings (B, **Figure 111**) are in place in the lower crankcase half. They must be in place to correctly locate the crankshaft and transmission bearings within the crankcase.
4. Install the internal shift mechanism as described in Chapter Six.
5. Install the oil pump and kickstarter assemblies as described in this chapter.
6. Install the transmission assemblies. Refer to Chapter Six for the correct procedure.
7. Install the crankshaft. Make sure the alignment lines (**Figure 112**) are aligned with the mating surface of the crankcase. This indicates that the locating dowels are correctly positioned into the locating holes in the crankshaft bearings.

NOTE
Make sure the mating surfaces are clean and free of all old gasket material. Make sure you get a leak-free seal.

8. Install the 2 locating dowels if they were removed.
9. Apply a light coat of gasker sealer to the sealing surfaces of both crankcase halves. Coat only the flat surfaces, not curved bearing surfaces. Make the coating as thin as possible or the case can shift and hammer out the bearings.

NOTE
Use Gasgacinch Gasket Sealer, 4-Three Bond or equivalent. When selecting an equivalent, avoid thick or hard setting materials.

10. Set the upper crankcase half onto the lower crankcase and tap it carefully into place with a plastic mallet.

CAUTION
Crankcase halves should fit together without force. If the crankcase halves do not fit together completely, do not attempt to pull them together with the crankcase screws. Separate the crankcase halves and investigate the cause of the interference. Do not risk damage by trying to force the cases together.

11. Install the upper crankcase bolts and tighten in a crisscross pattern in 2-3 steps to the final torque specification listed in **Table 2**. Refer to **Figure 104** for 175 cc engines or **Figure 105** for 250 and 350 cc engines.
12. On the TL250 engine, don't forget the one additional bolt. Its location is indicated by A, **Figure 105**.

13. In the following steps, set the crankcase assembly either on its side or on wood block(s) to prevent damage to the crankcase studs.
14. Install the lower crankcase bolts and tighten in a crisscross pattern in 2-3 steps to the final torque specification listed in **Table 2**. Refer to **Figure 106** for 175 cc engines or **Figure 107** for 250 and 350 cc engines.
15. After the crankcase halves are completely assembled, rotate the crankshaft and transmission shafts to make sure there is no binding. If any is present, disassemble the crankcase and correct the problem.
16. Feed the cam chain down through the top of the chain opening in the crankcase and install the cam chain onto the crankshaft sprocket. Make sure it is correctly engaged with the sprocket and install the set plate and bolt. Tighten the bolt securely.
17. Install all exterior engine assemblies as described in this chapter and other related chapters:
   a. External shift mechanism.
   b. Clutch.
   c. Alternator.
   d. Piston.
   e. Cylinder.
   f. Cylinder head.
   g. Cylinder head cover.

Crankcase and Crankshaft Inspection

1. Remove the securing bar (**Figure 113**) or bend up the locking tabs (**Figure 114**) and remove the bolts securing the oil baffle plate in the upper crankcase half. Remove the bolts and the baffle plate.
2. Clean the baffle plate and both crankcase halves inside and out with cleaning solvent. Thoroughly

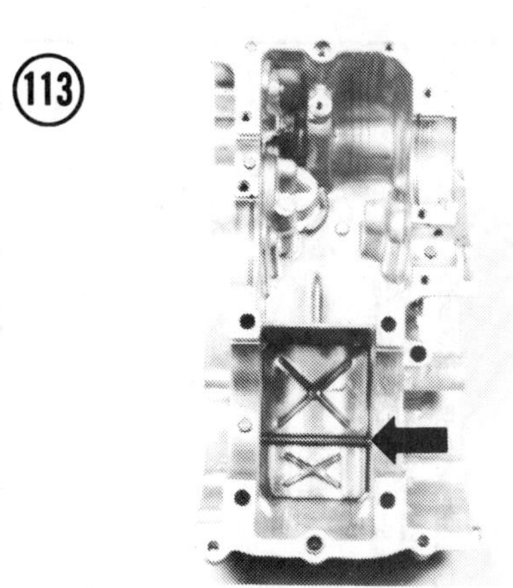

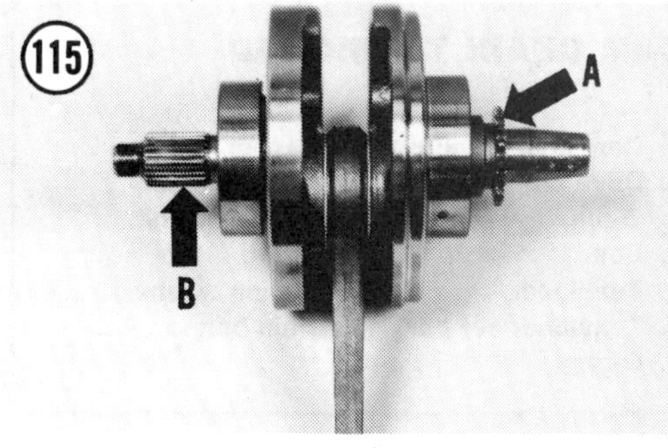

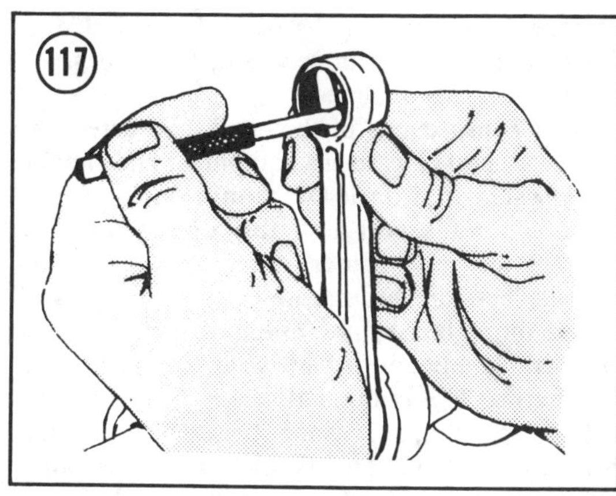

dry with compressed air and wipe off with a clean shop cloth. Be sure to remove all traces of old gasket material from all mating surfaces.

3. Carefully inspect the cases for cracks and fractures, especially in the lower areas; they are vulnerable to rock damage. Also check the areas around the stiffening ribs, around bearing bosses and threaded holes. If any are found, have them repaired by a shop specializing in the repair of precision aluminum castings or replace them.
4. Make sure the crankcase studs in the upper crankcase half are tight; retighten if necessary.
5. Inspect the cam chain sprocket (A, **Figure 115**) and the primary drive gear spline (B, **Figure 115**) for wear or missing teeth or spline damage. If either are damaged, replacement should be entrusted to a dealer.
6. Check both crankshaft main bearings (**Figure 116**) for roughness, pitting, galling and play by rotating them slowly by hand. If any roughness or play can be felt in the bearing it must be replaced. This must be entrusted to a dealer as special tools are required. The cam chain sprocket and primary drive gear must also be removed and realigned properly upon installation.
7. Measure the inside diameter of the connecting rod small end with a snap gauge and micrometer as shown in **Figure 117**. Compare to dimensions listed in **Table 1**. If worn to the service limit, the crankshaft assembly must be replaced.
8. Check the condition of the connecting rod big-end bearing by grasping the rod in one hand and lifting up on it. With the heel of your other hand, rap sharply on the top of the rod. A sharp metallic sound, such as a click, is an indication that the bearing or crankpin or both are worn and the crankshaft assembly should be replaced.
9. Check the connecting rod to crankshaft side clearance with a flat feeler gauge (**Figure 118**).

Compare to dimensions listed in **Table 1**. If the clearance is greater than specified, the crankshaft assembly must be replaced.

10. Other inspections of the crankshaft assembly involve accurate measuring equipment and should be entrusted to a dealer or competent machine shop. The crankshaft assembly operates under severe stress and dimensional tolerances are critical. These dimensions are listed in **Table 1**. If any are off by the slightest amount it may cause a considerable amount of damage or destruction of the engine. The crankshaft assembly must be replaced as a unit, as it cannot be serviced without the aid of a 10-12 ton (9,000-11,000 kilogram) capacity press, holding fixtures and crankshaft jig.

CAMSHAFT CHAIN AND TENSIONER

Refer to **Figure 119** for this procedure.

1. Remove the cam chain tensioner as described under *Crankcase Disassembly* in this chapter.
2. Inspect the surface of the chain guide and chain tensioner (A, **Figure 120**). If either part is worn (as shown in **Figure 121**) or disintegrating it must be replaced. This may indicate a worn cam chain or improper chain adjustment.
3. Check all the components (**Figure 122**) of the tensioner assembly; if any part is defective, replace the assembly.
4. Inspect the cam chain (B, **Figure 120**) for wear and damage. If the chain needs replacing, also check the drive sprocket on the crankshaft and cam sprocket. They also may be defective.

KICKSTARTER

Removal (175 cc Engine)

See **Figure 123**.

1. Remove the clutch assembly as described in Chapter Six.

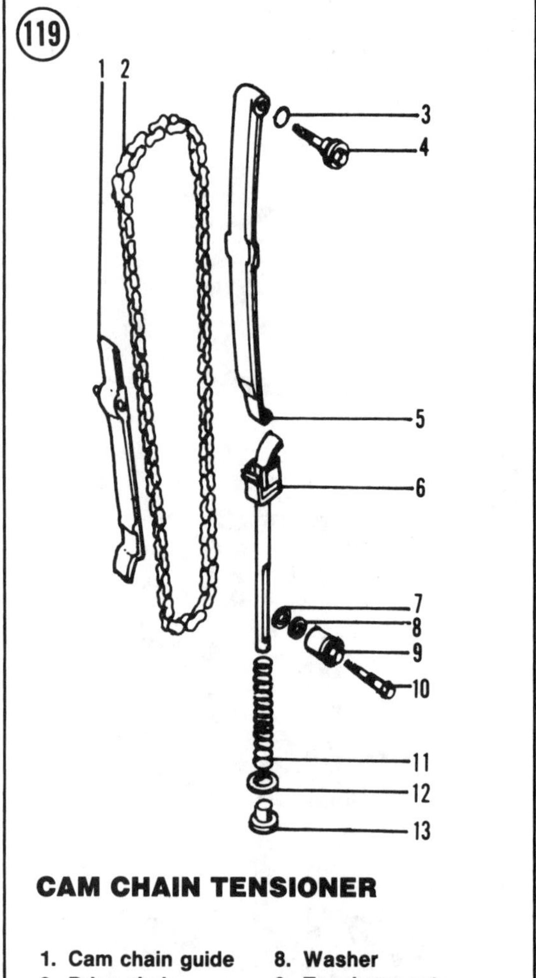

CAM CHAIN TENSIONER

1. Cam chain guide
2. Drive chain
3. O-ring
4. Bolt
5. Tensioner
6. Tensioner set bar
7. O-ring
8. Washer
9. Tensioner nut
10. Tensioner bolt
11. Spring
12. Sealing washer
13. Drain bolt

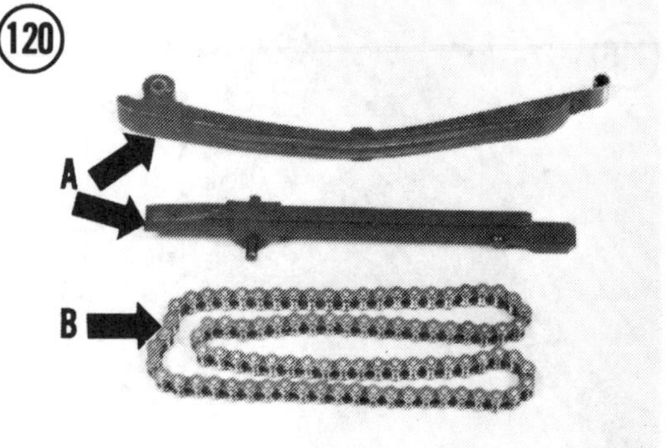

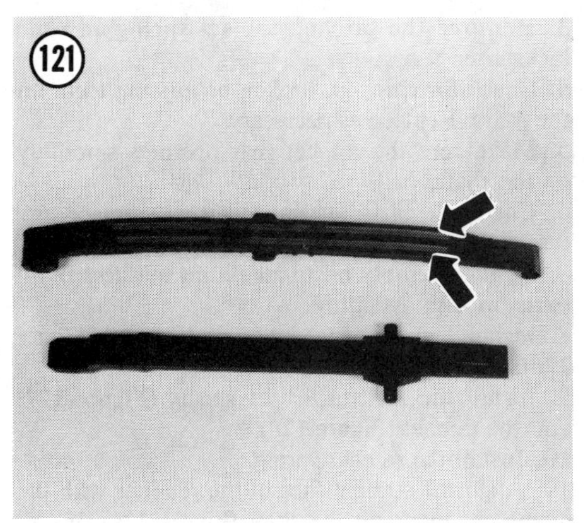

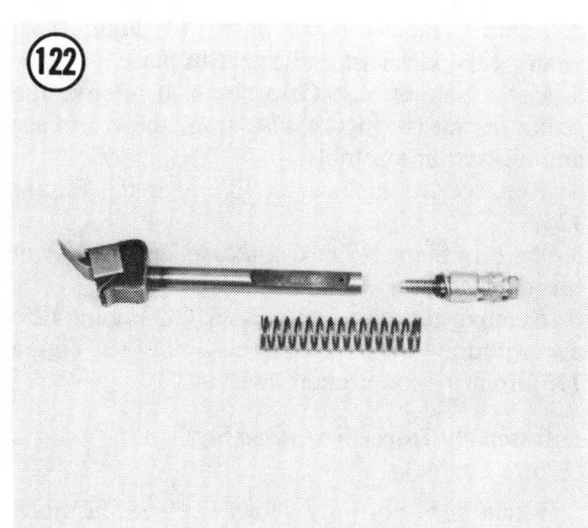

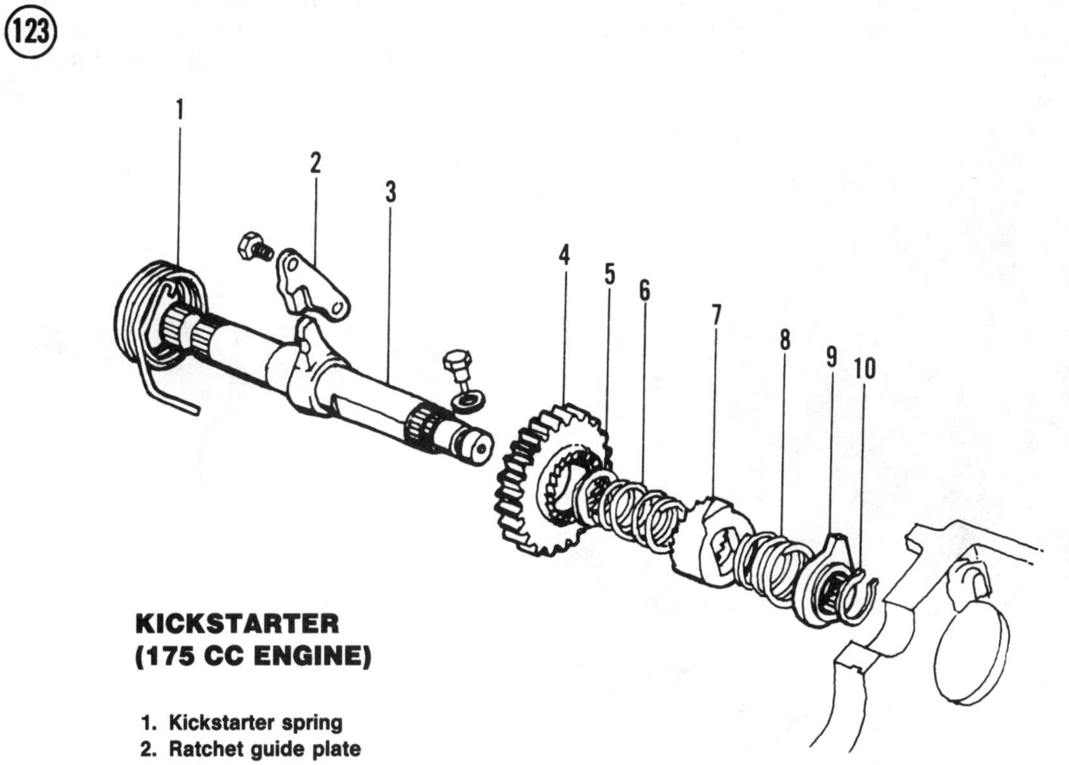

123

KICKSTARTER (175 CC ENGINE)

1. **Kickstarter spring**
2. **Ratchet guide plate**
3. **Kickstarter shaft**
4. **Kickstarter gear**
5. **Thrust washer**
6. **Set spring**
7. **Ratchet**
8. **Ratchet spring**
9. **Kickstarter retainer**
10. **Circlip**

2. Remove the circlip and washer (A, **Figure 124**) securing the kickstarter idle gear in place.
3. Use a pair of Vise Grip pliers to remove the return spring (B, **Figure 124**) from the crankcase and kickstarter assembly.
4. Remove the kickstarter idle gear (C, **Figure 124**).
5. Perform Steps 1-9 of *Crankcase Disassembly* in this chapter.
6. Remove the bolt and washer (A, **Figure 125**) and withdraw the kickstarter assembly (B, **Figure 125**) from the lower crankcase half.

Disassembly/Inspection/Assembly (175 cc Engine)

Honda does not provide service specifications for the kickstarter assembly.

1. Clean the assembled shaft in solvent and dry with compressed air.
2. Remove the circlip, the retainer and the ratchet spring.
3. Remove the ratchet, the set spring and the kickstarter gear.
4. Check for chipped, broken or missing teeth on the gears. Replace as necessary.
5. Make sure the ratchet gear operates smoothly on the shaft.
6. Check all parts for uneven wear; replace any that show signs of wear.
7. Apply assembly oil to all sliding surfaces of all parts prior to assembly.
8. Install the kickstarter gear onto the shaft (**Figure 126**).
9. Install the kickstarter set spring (**Figure 127**) and the ratchet (**Figure 128**).
10. Install the ratchet spring.
11. Align the straight face of the retainer with the alignment mark on the shaft (**Figure 129**). Install the retainer (A, **Figure 130**) onto the shaft and install the circlip (B, **Figure 130**).
12. After assembly is completed, refer to **Figure 131** for correct placement of all components.

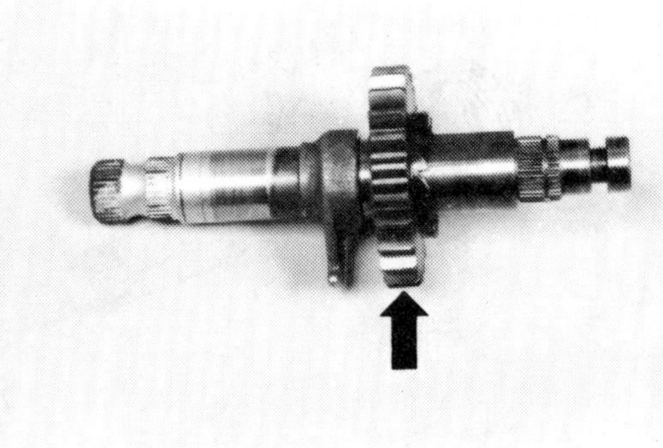

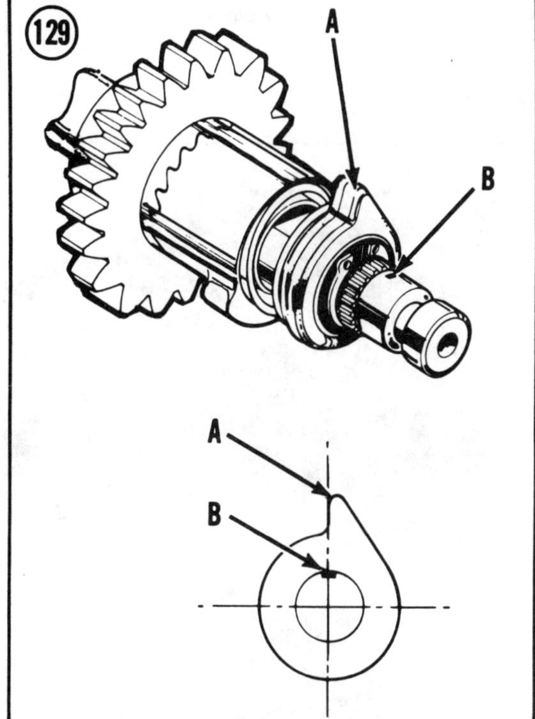

Installation (175 cc Engine)

1. Install the assembled shaft into the crankcase. Install the washer and bolt (A, **Figure 125**). Tighten the bolt securely.
2. Perform Steps 8-17 of *Crankcase Assembly* in this chapter.
3. Install the kickstarter idle gear (C, **Figure 124**) with the shaft hole shoulder side on first.
4. Install the washer and circlip (A, **Figure 124**).
5. Install the return spring. Engage the small end of the spring onto the retainer (A, **Figure 132**). Use a pair of Vise Grip pliers and install the other end of the return spring (B, **Figure 132**) onto the boss on the crankcase.
6. Install the clutch assembly as described in Chapter Six.

5

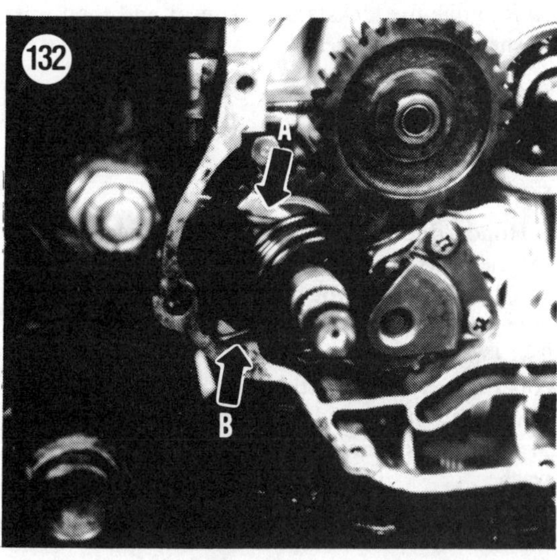

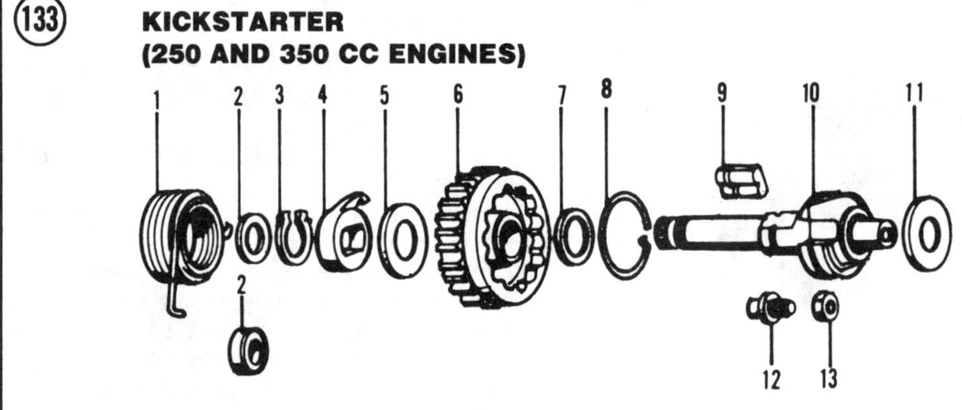

1. Kickstarter spring
2. Collar (XL350, XL350 K1)
   Washer (all other models)
3. Circlip
4. Spring retainer
5. Thrust washer
6. Kickstarter gear
7. Thrust washer
8. Ratchet spring
9. Starter pawl
10. Kickstarter shaft
11. Washer
12. Stopper pin
13. Nut

Removal
(250 and 350 cc Engines)

Refer to **Figure 133**.

The kickstarter can be removed with the engine in the frame. In this procedure the engine is shown removed from the frame for clarity.

1. Remove the clutch assembly as described in Chapter Six.
2. Use a pair of Vise Grip pliers to remove the kickstarter return spring from the crankcase and kickstarter assembly.
3. Withdraw the kickstarter assembly (**Figure 134**).
4. Remove the circlip and washer (**Figure 135**) securing the kickstarter idle gear in place.
5. Remove the kickstarter idle gear and the thrust washer behind the gear.

Disassembly/Inspection/Assembly
(250 and 350 cc Engines)

Honda does not provide service specifications for the kickstarter assembly.

1. Clean the assembled shaft in solvent and dry with compressed air.

2A. On XL350 and XL350 K1 models, slide the collar (**Figure 136**) off the shaft.

2B. On all other models, remove the washer.

3. Remove the circlip, the retainer and the thrust washer.
4. Remove the kickstarter gear and the thrust washer.

5. If necessary, remove the spring (A, **Figure 137**) and the starter pawl (B, **Figure 137**).
6. Remove the thrust washer off the other end of the shaft.
7. Check for chipped, broken or missing teeth on the gears. Replace as necessary.

(136)

(137)

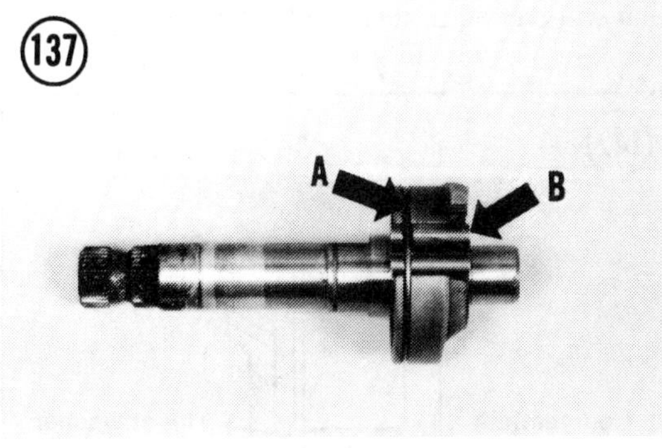

(138)

8. Make sure the starter pawl operates smoothly within the kickstarter gear.
9. Check all parts for uneven wear; replace any that show signs of wear.
10. Apply assembly oil to all sliding surfaces of all parts prior to assembly.
11. Install the thrust washer and the kickstarter gear onto the shaft.
12. Place the projection (A, **Figure 138**) on the back of the kickstarter shaft assembly in the 6 o'clock position. Install the thrust washer. Place the flat of the spring retainer (B, **Figure 138**) in the

(139)

(140)

9 o'clock position and install the spring retainer onto the shaft. This alignment is necessary for proper kickstarter operation.
13. Install the circlip (C, **Figure 138**).
14A. On XL350 and XL350 K1 models, slide the collar (**Figure 136**) onto the shaft.
14B. On all other models, install the washer.
15. Install the thrust washer onto the other end of the shaft.
16. After assembly is completed, refer to **Figure 139** for correct placement of all components.

Installation (250 and 350 cc Engines)

1. Install the thrust washer (**Figure 140**) onto the transmission shaft.
2. Install the kickstarter idle gear (**Figure 141**) onto the transmission shaft.
3. Install the washer and circlip (**Figure 135**) onto the transmission shaft.
4. The clearance between the thrust washer and the kickstarter idle gear must not exceed 0.76 mm

(0.03 in.) when installed (**Figure 142**). If the clearance is greater, add an additional 0.7 mm washer to reduce the clearance to 0.06-0.075 mm (0.002-0.03 in.).

5. Install the kickstarter assembly (**Figure 134**).
6. Install the return spring. Engage the small end of the spring onto the retainer (A, **Figure 143**). Use a pair of Vise Grip pliers to install the other end of the return spring (B, **Figure 143**) onto the boss on the crankcase.
7. Install the clutch assembly as described in Chapter Six.

BREAK-IN PROCEDURE

If the rings were replaced, a new piston installed, the cylinder rebored or honed or major lower end work performed, the engine should be broken in just as though it were new. The performance and service life of the engine depends greatly on a careful and sensible break-in.

For the first 800 km (100 miles), no more than one-third throttle should be used and speed should be varied as much as possible within the one-third throttle limit. Prolonged steady running at one speed, no matter how moderate, is to be avoided as well as hard acceleration.

Following the *800 km (500 Mile) Service* described in this chapter more throttle should not be used until the motorcycle has covered at least 1,600 km (1,000 miles) and then it should be limited to short bursts of speed until 2,400 km (500 miles) have been logged.

The mono-grade oils recommended for break-in and normal use provide a better bedding pattern for rings and cylinder than do multi-grade oils. As a result, piston ring and cylinder bore life are greatly increased. During this period, oil consumption will be higher than normal. It is therefore important to frequently check and correct oil level. At no time, during the break-in or later, should the oil level be allowed to drop below the bottom line on the dipstick; if the oil level is low, the oil will become overheated resulting in insufficient lubrication and increased wear.

800 km (500 Mile) Service

It is essential that the oil be changed and the oil filter rotor and filter screen be cleaned after the first 800 km (500 miles) . In addition, it is a good idea to change the oil and clean the oil filter rotor and filter screen at the completion of the 2,400 km (1,500 mile) break-in to ensure that all of the particles produced during break-in are removed from the lubrication system. The small added expense may be considered a smart investment that will pay off in increased engine life.

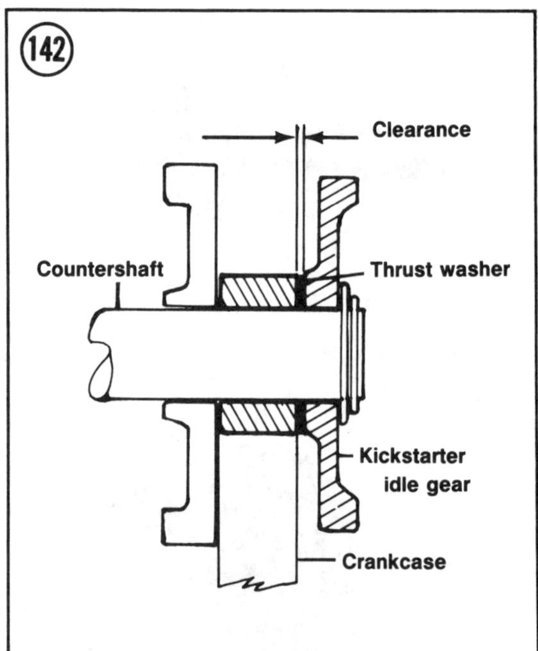

Table 1 ENGINE SPECIFICATIONS*

Item	Specification	Wear Limit
General		
Type	4-stroke, air-cooled, SOHC	
Number of cylinders	1	
Bore and stroke		
175 cc	64.0 x 54.0 mm (2.520 x 2.126 in.)	
250 cc	74.0 x 57.8 mm (2.913 x 2.276 in.)	
350 cc	79.0 x 71.0 mm (3.110 x 2.795 in.)	
Displacement		
175 cc	173 cc (10.6 cu. in.)	
250 cc	248 cc (15.1 cu. in.)	
350 cc	348 cc (21.2 cu. in.)	
Compression ratio		
175 cc	9.0 to 1	
250 cc	9.1 to 1	
350 cc	8.3 to 1	
Compression pressure		
XL175	171 psi (12 kg/cm²)	
TL250	156.4 psi (11.0 kg/cm²)	
XL250	199.13 psi (14.0 kg/cm²)	
XL350	170.4 psi (12.0 kg/cm²)	
Lubrication	Wet sump	
Cylinder		
Bore		
175 cc	64.0-64.01 mm (2.5197-2.5201 in.)	64.1 mm (2.5236 in.)
250 cc	74.00-74.01 mm (2.9134-2.9138 in.)	74.11 mm (2.918 in.)
350 cc	78.99-79.01 mm (3.1098-3.1106 in.)	79.11 mm (3.115 in.)
Out of round	N.A.	0.10 mm (0.004 in.)
Piston/cylinder clearance	N.A.	N.A.
Piston		
Diameter		
175 cc	63.970-63.990 mm (2.5185-2.5193 in.)	63.85 mm (2.514 in.)
250 cc	73.97-73.99 mm (2.912-2.913 in.)	73.88 mm (2.909 in.)
350 cc	78.97-79.01 mm (3.1091-3.1106 in.)	78.90 mm (3.106 in.)
Clearance in bore	N.A.	N.A.
Piston pin bore		
175 cc	15.002-15.008 mm (0.5906-0.5909 in.)	15.05 mm (0.593 in.)
250 cc	19.002-19.008 mm (0.7481-0.7483 in.)	19.08 mm (0.751 in.)
350 cc	20.994-21.000 mm (0.8265-0.8268 in.)	20.96 mm (0.825 in.)
Piston pin outer diameter		
175 cc	14.994-15.000 mm (0.5503-0.5906 in.)	14.9 mm (0.5866 in.)
250 cc	18.994-19.000 mm (0.7478-0.7480 in.)	18.96 mm (0.746 in.)
350 cc	20.994-21.000 mm (0.8265-0.8268 in.)	20.96 mm (0.825 in.)
Piston to pin clearance	N.A.	N.A.

(continued)

5

Table 1 ENGINE SPECIFICATIONS* (continued)

Item	Specification	Wear Limit
Piston rings		
Number of rings		
Compression	2	
Oil control	1	
Ring end gap		
Top and second ring		
175 cc	0.2-0.4 mm (0.0079-0.0157 in.)	0.75 mm (0.029 in.)
Top ring		
250 cc, 1974-1975 350 cc	0.15-0.35 mm (0.0059-0.0138 in.)	0.75 mm (0.029 in.)
1976-1978 350 cc	0.20-0.40 mm (0.0079-0.0157 in.)	0.80 mm (0.031 in.)
Second ring		
250 and 350 cc	0.20-0.40 mm (0.0079-0.0157 in.)	0.80 mm (0.031 in.)
Oil (side rail)		
175 cc, 250 cc	0.20-040 mm (0.0079-0.0157 in.)	0.80 mm (0.031 in.)
350 cc	0.20-090 mm (0.0079-0.0354 in.)	1.30 mm (0.051 in.)
Ring side clearance		
Top ring		
1972-1975	0.030-0.060 mm (0.0012-0.0024 in.)	0.15 mm (0.0059 in.)
1976-1978	0.03-0.06 mm (0.0012-0.0024 in.)	0.18 mm (0.007 in.)
Second ring		
1972-1975	0.015-0.045 mm (0.0006-0.0018 in.)	0.15 mm (0.0059 in.)
1976-1978	0.015-0.045 mm (0.0006-0.0018 in.)	0.165 mm (0.006 in.)
Connecting rod small end		
175 cc	15.016-15.034 mm (0.5912-0.5919 in.)	15.07 mm (0.593 in.)
250 cc	19.020-19.041 mm (0.7488-0.7496 in.)	19.07 mm (0.751 in.)
350 cc	21.020-21.041 mm (0.8276-0.8284 in.)	21.08 mm (0.829 in.)
Crankshaft		
Runout	N.A.	0.05 mm (0.002 in.)
Connecting rod big end side clearance		
XL175 and XL250	0.12-0.38 mm (0.0047-0.0150 in.)	0.60 mm (0.0236 in.)
TL250	0.22-0.68 mm (0.0087-0.0268 in.)	0.75 mm (0.0295 in.)
XL350	0.06-0.44 mm (0.0024-0.0173 in.)	0.94 mm (0.0370 in.)

(continued)

Table 1 ENGINE SPECIFICATIONS* (continued)

Item	Specification	Wear Limit
Camshaft		
Cam lobe height		
175 cc		
Intake	40.544 mm (1.5962 in.)	40.35 mm (1.5886 in.)
Exhaust	40.568 mm (1.5972 in.)	40.98 mm (1.5972 in.)
250 and 350 cc		
Intake	36.260 mm (1.4276 in.)	36.142 mm (1.4229 in.)
Exhaust	36.150 mm (1.4232 in.)	36.025 mm (1.4183 in.)
Cam journal OD		
175 cc		
Left-hand end	22.939-22.960 mm (0.9031-0.9039 in.)	22.92 mm (0.9024 in.)
Right-hand end	21.939-21.960 mm (0.8637-0.8646 in.)	21.92 mm (0.863 in.)
250 and 350 cc		
Left-hand end	23.939-23.960 mm (0.9425-0.9433 in.)	23.92 mm (0.9417 in.)
Right-hand end	21.939-21.960 mm (0.8637-0.8646 in.)	21.92 mm (0.863 in.)
Cam bearing surface in cylinder head	N.A.	N.A.
Valves		
Valve stem outer diameter		
175 cc		
Intake	6.975-6.990 mm (0.2746-0.2752 in.)	6.95 mm (0.2736 in.)
Exhaust	6.955-6.970 mm (0.2738-0.2744 in.)	6.93 mm (0.2728 in.)
250 and 350 cc		
Intake	5.480-5.490 mm (0.2157-0.2161 in.)	5.46 mm (0.215 in.)
Exhaust	5.460-5.470 mm (0.2149-0.2154 in.)	5.44 mm (0.2144 in.)
Valve guide inner diameter	N.A.	N.A.
Stem to guide clearance		
175 cc		
Intake	0.010-0.035 mm (0.0004-0.0014 in.)	0.08 mm (0.0032 in.)
Exhaust	0.030-0.055 mm (0.0012-0.0022 in.)	0.09 mm (0.0035 in.)
250 and 350 cc		
Intake	0.010-0.030 mm (0.0004-0.0012 in.)	0.06 mm (0.0024 in.)
Exhaust	0.030-0.050 mm (0.0012-0.0020 in.)	0.07 mm (0.0028 in.)
Valve seat width		
TL250	1.2 mm (0.0472 in.)	1.9 mm (0.0748 in.)
All other models	N.A.	N.A.
Valve face width	N.A.	N.A.

(continued)

5

Table 1 ENGINE SPECIFICATIONS* (continued)

Item	Specification	Wear Limit
Valve springs free length		
175 cc		
Inner	36.25 mm (1.427 in.)	36.0 mm (1.417 in.)
Outer	43.1 mm (1.697 in.)	41.9 mm (1.650 in.)
250 and 350 cc		
Inner	36.5 mm (1.43 in.)	36.0 mm (1.41 in.)
Outer	40.7 mm (1.610 in.)	39.7 mm (1.56 in.)
Rocker arm assembly		
Rocker arm to shaft clearance	0.016-0.052 mm (0.0006-0.0020 in.)	0.09 mm (0.0035 in.)
Oil pump		
XL175		
Inner to outer rotor tip clearance	0.15 (0.0059 in.)	0.30 mm (0.0118 in.)
Outer rotor to body clearance	0.15-0.21 mm (0.0059-0.0083 in.)	0.35 mm (0.0138 in.)
All other models	N.A.	N.A.

* Honda does not provide service information for all items nor all models. All available information is included in this table. "N.A." indicates that information is not available.

Table 2 ENGINE TORQUE SPECIFICATIONS

Item	N•m	ft.-lb.
Cylinder head cover		
175 cc	9-14	6-10
250 and 350 cc		
6 mm	8-12	5-9
8 mm	18-25	13-18
Cylinder head	18-20	13-14
175 cc	22-28	15-20
250 and 350 cc		
6 mm	8-12	5-9
8 mm	18-25	13-18
10 mm	30-36	22-26
Cylinder (250 and 350 cc)		
6 mm	8-12	5-9
8 mm	20-25	14-18
Crankcase bolts		
XL175		
6 mm	9-14	6-10
8 mm	22-28	15-20
TL250		
6 mm	8-12	5-9
8 mm	24-30	17-21
XL250, XL350 (8 mm)	24-30	17-21
Cam sprocket bolts	18-22	13-18
Ignition advance bolt	8-12	6-9
Oil filter rotor nut		
175 cc	50-60	36-43
250 and 350 cc	45-55	32-39
Alternator rotor bolt		
175 cc	35-45	25-32
250 and 350 cc	60-70	43-50

CHAPTER SIX

CLUTCH AND TRANSMISSION

6

Table 1 and **Table 2**, at the end of the chapter, contain clutch and shift mechanism specifications. Honda does not provide transmission specifications.

CLUTCH OPERATION

The clutch is a wet multi-plate type which operates immersed in the engine oil. It is mounted on the right-hand end of the transmission main shaft. The inner clutch hub is splined to the main shaft and the outer clutch housing can rotate freely on the main shaft. The outer clutch housing is geared to the crankshaft via the primary drive gear.

CLUTCH (100 AND 125 CC ENGINES)

The clutch shown in **Figure 1** is used on 100 and 125 cc models except the TL125. The TL125 clutch is shown in **Figure 2**.

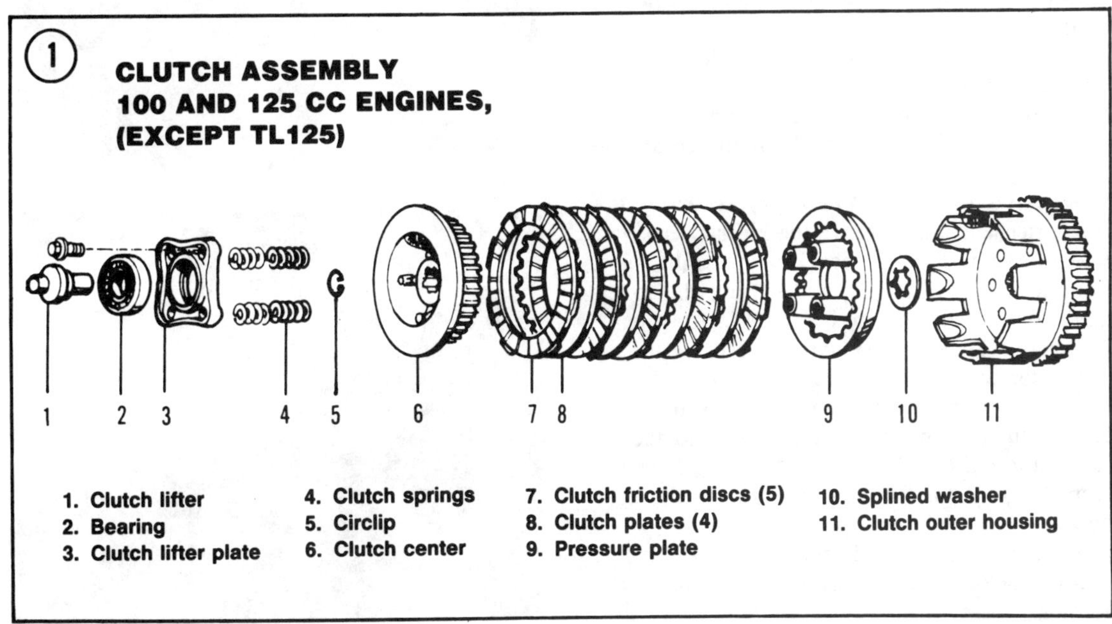

(2) CLUTCH ASSEMBLY (TL125)

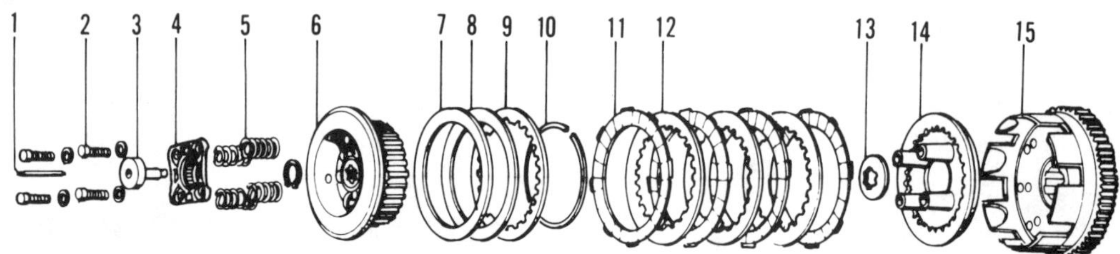

1. Clutch lifter rod
2. Bolt
3. Clutch lifter
4. Clutch lifter plate
5. Clutch springs
6. Clutch center
7. Disc spring seat*
8. Clutch spring*
9. Clutch disc spring*
10. Set spring*
11. Clutch friction discs (4)
12. Clutch plates (3)
13. Splined washer
14. Pressure plate
15. Clutch outer housing

*TL125, TL125 K1-K2 only

Removal/Disassembly

Refer to **Figure 1** and **Figure 2** for this procedure.

The clutch assembly can be removed with the engine in the frame. The following procedure shows the footpeg assembly and the exhaust system removed. It is not necessary to remove them for this procedure.

1. Drain the engine oil as described in Chapter Three.
2. Remove the rear brake pedal as described in Chapter Eleven.
3. Slacken the clutch cable at the hand lever.
4. Disconnect the clutch cable at the crankcase cover (**Figure 3**).
5. Remove the bolt (**Figure 4**) securing the kickstarter lever and remove the kickstarter lever.
6. Remove the bolts securing the right-hand crankcase cover (**Figure 5**) and remove the cover, gasket and 2 locating dowels.
7. Remove the screws (**Figure 6**) securing the oil filter rotor cover and remove the cover.
8. Place a copper washer (or copper penny) into mesh with the primary drive gear behind the oil filter rotor and the clutch outer housing. This will keep the oil rotor from turning during the next step.
9. Remove the nut and lockwasher (**Figure 7**) securing the oil rotor housing in place. Remove the housing.

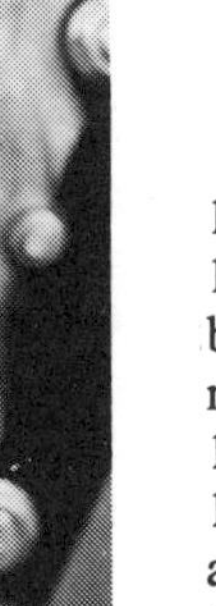

NOTE
Oil rotor nut removal requires a special tool available from a Honda dealer (Locknut Wrench 20 x 24, part No. 07716-0020100).

10. Remove the clutch lifter (**Figure 8**).
11. Using a crisscross pattern, remove the clutch bolts (**Figure 9**) securing the clutch lifter plate and remove the lifter plate.
12. Remove the clutch springs (**Figure 10**).
13. Remove the circlip securing the clutch assembly in place on the transmission shaft.
14. Remove the clutch center, plates, discs and pressure plate.
15. Remove the splined washer and the clutch outer housing.
16. Inspect all components as described under *Inspection (All Models)* in this chapter.

Assembly/Installation

NOTE
If new friction discs or clutch plates are being installed, apply new engine oil to all surfaces to avoid having the clutch lock up when used for the first time.

1. Install the clutch outer housing (**Figure 11**) and the splined washer (**Figure 12**).
2. Assemble the clutch center, friction discs, clutch plates and the pressure plate on your workbench. Onto the clutch center install first a friction disc and then a clutch plate. Continue to install a friction disc and then a clutch plate; alternate them until all are installed. The last item installed is a friction disc.
3. Install the pressure plate onto this assembly (**Figure 13**) and hold all components together with a clutch spring, bolt and large washer (**Figure 14**).
4. Slide on the clutch parts (clutch center, friction discs, clutch plates and pressure plate) assembled in Step 2 and Step 3. Push the assembly on slowly, carefully aligning the tabs of the friction discs with the slots in the clutch outer housing (**Figure 15**).
5. Install the circlip. Make sure that the circlip completely seats in the groove in the transmission shaft.
6. Remove the bolt and washer temporarily holding the clutch components together.
7. Install the remaining clutch springs.
8. Install the clutch lifter plate and the clutch bolts (**Figure 9**). Tighten the bolts securely in a crisscross pattern in 2 or 3 stages.
9. Install the clutch lifter (**Figure 8**).
10. Install the oil rotor housing. Install the lockwasher with the "OUTSIDE" marking facing toward the outside (**Figure 16**).
11. Install the locknut (**Figure** 7) and tighten to 40-50 N•m (29-36 ft.-lb.). Use the same tool setup as used in *Removal* Step 8.
12. Install the oil filter rotor cover and install the screws (**Figure 6**). Tighten the screws securely.
13. Install the dowel pins (A, **Figure 17**) and the gasket (B, **Figure 17**).

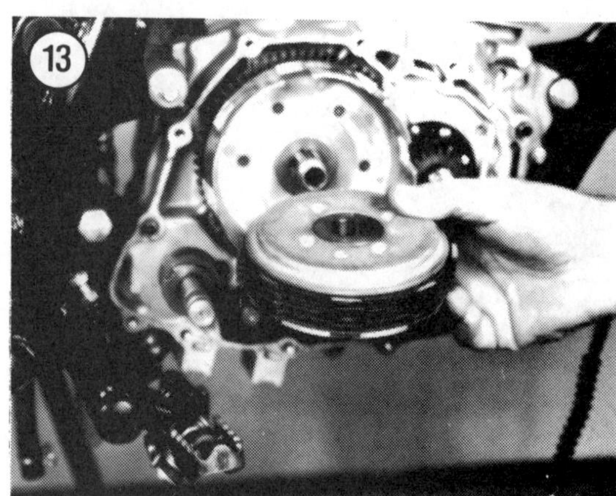

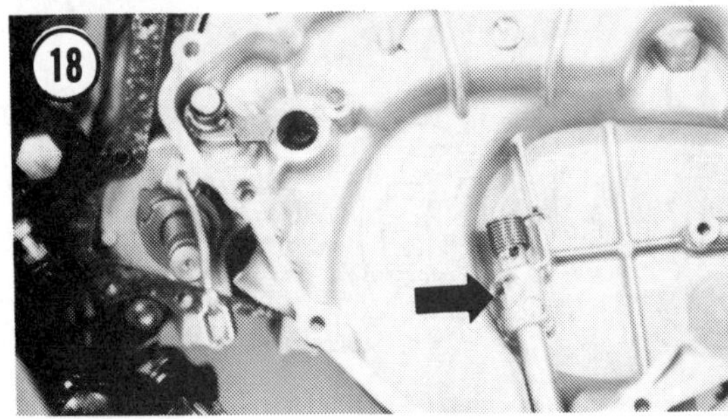

14. Hold the clutch actuating lever in the released position so the recess in the actuator (**Figure 18**) will mesh properly with the clutch lifter.
15. Install the right-hand crankcase cover. Push it all the way into place. Install the screws and tighten in a crisscross pattern until they are secure.

CAUTION
Do not install any of the crankcase cover screws until the crankcase cover is snug up against the crankcase surface. Do not try to force the cover into place with screw pressure. If the cover will not fit up against the crankcase, remove the crankcase cover and repeat Step 14.

16. Install the kickstarter lever and tighten the bolt securely.
17. Connect the clutch cable to the lever on the crankcase cover (**Figure 3**).
18. Install the rear brake pedal as described in Chapter Eleven.
19. Refill the engine with the recommended type and quantity of oil; refer to Chapter Three.
20. Adjust the clutch as described in Chapter Three.

CLUTCH (175, 250 AND 350 CC ENGINES)

Figure 19 shows the clutch used on 175 cc engines. **Figure 20** shows the TL250 clutch. **Figure 21** shows the clutch used on XL250 and all 350 cc models.

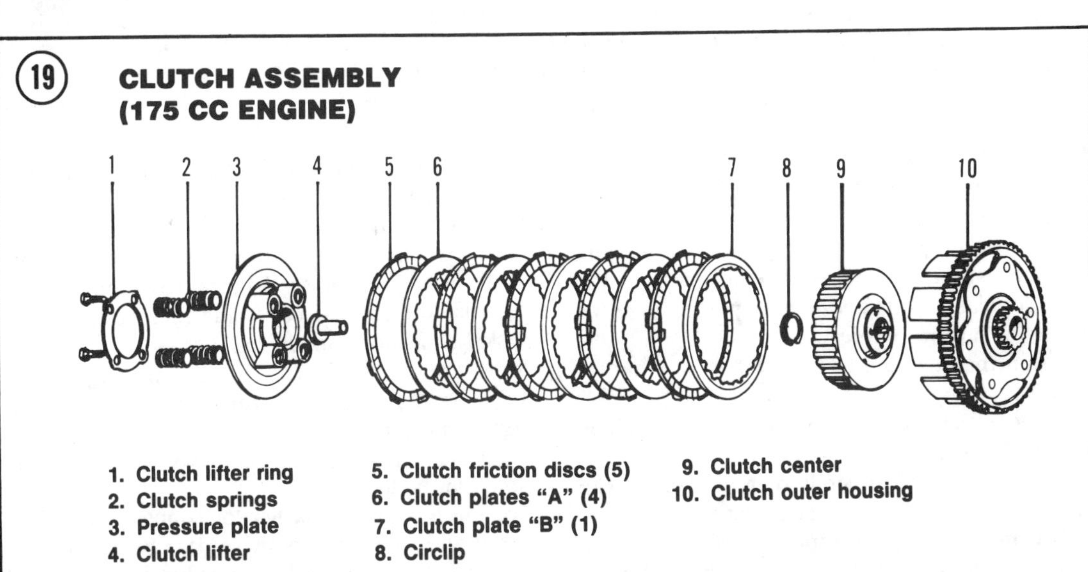

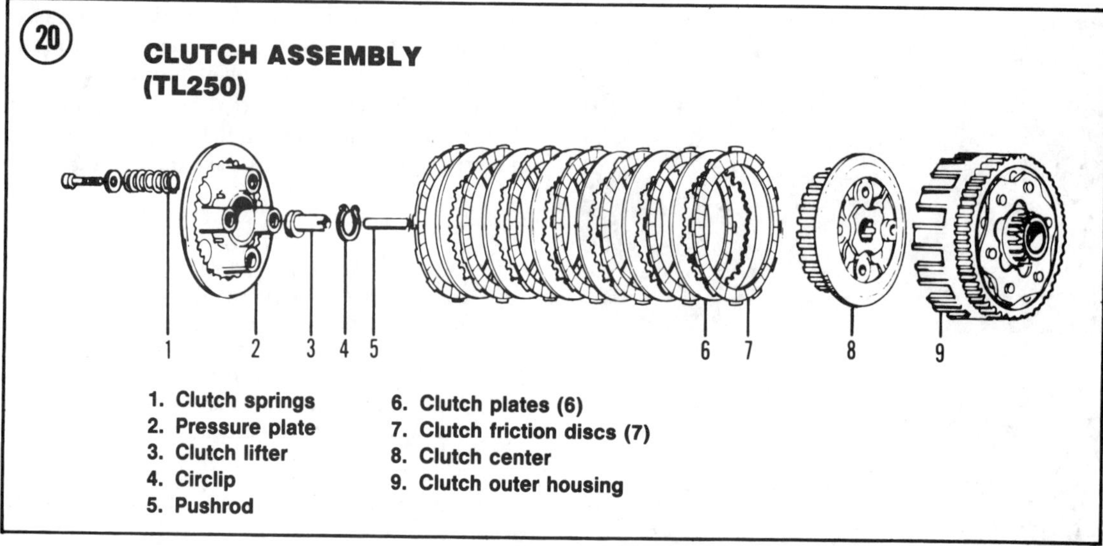

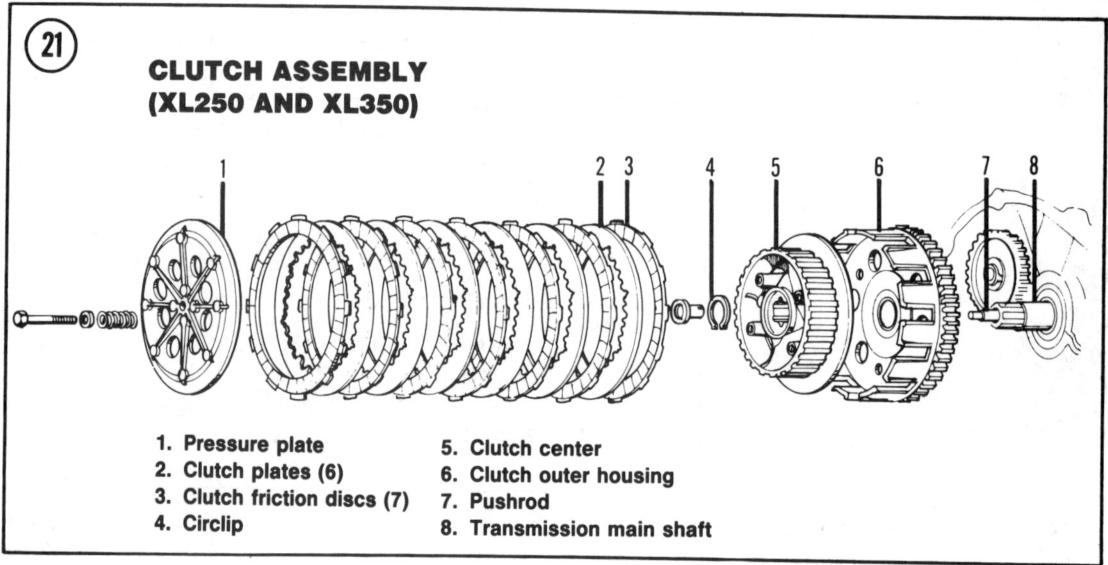

Removal/Disassembly

Refer to **Figures 19-21** for this procedure.

The clutch assembly can be removed with the engine in the frame. Portions of the following procedure show the engine is removed from the frame for clarity. It is not necessary to remove the engine for this procedure.

1. Drain the engine oil as described in Chapter Three.
2. Remove the rear brake pedal (A, **Figure 22**) as described in Chapter Eleven.
3. Slide back the rubber boot and slacken the clutch cable at the hand lever (**Figure 23**).
4. On models so equipped, disconnect the tachometer drive cable from the crankcase cover.
5. Disconnect the clutch cable at the crankcase cover (**Figure 24**).
6. Remove the bolt (B, **Figure 22**) securing the kickstarter lever and remove the kickstarter lever.
7. Remove the bolts (**Figure 25**) securing the right-hand crankcase cover and remove the cover, gasket and 2 locating dowels.
8. Remove the internal snap ring (**Figure 26**) securing the oil filter rotor cover. Remove the cover and O-ring seal.
9. Straighten the tab on the lockwasher from the notch in the locknut.
10. Place a copper washer (or copper penny) into mesh with the primary drive gear behind the oil filter rotor and the clutch outer housing. This will

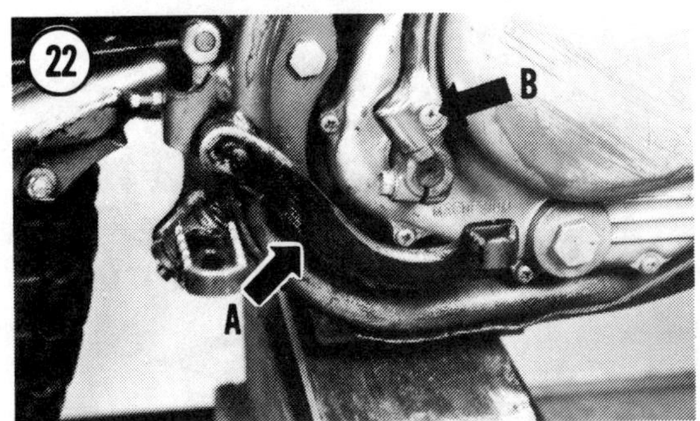

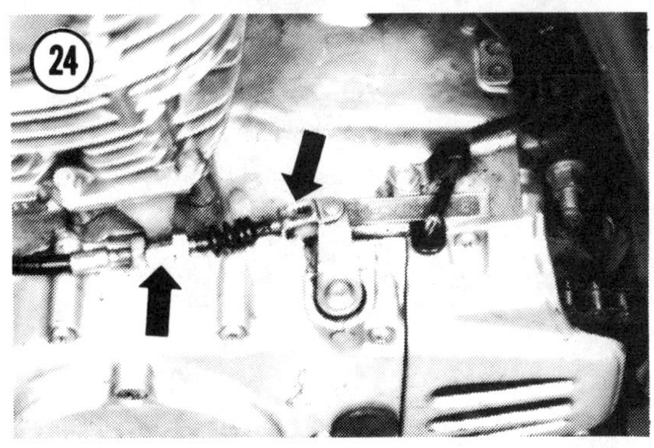

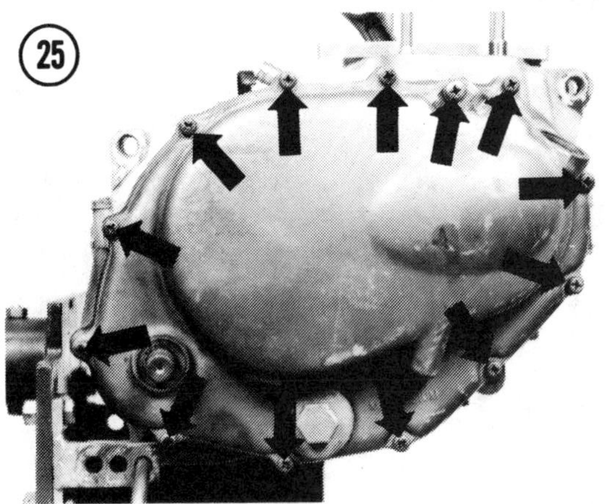

keep the oil rotor from turning during the next step.

11. Remove the nut (A, **Figure 27**), lockwasher and washer securing the oil rotor housing in place. Remove the housing.

NOTE
*Oil rotor nut removal requires a special tool (B, **Figure 27**) available from a Honda dealer (Locknut Wrench 20×24, part No. 07716-0020100).*

12A. On XL175 models, remove the clutch bolts (**Figure 28**) securing the clutch lifter ring and the clutch springs. Remove the lifter ring and the springs.

12B. On all other models, use a crisscross pattern to remove the clutch bolts (**Figure 29**) securing the clutch springs. Remove the springs (**Figure 30**).

14. Remove the pressure plate (**Figure 31**).

15. Remove the clutch plates and friction discs (**Figure 32**).

16. Remove the clutch lifter piece (**Figure 33**).

17. Remove the circlip (**Figure 34**) securing the clutch center assembly in place on the transmission shaft.

18. Remove the clutch center.

19. Remove the clutch outer housing.

20. On models so equipped, remove the tachometer driven gear (**Figure 35**).

21. On models so equipped, remove the tachometer drive gear (**Figure 36**).

22. Remove the primary drive gear and the thrust washer.

23. Inspect all components as described under *Inspection (All Models)* in this chapter.

Assembly/Installation

NOTE
If new friction discs or clutch plates are being installed, apply new engine oil to all surfaces to avoid having the clutch lock up when used for the first time.

1. Install the thrust washer (**Figure 37**) and the primary drive gear (**Figure 38**).
2. On models so equipped, install the tachometer drive gear (**Figure 36**).
3. On models so equipped, install the tachometer driven gear (**Figure 35**).
4. Install the clutch outer housing (**Figure 39**).
5. Install the clutch center (**Figure 40**).

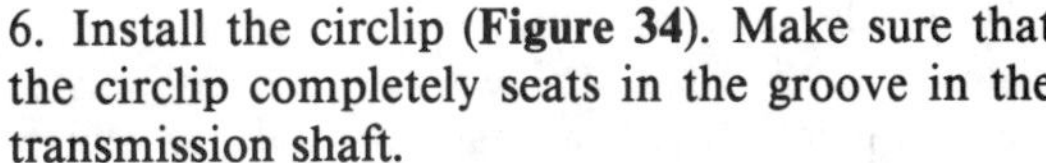

6. Install the circlip (**Figure 34**). Make sure that the circlip completely seats in the groove in the transmission shaft.

7. Install the clutch lifter piece (**Figure 33**).

8A. On 175 engines, install the clutch plate "B" first onto the clutch center. Install the plate with the formed shoulder side (**Figure 41**) facing toward the outside. Install a friction disc, a clutch plate, then a friction disc. Continue to install the clutch plates and friction discs, alternating them until all are installed. The last item installed is a friction disc (**Figure 42**).

8B. On all other models, onto the clutch center install a friction disc (**Figure 43**), a clutch plate, then a friction disc. Continue to install the clutch plates and friction discs alternating them until all are installed. The last item installed is a friction disc (**Figure 32**).
9. Install the pressure plate (**Figure 31**).
10. Install the clutch springs (**Figure 30**).
11A. On 175 models, install the clutch lifter ring and the clutch bolts (**Figure 28**).
11B. On all other models, install the clutch bolts and washers (**Figure 29**).
12. Tighten the clutch bolts securely in a crisscross pattern in 2 or 3 stages.
13. Install the oil rotor housing (**Figure 44**). Install the washer with the "OUTSIDE" marking facing toward the outside (**Figure 45**).
14. Install the lockwasher (**Figure 46**). Index it correctly into the locking section of the rotor housing.
15. Install the locknut (A, **Figure 27**) and tighten to 45-55 N•m (32-40 ft.-lb.). Use the same tool setup (B, **Figure 27**) as used in *Removal/ Disassembly* Step 10 and Step 11.
16. Bend one of the locking tabs down into one of the grooves in the locknut (**Figure 47**).
17. Inspect the O-ring seal (A, **Figure 48**) on the oil filter cover; replace if necessary.
18. Align one of the tabs on the oil filter cover with the groove (B, **Figure 48**) of the housing and install the cover.
19. Install the circlip (**Figure 26**). Make sure the circlip correctly seats into the groove in the rotor housing.
20. Install the dowel pins (A, **Figure 49**) and the gasket (B, **Figure 49**).
21. Install the right-hand crankcase cover. Push it all the way into place. Install the screws and tighten in a crisscross pattern until they are secure.

CAUTION
Do not install any of the crankcase cover screws until the crankcase cover is snug up against the crankcase surface. Do not try to force the cover into place with screw pressure.

22. Install the kickstarter lever and tighten the bolt securely.
23. Connect the clutch cable to the lever on the crankcase cover.
24. Install the rear brake pedal as described Chapter Eleven.

41

42

43

44

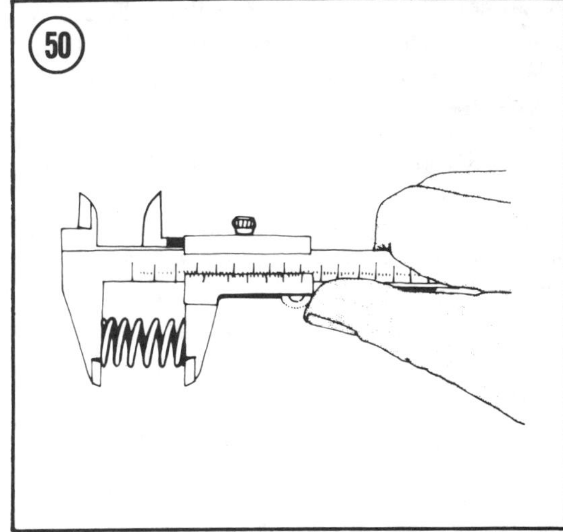

25. Refill the engine with the recommended type and quantity of oil; refer to in Chapter Three.
26. Adjust the clutch as described in Chapter Three.

CLUTCH INSPECTION (ALL MODELS)

1. Clean all parts in a petroleum based solvent such as kerosene and thoroughly dry with compressed air.
2. Measure the free length of each clutch spring as shown in **Figure 50**. If any of the springs are worn to the service limit in **Table 1**, they should be replaced. Replace all springs as a set.
3. Measure the thickness of each friction disc at several places around the disc as shown in **Figure 51**. Replace any disc that is worn to the service

limit listed in **Table 1**. For optimum performance, replace all discs as a set even if only a few need replacement.

4. Check the clutch plates for warpage on a surface plate such as a piece of plate glass (**Figure 52**). Replace any that are warped 0.20 mm (0.008 in.) or more. For optimum performance, replace all plates as a set even if only a few need replacement.

5. Inspect the grooves and studs in the pressure plate (A, **Figure 53**). If either show signs of wear or galling, the pressure plate should be replaced.

6. Inspect the inner splines and outer grooves in the clutch center (B, **Figure 53**). If damaged the clutch center should be replaced.

7. Inspect the teeth on the clutch outer housing (**Figure 54**). Remove any small nicks on the gear teeth with an oilstone. If damage is severe, the clutch housing should be replaced.

8. Inspect the slots in the clutch outer housing (**Figure 55**) for cracks, nicks or galling where they come in contact with the friction disc tabs. If any severe damage is evident, the clutch housing must be replaced.

9. On TL125 models, make sure the large set ring is correctly seated in the groove in the clutch center and that it is securely holding all 3 components in place. If the 3 components feel loose on the clutch center, remove the set ring and replace with a new one.

CLUTCH CABLE

Replacement

In time the clutch cable will stretch to the point that it will have to be replaced.

This procedure shows a typical clutch cable replacement. Minor variations exist among the different models.

1. Remove the side covers and the seat.
2. Remove the fuel tank as described in Chapter Seven.
3. At the clutch lever, pull back the rubber protective boot covering the cable adjuster.
4. Loosen the locknut and turn the adjuster barrel (**Figure 56**) all the way toward the cable sheath. Slip the cable end out of the hand lever.
5. At the right-hand crankcase cover, remove the cable end from the clutch lever (**Figure 57**). Remove the cable from any clamps on the frame.

NOTE

The piece of string attached in the next step will be used to pull the new clutch cable back through the frame so it will be routed in the exact same position.

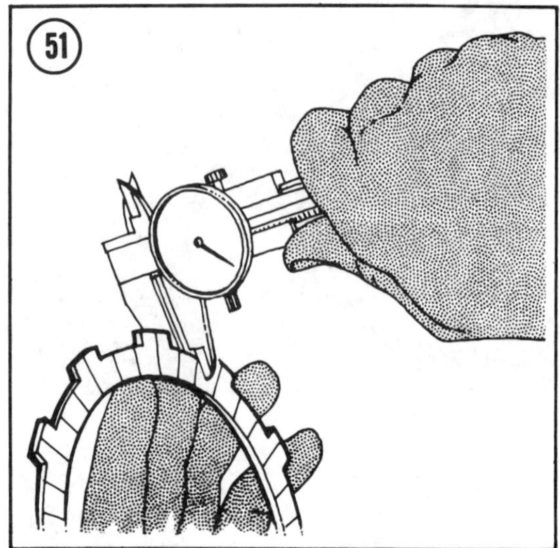

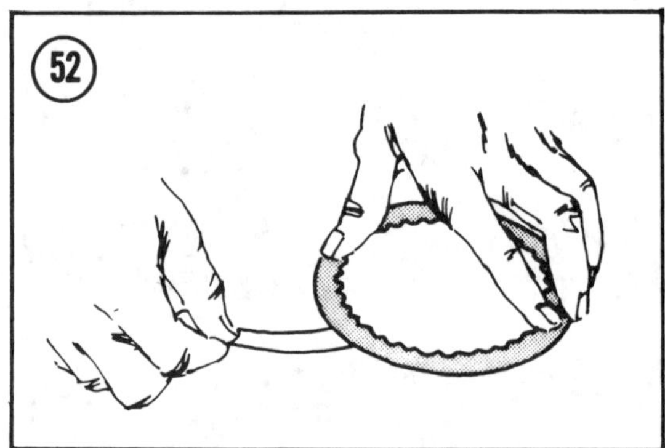

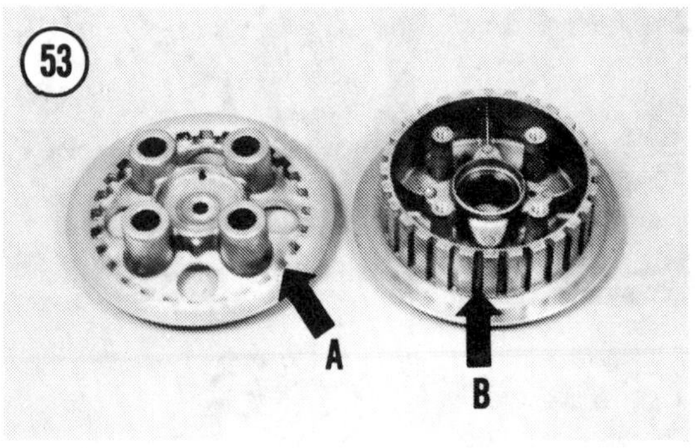

6. Tie a piece of heavy string or cord (approximately 1.8-2.4 m/6-8 ft. long) to the clutch mechanism end of the cable. Wrap this end with masking or duct tape. Do not use an excessive amount of tape. Tie the other end of the string to the footpeg or frame.
7. At the handlebar end of the cable, carefully pull the cable (and attached string) out through the frame and from behind the steering head area.

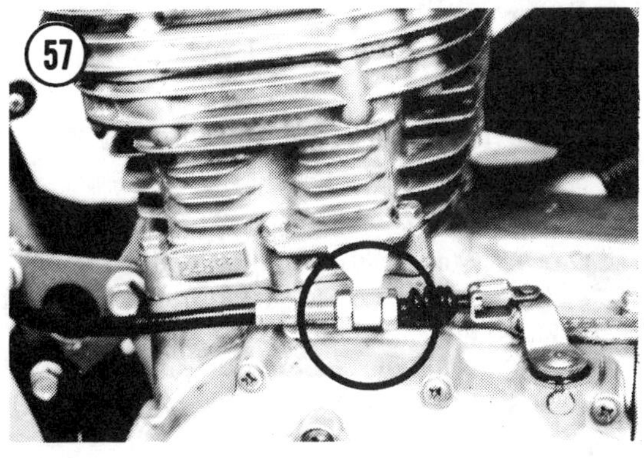

6

Make sure the attached string follows the same path of the cable through the frame (**Figure 58**).

8. Remove the tape and untie the string from the old cable.
9. Lubricate the new cable as described under *Control Cables* in Chapter Three.
10. Tie the string to the clutch mechanism end of the new clutch cable and wrap it with tape.
11. Carefully pull the string back through the frame, routing the new cable through the same path as the old cable.
12. Remove the tape and untie the string from the cable and the footpeg. Attach the new cable to the clutch lever and the clutch mechanism.
13. Install all components removed.
14. Adjust the clutch cable as described in Chapter Three.

EXTERNAL SHIFT MECHANISM

On 100 and 125 cc engines, the external shift mechanism is located on the same side of the crankcase as the clutch assembly (right-hand side). On 175, 250 and 350 cc engines, the gearshift mechanism is on the same side as the gearshift lever (left-hand side). On all models, the external shift mechanism can be removed with the engine in the frame. To remove the shift drum and shift forks, it is necessary to remove the engine and split the crankcase. This procedure is covered under *Internal Shift Mechanism* in this chapter.

The gearshift lever is subject to a lot of abuse. If the bike has been in a hard spill, the gearshift lever may have been hit and the shift shaft bent. It is very hard to straighten the shaft without subjecting the crankcase to abnormal stress where the shaft enters the case. If the shaft is bent enough to prevent it from being withdrawn from the

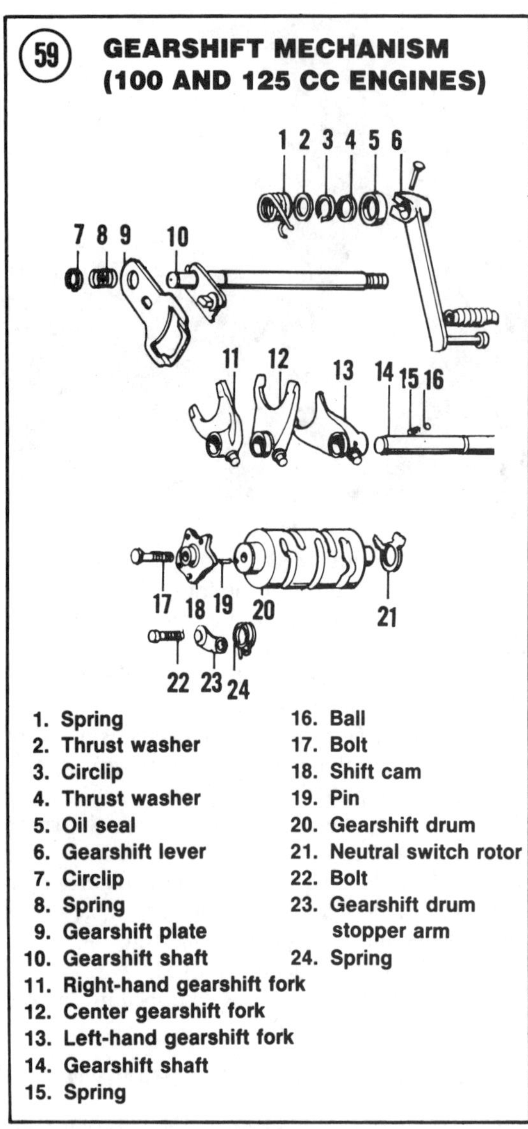

crankcase, there is little recourse but to cut the shaft off with a hacksaw very close to the crankcase. It is much cheaper in the long run to replace the shaft than risk damaging a very expensive crankcase.

EXTERNAL SHIFT MECHANISM (100 AND 125 CC ENGINES)

Removal

Refer to **Figure 59** for this procedure.

1. Drain the engine oil as described in Chapter Three.
2. Place a wood block(s) under the engine to support the bike securely.
3. Remove the clutch assembly as described in this chapter.

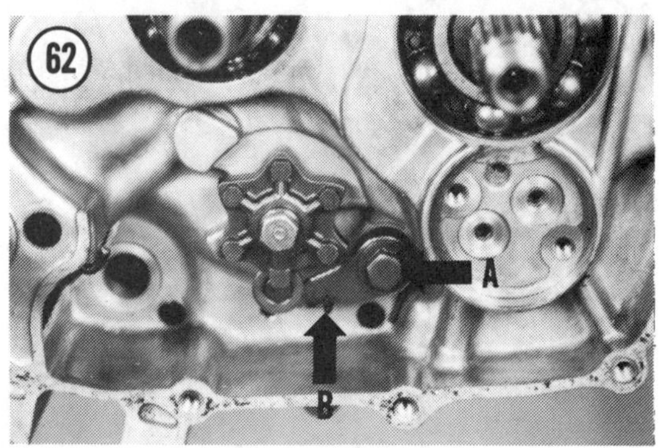

4. Remove the bolt on the gearshift lever (**Figure 60**) and remove the gearshift lever.

NOTE
See the introduction to this procedure if the assembly is difficult to remove.

5. Withdraw the gearshift spindle assembly (**Figure 61**). On models so equipped, don't lose the small thrust washer on the backside of the gearshift spindle assembly.
6. Remove the bolt (A, **Figure 62**) securing the stopper arm and remove the stopper arm (B, **Figure 62**).

63

66

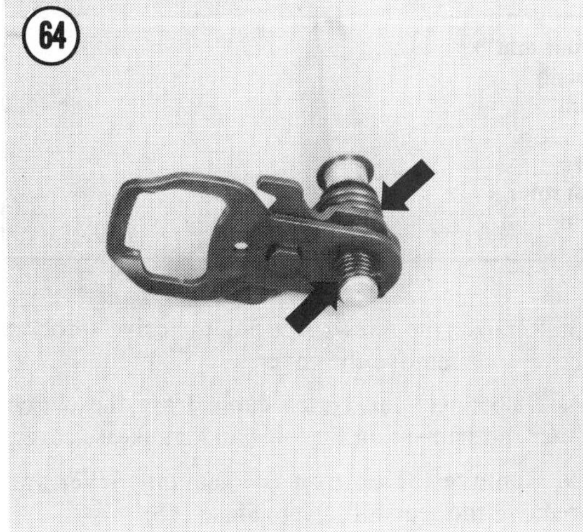

64

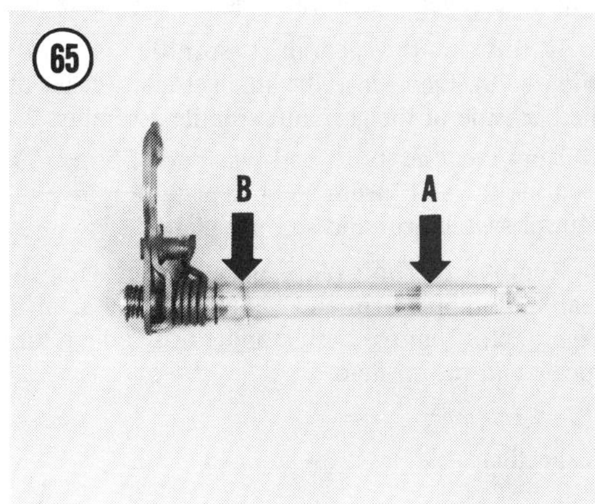

65

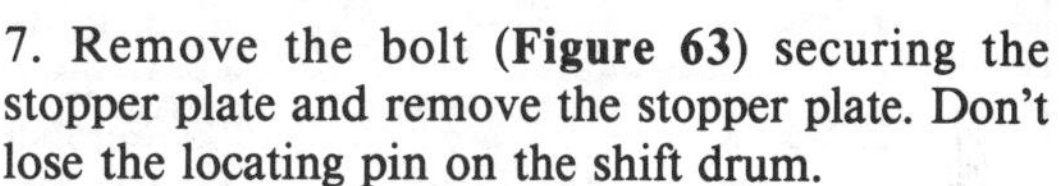

7. Remove the bolt (**Figure 63**) securing the stopper plate and remove the stopper plate. Don't lose the locating pin on the shift drum.

Inspection

1. Inspect the return springs on the gearshift spindle assembly (**Figure 64**). If broken or weak they must be replaced.
2. Inspect the gearshift lever assembly shaft (A, **Figure 65**) for bending, wear or other damage; replace if necessary.
3. Inspect the ramps on the stopper plate. They must be smooth and free of burrs or cracks. Replace if necessary.

Installation

1. Make sure the locating pin is installed in the shift drum. Align this pin with the hole in the backside of the stopper plate. Install the stopper plate and tighten the bolt securely (**Figure 63**).
2. Install the spring, stopper arm (B, **Figure 62**) and bolt (A, **Figure 62**). Tighten the bolt only finger-tight at this time.
3. Locate the stopper arm onto the stopper plate and tighten the stopper arm bolt securely.
4. Make sure the small thrust washer (B, **Figure 65**) is in place on the gearshift spindle.
5. Install the gearshift spindle assembly. Make sure the gearshift spindle assembly is correctly positioned onto the stopper plate (**Figure 66**).
6. Install the clutch assembly as described in this chapter.
7. Install the gearshift lever. Install the bolt and tighten securely.
8. Refill the engine with the correct type and quantity of oil. Refer to Chapter Three.
9. Adjust the clutch as described in Chapter Three.

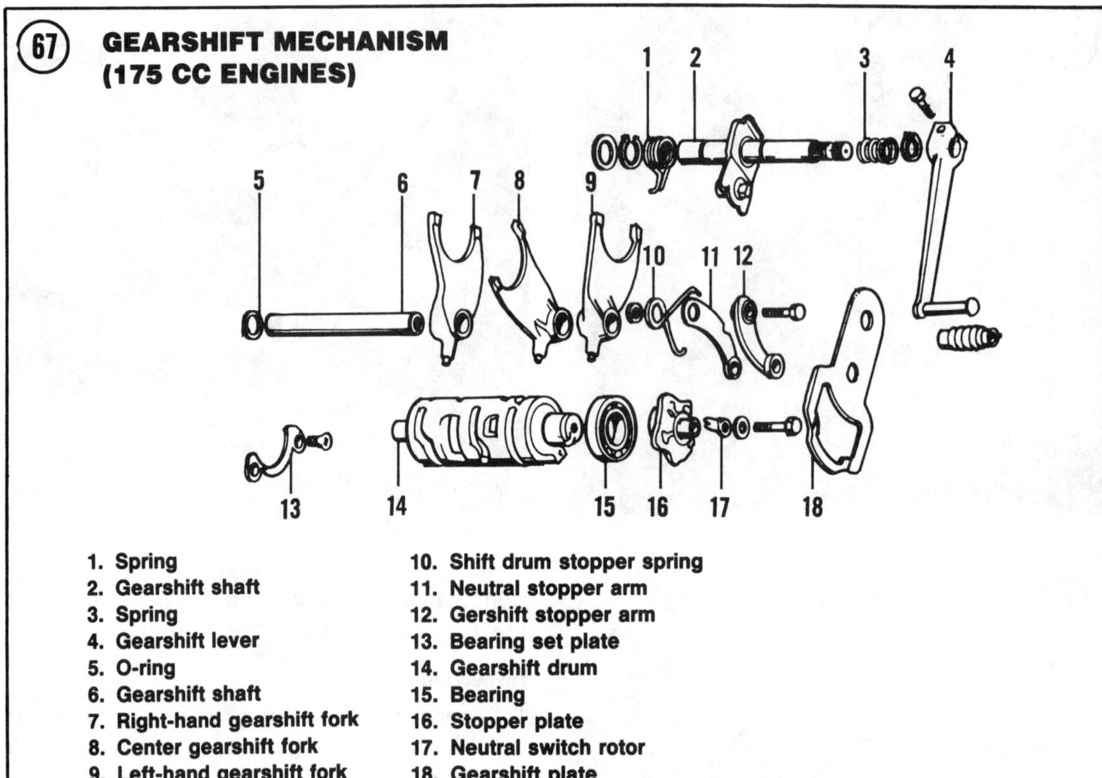

1. Spring
2. Gearshift shaft
3. Spring
4. Gearshift lever
5. O-ring
6. Gearshift shaft
7. Right-hand gearshift fork
8. Center gearshift fork
9. Left-hand gearshift fork
10. Shift drum stopper spring
11. Neutral stopper arm
12. Gershift stopper arm
13. Bearing set plate
14. Gearshift drum
15. Bearing
16. Stopper plate
17. Neutral switch rotor
18. Gearshift plate

EXTERNAL SHIFT MECHANISM (175 CC ENGINES)

NOTE

The gearshift lever is subject to a lot of abuse. If the bike has hit a large rock or other obstruction, the gearshift lever may have been hit and the shift shaft bent. It is very hard to straighten the shaft without subjecting the crankcase cover to abnormal stress where the shaft enters the case. If the shaft is bent enough to prevent the crankcase cover from being withdrawn over the shaft, there is little recourse but to cut the shaft off with a hacksaw very close to the crankcase cover. It is much cheaper in the long run to replace the shaft than risk damaging a very expensive crankcase cover.

Removal

Refer to **Figure 67** for this procedure.

1. Drain the engine oil as described in Chapter Three.
2. Place a wood block(s) under the engine to support the bike securely.
3. Remove the screws securing the drive sprocket cover and remove the cover.
4. Disconnect the clutch cable from the clutch lifter mechanism on the left-hand crankcase cover.
5. Remove the bolt on the gearshift lever and remove the gearshift lever (**Figure 68**).
6. Remove the screws securing the left-hand crankcase cover and remove the cover (**Figure 69**).
7. Withdraw the gearshift spindle assembly (**Figure 70**). Don't lose the small thrust washer on the backside of the gearshift spindle assembly.
8. Remove the bolt and washer (**Figure 71**) securing the shift drum stopper plate. Remove the neutral switch arm and stopper plate.
9. Remove the bolt (A, **Figure 72**) securing the gearshift stopper arm and neutral stopper arm (B, **Figure 72**). Remove both stopper arms, the return spring and the washer.

Inspection

1. Inspect the return springs on the gearshift spindle assembly (**Figure 73**). If broken or weak they must be replaced.

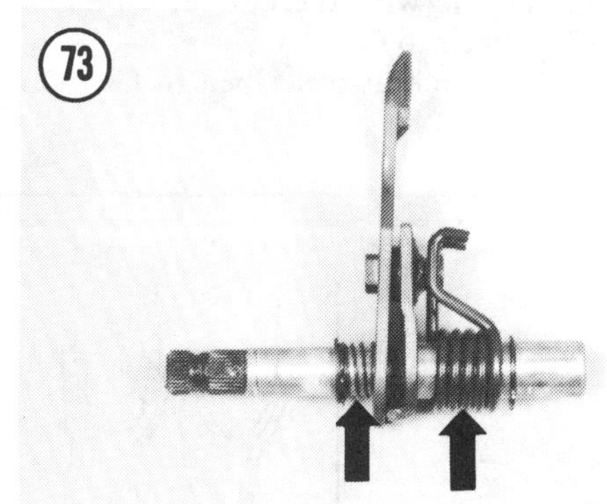

2. Inspect the gearshift lever assembly shaft for bending, wear or other damage; replace if necessary.

3. Inspect the ramps on the stopper plate. They must be smooth and free of burrs or cracks. Replace if necessary.

Installation

1. Onto the bolt install the gearshift stopper arm, the return spring, the washer, the neutral stopper arm, its return spring and the washer. Install this assembly into the crankcase and tighten the bolt securely (**Figure 74**).

6

2. Install the stopper plate and neutral switch arm. Tighten the bolt securely (**Figure 71**).
3. Make sure the small thrust washer is installed onto the backside of the gearshift spindle assembly.
4. Install the gearshift spindle assembly. Make sure the gearshift spindle assembly is correctly positioned onto the stopper plate.
5. Install the left-hand crankcase cover and tighten the screws securely.
6. Install the gearshift lever and tighten the bolt securely.
7. Attach the clutch cable onto the clutch lifter mechanism on the left-hand crankcase cover.
8. Install the drive sprocket cover.
9. Refill the engine with the correct type and quantity of oil. Refer to Chapter Three.
10. Adjust the clutch as described in Chapter Three.

EXTERNAL SHIFT MECHANISM (250 AND 350 CC ENGINES)

Removal

Refer to **Figure 75** for this procedure.

This procedure is shown with the engine removed and partially disassembled for clarity. It is not necessary to remove the engine from the frame for this procedure.

1. Drain the engine oil as described in Chapter Three.
2. Place a wood block(s) under the engine to support the bike securely.
3. Remove the screws securing the drive sprocket cover and remove the cover.
4. Disconnect the clutch cable from the actuating arm on the left-hand crankcase cover.

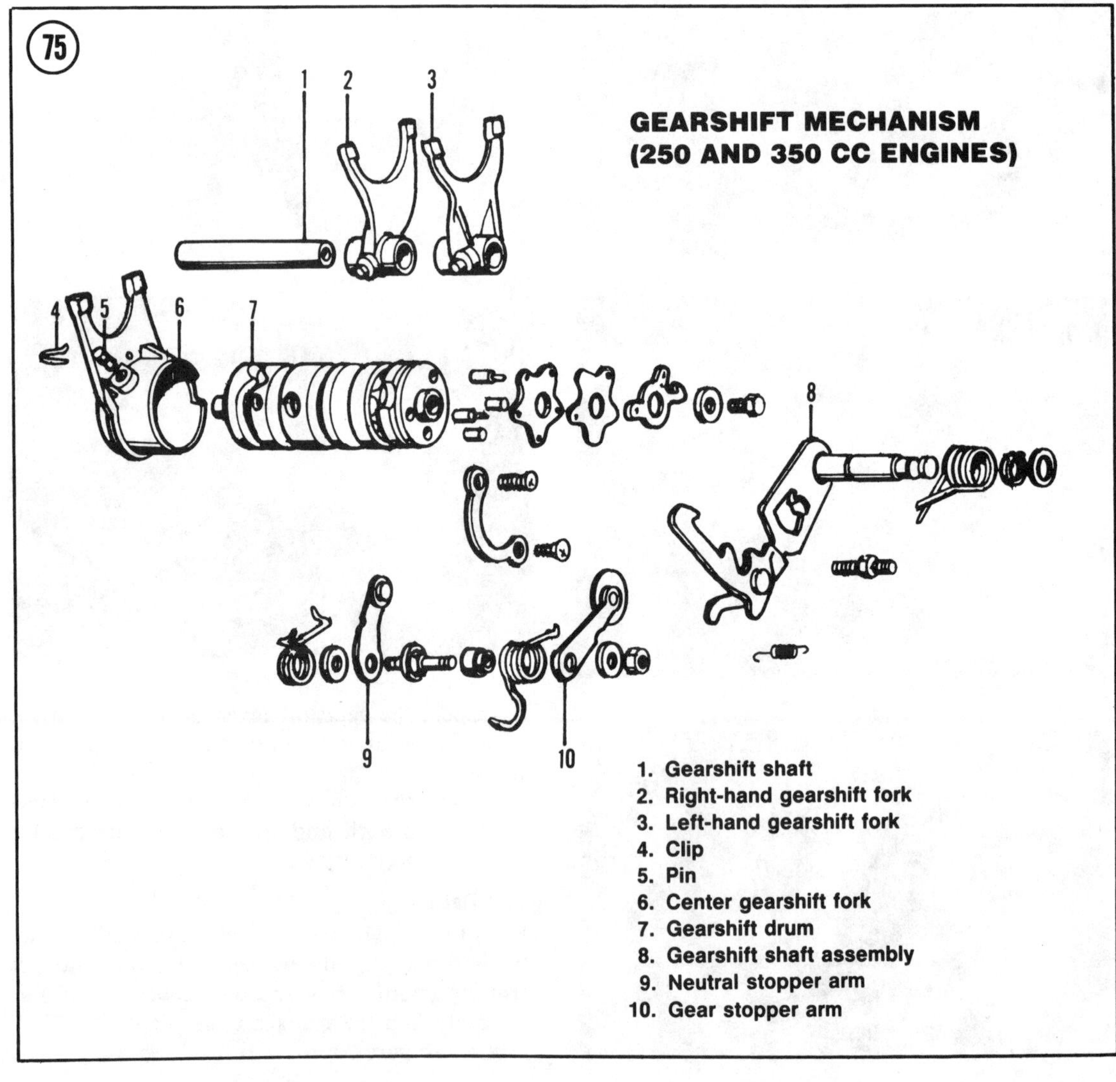

5. Remove the bolt on the gearshift lever and remove the gearshift lever.
6. Remove the screws securing the left-hand crankcase cover and remove the cover (**Figure 76**).
7. Disengage the gearshift spindle arm from the shift drum and withdraw the gearshift spindle assembly (**Figure 77**).
8. Don't lose the small thrust washer on the backside of the gearshift spindle assembly.
9. Remove the nut and washer (**Figure 78**) securing the gearshift stopper arm. Remove the gearshift stopper arm, its return spring and the collar.
10. Remove the threaded stud, neutral stopper arm, washer and the spring.
11. Remove the screws securing the shift drum retainer.
12. If necessary, remove the bolt and washer (A, **Figure 79**). Remove the neutral switch arm, both stopper plates and the shift drum pins.

Inspection

1. Inspect the return springs on the gearshift spindle assembly (**Figure 80**). If broken or weak they must be replaced.
2. Inspect the gearshift lever assembly shaft for bending, wear or other damage; replace if necessary.
3. Inspect ramps on the stopper plate. They must be smooth and free of burrs or cracks. Replace if necessary.

Installation

1. If removed, install the shift drum pins, the stopper plates, the neutral switch arm and the bolt and washer. Tighten the bolt securely.
2. Onto the threaded stud install the neutral stopper arm, the washer and the spring. Install this assembly into the crankcase. Correctly locate both

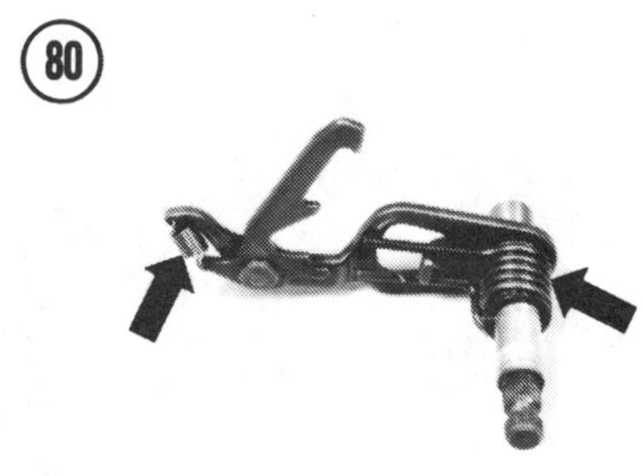

the arm and the spring (B, **Figure 79**). Tighten the threaded stud securely.

3. Install the collar (**Figure 81**), the return spring (**Figure 82**), the gearshift stopper arm (**Figure 83**), the washer and the nut (**Figure 78**). Tighten the nut securely.
4. Make sure the small thrust washer is installed onto the backside of the gearshift spindle assembly.
5. Install the gearshift spindle assembly. Make sure the gearshift spindle asembly is correctly positioned onto the shift drum stopper plate (**Figure 77**).
6. Install the left-hand crankcase cover and tighten the screws securely.
7. Install the gearshift lever and tighten the bolt securely.
8. Attach the clutch cable onto the clutch lifter mechanism on the left-hand crankcase cover.
9. Install the drive sprocket cover.
10. Refill the engine with the correct type and quantity of oil. Refer to Chapter Three.
11. Adjust the clutch as described in Chapter Three.

DRIVE SPROCKET

Removal/Installation

1. Shift the transmission into any gear. Push the bike forward until the master link is visible for removal.
2. Place a wood block(s) under the engine to support the bike securely.
3. Remove the bolt securing the shift lever (A, **Figure 84**) and remove the shift lever.
4. Remove the screws securing the drive sprocket cover (B, **Figure 84**) and remove the cover.
5. Have an assistant hold the rear brake on while you loosen the bolts securing the drive sprocket and drive sprocket holding plate.
6. Remove the drive chain master link clip (**Figure 85**) and remove the drive chain.

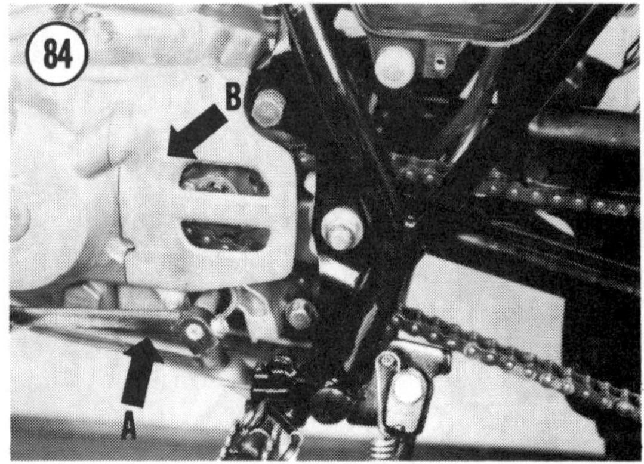

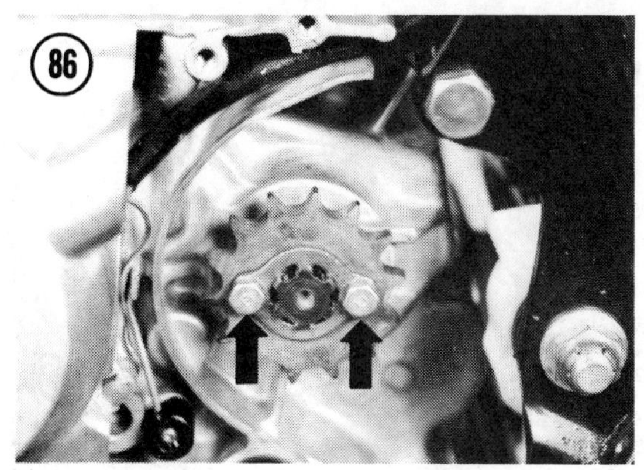

86

7. Remove the bolts (**Figure 86**) securing the drive sprocket and drive sprocket holding plate. Rotate the holding plate in either direction to disengage it from the splines on the shaft, then slide off the holding plate and drive sprocket.
8. Install by reversing these removal steps, noting the following.
9. Install a new drive chain master link so that the closed end of the clip is facing the direction of chain travel (**Figure 87**).
10. Adjust the drive chain as described in Chapter Three.

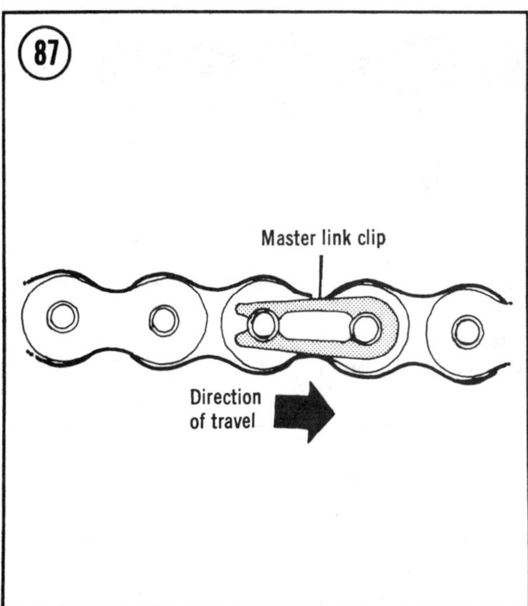

87

Inspection

Inspect the teeth on the drive sprocket. If the teeth are visibly worn (**Figure 88**), replace the sprocket with a new one. Also inspect the rear wheel driven sprocket as described in Chapter Ten.

If the sprocket requires replacement, the drive chain is probably worn also. Refer to Chapter Three.

TRANSMISSION AND INTERNAL SHIFT MECHANISM

To gain access to the transmission and internal shift mechanism it is necessary to remove the engine and split the crankcase. Once the crankcase has been split, removal of the transmission and shift drum and forks is a simple task of pulling the assemblies up and out of the crankcase. Installation is more complicated and is covered more completely than the removal sequence.

Refer to **Table 2** for specifications on the internal shift mechanism. There are no factory specifications for the transmission components.

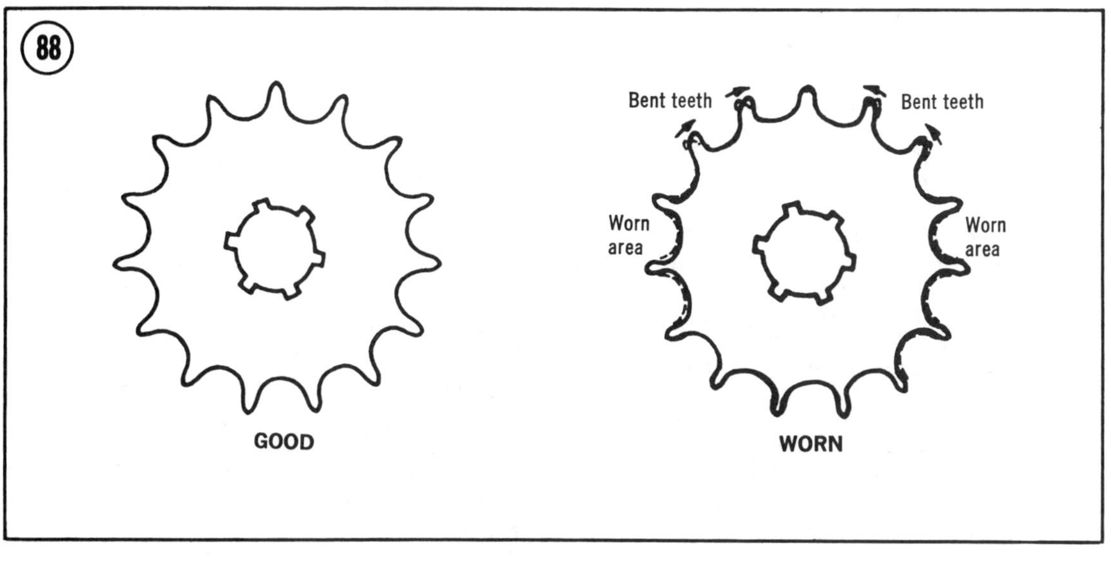

88

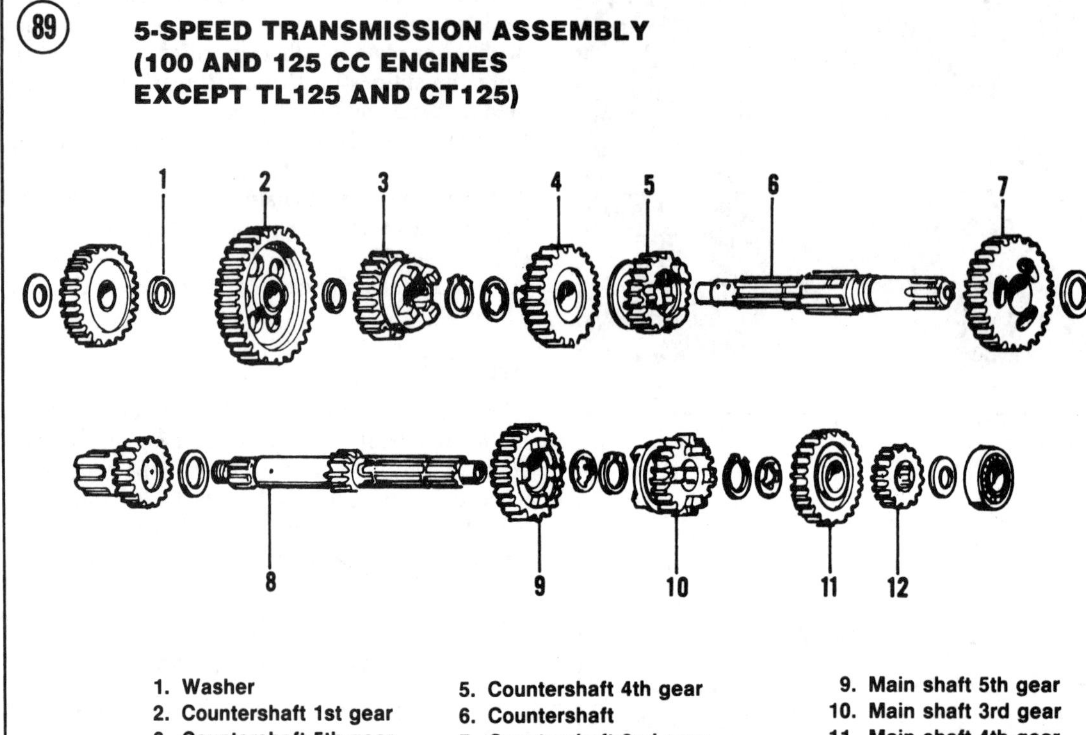

There are 4 types of 5-speed transmission used among the various models. The Type I and Type II transmissions are used with the 100 and 125 cc engines. The Type III transmission is used with the 175 cc engine and the Type IV transmission is used with the 250 and 350 cc engines.

NOTE
If disassembling a used, well run-in engine (high mileage) for the first time by yourself, pay particular attention to any additional shims that may have been added by a previous owner. These may have been added to take up the tolerance of worn components and must be reinstalled in the same position since the shims have developed a wear pattern. If new parts are going to be installed these shims may be eliminated. This is something you will have to determine upon reassembly.

5-SPEED TRANSMISSION AND INTERNAL SHIFT MECHANISM (100 AND 125 CC ENGINES)

The Type I transmission (**Figure 89**) is used on the following models:

a. All 100 cc models.
b. All CB125S.
c. All SL125.
d. All XL125.

The Type II transmission (**Figure 90**) is used on the following models:

a. All TL125.
b. All CT125.

Removal/Installation

1. Remove the engine and disassemble the crankcase as described in Chapter Four.
2. Remove the crankshaft assembly from the crankcase.
3. Pull the shift fork shaft (A, **Figure 91**) out of the crankcase.
4. Pivot the shift forks (B, **Figure 91**) away from the shift drum to allow shift drum removal.
5. Remove the shift drum (C, **Figure 91**).
6. Remove the shift forks and both transmission assemblies (D, **Figure 91**).
7. Disassemble and inspect the shift forks and transmission assemblies as described in this chapter.

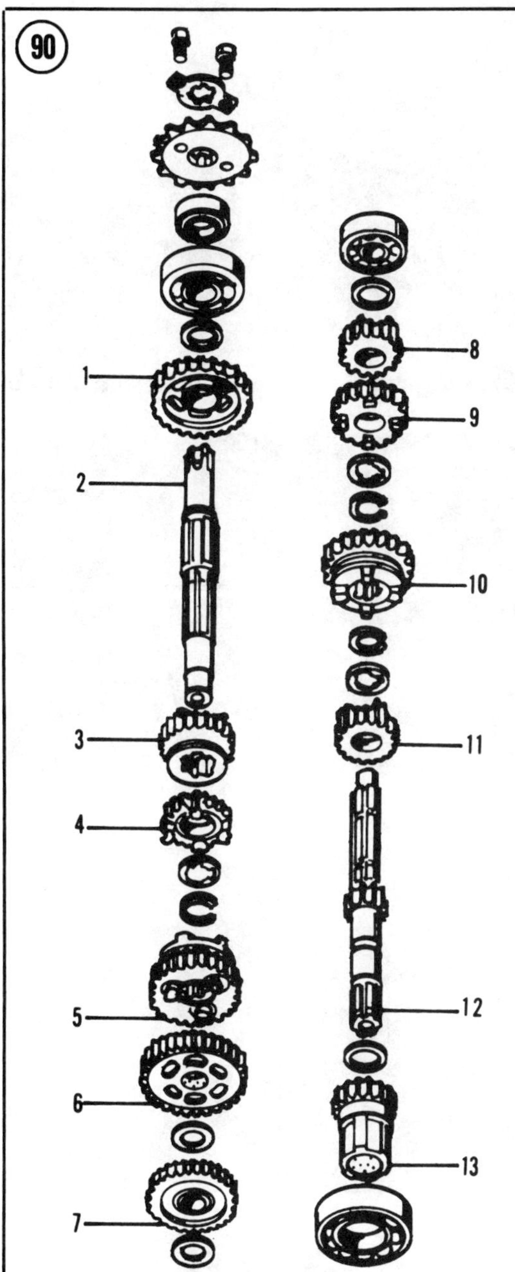

5-SPEED TRANSMISSION ASSEMBLY (TL125 AND CT125)

1. Countershaft 2nd gear
2. Countershaft
3. Countershaft 4th gear
4. Countershaft 5rd gear
5. Countershaft 3rd gear
6. Countershaft 1st gear
7. Kickstarter gear
8. Main shaft 2nd gear
9. Main shaft 4th gear
10. Main shaft 5th gear
11. Main shaft 3rd gear
12. Main shaft/1st gear
13. Kickstarter gear

8. Install the 2 transmission assemblies by meshing them together in their proper relationship. Install them in the left-hand crankcase. Hold the thrust washer and collar in place with your fingers on the countershaft (**Figure 92**). Make sure it is still positioned correctly after the assemblies are completely installed. After both assemblies are installed, tap on the end of each shaft with a plastic or rubber mallet to make sure it is completely seated.

NOTE
If the thrust washer on the end of the countershaft does not seat correctly, it will hold the transmission shaft up a little and prevent the crankcase halves from seating completely.

9. Each shift fork is marked with an "R" (right-hand side), "C" (center) or "L" (left-hand side). Install the shift forks with these marks facing *up*.

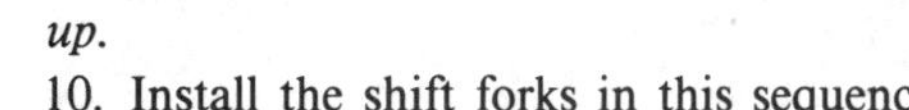

10. Install the shift forks in this sequence— "L," "C" then "R." Engage the shift forks into the

grooves in the gears (**Figure 93**) but do not insert the shift fork shaft.

11. Coat all bearing and sliding surfaces of the shift drum with assembly oil and install the shift drum (**Figure 94**). Rotate the shift drum to the neutral position by aligning the neutral switch rotor with the neutral switch in the crankcase (**Figure 95**). This will make it easier to insert the shift fork pin followers into the shift drum.
12. Pivot each shift fork into mesh with the shift drum.
13. Install the shift fork shaft (A, **Figure 96**). Make sure all 3 cam pin followers are in mesh with the shift drum grooves.
14. Spin the transmission shafts and shift through the gears using the shift drum. Make sure you can shift into all gears. This is the time to find that something may be installed incorrectly—not after the crankcase is completely assembled.

NOTE

This procedure is best done with the aid of a helper as the assemblies are loose and won't spin very easily. Have the helper spin the transmission shaft while you turn the shift drum through all the gears.

15. Make sure that the thrust washer (B, **Figure 96**) is installed on the countershaft.
16. On models so equipped, apply a light coat of multipurpose grease to the kickstarter shaft shim and position it onto the crankcase as shown in **Figure 97**.

NOTE

The kickstarter assembly is mounted in the right-hand crankcase half.

17. Install the crankshaft and assemble the crankcase as described in Chapter Four.

Preliminary Inspection

Prior to disassembling the transmission shaft assemblies they should be cleaned and inspected. Place the assembled shaft into a large can or plastic bucket and thoroughly clean with solvent and a stiff brush. Dry with compressed air or let it sit on rags to drip dry. Repeat for the other shaft assembly.

1. After they have been cleaned, visually inspect the components of the assemblies for excessive wear. Any burrs, pitting or roughness on the teeth of a gear will cause wear on the mating gear. Minor roughness can be cleaned up with an oilstone but there's little point in attempting to remove deep scars.

NOTE

Defective gears should be replaced. It's a good idea to replace the mating gear on the other shaft even though it may not show as much wear or damage.

2. Carefully check the engagement dogs. If any are chipped, worn, rounded or missing, the affected gear must be replaced.
3. If possible, check the runout of each transmission shaft. Mount the shaft being checked in a lathe, on V-blocks or on some other suitable centering device. Place a dial indicator so that its plunger contacts a constant surface near the center of the shaft. Rotate the shaft and record the extremes of the dial readings. The shaft should be replaced if the runout exceeds 0.04 mm (0.0016 in.).
4. Rotate the transmission bearings in the crankcases by hand. Refer to **Figure 98** and **Figure 99**. Check for roughness, noise and radial play. Any bearing that is suspect should be replaced. Refer to *Bearing Replacement* in Chapter Four.
5. If the transmission shafts are satisfactory and are not going to be disassembled, apply engine oil to all components and reinstall them in the crankcase as described in this chapter.

98

99

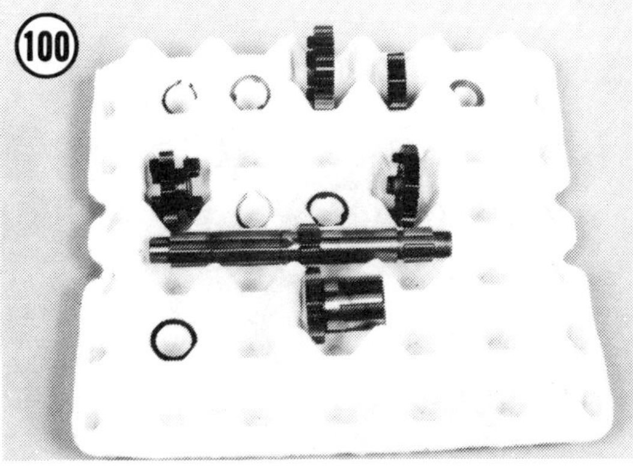

100

6

Main Shaft Disassembly/Inspection/Assembly

Refer to **Figure 89** for the Type I transmission or **Figure 90** for the Type II transmission during this procedure.

NOTE

*A helpful "tool" that should be used for transmission disassembly is a large egg flat (the type that restaurants get their eggs in). As you remove a part from the shaft set it in one of the depressions in the same position from which it was removed (**Figure 100**). This is an easy way to remember the correct relationship of all parts.*

1. If not cleaned in the *Preliminary Inspection* sequence, place the assembled shaft into a large can or plastic bucket and thoroughly clean with solvent and a stiff brush. Dry with compressed air or let it sit on rags to drip dry.

2A. On Type I transmissions, perform the following:

a. Slide off the thrust washer, the 2nd gear and the 5th gear.

b. Slide off the splined washer and remove the circlip.
c. Slide off the 3rd gear.
d. Remove the circlip and splined washer.
e. Slide off the 4th gear.

2B. On Type II transmissions, perform the following:

a. Slide off the thrust washer, the 2nd gear and the 4th gear.
b. Slide off the splined washer and remove the circlip.
c. Slide off the 5th gear.
d. Remove the circlip and splined washer.
e. Slide off the 3rd gear.

3. From the other end of the shaft, slide off the kickstarter idle gear and thrust washer.

4. Check each gear for excessive wear, burrs, pitting or chipped or missing teeth. Make sure the lugs on the gears are in good condition.

NOTE
Defective gears should be replaced. It is a good idea to replace the mating gear on the countershaft even though it may not show as much wear or damage.

NOTE
The 1st gear is part of the shaft. If the gear is defective the shaft must be replaced.

5. Make sure that all gears slide smoothly on the main shaft splines.

NOTE
It is a good idea to replace all circlips every other time the transmission is disassembled to ensure proper gear alignment.

6A. On Type I transmissions, perform the following:

a. Install the thrust washer and the kickstarter idle gear (**Figure 101**).
b. Slide on the 4th gear and install the splined washer and circlip (**Figure 102**).
c. Slide on the 3rd gear and install the circlip and splined washer (**Figure 103**).
d. Slide on the 5th gear, the 2nd gear and the thrust washer (**Figure 104**).

6B. On Type II transmissions, perform the following:

a. Install the thrust washer and the kickstarter idle gear.
b. Slide on the 3rd gear and install the splined washer and circlip.
c. Slide on the 5th gear and install the circlip and splined washer.

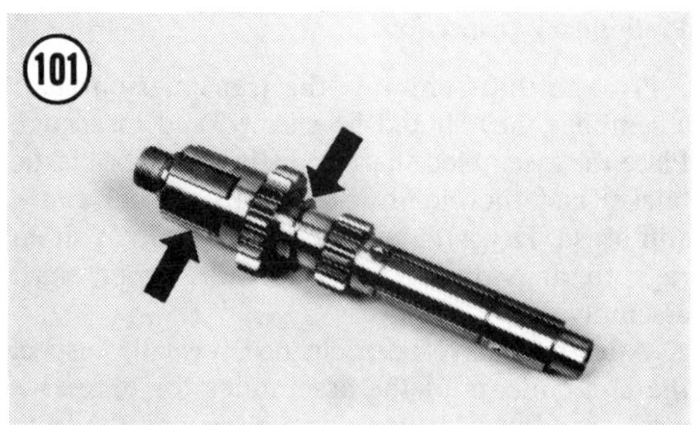
101

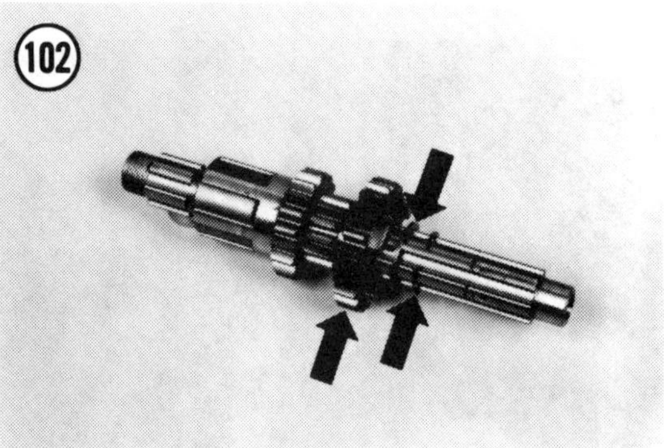
102

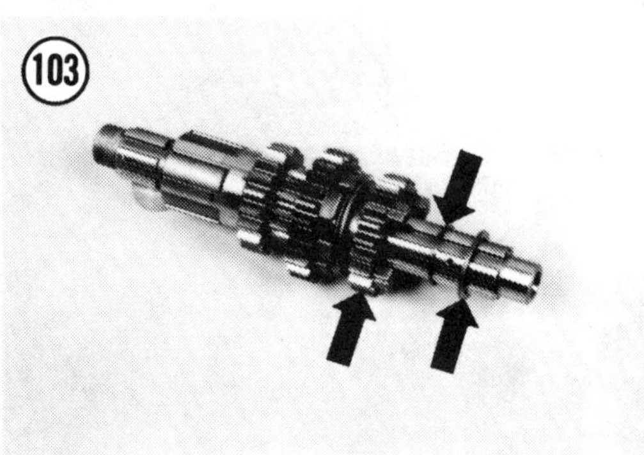
103

104

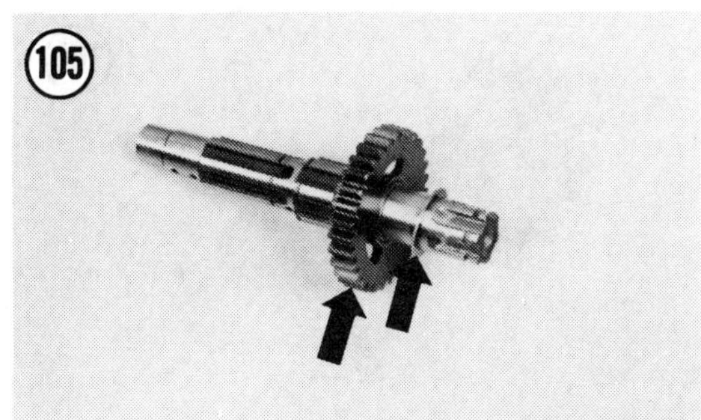

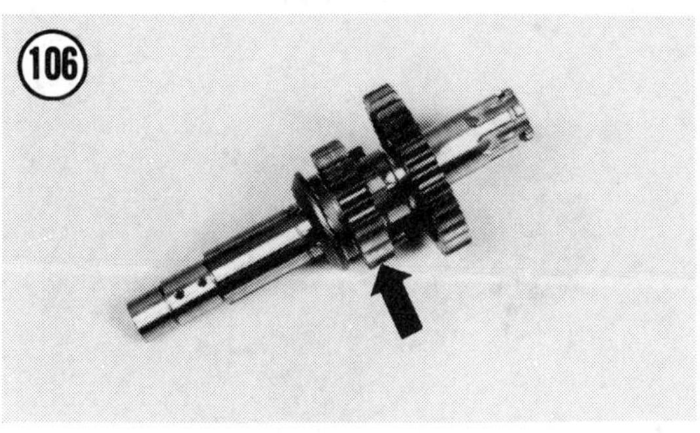

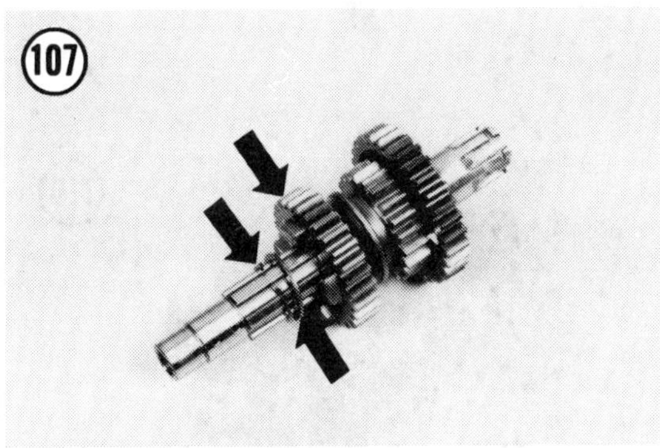

d. Slide on the 4th gear, the 2nd gear and the thrust washer.

7. Before installation, double-check the placement of all gears. Make sure all circlips are seated correctly in the main shaft grooves.

Countershaft Disassembly/ Inspection/Assembly

Refer to **Figure 89** for the Type I transmission or **Figure 90** for the Type II transmission during this procedure.

NOTE

Use the same large egg flat (used on the main shaft disassembly) during the countershaft disassembly. This is an easy way to remember the correct relationship of all parts.

1. If not cleaned in the *Preliminary Inspection* sequence, place the assembled shaft into a large can or plastic bucket and thoroughly clean with solvent and a stiff brush. Dry with compressed air or let it sit on rags to drip dry.

2A. On Type I transmissions, perform the following:

a. Remove the thrust washer and the kickstarter idle gear.
b. Slide off the thrust washer and the 1st gear.
c. Slide off the thrust washer and the 5th gear.
d. Remove the circlip and splined washer and slide off the 3rd gear.
e. Slide off the 4th gear.
f. From the other end of the shaft, remove the thrust washer and slide off the 2nd gear.

2B. On Type II transmissions, perform the following:

a. Remove the thrust washer and the kickstarter idle gear.
b. Slide off the thrust washer and the 1st gear.
c. Slide off the 3rd gear.
d. Remove the circlip and splined washer and slide off the 5th gear.
e. Slide off the 4th gear.
f. From the other end of the shaft, remove the thrust washer and slide off the 2nd gear.

3. Check each gear for excessive wear, burrs, pitting or chipped or missing teeth. Make sure the lugs on the gears are in good condition.

NOTE

Defective gears should be replaced. It is a good idea to replace the mating gear on the main shaft even though it may not show as much wear or damage.

4. Make sure that all gears slide smoothly on the countershaft splines.

NOTE

It is a good idea to replace the circlip every other time the transmission is disassembled to ensure proper gear alignment.

5A. On Type I transmissions, perform the following:

a. Slide on the 2nd gear (flush side on last) and install the thrust washer (**Figure 105**).
b. From the other side of the shaft, slide on the 4th gear (**Figure 106**).
c. Slide on the 3rd gear (flush side on first), splined washer and circlip (**Figure 107**).

6

d. Slide on the 5th gear and thrust washer (**Figure 108**).
e. Slide on the 1st gear (flush side on last) and install the thrust washer (**Figure 109**).
f. Slide on the kickstarter idle gear and thrust washer (**Figure 110**).

5B. On Type II transmissions, perform the following:

a. Slide on the 2nd gear (flush side on last) and install the thrust washer.
b. From the other side of the shaft, slide on the 4th gear.
c. Slide on the 5th gear, splined washer and circlip.
d. Slide on the 3rd gear.
e. Slide on the 1st gear (flush side on last) and install the thrust washer.
f. Slide on the kickstarter idle gear and thrust washer.

Before installation, double-check the placement of all gears. Make sure the circlip is seated correctly in the countershaft groove.

NOTE
*After both transmission shafts have been assembled, mesh the 2 assemblies together in the correct position (**Figure 111**, Type I shown). Check that all gears meet correctly. This is your last check prior to installing the assemblies into the crankcase; make sure they are correctly assembled.*

5-SPEED TRANSMISSION (175, 250 AND 350 ENGINES)

The Type III transmission (**Figure 112**) is used on all 175 cc models.

The Type IV transmission (**Figure 113**) is used on all 250 and 350 cc models.

NOTE
The internal shift mechanism is not removed during transmission removal. It is covered in a separate procedure in this chapter.

Removal/Installation

1. Remove the engine and disassemble the crankcase as described in Chapter Five.
2. Remove the crankshaft assembly from the crankcase.
3. Remove the main shaft assembly (A, **Figure 114**) and the countershaft assembly (B, **Figure 114**) from the lower crankcase half.

108

109

110

111

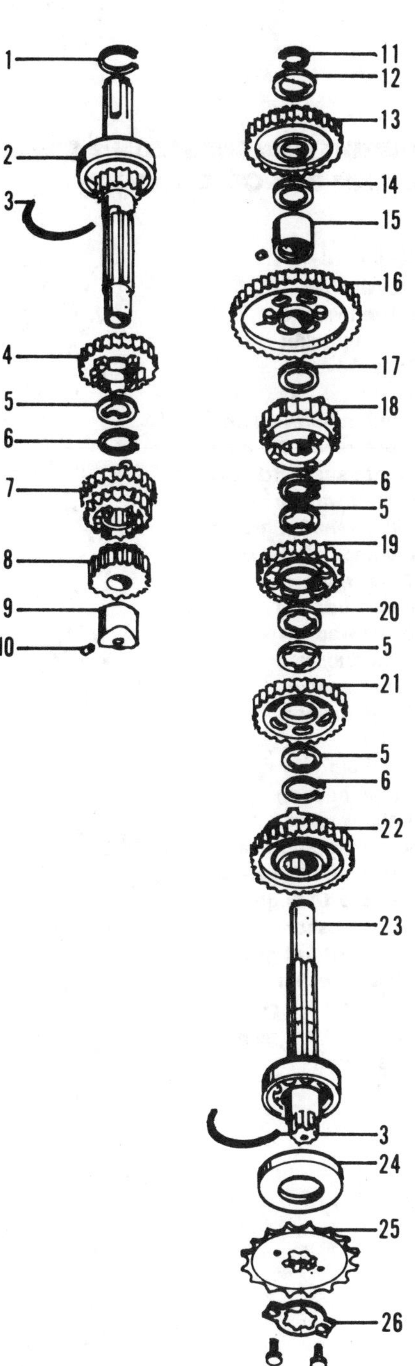

5-SPEED TRANSMISSION ASSEMBLY (175 CC ENGINE)

1. Circlip
2. Main shaft/1st gear
3. 1/2 set ring
4. Main shaft 5th gear
5. Splined washer
6. Circlip
7. Main shaft 3rd/4th combination gear
8. Main shaft 2nd gear
9. Needle bearing
10. Dowel pin
11. Circlip
12. Thrust washer
13. Kickstarter gear
14. Thrust washer
15. Bearing bushing
16. Countershaft 1st gear
17. Thrust washer
18. Countershaft 5th gear
19. Countershaft 4th gear
20. Splined lockwasher
21. Countershaft 2nd gear
22. Countershaft 2nd gear
23. Countershaft
24. Oil seal
25. Drive sprocket
26. Locking plate

6

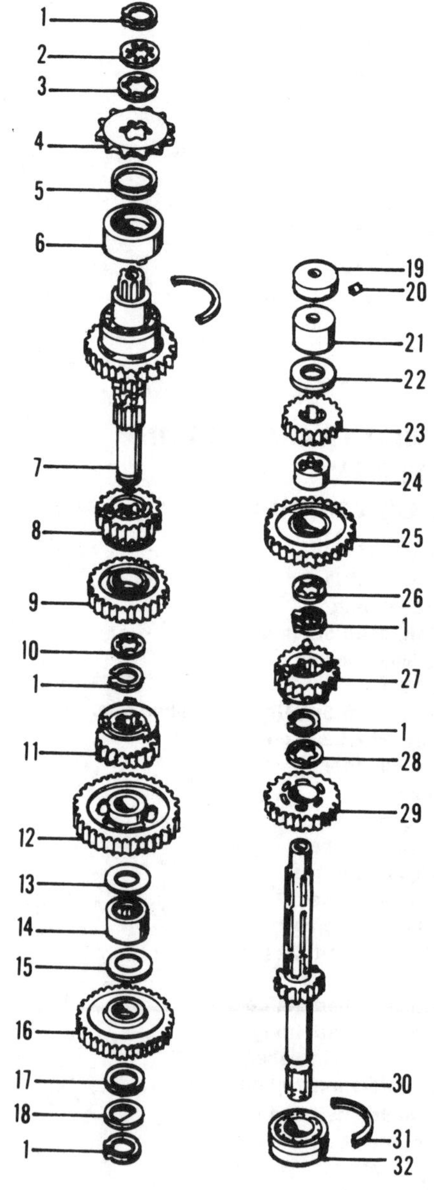

5-SPEED TRANSMISSION ASSEMBLY (250 AND 350 CC ENGINES)

1. Circlip
2. Lockwasher
3. Splined washer
4. Drive sprocket
5. Collar
6. Oil seal
7. Countershaft/2nd gear
8. Countershaft 5th gear
9. Countershaft 3rd gear
10. Splined washer
11. Countershaft 4th gear
12. Countershaft 1st gear
13. Thrust washer
14. Needle bearing
15. Thrust washer
16. Kickstarter gear
17. Thrust washer
18. Thrust washer
19. Oil seal
20. Dowel pin
21. Needle bearing
22. Thrust washer
23. Main shaft 2nd gear
24. Main shaft 5th gear bushing
25. Main shaft 5th gear
26. Thrust washer
27. Main shaft 3rd gear
28. Splined washer
29. Main shaft 4th gear
30. Main shaft/1st gear
31. 1/2 set ring
32. Bearing

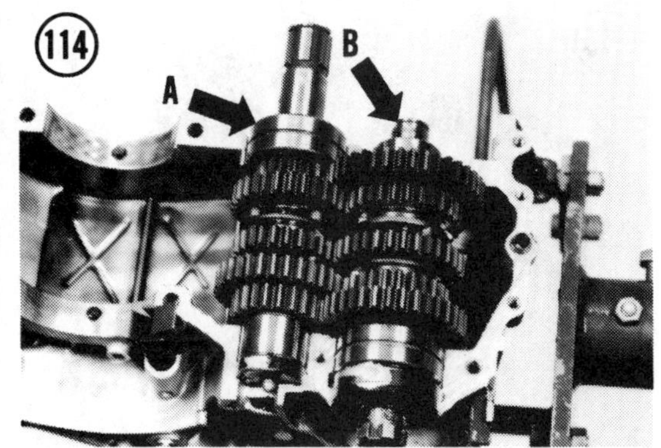

114

115

116

117

4. If necessary, disassemble and inspect the shift forks and transmission assemblies as described in this chapter.

> NOTE
> *Prior to installing the transmission assemblies, coat all bearings with assembly oil.*

5. Make sure that the bearing 1/2 set rings and locating dowels (**Figure 115**) are in place in the lower crankcase half.
6. Position the shift forks so they will engage correctly with the gears.

> NOTE
> *When a new oil seal is installed, apply a light coat of grease to the lips prior to installation.*

7. Install the main shaft assembly (**Figure 116**) and the countershaft assembly (**Figure 117**). Make sure the shift forks engage properly and that the bearings are properly indexed into the set rings and the locating dowels.
8. After the transmission shaft assemblies are installed rotate both by hand. Make sure there is no binding. Also shift through all 5 gears to make sure the shift forks are operating properly and that the transmission gears are properly installed on their respective shafts.
9. Install the crankshaft assembly. Make sure the bearings are indexed into the locating dowels in the crankcase.
10. Assemble the crankcase as described in Chapter Five.

Preliminary Inspection

Prior to disassembling the transmission shaft assemblies, they should be cleaned and inspected. Place the assembled shaft into a large can or plastic bucket and thoroughly clean with solvent and a stiff brush. Dry with compressed air or let it sit on rags to drip dry. Repeat for the other shaft assembly.

1. After they have been cleaned, visually inspect the components of the assemblies for excessive wear. Any burrs, pitting or roughness on the teeth of a gear will cause wear on the mating gear. Minor roughness can be cleaned up with an oilstone, but there's little point in attempting to remove deep scars.

> NOTE
> *Defective gears should be replaced. It's a good idea to replace the mating gear on the other shaft even though it may not show as much wear or damage.*

2. Carefully check the engagement dogs. If any are chipped, worn, rounded or missing, the affected gear must be replaced.
3. If possible, check the runout of each transmission shaft. Mount the shaft in a lathe, on V-blocks or on some other suitable centering device. Place a dial indicator so that its plunger contacts a constant surface near the center of the shaft. Rotate the shaft and record the extremes of the dial readings. The shaft should be replaced if the runout exceeds 0.04 mm (0.0016 in.).
4. Rotate the transmission bearings by hand. Check for roughness, noise and radial play. Any bearing that is suspect should be replaced.
5. If the transmission shafts are satisfactory and are not going to be disassembled, apply engine oil to all components and reinstall them in the crankcase as described.

Main Shaft Disassembly/Inspection/Assembly

Refer to **Figure 112** for the Type III transmission or **Figure 113** for Type IV transmission during this procedure.

NOTE

*A helpful "tool" that should be used for transmission disassembly is a large egg flat (the type that restaurants get their eggs in). As you remove a part from the shaft, set it in one of the depressions in the same position from which it was removed (**Figure 118**). This is an easy way to remember the correct relationship of all parts.*

1. If not cleaned in the *Preliminary Inspection* sequence, place the assembled shaft into a large can or plastic bucket and thoroughly clean with solvent and a stiff brush. Dry with compressed air or let it sit on rags to drip dry.
2A. On Type III transmissions perform the following:
   a. Slide off the needle bearing, the 2nd gear and the 3rd/4th combination gear.
   b. Remove the circlip and splined washer.
   c. Slide off the 5th gear.
2B. On Type IV transmissions, perform the following:
   a. Slide off the oil seal, the needle bearing, the thrust washer and the 2nd gear.
   b. Slide off the 5th gear and the 5th gear bushing.
   c. Slide off the splined washer and remove the circlip.
   d. Slide off the 3rd gear.

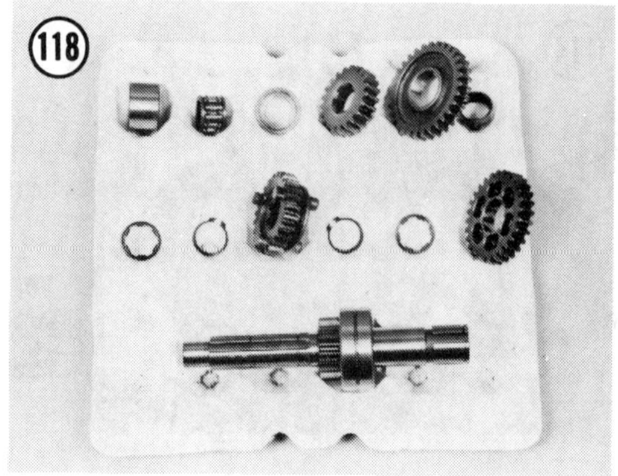
118

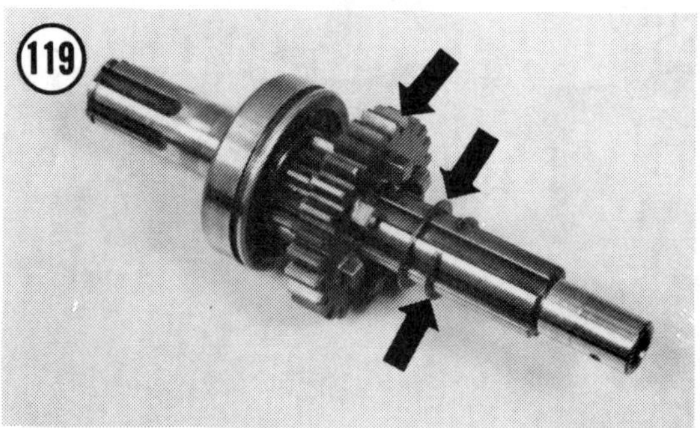
119

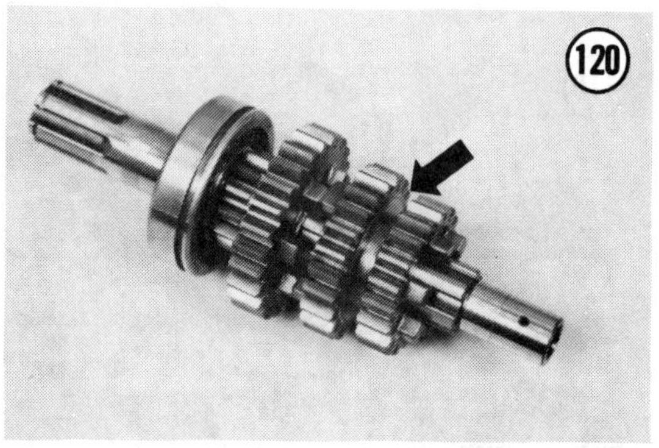
120

121

e. Remove the circlip and splined washer.

f. Slide off the 4th gear.

3. Check each gear for excessive wear, burrs, pitting or chipped or missing teeth. Make sure the lugs on the gears are in good condition.

NOTE

Defective gears should be replaced. It is a good idea to replace the mating gear on the countershaft even though it may not show as much wear or damage.

NOTE

The 1st gear is part of the shaft. If the gear is defective the shaft must be replaced.

4. Make sure that all gears slide smoothly on the main shaft splines.

NOTE

It is a good idea to replace all circlips every other time the transmission is disassembled to ensure proper gear alignment.

5A. On Type III transmissions, perform the following:

a. Slide on the 5th gear and install the splined washer and circlip (**Figure 119**).

b. Slide on the 3rd/4th combination gear with the larger diameter gear on first (**Figure 120**).

c. Slide on the 2nd gear, flush side on last (**Figure 121**).

d. Install the needle bearing assembly (**Figure 122**).

5B. On Type IV transmissions, perform the following:

a. Slide on the 4th gear and install the splined washer and circlip (**Figure 123**).

b. Slide on the 3rd gear and install the circlip and splined washer (**Figure 124**).

d. Align the oil hole in the 5th gear bushing with the oil hole in the main shaft (**Figure 125**). Slide the bushing into place.

e. Install the 5th gear onto the 5th gear bushing (A, **Figure 126**).

f. Slide on the 2nd gear (B, **Figure 126**).
g. Slide on the thrust washer (**Figure 127**).
h. Install the needle bearing assembly (**Figure 128**) and oil seal.

6. After assembly is complete, check for the correct placement of all gears. Refer to **Figure 129** for the Type III transmission or **Figure 130** for the Type IV transmission. Make sure all circlips are seated correctly in the main shaft grooves.

Countershaft Disassembly/Inspection/Assembly

Refer to **Figure 112** for the Type III transmission or **Figure 113** for the Type IV transmission during this procedure.

NOTE
Use the same large egg flat (used on the main shaft disassembly) during the countershaft disassembly. This is an easy way to remember the correct relationship of all parts.

1. If not cleaned in the *Preliminary Inspection* sequence, place the assembled shaft into a large can or plastic bucket and thoroughly clean with solvent and a stiff brush. Dry with compressed air or let it sit on rags to drip dry.

2A. On Type III transmissions, perform the following:

a. Remove the circlip and the thrust washer.
b. Slide off the kickstarter idle gear, the thrust washer and the bearing bushing.
c. Slide off the 1st gear, the thrust washer and the 5th gear.
d. Remove the circlip and splined washer and slide off the 4th gear.
e. Slide off the splined lockwasher. Rotate the splined washer in either direction to disengage the tangs from the raised splines on the transmission shaft. Slide off the splined washer.
f. Slide off the 3rd gear and the splined washer.
g. Remove the circlip and slide off the 2nd gear.

2B. On Type IV transmissions, perform the following:

a. Remove the circlip, the thrust washer with a flat on it, another thrust washer and the kickstarter idle gear.
b. Slide off the thrust washer, the needle bearing, the thrust washer and the 1st gear.
c. Slide off the 4th gear.
d. Remove the circlip and splined washer and slide off the 3rd gear.
e. Slide off the 5th gear.

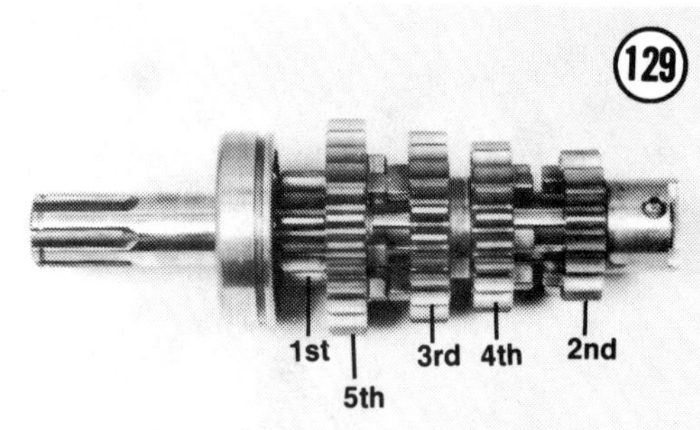

f. The 2nd gear is pressed onto the countershaft. If it is damaged, take the shaft to a dealer and have a new one installed.

3. Check each gear for excessive wear, burrs, pitting or chipped or missing teeth. Make sure the lugs on the gears are in good condition.

NOTE
Defective gears should be replaced. It is a good idea to replace the mating gear on the main shaft even though it may not show as much wear or damage.

4. Make sure that all gears slide smoothly on the countershaft splines.

NOTE
It is a good idea to replace the circlip every other time the transmission is disassembled to ensure proper gear alignment.

5A. On Type III transmissions, perform the following:

a. Slide on the 2nd gear and install the circlip and thrust washer (**Figure 131**).
b. Slide on the 3rd gear (A, **Figure 132**).
c. Slide on the splined washer (B, **Figure 132**). Rotate the washer in either direction so its tangs are engaged into the groove in the raised splines (**Figure 133**) of the countershaft.
d. Slide on the splined lockwasher (**Figure 134**) so that the tangs go into the open areas of the splined washer and lock the washer in place.
e. Slide on the 4th gear, the splined washer and circlip (**Figure 135**).

f. Slide on the 5th gear and thrust washer (**Figure 136**).
g. Slide on the 1st gear with the flush side on last (A, **Figure 137**).
h. Slide on the bearing bushing (B, **Figure 137**).
i. Slide on the thrust washer, kickstarter idle gear and thrust washer.
j. Install the circlip.

5B. On Type IV transmissions, perform the following:

a. Slide on the 5th gear (**Figure 138**).
b. Slide on the 3rd gear and and install the splined washer and the circlip (**Figure 139**).
c. Slide on the 4th gear (**Figure 140**).
d. Slide on the 1st gear, thrust washer and roller bearing (**Figure 141**).
e. Slide on the thrust washer, kickstarter idle gear, the thrust washer and the thrust washer with a flat on it.
f. Install the circlip.

6. After assembly is complete, check for the correct placement of all gears. Refer to **Figure 142** for the Type III transmission or **Figure 143** for the Type IV transmission. Make sure all circlips are seated correctly in the main shaft grooves.

NOTE
After both transmission shafts have been assembled, mesh the 2 assemblies together in the correct position. Refer to ***Figure 144*** *for Type III or* ***Figure 145*** *for Type IV transmissions. Check that all gears meet correctly. This is your last check prior to installing the assemblies into the crankcase; make sure they are correctly assembled.*

INTERNAL SHIFT MECHANISM

The internal shift mechanism for 100 and 125 cc models is removed during transmission shaft

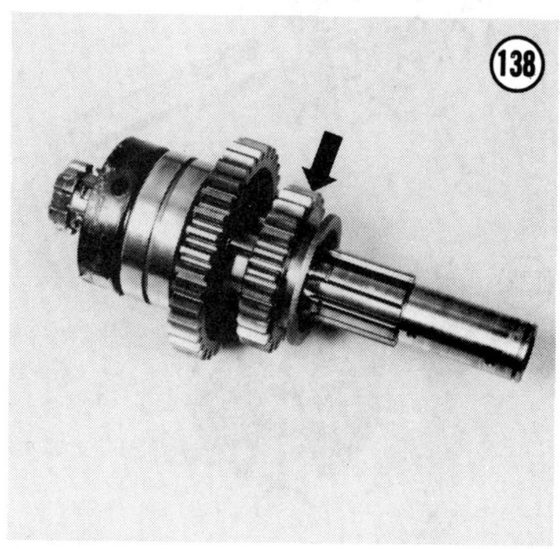

140

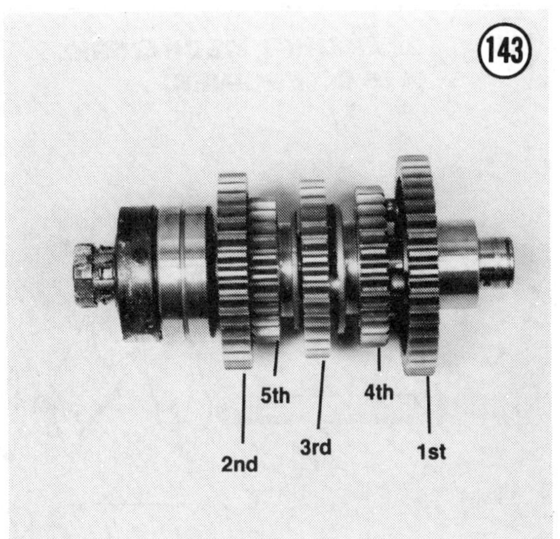
143
5th
4th
2nd
3rd
1st

141

144

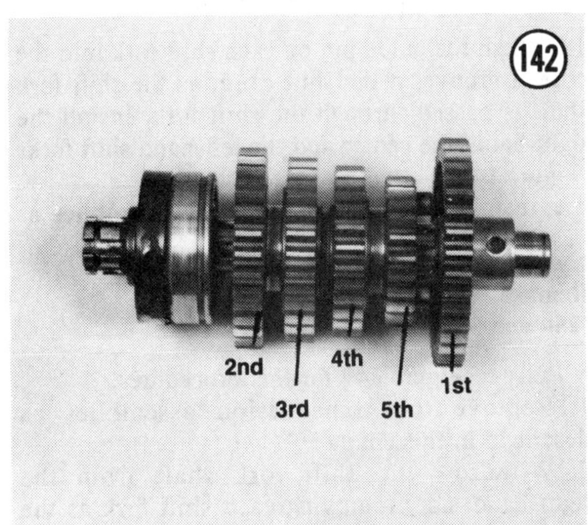
142
2nd
4th
1st
3rd
5th

145

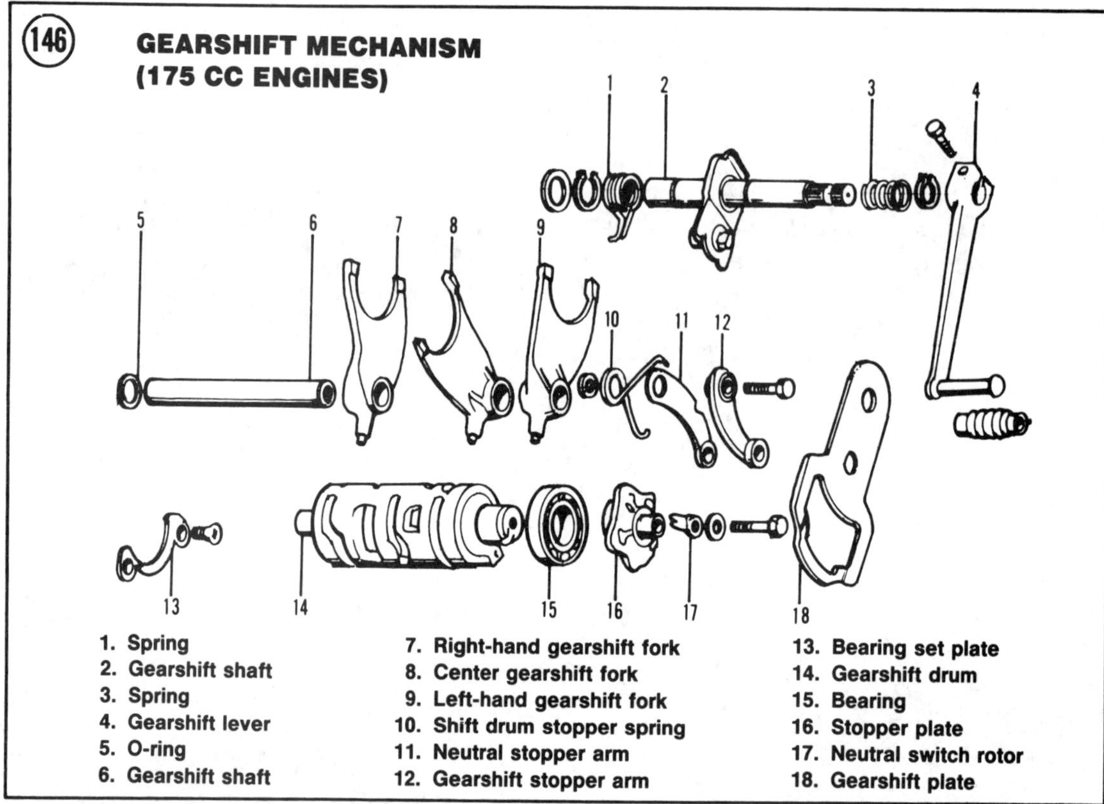

1. Spring
2. Gearshift shaft
3. Spring
4. Gearshift lever
5. O-ring
6. Gearshift shaft
7. Right-hand gearshift fork
8. Center gearshift fork
9. Left-hand gearshift fork
10. Shift drum stopper spring
11. Neutral stopper arm
12. Gearshift stopper arm
13. Bearing set plate
14. Gearshift drum
15. Bearing
16. Stopper plate
17. Neutral switch rotor
18. Gearshift plate

assembly removal; therefore, it is covered in the transmission procedure in this chapter. Once it is removed, inspect it as described here.

Removal/Installation (175 cc Engines)

Refer to **Figure 146** for this procedure.

1. Remove the transmission assemblies as described in this chapter.
2. Withdraw the shift fork shaft from the right-hand side, removing each shift fork as the shaft is withdrawn.
3. Remove the screws (A, **Figure 147**) securing the shift drum bearing set plate on the left-hand side of the crankcase. Remove the set plate.
4. Withdraw the shift drum (B, **Figure 147**) from the left-hand side.
5. Wash all parts in solvent and thoroughly dry.
6. Inspect all components as described in this chapter.
7. Coat all bearing surfaces with assembly oil.
8. Install the shift drum from the left-hand side and install the bearing set plate. Tighten the set plate screws securely.

NOTE
After the shift drum is installed, make sure it rotates smoothly with no binding.

9. Partially insert the shift fork shaft.

NOTE
Each shift fork is marked with an "R," "C" or "L" to identify its specific location. Do not interchange them.

10. Mesh the guide pin on each shift fork into the correct groove in the shift drum as the shift fork shaft is passed through the shift fork. Install the right-hand, the center and the left-hand shift forks (**Figure 148**).
11. Install the transmission shaft assemblies as described in this chapter.

Removal/Installation (250 and 350 cc Engines)

Refer to **Figure 149** for this procedure.

1. Remove the transmission assemblies as described in this chapter.
2. Withdraw the shift fork shaft from the right-hand side, removing each shift fork as the shaft is withdrawn.

147

148

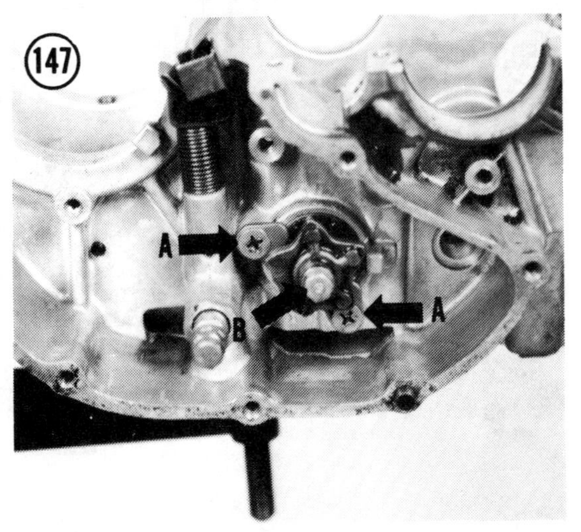

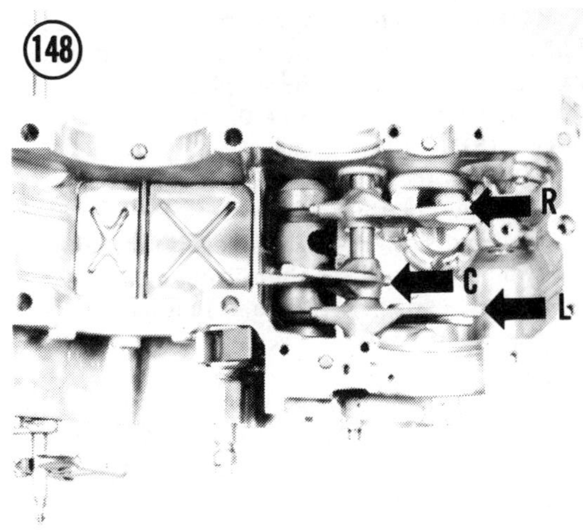

149

GEARSHIFT MECHANISM
(250 AND 350 CC ENGINES)

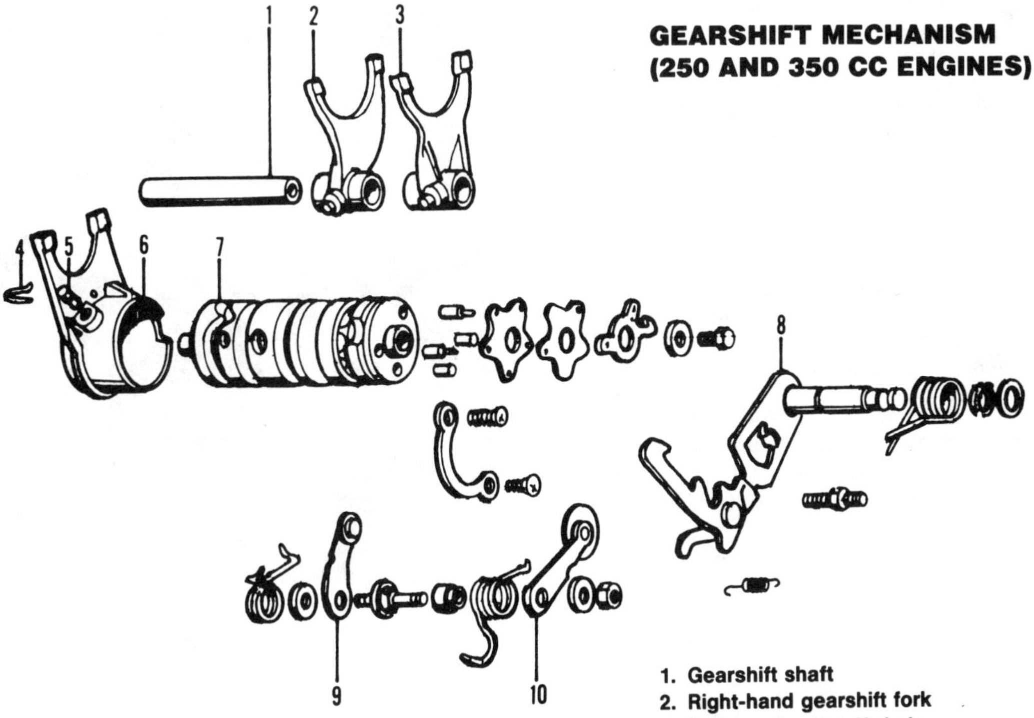

1. Gearshift shaft
2. Right-hand gearshift fork
3. Left-hand gearshift fork
4. Clip
5. Pin
6. Center gearshift fork
7. Gearshift drum
8. Gearshift shaft assembly
9. Neutral stopper arm
10. Gearshift stopper arm

3. Remove the screws (A, **Figure 150**) securing the shift drum bearing set plate on the left-hand side of the crankcase. Remove the set plate.
4. Remove the clip securing the shift fork set pin (**Figure 151**).
5. Withdraw the shift fork set pin.
6. Withdraw the shift drum (B, **Figure 150**) from the left-hand side. Hold onto the large center shift fork while removing the shift drum.
7. Wash all parts in solvent and thoroughly dry.
8. Inspect all components as described in this chapter.
9. Coat all bearing surfaces with assembly oil.
10. Partially install the shift drum. Position the large center shift fork (with the longer shoulder toward the left-hand side) and slide the shift drum all the way in until it seats completely in the crankcase.
11. Position the large center shift fork so the set pin hole is located on the middle shift drum groove.
12. Install the shift drum set pin and install the set pin clip (**Figure 151**).

NOTE
After the shift drum is installed, make sure it rotates smoothly with no binding.

13. Partially insert the shift fork shaft.

NOTE
Each shift fork is marked with an "R" or "L" to identify its specific location. Install the shift forks with the longer shoulder toward the left-hand side.

14. Mesh the guide pin on each shift fork into the correct groove in the shift drum as the shift fork shaft is passed through the shift fork. Install the right-hand and the left-hand shift forks (**Figure 152**).
15. Install the transmission shaft assemblies as described in this chapter.

Inspection (All Models)

NOTE
Prior to removal or disassembly of any of the components, lay the assembly down on a piece of paper or cardboard and carefully trace around it. Write down the identifying numbers and letter next to each item. This will take a little extra time now but it may save some time and frustration later.

1. Inspect each shift fork for signs of wear or cracking. Check for bending and make sure each

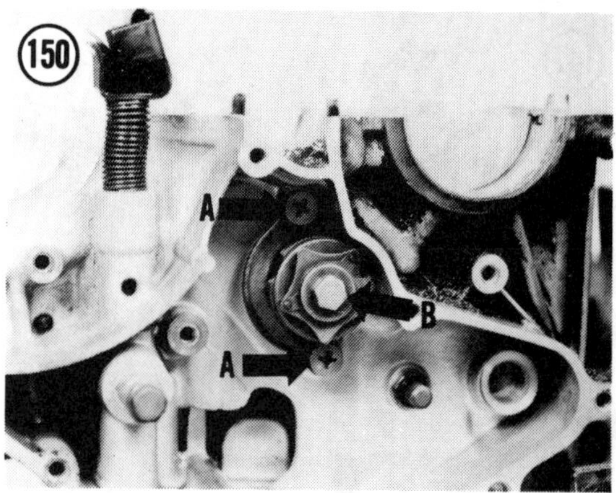

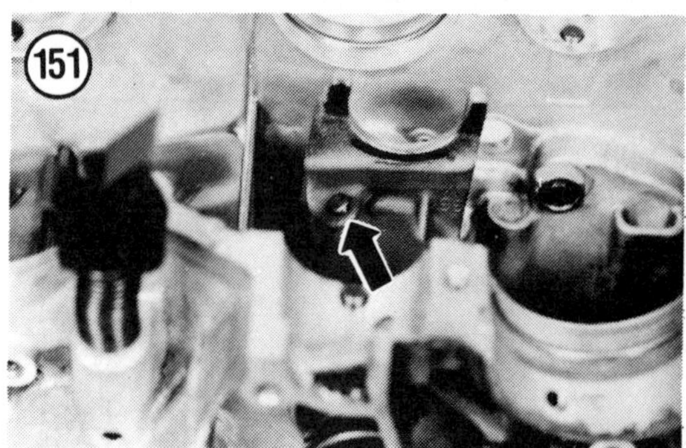

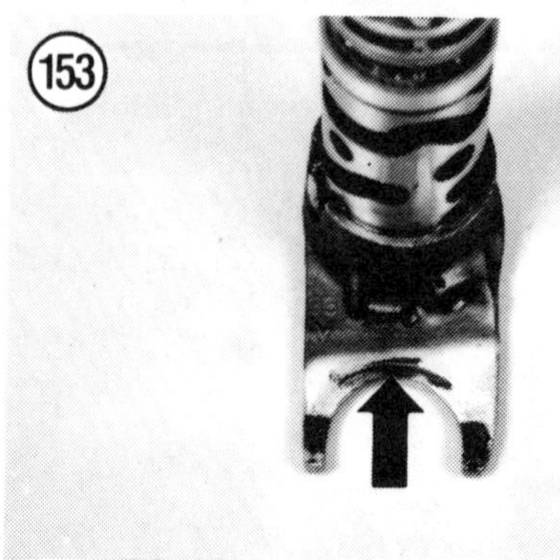

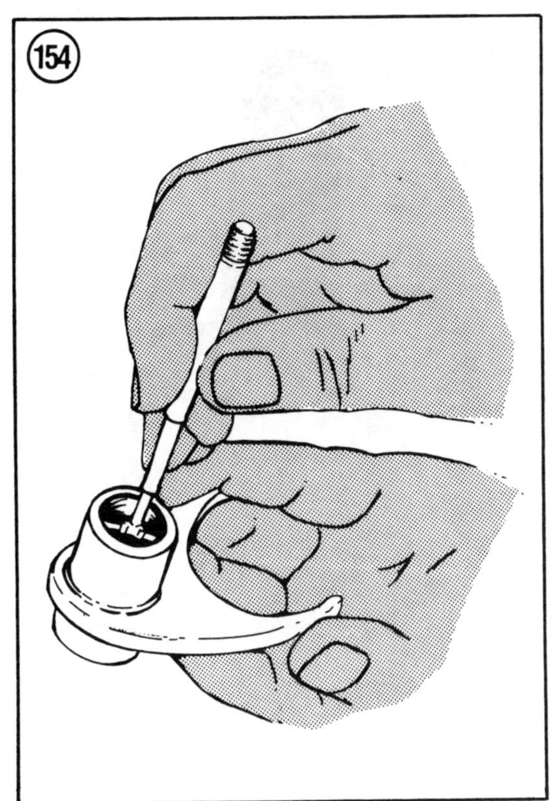

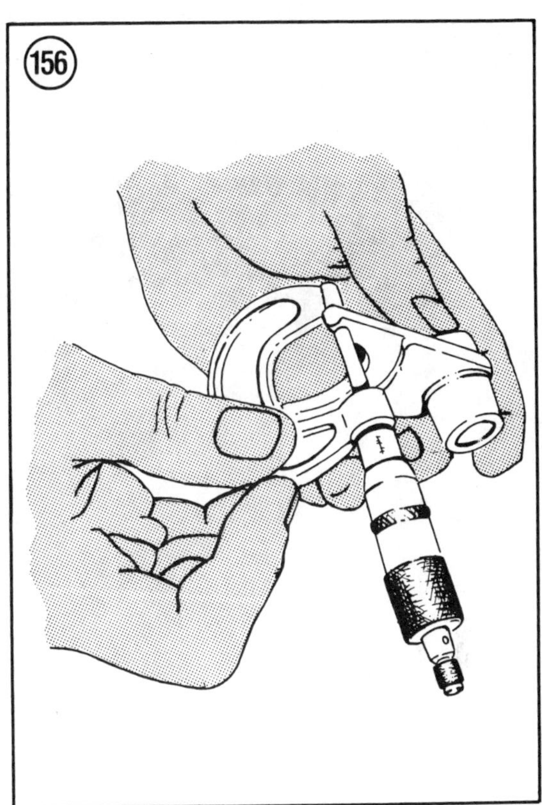

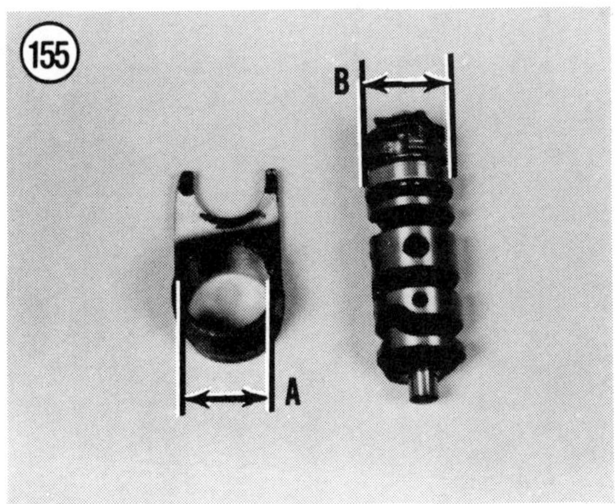

fork slides smoothly on the shaft. Replace any worn or damaged forks.

2. Check for any arc-shaped wear or burned marks on the shift forks (**Figure 153**). This indicates that the shift fork has come in contact with the gear. The fork fingers have become excessively worn and the fork must be replaced.

3. Measure the inside diameter of each shift fork with an inside micrometer or snap gauge (**Figure 154**). Replace any that are worn to the service limit listed in **Table 2**.

4. On Type IV transmissions, measure the inside diameter of the large center shift drum (A, **Figure 155**). Replace if worn to the dimension listed in **Table 2**.

5. On Type IV transmissions, measure the outside diameter of the shift drum (B, **Figure 155**). Replace if worn to the service limit listed in **Table 2**.

6. Measure the width of the gearshift fork fingers with a micrometer (**Figure 156**). Replace any that are worn to the service limit listed in **Table 2**.

7. Check the shift drum dowel pin on each shift fork for wear or damage; replace as necessary.

8. Roll the shift fork shaft on a flat surface such as a piece of plate glass and check for any bends. If the shaft is bent, it must be replaced.

9. Measure the outside diameter of the shift fork shaft with a micrometer. Replace if worn to the service limit listed in **Table 2**.

10. Check the grooves in the shift drum (**Figure 157**) for wear or roughness. If any of the groove profiles have excessive wear or damage, replace the shift drum.

11. Inspect the ramps of the stopper plate (**Figure 158**) for wear; replace if necessary.

12. Apply a light coat of oil to the shift fork shaft and the inside bores of the shift forks prior to installation.

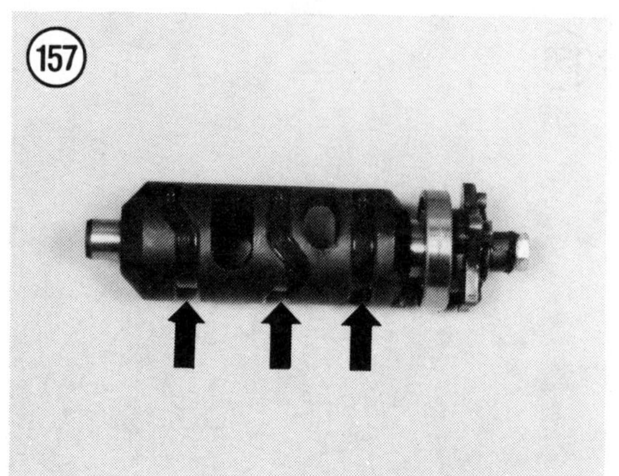
157

158

Table 1 CLUTCH SPECIFICATIONS

Item	Standard	Wear Limit
Friction disc thickness		
100 and 125 cc	2.9-3.0 mm (0.11-0.12 in.)	2.6 mm (0.10 in.)
250 and 350 cc	2.7 mm (0.106 in.)	2.3 mm (0.091 in.)
Clutch plate and disc warpage		
100 and 125 cc	0.1 mm (0.0039 in.)	0.20 mm (0.008 in.)
250 and 350 cc	0.15 mm (0.006 in.)	0.30 mm (0.012 in.)
Clutch springs free length		
XL100, XL125, CT125	35.5 mm (1.3976 in.)	32 mm (1.260 in.)
All other 100 and 125 cc	N.A.	N.A.
XL175	28.26 mm (1.113 in.)	27.0 mm (1.063 in.)
250 and 350 cc	35.5 mm (1.40 in.)	34.2 mm (1.35 in.)

N.A. = Information not available.

6

Table 2 SHIFT FORK AND SHAFT SPECIFICATIONS

Item	Specifications	Wear Limit
Shift fork ID		
XL100, XL125, CT125	12.000-12.018 mm (0.4724-0.4731 in.)	12.05 mm (0.474 in.)
All other 100 and 125 cc	N.A.	N.A.
175 cc	13.000-13.018 mm (0.5118-0.5125 in.)	12.95 mm (0.5098 in.)
250 and 350 cc		
Left and right	13.000-13.018 mm (0.5118-0.5125 in.)	12.95 mm (0.5098 in.)
Center	36.00-36.025 mm (1.4173-1.4183 in.)	36.075 mm (1.4203 in.)
Shift fork finger thickness		
XL100, XL125, CT125	4.93-5.00 mm (0.1941-0.1969 in.)	4.70 mm (0.1859 in.)
All other 100 and 125 cc	N.A.	N.A.
175 cc	5.36-5.44 mm (0.2110-0.2142 in.)	5.0 mm (0.1969 in.)
250 and 350 cc	4.93-5.00 mm (0.1941-0.1969 in.)	4.70 mm (0.1859 in.)
Shift fork shaft OD		
XL100, XL125, CT125	11.976-11.994 mm (0.4715-0.4722 in.)	11.96 mm (0.471 in.)
All other 100 and 125 cc	N.A.	N.A.
175 cc	12.966-12.984 mm (0.5117-0.5118 in.)	12.90 mm (0.5079 in.)
Gear shift drum OD		
250 and 350	35.950-35.975 mm (1.4153-1.4163 in.)	35.9 mm (1.1413 in.)

N.A. = Information not available.

CHAPTER SEVEN

FUEL AND EXHAUST SYSTEMS

The fuel system consists of the fuel tank, the shutoff valve, a single carburetor and the air cleaner. Shutoff valve service is described in Chapter Three.

The exhaust system consists of an exhaust pipe, muffler and a tail pipe.

This chapter includes service procedures for all parts of the fuel system and exhaust system. Carburetor specifications are in **Table 1** at the end of the chapter.

AIR CLEANER

The air cleaner must be cleaned frequently. Refer to Chapter Three for specific procedures and service intervals.

CARBURETOR OPERATION

For proper operation a gasoline engine must be supplied with fuel and air mixed in proper proportions by weight. A mixture in which there is an excess of fuel is said to be rich. A lean mixture is one which contains insufficient fuel. A properly adjusted carburetor supplies the proper mixture to the engine under all operating conditions.

The carburetor consists of several major systems. A float and float valve mechanism maintain a constant fuel level in the float bowl. The pilot system supplies fuel at low speeds. The main fuel system supplies fuel at medium and high speeds. A starter (choke) system supplies the very rich mixture needed to start a cold engine.

CARBURETOR SERVICE

Major carburetor service (removal and cleaning) should be performed at the intervals indicated in Table 1 in Chapter Three or when poor engine performance, hesitation and little or no response to mixture adjustment is observed. Alterations in jet size and throttle slide cutaway and changes in jet needle position, etc., should be attempted only if you're experienced in this type of "tuning" work; a bad guess could result in costly engine damage or, at least, poor performance. If, after servicing the carburetor and making the adjustments described in this chapter, the bike does not perform correctly (and assuming that other factors affecting performance are correct, such as ignition timing and condition, etc.), the bike should be checked by a dealer or a qualified performance tuning specialist.

Removal/Installation

1. Place a wood block(s) under the engine to support it securely.
2. Remove both side covers and the seat.
3. Turn the fuel shutoff valve to the S or OFF position and remove the fuel line to the carburetor.
4. Remove the fuel tank as described in this chapter.
5. Place a metal container under the drain tube and open the drain screw on the carburetor. Drain out all fuel from the float bowl.

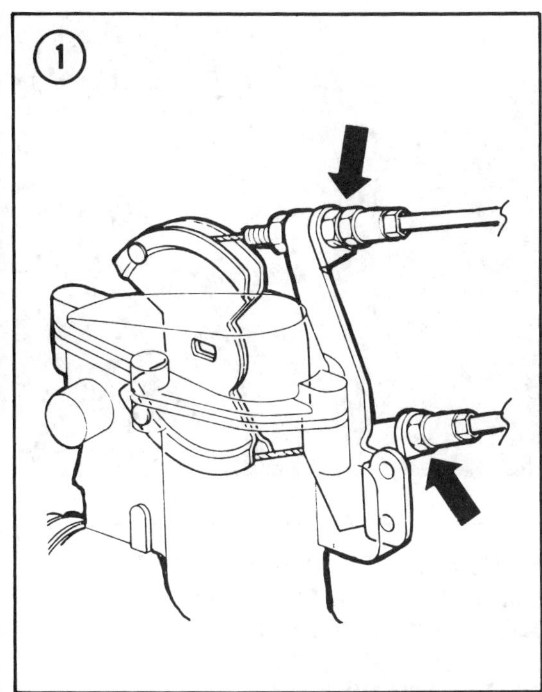

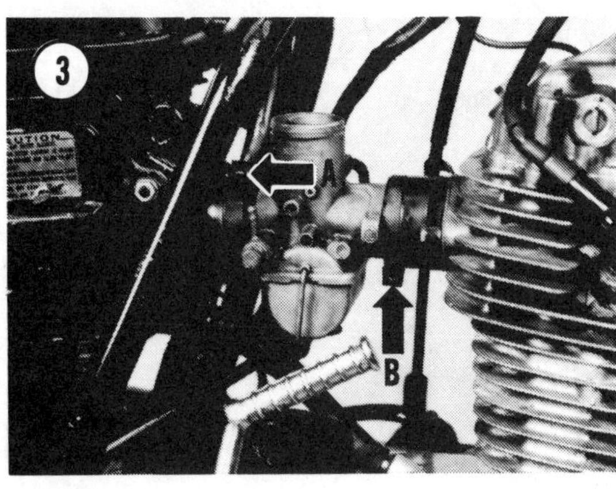

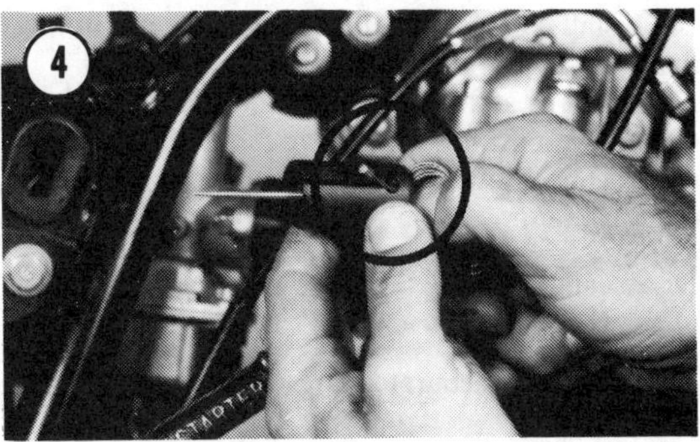

6A. On 250 and 350 cc models, loosen the locknuts on both cables and disconnect the throttle cables from the carburetor (**Figure 1**).

NOTE
Prior to removing the top cap, thoroughly clean the area around it so no dirt will fall into the carburetor.

6B. On all other models, unscrew the carburetor top cap (**Figure 2**) and pull the throttle valve assembly up and out of the carburetor.

NOTE
If the top cap and throttle valve assembly are not going to be removed from the throttle cable for cleaning, wrap them in a clean shop cloth or place them in a plastic bag to help keep them clean.

7. On models equipped with a choke cable, remove the choke cable from the carburetor and tie the loose end up and out of the way.
8. Loosen the clamping screw (A, **Figure 3**) on the rubber boot going to the air cleaner assembly. Slide the clamp off and away from the carburetor.
9. Either remove the nuts securing the carburetor to the rubber intake tube or loosen the clamping screws (B, **Figure 3**) securing the carburetor to the rubber intake tube on the cylinder head.
10. Note the routing of the carburetor overflow and vent tubes through the frame, then carefully pull all of them free. Leave them attached to the carburetor.
11. Carefully work the carburetor free from the rubber boot and remove it.
12. Take the carburetor to a workbench for disassembly and cleaning.
13. To remove the throttle valve from the throttle cable, depress the throttle spring away from the throttle valve. Push the throttle cable end down and out along the groove in the side of the throttle valve (**Figure 4**). Remove the throttle valve and needle jet assembly.

14. Install by reversing these removal steps, noting the following.
15. When installing the throttle valve into the carburetor, position the groove in the throttle slide toward the throttle adjust screw (**Figure 5**) side of the carburetor.

Disassembly (Type I)

The Type I carburetor is used on the following models:

a. **Figure 6**—All CB100, all CL100, all SL100, XL100 through 1976, CB125S through 1978, all SL125, TL125 and TL125 K1-K2.
b. **Figure 7**—All CT125 and XL125.
c. **Figure 8**—1976 TL125.

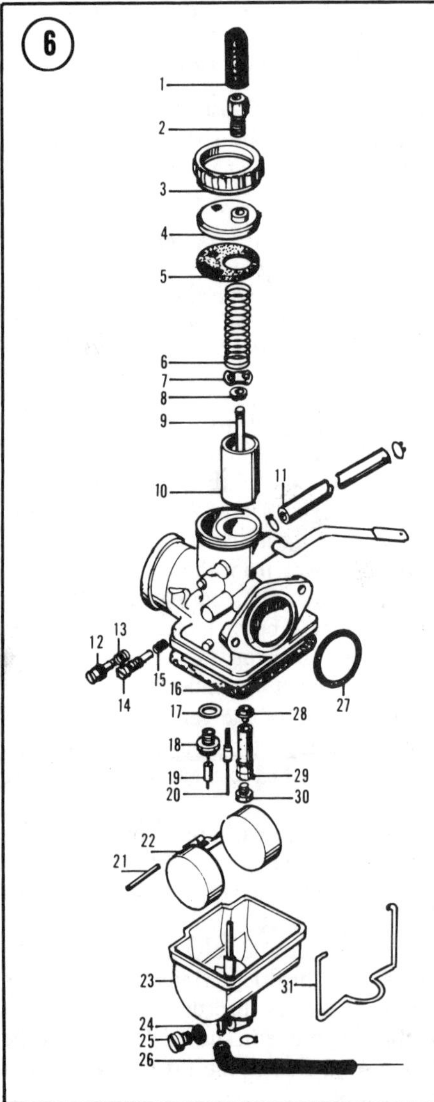

CARBURETOR ASSEMBLY TYPE I (ALL CB100, ALL CL100, ALL SL100, XL100 THROUGH 1976, CB125S THROUGH 1978, ALL SL125, TL125 AND TL125 K1-K2)

1. Cap
2. Cable adjuster
3. Cap
4. Lid
5. Gasket
6. Spring
7. Needle clip plate
8. Needle clip
9. Jet needle
10. Throttle valve
11. Fuel line
12. Air screw
13. Spring
14. Throttle adjust screw
15. Spring
16. Float bowl gasket
17. Gasket
18. Valve seat
19. Float valve
20. Slow jet
21. Float pivot pin
22. Float assembly
23. Float bowl
24. Gasket
25. Drain screw
26. Drain tube
27. O-ring
28. Needle jet
29. Needle jet holder
30. Main jet
31. Float bowl clip

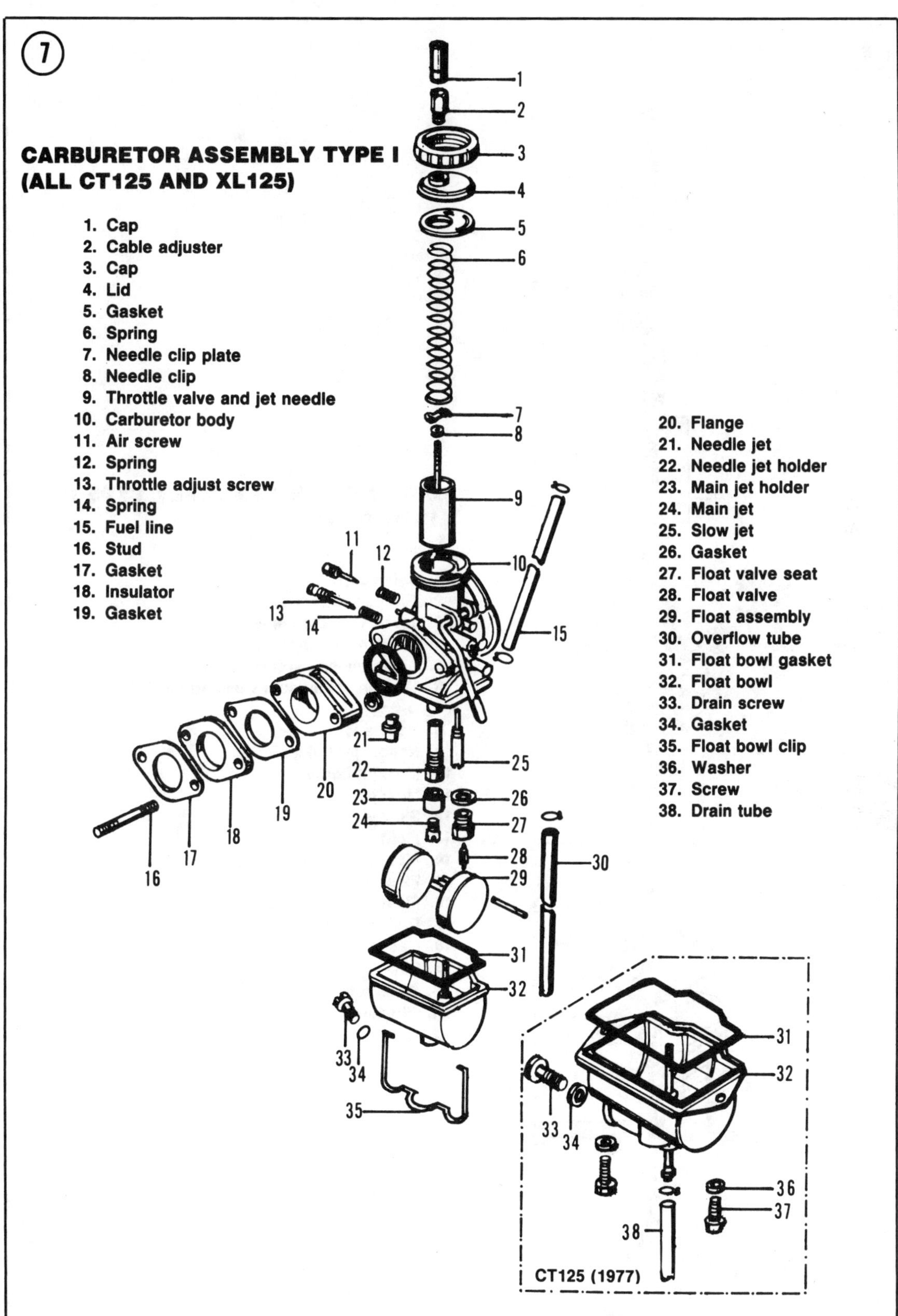
7
CARBURETOR ASSEMBLY TYPE I
(ALL CT125 AND XL125)
1. Cap
2. Cable adjuster
3. Cap
4. Lid
5. Gasket
6. Spring
7. Needle clip plate
8. Needle clip
9. Throttle valve and jet needle
10. Carburetor body
11. Air screw
12. Spring
13. Throttle adjust screw
14. Spring
15. Fuel line
16. Stud
17. Gasket
18. Insulator
19. Gasket
20. Flange
21. Needle jet
22. Needle jet holder
23. Main jet holder
24. Main jet
25. Slow jet
26. Gasket
27. Float valve seat
28. Float valve
29. Float assembly
30. Overflow tube
31. Float bowl gasket
32. Float bowl
33. Drain screw
34. Gasket
35. Float bowl clip
36. Washer
37. Screw
38. Drain tube
CT125 (1977)

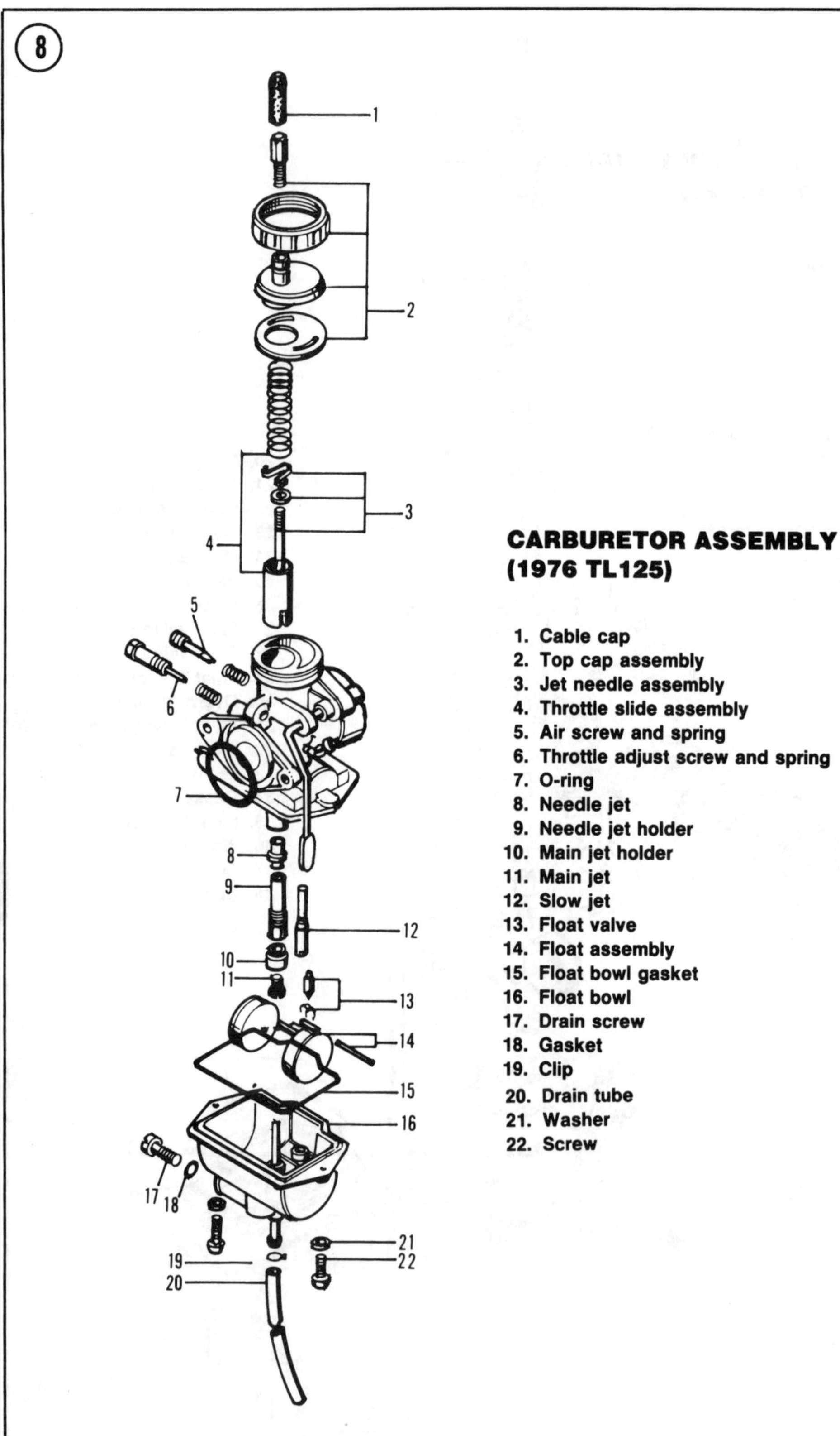

CARBURETOR ASSEMBLY TYPE I (1976 TL125)

1. Cable cap
2. Top cap assembly
3. Jet needle assembly
4. Throttle slide assembly
5. Air screw and spring
6. Throttle adjust screw and spring
7. O-ring
8. Needle jet
9. Needle jet holder
10. Main jet holder
11. Main jet
12. Slow jet
13. Float valve
14. Float assembly
15. Float bowl gasket
16. Float bowl
17. Drain screw
18. Gasket
19. Clip
20. Drain tube
21. Washer
22. Screw

d. **Figure 9**—All XL175.
e. **Figure 10**—All TL250.

1. Remove the drain tube.
2. Slide off the clip (**Figure 11**) or remove the screws securing the float bowl and remove the float bowl.
3. Remove the float pin and remove the float (**Figure 12**).
4. Remove the float valve (A, **Figure 13**).
5. If necessary, remove the float valve assembly (B, **Figure 13**).
6. Remove the main jet and the main jet holder (**Figure 14**).
7. Remove the needle jet holder (**Figure 15**) and needle jet.

NOTE
Turn the carburetor over and catch the needle jet as it falls out into your hand.

8. Remove the slow jet (**Figure 16**).

NOTE
*Prior to removing the air screw, carefully screw it in until it **lightly** seats. Count and record the number of turns so it can be installed in the same position.*

9. Unscrew the air screw (A, **Figure 17**) and remove the spring washer and the O-ring seal.
10. Remove the throttle adjust screw and spring (B, **Figure 17**).

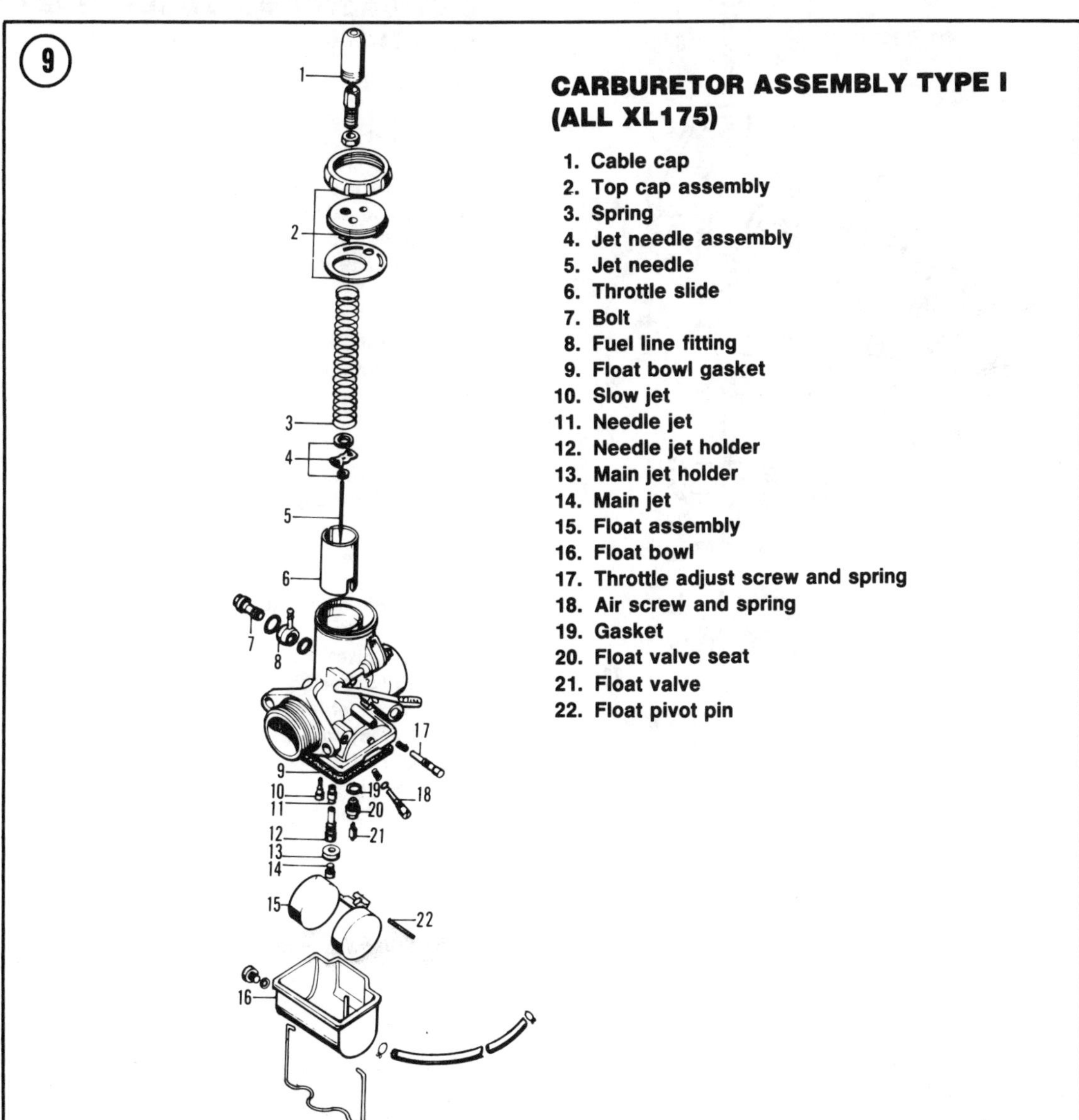

CARBURETOR ASSEMBLY TYPE I (ALL XL175)

1. Cable cap
2. Top cap assembly
3. Spring
4. Jet needle assembly
5. Jet needle
6. Throttle slide
7. Bolt
8. Fuel line fitting
9. Float bowl gasket
10. Slow jet
11. Needle jet
12. Needle jet holder
13. Main jet holder
14. Main jet
15. Float assembly
16. Float bowl
17. Throttle adjust screw and spring
18. Air screw and spring
19. Gasket
20. Float valve seat
21. Float valve
22. Float pivot pin

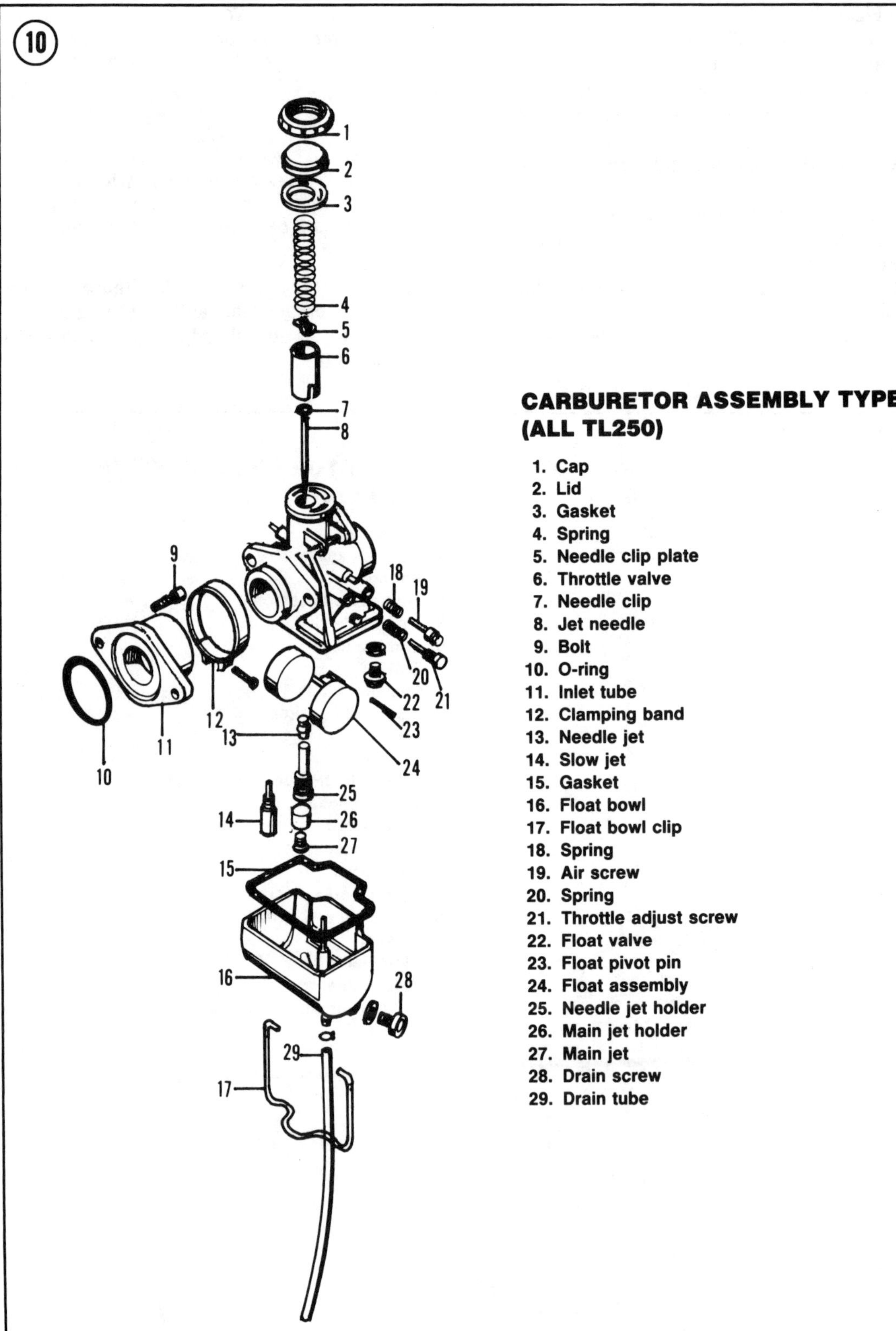

CARBURETOR ASSEMBLY TYPE I (ALL TL250)

1. Cap
2. Lid
3. Gasket
4. Spring
5. Needle clip plate
6. Throttle valve
7. Needle clip
8. Jet needle
9. Bolt
10. O-ring
11. Inlet tube
12. Clamping band
13. Needle jet
14. Slow jet
15. Gasket
16. Float bowl
17. Float bowl clip
18. Spring
19. Air screw
20. Spring
21. Throttle adjust screw
22. Float valve
23. Float pivot pin
24. Float assembly
25. Needle jet holder
26. Main jet holder
27. Main jet
28. Drain screw
29. Drain tube

11

12

13
A
B

14

15

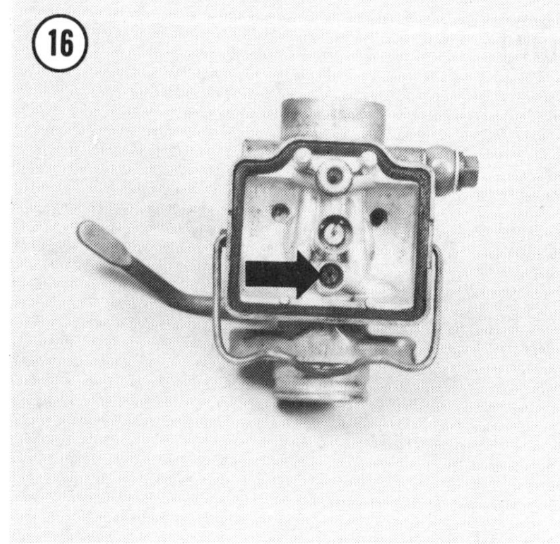
16

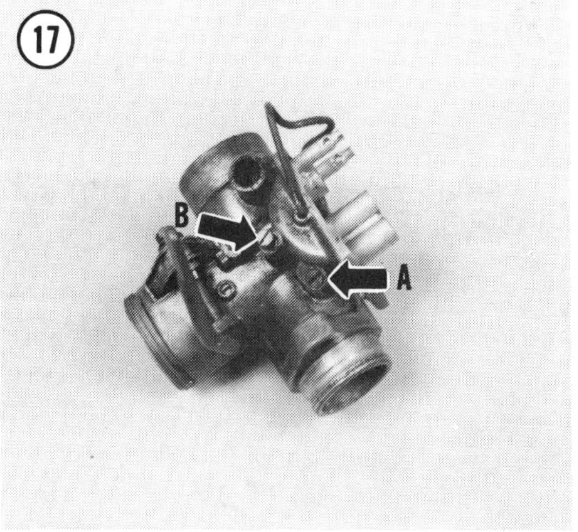
17
B
A

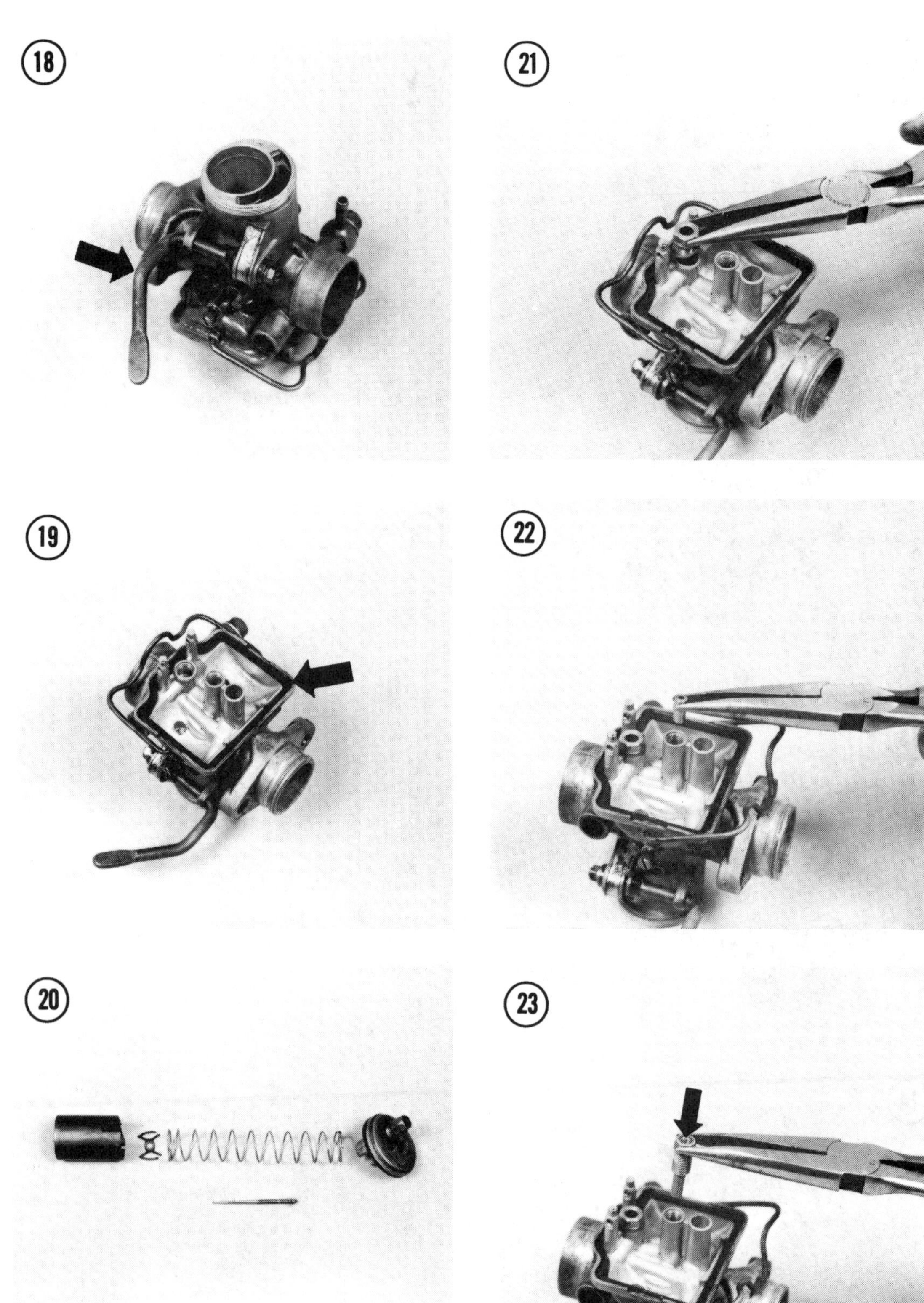
18
21
19
22
20
23

24

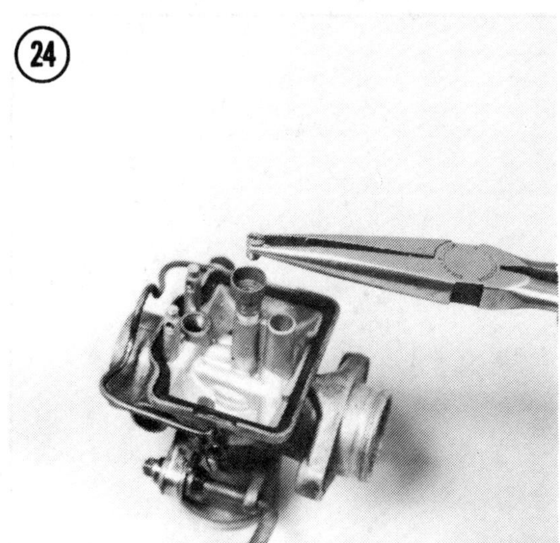

11. Remove the choke assembly (**Figure 18**).
12. Remove the float bowl seal from the carburetor body (**Figure 19**).
13. Disassemble the throttle valve assembly (**Figure 20**).

NOTE
If the needle jet clip is going to be removed, record the clip position on the needle prior to removal.

NOTE
Further disassembly is neither necessary nor recommended. If throttle or choke shafts or butterflies are damaged, take the carburetor body to a dealer for replacement.

14. Clean and inspect the carburetor components as described in this chapter.

Assembly

1. Install a new float bowl seal in the carburetor body.

NOTE
*Install the air screw to its original position as noted in **Disassembly** Step 9.*

2. Install the throttle adjust screw, the air screw and the choke assembly.
3. Install the float valve assembly and gasket (**Figure 21**).
4. Install the needle jet (**Figure 22**) with the chamfered side facing *up* toward the needle jet holder.
5. Install the needle jet holder (**Figure 23**).
6. Install the main jet holder and the main jet (**Figure 24**).
7. Install the slow jet (**Figure 16**).
8. Install the float assembly and the float pin (**Figure 12**).
9. Install the needle jet clip in the correct groove; refer to **Table 1** at the end of this chapter. Assemble the throttle valve assembly.
10. Check the float height and adjust if necessary as described in this chapter.
12. After the carburetor has been disassembled, the idle speed and mixture should be adjusted. Refer to *Idle Speed and Mixture Adjustment* in this chapter.

7

Disassembly/Assembly (Type II)

The Type II carburetor is used on the following models:
a. **Figure 25**—1977-1978 XL100.
b. **Figure 26**—1979-on CB125S.
1. Remove the drain tube.
2. Remove the screws (**Figure 27**) securing the float bowl and remove the float bowl.
3. Remove the main jet holder.
4. Remove the main jet (**Figure 28**).
5. Remove the needle jet holder (**Figure 29**) and needle jet.

NOTE
Turn the carburetor over and catch the needle jet as it falls out into your hand.

6. Remove the float pivot pin (**Figure 30**) and remove the float.

NOTE
*Prior to removing the pilot screw, carefully screw it in until it **lightly** seats. Count and record the number of turns so it can be installed in the same position.*

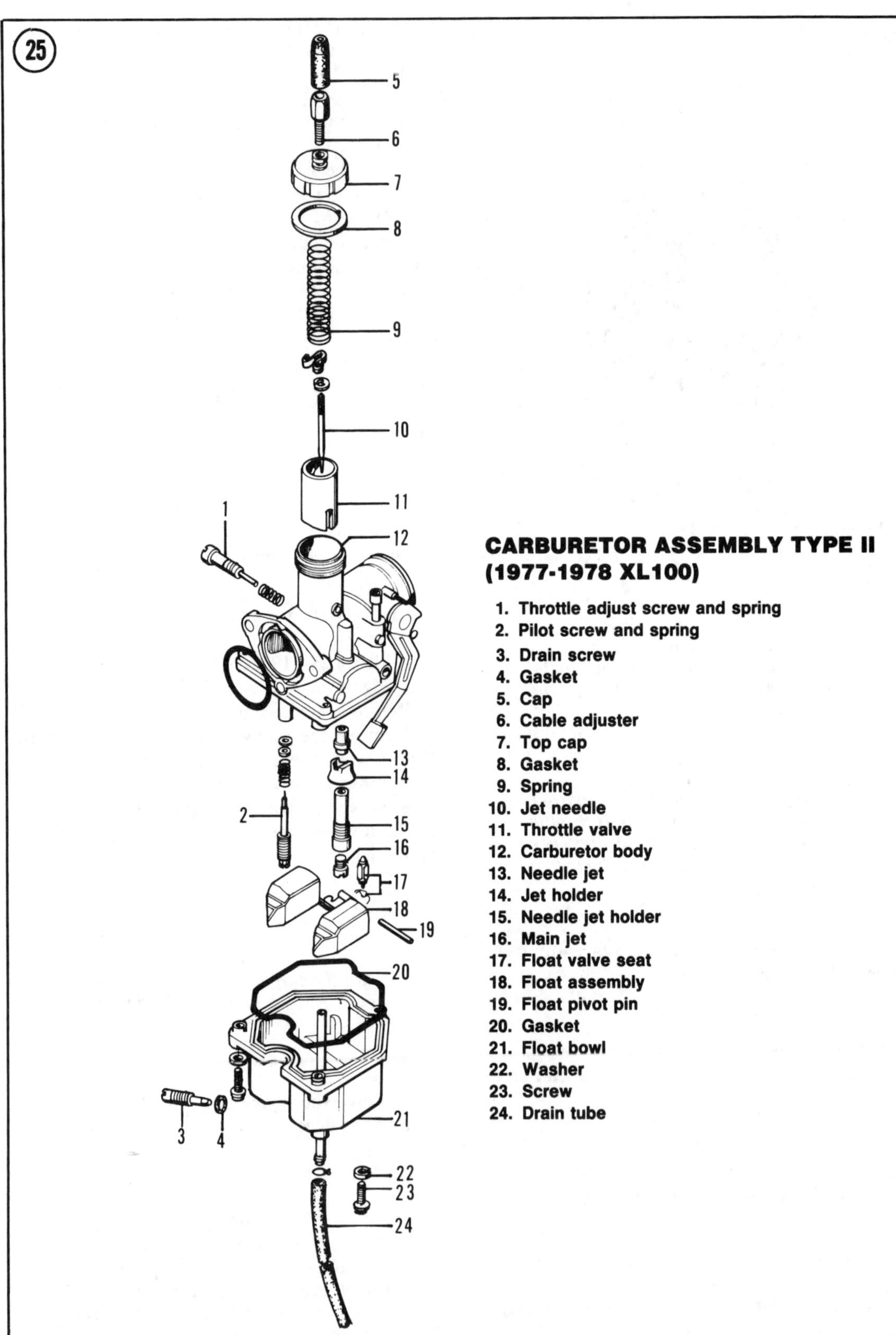

CARBURETOR ASSEMBLY TYPE II (1977-1978 XL100)

1. Throttle adjust screw and spring
2. Pilot screw and spring
3. Drain screw
4. Gasket
5. Cap
6. Cable adjuster
7. Top cap
8. Gasket
9. Spring
10. Jet needle
11. Throttle valve
12. Carburetor body
13. Needle jet
14. Jet holder
15. Needle jet holder
16. Main jet
17. Float valve seat
18. Float assembly
19. Float pivot pin
20. Gasket
21. Float bowl
22. Washer
23. Screw
24. Drain tube

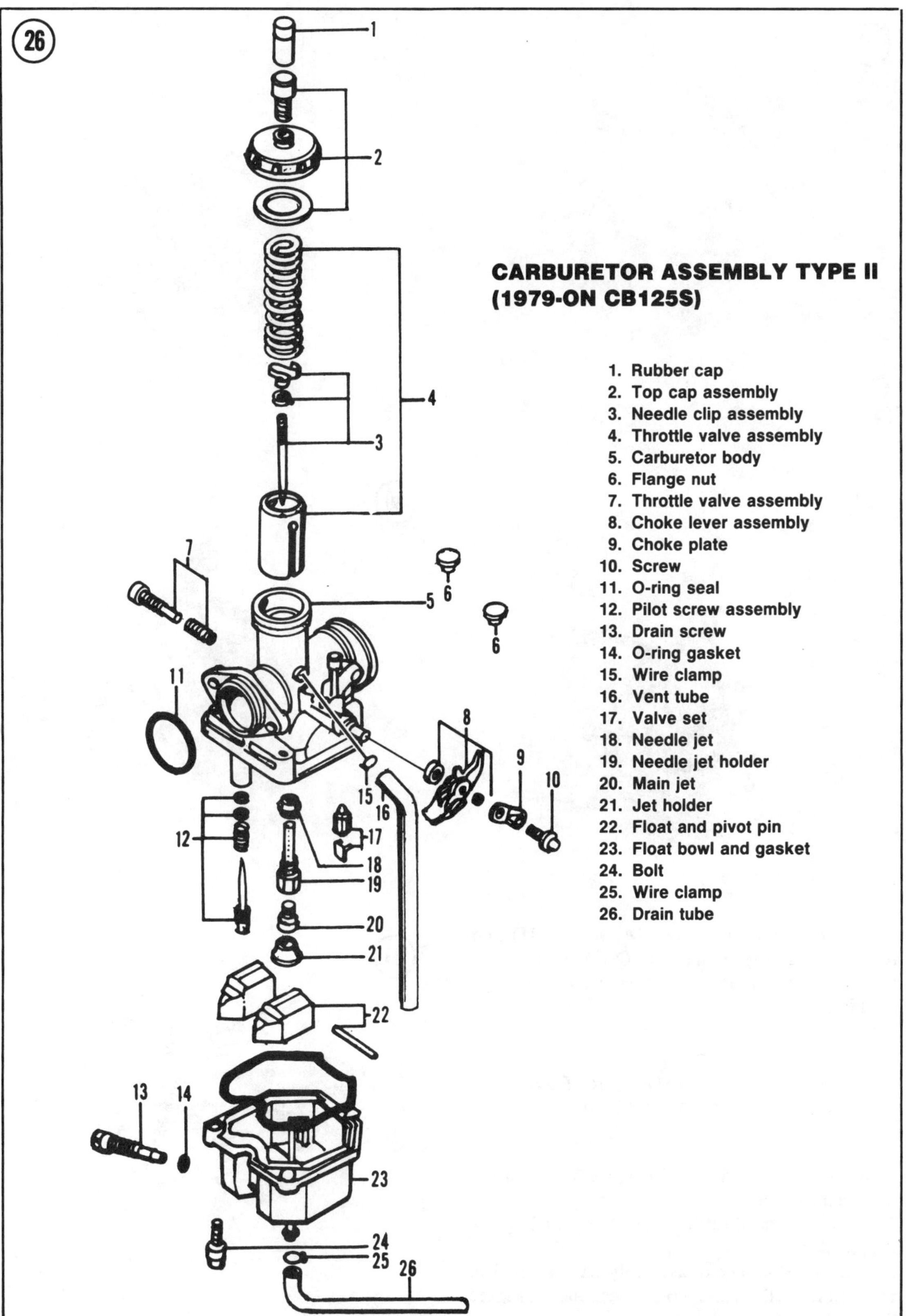
26
CARBURETOR ASSEMBLY TYPE II
(1979-ON CB125S)
1. Rubber cap
2. Top cap assembly
3. Needle clip assembly
4. Throttle valve assembly
5. Carburetor body
6. Flange nut
7. Throttle valve assembly
8. Choke lever assembly
9. Choke plate
10. Screw
11. O-ring seal
12. Pilot screw assembly
13. Drain screw
14. O-ring gasket
15. Wire clamp
16. Vent tube
17. Valve set
18. Needle jet
19. Needle jet holder
20. Main jet
21. Jet holder
22. Float and pivot pin
23. Float bowl and gasket
24. Bolt
25. Wire clamp
26. Drain tube
1
2
3
4
5
6
6
7
8
9
10
11
12
13
14
15
16
17
18
19
20
21
22
23
24
25
26

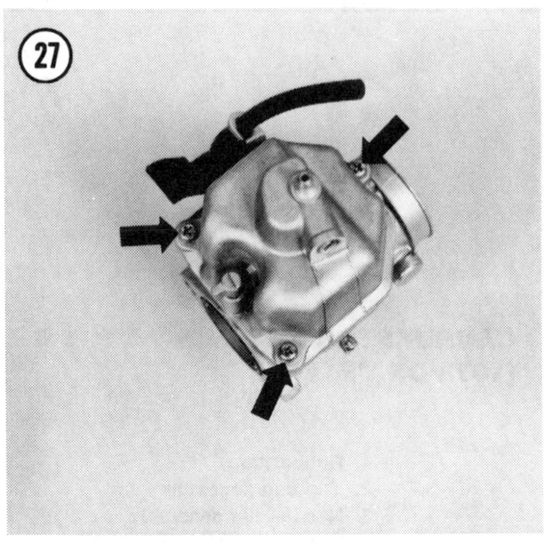

7. Unscrew the pilot screw (A, **Figure 31**) and remove the spring, washer and O-ring seal.
8. If necessary, remove the float valve assembly (B, **Figure 31**).

NOTE

*On most models, the slow jet (C, **Figure 31**) is pressed into place and cannot be removed.*

9. Remove the O-ring seal (**Figure 32**) from the carburetor flange.
10. Remove the throttle adjust screw and spring (**Figure 33**).
11. Remove the choke assembly (A, **Figure 34**), the vent tube (B, **Figure 34**) and fuel line (C, **Figure 34**).

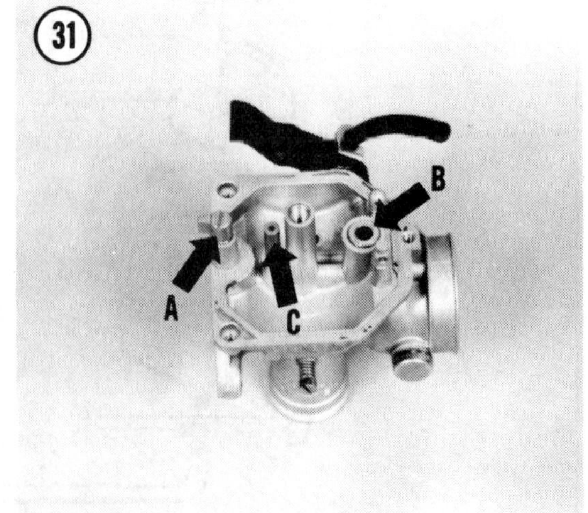

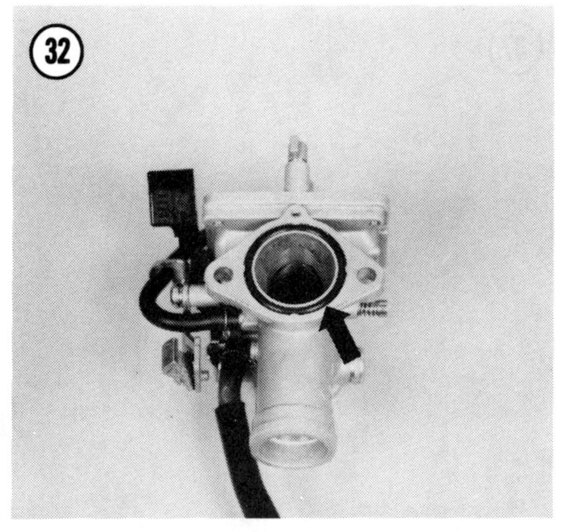
32

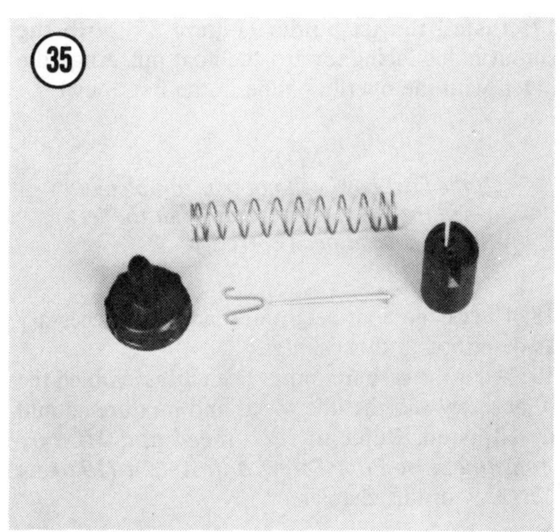
35

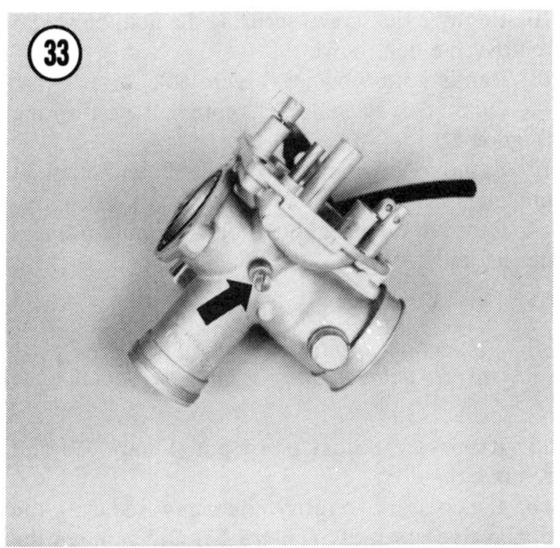
33

36

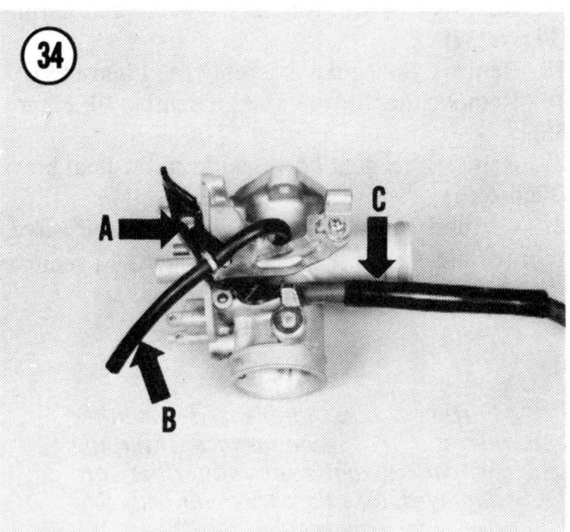

34

12. Remove the float bowl seal from the float bowl.

13. Remove the needle clip retainer and remove the jet needle (**Figure 35**).

NOTE

Further disassembly is neither necessary nor recommended. If throttle or choke shafts or butterflies are damaged, take the carburetor body to a dealer for replacement.

14. Clean and inspect the carburetor components as described in this chapter.

15. Assembly is the reverse of these disassembly steps, noting the following.

16. Install the needle jet (**Figure 36**) with the chamfered end facing *up* toward the needle jet holder.

17. Install the jet holder (**Figure 37**) with the cutout notch facing toward the float pin. Align the notch with the overflow tube in the float bowl.

NOTE
If the float bowl will not seat completely when installed, check again that the jet holder is positioned correctly.

18. Check the float height and adjust if necessary as described in this chapter.
19. After the carburetor has been disassembled the pilot screw and the idle speed and mixture should be adjusted. Refer to *Idle Speed and Mixture Adjustment* or *Pilot Screw Adjustment (1980-on CB125S)* in this chapter.

Disassembly/Assembly (Type III)

The Type III carburetor is used on the following models:

a. **Figure 38**—All XL250.
b. **Figure 39**—XL350, XL350 K1.
c. **Figure 40**—1976 XL350.
d. **Figure 41**—1977-1978 XL350.

1. Remove the drain tube.
2. Remove the screws (**Figure 42**) securing the top cap and remove the top cap and gasket.
3. Straighten the locking tab on the lockwasher under the bolt (**Figure 43**) and remove the bolt.
4. Pivot the link arm up, straighten the locking tab on the other bolt (**Figure 44**) and remove the bolt.
5. Pivot the link arm up and disengage the link arm from the slide mechanism (**Figure 45**).
6. Withdraw the slide mechanism from the carburetor.
7. Remove the screws (A, **Figure 46**) securing the plate to the slide.
8. Remove the plate and withdraw the needle (B, **Figure 46**).

NOTE
*Prior to removing the air screw, carefully screw it in until it **lightly** seats. Count and record the number of turns so it can be installed in the same position.*

9A. On 1977-1978 XL350 models, unscrew the air screw and remove the spring, washer and O-ring seal. The air (or pilot) screw is located on the base of the carburetor on these models.
9B. On all other models, unscrew the air screw (**Figure 47**) and remove the spring, washer and O-ring seal.

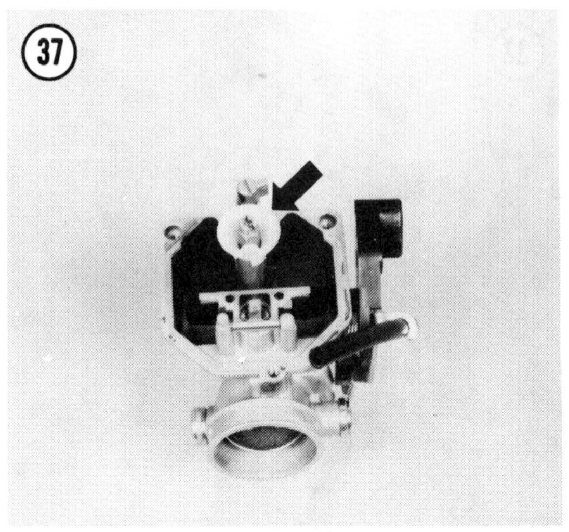
37

10. Remove the screws securing the float bowl and remove the float bowl.
11. Remove the slow jet (**Figure 48**).
12. On models so equipped, remove the leaf spring (**Figure 49**).
13. Remove the main jet (**Figure 50**) and main jet holder.
14. Remove the needle jet holder (**Figure 51**) and needle jet.

NOTE
Turn the carburetor over and catch the needle jet as it falls out into your hand.

15. Remove the float pivot pin (**Figure 52**) and remove the float.
16. If necessary, remove the screw securing the float valve assembly (**Figure 53**) and remove the float valve assembly.
17. Remove the throttle adjust screw and spring (**Figure 54**).
18. Remove the choke assembly (A, **Figure 55**).
19. Remove the throttle wheel assembly (B, **Figure 55**).
20. Remove the float bowl seal from the float bowl (**Figure 56**).
21. On models equipped with the air cut-off valve, remove the screws securing the cover and remove the cover. Remove the diaphragm and spring.

NOTE
Further disassembly is neither necessary nor recommended. If throttle or choke shafts or butterflies are damaged, take the carburetor body to a dealer for replacement.

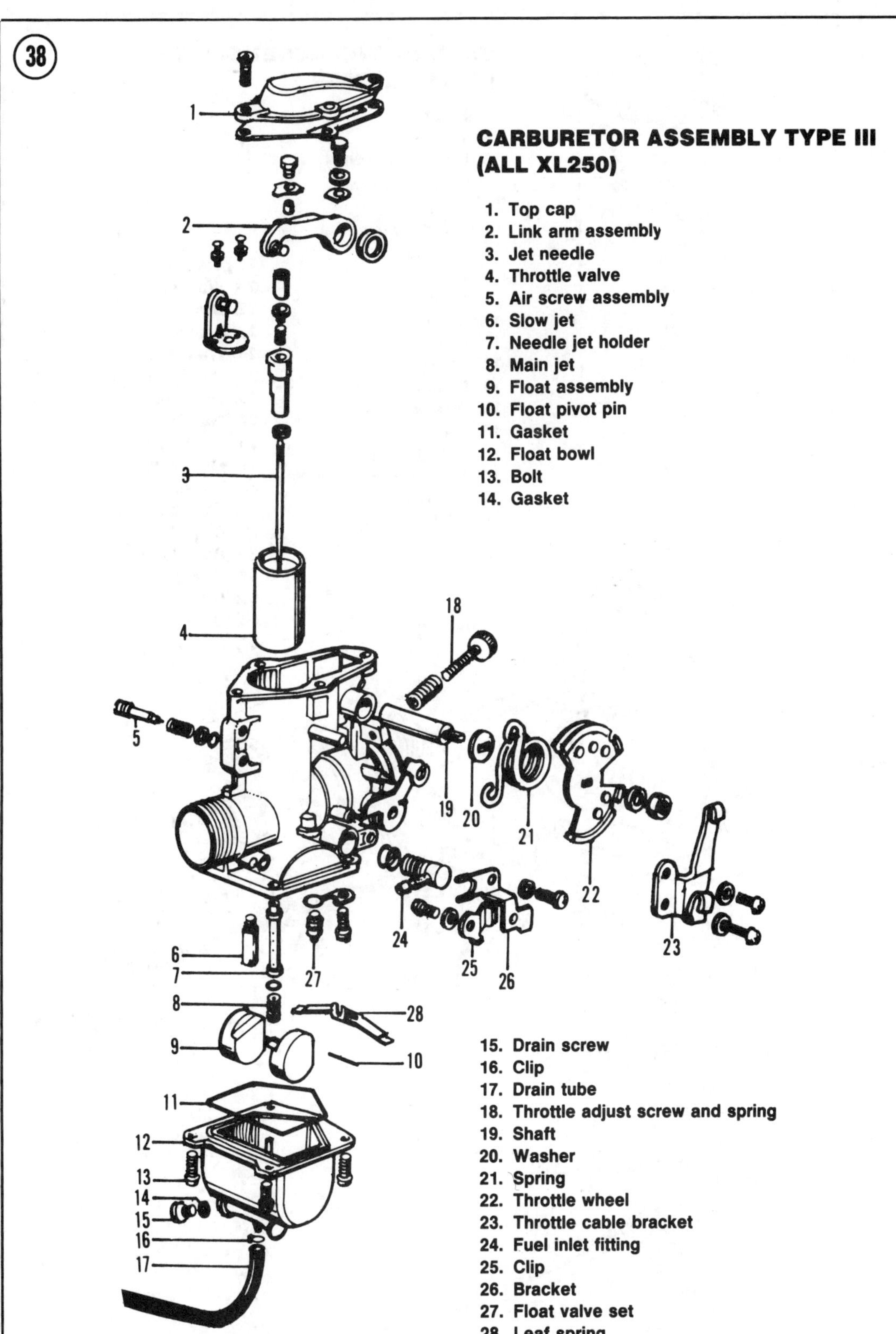
38
1
2
3
4
5
6
7
8
9
10
11
12
13
14
15
16
17
18
19
20
21
22
23
24
25
26
27
28
CARBURETOR ASSEMBLY TYPE III (ALL XL250)
1. Top cap
2. Link arm assembly
3. Jet needle
4. Throttle valve
5. Air screw assembly
6. Slow jet
7. Needle jet holder
8. Main jet
9. Float assembly
10. Float pivot pin
11. Gasket
12. Float bowl
13. Bolt
14. Gasket
15. Drain screw
16. Clip
17. Drain tube
18. Throttle adjust screw and spring
19. Shaft
20. Washer
21. Spring
22. Throttle wheel
23. Throttle cable bracket
24. Fuel inlet fitting
25. Clip
26. Bracket
27. Float valve set
28. Leaf spring

7

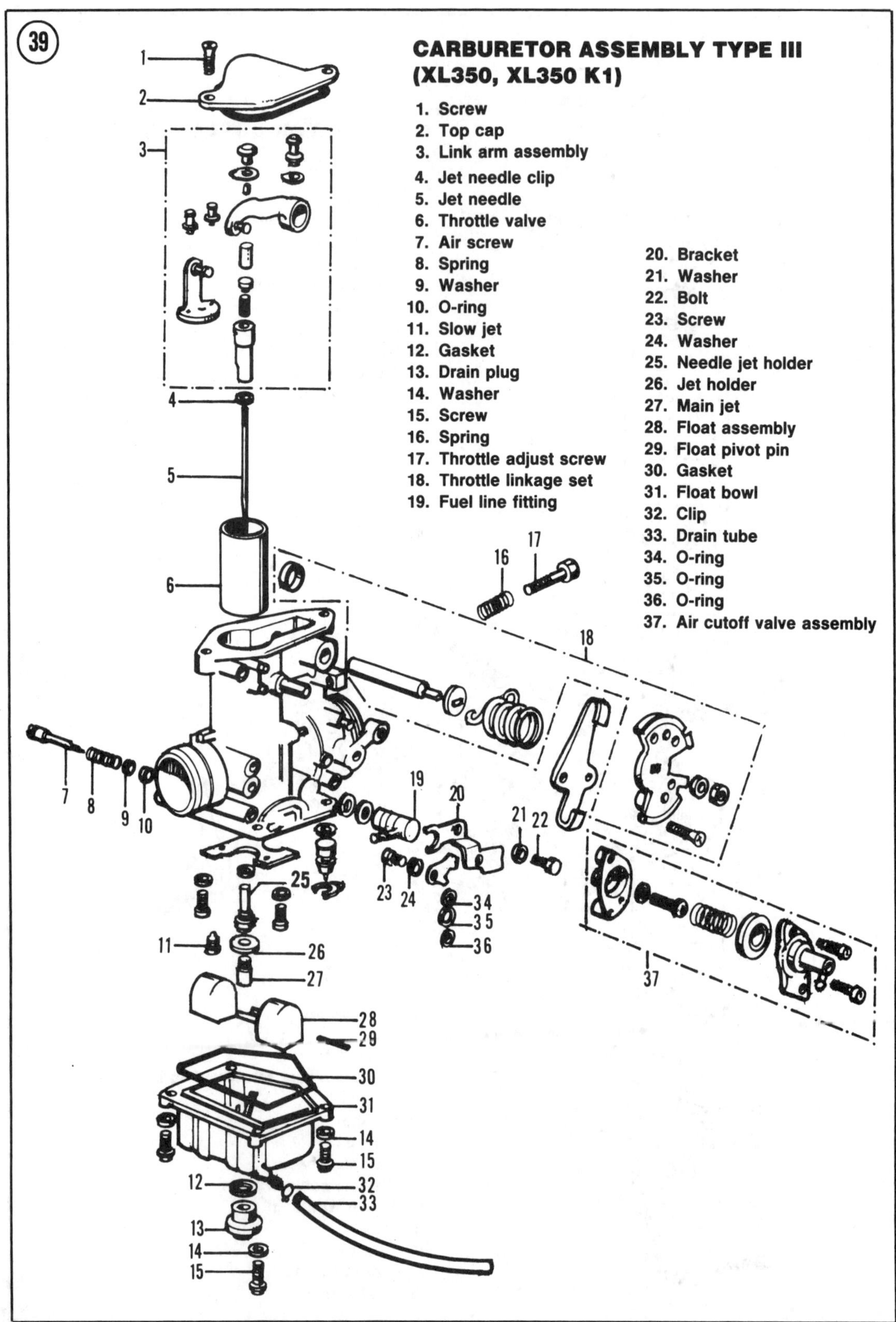
39
CARBURETOR ASSEMBLY TYPE III
(XL350, XL350 K1)
1. Screw
2. Top cap
3. Link arm assembly
4. Jet needle clip
5. Jet needle
6. Throttle valve
7. Air screw
8. Spring
9. Washer
10. O-ring
11. Slow jet
12. Gasket
13. Drain plug
14. Washer
15. Screw
16. Spring
17. Throttle adjust screw
18. Throttle linkage set
19. Fuel line fitting
20. Bracket
21. Washer
22. Bolt
23. Screw
24. Washer
25. Needle jet holder
26. Jet holder
27. Main jet
28. Float assembly
29. Float pivot pin
30. Gasket
31. Float bowl
32. Clip
33. Drain tube
34. O-ring
35. O-ring
36. O-ring
37. Air cutoff valve assembly

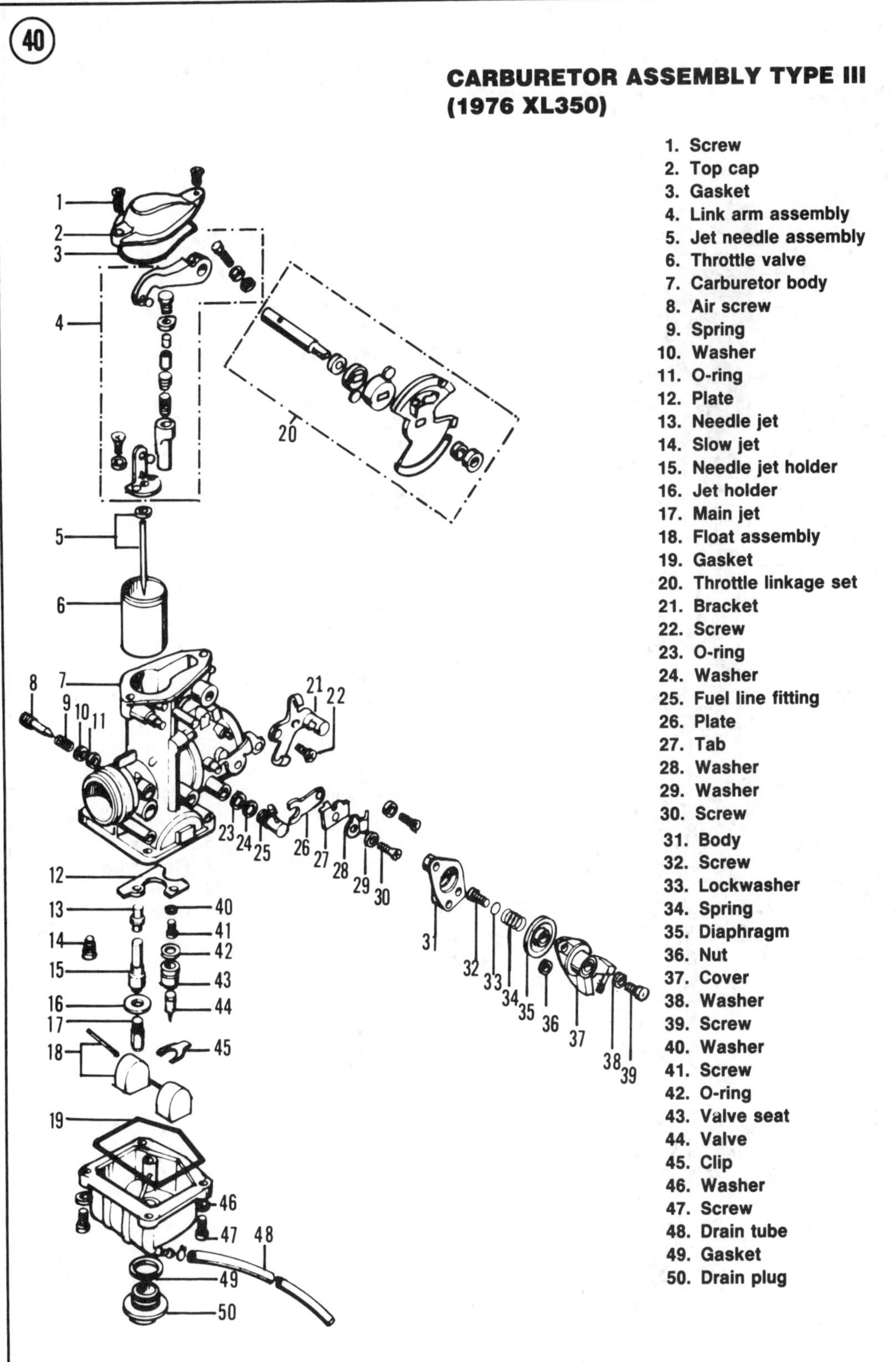
40
CARBURETOR ASSEMBLY TYPE III
(1976 XL350)
1. Screw
2. Top cap
3. Gasket
4. Link arm assembly
5. Jet needle assembly
6. Throttle valve
7. Carburetor body
8. Air screw
9. Spring
10. Washer
11. O-ring
12. Plate
13. Needle jet
14. Slow jet
15. Needle jet holder
16. Jet holder
17. Main jet
18. Float assembly
19. Gasket
20. Throttle linkage set
21. Bracket
22. Screw
23. O-ring
24. Washer
25. Fuel line fitting
26. Plate
27. Tab
28. Washer
29. Washer
30. Screw
31. Body
32. Screw
33. Lockwasher
34. Spring
35. Diaphragm
36. Nut
37. Cover
38. Washer
39. Screw
40. Washer
41. Screw
42. O-ring
43. Valve seat
44. Valve
45. Clip
46. Washer
47. Screw
48. Drain tube
49. Gasket
50. Drain plug

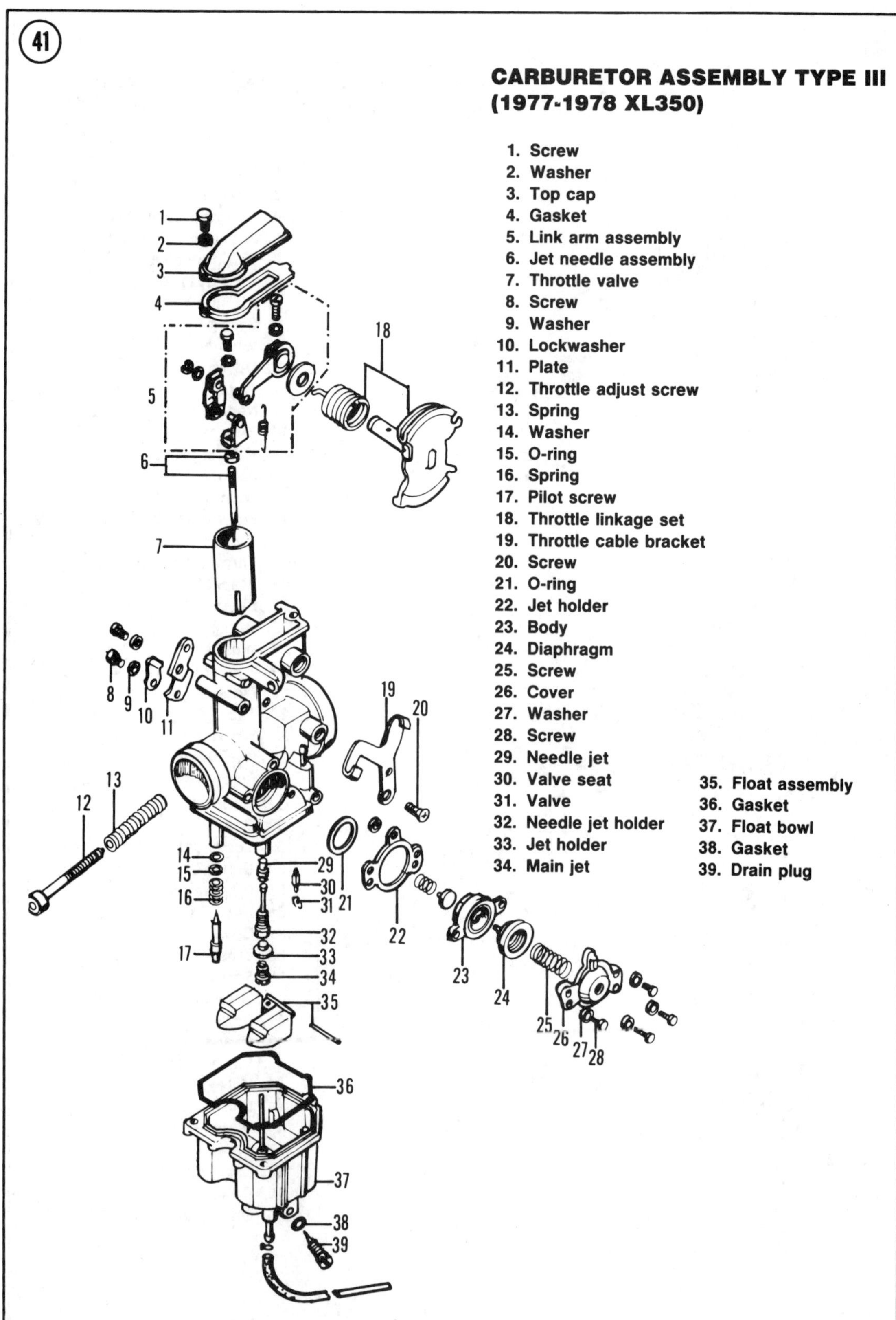
41
CARBURETOR ASSEMBLY TYPE III
(1977-1978 XL350)
1. Screw
2. Washer
3. Top cap
4. Gasket
5. Link arm assembly
6. Jet needle assembly
7. Throttle valve
8. Screw
9. Washer
10. Lockwasher
11. Plate
12. Throttle adjust screw
13. Spring
14. Washer
15. O-ring
16. Spring
17. Pilot screw
18. Throttle linkage set
19. Throttle cable bracket
20. Screw
21. O-ring
22. Jet holder
23. Body
24. Diaphragm
25. Screw
26. Cover
27. Washer
28. Screw
29. Needle jet
30. Valve seat
31. Valve
32. Needle jet holder
33. Jet holder
34. Main jet
35. Float assembly
36. Gasket
37. Float bowl
38. Gasket
39. Drain plug

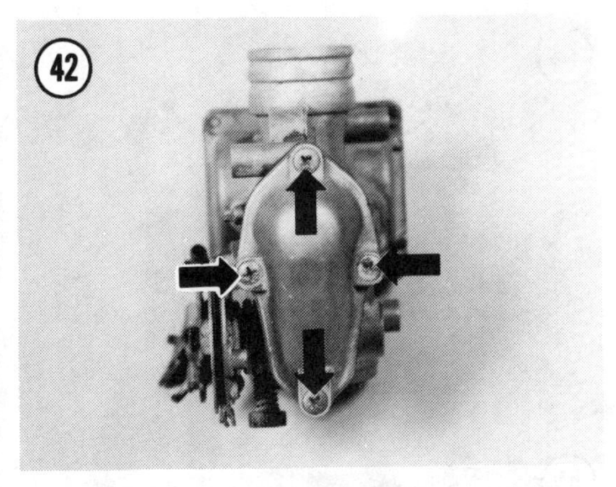

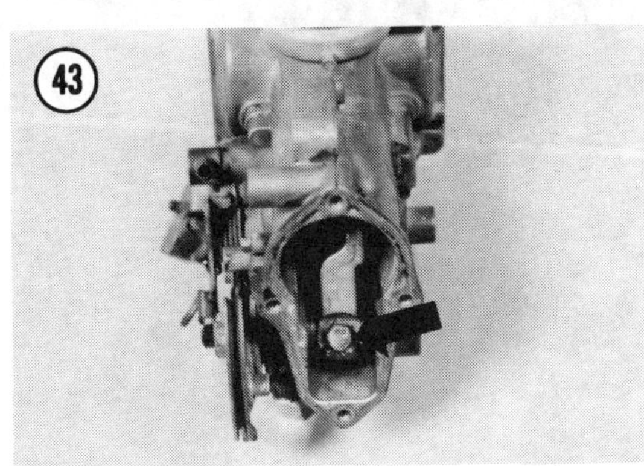

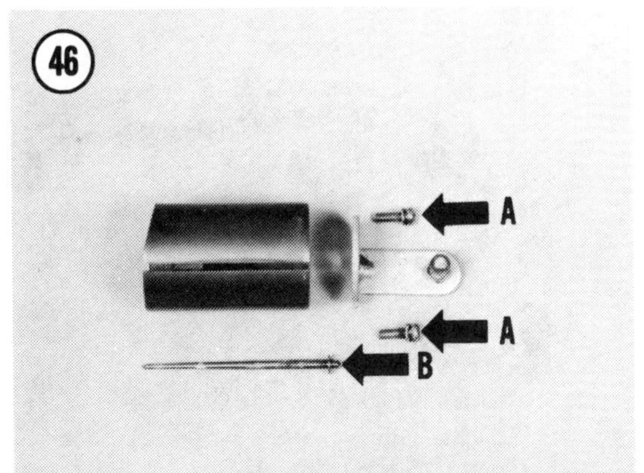

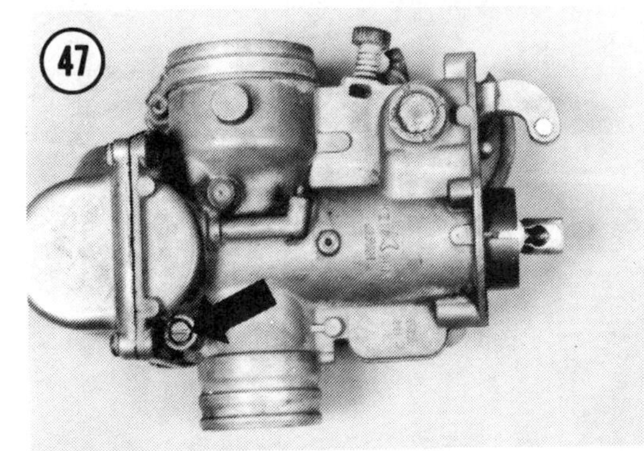

7

50

54

51

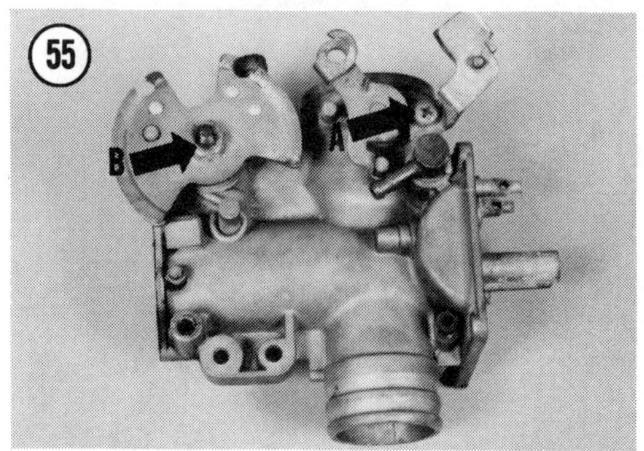
55
B
A

52

56

53

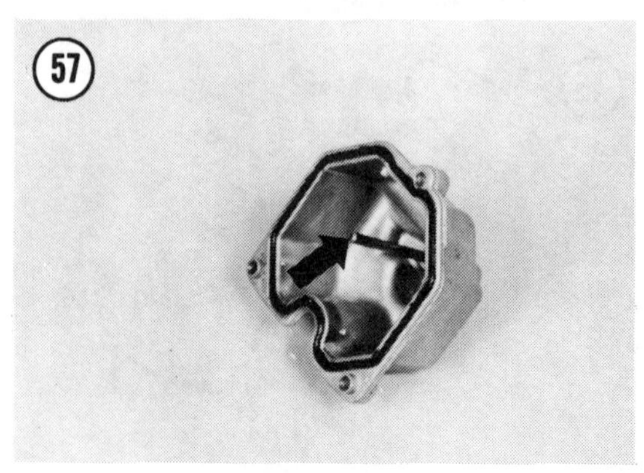
57

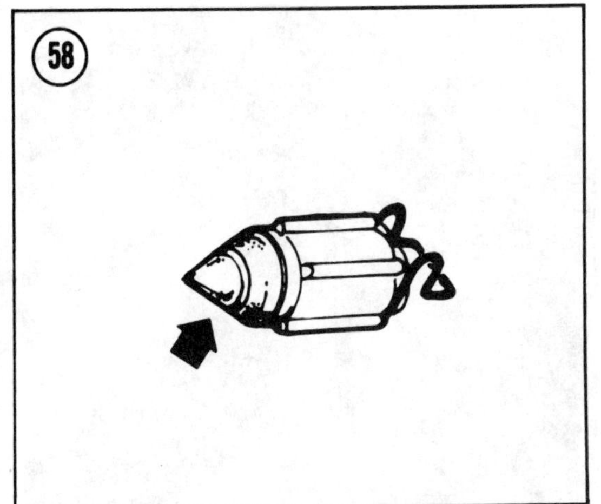

58

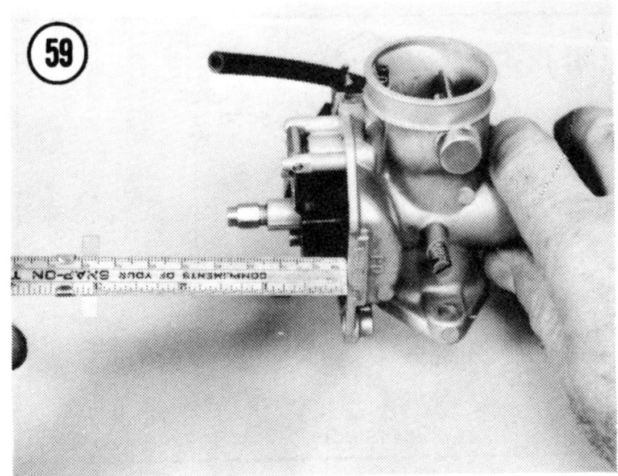

59

22. Inspect the carburetor components as described in this chapter.
23. Assembly is the reverse of these steps, noting the following.
24. Install the needle jet with the chamfered end facing *up* toward the needle jet holder.
25. Check the float height and adjust if necessary as described in this chapter.
26. After the carburetor has been disassembled, the idle speed and mixture should be adjusted. Refer to *Idle Speed and Mixture Adjustment* in this chapter.

Cleaning and Inspection

1. Clean all parts, except rubber or plastic parts, in a good grade of carburetor cleaner. This solution is available at most automotive or motorcycle supply stores in a small, resealable tank with a dip basket for just a few dollars. If it is tightly sealed when not in use, the solution will last for several cleanings. Follow the manufacturer's instructions for correct soak time (usually about 1/2 hour).
2. Remove all parts from the cleaner and blow dry with compressed air. Blow out the jets with compressed air. *Do not* use a piece of wire to clean them as minor gouges in the jet can alter flow rate and upset the fuel-air mixture.
3. Be sure to clean out the overflow tube **(Figure 57)** from both ends.
4. Inspect the end of the float valve needle **(Figure 58)** and seat for wear or damage; replace either or both parts if necessary.
5. Inspect all O-ring seals. O-ring seals tend to become hardened after prolonged use and heat and therefore lose their ability to seal properly.

CARBURETOR ADJUSTMENTS

Float Adjustment

The carburetor assembly has to be removed and partially disassembled for this adjustment.

1. Remove the carburetor as described in this chapter.
2. Remove the float bowl from the main body.
3. Hold the carburetor so the float arm is just touching the float needle, not pushing it down. Use a float level gauge, vernier caliper or small ruler **(Figure 59)** and measure the distance from the carburetor body to the float. The correct height is listed in **Table 1**.
4. Adjust by carefully bending the tang on the float arm. If the float level is set too high, the result will be a rich fuel-air mixture. If it is set too low, the mixture will be too lean.

NOTE
Both float chambers must be at the same height.

5. Reassemble and install the carburetor.

Needle Jet Adjustment

On most models the position of the needle jet can be adjusted to affect the fuel-air mixture for medium throttle openings.

The top of the carburetor must be removed for this adjustment. It is not necessary to remove the carburetor but the fuel tank must be removed.

1. Place a wood block(s) under the engine to support it securely.
2. Remove the side covers and seat.
3. Turn the fuel shutoff valve to the S or OFF position and remove the fuel line to the carburetor.

7

4. Remove the fuel tank as described in this chapter.

NOTE
Prior to removing the top cap, thoroughly clean the area around it so no dirt will fall into the carburetor.

5A. On Type I and Type II carburetors, perform the following:

a. Unscrew the carburetor top cap and pull the throttle valve assembly up and out of the carburetor.
b. Depress the throttle valve spring and remove the throttle cable from the throttle valve (**Figure 60**).
c. Remove the needle clip retainer and remove the jet needle.

5B. On Type III carburetors, perform the following:

a. Remove the screws (**Figure 42**) securing the top cap and remove the top cap and gasket.
b. Straighten the locking tab on the lockwasher under the bolt (**Figure 43**) and remove the bolt.
c. Pivot the link arm up, straighten the locking tab on the other bolt (**Figure 44**) and remove the bolt.
d. Pivot the link arm up and disengage the link arm from the slide mechanism (**Figure 45**).
e. Withdraw the slide mechanism from the carburetor.
f. Remove the screws (A, **Figure 46**) securing the plate to the slide.
g. Remove the plate and withdraw the needle (B, **Figure 46**).

6. Record the clip position prior to removal. Remove the needle clip and install it in the new position. Raising the needle (lowering the clip) will enrich the mixture during mid-throttle opening, while lowering the needle (raising the clip) will lean the mixture. Refer to **Figure 61**.

7A. On Type I and Type II carburetors, reassemble and install the top cap. When installing the throttle valve into the carburetor, position the groove in the throttle slide toward the throttle adjust screw side of the carburetor.

7B. On Type III carburetors, reverse Step 5B to install.

8. Refer to **Table 1** for standard clip position for all models.

NOTE

*Honda does not provide service specifications for all models. **Table 1** lists all specifications that are available.*

60

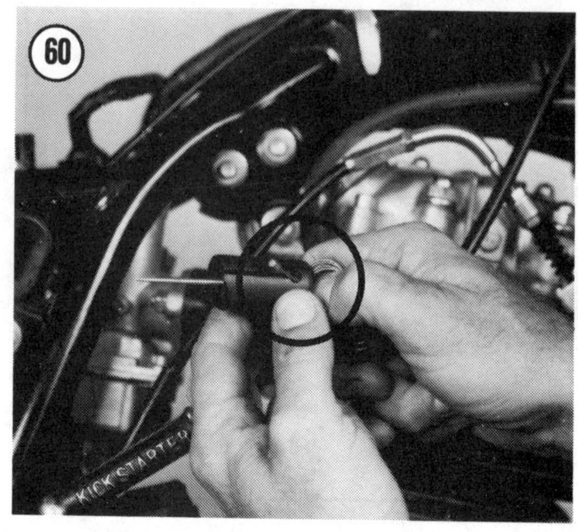

61

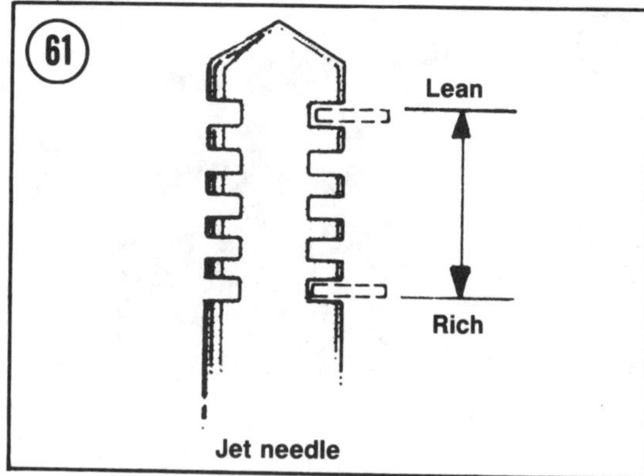

Idle Speed and Mixture Adjustment (Model Group A)

Model group A consists of the following models:

a. All CB100.
b. All CL100.
c. All SL100.
d. CB125 S, CB125 S1-S2, 1976-1978 CB125.
e. All SL125.
f. All TL125.
g. All XL175.

The air cleaner must be cleaned before starting this procedure or the results will be inaccurate.

1. Place a wood block(s) under the engine to support it securely.
2. Start the engine and let it reach normal operating temperature. Ten minutes at idle is usually sufficient. Shut off the engine.
3. Connect a portable tachometer following the manufacturer's instructions. Restart the engine.
4. Turn the idle adjust screw (A, **Figure 62**) in or out to achieve the specified idle speed as listed in **Table 1** for your specific model.

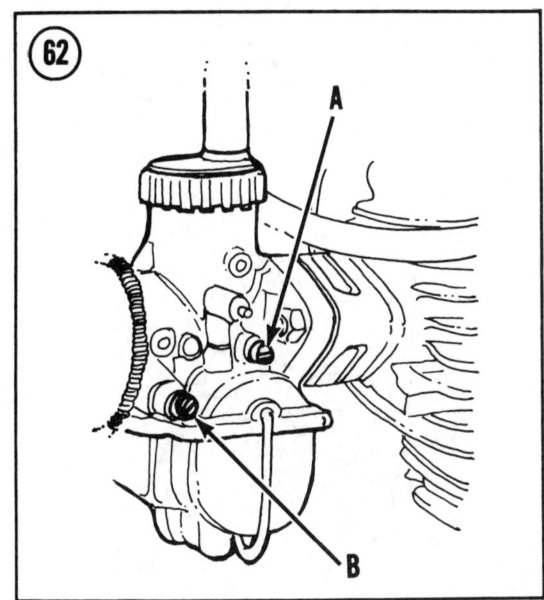

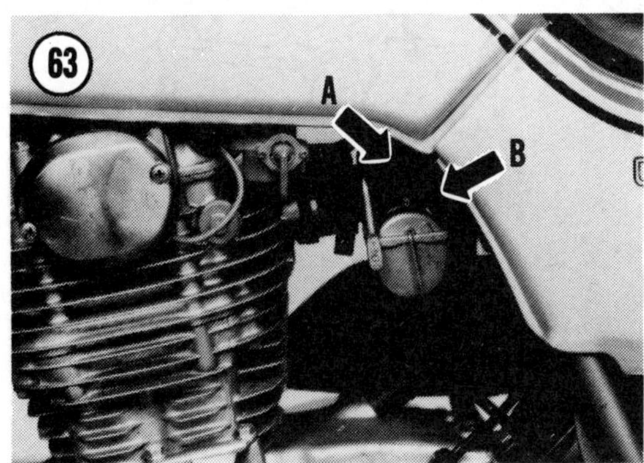

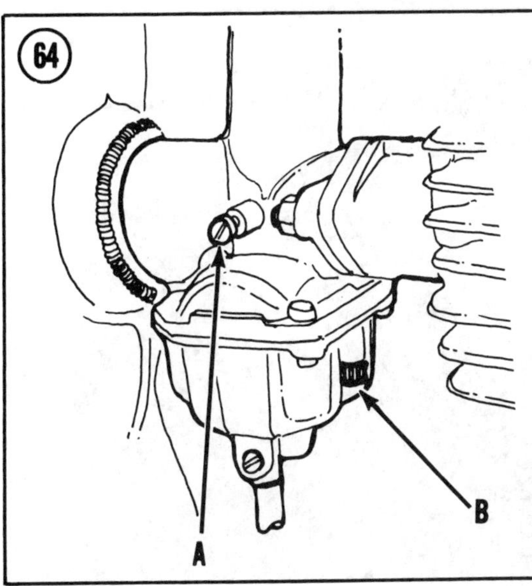

5. Turn the pilot air screw (B, **Figure 63**) in or out to achieve the highest engine rpm.
6. If necessary, repeat Step 4 to achieve the specified idle speed.
7. From this point turn the pilot screw in or out 1/8 to 1/4 turn to achieve the smoothest idle condition.
8. Open and close the throttle a couple of times and check for variations in idle speed. Readjust if necessary.
9. Turn the engine off and disconnect the portable tachometer.

Idle Speed and Mixture Adjustment (Model Group B)

Model group B consists of the following models:

a. XL100, XL100 K1, 1976 XL100.
b. All XL125.
c. All CT125.
d. All TL250.

The air cleaner must be cleaned before starting this procedure or the results will be inaccurate.

1. Place a wood block(s) under the engine to support it securely.
2. Start the engine and let it reach normal operating temperature. Ten minutes at idle is usually sufficient. Shut off the engine.
3. Connect a portable tachometer following the manufacturer's instructions.
4. Turn the pilot air screw (A, **Figure 63**) in until it lightly seats. Back it out 1 1/2 turns. Restart the engine.
5. Turn the idle adjust screw (B, **Figure 64**) to achieve the lowest stable idle speed.
6. Turn the pilot air screw in or out to achieve the highest idle speed.
7. Turn the idle adjust screw to achieve the specified idle speed listed in **Table 1** for your specific model.
8. Open and close the throttle a couple of times and check for variations in idle speed. Readjust if necessary.
9. Turn the engine off and disconnect the portable tachometer.

Idle Speed and Mixture Adjustment (Model Group C)

Model group C consists of the following models:

a. 1977-1978 XL100.
b. All XL250.
c. All XL350.

7

Refer to **Figure 64** for XL100 models or **Figure 65** for XL250 and XL350 models.

The air cleaner must be cleaned before starting this procedure or the results will be inaccurate.

1. Place a wood block(s) under the engine to support it securely.
2. Start the engine and let it reach normal operating temperature. Ten minutes at idle is usually sufficient. Shut off the engine.
3. Connect a portable tachometer following the manufacturer's instructions. Restart the engine.
4. Turn the idle adjust screw (A, **Figure 64** or A, **Figure 65**) in or out to achieve the specified idle speed as listed in **Table 1** for your specific model.
5. Turn the pilot air screw (B, **Figure 64** or B, **Figure 65**) clockwise until the engine misses or decreases in engine speed. Note that position.
6. Turn the pilot air screw counterclockwise until the engine misses or decreases in engine speed. Note that position.
7. Position the pilot air screw at the mid-point of the 2 previously noted settings. This point is usually:
   a. XL100 models—1 1/2 turns from the fully closed position.
   b. XL250 and XL350 models—7/8-1 5/8 turns from the fully closed position.
8. If necessary, repeat Step 4 to achieve the specified idle speed.
9. Open and close the throttle a couple of times and check for variations in idle speed. Readjust if necessary.
10. Turn the engine off and disconnect the portable tachometer.

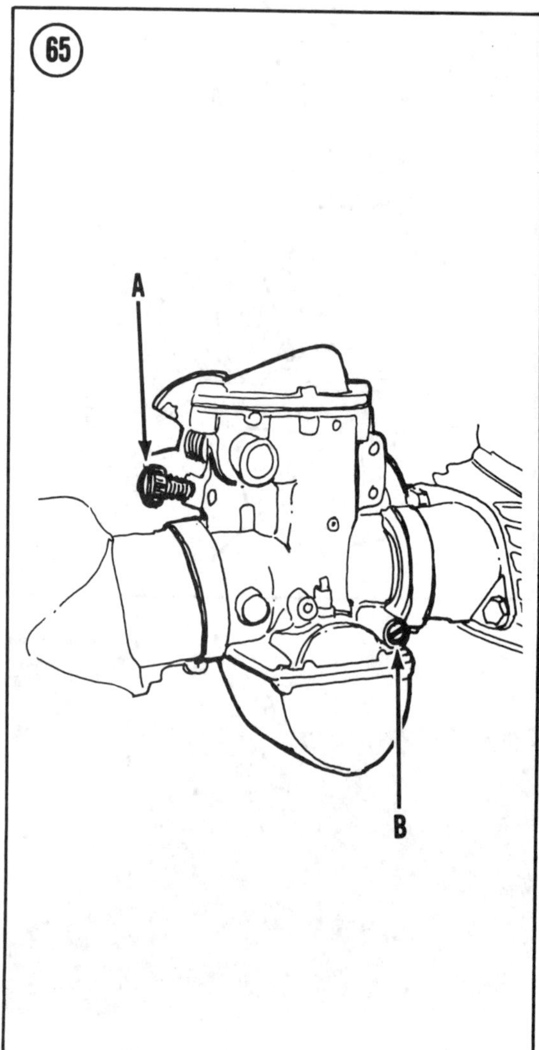

Pilot Screw Adjustment (1979 CB125S)

NOTE

The pilot jet is pre-set at the factory. Adjustment is not necessary unless the carburetor has been overhauled or someone has misadjusted it.

1. Place a wood block(s) under the engine to support the bike securely.
2. For the preliminary adjustment, carefully turn the pilot screw (A, **Figure 66**) in until it seats *lightly* and then back it out 1 full turn.

CAUTION

The pilot screw seat can be damaged if the pilot screw is tightened too hard against the seat.

3. Start the engine and let it reach normal operating temperature. Ten minutes at idle is usually sufficient.

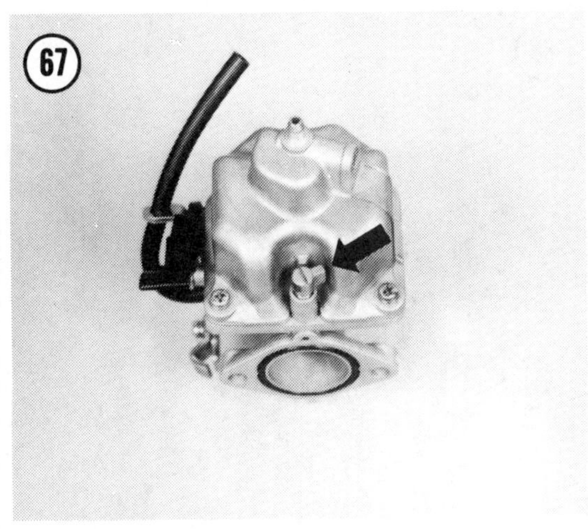

4. Turn the engine off and connect a portable tachometer following the manufacturer's instructions.
5. Start the engine and turn the throttle adjust screw to obtain an idle speed of 1,300 ±100 rpm.
6. Turn the idle adjustment (B, **Figure 66**) *clockwise slowly* until the engine stops running.
7. From this setting back out the pilot screw 3/4 turn.
8. Restart the engine and reset the idle speed (1,300 ±100 rpm) if necessary.
9. Open and close the throttle a couple of times and check for variations in idle speed. Readjust if necessary.
10. Disconnect the portable tachometer.

Pilot Screw Adjustment And New Limiter Cap Installation (1980-on CB125S, U.S. Models)

To comply with U.S. emission control standards, a limiter cap is attached to the pilot screw. This is to prevent the owner from readjusting the factory setting. The limiter cap will allow a maximum of 7/8 of a turn of the pilot screw *to a leaner mixture only.* The pilot screw is preset at the factory and should not be reset unless the carburetor has been overhauled.

CAUTION
Do not try to remove the limiter cap from the pilot screw, as it is bonded in place and will break off and damage the pilot screw if removal is attempted.

The air cleaner must be cleaned before starting this procedure or the results will be inaccurate.

1. For the preliminary adjustment, carefully turn the pilot screw in until it *lightly seats* and then back it out 2 full turns.
2. Perform *Pilot Screw Adjustment (1979 CB125S)* in this chapter.
3. Perform this step only if a new limiter cap is to be installed. Apply Loctite No. 601 or equivalent to the limiter cap and install it on the pilot screw. Make sure the pilot screw does not move while installing the limiter cap. Position the limiter cap against the stop on the float bowl (**Figure 67**) so that the pilot screw can *only turn clockwise*, not counterclockwise.

WARNING
With the engine idling, move the handlebar from side to side. If idle speed increases during this movement, the throttle cable needs adjustment or it may be incorrectly routed through the frame. Correct this problem immediately. Do not ride the bike in this unsafe condition.

4. Turn the engine off and disconnect the portable tachometer.
5. After this adjustment is completed, test ride the bike. Throttle response from idle should be rapid and without any hesitation.

High-altitude Adjustment (1980-on CB125S)

If the bike is going to be ridden for any sustained period at elevations above 2,000 m (5,600 ft.), the main jet should be changed. Never change the jet by more than one size at a time. Always test ride the bike and run a spark plug test. Refer to *Reading Spark Plugs* in Chapter Three.

The carburetor is set with the standard jet for normal sea level conditions. If the bike is run at higher altitudes the main jet should be replaced with a one-step smaller size to prevent the engine from running too rich and carboning up quickly.

CAUTION
If the carburetor has been adjusted for high-altitude operation (smaller jet installed), it must be changed back to standard settings when ridden at altitudes below 1,500 m (5,000 ft.). Engine overheating and piston seizure will occur if the engine runs too lean with the smaller jet installed.

1. Remove the carburetor as described in this chapter.
2. Remove the screws securing the float bowl and remove the float bowl.

3. Remove the main jet holder and remove the main jet (**Figure 68**). Replace it with the factory recommended high altitude size listed in **Table 1**.
4. Install the float bowl.
5. Reinstall the carburetor as described in this chapter.
6. Start the engine and adjust the pilot screw as described under *Idle Speed Adjustment* in this chapter.
7. Test ride the bike and perform a spark plug test; refer to *Reading Spark Plugs* in Chapter Three.

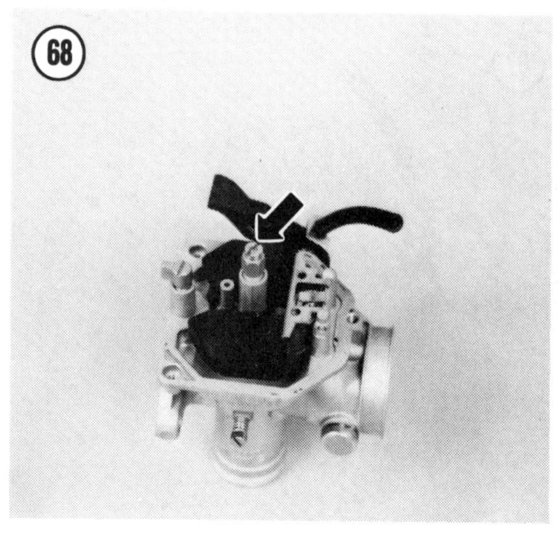

THROTTLE CABLE

Removal

1. Place a wood block(s) under the engine to support the bike securely.
2. Remove the side covers and the seat.
3. Remove the fuel tank as described in this chapter.

NOTE

Prior to removing the top cap, thoroughly clean the area around it so no dirt will fall into the carburetor.

4A. On Type I and Type II carburetors, unscrew the carburetor top cap and pull the throttle valve assembly up and out of the carburetor. Depress the throttle valve spring and remove the throttle cable from the throttle valve.

NOTE

Place a clean shop rag over the top of the carburetor to keep any foreign matter from falling into the throttle slide area.

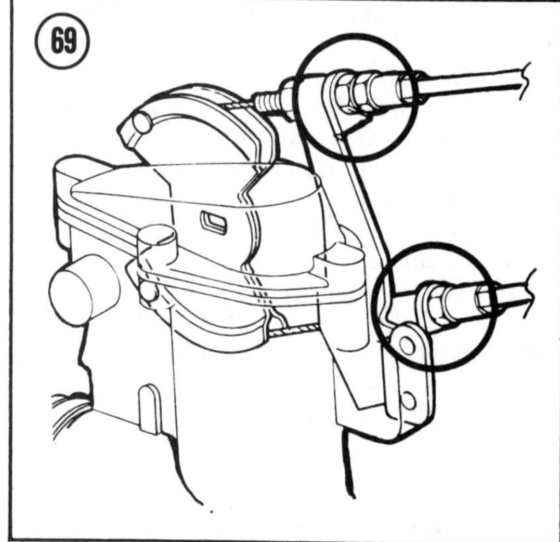

4B. On Type III carburetors, loosen the locknuts on both throttle cables (**Figure 69**) and remove the throttle cables from the link plate on the carburetor assembly. Note which cable is attached to the upper and lower portion of the link plate. The new cables must be reinstalled into the correct notch of the link plate.
5. Disassemble the throttle lever assembly. Remove the screws (**Figure 70**) securing the throttle cover and separate the 2 halves of the assembly. Remove the assembly from the handlebar.
6. Remove the throttle cable(s) from the throttle lever.

NOTE

On Type III carburetors, note which cable is attached to the front and rear portion of the throttle grip receptacles.

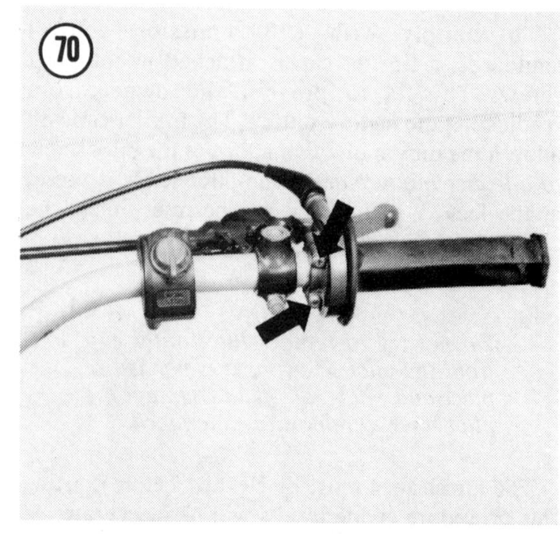

71

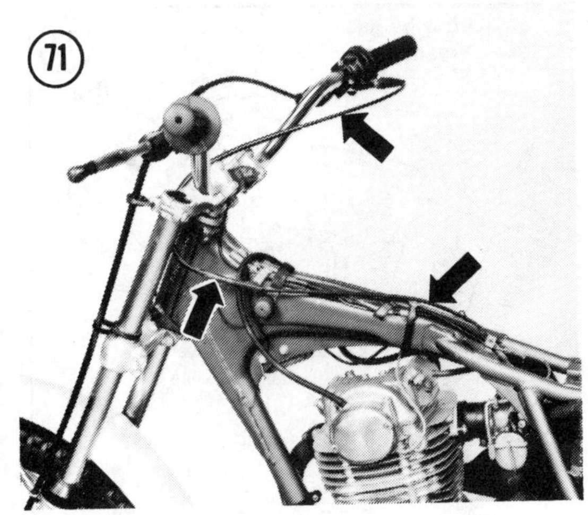

The new cables must be reinstalled to the correct receptacle.

NOTE
The piece of string attached in the next step will be used to pull the new throttle cable(s) back through the frame so it will be routed in the same position.

7. Tie a piece of heavy string or cord approximately 2 m (6-8 ft.) long to the carburetor end of the throttle cable(s). Wrap this end with masking or duct tape. Do not use an excessive amount of tape, as it will be pulled through the frame loop during removal. Tie the other end of the string to the frame.
8. At the throttle lever end of the cable(s), carefully pull the cable (and attached string) out through the frame (**Figure 71**). Make sure the attached string follows the same path of the cable(s) through the frame and behind the headlight.
9. Remove the tape and untie the string from the old cable.
10. Lubricate the new cable as described under *Control Cables* in Chapter Three.
11. Tie the string to the new throttle cable(s) and wrap it with tape.
12. Carefully pull the string back through the frame routing the new cable(s) through the same path as the old cable(s).
13. Remove the tape and untie the string from the cable(s) and the frame.

Installation

1. Install the new throttle cable(s) by reversing Steps 1-6, noting the following.
2. On Type III carburetors, make sure to install the cable to the correct notch of the link plate as noted in *Removal* Step 4B.
3. Apply grease to the sliding surface of the throttle grip and install it onto the handlebar. Align the punch mark on the handlebar with the slit in the throttle cover and tighten the forward screw first.
4. Operate the throttle grip and make sure the carburetor throttle linkage is operating correctly and with no binding. If operation is incorrect or there is binding carefully check that the cable(s) is attached correctly and there are no tight bends in the cable(s).
5. Adjust the throttle cable as described in Chapter Three.
6. Test ride the bike and make sure the throttle is operating correctly.

FUEL TANK

Removal/Installation

1. Place a wood block(s) under the engine to support the bike securely.
2. Turn the fuel shutoff valve to the S or OFF position and remove the fuel line to the carburetor.
3. Remove the side covers and the seat.
4A. On models equipped with a rubber retaining bar, pull the bar toward the rear and pull the rear of the fuel tank up and out of the retaining bar. Pull the tank to the rear and remove the tank.
4B. On models equipped with a bolt and washer retainer, remove the bolt securing the rear of the fuel tank. Pull the fuel fill cap vent tube free from the steering head area. Pull the tank up and toward the rear and remove the tank.
5. Inspect the rubber cushions on the frame where the fuel tank is held in place. Replace as a set if either is damaged or starting to deteriorate.
6. Install by reversing these removal steps.

FUEL FILTER

The bike is fitted with a small fuel filter screen in the shutoff valve as described in Chapter Three. Considering the dirt and residue that is often found in today's gasoline, it is a good idea to install an inline fuel filter to help keep the carburetor clean.

A good quality inline fuel filter (A.C. part No. GF453 or equivalent) is available at most auto and motorcycle supply stores. Just cut the flexible fuel line from the fuel tank to the carburetor and install the filter. Cut out a section of the fuel line the length of the filter so the fuel line does not kink and restrict fuel flow.

CRANKCASE BREATHER SYSTEM (1979-ON CB125S, U.S. MODELS)

In order to comply with air pollution standards, the 1979-on CB125S is equipped with a crankcase breather system. The system is shown in **Figure 72**. It draws blow-by gases from the crankcase and recirculates them into the fuel-air mixture to be burned.

The system used on some earlier model bikes differs in that the gases are not routed into the air box for burning. They are routed as shown in **Figure 73** and are vented to atmosphere under the seat.

Inspection

Make sure all hose clamps are tight and check all hoses for deterioration. Replace as necessary. Check that all hoses are not clogged or crimped.

Remove the plug from the drain hose and clean out all residue. This cleaning procedure is needed more frequently if a considerable of riding is done at full throttle or in the rain.

NOTE
Be sure to install the plug and clamps.

EXHAUST SYSTEM

The exhaust system is a vital performance component and frequently, because of its design, it is a vulnerable piece of equipment. Check the exhaust system for deep dents and fractures and repair or replace them immediately. Check the muffler frame mounting flanges for fractures and loose bolts. Check the cylinder head mounting flange for tightness. A loose exhaust pipe connection will not only rob the engine of power, it could also damage the piston and cylinder.

The exhaust system consists of an exhaust pipe, muffler and tail pipe.

Removal/Installation

The following represents a typical removal and installation procedure. Minor variations exist among the various models.

1. Place a wood block(s) under the engine to support the bike securely.
2. Remove the side covers and the seat.
3. Remove the fuel tank as described in this chapter.
4. Remove the nuts (**Figure 74**) securing the exhaust pipe to the cylinder head.
5. Loosen the clamping bolt (**Figure 75**) at the muffler joint.
6. Carefully pull the exhaust pipe out of the front of the muffler. On a well run-in bike (or rusty one)

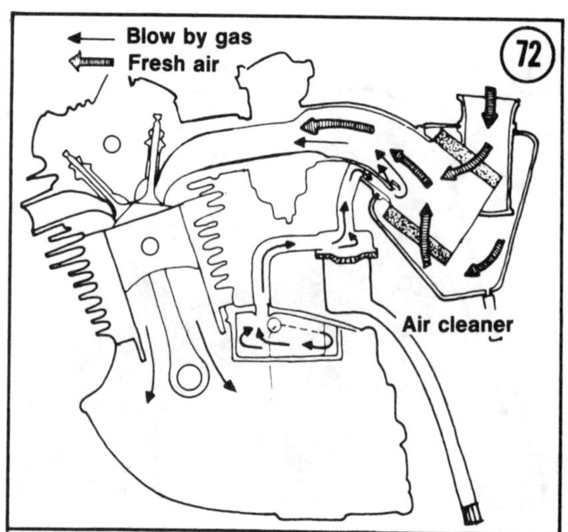

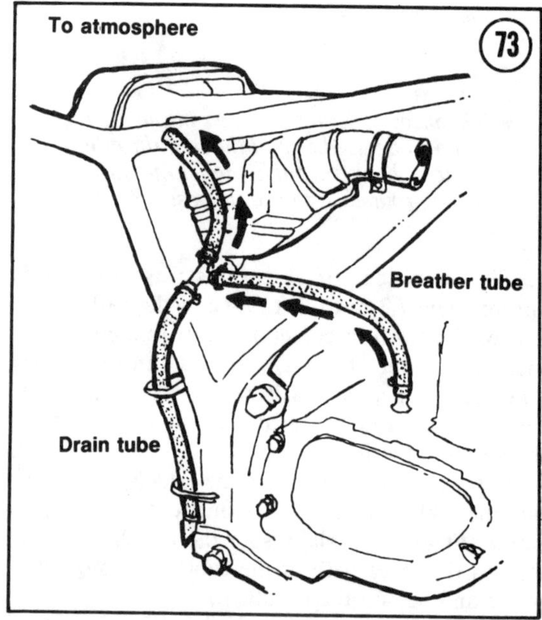

spray some WD-40 into the joint and let it set for 10 minutes. Gently twist and carefully pull the exhaust pipe loose. Remove the exhaust pipe.

7. Remove the bolts and washers securing the muffler and tail pipe to the frame (**Figure 76**).

8. Remove the exhaust system out through the rear and remove it.

9. Inspect the gaskets at all joints; replace as necessary.

10. Make sure the cylinder head exhaust port gasket is in place.

11. Install the exhaust system into the frame.

12. Install the muffler and tail pipe into position and install the attachment bolts only finger-tight at this time.

13. Install the exhaust pipe into the muffler front joint and into place on the cylinder head. Tighten the nuts securely.

NOTE

Tightening the cylinder head nuts first will minimize an exhaust leak at the cylinder head.

14. Tighten the muffler clamping joint and then the frame bolts securely.

15. Install the fuel tank, the seat and side covers.

16. After installation is complete, start the engine and make sure there are no exhaust leaks.

7

Table 1 is on the following pages.

Table 1 CARBURETOR SPECIFICATIONS*

Item	CB100, CL100	SL100, 1969-1975 XL100
Model No.	667A, 658A, 659A, 671A, GB10A, SL10A	658A, SL10A
Main jet No.		
	667A; 100 658A, 659A, 671A, GB10A; 105 SL10A; 110	658A; 105 SL10A, 110
Air jet	100	100
Slow jet	38	38
Initial pilot screw opening		
	GB10A, SL10A: 1 1/4 658A, 659A, 667A 671A; 1 5/8	SL10A, 1 1/4 658A, 1 5/8
Needle jet clip position from top		
	671A; 2nd groove All others; 3rd groove	2nd groove
Float level	24 mm (0.945 in.)	12.5 mm (0.49 in.)
Idle speed	1,200 ±100 rpm	1,400 ±100 rpm
Item	**1976-1978 XL100**	**CL125, 1973-1975 CB125S**
Model No.	PD90A, PD90D	660B
Main jet No.	95	105
Air jet	N.A.	100
Slow jet	38	38
Initial pilot screw opening		
	PD90A; 1 1/2 PD90D; 1	1 3/8
Needle jet clip position from top	2nd groove	3rd groove
Float level	12.5 mm (0.49 in.)	24 mm (0.945 in.)
Idle speed	1,300 ±100 rpm	1,200 ±100 rpm
Item	**1976-1977 CB125S**	**1978-1979 CB125S**
Model No.	066B	1978: PD66B 1979: PD68B
Main jet No.	110	110
High altitude main jet	N.A.	1978: N.A. 1979: 100
Air jet	N.A.	N.A.
Slow jet	40	40
Initial pilot screw opening	1 1/2	1
Needle jet clip position from top	2nd groove	3rd groove
Float level	24 mm (0.945 in.)	18.5 mm (0.728 in.)
Idle speed	1,300 ±100 rpm	1,300 ±100 rpm

(continued)

Table 1 CARBURETOR SPECIFICATIONS* (continued)

Item	1980-on CB125S	SL125
Model No.	PD24A	662A, 660A, 648A
Main jet No.	88	662A; 92 660A; 98 648A; 100
High altitude main jet	85	N.A.
Slow jet	N.A.	38
Initial pilot screw opening	2	648A; 1 1/2 660A, 622A; 1 5/8
Needle jet clip position from top	Fixed	3rd groove
Float level	12.5 mm (0.49 in.)	24 mm (0.945 in.)
Idle speed	1,300 ±100 rpm	1,200 ±100 rpm
Item	**TL125**	**XL125**
Model No.	N.A.	017A
Main jet No.	1972-1975; 95 1976; 92	110
Slow jet	1972-1975; 38 1976; 35	42
Initial pilot screw opening	1972-1975; 7/8 1976; 1 1/4	1 1/2
Needle jet clip position from top	1972-1975; 3rd groove 1976; 2nd groove	2nd groove
Float level	1972-1975; 21.5 mm (0.846 in) 1976; 20 mm (0.787 in.)	24 mm (0.945 in.)
Idle speed	1,300 ±100 rpm	1,300 ±100 rpm
Item	**XL125**	**CT125**
Model no.	PC04A	662A, 660A, 648A
Main jet no.	105	662A; 92 660A; 98 648A; 100
Slow jet	35	38
Initial pilot screw opening	1 7/8	648A; 1 1/2 660A, 622A; 1 5/8
Needle jet clip position from top	2nd groove	3rd groove
Float level	20 mm (0.787 in.)	24 mm (0.945 in.)
Idle speed	1,300 ±100 rpm	1,200 ±100 rpm

(continued)

Table 1 CARBURETOR SPECIFICATIONS* (continued)

Item	XL175	TL250
Model No.		X057A
	1973-1975; 697A	
	1976-1978; 697B	
Main jet No	110	115
Air jet	N.A.	150
Slow jet		38
	1973-1975; 40	
	1976-1978; 38	
Initial pilot screw opening		1 1/4
	1973-1975; 1 1/8	
	1976-1978; 1	
Needle jet clip position from top		4th groove
	1973-1975; 2nd groove	
	1976-1978; 4th groove	
Float level	22.5 mm (0.885 in.)	24 mm (0.945 in.)
Idle speed	1,200 ±100 rpm	1,000 ±100 rpm
Item	**XL250**	**XL350**
Model No.		
	1972-1975; 645B	1974-1975; 699A
	1976-1978; 074A	1976; 075A
		1977-1978; PD01A
Main jet No.		
	1972-1975; 120	1974-1975; 130
	1976-1978; 125	1976; 125
		1977-1978; 115
Air jet	N.A.	N.A.
Slow jet	45	
		1974-1976; 48
		1977-1978; 45
Initial pilot screw opening	1 1/4	
		1974-1976; 1 1/4
		1977-1978; 1
Needle jet clip position from top	3rd groove	
		1974-1975; 3rd groove
		1976-1978; 4th groove
Float level	24 mm (0.945 in.)	
		1974-1976 18 mm (0.709 in.)
		1977-1978 14.5 mm (0.571 in.)
Idle speed	1,200 ±100 rpm	1,200 ±100 rpm

* Honda does not provide service specifications for all items nor all models. All available information is included in this table. "N.A." indicates that information is not available.

CHAPTER EIGHT

ELECTRICAL SYSTEM

This chapter describes operating principles and service procedures for all electrical systems. The electrical systems vary from model to model, but generally include:

a. Charging system with battery (except TL125 and TL250).
b. Ignition system (breaker point or capacitor discharge).
c. Lighting system (including directional signals on some models).
d. Horn.

Tables 1-5 are at the end of the chapter.

CHARGING SYSTEM (EXCEPT TL 125 AND TL250)

The charging system includes the battery, the alternator and a solid-state current rectifier. CB125S models from 1981-on have a solid-state combination rectifier/voltage regulator. The various charging system designs are shown in **Figures 1-5**.

All battery testing and service is described in Chapter Three.

Alternating current generated by the alternator is rectified to direct current by the rectifier. On models so equipped, the voltage regulator maintains the voltage to the battery and additional electrical load (lights, ignition, etc.) at a constant voltage regardless of variations in engine speed and load.

Output Test

Whenever a charging system trouble is suspected, make sure the battery is fully charged and in good condition before going any further. Clean and test the battery as described in Chapter Three.

Prior to starting the test, start the bike and let it reach normal operating temperature; shut off the engine.

To test the charging system, disconnect the battery wires. Connect a 0-15 *DC* voltmeter and 0-10 *DC* ammeter into the circuit as shown in **Figure 6**.

NOTE
During the test, if the needle of the ammeter reads in the opposite direction on the scale, reverse the polarity of the test leads.

Start the engine and let it idle. Check the output at the different engine speeds with the headlight either ON or OFF as listed in **Table 1**.

If the charging current is considerably lower than specified, check the alternator, the rectifier or the voltage regulator/rectifier. Less likely is the possibility that the voltage is too high; in that case the voltage regulator/rectifer (if so equipped) is probably at fault.

Test the separate charging system components as described under the appropriate headings in this chapter.

1

CHARGING CIRCUIT (CB100, CL100, SL100, XL100, 1973-1980 CB125, SL125)

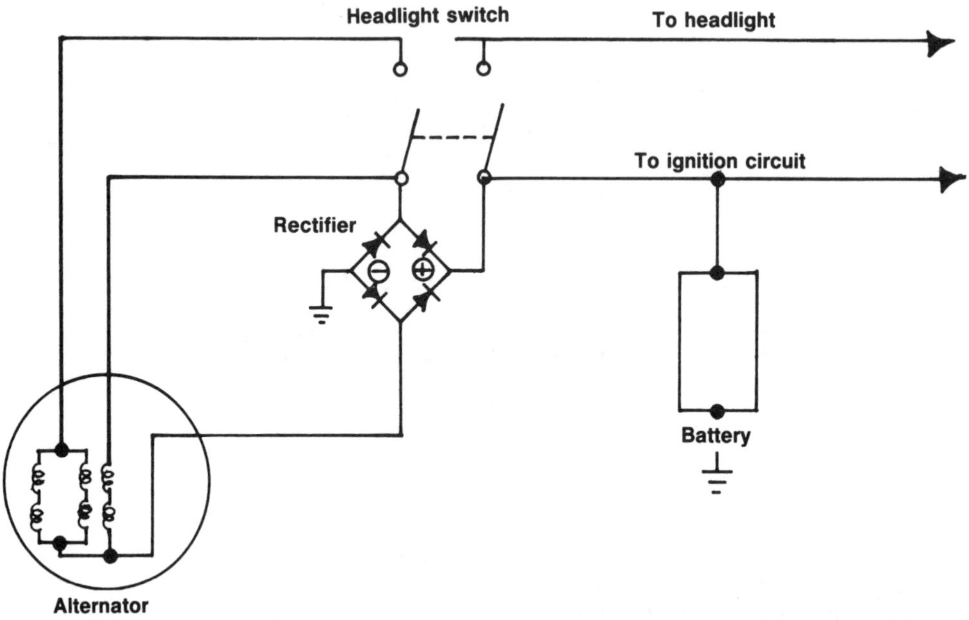

Headlight switch
To headlight
To ignition circuit
Rectifier
Battery
Alternator

2

CHARGING CIRCUIT (XL125, CT125)

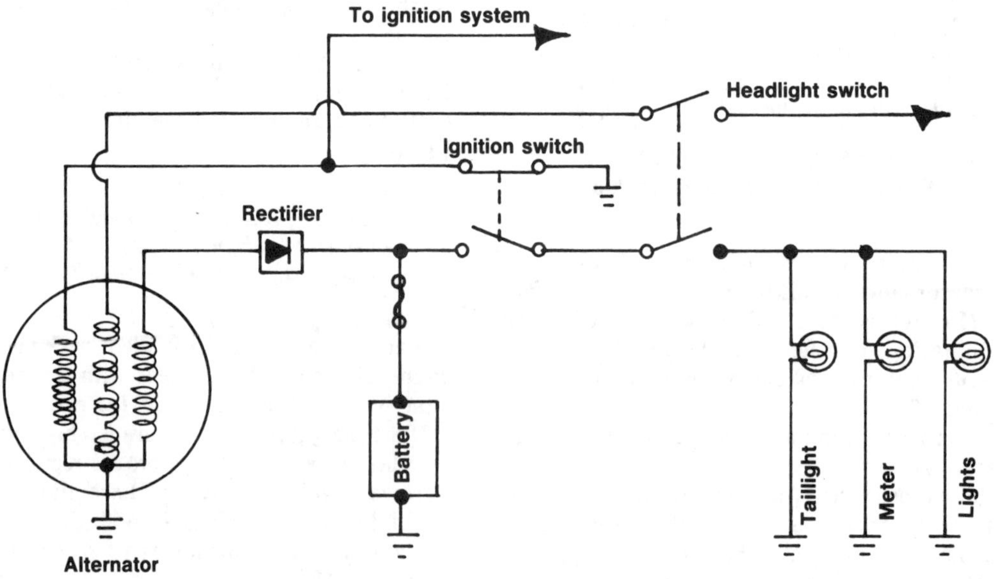

To ignition system
Headlight switch
Ignition switch
Rectifier
Battery
Taillight
Meter
Lights
Alternator

③ CHARGING CIRCUIT (XL125)

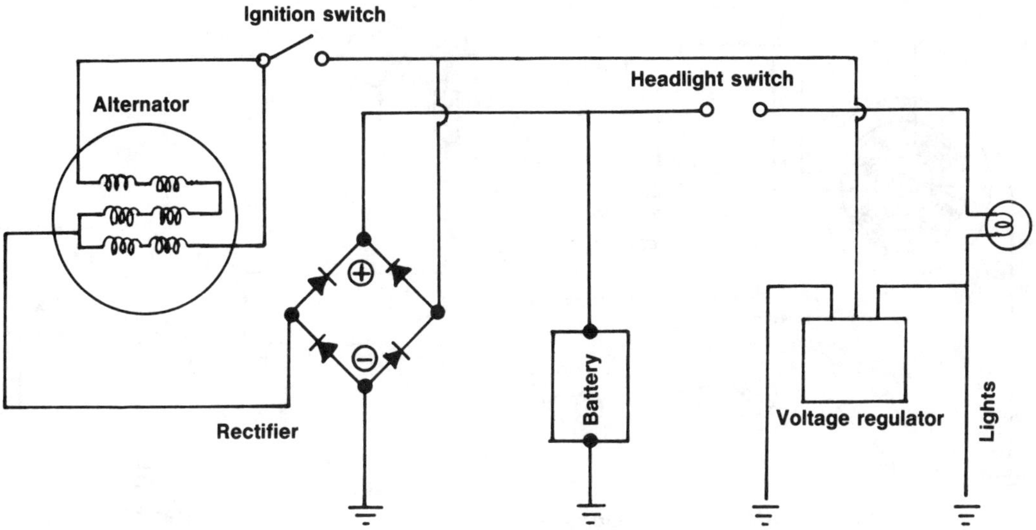

④ CHARGING CIRCUIT (XL250, XL350)

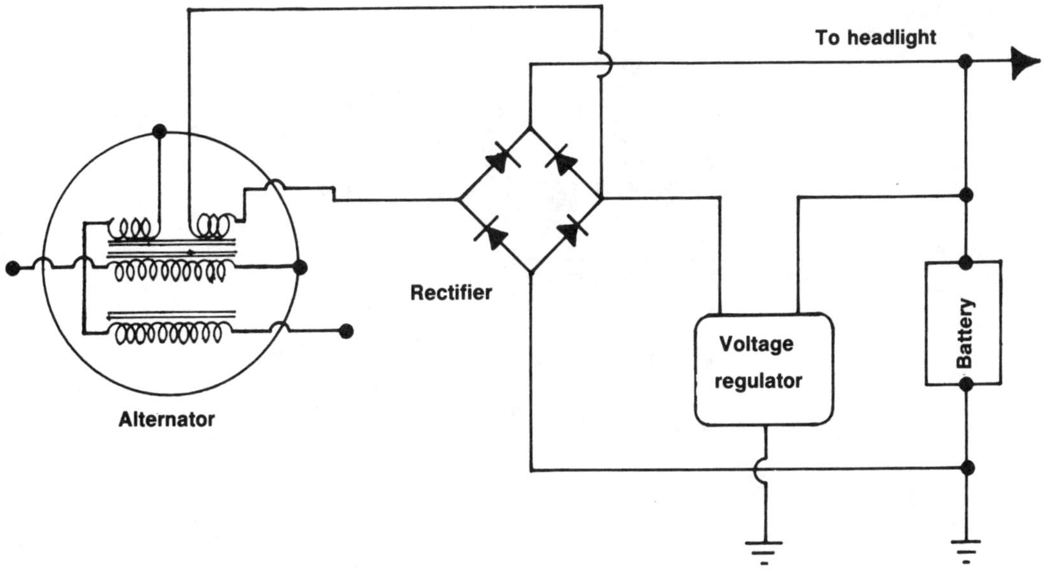

5

CHARGING CIRCUIT (1981-ON CB125)

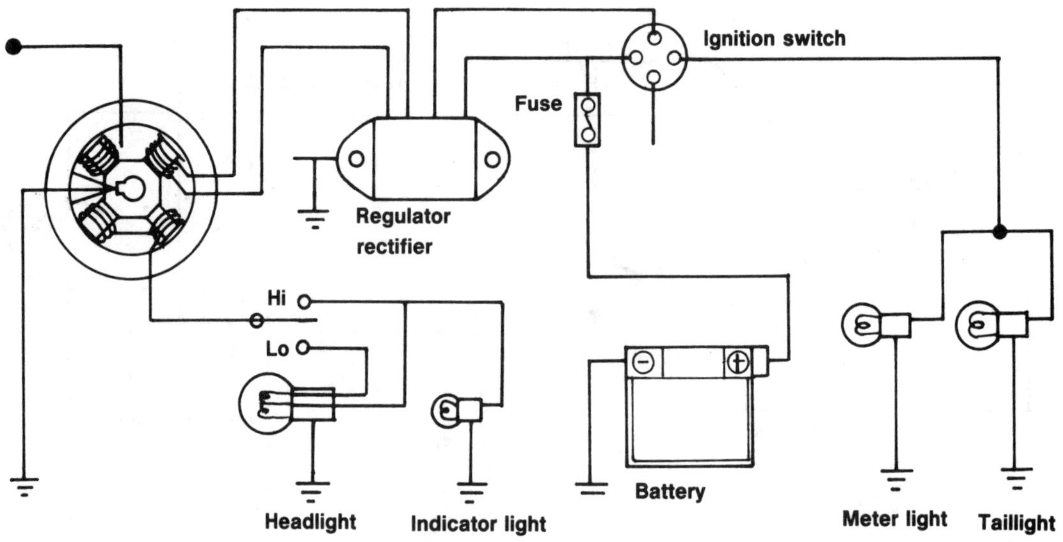

6

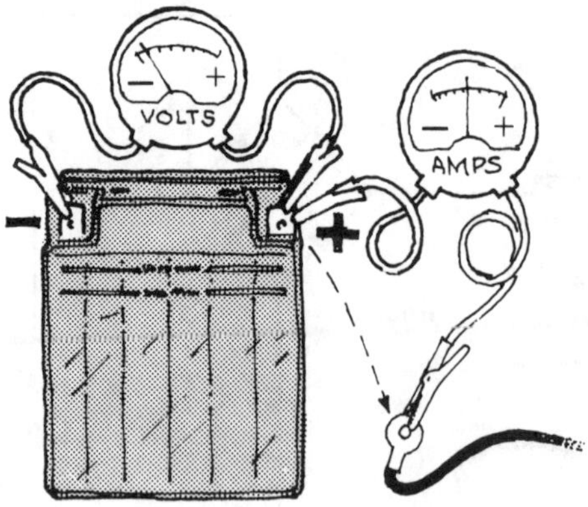

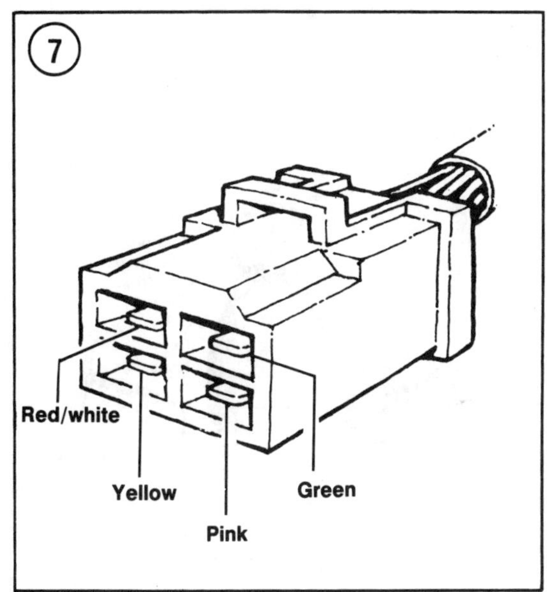

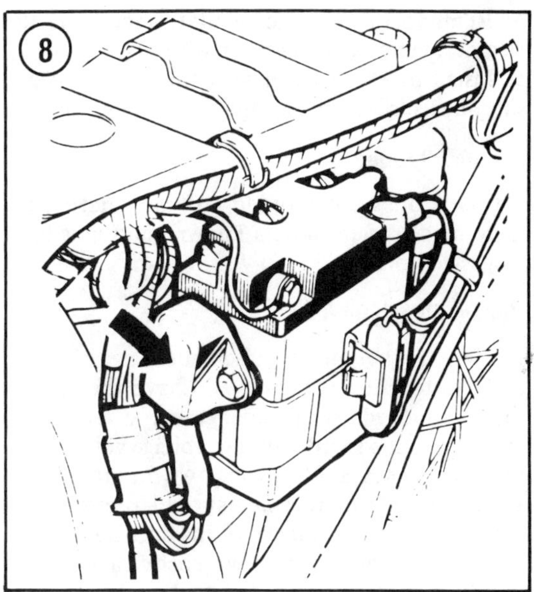

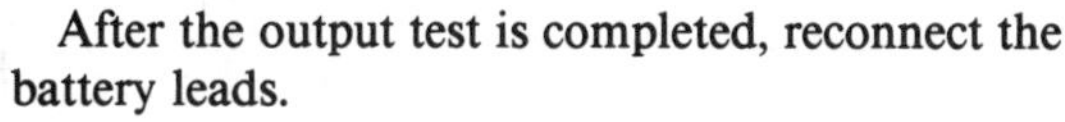

After the output test is completed, reconnect the battery leads.

RECTIFIER

Removal/Installation

1. Remove the seat and the left-hand side cover.
2. Remove the fuel tank as described in Chapter Seven.
3. Disconnect the battery negative lead.
4. Disconnect the electrical connection coming from the rectifier.
5. Remove the bolt securing the rectifier to the mounting bracket and remove the rectifier.
6. Install by reversing these removal steps. Make sure all electrical connections are tight.

Testing (4-terminal Rectifier)

Make the following test using an ohmmeter with a positive ground. If a negative ground ohmmeter is used, reverse the test leads in the following test. Refer to **Figure 7** for this procedure.

1. Disconnect the electrical connector coming from the rectifier. This connection contains 4 wires (one green, one pink, one yellow and one red/white).
2. Connect the ohmmeter positive (+) lead to the red/white wire and the negative (-) lead first to the pink wire, then to the green wire and finally to the yellow wire. All 3 readings should show continuity (low resistance).
3. Reverse the ohmmeter leads and repeat Step 2. This time all readings should show no continuity (infinite resistance).
4. There should be no continuity between any other wire pairs other than those tested in Step 2.
5. If the rectifier fails to pass any of these tests the unit is defective and must be replaced.

Testing (2-terminal Rectifier)

Make the following test using an ohmmeter with a positive ground. If a negative ground ohmmeter is used, reverse the test leads in the following test.

1. Disconnect the rectifier from the electrical connector on the wiring harness. This connector contains 2 wires (one red and one white).
2. Connect the ohmmeter positive (+) lead to the red wire and the negative (-) lead to the white wire. There should be continuity (low resistance).
3. Reverse the ohmmeter leads and repeat Step 1. This time there should be no continuity (infinite resistance).
4. If the rectifier fails to pass these tests the unit is defective and must be replaced.

VOLTAGE REGULATOR/RECTIFIER (1981-ON CB125S)

Removal/Installation

1. Remove the seat and the left-hand side cover.
2. Disconnect the battery negative lead.
3. Disconnect the electrical connectors. Remove the nuts securing the voltage regulator/rectifier to the battery holder (**Figure 8**).

4. Remove the voltage regulator/rectifier, the electrical connector and the 2 wires.
5. Install by reversing these removal steps. Make sure all electrical connections are tight and correct.

Rectifier Testing

Honda does not provide test information for these models. Substitute a known good unit for a suspected one.

Voltage Regulator Test

Connect a voltmeter to the battery negative and positive terminals (**Figure 9**). Leave the battery cables attached. Start the engine and let it idle; increase engine speed until the voltage going to the battery reaches 8.0-9.0 volts. At this point, the voltage regulator/rectifier should prevent any further increase in voltage. If this does not happen and voltage increases above specifications, the voltage regulator/rectifier is faulty and must be replaced.

ALTERNATOR

The alternator is a form of electrical generator in which a magnetized field called a rotor revolves within a set of stationary coils called a stator. As the rotor revolves, alternating currect is induced in the stator. The current is then rectified and used to operate the electrical accessories on the motorcycle and for charging the battery (except TL125 and TL250 models). The rotor is permanently magnetized.

ALTERNATOR (INNER ROTOR TYPE)

An inner-rotor alternator (**Figure 10**) is used on the following models:

a. All CB100.
b. All CL100.
c. All SL100.
d. All XL100.
e. CB125 S, CB125 S1-S2, 1976-1980 CB125S.
f. All SL125.
g. All XL125.
h. All XL175.

Rotor Removal/Installation

1. Place a wood block(s) under the engine to support the bike securely.
2. Drain the engine oil as described in Chapter Three.
3. Remove the left-hand rear side cover (**Figure 11**).

9

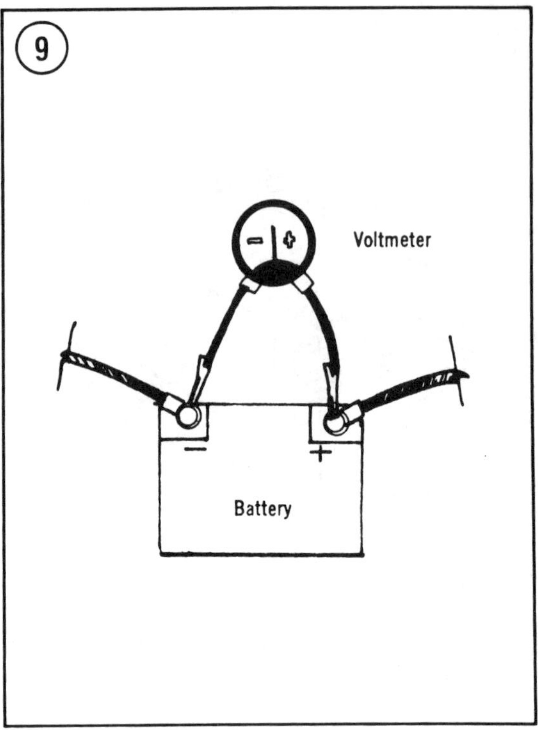

4. Shift the transmission into 5th gear.
5. Remove the bolt securing the gearshift lever (A, **Figure 12**) and remove the gearshift lever.

NOTE
Move the oil drain pan (used in Step 2) under the left-hand crankcase cover as additional oil will drain out when the cover is removed.

6. Remove the bolts securing the left-hand crankcase cover (B, **Figure 12**) and remove the cover.
7. Remove the bolt and washer securing the alternator rotor (**Figure 13**).
8. Screw in a flywheel puller (**Figure 14**) until it stops. Use the Honda flywheel puller (part No. 07933-200000), K & N flywheel puller (part No. 82-015) or equivalent.

CAUTION
Don't try to remove the rotor without a puller; any attempt to do so will ultimately lead to some form of damage to the engine and/or rotor. Many aftermarket pullers are available from motorcycle dealers or mail order houses. The cost of one of these pullers is about $10 and it makes an excellent addition to any mechanic's tool box. If you can't buy or borrow one, have a dealer remove the rotor.

(10)

ALTERNATOR ASSEMBLY (ALL CB100, CL100, SL100, XL100, SL125, XL125, XL175; CB125 S, CB125 S1-S2, 1976-1980 CB125S)

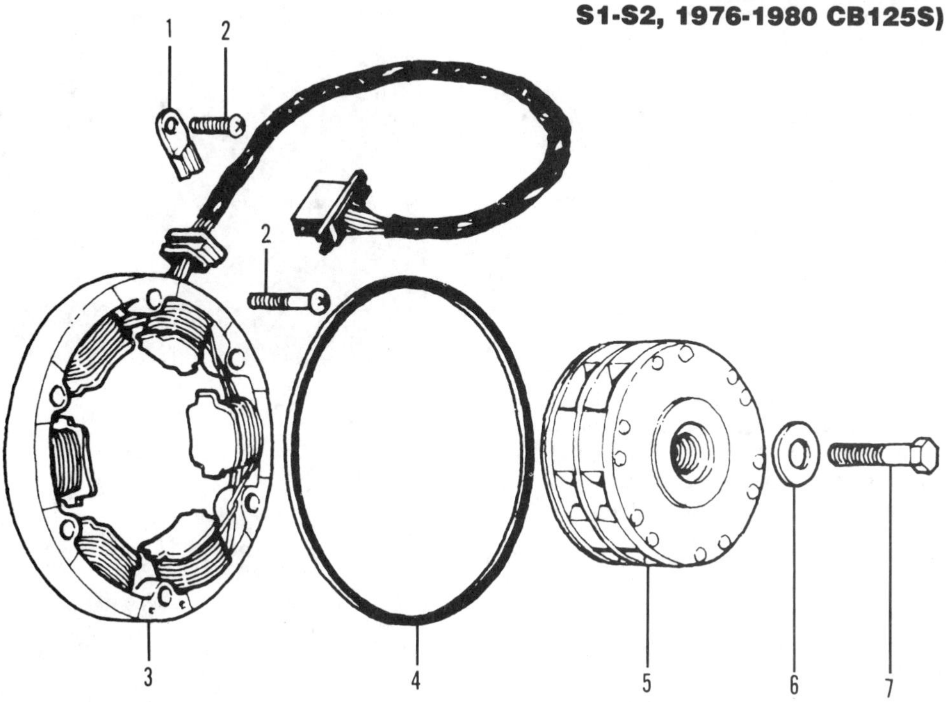

1 2

2

3 4 5 6 7

1. Bracket
2. Screw
3. Stator assembly
4. O-ring seal
5. Rotor
6. Washer
7. Bolt

9. With the transmission in gear, have an assistant hold the rear brake on. Gradually tighten the puller until the rotor disengages from the crankshaft.

NOTE
If the rotor is difficult to remove, strike the puller with a hammer a few times. This will usually break it loose.

CAUTION
If normal rotor removal attempts fail, do not force the puller as the threads may be stripped out of the rotor causing expensive damage. Take it to a dealer and have it removed.

10. Remove the rotor and puller. Don't lose the Woodruff key on the crankshaft.

CAUTION
*Carefully inspect the outside of the rotor (**Figure 15**) for small bolts, washers or other metal "trash" that may have been picked up by the magnets. These small metal bits can cause severe damage to the stator ring components.*

11. Install by reversing these removal steps, noting the following.
12. Make sure the Woodruff key is in place on the crankshaft and align the keyway in the rotor with the key when installing the rotor.
13. Be sure to install the washer prior to installing the rotor bolt. Install the rotor bolt.
14. To keep the rotor from turning, hold it as described in Step 9.
15. Tighten the rotor bolt to the torque specifications listed in **Table 2**.
16. Fill the engine with the recommended type and quantity of oil; refer to Chapter Three.

Rotor Testing

The rotor is permanently magnetized and cannot be tested except by replacement with a rotor known to be good. A rotor can lose magnetism from old age or a sharp blow. If defective, the rotor must be replaced; it cannot be remagnetized.

Stator Assembly Removal/Installation

1. Remove the alternator rotor, as described in this chapter.
2. Disconnect the alternator electrical connector (**Figure 16**).
3A. On 100 and 125 cc engines, remove the screws (**Figure 17**) securing the stator ring assembly to the left-hand crankcase and remove the stator

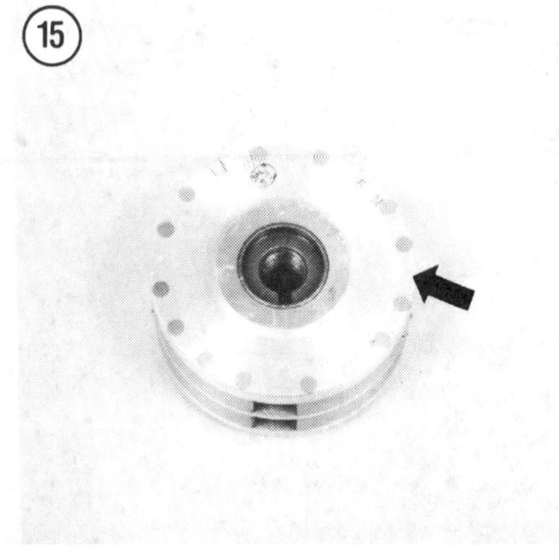

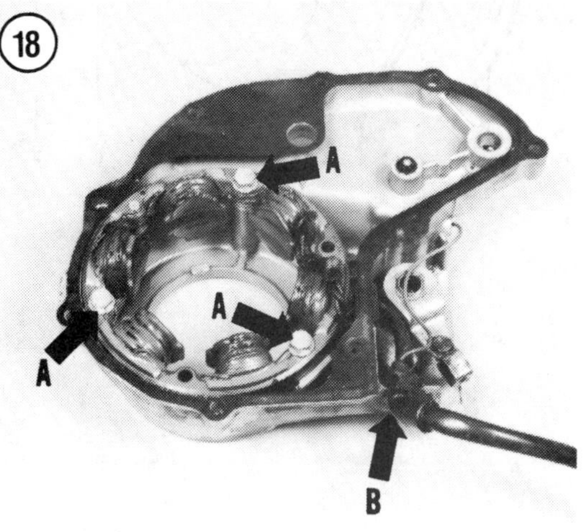

assembly. Pull the grommet and electrical harness out of the left-hand crankcase.

3B. On 175 cc engines, remove the screws (A, **Figure 18**) securing the stator ring assembly to the left-hand crankcase cover and remove the stator assembly. Pull the grommet (B, **Figure 18**) and electrical harness out of the left-hand crankcase cover.

4. Install by reversing these removal steps, noting the following.

5. On 100 and 125 cc engines, make sure the large O-ring is in place on the left-hand crankcase cover.

6. Fill the engine with the recommended type and quantity of oil; refer to Chapter Three.

Stator Coil Testing

It is not necessary to remove the stator assembly to perform the following tests.

In order to get accurate resistance measurements the stator assembly and coil must be warm; minimum temperature is 20° C (68° F). If necessary, start the engine and let it warm up to normal operating temperature, then shut it off.

Use an ohmmeter set at R×1 and check for continuity between each of the terminals of the alternator connector (**Figure 16**). There should be continuity (low resistance). If there is infinite resistance, this indicates there is an open in the circuit. Honda does not provide the specific resistance value.

Also check that there is no continuity between the yellow wire and the stator core (ground). If there is continuity (low resistance), the coil is shorted to ground.

If any of these continuity tests are not met, the coil is bad and the stator assembly must be replaced.

Visually inspect the stator assembly for breaks or cracks in the insulation or other visible damage. Replace if necessary.

8

ALTERNATOR (OUTER ROTOR TYPE)

An outer-rotor alternator is used on the following models:

a. **Figure 19**—1981-on CB125S.
b. **Figure 20**—All TL125.
c. **Figure 21**—All CT125 and TL250.
d. **Figure 22**—All XL250 and XL350.

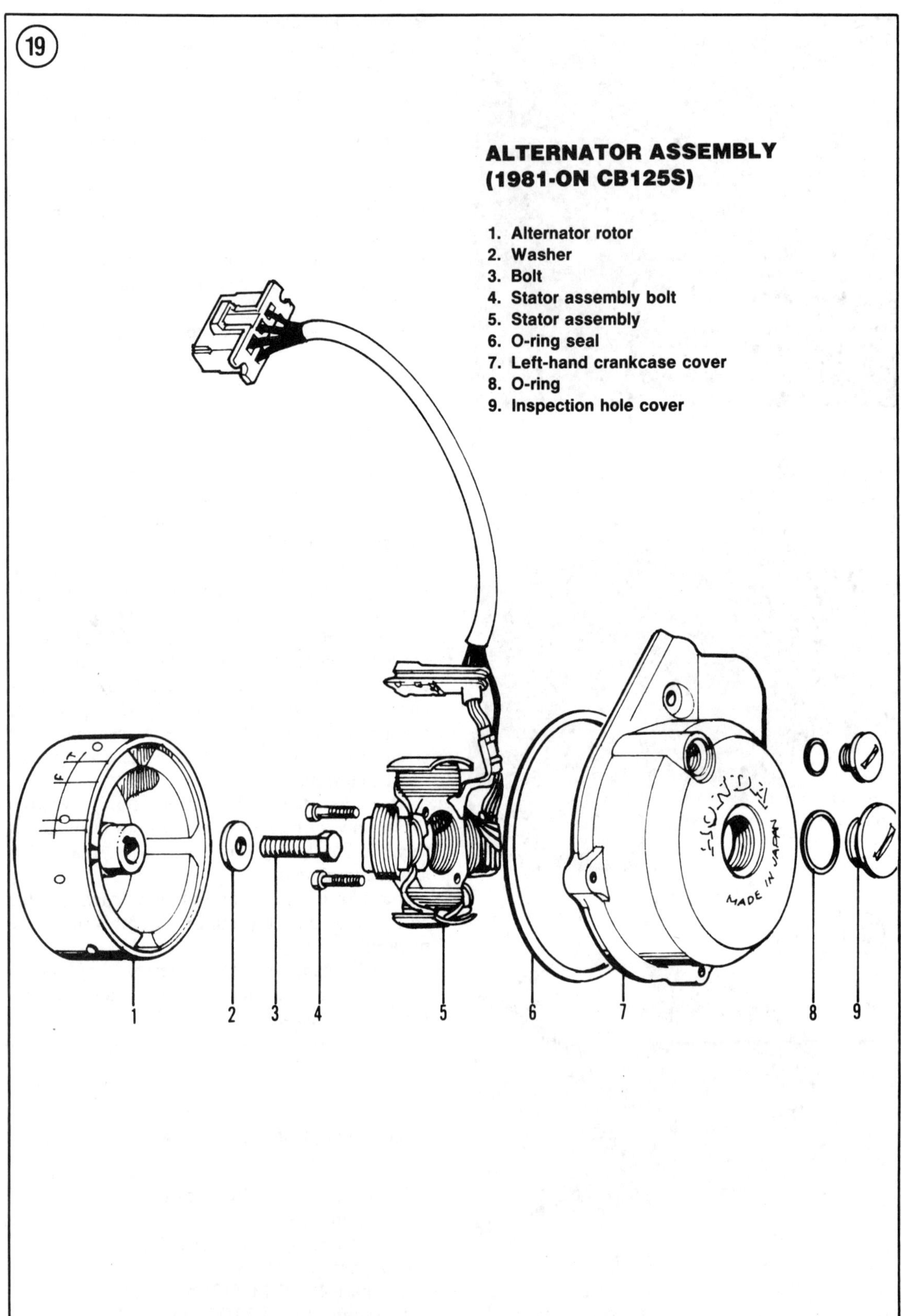
19
ALTERNATOR ASSEMBLY
(1981-ON CB125S)
1. Alternator rotor
2. Washer
3. Bolt
4. Stator assembly bolt
5. Stator assembly
6. O-ring seal
7. Left-hand crankcase cover
8. O-ring
9. Inspection hole cover
HONDA
MADE IN JAPAN
F
T
1
2
3
4
5
6
7
8
9

ALTERNATOR ASSEMBLY
(All TL125)

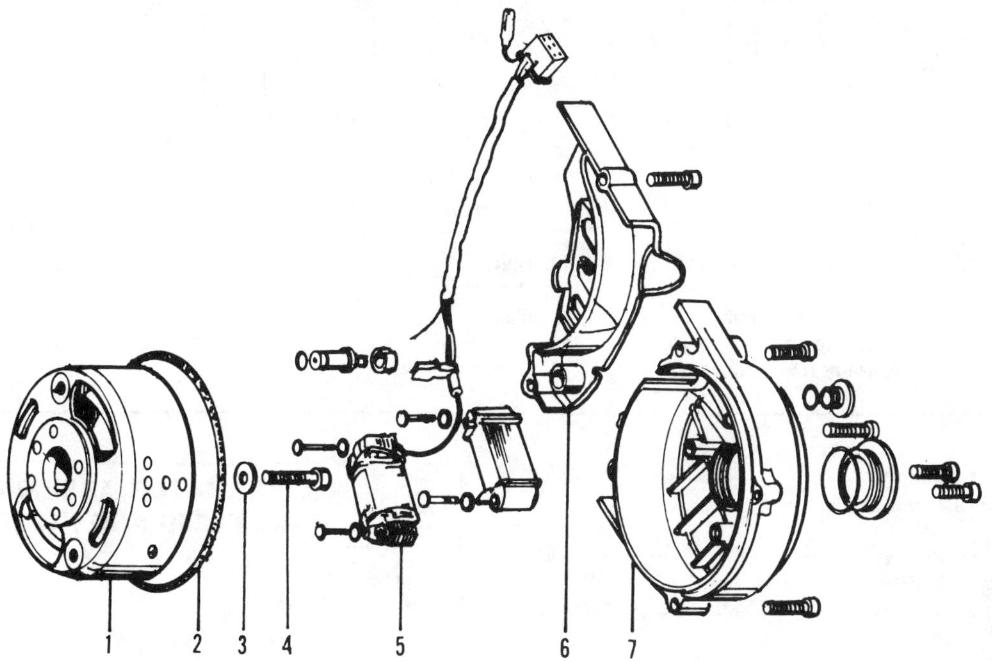

1. Rotor
2. O-ring seal
3. Washer
4. Bolt
5. Stator assembly
6. Left-hand rear crankcase cover
7. Left-hand crankcase cover

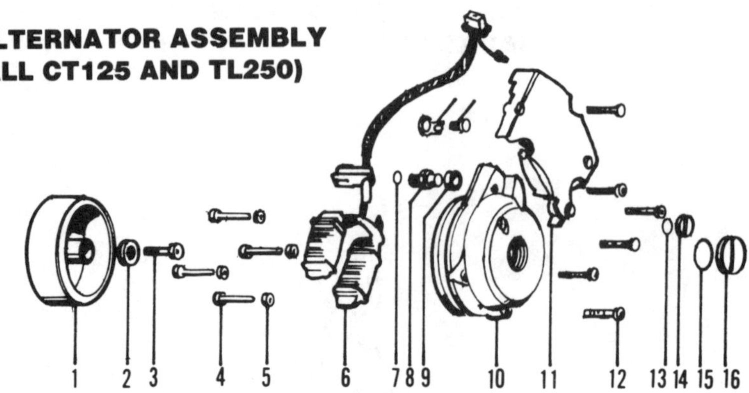

1. Alternator rotor
2. Washer
3. Bolt
4. Stator assembly bolt
5. Washer
6. Stator assembly
7. O-ring seal
8. Neutral indicator switch
9. Spacer
10. Left-hand crankcase cover
11. Left-hand rear crankcase cover
12. Bolt
13. O-ring
14. Cap
15. O-ring
16. Cap

Stator Assembly Removal/Installation

This procedure is shown with the engine removed from the frame for clarity. It is not necessary to remove the engine to perform this procedure.

1. Place a wood block(s) under the engine to support the bike securely.
2. Drain the engine oil as described in Chapter Three.
3. Remove the left-hand rear side cover.
4. Shift the transmission into 5th gear.
5. Remove the gearshift lever (A, **Figure 23**).
6. Disconnect the alternator electrical connector.
7. On models so equipped, disconnect the wire to the neutral switch.

NOTE
Move the oil drain pan (used in Step 2) under the left-hand crankcase cover as additional oil will drain out when the cover is removed.

8. Remove the bolts securing the left-hand crankcase cover (B, **Figure 23**) and remove the cover.
9. If necessary, remove the screws securing the stator assembly (A, **Figure 24**) to the left-hand

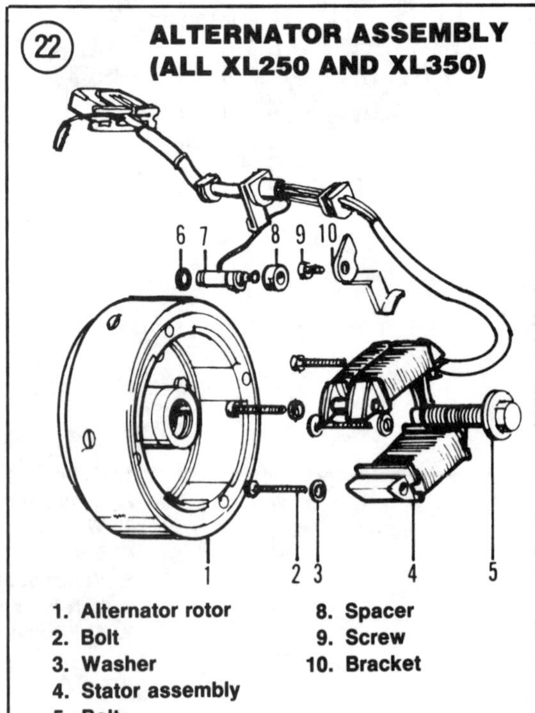

1. Alternator rotor
2. Bolt
3. Washer
4. Stator assembly
5. Bolt
6. O-ring seal
7. Neutral indicator switch
8. Spacer
9. Screw
10. Bracket

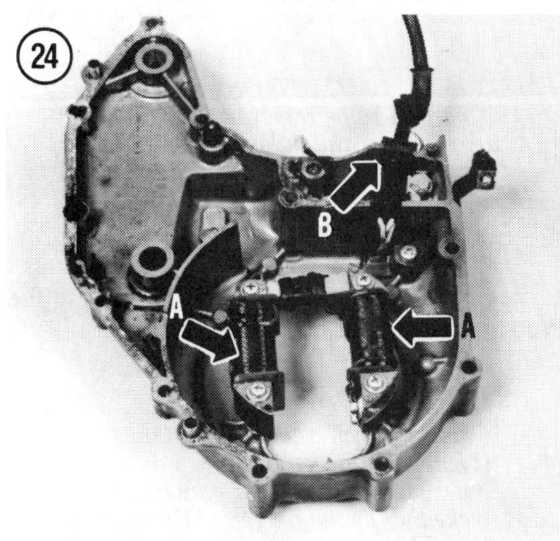

crankcase housing and remove the stator assembly. Pull the grommet (B, **Figure 24**) and electrical harness out of the left-hand crankcase housing.

10. Install by reversing these removal steps, noting the following.
11. On models so equipped, make sure the large O-ring or gasket is in place on the left-hand crankcase cover.
12. Fill the engine with the recommended type and quantity of oil; refer to Chapter Three.

Stator Coil Testing

It is not necessary to remove the stator assembly to perform the following tests.

In order to get accurate resistance measurements the stator assembly and coil must be warm; minimum temperature is 20° C (68° F). If necessary, start the engine and let it warm up to normal operating temperature, then shut it off.

1981-on CB125

Use an ohmmeter set at R×1 and check for continuity between the white/yellow wire and ground. The specified resistance is 0.47 ohms.

Check resistance between the yellow wire and the pink wire; the specified resistance is 0.58 ohms.

If either of these tests are not met, one of the coils is bad and the stator assembly must be replaced (the individual coil cannot be replaced).

Use an ohmmeter set at R×1 and check for continuity between the black/white wire and ground. The specified resistance is 2.29 ohms.

Check between the white/yellow wire and ground; the specified resistance is 0.36 ohms.

Check between the yellow wire and the pink wire; the specified resistance is 0.57 ohms.

If any of these resistance values are not met, one of the coils is bad and the stator assembly must be replaced (the individual coil cannot be replaced).

All TL125

Use an ohmmeter set at R×1 and check for continuity between the black/white wire and ground. There should be continuity (low resistance). Honda does not provide specific resistance values.

If there is no continuity (infinite resistance), there is an open in the coil and the stator assembly must be replaced.

All CT125

Use an ohmmeter set at R×1 and check for continuity between each of the following points:

a. Black/white wire to yellow wire.
b. Pink wire to ground.
c. White/yellow wire to pink wire.
d. Yellow wire to ground.

There should be continuity (low resistance) between each of these points. Honda does not provide specific resistance values.

If there is no continuity (infinite resistance) there is an open in the coil(s) and the stator assembly must be replaced (individual coils cannot be replaced).

All TL250

Use an ohmmeter set at R×1 and check for continuity between the black wire and the yellow wire. There should be continuity (low resistance). Honda does not provide specific resistance values.

If there is no continuity (infinite resistance) there is an open in the coil and the stator assembly must be replaced.

All XL250 and XL350

Use an ohmmeter set at R×1 and check for continuity between the black/white wire and ground. The specified resistance is 2.29 ohms.

Check between the white/yellow wire and ground; the specified resistance is 0.36 ohms.

Check between the yellow wire and the pink wire; the specified resistance is 0.57 ohms.

If any of these resistance values are not met, one of the coils is bad and the stator assembly must be replaced (the individual coil cannot be replaced).

Rotor
Removal/Installation

1. Remove the stator assembly, as described in this chapter.
2. Remove the bolt securing the alternator rotor (**Figure 25**).
3. Screw in a flywheel puller (**Figure 26**) until it stops:
   a. On 125 cc engines, use the Honda flywheel puller (part No. 07933-2000000) or equivalent.
   b. On 250 and 350 cc engines, use a Honda flywheel puller (part No. 07933-3290000), K & N flywheel puller (part No. 81-0170) or equivalent.

CAUTION
Don't try to remove the rotor without a puller; any attempt to do so will ultimately lead to some form of damage to the engine and/or rotor. Many aftermarket pullers are available from most motorcycle dealers or mail order houses. The cost of one of these pullers is about $10 and it makes an excellent addition to any mechanic's tool box. If you can't buy or borrow one, have a dealer remove the rotor.

4. With the transmission in gear, have an assistant hold the rear brake on and gradually tighten the puller until the rotor disengages from the crankshaft.

NOTE
If the rotor is difficult to remove, strike the puller with a hammer a few times. This will usually break it loose.

CAUTION
If normal rotor removal attempts fail, do not force the puller as the threads may be stripped out of the rotor causing expensive damage. Take it to a dealer and have it removed.

5. Remove the rotor and puller. Don't lose the Woodruff key on the crankshaft.

CAUTION
*Carefully inspect the inside of the rotor (**Figure 27**) for small bolts, washers or other metal "trash" that may have been picked up by the magnets. These small metal bits can cause severe damage to the stator plate components.*

25

26

6. Install by reversing these removal steps, noting the following.
7. Make sure the Woodruff key (**Figure 28**) is in place on the crankshaft and align the keyway in the rotor with the key when installing the rotor.
8. Be sure to install the washer prior to installing the rotor bolt. Install the rotor bolt.
9. To keep the rotor from turning, hold it as described in Step 4.
10. Tighten the rotor nut to the torque specification listed in **Table 2**.
11. Fill the engine with the recommended type and quantity of oil; refer to Chapter Three.

Rotor Testing

The rotor is permanently magnetized and cannot be tested except by replacement with a rotor known to be good. A rotor can lose magnetism from old age or a sharp blow. If defective, the rotor must be replaced; it cannot be remagnetized.

BREAKER POINT IGNITION

Contact breaker point ignition is used on all models except the 1981-on CB125S. This model is equipped with an electronic ignition system that is covered separately in this chapter.

As the alternator rotor turns, magnets located in it move past a stationary ignition source coil on the stator, inducing a current in the coil. A cam on the end of the camshaft opens the contact breaker point assembly at the precise instant the piston reaches its firing position.

Figure 29 shows a typical contact breaker point ignition system. Variations exist among the

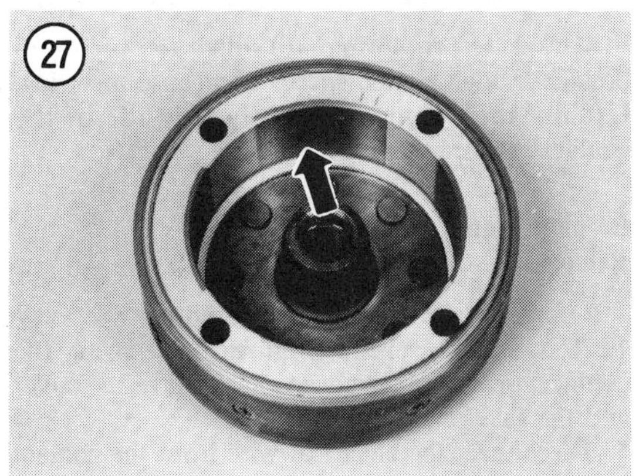

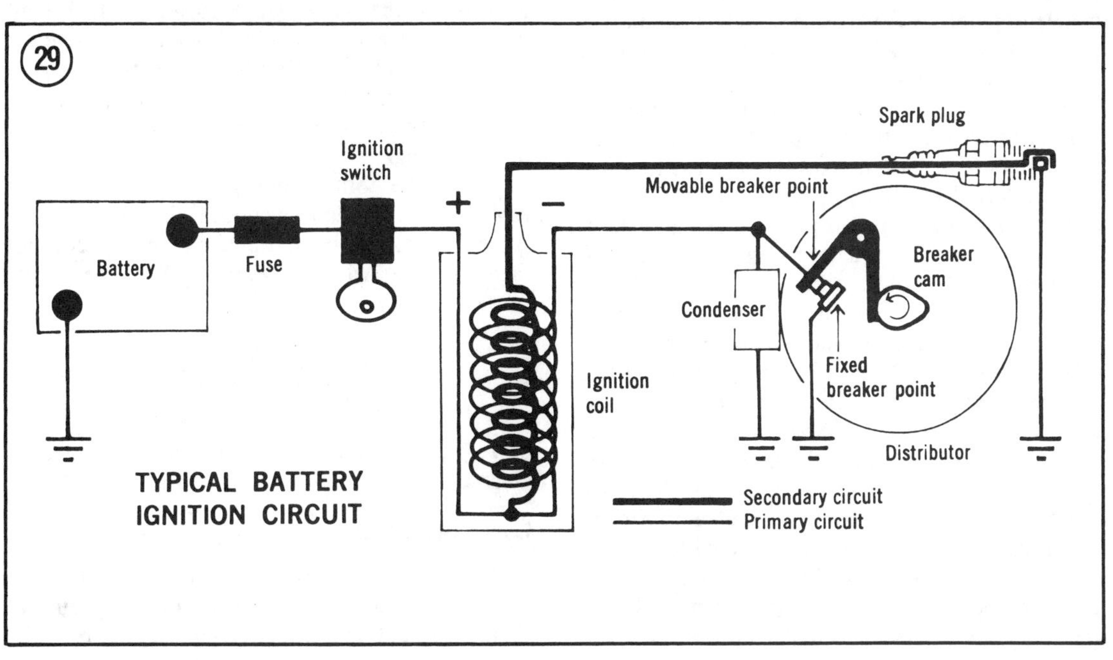

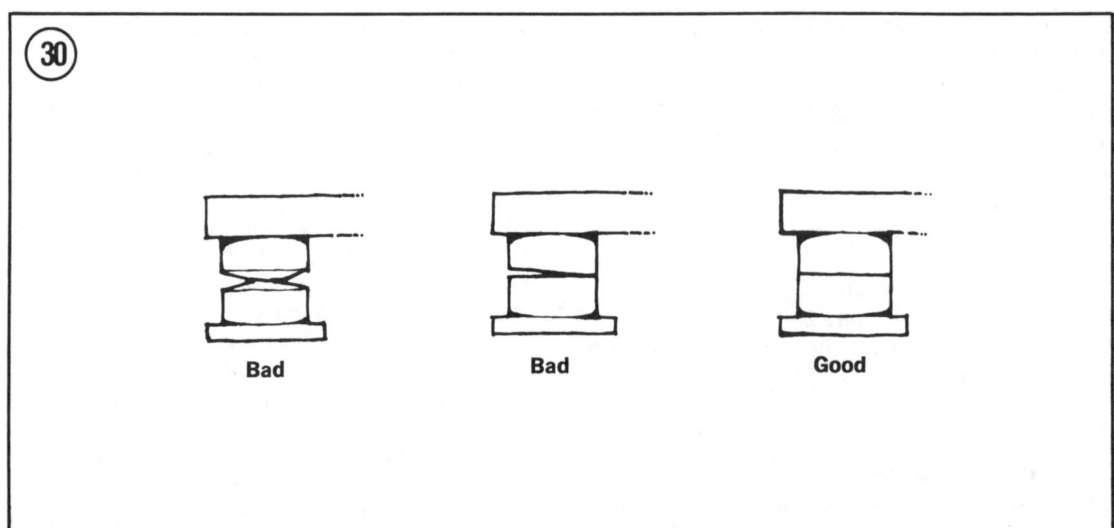

various models but servicing procedures are the same.

Spark plug service is described in Chapter Three.

Breaker Point Inspection/Cleaning

During normal operation, the contact surfaces of the points gradually pit and burn. If the points are not too badly pitted, they can be dressed with a few strokes of a clean point file or Flexstone (available as most auto supply stores). Do not use emery cloth or sandpaper, as particles will remain on the points and cause arcing and burning. If a few strokes of the file do not smooth the points completely, replace them with a new set. If the points are still serviceable after filing, remove all residue with electrical contact cleaner or lacquer thinner. Close the points on a piece of white paper such as a business card. Continue to pull the card through the closed points until no particles or discoloration are transferred to the card. Finally, rotate the engine and observe the points as they open and close. If they do not meet squarely (**Figure 30**), replace them as described in this chapter.

Oil or dirt may get on the points, creating electrical resistance or resulting in their failure. This can be caused by a defective camshaft seal or incorrect breaker cam lubricant. To correct this condition, remove the contact breaker assembly and dress the points. Clean the assembly in lacquer thinner (or aerosol contact cleaner) and lubricate the breaker cam with contact breaker lubricant. Never use oil or common grease; they break down under high temperature and frictional load and are likely to find their way to the point surface. Check the camshaft end seal and replace if necessary.

A weak return spring will allow the points to bounce at high engine speeds and cause misfiring. Usually the spring will last for the life of the contact breaker asembly.

Breaker Point Removal/Installation

Refer to **Figure 31** for this procedure.

1. Remove the screws (**Figure 32**) securing the contact breaker point cover and remove the cover and the gasket.
2. Disconnect the electrical wire from the contact breaker point assembly to the wiring harness.
3. Remove the screws (A, **Figure 33**) which hold the contact breaker assembly in place. Remove the rubber grommet (B, **Figure 33**) from the engine housing and remove the breaker point assembly.
4. Install by reversing these removal steps, noting the following.
5. When the contact breaker point assembly is replaced the condenser should also be replaced. Apply breaker point lubricant to the contact breaker point wick (C, **Figure 33**) and coat the brcakcr cam.

NOTE
The condenser is located next to the ignition coil.

6. Adjust the ignition timing as described in Chapter Three.

Condenser Testing

The condenser requires no service other than checking to see that its connections is clean and tight. It should be routinely replaced each time the

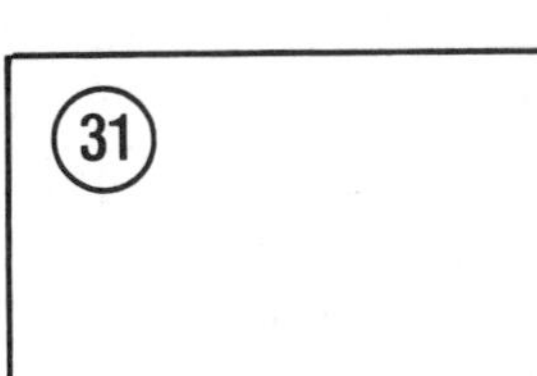

(31)

BREAKER POINT ASSEMBLY

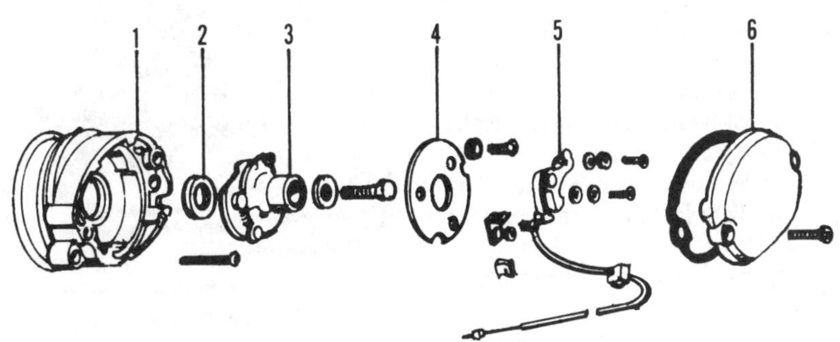

1. Breaker point case
2. Oil seal
3. Ignition advance mechanism
4. Base plate
5. Contact breaker points
6. Cover and gasket

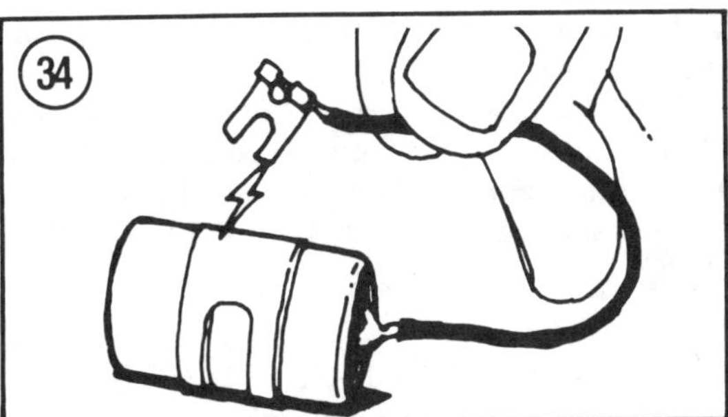

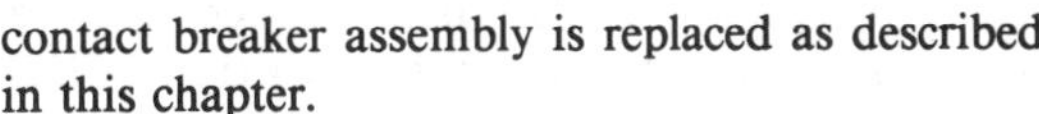

contact breaker assembly is replaced as described in this chapter.

NOTE

On all 250 cc and some 350 cc engines, the condenser is an integral part of the ignition coil. Only replace the condenser on these models if it fails to pass its test.

To test the condenser remove it from the ignition coil mounting area and connect it to a 6-volt battery. Connect the battery negative lead (-) to the condenser lead and the battery positive lead (+) to the condenser case. Allow it to charge for a few seconds. Then, quickly disconnect it and touch the lead to the condenser case (**Figure 34**). If there is a spark as the lead touches the case, you may assume that the condenser is good. If not, replace the condenser.

Ignition Advance Mechanism Removal/Inspection/Installation

The ignition advance mechanism advances the ignition (fires the spark plug sooner) as engine speed increases. If it does not advance properly and smoothly, ignition timing will be incorrect at high engine rpm. It must be inspected periodically to make certain it operates smoothly.

The ignition advance mechanism is located in the cylinder head just behind the contact breaker point assembly.

1. Remove the contact breaker point assembly as described in this chapter.
2. Remove the bolt and washer (**Figure 35**) securing the ignition advance unit to the camshaft and remove the unit.
3. Inspect the pivot points (A, **Figure 36**) of each weight. The arms must rotate freely to maintain proper ignition advance.
4. Inspect the return springs (B, **Figure 36**). Make sure they are taut and that they completely return the arms to their fully retarded position.
5. If the unit fails either of these inspections, it must be replaced.
6. Install by reversing these removal steps, noting the following.
7. Index the dowel pin on the camshaft (A, **Figure 37**) with the notch (B, **Figure 37**) on the backside of the ignition advance unit. Install the bolt and washer and tighten the bolt to 8-12 N•m (6-9 ft.-lb.).

CAPACITOR DISCHARGE IGNITION (1981-ON CB125S)

The 1981-on CB125S is equipped with a solid-state capacitor discharge ignition (CDI) system that uses no breaker points (**Figure 38**).

Alternating current from the alternator is rectified to direct current and is used to charge the capacitor. As the piston approaches the firing position, a pulse from the exciter coil is used to trigger the silicone controlled rectifier. The rectifier in turn allows the capacitor to discharge quickly into the primary circuit of the ignition coil, where the voltage is stepped up in the secondary circuit to a value sufficient to fire the spark plug.

Spark plug service is described in Chapter Three.

CDI Precautions

Certain measures must be taken to protect the capacitor discharge system. Instantaneous damage

35

36

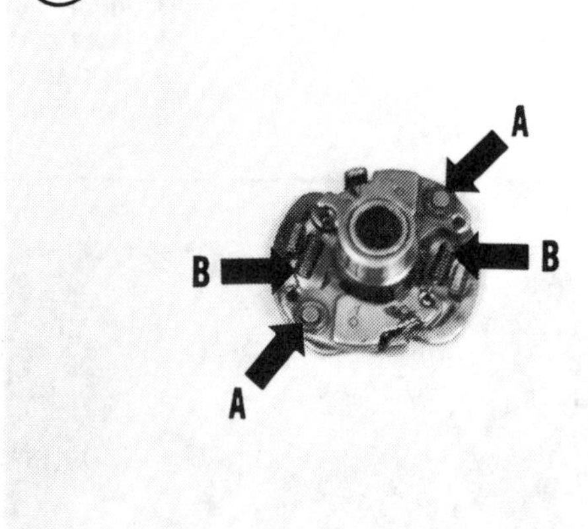

37

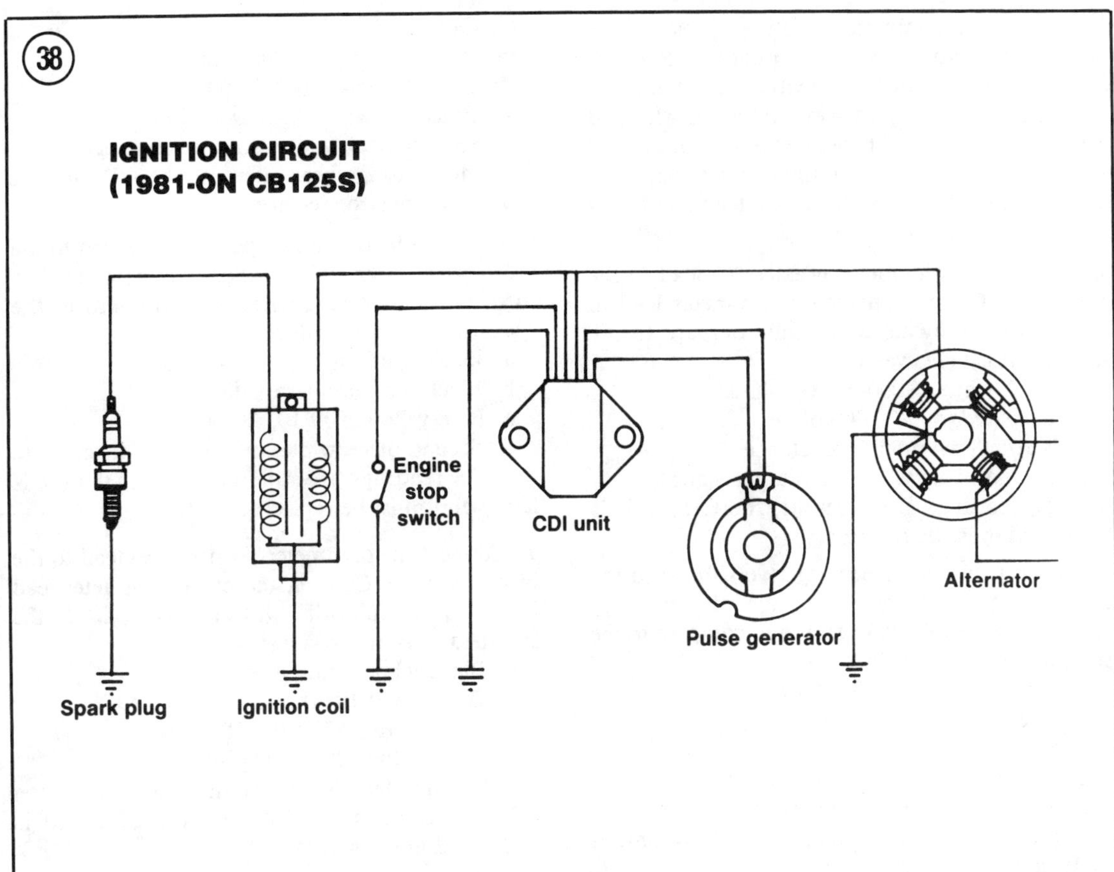

to the semiconductors in the system will occur if the following precautions are not observed.

1. Never disconnect any of the electrical connections while the engine is running.
2. Keep all connections between the various units clean and tight. Be sure that the wiring connectors are pushed together firmly to help keep out moisture.
3. Do not substitute another type of ignition coil.
4. The CDI unit is mounted within a rubber vibration isolator. Always be sure that the isolator is in place when installing the unit.
5. Never connect the battery backwards. If the battery polarity is wrong, damage will occur to the voltage regulator/rectifier, the alternator and the CDI unit.

CDI Troubleshooting

Problems with the capacitor discharge system fall into one of the following categories. See **Table 3**.

a. Weak spark.
b. No spark.

CDI Testing

To test the CDI unit, remove the unit from the frame as described in this chapter.

CAUTION

Tests may be performed on the CDI unit but a good one may be damaged by someone unfamiliar with the test equipment. If you feel unqualified to perform the test, have the test made by a Honda dealer or substitute a known good unit for a suspected one.

NOTE

Tests must be made with an accurate ohmmeter or the test readings may be false.

1. Connect the ohmmeter negative (-) lead to the black/white wire. Connect the other ohmmeter lead in turn to the green wire, the black/red wire, the second green wire, the blue/yellow wire and the second black/white wire. There must be no continuity. If the readings are different, the CDI unit is faulty and must be replaced.

8

2. Connect the ohmmeter negative (-) lead to the other black/white wire. Connect the other ohmmeter lead to the black/white wire, the green wire, the other black/red wire, the green wire and the blue/yellow wire. There must be continuity and all readings must the same (infinite resistance). If the readings are different, the CDI unit is faulty and must be replaced.

3. Connect the ohmmeter negative (-) lead to the green wire. Connect the other ohmmeter lead in turn to the following wires and compare to the specified resistance values:

a. Black/white: 2,000-50,000 ohms.
b. Black/red: 500-10,000 ohms.
c. Blue/yellow: infinite resistance.
d. Second black/white: infinite resistance.

If the readings are different, the CDI unit is faulty and must be replaced.

4. Connect the ohmmeter negative (-) lead to the black/red wire. Connect the other ohmmeter in turn lead to the following wires and compare to the specified resistance values:

a. Black/white: 500-10,000 ohms.
b. Green: infinite resistance.
c. Second green: infinite resistance.
d. Blue/yellow: infinite resistance.
e. Second black/white: infinite resistance.

If the readings are different, the CDI unit is faulty and must be replaced.

5. Connect the ohmmeter negative (-) lead to the second green wire. Connect the other ohmmeter lead in turn to the following wires and compare to the specified resistance values:

a. Black/white: 2,000-50,000 ohms.
b. Black/red: 500-10,000 ohms.
c. Blue/yellow: infinite resistance.
d. Second black/white: infinite resistance.

If the readings are different, the CDI unit is faulty and must be replaced.

6. Connect the ohmmeter negative (-) lead to the blue/yellow wire. Connect the other ohmmeter lead in turn to the following wires and compare to the specified resistance values:

a. Black/white: 2,000-50,000 ohms.
b. Green: 500-10,000 ohms.
c. Black/red: 2,000-50,000 ohms.
b. Second green: 500-10,000 ohms.
e. Second black/white: infinite resistance.

If the readings are different, the CDI unit is faulty and must be replaced.

7. Connect the ohmmeter positive (+) lead to the black/white wire. Connect the other ohmmeter lead in turn to the following wires and compare to the specified resistance values:

a. Green: 2,000-50,000 ohms.
b. Black/red: 500-10,000 ohms.
c. Second green: 2,000-50,000 onms.
d. Blue/yellow: 2,000-50,000 ohms.
e. Second black/white: infinite resistance.

If the readings are different, the CDI unit is faulty and must be replaced.

8. Connect the ohmmeter positive (+) lead to the green wire. Connect the other ohmmeter lead in turn to the following wires and compare to the specified resistance values:

a. Black/white: infinite resistance.
b. Black/red: infinite resistance.
c. Blue/yellow: 500-10,000 ohms.
d. Second black/white: infinite resistance.

If the readings are different, the CDI unit is faulty and must be replaced.

9. Connect the ohmmeter positive (+) lead to the black/red wire. Connect the other ohmmeter lead in turn to the following wires and compare to the specified resistance values:

a. Black/white: infinite resistance.
b. Green: 500-10,000 ohms.
c. Second green: 500-10,000 ohms.
d. Blue/yellow: 200-50,000 ohms.
e. Second black/white: infinite resistance.

If the readings are different, the CDI unit is faulty and must be replaced.

10. Connect the ohmmeter positive (+) lead to the green wire. Connect the other ohmmeter lead in turn to the following wires and compare to the specified resistance values:

a. Black/white: infinite resistance.
b. Black/red: infinite resistance.
c. Blue/yellow: 500-10,000 ohms.
d. Second black/white: infinite resistance.

If the readings are different, the CDI unit is faulty and must be replaced.

11. Connect the ohmmeter positive (+) lead to the blue/yellow terminal. Connect the other ohmmeter lead in turn to the black/white wire, the green wire, the black/red wire, the second green wire and the second black/white wire. There must be no continuity. If the readings are different, the CDI unit is faulty and must be replaced.

12. Connect the ohmmeter positive (+) lead to the black/white wire. Connect the other ohmmeter lead to the other black/white wire, the green wire, the black/red wire, the other green wire and to the blue/yellow wire. There must be continuity and all readings must the same (infinite resistance). If the readings are different or there is no continuity the CDI unit is faulty and must be replaced.

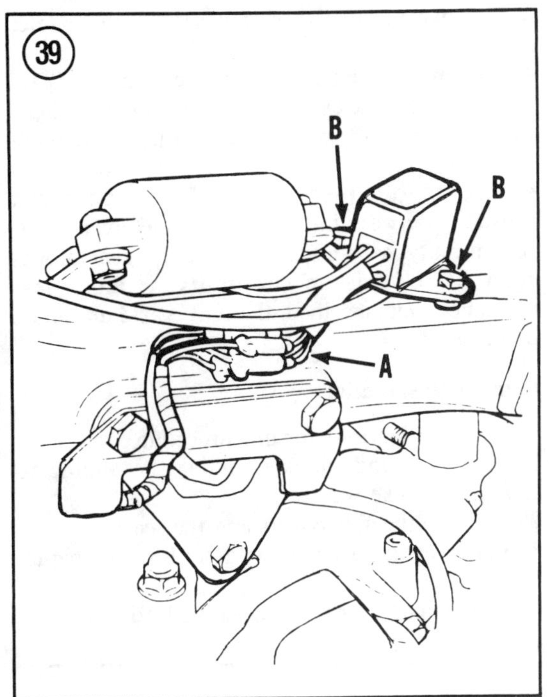

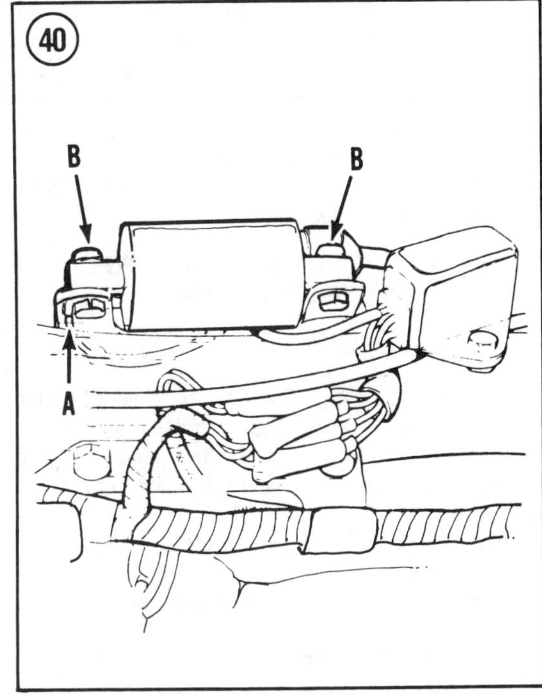

CDI Replacement

1. Remove the side covers and the seat.
2. Remove the fuel tank as described in Chapter Seven.
3. Disconnect the electrical wires from the CDI unit to the electrical harness and the wire going to the ignition coil (A, **Figure 39**).
4. Remove the bolts securing the CDI unit to the mounting bracket (B, **Figure 39**) on the frame just behind the ignition coil.
5. Install a new CDI unit and attach the electrical wires to it. Make sure all electrical connections are tight.
6. Reinstall the fuel tank, seat and side covers.

IGNITION COIL

Removal/Installation

1. Remove the side covers and the seat.
2. Remove the fuel tank as described in Chapter Seven.
3. On models so equipped, disconnect the battery negative lead.
4. Disconnect the high voltage lead from the spark plug.

5A. On 1981-on CB125S, disconnect the electrical wire (A, **Figure 40**) from the CDI unit to the ignition coil.

5B. On all other models, disconnect the secondary electrical wires from the ignition coil.

6. Remove the bolts (B, **Figure 40**) securing the ignition coil to the frame and remove the coil.
7. Install by reversing these removal steps, noting the following.
8. Make sure all electrical connections are tight and free of corrosion.

Testing

The ignition coil is a form of transformer which develops the high voltage required to jump the spark plug gap. The only maintenance required is that of keeping the electrical connections clean and tight and occasionally checking to see that the coil is mounted securely.

If the condition of the coil is doubtful, disconnect the high voltage lead from the spark plug. Remove the spark plug from the cylinder head. Connect a new or known good spark plug to the high voltage lead and place the spark plug base on a good ground such as the engine cylinder head. Position the spark plug so you can see the electrode.

WARNING
On the 1981-on CB125S, if it is necessary to hold the high voltage lead, do so with an insulated pair of pliers. The high voltage generated by the CDI could produce serious or fatal shocks.

Turn the engine over with the kickstarter. If a fat blue spark occurs, the coil is in good condition. Make sure that you are using a known good spark plug for this test. If the spark plug used is defective the test results will be incorrect. Also make sure the spark plug lead is not defective.

Reinstall the spark plug in the cylinder head and connect the spark plug lead.

IGNITION PULSE GENERATOR (1981-ON CB125S)

Inspection

In order to get accurate resistance measurements the unit must be warm; minimum temperature is 20° C (68° F). If necessary, start the engine and let it warm up to normal operating temperature, then shut it off.

1. Place a wood block(s) under the engine to support the bike securely.
2. Remove the side covers and the seat.
3. Remove the fuel tank as described in Chapter Seven.
4. Disconnect the battery negative lead.
5. Disconnect the electrical connector containing 2 wires (one green, one blue/yellow) from the pulse generator.
6. Use an ohmmeter set at R×1 and check resistance between the blue/yellow and green wires. If continuity is 20-60 ohms, the pulse generator is good. If there is no continuity or much less resistance than specified, the unit is bad and must be replaced.

Removal/Installation

Refer to **Figure 41** for this procedure.

1. Place a wood block(s) under the engine to support the bike securely.
2. Remove the side covers and the seat.
3. Remove the fuel tank as described in Chapter Seven.
4. Disconnect the battery negative lead.

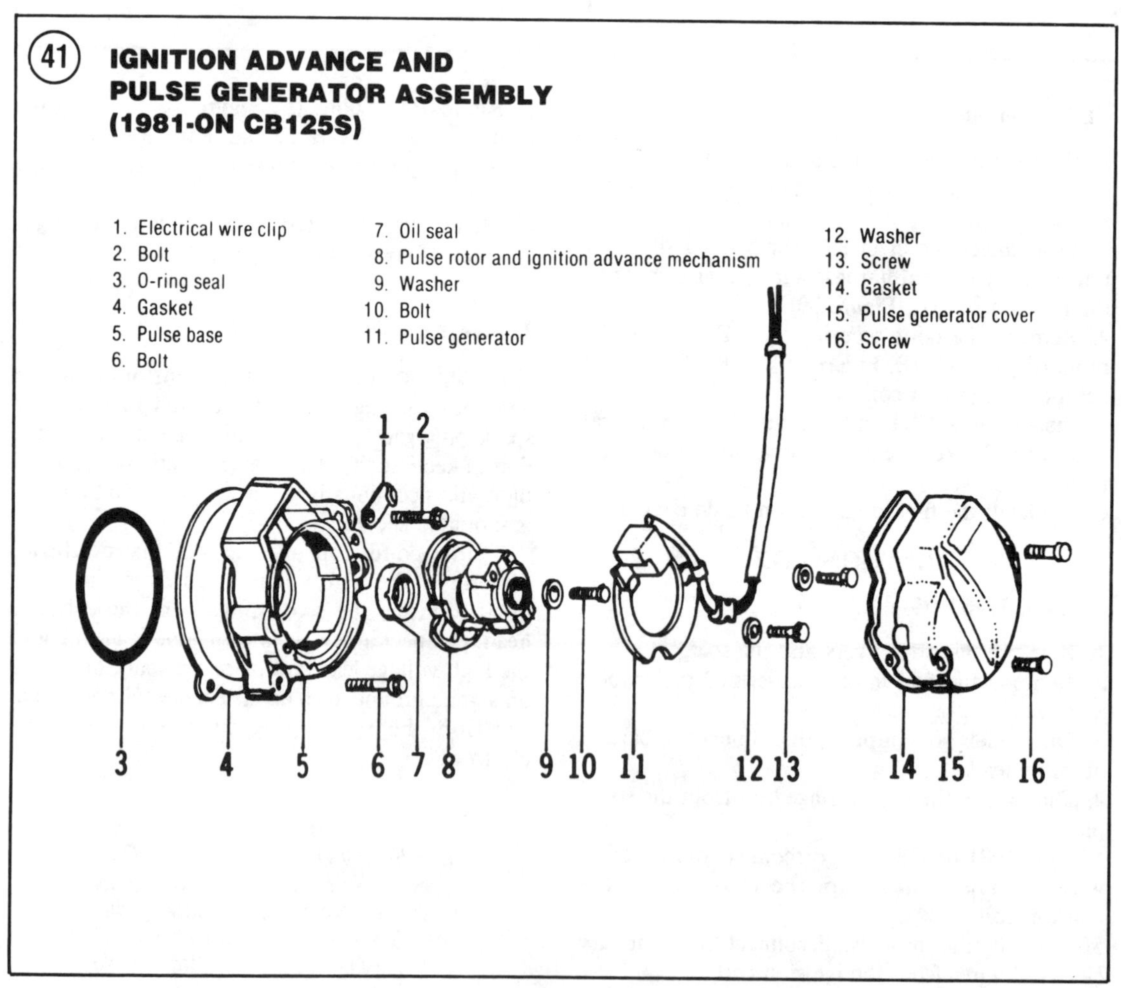

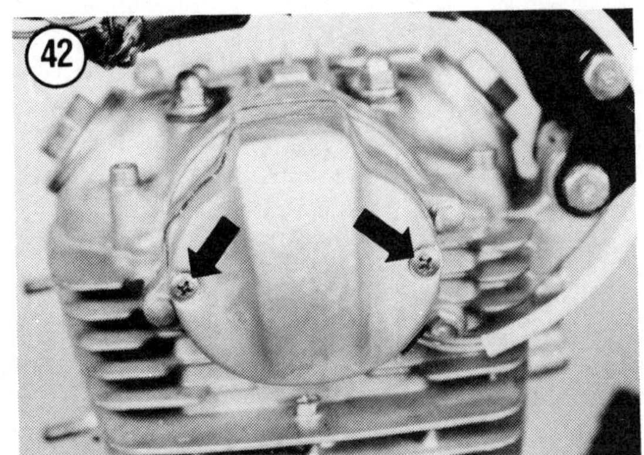

5. Remove the screws (**Figure 42**) securing the pulse generator cover and remove the cover and the gasket.
6. Disconnect the electrical connector from the pulse generator.

NOTE
Prior to removing the pulse generator assembly, make a mark on the backing plate at the centerline of one of the attachment screws. That way the assembly can be installed in the same position and ignition timing will be correct (providing it was correct prior to removal).

7. Remove the screws (**Figure 43**) securing the pulse generator assembly to the cylinder head and remove the assembly.
8. If necessary, remove the dowel pin (A, **Figure 44**) on the camshaft. Remove the bolts (B, **Figure 44**) securing the pulse generator base and remove the base and the gasket.
9. If removed, inspect the O-ring and the gasket (**Figure 45**) on the back of the base. Also inspect the oil seal (**Figure 46**) in the pulse base. Replace all 3 if any need replacing.
10. Install by reversing these removal steps, noting the following.
11. Make sure the dowel pin is in place in the camshaft.
12. Make sure all electrical connections are tight.
13. Adjust ignition timing as described in Chapter Three.

8

IGNITION ADVANCE MECHANISM (1981-ON CB125S)

The ignition advance mechanism advances the ignition timing (fires the spark plug sooner) as engine speed increases. If it does not advance properly and smoothly, the ignition timing will be

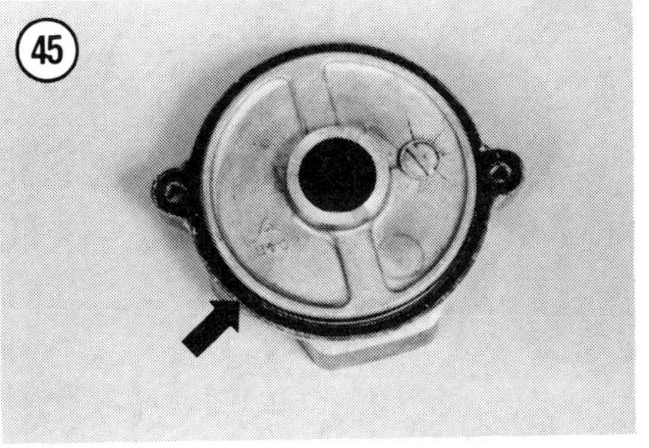

incorrect at high engine rpm. It must be inspected periodically to make certain it operates freely.

Inspection

1. Remove the ignition advance mechanism as described in this chapter.
2. Inspect both rotor pivot points (A, **Figure 47**) of each weight. The rotor must pivot freely to maintain proper ignition advance. Apply lightweight grease to the pivot pins.
3. Inspect both rotor return springs (B, **Figure 48**). Make sure they are taut and return the rotor to its fully retarded position.
4. If the rotor was removed from the base, align the punch mark (A, **Figure 48**) with the index mark on the base (B, **Figure 48**) when installing it.
5. If the unit fails any of these inspections it must be replaced.
6. Install the ignition advance mechanism as described in this chapter.

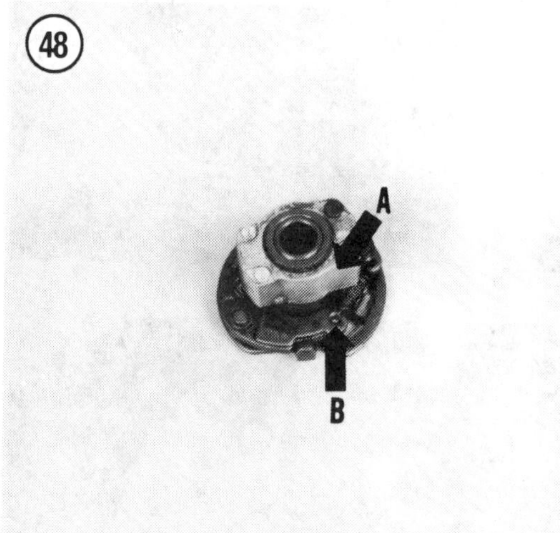

LIGHTING SYSTEM

The lighting system consists of a headlight, a taillight/brakelight combination, directional signals, indicator lights and a meter illumination light. **Table 4** lists replacement bulbs for these components.

Not all models covered in this book have all of these components. The TL250 is not equipped with a headlight or taillight as standard equipment, but both items are available as optional equipment.

Always use the correct wattage bulb as indicated in this section. The use of a larger wattage bulb will give a dim light and a smaller wattage bulb will burn out prematurely.

Each procedure in this section represents a typical bike. Minor variations exist among the various models.

Headlight Replacement

1. Remove the screws (**Figure 49**) on each side securing the headlight assembly.
2. Pull out on the bottom of the headlight assembly and disengage it from the locating tab on top of the headlight housing.
3. Disconnect the electrical connector from the headlight unit.
4. Remove the horizontal adjust screw and the 2 headlight retaining screws. Remove the sealed beam unit. Assemble by reversing this sequence.
5. Install by reversing these removal steps.
6. Adjust the headlight as described in this chapter.

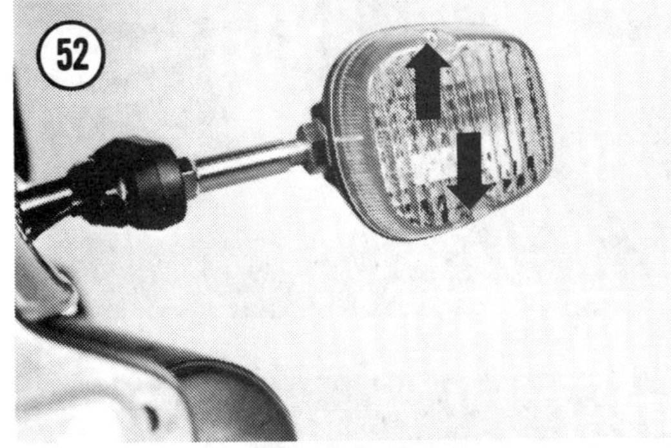

Headlight Adjustment

Adjust the headlight horizontally and vertically according to Department of Motor Vehicle regulations in your area.

To adjust the headlight horizontally, turn the screw (A, **Figure 50**) on the right-hand side of the headlight trim bezel. Screwing in turns the light toward the right-hand side of the rider and loosening the screw will direct the light to the left-hand side of the rider.

To adjust the headlight vertically, remove the side reflex reflector (if so equipped) on each side of the headlight assembly. Loosen the mounting bolt (B, **Figure 50**) on each side and position the headlight correctly. Retighten the bolts and reinstall the reflex reflectors (if so equipped).

Taillight/Brakelight Replacement

1. Remove the screws securing the lens (**Figure 51**) and remove the lens.
2. Wash the inside and outside of the lens with a mild detergent and wipe dry. Wipe off the reflective base surrounding the bulbs with a soft cloth.
3. Inspect the lens gasket and replace if it is damaged or deteriorated.
4. Replace the bulb(s) and install the lens; do not overtighten the screws as the lens may crack.

Directional Signal Light Replacement

1. Remove the screws securing the lens (**Figure 52**) and remove the lens.
2. Wash out the inside and outside of the lens with a mild detergent and wipe dry.
3. Inspect the condition of the lens gasket and replace if it is damaged or deteriorated.
4. Replace the bulb and install the lens; do not overtighten the screws as the lens may crack.

Meter Illumination Light Replacement

1. Disconnect the meter drive cable (A, **Figure 53**).
2. Unscrew the nuts and washers (B, **Figure 53**) securing the meter housing.

NOTE
In the next step, do not pull up too hard on the housing as there is very little slack in the electrical wires, they are very short.

3. Carefully pull the housing up and off of the mounting bracket. Carefully pull the socket/bulb assembly out of the backside of the meter housing.

4. Replace the defective bulb(s).
5. Install by reversing these removal steps.

SWITCHES

NOTE
Each procedure in this section represents a typical switch removal and installation procedure. Minor variations exist among the various models.

Engine Kill Switch Removal/Installation (Except TL250)

1. Remove the seat.
2. Remove the fuel tank as described in Chapter Seven.
3. On models so equipped, remove the right-hand rear view mirror.
4. Unhook the plastic straps securing the electrical wires to the handlebar.
5. Disconnect the electrical wire connectors going to the engine kill switch.
6. Remove the screws (**Figure 54**) securing the kill switch to the handlebar. Remove the switch assembly.
7. Install a new switch assembly by reversing these removal steps.

Engine Kill Switch Removal/Installation (TL250)

1. Remove the seat.
2. Remove the fuel tank as described in Chapter Seven.
3. Disconnect the electrical wire connector going to the engine kill switch.
4. Remove the nut and washer (**Figure 55**) securing the kill switch to the handlebar.
5. Remove the engine kill switch and electrical wires from the frame.
6. Install a new switch assembly by reversing these removal steps.

Front Brake Light Switch Removal/Installation

1. Remove the seat.
2. Remove the fuel tank as described in Chapter Seven.
3. Pull back the rubber protective boot on the brake lever.
4. Unhook the plastic straps securing the electrical wires to the handlebar.

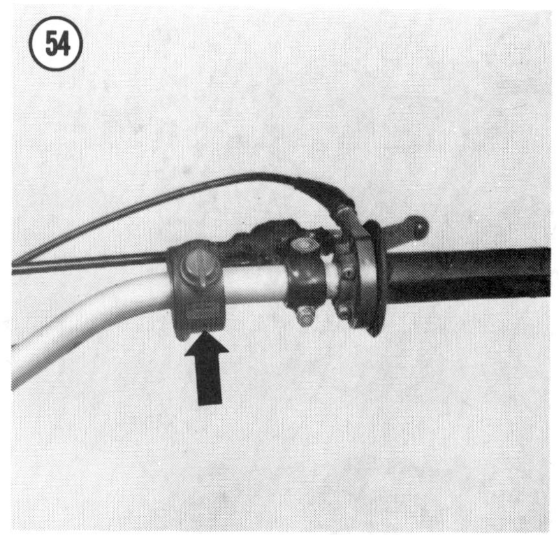
54

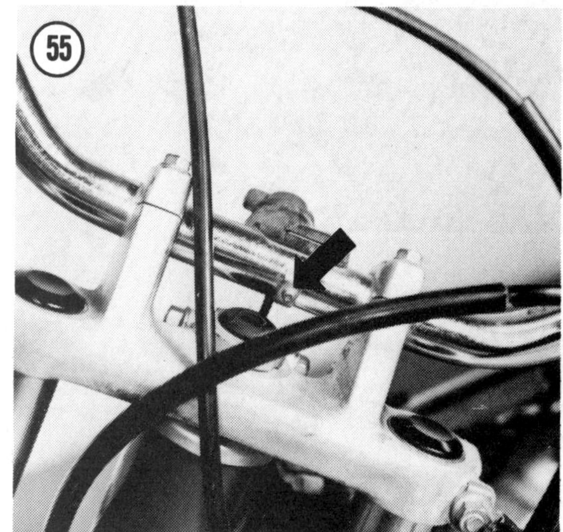
55

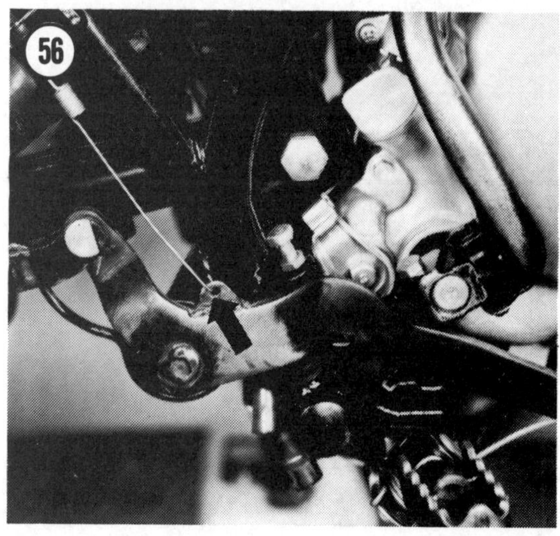
56

5. Disconnect the electrical connector going to the front brake light switch.
6. Carefully remove the switch assembly from the brake lever.
7. Remove the brake switch and electrical wires from the frame.
8. Install a new switch assembly by reversing these removal steps.

Rear Brake Light Switch Removal/Installation

1. Remove the right-hand side cover.
2. Unhook the switch spring from the brake arm (**Figure 56**).
3. Unscrew the switch housing and adjust nut (**Figure 57**) from the frame bracket.
4. Disconnect the electrical connectors from the wiring harness.
5. Install a new switch by reversing these removal steps, noting the following.
6. Adjust the switch as described in this chapter.

Rear Brake Light Switch Adjustment

1. Turn the ignition switch ON.
2. Depress the brake pedal. The light should come on just as the brake begins to work.
3. To make the light come on earlier, hold the switch body and turn the adjusting nut *clockwise* as viewed from the top. Turn *counterclockwise* to delay the light from coming on. Refer to **Figure 57**.

NOTE
Some riders prefer the light to come on a little early. This way, they can tap the pedal without braking to warn drivers who are following too closely.

Turn Signal Relay Removal/Installation

1. Remove the left-hand side cover.
2. Pull the turn signal relay out of the rubber mount located next to the battery.
3. Transfer the electrical wires (one green, one black) to the new relay.
4. Install the relay in the rubber mount.
5. Install the side cover.

8

HORN

Removal/Installation

1. Disconnect the electrical connectors (A, **Figure 58**) from the horn.
2. Remove the screw and washer (B, **Figure 58**) securing the horn to the frame and remove the horn.
3. Install by reversing these removal steps.

Horn Testing

Remove the horn as described in this chapter. Connect a 6-volt battery to the horn; positive terminal to the horn wire, negative terminal to the horn mounting flange. If the horn is good, it will sound. If not; replace it.

METERS

Removal/Installation

1. Disconnect the speedometer and/or tachometer drive cable(s).
2. Unscrew the nuts (or bolts), washers and rubber dampers securing the instrument(s) to the upper fork bridge or mounting bracket(s).
3. Remove the headlight as described in this chapter.

4. Within the headlight housing, disconnect all electrical connectors going to the instrument(s).
5. Carefully pull the electrical wires out through the back of the headlight housing. Pull the instrument(s) up and off of the upper fork bridge or mounting bracket(s).
6. Install by reversing these removal steps. Be sure to install all rubber dampers (if so equipped).

FUSE

There is one fuse used on models equipped with a battery. It is located next to the battery in a fuse holder. See **Table 5** for specified fuse amperage.

NOTE
Always carry a spare fuse.

Whenever a fuse blows, find out the reason for the failure before replacing the fuse. Usually the trouble is a short circuit in the wiring. This may be caused by worn-through insulation or a disconnected wire shorted to ground.

CAUTION
Never substitute metal foil or wire for a fuse. Never use a higher amperage fuse than specified. An overload could cause a fire and complete loss of the motorcycle.

Table 1 CHARGING CURRENT

Model	Headlight Switch Position	Engine rpm/ Voltage	Engine rpm/ Amperage/Voltage
CL100, CB100, SL100	OFF	1,000/6.8 V	5,000/1.3 A/7.8 V
	ON-high beam	3,500/6.8 V	5,000/1.3 A/7.8 V
	ON-low beam	2,200/6.8 V	5,000/1.3 A/7.2 V
XL100	OFF	1,000/6.8 V	5,000/1.3 A/7.8 V
	ON-high beam	3,500/6.8 V	5,000/0.2 A/7.2 V
	ON-low beam	2,200/6.8 V	5,000/1.3 A/7.8 V
1973-1980 CB125S, SL125	ON-low beam	2,000/6.8 V	5,000/1.3 A/7.8 V
Model	**Headlight Switch Position**	**Engine rpm/ Amp/Volt**	**Engine rpm/ Amp/Volt**
1981-1982 CB125S	ON-high beam	4,000/1.2A/8.0V	8,000/3.4A/9.0 V
XL125	OFF	5,000/1.7-2.3 A/6.8 V	10,000/3.1 A/9.0 V
	ON	5,000/0.5-1.1 A/6.8 V	10,000/0.7-1.6 A/8.8 V
CT125	Not equipped	5,000/1 A/7.8-8.2 V	8,000 2 A/8.2-8.6 V
XL175	OFF	5,000/1.3 A/7.8 V	10,000/2.2 A/8.8 V
	ON-high	5,000/0.2 A/7.2 V	10,000/1.5 A/8.8 V
	ON-low	5,000/1.3 A/7.8 V	10,000/2.5 A/8.8 V
XL250, XL350	OFF	5,000/1.2 A/7.5 V	8,000/1.3 A/8.3 V
	ON	5,000/1.5 A/8.0 V	8,000/4 A/8.9 V

Table 2 ALTERNATOR ROTOR NUT TORQUE

Model	N•m	ft.-lb.
100 and 125 cc		
Through 1980	26-32	19-23
1981-on	40-50	29-36
175 cc	35-45	25-32
250 and 350 cc	60-70	43-50

Table 3 CDI TROUBLESHOOTING

Symptoms	Probable cause	Cure
Weak spark	Poor connections	Clean and retighten
	High voltage leak	Replace defective wire
	Defective coil	Replace ignition coil
No spark	Wiring broken	Replace wire
	Defective ignition	Replace coil
	Defective pulser coil in magneto	Replace coil

Table 4 REPLACEMENT BULB NUMBERS

Item	Voltage/Wattage
Headlight	
100 and 125 cc	
1969-1978	6V 35/25W
1979-on	6V 35/36.5 W
175 cc	6V 35/25 W
TL250	6V 25/25 W
250 and 350 cc	6V 25/25 W
Taillight/brakelight	
CB100, CL100, SL100, SL125, 1974 XL350	6V 5.3/17 W
1974 XL100	6V 5.3/2.5 W
1973-1974 CB125	6V 3/10 W
1975-1978 XL100, 1975-on CB125S, XL125, CT125, XL175, XL250, 1975-1978 XL350	6V 5.3/25 W
Turn signal	
1973-1974 CB125S	6V 8 W
1974 XL350	6V 17 W
All other models	6V 18 W
Neutral indicator	6V 3 W
Speedometer illumination, turn signal and high beam indicator	
CB100, CL100, 1974 XL100, 1973-1974 CB125S, SL125, 1974 XL125, 1973 and 1975 XL250, 1974 XL350	6V 1.5 W
All other models	6V 1.7 W

8

Table 5 FUSE AMPERAGE

Model	Specified Amperage
All CB100, CL100, SL100	15
XL100	10
XL100 K1	15
1976 XL100	10
1977-1978 XL100	15
CB125 S, CB125 S1	10
CB125 S2, 1976-1980 CB125 S	15
1981-on CB125 S	10
All SL125	15
XL125	10
XL125 K1	15
CT125	10
XL175, XL175 K1-K2	15
1976-1978 XL175	10
All XL250, XL350	10

CHAPTER NINE

FRONT SUSPENSION AND STEERING

This chapter describes repair and maintenance of the front wheel, forks and steering components.

Tables 1-6 are at the end of the chapter.

FRONT WHEEL

Removal

1. Place a wood block(s) under the engine to support it securely with the front wheel off the ground.
2. Slacken the brake cable at the hand lever (**Figure 1**).
3. On models so equipped, unscrew the speedometer cable set screw. Pull the speedometer cable free from the hub.
4. At the brake panel, loosen the locknut (A, **Figure 2**) and remove the cable end from the brake arm (B, **Figure 2**). Remove the brake cable from the bracket on the brake panel (C, **Figure 2**).

5A. On XL250 and XL350 models, remove the axle holder nuts, lockwashers and washers. Remove the axle holders.

5B. On all other models, remove the cotter pin and discard it. Unscrew the axle nut and remove the axle (D, **Figure 2**).

6. Pull the wheel down and forward. This allows the brake panel to disengage from the boss on the left-hand fork slider. Remove the wheel. Don't lose any axle spacer(s).

NOTE

On disc brake models, insert a piece of wood between the brake pads in place of the disc. If the brake lever is inadvertently squeezed, the automatic adjuster may advance and leave no room for the brake disc. If this does happen, remove the caliper cover and back off the adjuster bolt as necessary until the disc can be reinstalled. Then squeeze the brake lever several times so the automatic adjuster will take up the slack between the pads and the disc.

Installation

1. Make sure the axle bearing surfaces of the fork sliders (and axle holders on XL250 and XL350 models) are free from burrs and nicks.
2. Clean the axle in solvent and thoroughly dry. Make sure all surfaces that the axle comes in contact with are clean and free from road dirt and old grease prior to installation.
3. Position the wheel, carefully inserting the groove in the brake panel into the groove in the left-hand fork slider. This is necessary for proper brake operation.
4A. On XL175 models, install the axle from the left-hand side through the wheel hub.
4B. On all other models, install the axle from the right-hand side through the wheel hub.
5A. On XL250 and XL350 models, install the axle holders with the "F" mark facing toward the front. Install the washers, lockwashers and nuts. Tighten the front nuts first and then the rear nuts to the torque specification listed in **Table 1**.

NOTE
The axle holder nuts must be tightened in this manner and to this torque specification. After installation is complete, there will be a slight gap at the rear and no gap at the front. If done incorrectly the studs may fail, resulting in loss of control of the bike when riding.

5B. On all other models, install the axle nut and tighten to the torque specification listed in **Table 1**. Install a new cotter pin and bend the ends over completely. Never reuse a cotter pin as it may break and fall out.
6. On models so equipped, slowly rotate the wheel and install the speedometer cable into the speedometer housing. Install and tighten the cable set screw.
7. After the wheel is completely installed, rotate it several times and apply the brakes a couple of times to make sure that it rotates freely and that the brake is operating correctly.

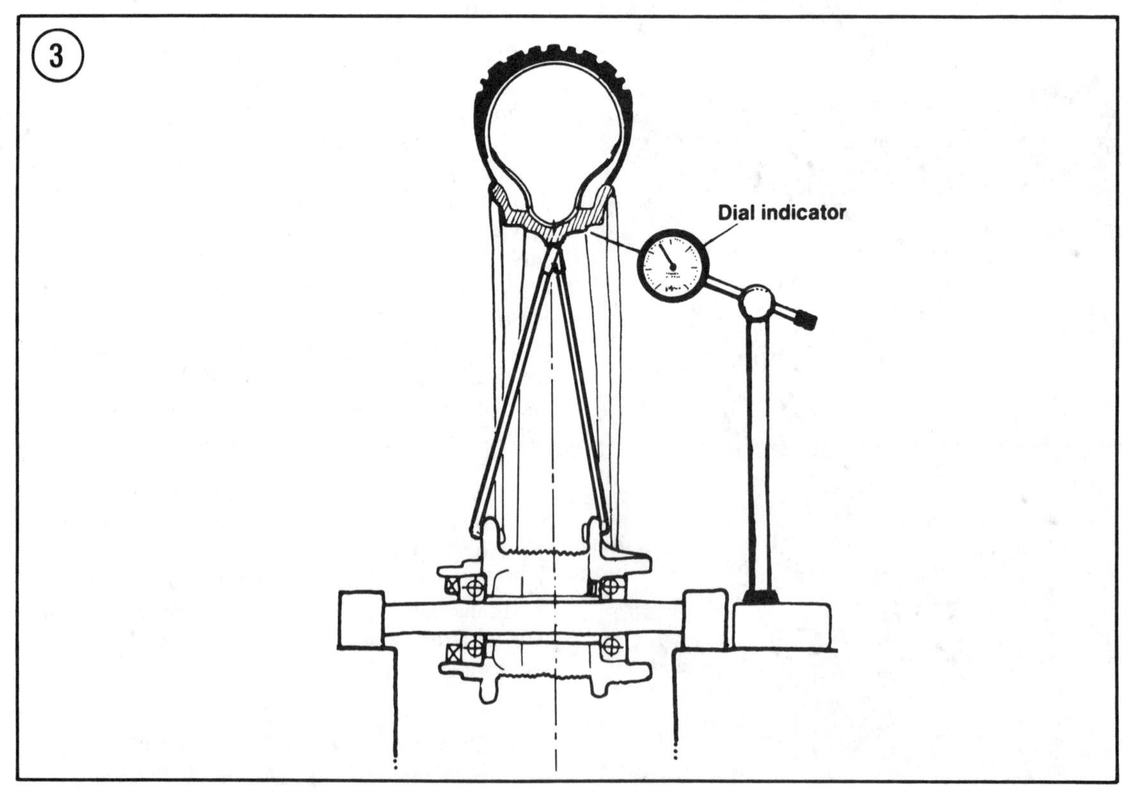

8. Adjust the front brake as described in Chapter Three.

Inspection

Measure the radial and axial runout of the wheel rim with a dial indicator as shown in **Figure 3**. The maximum service limit for both radial and axial runout is 2.0 mm (0.08 in.).

Some of this condition can be corrected by either tightening or replacing any loose or bent spokes. Refer to *Spoke Adjustment* or *Spoke Inspection and Replacement* in this chapter.

Check the axle runout as described under *Front Hub Inspection* in this chapter.

FRONT HUB

Refer to **Figures 4-7** for this procedure.

Disassembly (Drum Brake Models)

1. Remove the front wheel as described in this chapter.
2. Pull the brake panel assembly straight up and out of the brake drum.
3. On XL250 and XL350 models, remove the speedometer housing. Remove the screws securing the bearing retainer and remove the bearing retainer.

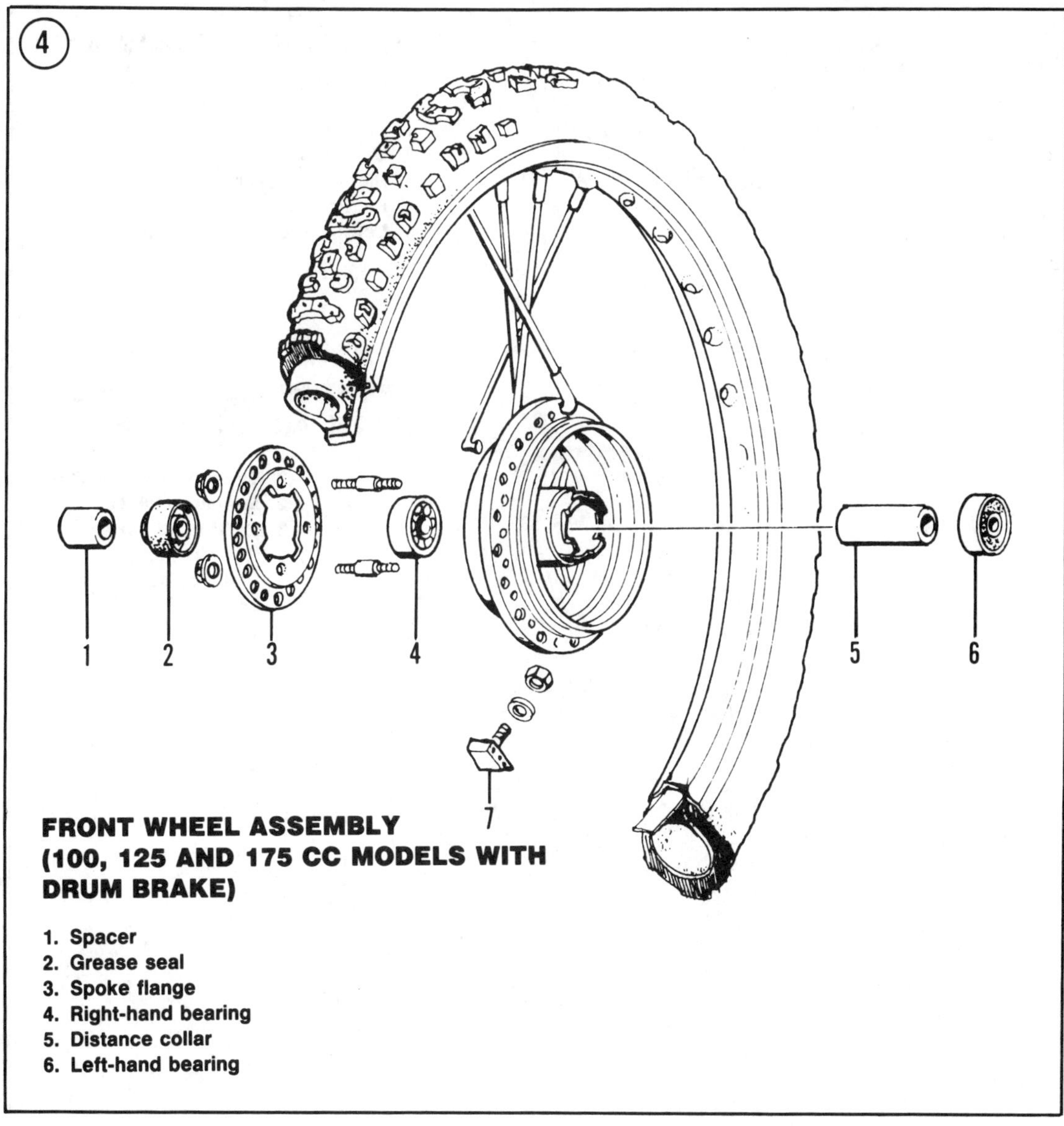

FRONT WHEEL ASSEMBLY (100, 125 AND 175 CC MODELS WITH DRUM BRAKE)

1. Spacer
2. Grease seal
3. Spoke flange
4. Right-hand bearing
5. Distance collar
6. Left-hand bearing

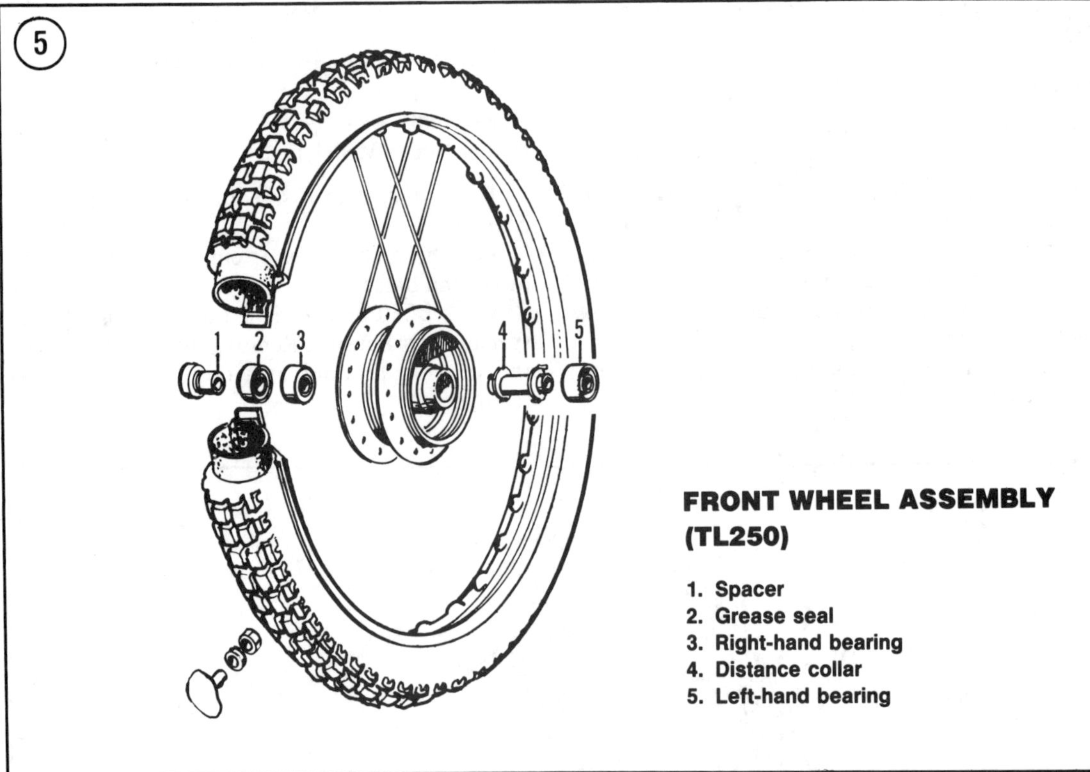

FRONT WHEEL ASSEMBLY (TL250)

1. Spacer
2. Grease seal
3. Right-hand bearing
4. Distance collar
5. Left-hand bearing

6

FRONT WHEEL ASSEMBLY (XL250 AND XL350)

1. Speedometer housing
2. Bearing retainer
3. Right-hand bearing
4. Hub assembly
5. Distance collar
6. Left-hand bearing

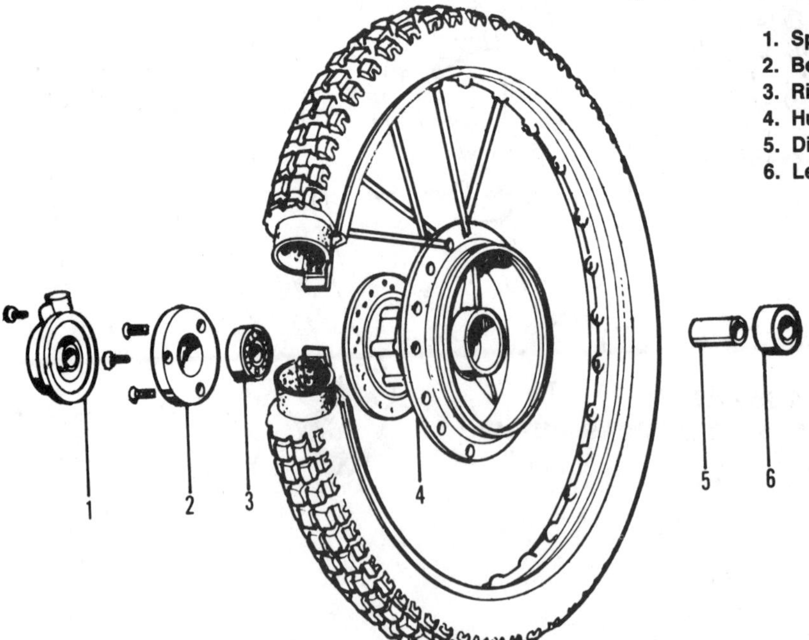

(7)

FRONT WHEEL ASSEMBLY (CB125 WITH DISC BRAKE)

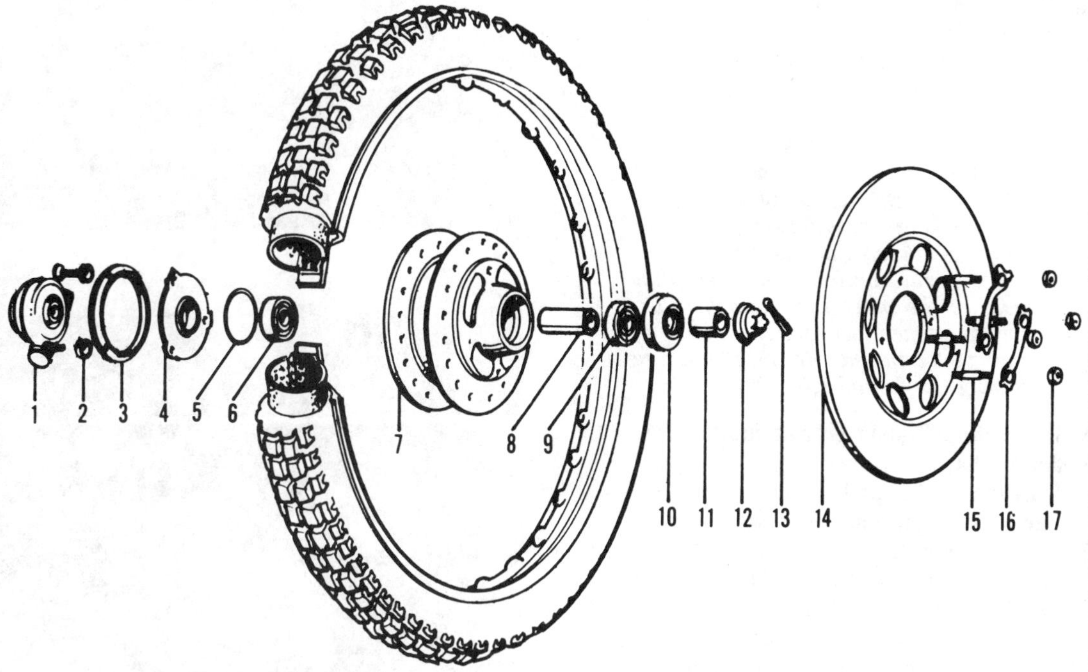

1. Speedometer housing
2. Screw and washer
3. Speedometer gear box retainer cover
4. Speedometer gear box retainer
5. O-ring
6. Right-hand bearing
7. Hub assembly
8. Distance collar
9. Left-hand bearing
10. Grease seal
11. Spacer
12. Axle nut
13. Cotter pin
14. Brake disc
15. Stud
16. Lockwasher
17. Nut

4. On models so equipped, remove the spacer (**Figure 8**) from either or both sides of the wheel.
5. On models so equipped, remove the dust seal (**Figure 9**) from the right-hand side.
6. To remove the right- and left-hand bearings and distance collar, insert a soft aluminum or brass drift into one side of the hub. Push the distance collar over to one side and place the drift on the inner race of the lower bearing. Tap the bearing out of the hub with a hammer working around the perimeter of the inner race.
7. Remove the distance collar and tap out the opposite bearing in the same manner.
8. Inspect the hub as described in this chapter.

Assembly (Drum Brake Models)

1. On non-sealed bearings, pack the bearings with a good quality bearing grease. Work the grease in between the balls thoroughly. Turn the bearing by hand a couple of times to make sure the grease is distributed evenly inside the bearing.
2. Pack the wheel hub and distance collar with multipurpose grease.

CAUTION

*Install the stock Honda wheel bearings with the sealed side facing out (**Figure 10**). During installation, tap the bearings squarely into place and tap on the outer race only. Use a socket that matches the outer race diameter. Do not tap on the inner race or the bearing may be damaged. Be sure that the bearings are completely seated.*

3. Install the left-hand bearing first and press the distance collar into place.
4. Install the right-hand bearing.
5. Lubricate the dust seal with grease.
6. On models so equipped, install the dust seal (**Figure 9**) into the right-hand side of the hub.
7. On XL250 and XL350 models, install the bearing retainer. Install the screws securing the bearing retainer and tighten the screws securely. Install the speedometer housing.
8. On models so equipped, install the spacer (**Figure 8**) onto the correct side of the wheel.
9. Install the front wheel as described in this chapter.

Disassembly (Disc Brake Models)

1. Remove the front wheel as described in this chapter.
2. Pull the brake panel assembly straight up and out of the brake drum.
3. Remove the speedometer housing. Remove the screws securing the speedometer gearbox retainer cover, the gearbox retainer and the O-ring.
4. On models so equipped, remove the spacer (**Figure 8**) from either or both sides of the wheel.
5. Remove the dust seal from the left-hand side of the hub.
6. To remove the right- and left-hand bearings and distance collar, insert a soft aluminum or brass drift into one side of the hub. Push the distance collar over to one side and place the drift on the inner race of the lower bearing. Tap the bearing out of the hub with a hammer working around the perimeter of the inner race.

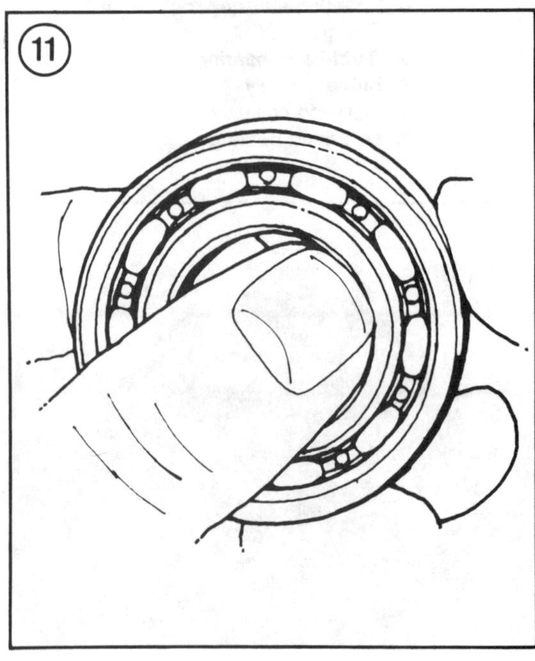

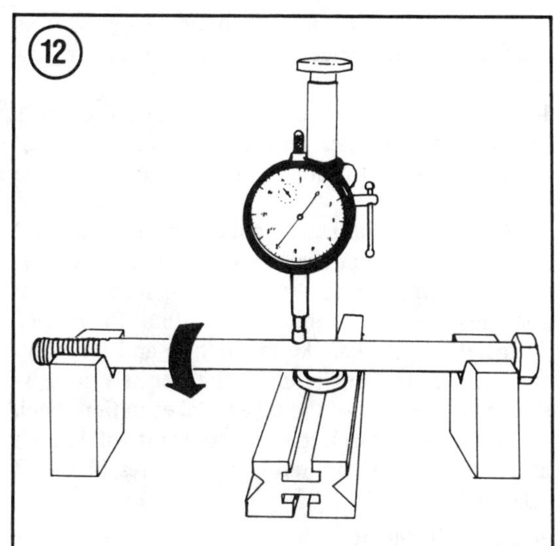

7. Remove the distance collar and tap out the opposite bearing in the same manner.
8. Inspect the hub as described in this chapter.

Assembly (Disc Brake Models)

1. On non-sealed bearings, pack the bearings with a good quality bearing grease. Work the grease in between the balls thoroughly. Turn the bearing by hand a couple of times to make sure the grease is distributed evenly inside the bearing.
2. Pack the wheel hub and distance collar with multipurpose grease.

CAUTION
*Install the stock Honda wheel bearings with the sealed side facing out (**Figure 10**). During installation, tap the bearings squarely into place and tap on the outer race only. Use a socket that matches the outer race diameter. Do not tap on the inner race or the bearing may be damaged. Be sure that the bearings are completely seated.*

3. Install the left-hand bearing first and press the distance collar into place.
4. Install the right-hand bearing.
5. Lubricate the dust seal with grease.
6. Install the dust seal into the left-hand side of the hub.
7. Install the new O-ring seal, the gearbox retainer and the gearbox retainer cover. Install the screws securing the speedometer gearbox retainer cover and tighten the screws securely.
8. On models so equipped, install the spacer (**Figure 8**) onto the correct side of the wheel.
9. Install the front wheel as described in this chapter.

Inspection (All Models)

1. Thoroughly clean out the inside of the hub with solvent and dry with compressed air or a shop cloth.
2. Do not clean sealed bearings. If non-sealed bearings are installed, thoroughly clean them in solvent and thoroughly dry with compressed air. Do not let the bearing spin while drying.
3. Turn each bearing by hand (**Figure 11**). Make sure the bearings turn smoothly.

NOTE
Some axial play is normal, but radial play should be negligible. The bearing should turn smoothly.

4. On non-sealed bearings, check the balls for evidence of wear, pitting or excessive heat (bluish tint). Replace bearings if necessary; always replace as a complete set. When replacing, be sure to take your old bearings along to ensure a perfect matchup.

NOTE
Fully sealed bearings are available from many bearing specialty shops. Fully sealed bearings provide better protection from dirt and moisture that may get into the hub.

5. Check the axle for wear and straightness. Use V-blocks and a dial indicator as shown in **Figure 12**. If the runout is 0.2 mm (0.008 in.) or greater, the axle should be replaced.

WHEELS

Wheels should be inspected prior to a long ride. This little time spent will help keep you out of trouble on the highway or trail.

Wheel Balance

An unbalanced wheel is unsafe. Depending on the degree of unbalance and the speed of the bike, the rider may experience anything from a mild vibration to a violent shimmy and loss of control.

The balance weights are applied to the spokes on the light side of the wheel to correct the condition.

NOTE
Be sure to balance the rear wheel with the driven sprocket assembly attached as it will affect the balance.

Before you attempt to balance the wheel, check to be sure that the wheel bearings are in good condition and properly lubricated. The wheel must rotate freely.

1. Remove the wheel as described in this chapter or in Chapter Ten. On models with a front disc brake, leave the disc attached to the wheel for this test.
2. Mount the wheel on a fixture such as the one shown in **Figure 13** so it can rotate freely.
3. Give the wheel a spin and let it coast to a stop. Mark the tire at the lowest point.
4. Spin the wheel several more times. If the wheel keeps coming to rest at the same point, it is out of balance.
5. Attach a weight to the upper (or light) side of the wheel on the spoke (**Figure 14**). Weights come in 4 sizes: 5, 10, 15 and 20 grams. Crimp the weights onto the spoke with ordinary gas pliers.
6. Experiment with different weights until the wheel comes to rest at a different position each time it is spun. When this happens, consider the wheel balanced. Tighten the weights so they won't be thrown off.

Spoke Inspection and Replacement

Spokes loosen with use and should be checked periodically. The "tuning fork" method for checking spoke tightness is simple and works well. Tap each spoke with a spoke wrench (**Figure 15**) or the shank of a screwdriver and listen for a tone. A tight spoke will emit a clear, ringing tone while a loose spoke will sound flat. All the spokes in a correctly tightened wheel will emit tones of similar pitch but not necessarily the same precise tone.

Bent or stripped spokes should be replaced as soon as they are detected, as they can destroy an expensive hub.

1. Unscrew the nipple from the spoke and depress the nipple into the rim far enough to free the end of the spoke; take care not to push the nipple all the way in.
2. Remove the damaged spoke from the hub and use it to match a new spoke of identical length. If necessary, trim the new spoke to match the original and dress the end of the thread with a thread die.
3. Install the new spoke in the hub and screw on the nipple; tighten it until the spoke's tone is similar to the tone of the other spokes in the wheel.
4. Periodically check the new spoke; it will stretch and must be retightened several times before it takes a final set.

Spoke Adjustment

If all spokes appear loose, tighten all on one side of the hub then tighten all on the other side. One-half to one turn should be sufficient; do not overtighten.

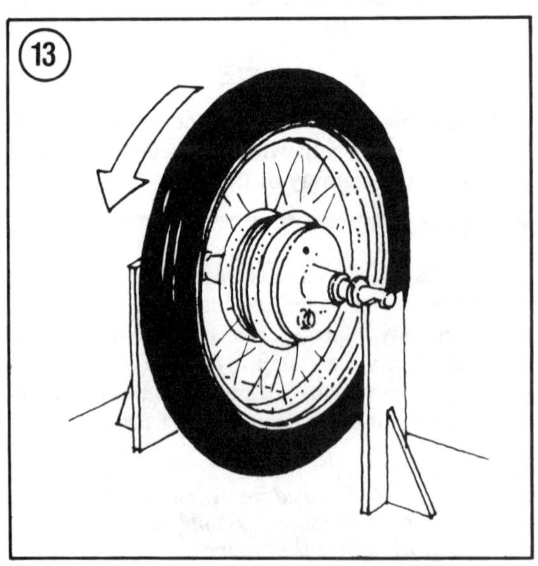

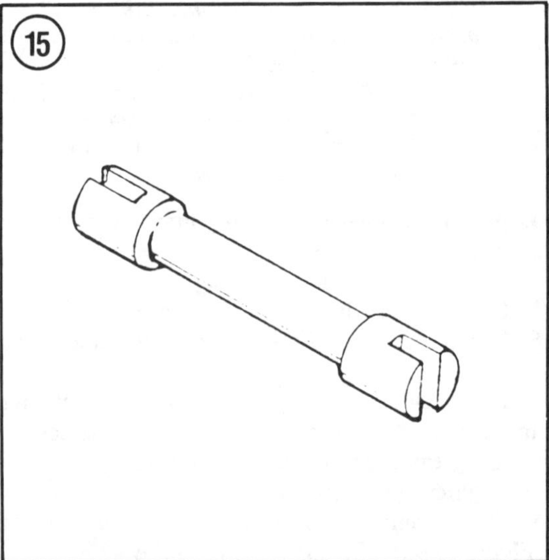

After tightening the spokes, check rim runout to be sure you haven't pulled the rim out of shape.

One way to check rim runout is to mount a dial indicator on the front fork or swing arm, so that it bears against the rim.

If you don't have a dial indicator, improvise one as shown in **Figure 16**. Adjust the position of the bolt until it just clears the rim. Rotate the rim and note whether the clearance increases or decreases. Mark the tire with chalk or light crayon at areas that produce significantly large or small clearance. Clearance must not change by more than 2.0 mm (0.08 in.).

To pull the rim out, tighten spokes which terminate on the same side of the hub and loosen spokes which terminate on the opposite side of the hub (**Figure 17**). In most cases, only a slight amount of adjustment is necessary to true a rim.

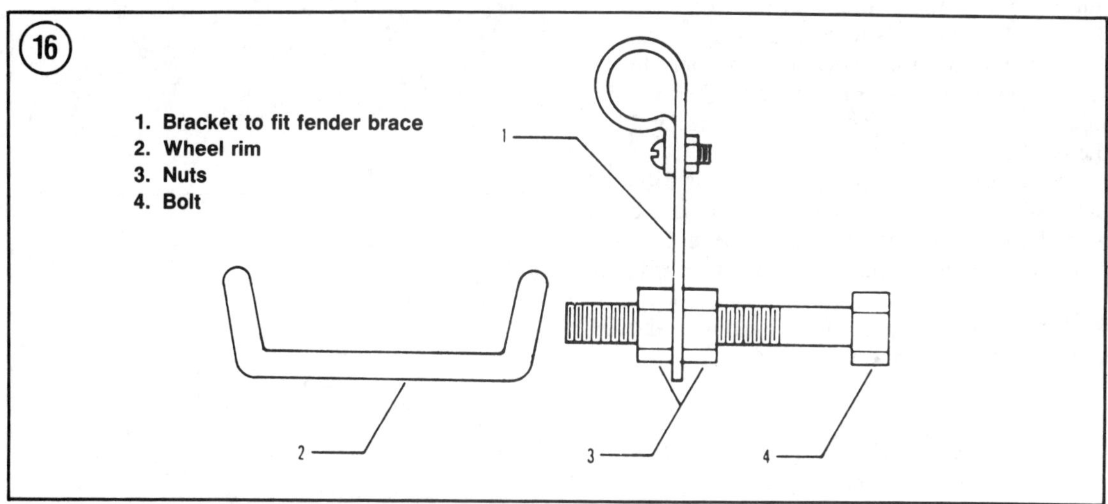

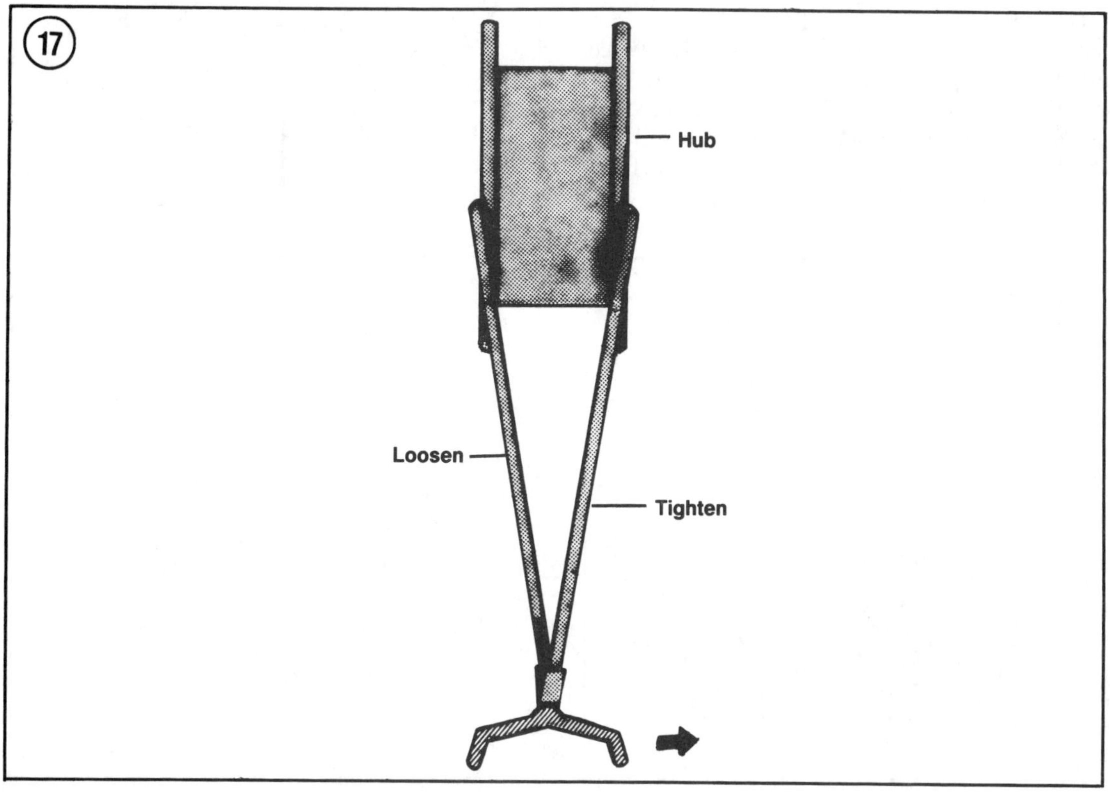

17

Hub

Loosen

Tighten

After adjustment, rotate the rim and make sure another area has not been pulled out of true. Continue adjustment and checking until runout is less than 2.0 mm (0.08 in.).

TIRE CHANGING

Removal

1. Remove the valve core and deflate the tire.
2. Press the entire bead on both sides of the tire into the center of the rim.
3. Lubricate the beads with soapy water.
4. Insert the tire iron under the bead next to the valve (**Figure 18**). Force the bead on the opposite side of the tire into the center of the rim and pry the bead over rim with the tire iron.
5. Insert a second tire iron next to the first to hold the bead over the rim. Then work around the tire with the first tire iron, prying the bead over the rim. Be careful not to pinch the inner tube with the tire irons.
6. Remove the valve stem from the hole in the rim and remove the tube from the tire.

NOTE
Step 7 is required only if it is necessary to completely remove the tire from the rim, such as for tire replacement.

7. Stand the tire upright. Insert the tire iron between the second bead and the side of the rim that the first bead was pried over (**Figure 19**). Force the bead on the opposite side from the tire iron into the center of the rim. Pry the second bead off of the rim, working around the wheel wih 2 tire irons as with the first bead. Remove the tire from the rim.

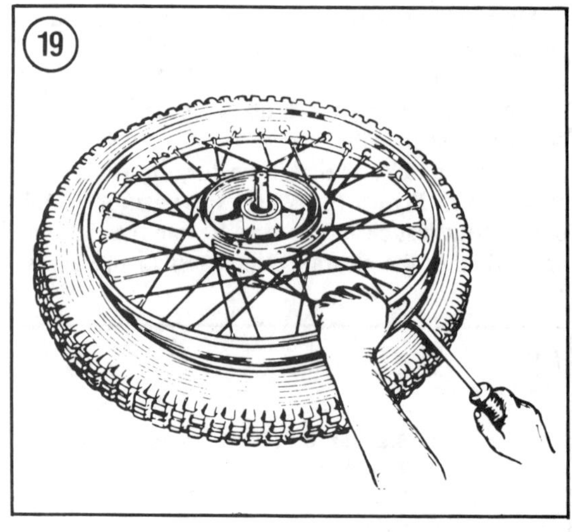

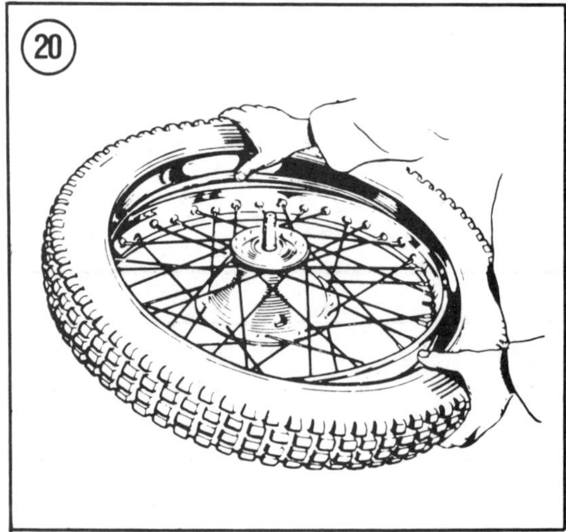

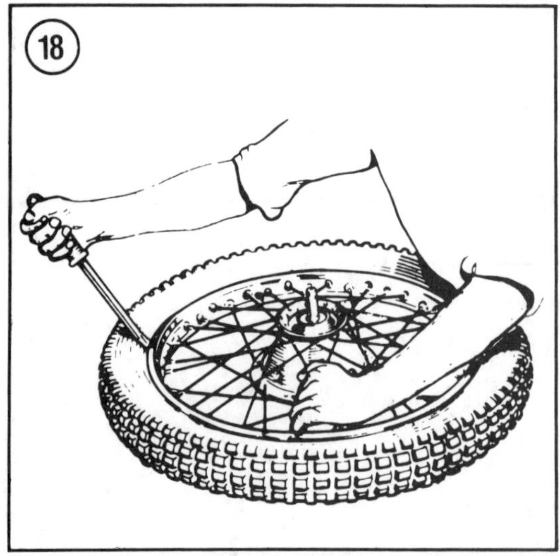

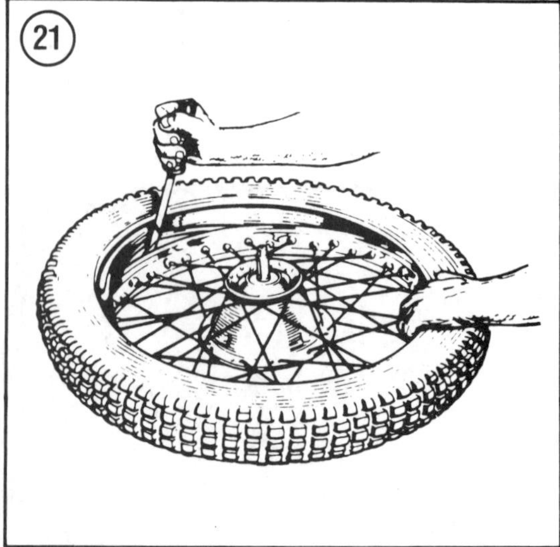

Installation

1. Carefully check the tire for any damage, especially inside.
2. A new tire may have balancing rubbers inside. These are not patches and should not be disturbed. A colored spot near the bead indicates a lighter point on the tire. This should be placed next to the valve.
3. Check that the spoke ends do not protrude through the nipples into the center of the rim where they can puncture the tube. File off any protruding spoke ends. Be sure the rim rubber tape is in place with the rough side toward the rim.
4. Install the valve stem core and tighten securely.
5. Inflate the tube just enough to round it out. Too much air will make it difficult to install it in the tire and too little will increase the chances of pinching the tube with the tire irons. Install the tube into the tire.

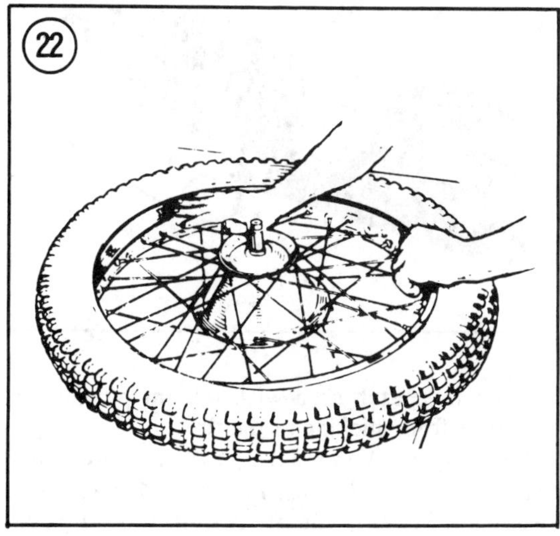

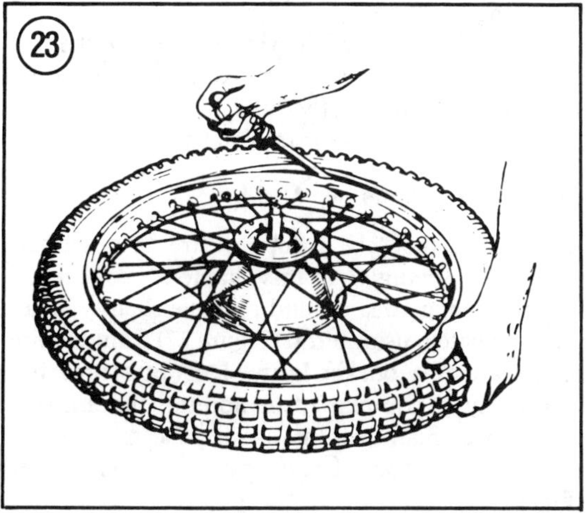

6. Lubricate the tire beads and rim with soapy water.
7. Pull the tube partly out of the tire at the valve stem. Squeeze the beads together to hold the tube and insert the valve stem into the hole in the rim. The lower bead should go into the center of the rim with the upper bead outside it.
8. Press the lower bead into the rim center on each side of the valve, working around the tire in both directions (**Figure 20**). Use a tire iron for the last few inches of the bead (**Figure 21**).
9. Press the upper bead into the rim opposite the valve stem (**Figure 22**). Pry the bead into the rim on both sides of the initial point with a tire iron, working around the rim to the valve stem (**Figure 23**).
10. Wiggle the valve stem to be sure the tube is not trapped under the bead. Set the valve stem squarely in its hole before screwing on the valve nut to hold it against the rim.
11. Check the bead on both sides of the tire for even fit around the rim.
12. Inflate the tire slowly to seat the beads in the rim. It may be necessary to bounce the tire to complete the seating. Inflate to the required pressure; refer to **Table 2**. Balance the wheel as described in this chapter.

TIRE REPAIRS

Every rider will eventually experience trouble with a tire or tube. Repairs and replacement are fairly simple and every rider should know the techniques.

Patching a motorcycle tube is only a temporary fix. The tire flexes too much and the patch could rub right off. However, a patched tire will get you far enough to buy a new tube.

NOTE
A can of pressurized tire sealant and inflation air can be carried in your tool box or tow vehicle. It may be able to inflate and seal the hole. This is only a temporary fix.

Tire Repair Kits

Tire repair kits can be purchased from motorcycle dealers and some auto supply stores. When buying, specify that the kit you want is for motorcycles.

There are 2 types of tire repair kits:

a. Hot patch.
b. Cold patch.

Hot patches are stronger because they actually vulcanize to the tube, becoming part of it.

9

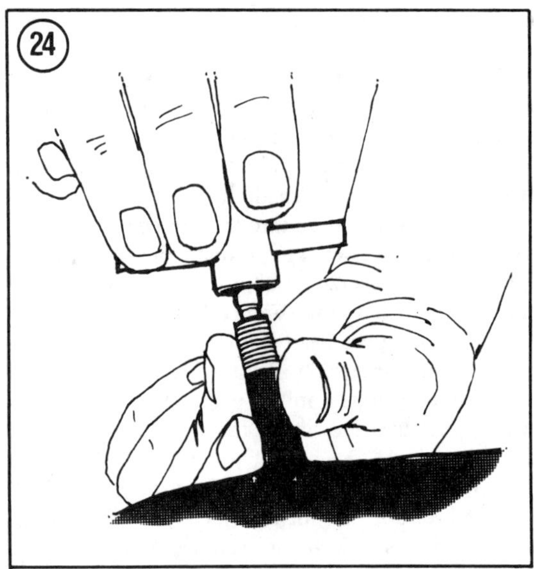

However, they are far too bulky to carry for roadside repairs and the strength is unnecessary for a temporary repair.

Cold patches are not vulcanized to the tube; they are simply glued to it. Though not as strong as hot patches, cold patches are still very durable. Cold patch kits are less bulky than hot and more easily applied under adverse conditions. A cold patch kit contains everything necessary and tucks easily into your emergency tool kit.

Tube Inspection

1. Remove the inner tube as described under *Tire Changing* in this chapter.
2. Install the valve core into the valve stem (**Figure 24**) and inflate the tube slightly. Do not overinflate.
3. Immerse the tube in water a section at a time (**Figure 25**). Look carefully for bubbles indicating a hole. Mark each hole and continue checking until you are certain that all holes are discovered and marked. Also make sure that the valve core is not leaking; tighten it if necessary.

NOTE

*If you do not have enough water to immerse sections of the tube, try running your hand over the tube slowly and very close to the surface. If your hand is damp, it works even better. If you suspect a hole anywhere, apply some saliva to the area to verify it (**Figure 26**).*

4. Apply a cold patch using the techniques described under *Cold Patch Repair* in this chapter.

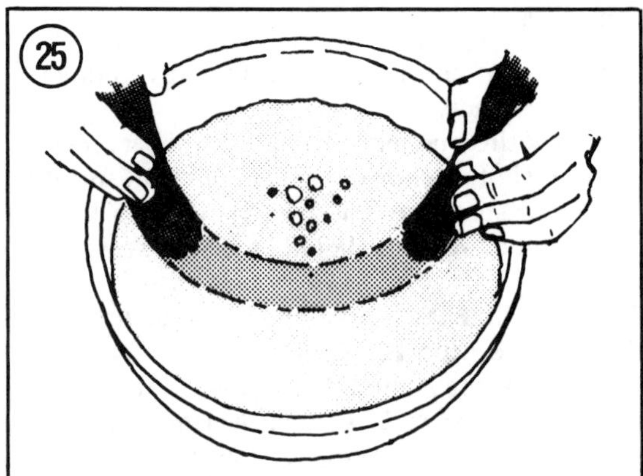

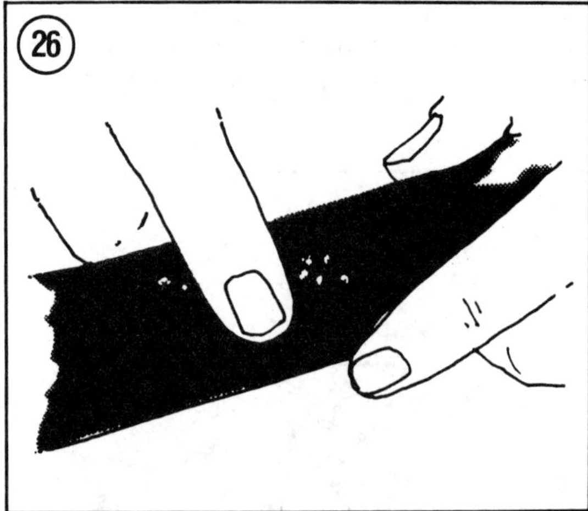

5. Dust the patch area with talcum powder to prevent it from sticking to the tire.
6. Carefully check the inside of the tire casing for small rocks or sand which may have damaged the tube. If the inside of the tire is split, apply a patch to the area to prevent it from pinching and damaging the tube again.
7. Check the inside of the rim. Make sure the rim band is in place, with no spoke ends protruding which could puncture the tube.
8. Deflate the tube prior to installation in the tire.

Cold Patch Repairs

1. Remove the tube from the tire as described under *Tire Changing* in this chapter.
2. Roughen an area around the hole slightly larger than the patch, using a cap (**Figure 27**) from the tire repair kit or a pocket knife. Do not scrape too vigorously or you may cause additional damage.
3. Apply a small quantity of special cement to the puncture and spread it evenly with your finger (**Figure 28**).

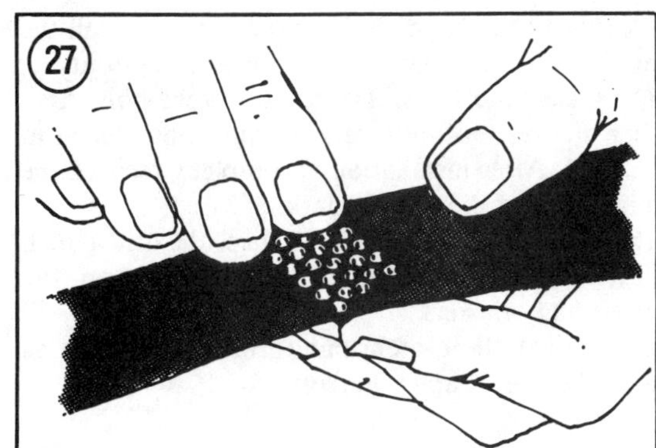

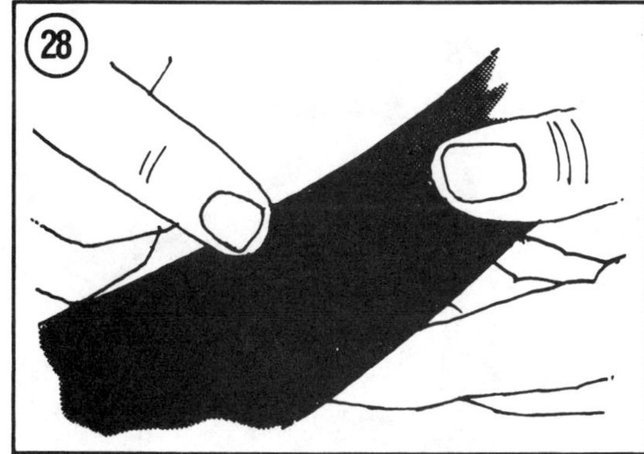

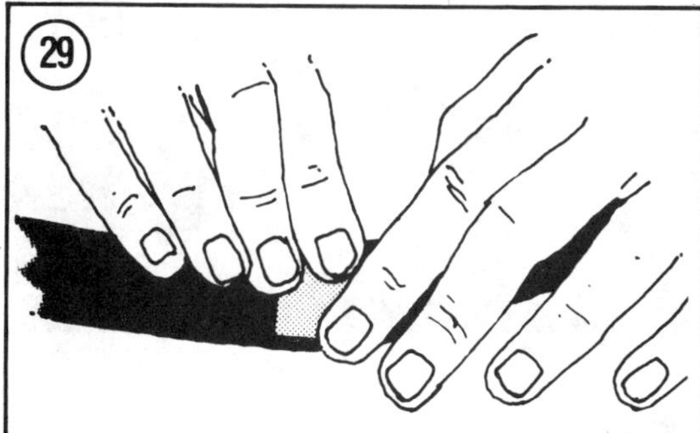

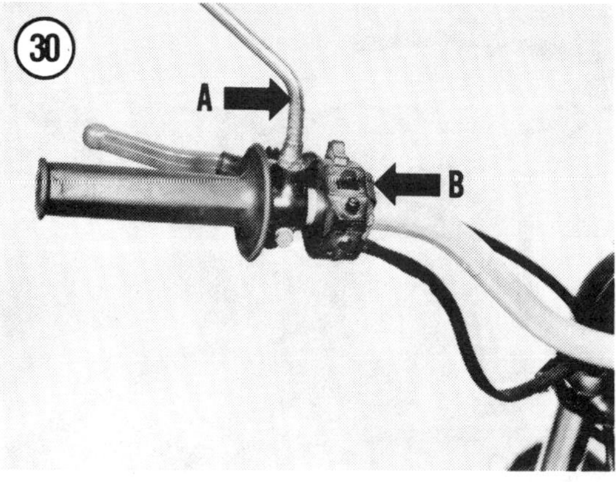

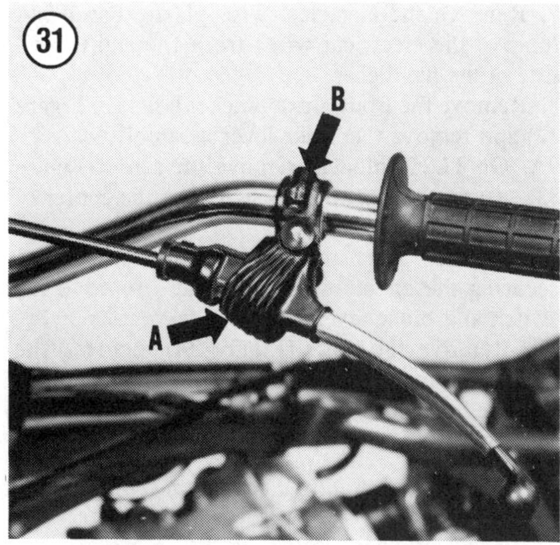

4. Allow the cement to dry until tacky—usually 30 seconds or so is sufficient.
5. Remove the backing from the patch.

CAUTION
Do not touch the newly exposed rubber with your fingers or the patch will not stick firmly.

6. Center the patch over the hole. Hold the patch firmly in place for about 30 seconds to allow the cement to set (**Figure 29**).
7. Dust the patched area with talcum powder to prevent sticking.
8. Install the tube as described in this chapter.

9

HANDLEBAR

Removal/Installation

1. On models so equipped, remove the rear view mirrors (A, **Figure 30**).
2. Remove the screws securing the left-hand handlebar switch assembly (B, **Figure 30**) and remove the switch assembly.
3. Remove the electrical wire plastic band and remove the electrical wires from the left-hand side of the handlebar.
4. Slacken the clutch cable (A, **Figure 31**) and disconnect the cable from the clutch hand lever.
5. Loosen the clutch bracket bolt (B, **Figure 31**) and remove the clutch lever assembly.
6. Remove the screws (A, **Figure 32**) securing the throttle assembly. Slide off the assembly and carefully lay the throttle assembly and cable over the fender or back over the fuel tank. Be careful that the cable does not get crimped or damaged.

7. Remove the electrical wire plastic band and remove the electrical wires from the right-hand side of the handlebar.
8. Remove the front brake bracket bolts (B, **Figure 32**) and remove the brake lever assembly.
9A. On TL250 models, remove the screw (**Figure 33**) securing the engine kill switch to the center of the handlebar.
9B. On all other models, remove the screw securing the engine stop switch and remove the switch and brake lever assembly.
10. Remove the bolts (**Figure 34**) securing the handlebar upper holders and remove the holders and the handlebar.

NOTE
Some models have a cable bracket that is attached to the front bolts of the upper holders. Move the bracket and cable(s) out of the way.

11. To maintain a good grip on the handlebar and to prevent it from slipping down, clean the knurled section of the handlebar with a wire brush. It should be kept rough so it will be held securely by the holders. The upper and lower holders should also be kept clean and free of any metal that may have been gouged loose by handlebar slippage.
12. Install by reversing these removal steps, noting the following.
13. Position the handlebar in the lower holders on the fork bridge so the punch mark on the handlebar is aligned with the top surface of the lower holders (**Figure 35**).

NOTE
On models so equipped, install the cable bracket under the front bolts prior to installing the bolts.

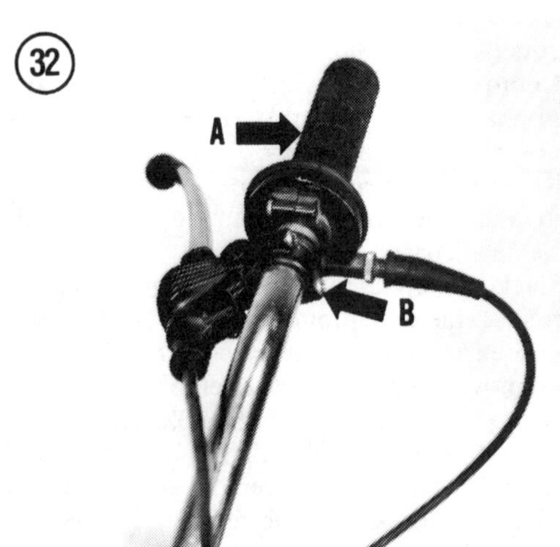

32

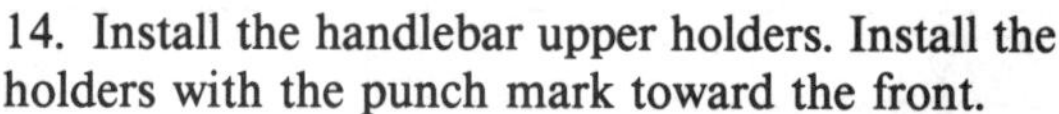

14. Install the handlebar upper holders. Install the holders with the punch mark toward the front.
15. Install the bolts. Tighten the front bolts first, then the rear to the torque specifications listed in **Table 1**. After installation is complete, recheck the alignment of the punch mark.
16. When installing all assemblies, align the punch mark on the handlebar with the slit on the mounting brackets.
17. Adjust the clutch and throttle operation as described in Chapter Three.

STEERING HEAD

Refer to **Figures 36-44** for this procedure.

33

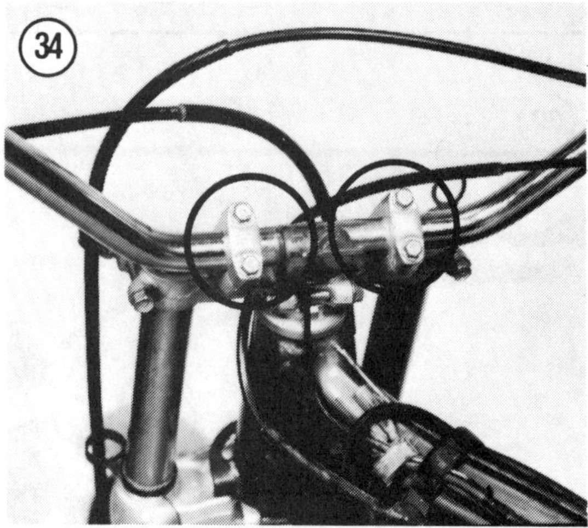

34

35

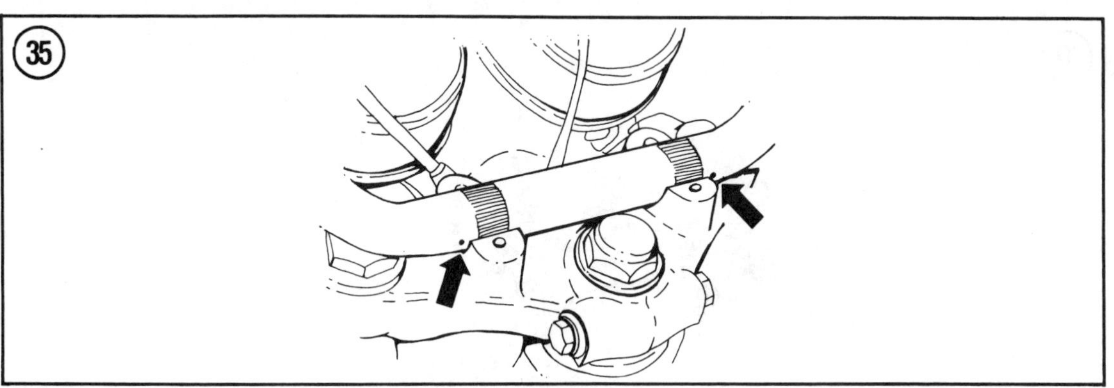

36

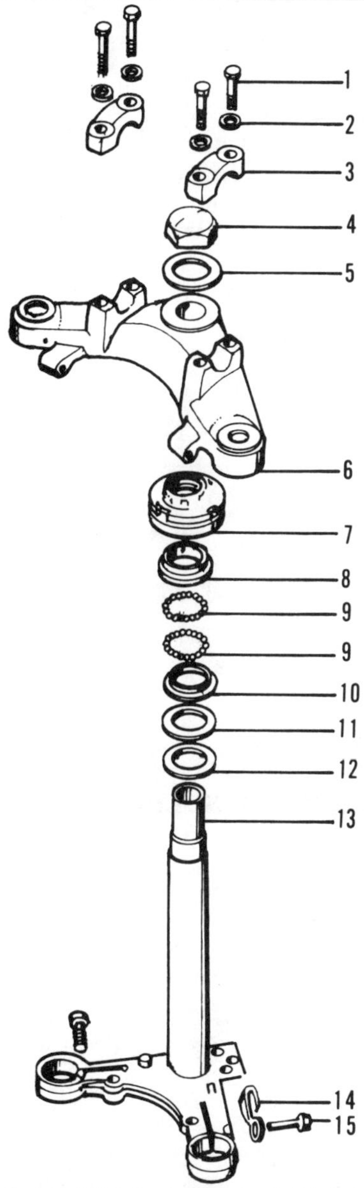

STEERING STEM ASSEMBLY (CB100, CL100, CB125S, CB125 S1-S2)

1. Bolt
2. Washer
3. Handlebar holder
4. Steering stem nut
5. Washer
6. Upper fork bridge
7. Steering stem adjust nut
8. Upper bearing race
9. Ball bearings (21 balls each bearing No. 6)
10. Lower bearing race
11. Dust seal
12. Washer
13. Steering stem
14. Clip
15. Bolt

37

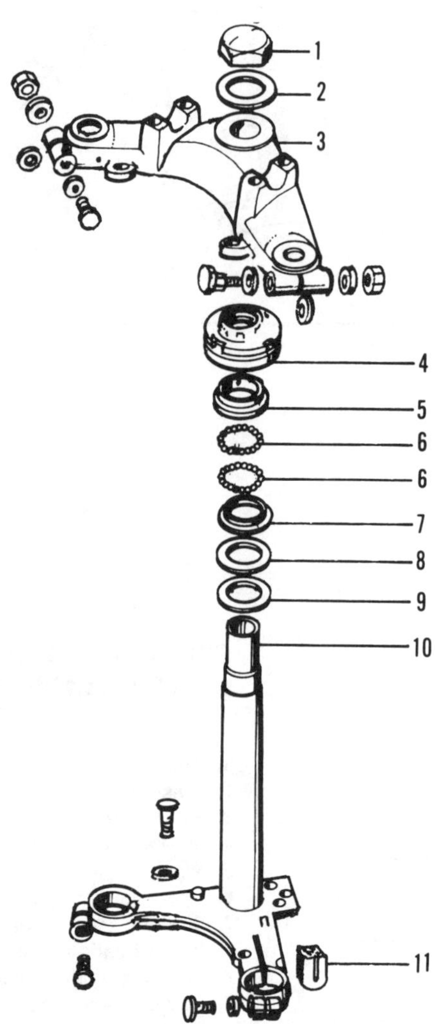

STEERING STEM ASSEMBLY (SL100, XL100, XL100 K1, 1976, XL100 SL125)

1. Steering stem nut
2. Washer
3. Upper fork bridge
4. Steering stem adjust nut
5. Upper bearing race
6. Ball bearings (21 balls each bearing No. 6)
7. Lower bearing race
8. Dust seal
9. Washer
10. Steering stem
11. Lock

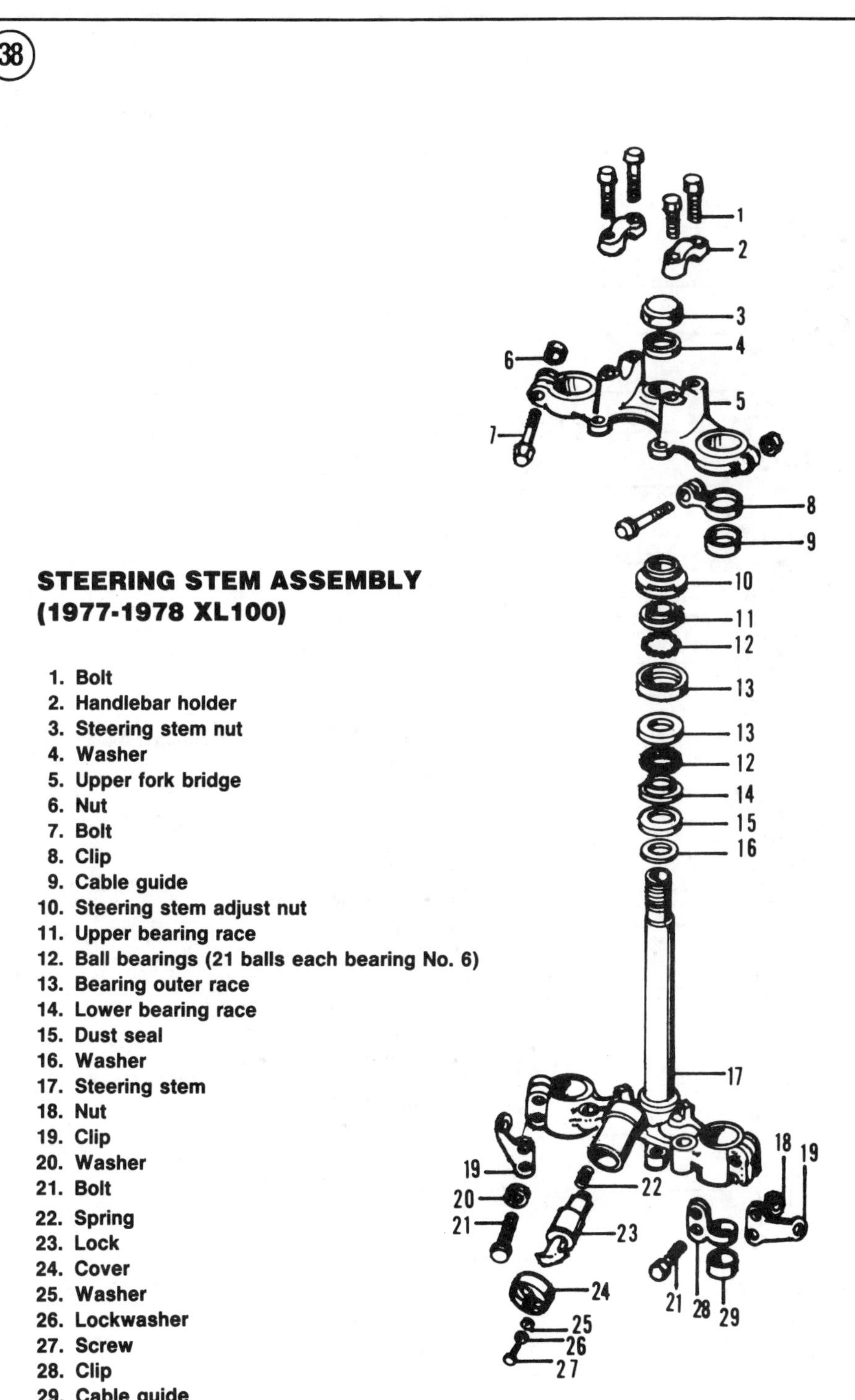
38
STEERING STEM ASSEMBLY
(1977-1978 XL100)
1. Bolt
2. Handlebar holder
3. Steering stem nut
4. Washer
5. Upper fork bridge
6. Nut
7. Bolt
8. Clip
9. Cable guide
10. Steering stem adjust nut
11. Upper bearing race
12. Ball bearings (21 balls each bearing No. 6)
13. Bearing outer race
14. Lower bearing race
15. Dust seal
16. Washer
17. Steering stem
18. Nut
19. Clip
20. Washer
21. Bolt
22. Spring
23. Lock
24. Cover
25. Washer
26. Lockwasher
27. Screw
28. Clip
29. Cable guide

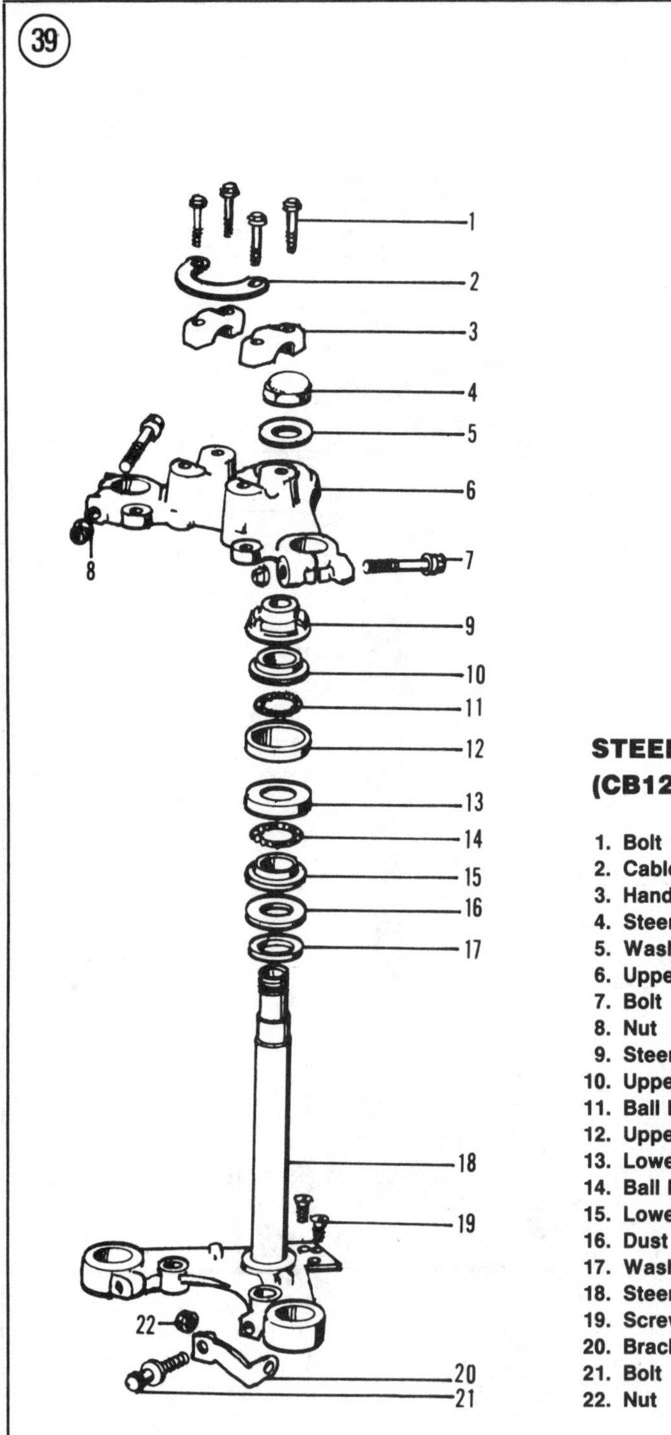

STEERING STEM ASSEMBLY (CB125S)

1. Bolt
2. Cable holder
3. Handlebar holder
4. Steering stem nut
5. Washer
6. Upper fork bridge
7. Bolt
8. Nut
9. Steering stem adjust nut
10. Upper bearing race
11. Ball bearings (21 ball bearings No. 6)
12. Upper bearing outer race
13. Lower bearing outer race
14. Ball bearings (21 ball bearings No. 6)
15. Lower bearing race
16. Dust seal
17. Washer
18. Steering stem
19. Screw
20. Bracket
21. Bolt
22. Nut

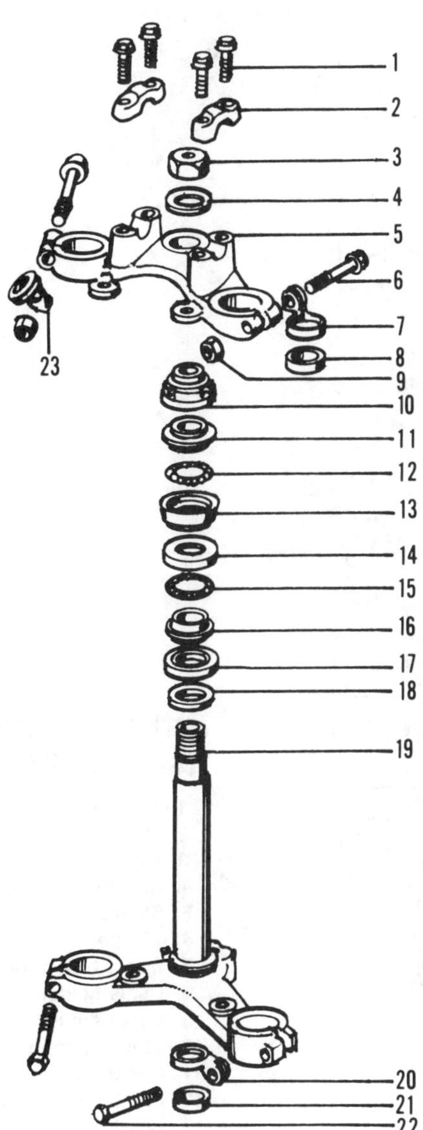

STEERING STEM ASSEMBLY (TL125)

1. Bolt
2. Handlebar holder
3. Steering stem nut
4. Washer
5. Upper fork bridge
6. Bolt
7. Cable holder
8. Cable guide
9. Nut
10. Steering stem adjust nut
11. Upper bearing race
12. Ball bearings (21 ball bearings No. 6)
13. Upper bearing outer race
14. Lower bearing outer race
15. Ball bearings (21 ball bearings No. 6)
16. Lower bearing race
17. Dust seal
18. Washer
19. Steering stem
20. Cable holder
21. Cable guide
22. Bolt

9

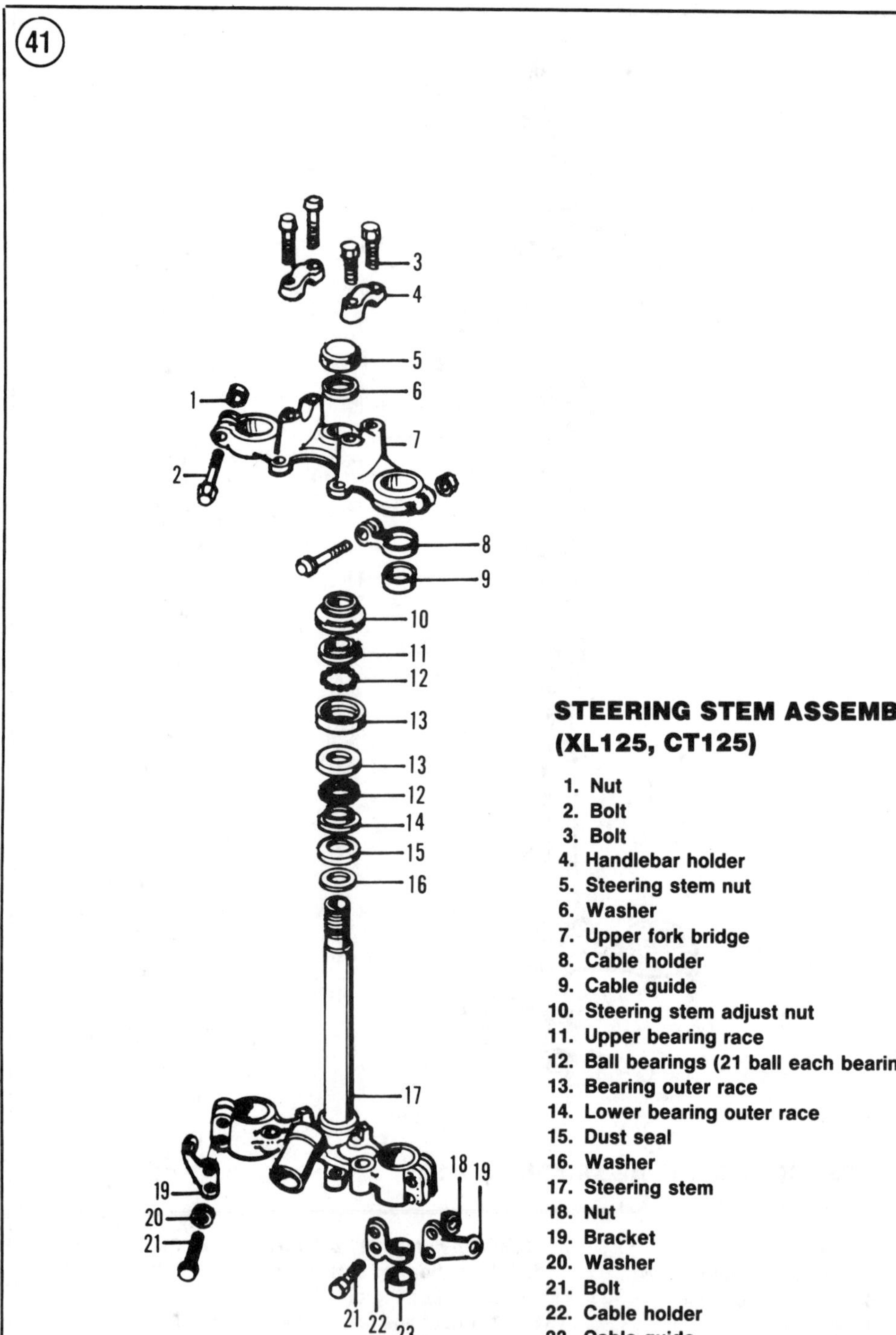

STEERING STEM ASSEMBLY (XL125, CT125)

1. Nut
2. Bolt
3. Bolt
4. Handlebar holder
5. Steering stem nut
6. Washer
7. Upper fork bridge
8. Cable holder
9. Cable guide
10. Steering stem adjust nut
11. Upper bearing race
12. Ball bearings (21 ball each bearing No. 6)
13. Bearing outer race
14. Lower bearing outer race
15. Dust seal
16. Washer
17. Steering stem
18. Nut
19. Bracket
20. Washer
21. Bolt
22. Cable holder
23. Cable guide

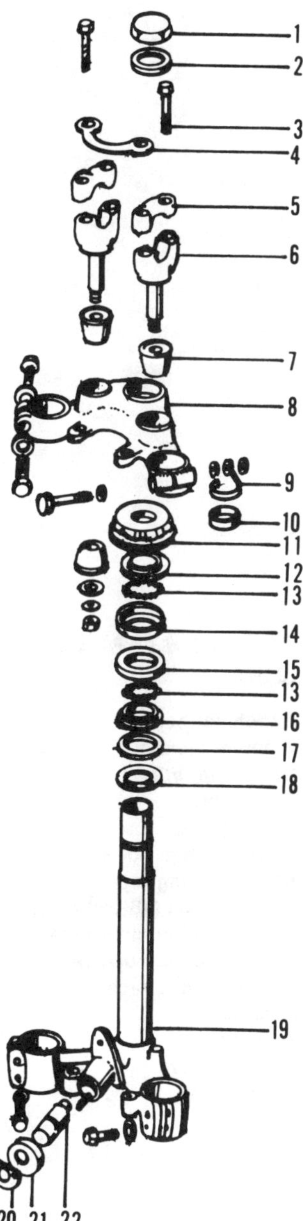

STEERING STEM ASSEMBLY (XL175, XL250)

1. Steering stem nut
2. Washer
3. Bolt
4. Cable bracket
5. Handlebar upper holder
6. Handlebar lower holder
7. Rubber damper
8. Upper fork bridge
9. Cable holder
10. Cable guide
11. Steering stem adjust nut
12. Upper bearing race
13. Ball bearings (18 ball each bearing No. 8)
14. Upper bearing outer race
15. Lower bearing outer race
16. Lower bearing race
17. Dust seal
18. Washer
19. Steering stem
20. Plate
21. Cover
22. Lock

9

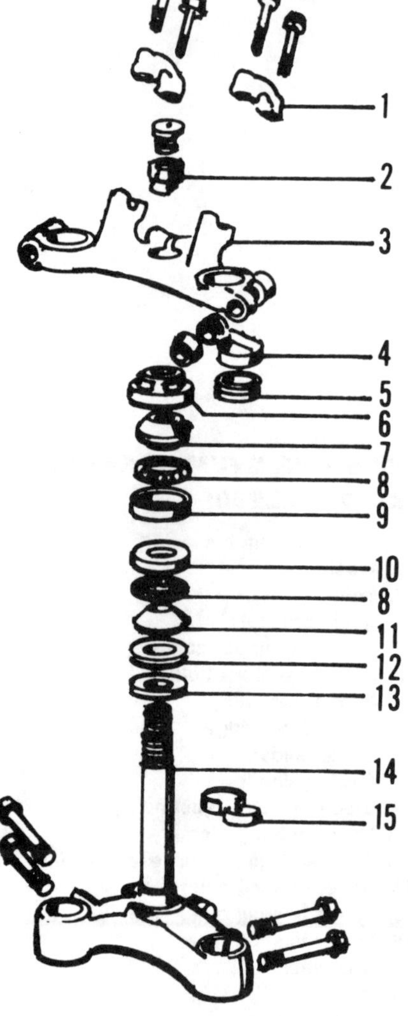

STEERING STEM ASSEMBLY (TL250)

1. Handlebar holder
2. Steering stem nut
3. Upper fork bridge
4. Cable holder
5. Cable guide
6. Steering stem adjust nut
7. Upper bearing race
8. Ball bearings (18 ball each bearing No. 6)
9. Upper bearing outer race
10. Lower bearing outer race
11. Lower bearing race
12. Dust seal
13. Washer
14. Steering stem
15. Strap

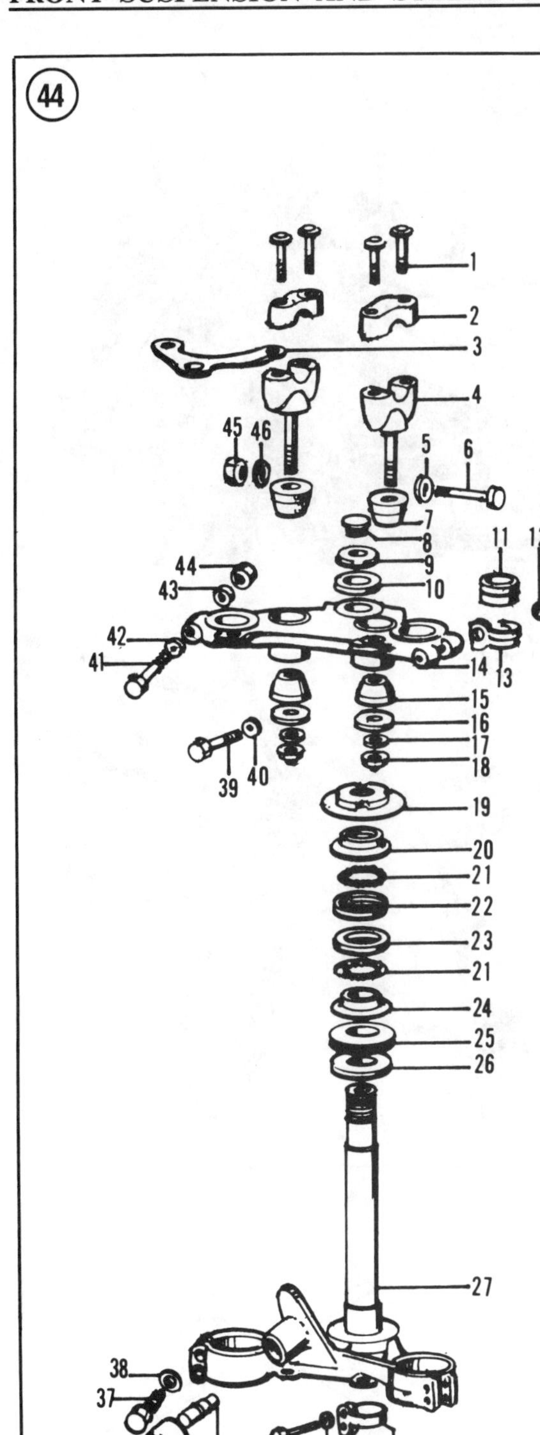

STEERING STEM ASSEMBLY (XL350)

1. Bolt
2. Handlebar upper holder
3. Cable bracket
4. Handlebar lower holder
5. Washer
6. Bolt
7. Rubber damper
8. Steering stem nut trim cap
9. Washer
10. Washer
11. Cable holder
12. Nut
13. Cable guide
14. Upper fork bridge
15. Rubber damper
16. Washer
17. Lockwasher
18. Nut
19. Steering stem adjust nut
20. Upper bearing race
21. Ball bearings (18 ball each bearing No. 8)
22. Upper bearing outer race
23. Lower bearing outer race
24. Lower bearing race
25. Dust seal
26. Washer
27. Steering stem
28. Cable holder
29. Cable guide
30. Washer
31. Bolt
32. Screw
33. Lockwasher
34. Plate
35. Cover
36. Lock
37. Bolt
38. Washer
39. Bolt
40. Washer
41. Bolt
42. Washer
43. Lockwasher
44. Nut
45. Nut
46. Lockwasher

Disassembly

1. Remove the front wheel as described in this chapter.
2. Remove the handlebar (A, **Figure 45**) as described in this chapter.
3. Remove the headlight assembly (B, **Figure 45**) as described in Chapter Eight.
4. Remove the bolts securing the front fender and remove the fender.
5. Remove the front forks (C, **Figure 45**) as described in this chapter.
6. Remove the steering stem nut and washer (D, **Figure 45**).
7. On models so equipped, loosen the steering stem clamp bolt and nut **(Figure 46)** on the upper fork bridge.
8. Remove the upper fork bridge assembly (E, **Figure 45**).
9. Remove the steering head adjusting nut. Use a large drift and hammer or the easily improvised tool shown in **Figure 47**.

NOTE
Have an assistant hold a large pan under the steering stem to catch the loose ball bearings while you carefully lower the steering stem.

10. Lower the steering stem assembly down and out of the steering head **(Figure 48)**.
11. Remove the ball bearings from the upper and lower race.

NOTE
All models have the same number of balls in each race.

Inspection

1. Clean the bearing races in the steering head, the steering stem races and the bearings with solvent.
2. Check the welds around the steering head for cracks and fractures. If any are found, have them repaired by a competent frame shop or welding service.
3. Check the balls or rollers for pitting, scratches or discoloration indicating wear or corrosion. Replace them in sets if any are bad.
4. Check the races for pitting, galling and corrosion. If any of these conditions exist, replace the races as described in this chapter.
5. Check the steering stem for cracks and check its race for damage or wear. If this race or any race is damaged, the bearings should be replaced as a complete bearing set. Take the old races and bearings to your dealer to ensure accurate replacement.

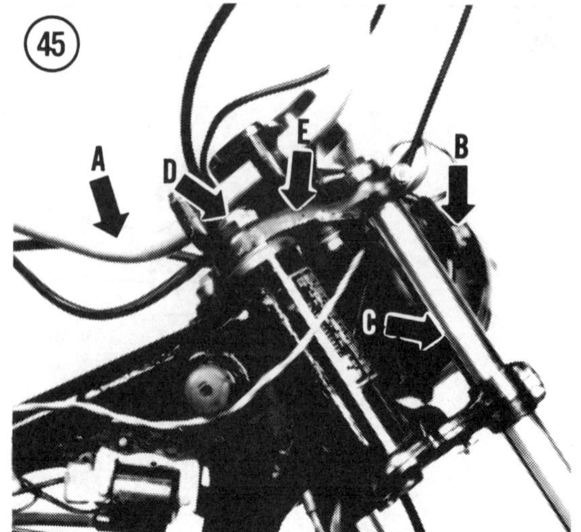

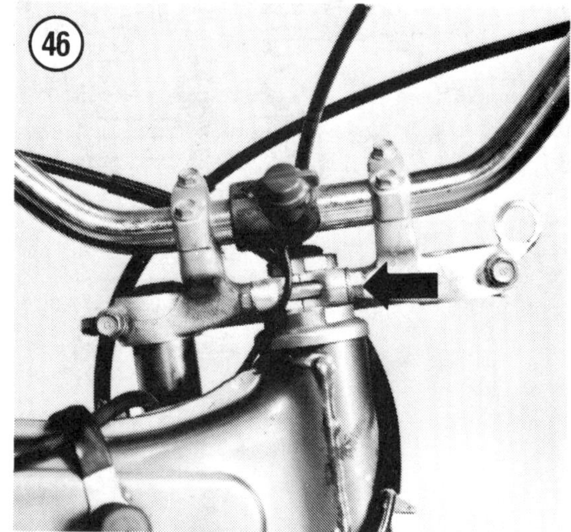

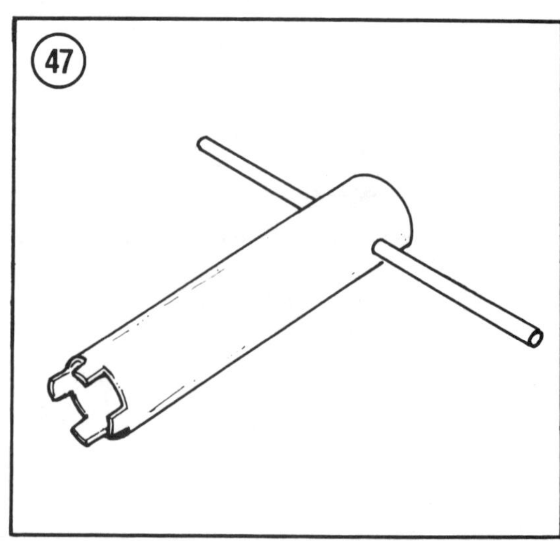

48

1. Adjuster nut
2. Head pipe
3. Steel balls
4. Steering stem

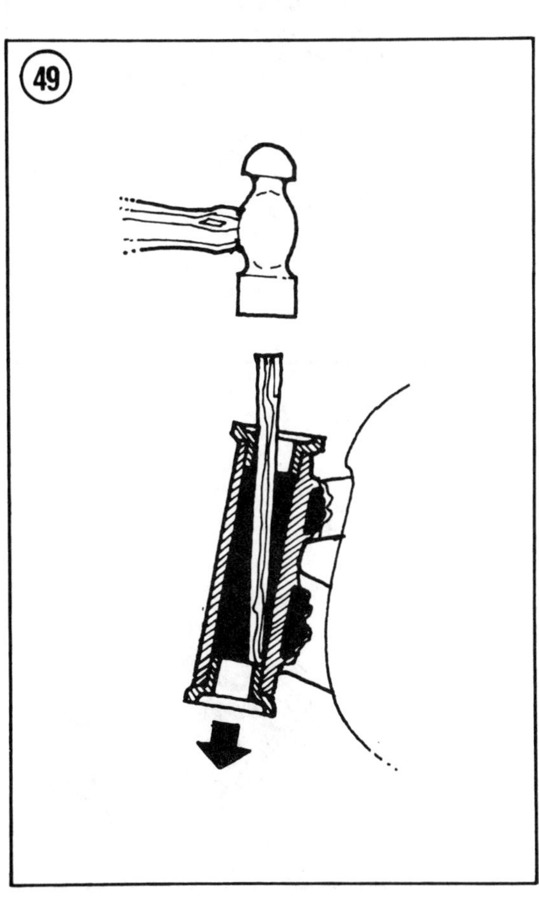

Steering Head Bearing Races

The headset and steering stem bearing races are pressed into place. Because they are easily bent, do not remove them unless they are worn and require replacement.

Headset bearing race removal/installation

To remove the headset race, insert a hardwood stick or soft punch into the head tube (**Figure 49**) and carefully tap the race out from the inside. After it is started, tap around the race so that neither the race nor the head tube is damaged.

To install the headset race, tap it in slowly with a block of wood, a suitable size socket or piece of pipe (**Figure 50**). Make sure that the race is squarely seated in the headset race bore before tapping it into place. Tap the race in until it is flush with the steering head surface.

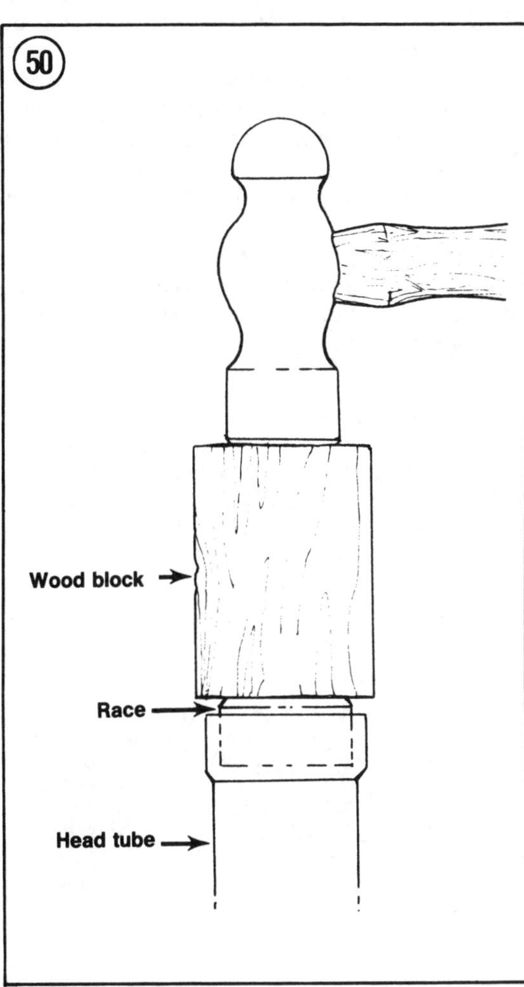

Steering stem bearing race and grease seal removal/installation

1. To remove the steering stem race, try twisting and pulling it up by hand. If it will not come off, carefully pry it up with a screwdriver; work around in a circle, prying a little at a time.
2. Remove the lower bearing race, dust seal and dust seal washer.
3. Install the dust seal washer, dust seal and race. Slide the lower race over the steering stem with the bearing surface pointing up.
4. Tap the race down with a piece of hardwood; work around in a circle so the race will not be bent. Make sure it is seated squarely and is all the way down.

Assembly

1. Make sure the steering head and stem races are properly seated.
2. Apply a coat of cold grease to the upper bearing race cone and fit the ball bearings around it (**Figure 51**). Refer to **Table 3** for the correct number of balls required.
3. Apply a coat of cold grease to the lower bearing race cone and fit the ball bearings around it (**Figure 52**). Refer to **Table 3** for the correct number of balls required.
4. Install the steering stem into the head tube and hold it firmly in place.
5. Install the upper bearing race.
6. Install the steering stem adjusting nut (**Figure 53**) and tighten it until it is snug against the upper race, then back it off 1/8 turn.

NOTE
The adjusting nut should be just tight enough to remove both horizontal and vertical play, yet loose enough so that the assembly will turn to both lock positions under its own weight after an assist.

51

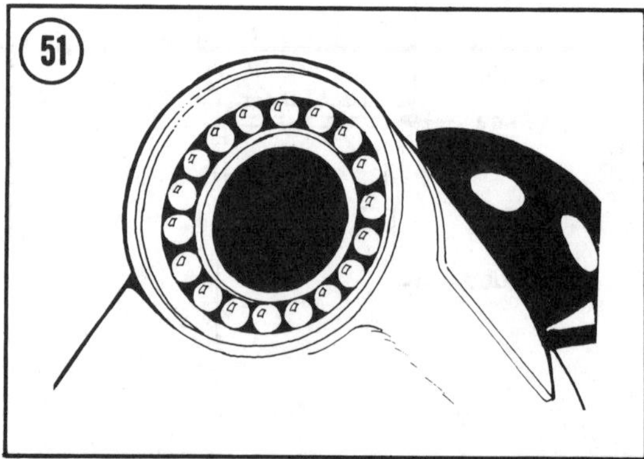

52

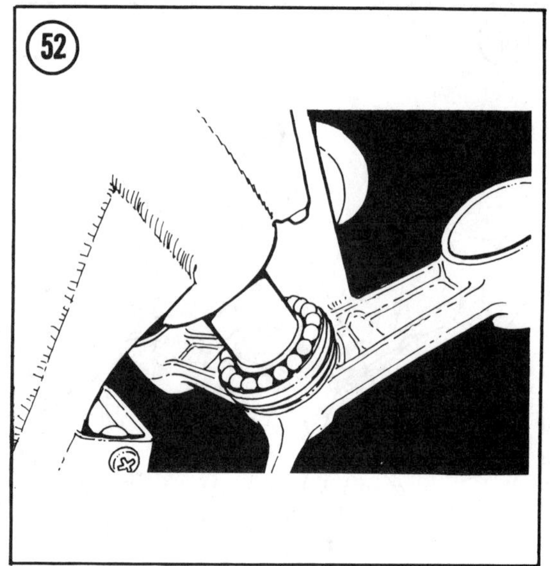

53

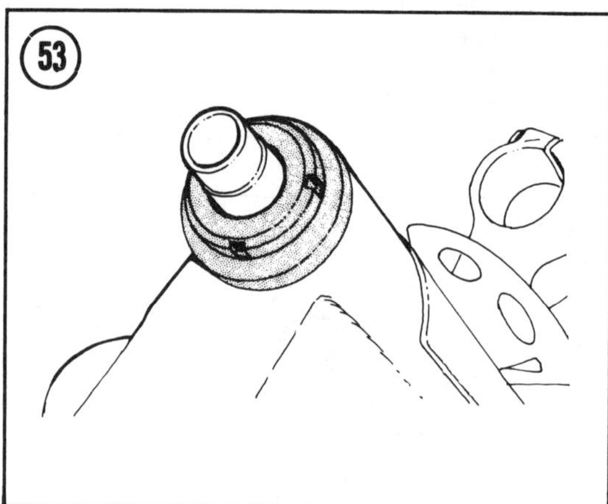

54

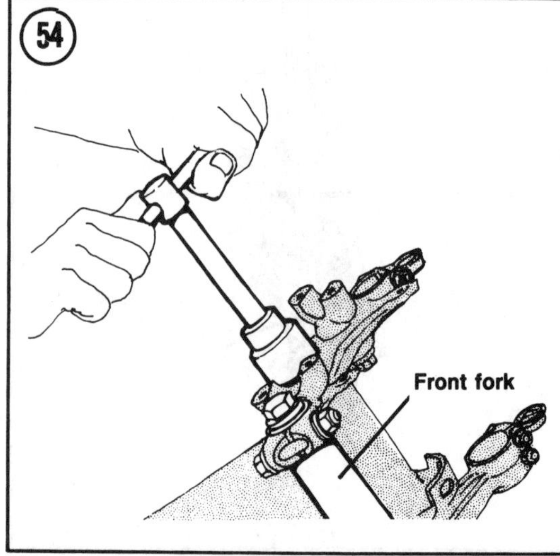

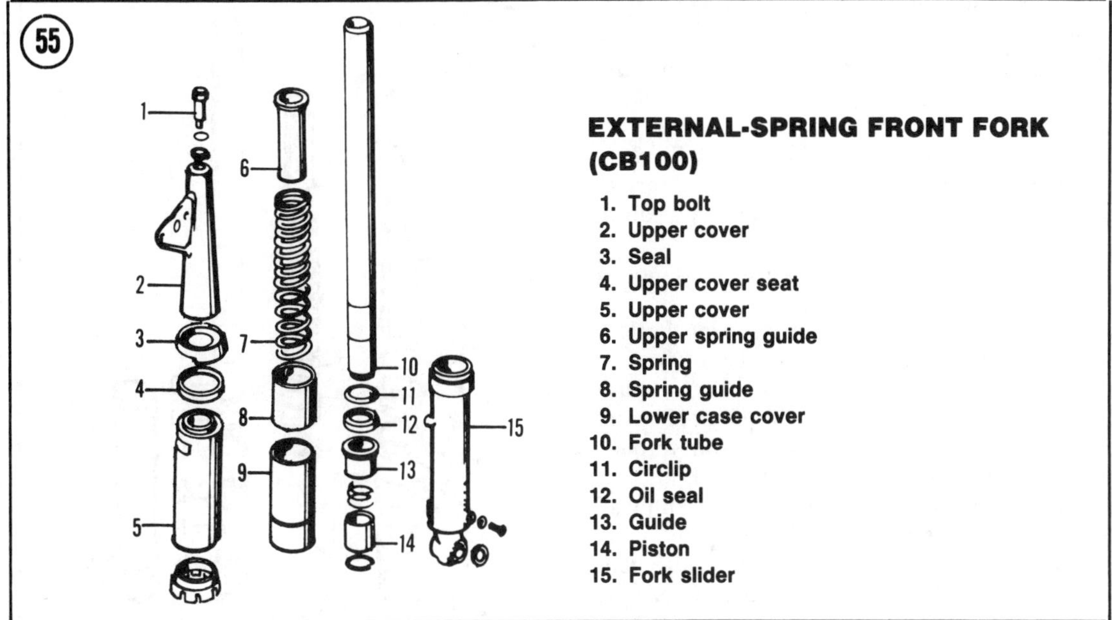

EXTERNAL-SPRING FRONT FORK (CB100)

1. Top bolt
2. Upper cover
3. Seal
4. Upper cover seat
5. Upper cover
6. Upper spring guide
7. Spring
8. Spring guide
9. Lower case cover
10. Fork tube
11. Circlip
12. Oil seal
13. Guide
14. Piston
15. Fork slider

7. Install the upper fork bridge, washer and steering stem flange bolt finger-tight.

NOTE
Steps 9-11 must be performed in this order to assure proper upper and lower fork bridge to fork alignment.

8. Slide the fork tubes into position and tighten the lower fork bridge bolts to the torque specifications listed in **Table 1**.
9. Tighten the steering stem nut (**Figure 54**) to the torque specifications in **Table 1**.
10. Tighten the upper fork bridge bolts to the torque specifications in **Table 1**.
11. On models so equipped, tighten the upper fork bridge steering stem clamp bolt securely.
12. Install the headlight assembly as described in Chapter Eight.
13. Install the handlebar assembly as described in this chapter.
14. Install the front wheel as described in this chapter.
15. After a few hours of riding, the bearings have had a chance to seat; readjust the free play in the steering stem with the steering stem adjusting nut. Refer to Step 6.

Steering Stem Adjustment

If play develops in the steering system, it may only require adjustment. However, don't take a chance on it. Disassemble the stem and look for possible damage. Then reassemble and adjust as described in Step 6 of the *Steering Head Assembly* procedure.

FRONT FORK

The front suspension uses a spring controlled, hydraulically damped, telescopic fork. The front fork used on various models differ in construction and operation, but can be grouped into 3 general types:

a. External spring.
b. Internal spring, Type I.
c. Internal spring, Type II.

Service procedures for these three types are covered separately.

Before suspecting major trouble, drain the front fork oil and refill with the proper type and quantity; refer to Chapter Three. If you still have trouble, such as poor damping, a tendency to bottom or top out or leakage around the rubber seals, follow the service procedures in this chapter.

To simplify fork service and to prevent the mixing of parts, the legs should be removed, serviced and installed individually.

External-spring Front Fork

This type of fork has a spring that travels on the outside of the fork tube. External-spring forks are used on the following models:

a. **Figure 55**-All CB100.
b. **Figure 56**-All CL100; CB125 S, CB125 S1-S2.

1. Remove the front wheel as described in this chapter.
2. Remove the bolts securing the front fender and remove the fender.
3. Loosen the lower fork bridge bolts.
4. Remove the top fork bolt and washer.
5. Remove the fork tube. It may be necessary to slightly rotate the fork tube while pulling it down and out.
6. Install by reversing these removal steps, noting the following.
7. Be sure the fork cover is in place on the fork bridge prior to installing the fork tube.
8. Insert the fork tube into the fork cover and push it up as far as it will go. Insert a long bolt (with threads that match the top fork bolt) down through the hole in the upper fork bridge. Screw it into the top of the fork tube and pull the fork assembly all the way up into position.
9. Temporarily tighten the lower fork bridge bolt.
10. Remove the long bolt and install the fork top bolt and washer. Loosen the lower fork bridge bolt.
11. Tighten the top fork bolt securely.
12. Tighten the lower fork bridge bolt to the torque specifications listed in **Table 1**.

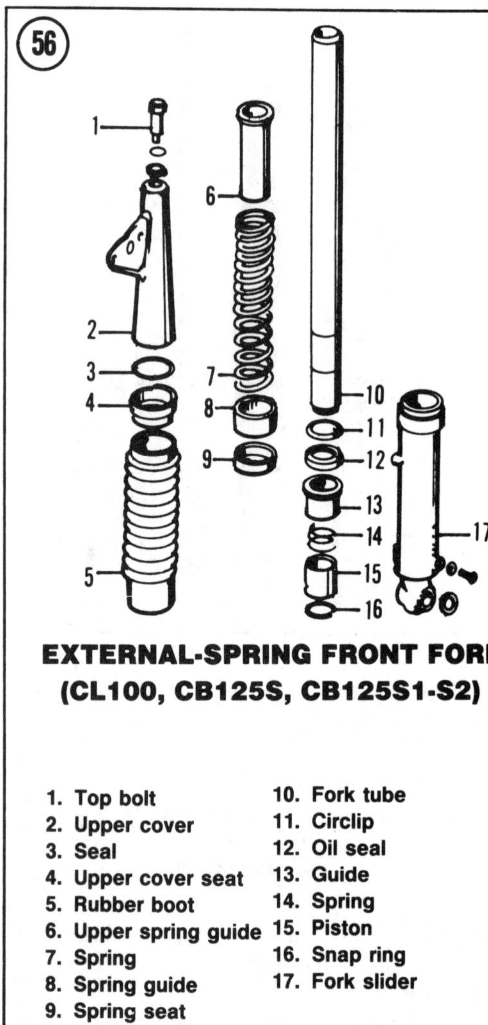

EXTERNAL-SPRING FRONT FORK (CL100, CB125S, CB125S1-S2)

1. Top bolt
2. Upper cover
3. Seal
4. Upper cover seat
5. Rubber boot
6. Upper spring guide
7. Spring
8. Spring guide
9. Spring seat
10. Fork tube
11. Circlip
12. Oil seal
13. Guide
14. Spring
15. Piston
16. Snap ring
17. Fork slider

Disassembly

Refer to **Figure 55** and **Figure 56** during the disassembly procedure.

The following procedure represents a typical fork disassembly. Minor variations exist among the different models and years. Pay particular attention to the location and positioning of spacers, washers and springs to make sure they are assembled in the correct location.

1. Remove the fork cap bolt and the drain screw on the bottom of the fork slider. Pour the fork oil out and discard it. Pump the fork several times by hand to expel most of the remaining oil. Reinstall the drain screw and washer.
2. On models so equipped, slide the rubber boot and the upper and lower spring seats (**Figure 57**) off of the fork tube.
3. Clamp the slider in a vise with soft jaws (**Figure 58**).
4. Remove the circlip (**Figure 59**) from the slider.
5. There is an interference fit between the oil seal and the fork tube guide. In order to remove the oil seal from the slider, pull hard on the fork tube using quick in and out strokes. Doing this will withdraw the oil seal.

NOTE
It may be necessary to slightly heat the area on the slider around the oil seal

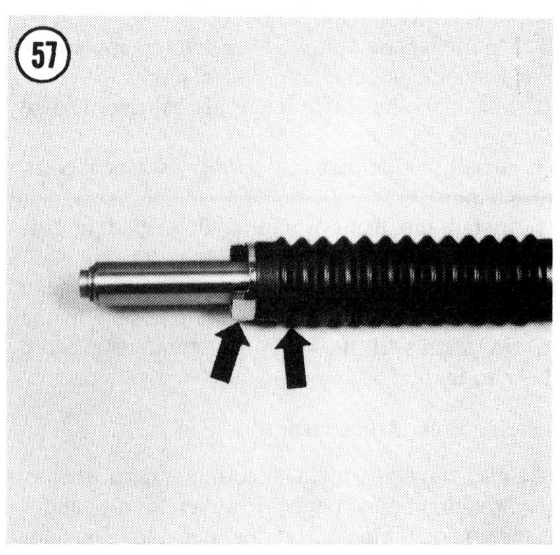

58

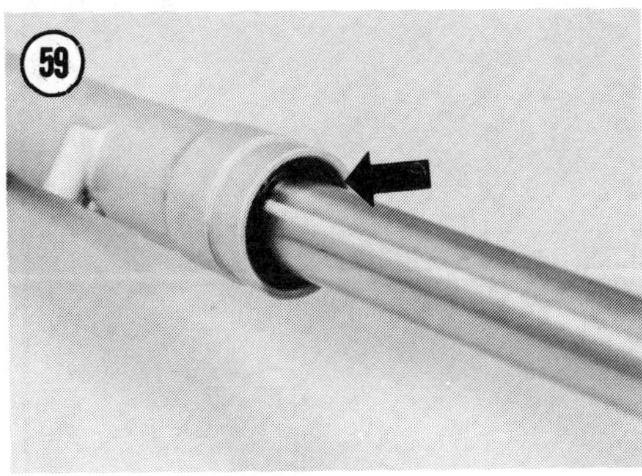
59

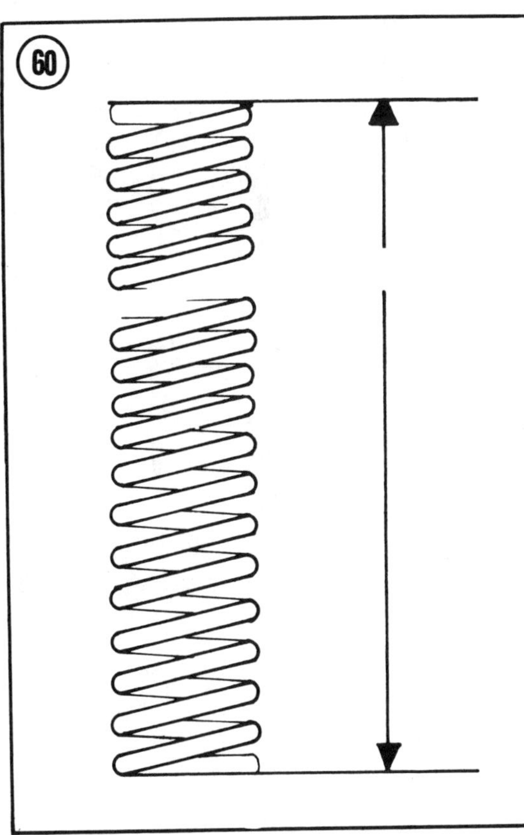
60

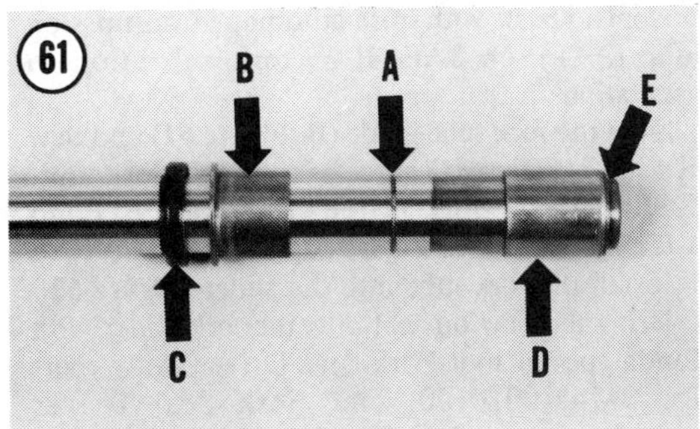

61

prior to removal. Use a rag soaked in hot water; do not apply a flame directly to the fork slider.

6. Remove the circlip at the base of the fork tube and slide off the fork piston.
7. Slide off the oil seal and the fork tube guide from the top of the fork tube.

Inspection

1. Thoroughly clean all parts in solvent and dry them.
2. Inspect the oil seal for scoring, nicks and loss of resiliency. Replace if its condition is questionable.
3. Check the fork tube for straightness. If bent or severely scratched, it should be replaced. Also check the fork tube for signs of wear or scratches.
4. Check the lower slider for dents or exterior damage that may cause the upper fork tube to hang up during riding. Replace if necessary.

NOTE
Honda does not provide fork specifications for all models. ***Table 4*** *and* ***Table 5*** *list all service limit specifications that are available.*

5. Measure the uncompressed length of the fork spring as shown in **Figure 60**. If the spring has sagged to the service limit dimensions in **Table 4** it must be replaced.
6. Measure the outside diameter of the fork piston with a micrometer. If it is worn to less than the service limit in **Table 5**, the piston must be replaced.
7. Any parts that are worn or damaged should be replaced. Simply cleaning and reinstalling unserviceable components will not improve performance of the front suspension.

Assembly

Refer to **Figure 55** and **Figure 56**.

1. Make sure the snap ring (A, **Figure 61**) is in place on the fork tube.

9

2. Coat all parts with fresh automatic transmission fluid (ATF) or SAE 10W fork oil prior to installation.
3. Slide the fork tube guide (B, **Figure 61**) and new oil seal (C, **Figure 61**) onto the top of the fork tube.
4. Slide on the fork piston (D, **Figure 61**) and install the circlip (E, **Figure 61**).
5. Install the fork tube into the slider (**Figure 62**).
6. Drive the new oil seal into the fork slider with Honda special tool Fork Seal Driver Body (part No. 07747-0010100) and Fork Seal Driver Attachment (part No. 07947-1180001). Refer to **Figure 63**. Drive the oil seal in until the circlip groove in the slider can be seen above the top surface of the backup ring.
7. Install the circlip (**Figure 59**) with the sharp edge facing up. Make sure the circlip is correctly seated in the groove in the fork slider.

NOTE
Install the fork spring with the narrow pitch (closer wound) coils toward the top of the fork.

8. Install the fork spring lower seat (A, **Figure 64**) and the fork spring and spring guide (B, **Figure 64**) onto the fork tube.
9. Install the rubber boot and upper spring seat (**Figure 57**).
10. Remove the fork cap bolt and fill each fork tube with DEXRON ATF or SAE 10W fork oil. Refer to **Table 6** for the specific quantity for each fork leg.

NOTE
In order to measure the correct amount of fluid, use a plastic baby bottle. These have graduations in fluid ounces (oz.) and cubic centimeters (cc) on the side. Many fork oil containers have a semi-transparent strip on the side of the bottle to aid in measuring.

11. Insect the O-ring seal on the fork cap bolt (**Figure 65**). If it is damaged or starting to deteriorate, it must be replaced.

Internal-spring Front Fork (Type I)

On this type of fork, the spring travels on the inside of the fork tube and slides. Type I internal-spring forks are used on the following models:

a. **Figure 66**—All SL100.
b. **Figure 67**—SL125.
c. **Figure 68**—1976-1978 CB125.

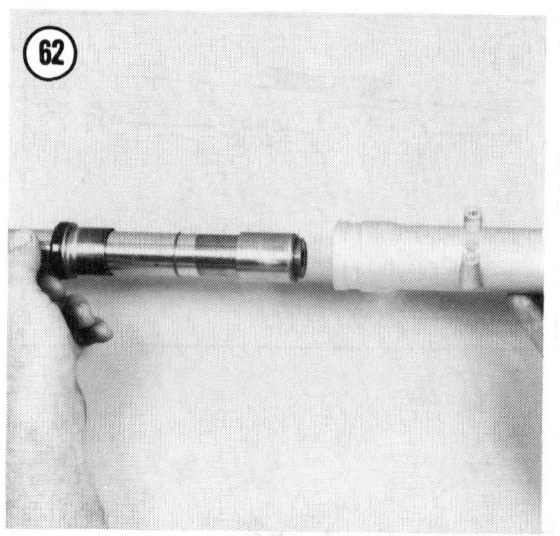

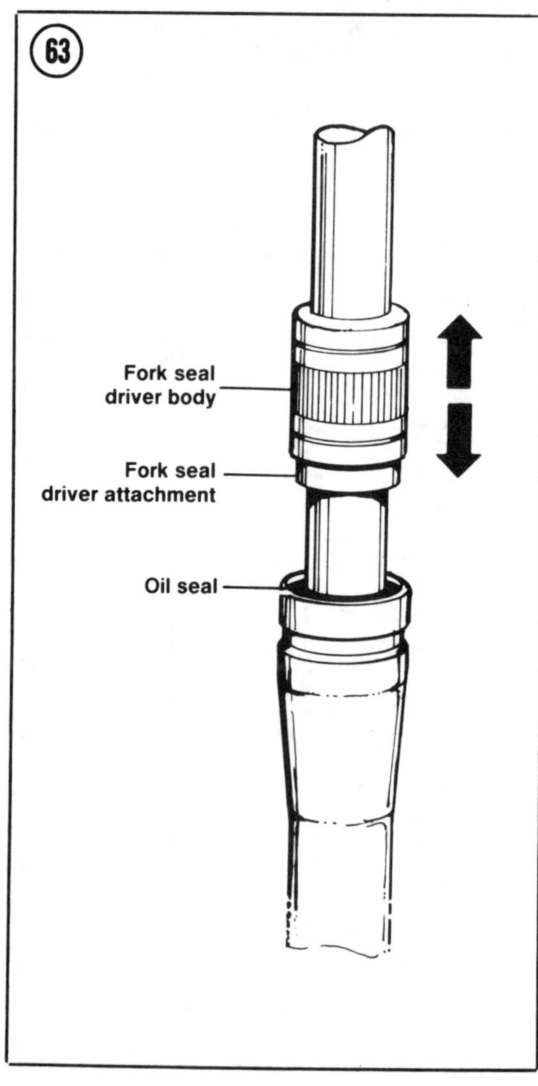

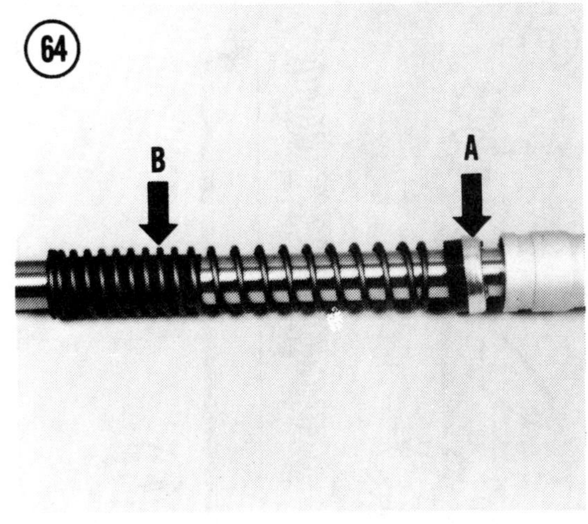

Removal/Installation

1. Remove the front wheel as described in this chapter.
2. Remove the bolts securing the front fender and remove the fender.
3. Loosen the lower fork bridge bolts.
4. Remove the top fork bolt and washer.
5. Remove the fork tube. It may be necessary to slightly rotate the fork tube while pulling it down and out.
6. Install by reversing these removal steps, noting the following.
7. Tighten the top fork bolt and the lower fork bridge bolt to the torque specifications in **Table 1**.

Disassembly

Refer to **Figures 66-68** during the disassembly and assembly procedure.

The following procedure represents a typical fork disassembly. Minor variations exist among the different models and years. Pay particular attention to the location and positioning of spacers, washers and springs to make sure they are assembled in the correct location.

1. Remove the fork cap bolt and the drain screw on the bottom of the fork slider. Pour the fork oil out and discard it. Pump the fork several times by hand to expel most of the remaining oil. Reinstall the drain screw and washer.
2. Clamp the slider in a vise with soft jaws (**Figure 58**).
3. Remove the circlip and oil seal backup ring from the slider (**Figure 69**).

NOTE
On SL125 models, there is no oil seal backup ring.

4. There is an interference fit between the oil seal and the fork tube guide. In order to remove the oil seal from the slider, pull hard on the fork tube using quick in and out strokes. Doing this will withdraw the oil seal and backup ring from the slider.

NOTE
It may be necessary to slightly heat the area on the slider around the oil seal prior to removal. Use a rag soaked in hot water; do not apply a flame directly to the fork slider.

5. Withdraw the fork tube from the slider.
6. Withdraw the fork spring from the slider.
7. Remove the circlip at the base of the fork tube and slide off the fork piston.
8. Slide off the oil seal and the fork tube guide from the top of the fork tube.

Inspection

1. Thoroughly clean all parts in solvent and dry them.
2. Inspect the oil seal for scoring, nicks and loss of resiliency. Replace if its condition is questionable.
3. Check the fork tube for straightness. If bent or severely scratched, it should be replaced. Also check the fork tube for signs of wear or scratches.
4. Check the slider for dents or exterior damage that may cause the fork tube to hang up during riding. Replace if necessary.

NOTE
Honda does not provide fork specifications for all models. ***Table 4*** *and* ***Table 5*** *list all service limit specifications that are available.*

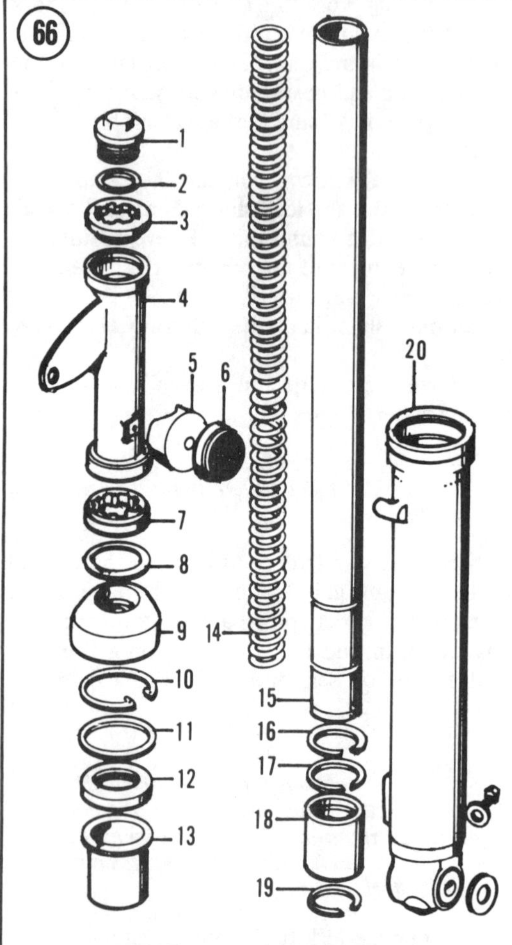

INTERNAL-SPRING FRONT FORK, TYPE I (SL100)

1. Top bolt
2. O-ring seal
3. Upper cover top seal
4. Upper cover
5. Bracket
6. Side reflex reflector
7. Upper cover lower seal
8. Washer
9. Dust seal
10. Circlip
11. Backup ring
12. Oil seal
13. Guide
14. Fork spring
15. Fork tube
16. Snap ring
17. Snap ring
18. Piston
19. Snap ring
20. Fork slider

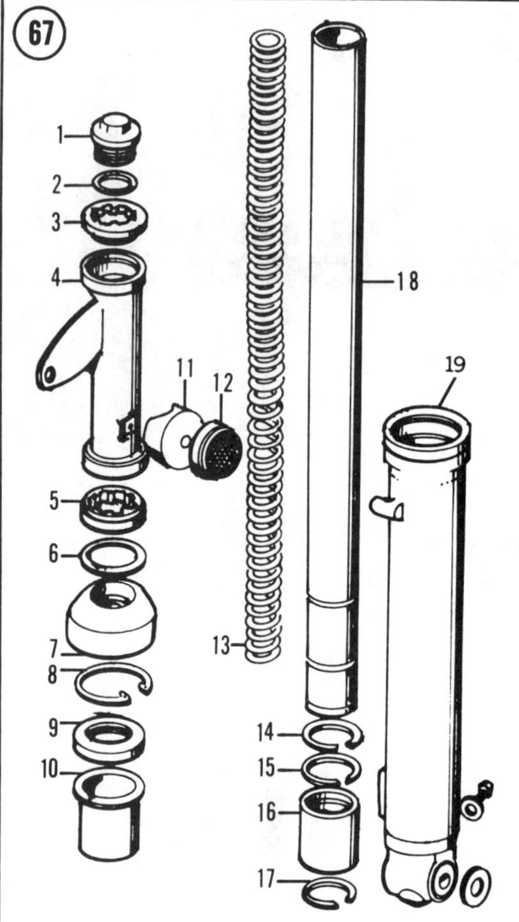

INTERNAL-SPRING FRONT FORK, TYPE I (SL125)

1. Top bolt
2. O-ring seal
3. Upper cover top seal
4. Upper cover
5. Upper cover lower seal
6. Washer
7. Dust seal
8. Circlip
9. Oil seal
10. Guide
11. Bracket
12. Side reflex reflector
13. Fork spring
14. Snap ring
15. Snap ring
16. Piston
17. Snap ring
18. Fork tube
19. Fork slider

68

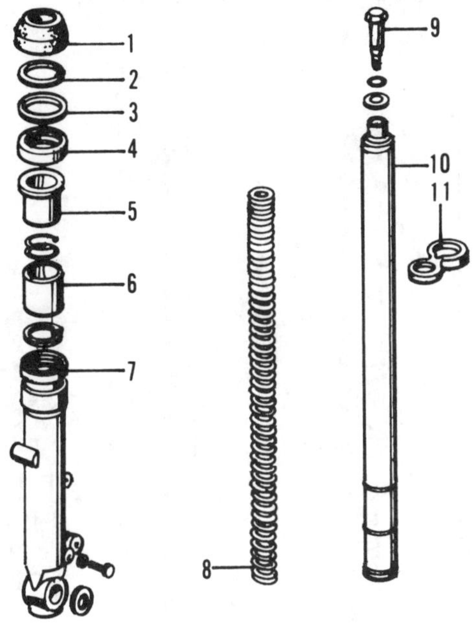

INTERNAL-SPRING FRONT FORK, TYPE I (1976-1978 CB125)

1. Dust seal
2. Circlip
3. Backup ring
4. Oil seal
5. Guide
6. Piston
7. Fork slider
8. Fork spring
9. Fork top bolt
10. Fork tube
11. Bracket

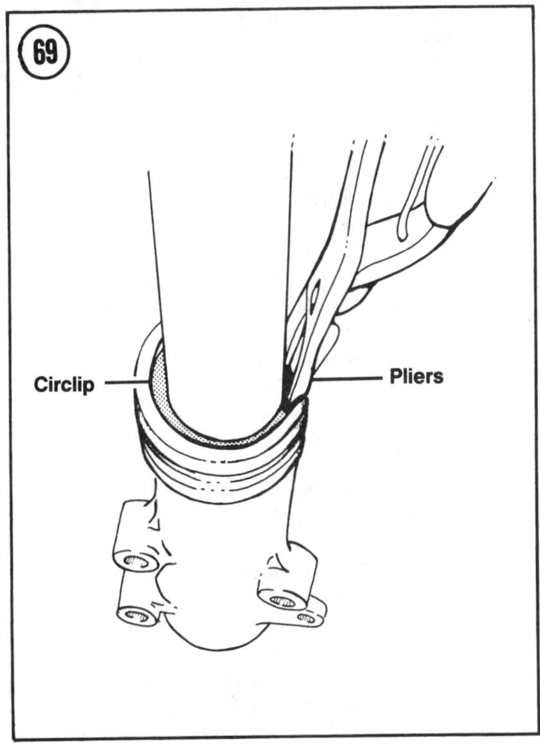

5. Measure the uncompressed length of the fork spring as shown in **Figure 60**. If the spring has sagged to less than the service limit in **Table 4**, it must be replaced.
6. Measure the outside diameter of the fork piston with a micrometer. If the piston is worn to less than the service limit in **Table 5**, the piston must be replaced.
7. Any parts that are worn or damaged should be replaced. Simply cleaning and reinstalling unserviceable components will not improve performance of the front suspension.

Assembly

Refer to **Figures 66-68**.

1. Make sure the snap ring (A, **Figure 61**) is in place on the fork tube.
2. Coat all parts with fresh automatic transmission fluid (ATF) or SAE 10W fork oil prior to installation.
3. Slide on the fork tube guide (B, **Figure 61**) and new oil seal (C, **Figure 61**) from the top of the fork tube.
4. Slide on the fork piston (D, **Figure 61**) and install the circlip (E, **Figure 61**).

5. Install the fork spring into the fork tube with the narrow pitch (closer wound) coils toward the top of the fork assembly.
6. Install the fork tube into the slider (**Figure 62**).

NOTE
On SL125 models, there is no oil seal backup ring.

7. Install the backup ring on top of the new oil seal. Drive the oil seal into the fork slider with Honda special tool Fork Seal Driver Body (part No. 07747-0010100) and Fork Seal Driver Attachment (part No. 07747-0010200). Refer to **Figure 63**. Drive the backup ring and oil seal in until the snap ring groove in the slider can be seen above the top surface of the backup ring.
8. Install the circlip with the sharp edge up. Make sure the circlip is completely seated in the groove in the fork slider.
9. Remove the top fork bolt and fill each fork tube with DEXRON ATF or SAE 10W fork oil. Refer to **Table 6** for the specific quantity for each fork leg.

NOTE
In order to measure the correct amount of fluid, use a plastic baby bottle. These have graduations in fluid ounces (oz.) and cubic centimeters (cc) on the side. Many fork oil containers have a semi-transparent strip on the side of the bottle to aid in measuring.

10. Inspect the O-ring seal on the fork cap bolt. If it is damaged or starting to deteriorate, it must be replaced.
11. Repeat for the other fork assembly.

Internal-spring Front Fork (Type II)

This type of fork has a spring that travels on the inside of the fork tube and slides. Type II internal-spring fork are used on the following models:

a. **Figure 70**—XL100, XL100 K1, 1976 XL100.
b. **Figure 71**—1977-1978 XL100, XL125, XL125 K1, all CT125.
c. **Figure 72**—1979-on CB125S.
d. **Figure 73**—SL125 K1-K2.
e. **Figure 74**—TL125, TL125 K1-K2.
f. **Figure 75**—1976 TL125.
g. **Figure 76**—All XL175.
h. **Figure 77**—All TL250.
i. **Figure 78**—All XL250.
j. **Figure 79**—All XL350.

(70)

INTERNAL-SPRING FRONT FORK, TYPE II (XL100, XL100 K1, 1976 XL100)

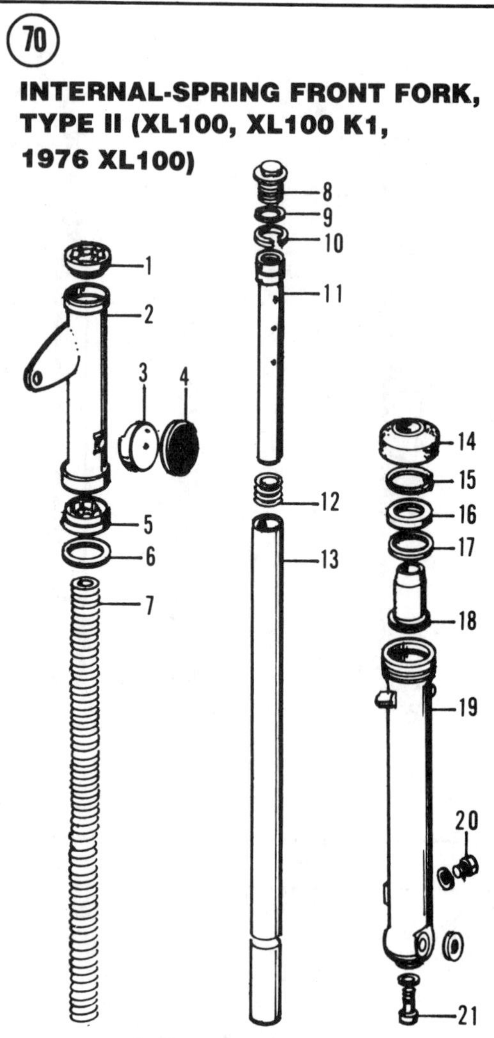

1. Upper cover top seal
2. Upper cover
3. Bracket
4. Side reflex reflector
5. Upper cover lower seal
6. Headlight stay
7. Fork spring
8. Fork top cap
9. O-ring seal
10. Piston ring
11. Damper rod
12. Rebound spring
13. Fork tube
14. Dust seal
15. Snap ring
16. Backup ring
17. Oil seal
18. Oil lock piece
19. Fork slider
20. Drain screw and gasket
21. Allen bolt and gasket

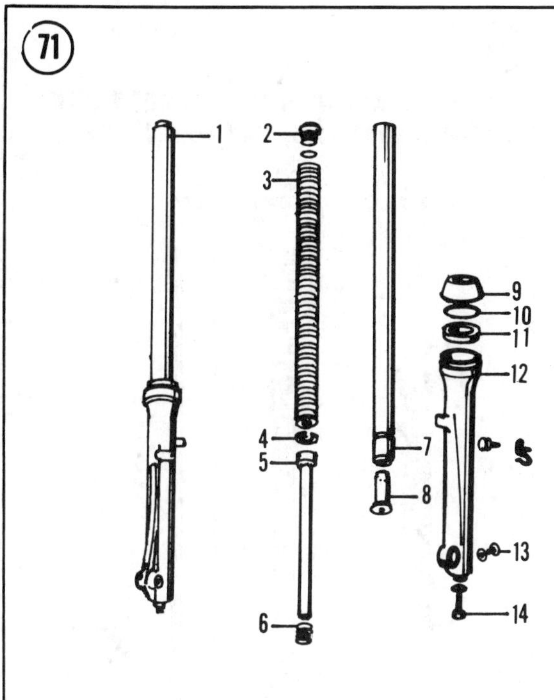

INTERNAL-SPRING FRONT FORK, TYPE II (1977-1978 XL100, XL125, XL125 K1, 1977 CT125)

1. Fork assembly
2. Fork top bolt
3. Fork spring
4. Piston seal
5. Damper rod
6. Rebound spring
7. Fork tube
8. Oil lock piece
9. Dust seal
10. Circlip
11. Fork seal
12. Fork slider
13. Drain screw and gasket
14. Allen bolt and gasket

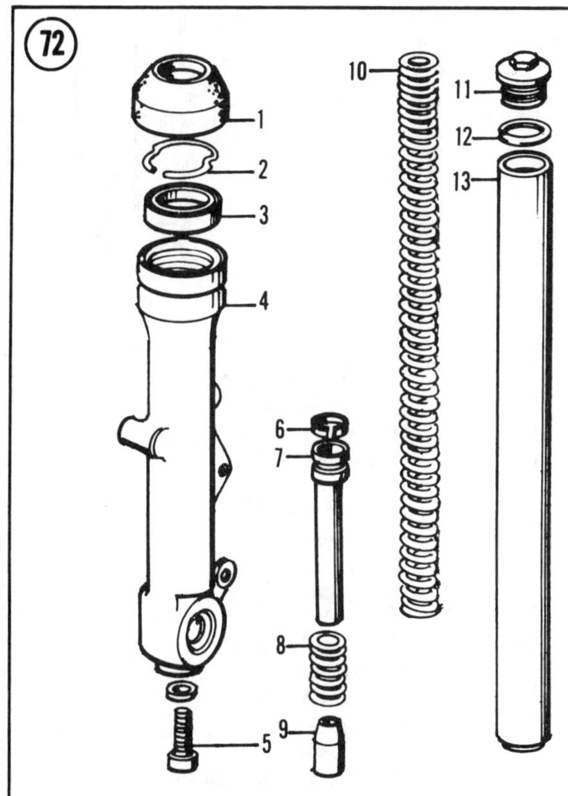

INTERNAL-SPRING FRONT FORK, TYPE II (1979-ON CB125)

1. Dust seal
2. Circlip
3. Fork seal
4. Fork slider
5. Allen screw and gasket
6. Piston seal
7. Damper rod
8. Rebound spring
9. Oil lock piece
10. Fork spring
11. Fork top bolt
12. O-ring seal
13. Fork tube

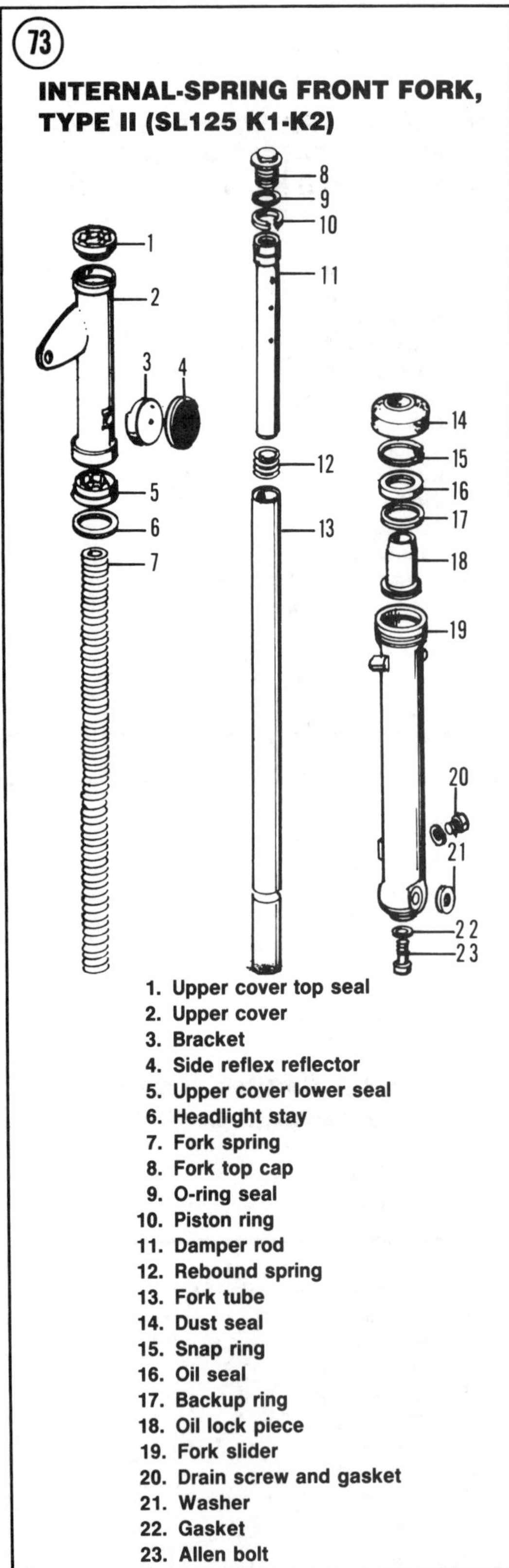

INTERNAL-SPRING FRONT FORK, TYPE II (SL125 K1-K2)

1. Upper cover top seal
2. Upper cover
3. Bracket
4. Side reflex reflector
5. Upper cover lower seal
6. Headlight stay
7. Fork spring
8. Fork top cap
9. O-ring seal
10. Piston ring
11. Damper rod
12. Rebound spring
13. Fork tube
14. Dust seal
15. Snap ring
16. Oil seal
17. Backup ring
18. Oil lock piece
19. Fork slider
20. Drain screw and gasket
21. Washer
22. Gasket
23. Allen bolt

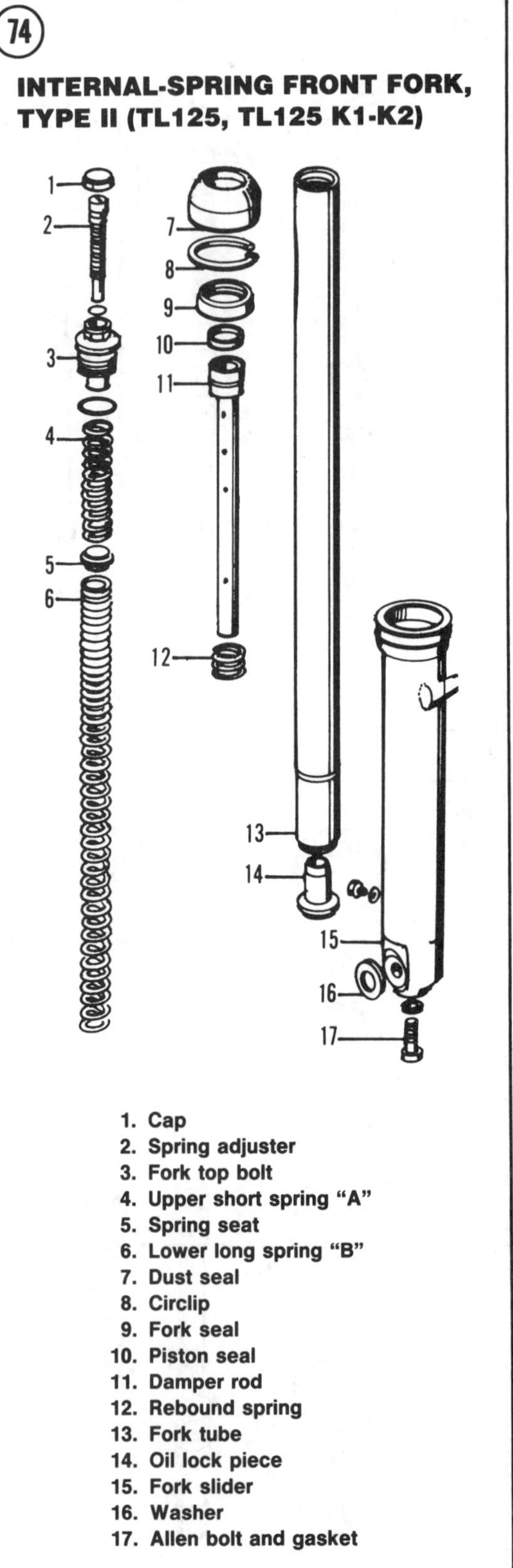

INTERNAL-SPRING FRONT FORK, TYPE II (TL125, TL125 K1-K2)

1. Cap
2. Spring adjuster
3. Fork top bolt
4. Upper short spring "A"
5. Spring seat
6. Lower long spring "B"
7. Dust seal
8. Circlip
9. Fork seal
10. Piston seal
11. Damper rod
12. Rebound spring
13. Fork tube
14. Oil lock piece
15. Fork slider
16. Washer
17. Allen bolt and gasket

75

INTERNAL-SPRING FRONT FORK, TYPE II (TL125)

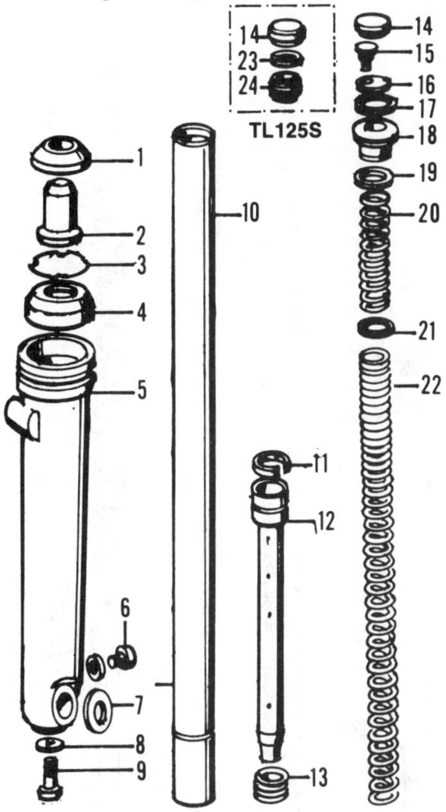

TL125S

1. Dust seal
2. Oil lock piece
3. Oil seal stop ring
4. Oil seal
5. Fork slider
6. Drain screw and gasket
7. Washer
8. Gasket
9. Allen bolt
10. Fork tube
11. Piston seal
12. Damper rod
13. Rebound spring
14. Cap
15. Bolt
16. Support washer
17. Support ring
18. Upper spring seat
19. O-ring seal
20. Upper short spring "A"
21. Spring seat
22. Lower long spring "B"
23. Circlip
24. Oil seal

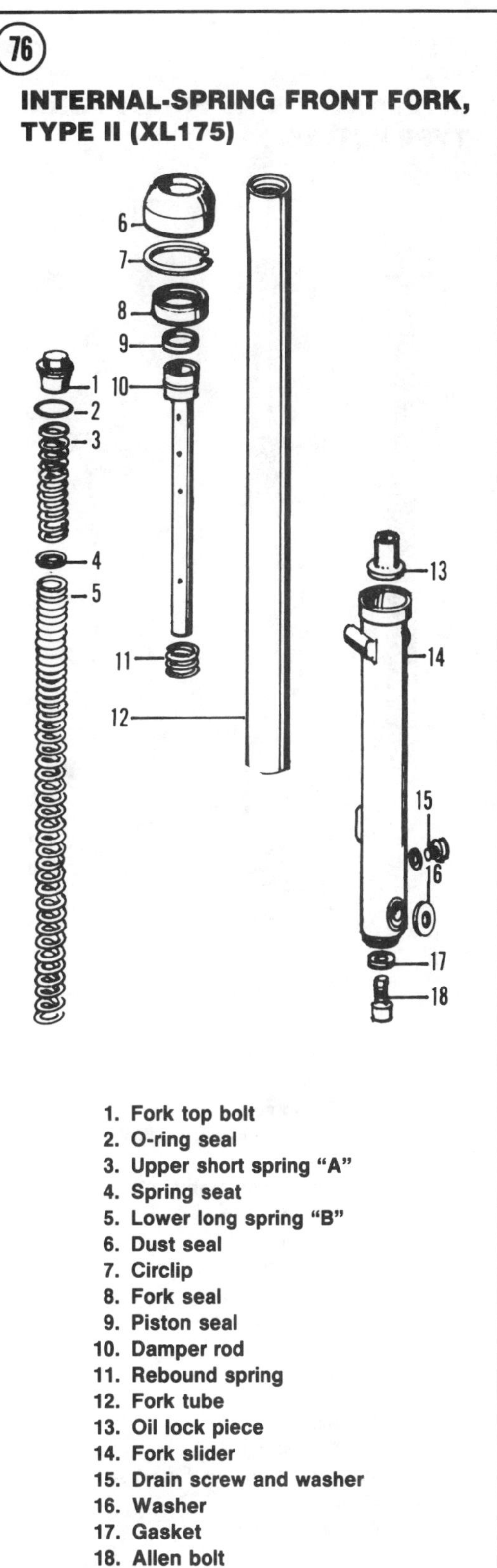

76

INTERNAL-SPRING FRONT FORK, TYPE II (XL175)

1. Fork top bolt
2. O-ring seal
3. Upper short spring "A"
4. Spring seat
5. Lower long spring "B"
6. Dust seal
7. Circlip
8. Fork seal
9. Piston seal
10. Damper rod
11. Rebound spring
12. Fork tube
13. Oil lock piece
14. Fork slider
15. Drain screw and washer
16. Washer
17. Gasket
18. Allen bolt

INTERNAL-SPRING FRONT FORK, TYPE II (TL250)

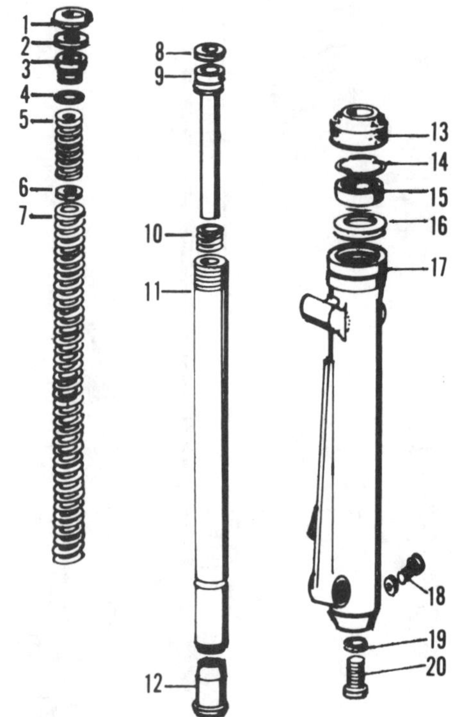

1. Cap
2. Fork top bolt
3. Upper spring seat
4. O-ring seal
5. Upper short spring "A"
6. Spring seat
7. Lower long spring "B"
8. Piston seal
9. Damper rod
10. Rebound spring
11. Fork tube
12. Oil lock piece
13. Dust seal
14. Circlip
15. Fork seal
16. Spacer
17. Fork slider
18. Drain screw and washer
19. Gasket
20. Allen bolt

INTERNAL-SPRING FRONT FORK, TYPE II (XL250)

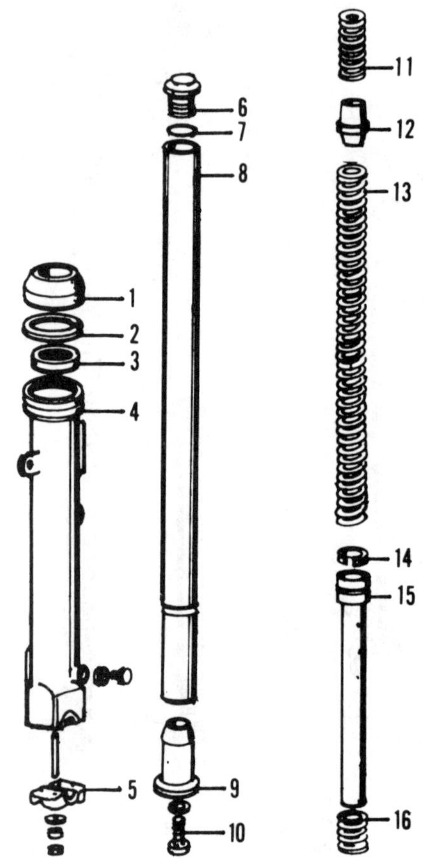

1. Dust seal
2. Circlip
3. Fork seal
4. Fork slider
5. Axle holder
6. Fork top bolt
7. O-ring seal
8. Fork tube
9. Oil lock piece
10. Allen bolt and gasket
11. Upper short spring "A"
12. Spring seat
13. Lower long spring "B"
14. Piston seal
15. Damper rod
16. Rebound spring

(79)

INTERNAL-SPRING FRONT FORK, TYPE II (XL350)

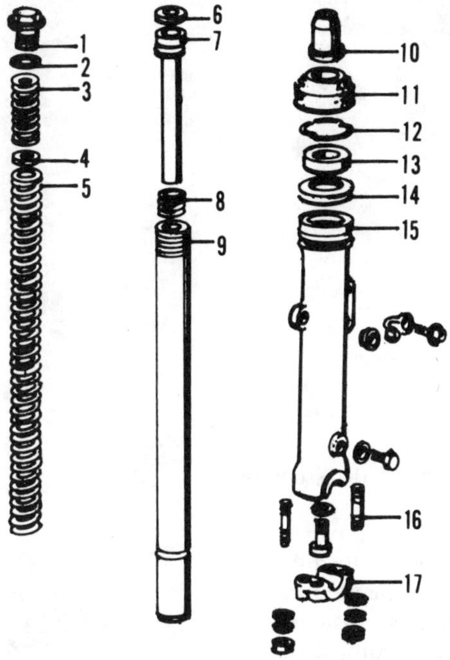

1. Fork top bolt
2. O-ring seal
3. Upper short spring "A"
4. Spring seat
5. Lower long spring "B"
6. Piston seal
7. Damper rod
8. Rebound spring
9. Fork tube
10. Oil lock piece
11. Dust seal
12. Circlip
13. Fork seal
14. Spacer
15. Fork slider
16. Threaded stud
17. Axle holder

Removal/Installation

1. Remove the front wheel as described in this chapter.
2. On models so equipped disconnect the speedometer and brake cables from the wire brackets on the fork slider.
3. Remove the bolts securing the front fender and remove the fender.
4. Loosen the upper and lower fork bridge bolts (**Figure 80**).
5. Remove the fork tube. It may be necessary to slightly rotate the fork tube while pulling it down and out.
6. Install by reversing these removal steps, noting the following.
7. Tighten the bolts to the torque specifications listed in **Table 1**.

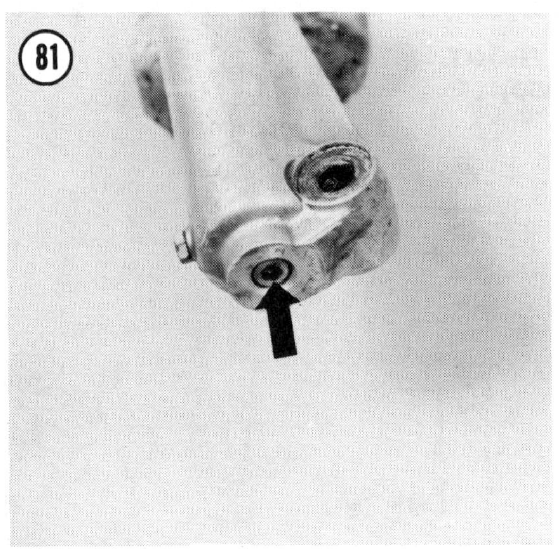
81

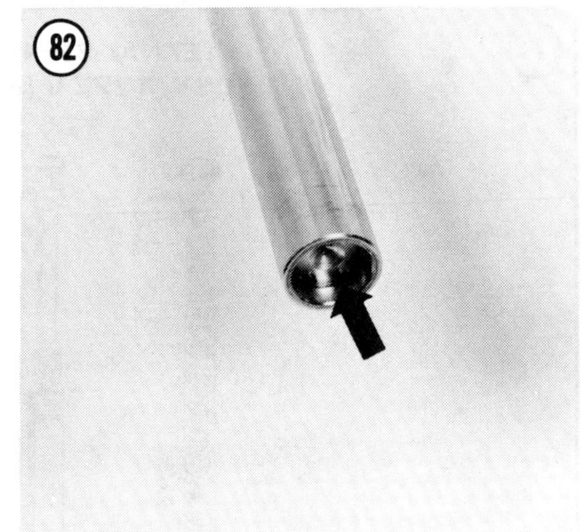
82

Disassembly

Refer to **Figures 70-79** during the disassembly procedure.

This disassembly procedure is shown on a TL250. Minor variations exist among the different models and years. Pay particular attention to the location and positioning of spacers, washers and springs to make sure they are assembled in the correct location.

1. Clamp the slider in a vise with soft jaws (**Figure 58**).
2. Remove the Allen head screw and gasket (**Figure 81**) from the bottom of the slider.

NOTE
This screw has been secured with Loctite and is often very difficult to remove because the damper rod will turn inside the slider. It sometimes can be removed with an air impact driver. If you are unable to remove it, take the fork tubes to a dealer and have the screws removed.

3. Hold the upper fork tube in a vise with soft jaws and remove the top cap or cap bolt.

WARNING
Be careful when removing the cap bolt as the spring(s) is under pressure.

4A. On TL250 models, remove the circlip and top cap (**Figure 82**) from the fork tube.
4B. On all other models, remove the cap bolt from the fork tube.
5. Remove the fork spring(s). On models with 2 springs, also remove the spacer between the 2 springs.

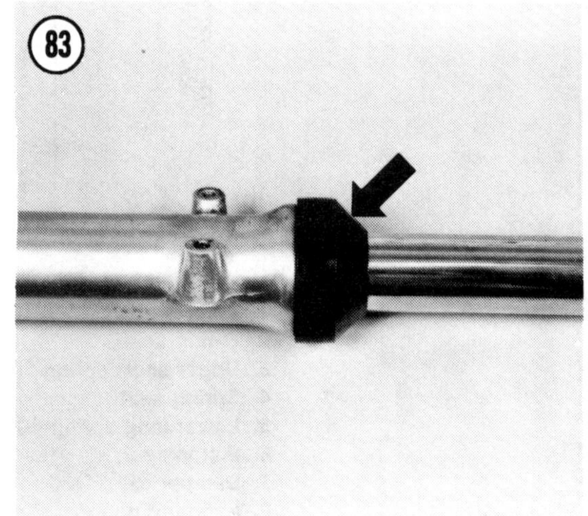
83

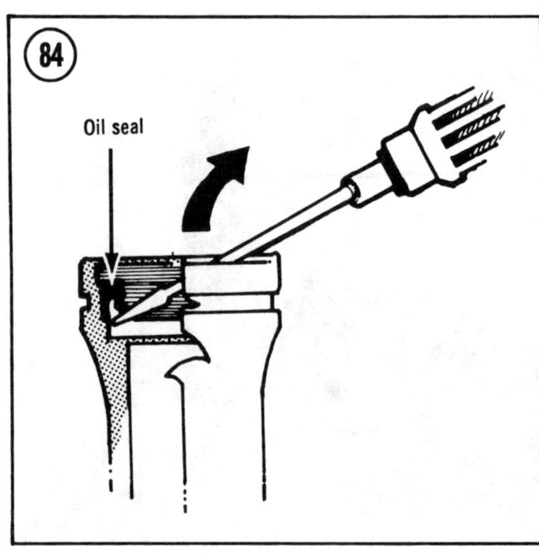

84

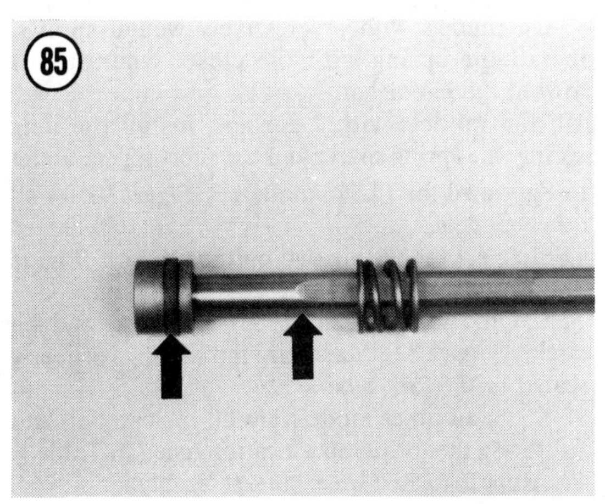

85

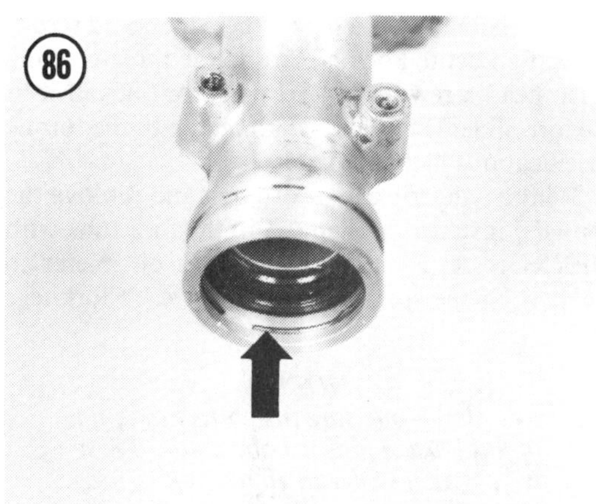

86

6. Remove the fork from the vise, pour the fork oil out and discard it. Pump the fork several times by hand to expel most of the remaining oil.
7. Pull the fork tube out of the slider.
8. Remove the oil lock piece, the damper rod and rebound spring.
9. If oil has been leaking from the top of the slider, remove the dust seal (**Figure 83**), the circlip, the oil seal and, on models so equipped, the oil seal spacer.

CAUTION
*Use a dull screwdriver blade to remove the oil seal (**Figure 84**). Do not damage the outer edge or inner surface of the slider.*

NOTE
It may be necessary to slightly heat the area on the slider around the oil seal prior to removal. Use a rag soaked in hot water; do not apply a flame directly to the fork slider.

Inspection

1. Thoroughly clean all parts in solvent and dry them.
2. Inspect the oil seal for scoring, nicks and loss of resiliency. Replace if its condition is questionable.
3. Check the fork tube for straightness. If bent or severely scratched, it should be replaced. Also check the fork tube for signs of wear or scratches.
4. Check the slider for dents or exterior damage that may cause the fork tube to hang up during riding. Replace if necessary.

NOTE
*Honda does not provide fork specifications for all models. **Table 4** and **Table 5** list all service limit specifications that are available.*

5. Carefully check the damper rod and piston ring (**Figure 85**) for wear or damage.
6. Inspect the oil seals for scoring, nicks and loss of resiliency. Replace if their condition is questionable.
7. Measure the uncompressed length of the fork spring(s) (not rebound spring) as shown in **Figure 60**. If the spring has sagged to less than the service limit in **Table 4**, it must be replaced.
8. Any parts that are worn or damaged should be replaced. Simply cleaning and reinstalling unserviceable components will not improve performance of the front suspension.

9

Assembly

Refer to **Figures 70-79**.

1. Coat all parts with fresh automatic transmission fluid (ATF) or fork oil prior to installation. If removed, install a new seal spacer and (on models so equipped) a new oil seal. Drive the seal into the slider (**Figure 63**) with Honda special tools Fork Seal Driver Body (part No. 07747-0010100) and Fork Seal Driver Attachment (part No. 07747-0010300) or a suitable size socket. Drive the oil seal in until the groove in the slider can be seen above the top surface of the oil seal.
2. Install the circlip (**Figure 86**). Make sure that the circlip is completely seated in the groove in the slider.
3. Install the rebound spring onto the damper rod and insert this assembly into the fork tube (**Figure 87**).
4. Temporarily install the fork spring(s) and top cap or cap bolt to hold the damper rod in place.
5. Install the oil lock piece onto the damper rod (**Figure 88**) and install the upper fork assembly into the slider (**Figure 89**).

6. Make sure the gasket is on the Allen head screw.
7. Apply Loctite Lock N' Seal to the threads of the Allen head screw prior to installation. Install it in the fork slider (**Figure 81**) and tighten to the torque specifications listed in **Table 1**.
8. Remove the top cap or cap bolt and remove the spring(s) installed in Step 4. Fill the fork tube with DEXRON ATF or SAE 10W fork oil. Refer to **Table 6** for the specific quantity for each fork leg.

NOTE
In order to measure the correct amount of fluid, use a plastic baby bottle. These have graduations in fluid ounces (oz.) and cubic centimeters (cc) on the side. Many fork oil containers have a semi-transparent strip on the side of the bottle to aid in measuring.

9. On models with progressively wound springs, install the spring with the closer wound coils toward the handlebar.
10. On models with 2 springs, install the long spring, the spring spacer and the short spring. Refer to **Figure 90** for TL250 models or **Figure 91** for all other models.
11. Inspect the O-ring seal on the top bolt (**Figure 92**) or cap (**Figure 93**); replace if necessary.
12A. On TL250 models, install the top cap and the circlip (**Figure 82**). Make sure the circlip is properly seated in the fork tube.
12B. On all other models, install the cap bolt and tighten to the torque specification listed in **Table 1**.
13. Repeat for the other fork assembly.

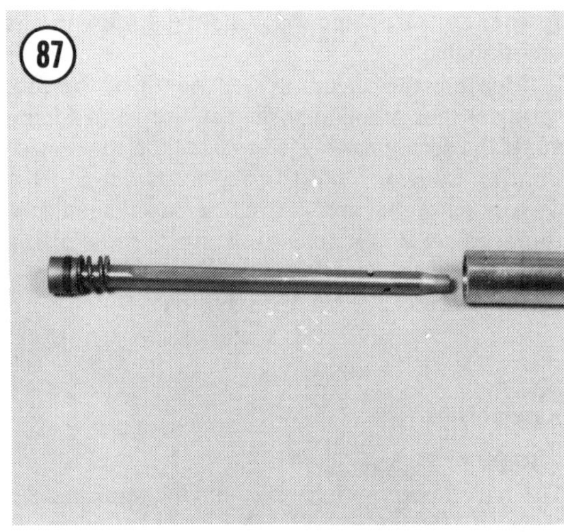

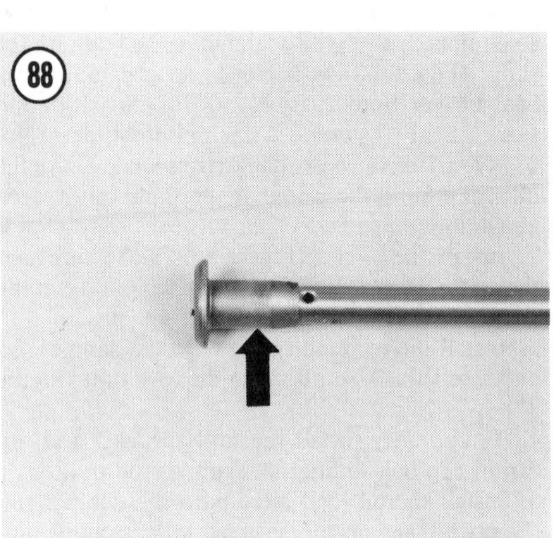

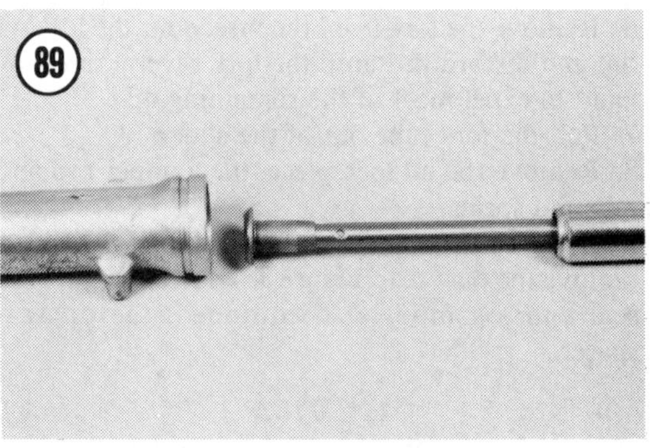

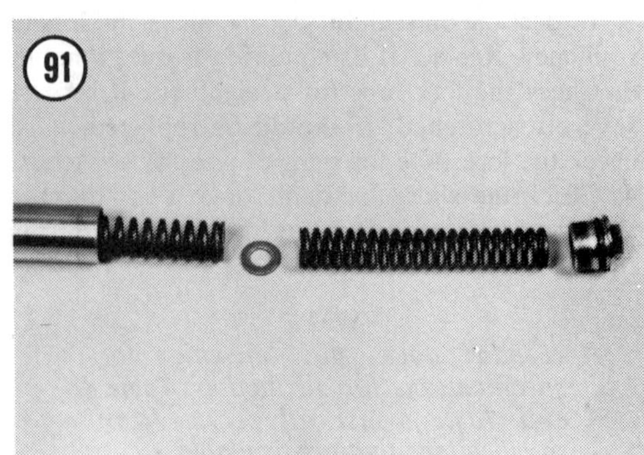

Table 1 FRONT SUSPENSION TORQUE SPECIFICATIONS*

Item	N•m	ft.-lb.
Front axle nut		
CB100, CL100, SL100, CB125S, SL125	40-50	29-36
XL100, XL125, CT125	35-50	25-36
XL175	60-80	43-58
TL250, XL250, XL350	55-65	40-47
Front axle clamp nuts		
XL250, XL350	18-23	13-17
Handlebar holder bolts		
CB100, CL100, SL100, CB125S, SL125	9-11	6-8
XL100, XL125, CT125	8-12	5-9
XL175	18-25	13-18
TL250	3-5	2.2-3.6
XL250, XL350	18-23	13-16
Fork top mounting bolt		
CB100, CL100, SL125, 1973-1978 CB125S	40-50	29-36
XL125, CT125	25-30	18-21
Upper fork bridge bolts		
1979-on CB125S	12-16	9-12
TL125	N.A.	N.A.
XL175, TL250	18-25	13-18
XL250, XL350	18-23	13-16
Lower fork bridge bolts		
1979-on CB125S	20-25	15-18
TL125	N.A.	N.A.
XL175, TL250	18-25	13-18
XL250, XL350	18-23	13-16
Steering stem nut		
CB100, CL100, SL100, XL100, CB125S, SL125, XL125	60-80	43-58
CT125	60-90	43-65
XL175, TL250, XL250, XL350	80-120	58-87
Fork cap bolt		
1979-on CB125S	15-30	11-22
All other models	N.A.	N.A

*Honda does not provide service information for all items nor all models. All available information is included in this table. "N.A." indicates that the information is not available.

9

Table 2 TIRE INFLATION PRESSURE

Model	Front psi	Front kg/cm²	Rear psi	Rear kg/cm²
CB100, CL100, SL100, CB125, SL125	26	1.8	28	2.0
XL100	28	2.0	21	1.5
CT125	25	1.8	32	2.5
XL125, TL125, XL175, XL250, XL350	21	1.5	21	1.5
TL250	5.7	0.4	4.3	0.3

Table 3 STEERING STEM BALL BEARINGS

Model	Quantity (top and bottom)	Size*
CB100, CL100, XL100, CB125S, SL125, TL125, CT125	21 balls	No. 6
TL250	18 balls	No. 6
XL175, XL250, XL350	18 balls	No. 8

* A No. 6 ball is 3/16 in. in diameter. A No. 8 ball is 1/4 in. in diameter

Table 4 FRONT FORK SPRING FREE LENGTH*

Model	Standard Length	Service Limit
CB100, CL100	184 mm (7.24 in.)	160 mm (6.30 in.)
SL100	484.2 mm (19.06 in.)	460 mm (18.11 in.)
1973-1975 CB125S	205.5 mm (8.09 in.)	180 mm (7.09 in.)
1976-1978 CB125S	411.6 mm (16.20 in.)	390 mm (15.35 in.)
1979-on CB125S	457 mm (18.0 in.)	448 mm (17.6 in.)
SL125	482.3 mm (18.99 in.)	460 mm (18.11 in.)
XL100	491.7 mm (19.358 in.)	470 mm (18.504 in.)
TL125	N.A.	N.A.
XL125, CT125	550.7 mm (21.682 in.)	530 mm (20.866 in.)
XL175		
Spring A	140.1 mm (5.516 in.)	132 mm (5.197 in.)
Spring B	320.7 mm (12.626 in.)	302 mm (11.980 in.)
TL250		
Spring A	77.7 mm (3.06 in.)	76 mm (3.0 in.)
Spring B	476.5 mm (18.76 in.)	466 mm (18.35 in.)
1972-1975 XL250, XL350		
Spring A and B combined	481.1 mm (18.94 in.)	470 mm (18.50 in.)
1976-1978 XL250, XL350		
Spring A	53.5 mm (2.11 in.)	52.5 mm (2.07 in.)
Spring B	431 mm (16.97 in.)	420 mm (16.54 in.)

*Honda does not provide service information for all items nor all models. All available information is included in this table. "N.A." indicates that the information is not available.

Table 5 FRONT FORK PISTON OD*

Model	Standard	Service Limit
CB100, CL100, 1973-1975 CB125S	30.936-30.975 mm (1.2174-1.2194 in.)	30.9 mm (1.2165 in.)
1976-1978 CB125S	30.936-30.975 mm (1.21795-1.2195 in.)	309.0 mm (1.216 in.)
SL100, SL125	35.425-35.450 mm (1.3946-1.3956 in.)	35.4 mm (1.2937 in.)

* The models listed are the only ones on which this measurement is required.

Table 6 DRIVE CHAIN REPLACEMENT NUMBERS

Model	Standard	Optional
CB100	RK428-102L	DK428-102L
CL100	DK428-104L	DK428-103L
SL100	DK428-104L	
SL100 K1	DK428-104L	DID428-108L
SL100 K2-K3, XL100, XL100 K1	DK428-110L	
1976 XL100	DK 428H-110L	
1977-1978 XL100	N.A.	
CB125 S, CB125 S1-S2	RK428D-102L	DID428D-102L
1976-on CB125 S	DID428D-100L	
SL125	DK428-110L	
CT125	DID428H-102L	DID428-118L
TL125, TL125 K1-K2	DID428H-120L	
1976 TL125	N.A.-102L	
XL125	N.A.	
XL175	N.A.	
TL250	Diado-102L	Diado-122L
XL250, XL250 K1	N.A.-100L	N.A.-98L
1976 XL250 K2, XL250	N.A.-102L	
XL350	DID500DS-100L	

N.A. = Honda does not provide information for all models.

CHAPTER TEN

REAR SUSPENSION

This chapter contains repair and replacement procedures for the rear wheel, rear hub and rear suspension components. Service to the rear suspension consists of periodically checking bolt tightness, replacing swing arm bushings and checking the condition of the shock absorbers and replacing them as necessary.

Wheel balancing, tire changing and tire repairs are described in Chapter Nine.

Tables 1-3 are at the end of this chapter.

REAR WHEEL

Removal/Installation

1. Place a wood block(s) under the engine to support the bike securely so that the rear wheel is off the ground.
2. Remove the cotter pin and axle nut (A, **Figure 1**). Discard the old cotter pin.
3. On CT125 models, remove the drive chain case as described in this chapter.
4. On all models except the TL250, loosen the drive chain adjuster locknuts (B, **Figure 1**) and screw the adjuster out on each side of the wheel. On TL250 models, turn the snail adjuster to allow maximum chain slack.
5. Unscrew the rear brake adjust nut completely from the brake rod (A, **Figure 2**). Depress the brake pedal and withdraw the brake rod from the brake lever. Pivot the rod out of the way and reinstall the adjust nut to avoid misplacing it.
6. Remove the cotter pin and then remove the nut and washer (B, **Figure 2**) securing the rear brake torque link. Let it pivot down out of the way.

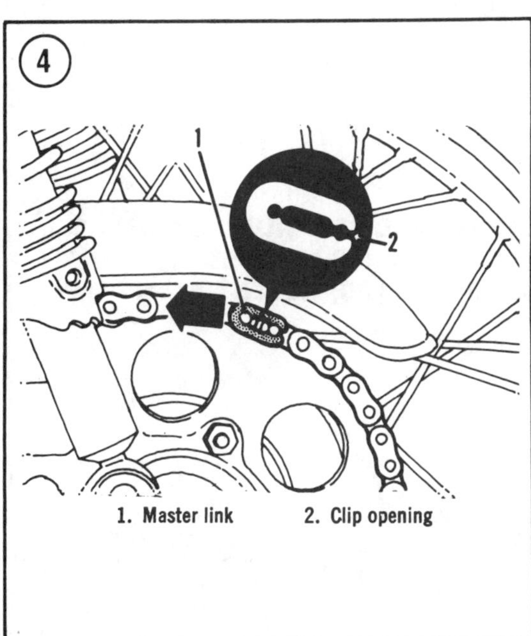

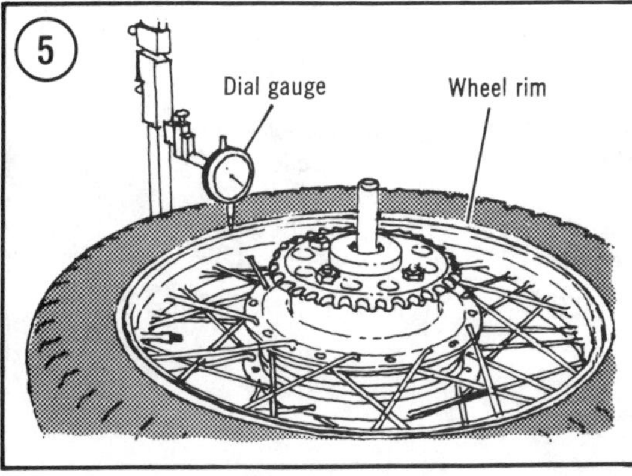

7. Push the wheel forward until there is slack in the drive chain. Remove the master link clip and remove the master link. Remove the drive chain from the driven sprocket.

NOTE
Some models have an axle spacer on the right-hand side of the wheel only while others also have a spacer on the left-hand side.

8. Withdraw the axle from the right-hand side of the wheel. Do not lose the wheel spacer(s).
9. Pull the wheel to the rear and remove it.
10. Install by reversing these removal steps, noting the following.
11. Inspect wheel components as described in this chapter.
12. Be sure to install the axle spacer(s) (**Figure 3**).

CAUTION
Rear wheel spacers should be periodically replaced. Frequent tightening of the rear axle nut causes the spacer to compress slightly. A compressed spacers alters swing arm to rear wheel clearance.

NOTE
Make sure the drive chain adjusters are in place prior to installing the axle.

13. Install the axle from the right-hand side and install the axle nut finger-tight.
14. Make sure the drive chain adjuster stoppers are in place on the swing arm.
15. Install a new drive chain master link clip with the closed end facing in the direction of chain travel (**Figure 4**).
16. Adjust the drive chain tension as described in Chapter Three.
17. Tighten the axle nut and brake torque link nut to the torque specifications listed in **Table 1**. Install a new cotter pin on the axle nut and torque link nut; never reuse an old one as it may break and fall off. Bend the ends over completely.

18. After the wheel is completely installed, rotate it several times to make sure it rotates smoothly. Apply the brake several times to make sure it operates correctly.
19. Adjust the rear brake as described under *Rear Brake Pedal Adjustment* in Chapter Three.

Inspection

Measure the radial and axial runout of the wheel rim with a dial indicator as shown in **Figure 5**. The maximum radial and axial runout is 2.0 mm (0.08

in.). If the runout exceeds this dimension, check the condition of the wheel bearings. Some of this condition can be corrected as described under *Spoke Inspection and Replacement* in Chapter Nine.

Check axle runout as described under *Rear Hub Inspection* in this chapter.

REAR HUB AND DRIVEN SPROCKET

Disassembly

Refer to **Figures 6-10** for this procedure.

1. Remove the rear wheel as described in this chapter.
2. Pull the rear brake panel straight up and out of the brake drum.
3. Remove the dust cover from the left-hand side of the wheel.

4A. On 100, 125 and 175 cc models, remove the circlip (A, **Figure 11**) and remove the driven sprocket assembly.

4B. On 250 and 350 cc models, straighten the locking tabs on the lockwashers and remove the nuts securing the driven sprocket assembly. Discard the lockwashers.

NOTE
If it is difficult to remove, tap on the backside of the sprocket (from the opposite side of the wheel through the spokes) with the wooden handle of a hammer. Tap evenly around the perimeter of the sprocket until the assembly is free.

5. Remove the dust seal from the left-hand side (B, **Figure 11**).

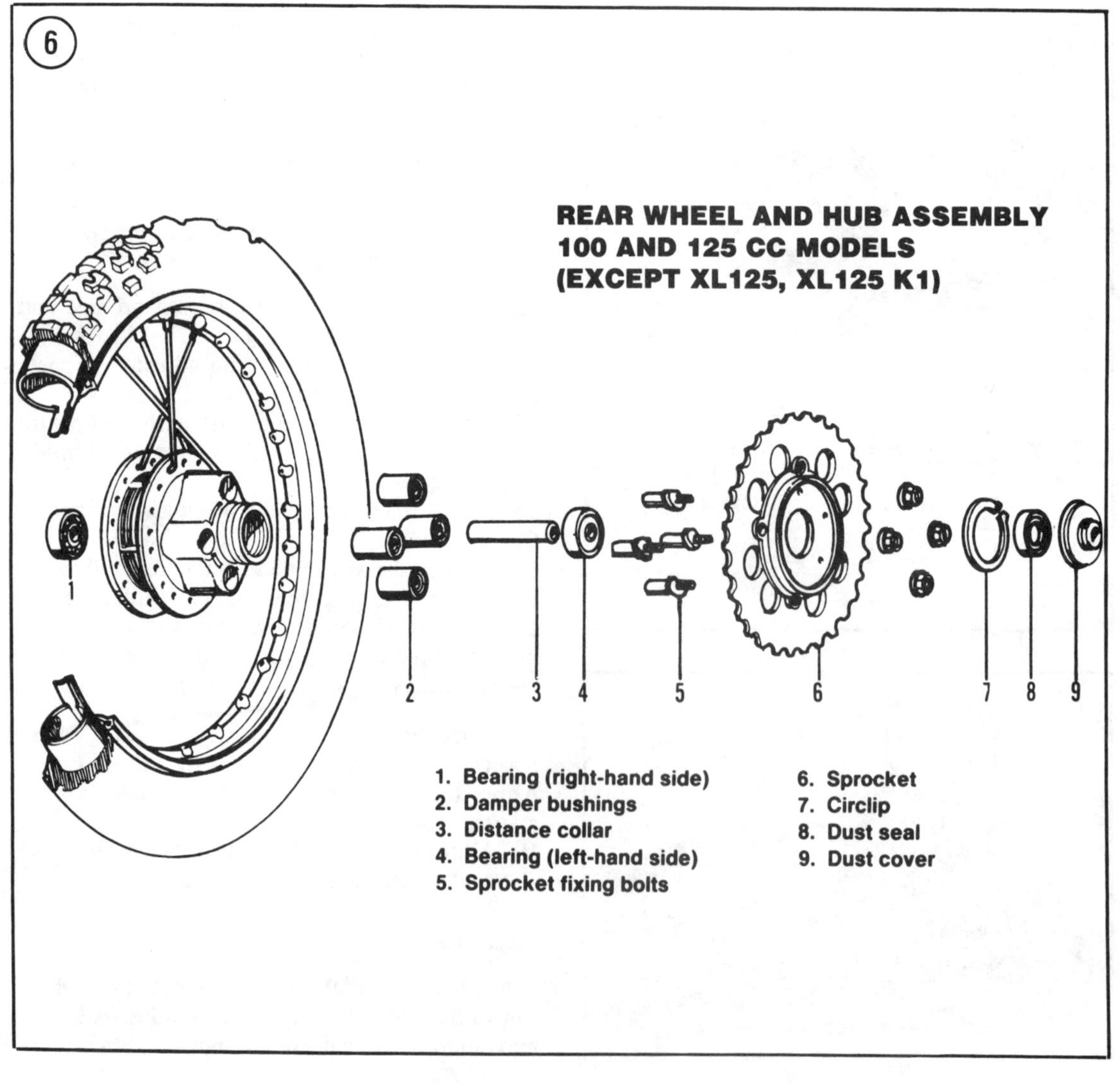

(7)

REAR WHEEL AND HUB ASSEMBLY (XL125)

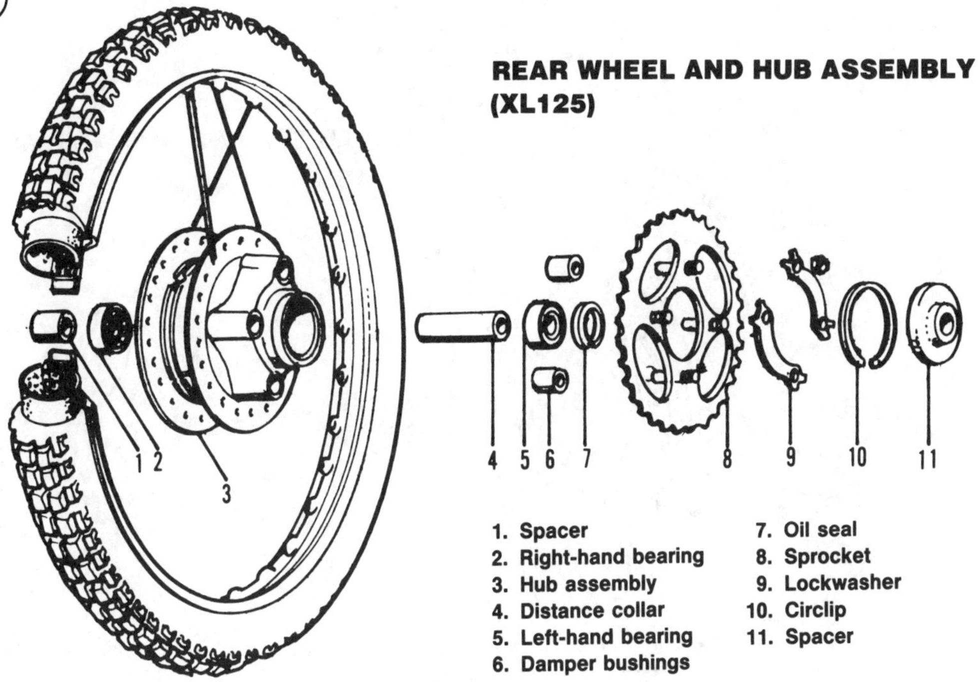

1. Spacer
2. Right-hand bearing
3. Hub assembly
4. Distance collar
5. Left-hand bearing
6. Damper bushings
7. Oil seal
8. Sprocket
9. Lockwasher
10. Circlip
11. Spacer

(8)

REAR WHEEL AND HUB ASSEMBLY (XL175)

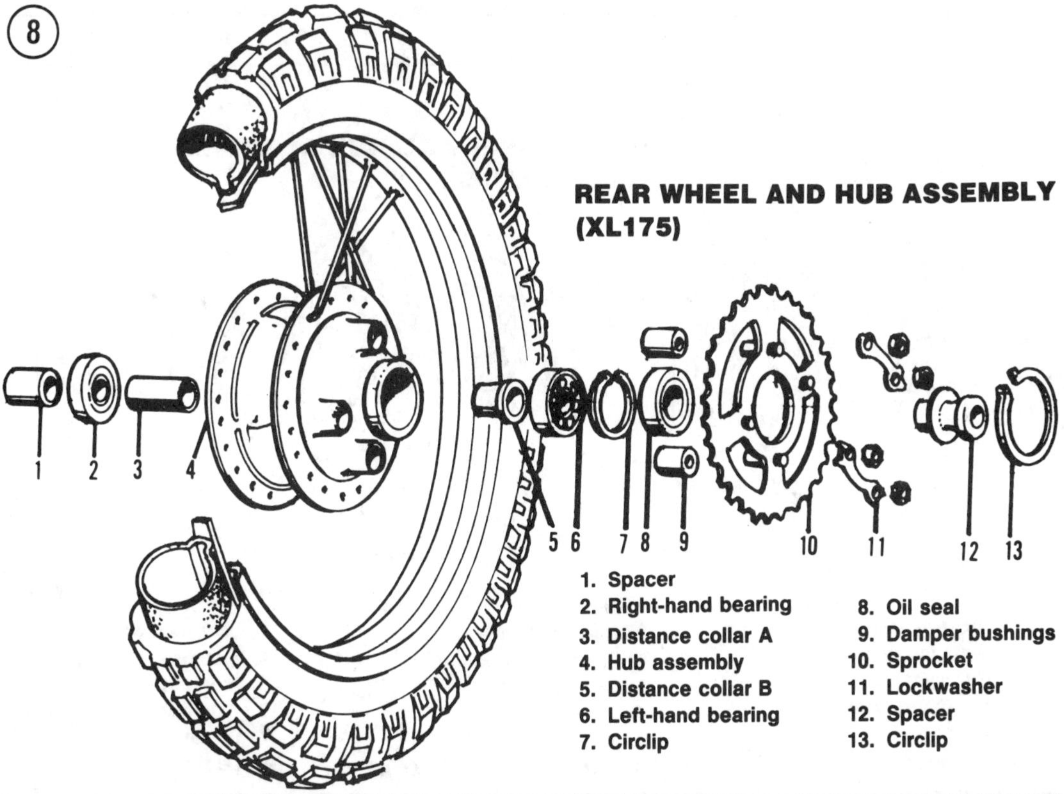

1. Spacer
2. Right-hand bearing
3. Distance collar A
4. Hub assembly
5. Distance collar B
6. Left-hand bearing
7. Circlip
8. Oil seal
9. Damper bushings
10. Sprocket
11. Lockwasher
12. Spacer
13. Circlip

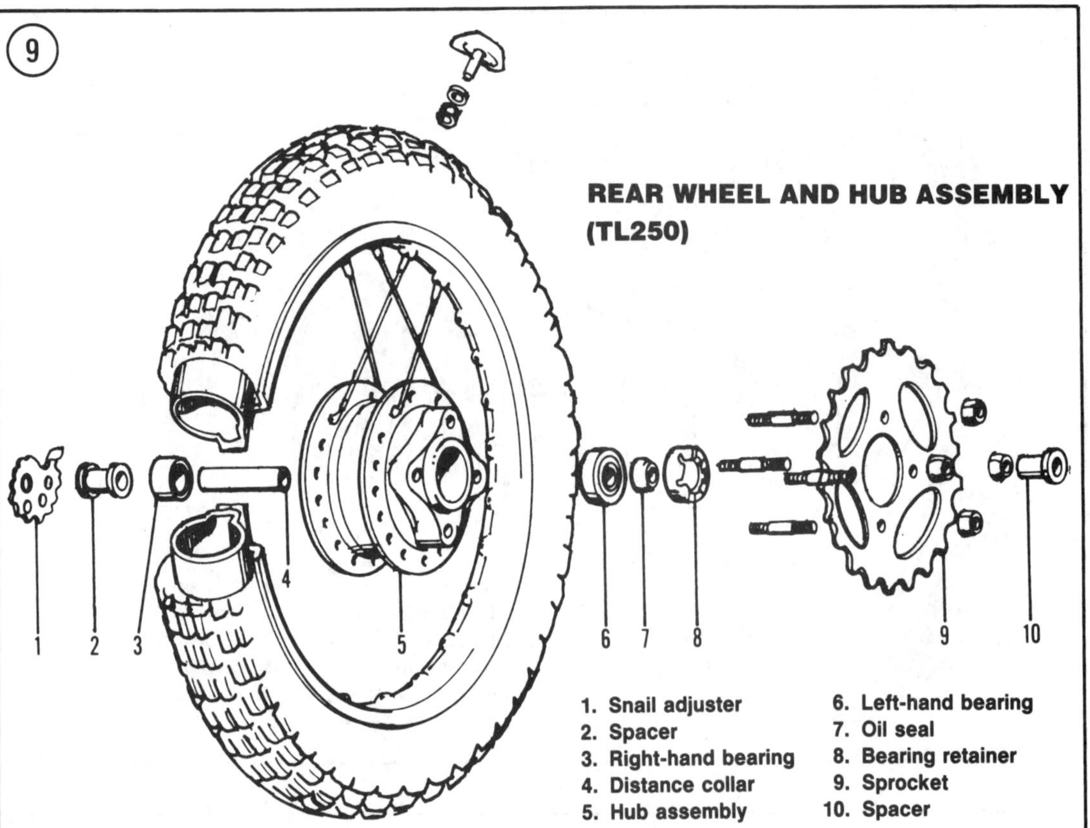

9

REAR WHEEL AND HUB ASSEMBLY (TL250)

1. Snail adjuster
2. Spacer
3. Right-hand bearing
4. Distance collar
5. Hub assembly
6. Left-hand bearing
7. Oil seal
8. Bearing retainer
9. Sprocket
10. Spacer

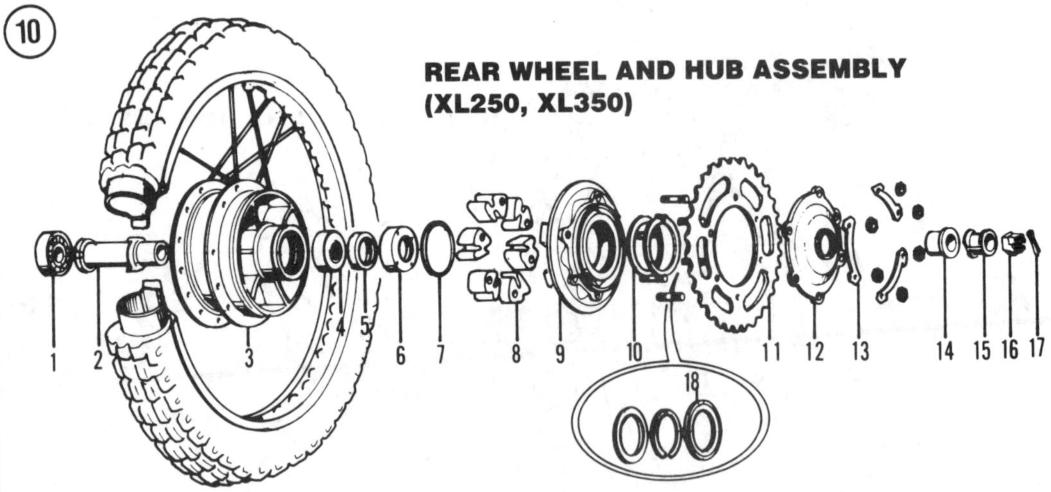

10

REAR WHEEL AND HUB ASSEMBLY (XL250, XL350)

1. Right-hand bearing
2. Distance collar
3. Hub assembly
4. Left-hand bearing
5. Oil seal
6. Bearing retainer
7. O-ring seal
8. Rubber dampers
9. Final driven flange
10. 66 mm washer
11. Driven sprocket
12. Hub dust cover
(not used on 1976-1978 XL350)
13. Lockwasher
14. Spacer
15. Axle collar
16. Axle nut
17. Cotter pin
18. Dust seal

6. On 250 and 350 cc models, unscrew the bearing retainer on the left-hand side. See **Figure 12** for XL250 and XL350 models; see **Figure 13** for TL250 models. Use a small drift and a hammer or use the following Honda special retainer wrench:
   a. XL250—part No. 07910-3290000.
   b. XL350—part No. 07910-360000.
   c. TL250—no special tool available.
7. To remove the hub right- and left-hand bearings and distance collar, insert a soft aluminum or brass drift into one side of the hub. Push the distance collar over to one side and place the drift on the inner race of the lower bearing. Tap the bearing out of the hub with a hammer, working around the perimeter of the inner race.
8. Remove the distance collar and tap out the opposite bearing.

Assembly

1. On non-sealed bearings, pack the bearings with a good quality bearing grease. Work the grease in between the balls thoroughly. Turn the bearing by hand a couple of times to make sure the grease is distributed evenly inside the bearing.
2. Blow any dirt or foreign matter out of the hub prior to installing the bearings.
3. Pack the wheel hub with multipurpose grease.
4. Install the right-hand bearing into the hub.

CAUTION
*Install stock Honda bearings with the sealed side facing out (**Figure 14**).*

5. Tap the bearing squarely into place and tap on the outer race only. Use a socket (**Figure 15**) that matches the outer race diameter. Do not tap on the inner race or the bearing might be damaged. Be sure that the bearing is completely seated.

6. Press the distance collar into the hub from the left-hand side.
7. Install the left-hand bearing into the hub.
8. On 250 and 350 cc models, inspect the threads on the bearing retainer; replace if the threads are damaged. Screw the bearing retainer into the hub. After the bearing retainer has been screwed in securely, lock it into place by staking it with a center punch and hammer.
9. Install the driven sprocket assembly (**Figure 16**).
10A. On 100, 125 and 175 cc models, install the circlip (A, **Figure 11**) securing the driven sprocket assembly.
10B. On 250 and 350 cc models, install new lockwashers. Install the nuts securing the driven sprocket assembly and tighten to the torque specifications listed in **Table 1**.
11. Lubricate the new oil seal with fresh multipurpose grease and tap it gently into place.
12. Install the rear wheel as described this chapter.

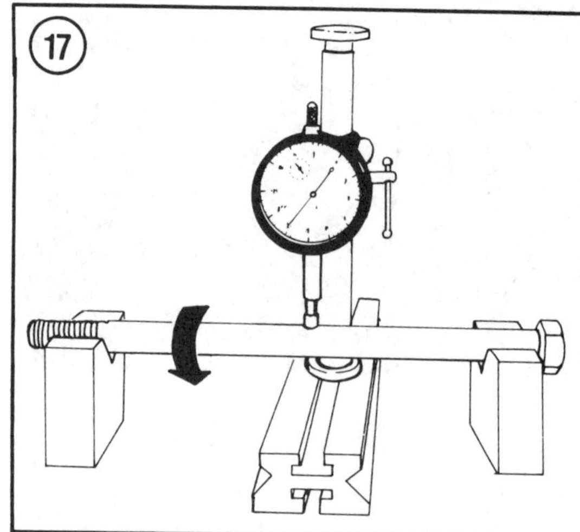

Inspection

1. Thoroughly clean out the inside of the hub with solvent and dry with compressed air or a shop cloth.

NOTE
Avoid getting any greasy solvent residue on the brake drum during this procedure. If this happens, clean it off with a clean shop cloth and lacquer thinner.

2. Do not clean sealed bearings. If non-sealed bearings are installed, thoroughly clean them in solvent and thoroughly dry with compressed air. Do not let the bearing spin while drying.
3. Turn each bearing by hand. Make sure the bearings turn smoothly.
4. On non-sealed bearings, check the balls for evidence of wear, pitting or excessive heat (bluish tint). Replace the bearing if necessary; always replace as a complete set. When replacing, be sure to take your old bearings along to ensure a perfect matchup.

NOTE
Fully sealed bearings are available from many bearing specialty shops. Fully sealed bearings provide better protection from dirt and moisture that may get into the hub.

5. Check the axle for wear and straightness. Use V-blocks and a dial indicator as shown in **Figure 17**. If the runout is 0.2 mm (0.008 in.) or greater, the axle should be replaced.
6. Inspect the driven sprocket rubber dampers for signs of damage or deterioration. Replace as a complete set even though only one may require replacement.
7. Inspect the teeth on the sprocket. If they are visibly worn as shown in **Figure 18**, replace the sprocket.
8. If the sprocket requires replacement, the drive chain is probably worn also and may need replacement. Refer to *Drive Chain Removal/ Installation* in this chapter.

DRIVE CHAIN

Removal/Installation

1. Place a wood block(s) under the engine to support the bike securely so that the rear wheel is off the ground.
2. Remove the gearshift pedal (A, **Figure 19**).
3. Remove the bolts securing the left-hand rear crankcase cover (B, **Figure 19**) and remove the cover.

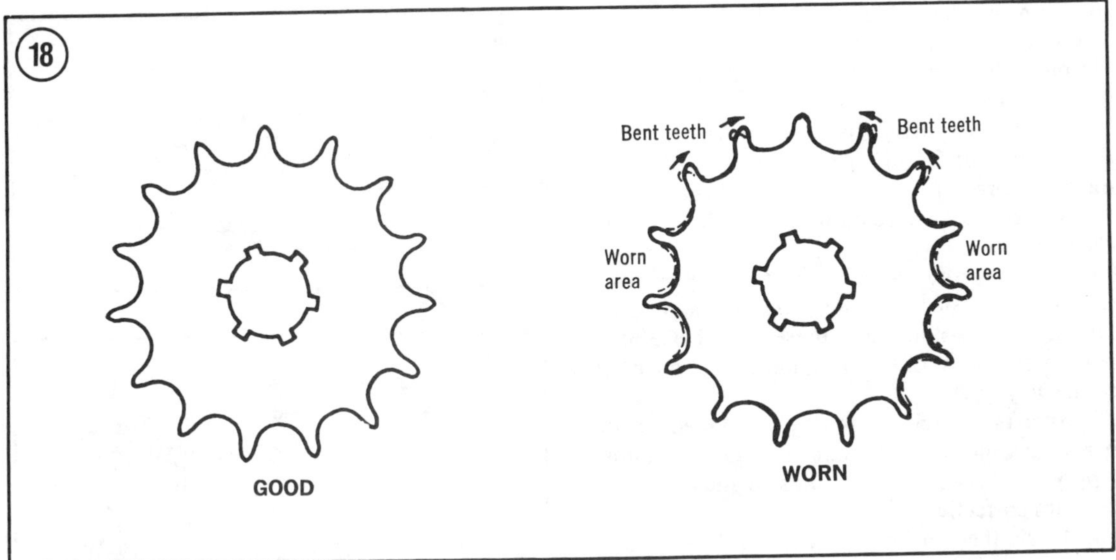

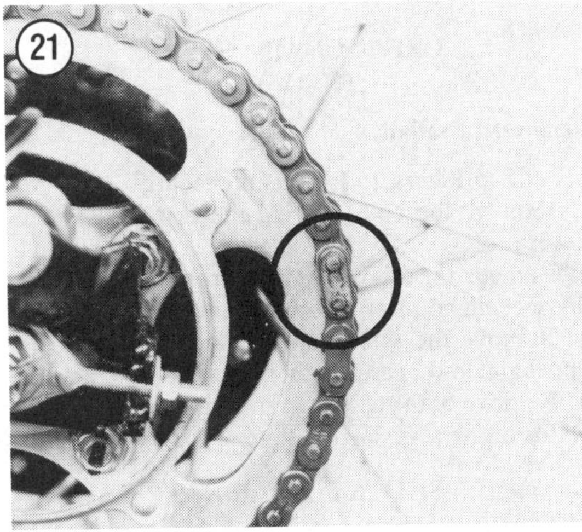

4. On CT125 models, remove the drive chain case as described in this chapter.
5. Remove the cotter pin and axle nut (A, **Figure 20**). Discard the old cotter pin.
6A. On TL250 models, rotate both drive chain snail adjusters (B, **Figure 20**) toward the front so the wheel can be moved forward for maximum chain slack.
6B. On all other models, loosen the drive chain adjuster locknuts on each side of the wheel and screw the adjuster out.
7. Push the rear wheel forward for maximum chain slack.
8. Rotate the rear wheel until the drive chain master link is visible.
9. Remove the clip on the master link (**Figure 21**) and remove the master link from the chain.

10. Remove the drive chain and inspect it as described in Chapter Three.
11. Install by reversing these removal steps, noting the following.
12. Install a new drive chain master link clip with the closed end facing in the direction of chain travel (**Figure 22**).
13. Adjust the drive chain tension as described in Chapter Three.
14. Tighten the axle nut to the torque specifications listed in **Table 1**. Install a new cotter pin on the axle nut; never reuse an old one as it may break and fall off. Bend the ends over completely.
15. After the wheel is completely installed, rotate it several times to make sure it rotates smoothly. Apply the brake several times to make sure it operates correctly.
16. Adjust the rear brake as described in Chapter Three.

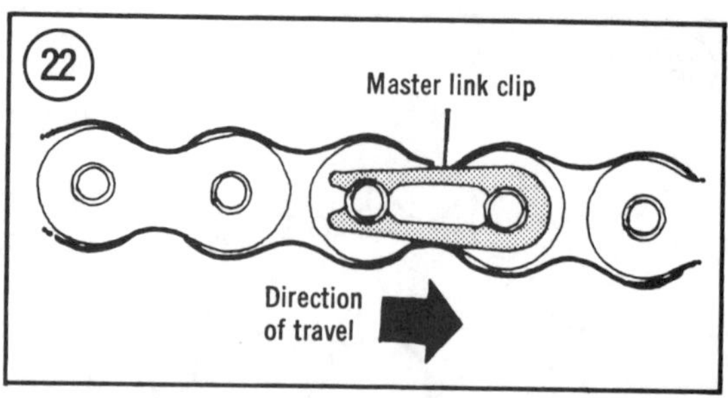

DRIVE CHAIN CASE (CT125)

Removal/Installation

Refer to **Figure 23** for this procedure.

1. Remove the bolt securing the rear case to the lower case.
2. Remove the adjustment nut from the left-hand drive chain adjuster and remove the rear case.
3. Remove the screws and washers securing the upper and lower cases to their attachment brackets.
4. Remove both the upper and lower cases.
5. Install by reversing these removal steps.

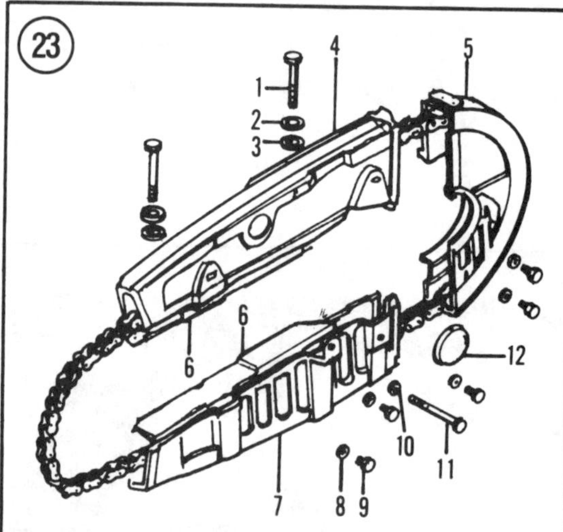

CHAIN CASE (CT125)

1. Bolt
2. Lockwasher
3. Washer
4. Upper case
5. Rear case
6. Attachment brackets
7. Lower case
8. Washer
9. Screw
10. Washer
11. Bolt
12. Inspection cap

SHOCK ABSORBERS

The rear shocks are spring controlled and hydraulically damped. The units are sealed and cannot be serviced. Service is limited to removal and replacement of the damper unit or the spring. If either shock fails to dampen adequately, replace them as a set.

Spring Pre-load Adjustment

NOTE
Not all models covered in this book have this adjustment feature.

Spring pre-load can be adjusted by rotating the cam ring (**Figure 24**) at the bottom of the spring. Looking down onto the shock, turn the cam ring *counterclockwise* to decrease preload (or soften) or *clocwise* to increase preload (or hard). Use the spanner wrench provided in the owner's tool kit for this adjustment.

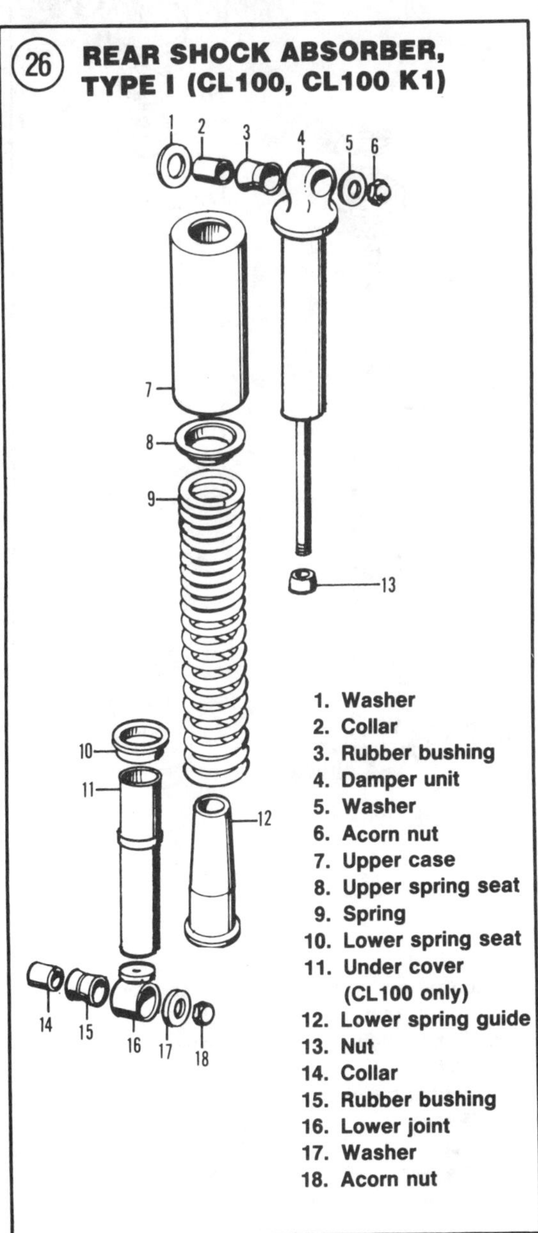

The cam ring must be indexed on the same detent on both shocks.

Removal/Installation

Removal and installation of the rear shocks is easier if they are done separately. The remaining unit will support the rear of the bike and maintain the correct relationship between the top and bottom mounts.

1. Place a wood block(s) under the engine to support the bike securely with the rear wheel off the ground.
2. Adjust both shocks to the softest setting, if applicable.
3. Remove the upper and lower nut or bolt and washers securing the shock absorber to the frame and to the swing arm (**Figure 25**).

NOTE
***Figure 25** is shown with the rear wheel removed for clarity. It is not necessary to remove the wheel for this procedure.*

4. Pivot the lower end of the shock to the rear and pull the shock off of the upper stud.
5. Install by reversing these removal steps, noting the following.
6. Be sure to install a washer behind the bolt and the nut.
7. Tighten the nut and mounting bolt to the torque specifications listed in **Table 1**.
8. Repeat Steps 3-7 for the other shock.
9. Adjust the shocks as described in this chapter, if applicable.

Disassembly/Assembly (Type I)

Type I shock absorbers are used on the following models:

a. CL100, CL100 K1.

Refer to **Figure 26** when disassembling and assembling this type of shock absorber.

Disassembly/Inspection/Assembly (Type II)

Type II shock absorbers are used on the following models:

a. **Figure 27**—All CB100, CB125S, CB125S1.
b. **Figure 28**—CL100 K2, CL100 S, CL100 SK2, CL100 S3.
c. **Figure 29**—CB125 S2, 1976-1978 CB125S.
d. **Figure 30**—1979-on CB125S.
e. **Figure 31**—All TL125.

27

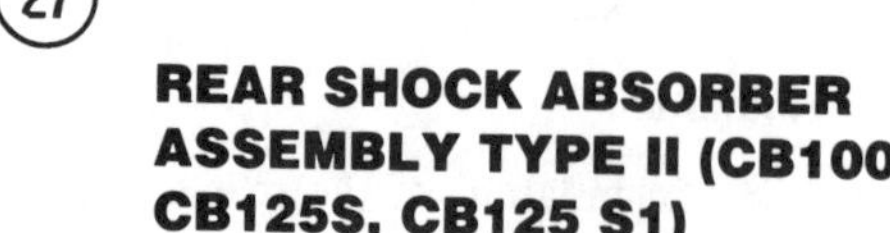

REAR SHOCK ABSORBER ASSEMBLY TYPE II (CB100 CB125S, CB125 S1)

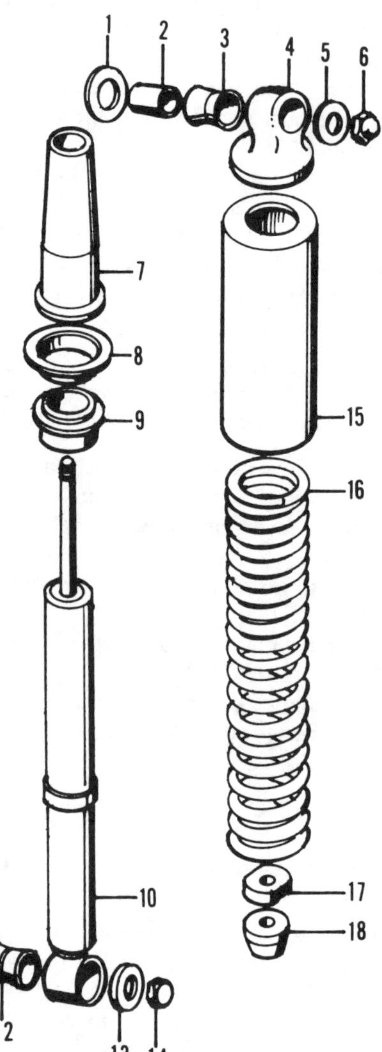

1. Washer
2. Collar
3. Rubber bushing
4. Upper joint
5. Washer
6. Acorn nut
7. Lower spring guide
8. Upper spring seat
9. Lower spring seat
10. Damper unit
11. Collar
12. Rubber bushing
13. Washer
14. Acorn nut
15. Outer case
16. Spring
17. Locknut
18. Rubber stopper

28

REAR SHOCK ABSORBER, TYPE II (CL100 K2, CL100 S, CL100 SK2, CL100 S3)

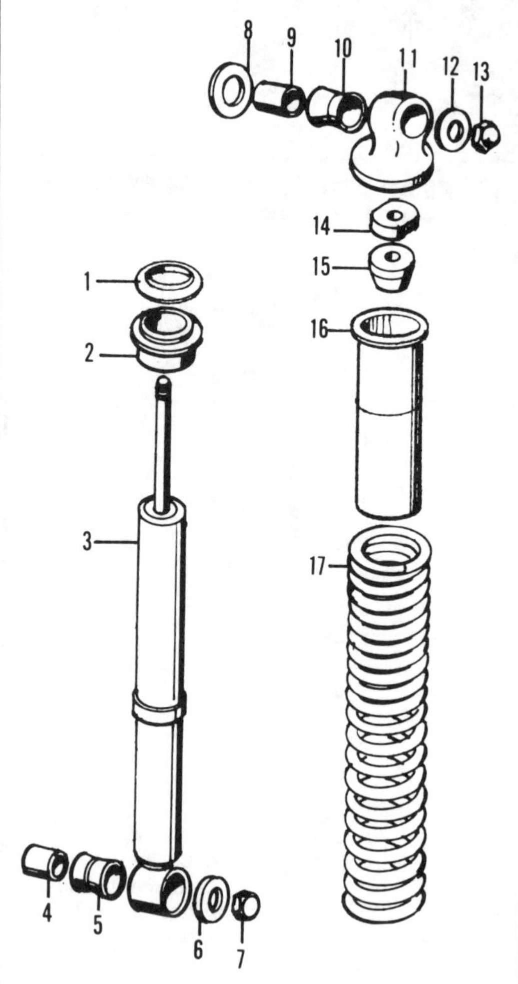

1. Lower spring seat
2. Spring seat
3. Damper unit
4. Collar
5. Rubber bushing
6. Washer
7. Acorn nut
8. Washer
9. Collar
10. Rubber bushing
11. Upper joint
12. Washer
13. Acorn nut
14. Locknut
15. Rubber stopper
16. Spring guide
17. Spring

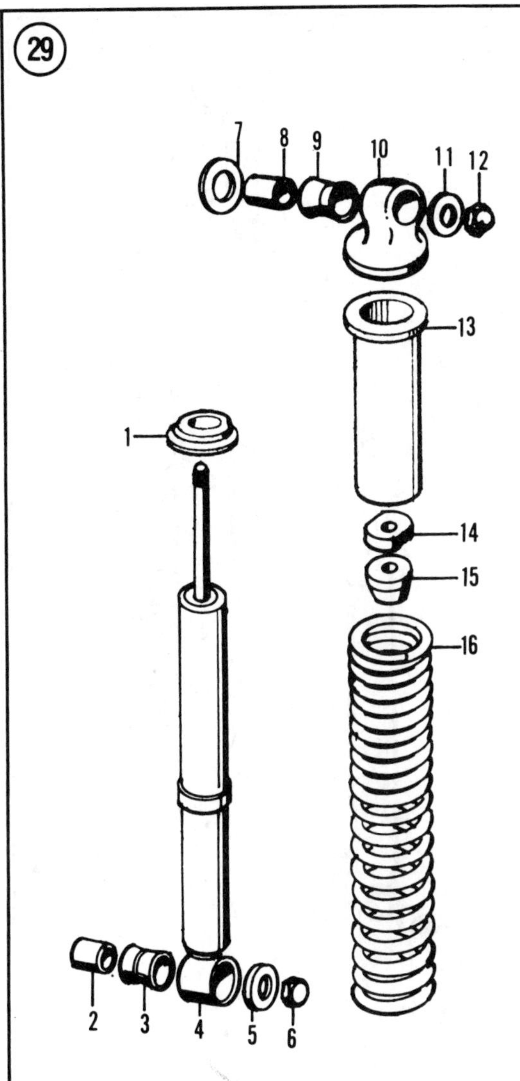

REAR SHOCK ABSORBER, TYPE II (CB125 S2, 1976-1978 CB125S)

1. Lower spring seat
2. Collar
3. Rubber bushing
4. Damper unit
5. Washer
6. Acorn nut
7. Washer
8. Collar
9. Rubber bushing
10. Upper joint
11. Washer
12. Acorn nut
13. Spring guide
14. Locknut
15. Rubber stopper
16. Spring

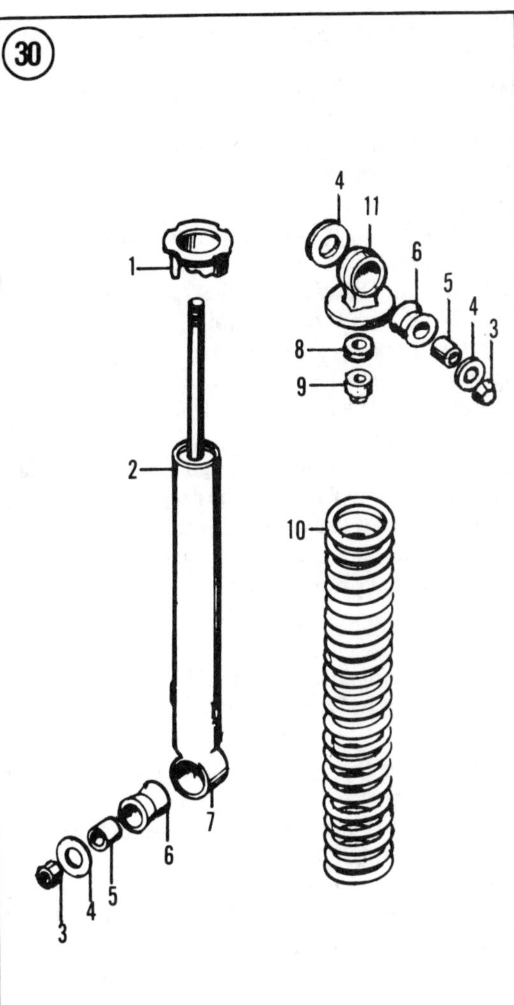

REAR SHOCK ABSORBER TYPE II (1979-ON CB125)

1. Spring adjuster
2. Damper unit
3. Nut
4. Washer
5. Collar
6. Rubber damper
7. Damper unit
8. Locknut
9. Rubber stopper
10. Spring
11. Upper joint

The following procedure represents a typical shock absorber disassembly, inspection and assembly. Minor variations exist among the different models and years. Pay particular attention to the location of washers, rubber stoppers, spring seats and guides to make sure they are positioned correctly.

1. Install the upper joint of the shock absorber in a vise equipped with soft jaws.
2. With your hands, pull the spring and spring guide away from the upper joint.
3. Loosen the locknut next to the upper joint. Unscrew the upper joint from the damper rod.
4. Slide off the spring and all other components from the damper unit.
5. Measure the spring free length (**Figure 32**). The spring must be replaced if it has sagged to less than the service limit listed in **Table 2.**
6. Check the damper unit for leakage and make sure the damper rod is straight.

NOTE
The damper unit cannot be rebuilt; it must be replaced as a unit.

7. Make sure the spring guide is not cracked or damaged. Replace if necessary.
8. Assembly is the reverse of these disassembly steps, noting the following.
9. On models with a variable rate spring, be sure to install the spring with the closer wound coil toward the top of the shock.
10. Apply Loctite Lock N' Seal to the threads prior to installing the lower joint. Screw on the lower joint until it stops. Tighten the locknut securely.

Disassembly/Inspection/Assembly (Type III)

Type III shock absorbers are used on the following models:

a. SL100, SL100 K1 (**Figure 33**).
b. SL100 K2-K3, XL100 (all years), SL125 (all years) (**Figure 34**).
c. XL125 (all years) (**Figure 35**).
d. CT125 (**Figure 36**).
e. XL175 (all years), XL250, XL250 K1-K2, XL350, XL350 K1 (**Figure 37**).
f. TL250 (all years) (**Figure 38**).
g. 1976 XL250, 1976-1978 XL350 (**Figure 39**).

The following procedure represents a typical shock absorber disassembly, inspection and assembly. Minor variations exist among the different models and years. Pay particular attention to the location of washers, rubber stoppers, spring

31

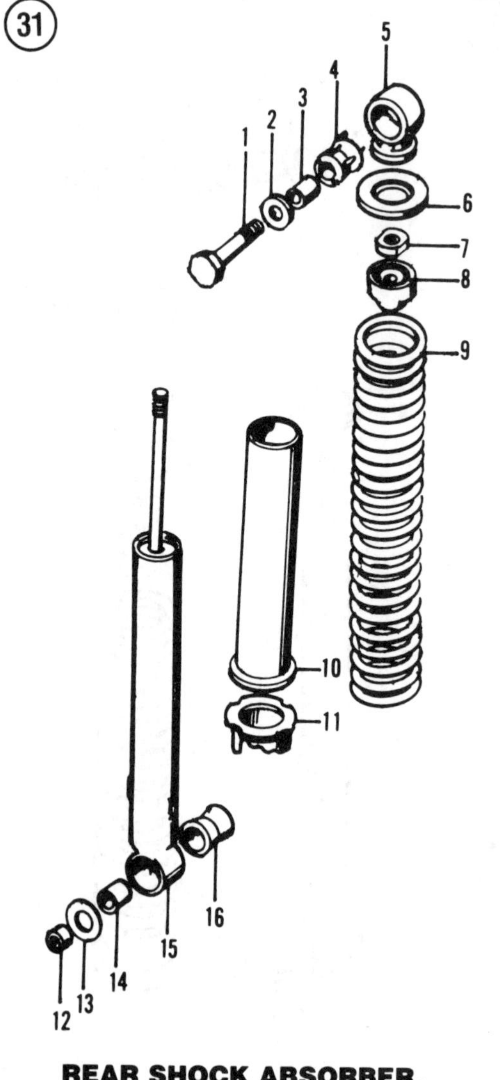

REAR SHOCK ABSORBER, TYPE II (TL125)

1. Bolt
2. Washer
3. Collar
4. Rubber bushing
5. Upper joint
6. Spring seat
7. Locknut
8. Rubber stopper
9. Spring
10. Spring guide
11. Spring adjuster
12. Nut
13. Washer
14. Collar
15. Damper unit
16. Rubber bushing

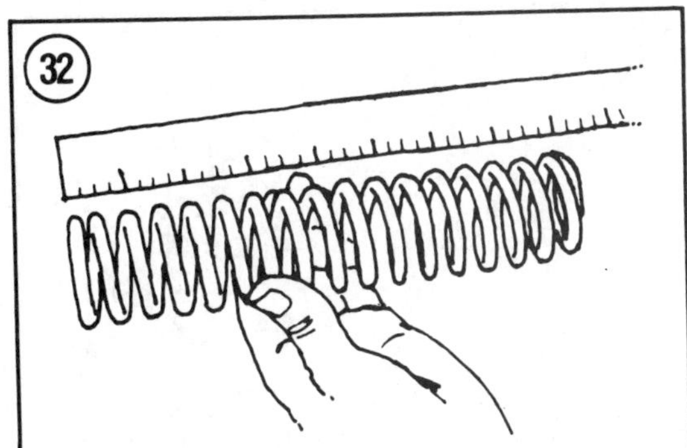

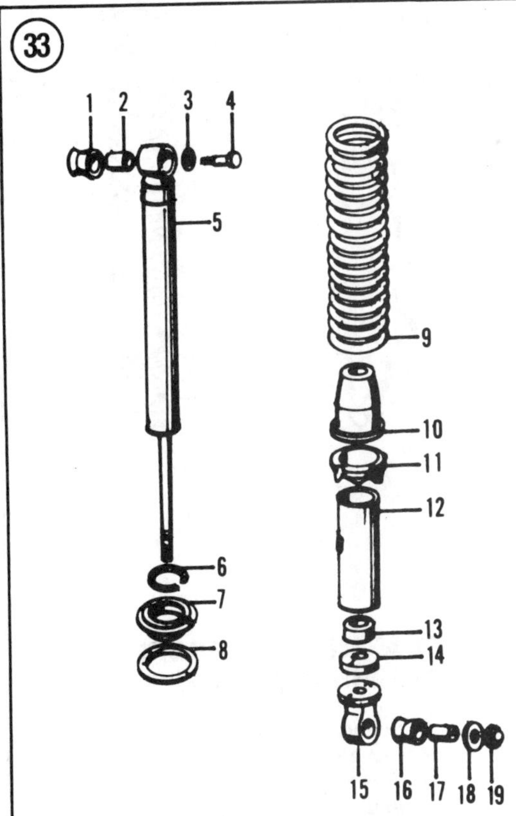

REAR SHOCK ABSORBER, TYPE III (SL100, SL100 K1)

1. Rubber bushing
2. Collar
3. Washer
4. Bolt
5. Damper unit
6. Snap ring
7. Spring stopper
8. Upper spring seat
9. Spring
10. Spring guide
11. Spring adjuster
12. Case
13. Rubber stopper
14. Locknut
15. Lower joint
16. Rubber bushing
17. Collar
18. Washer
19. Acorn nut

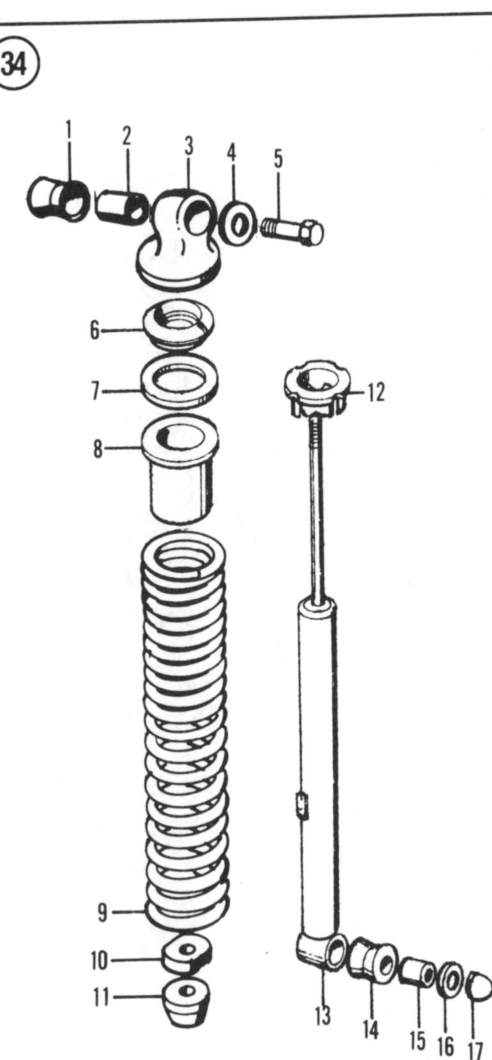

REAR SHOCK ABSORBER, TYPE III (SL100 K2-K3, XL100, SL125)

1. Rubber bushing
2. Collar
3. Upper joint
4. Washer
5. Bolt
6. Spring stopper
7. Upper spring seat
8. Spring guide
9. Spring
10. Locknut
11. Rubber stopper
12. Spring adjuster
13. Damper unit
14. Rubber bushing
15. Collar
16. Washer
17. Acorn nut

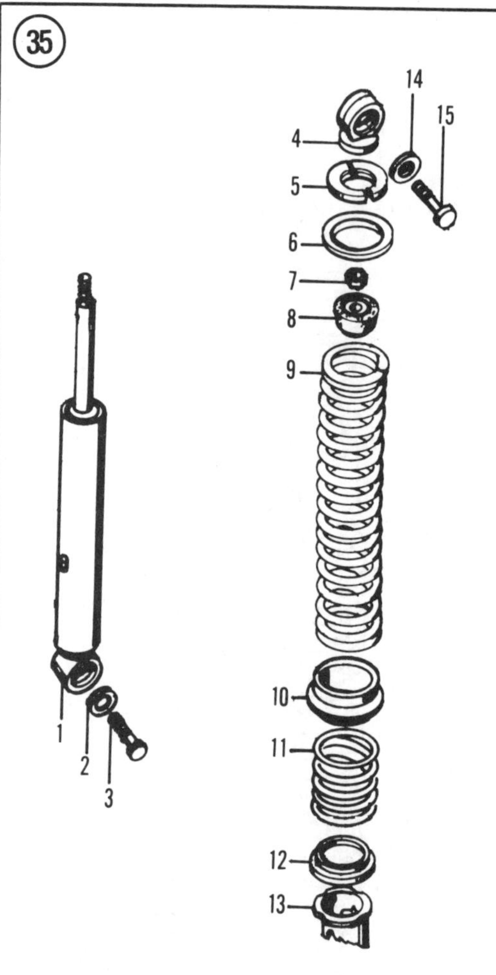

REAR SHOCK ABSORBER, TYPE III (XL125)

1. Damper unit
2. Washer
3. Bolt
4. Upper joint
5. Spring seat
6. Washer
7. Locknut
8. Rubber stopper
9. Upper long spring
10. Spring seat
11. Lower short spring
12. Spring seat
13. Spring adjuster
14. Washer
15. Bolt

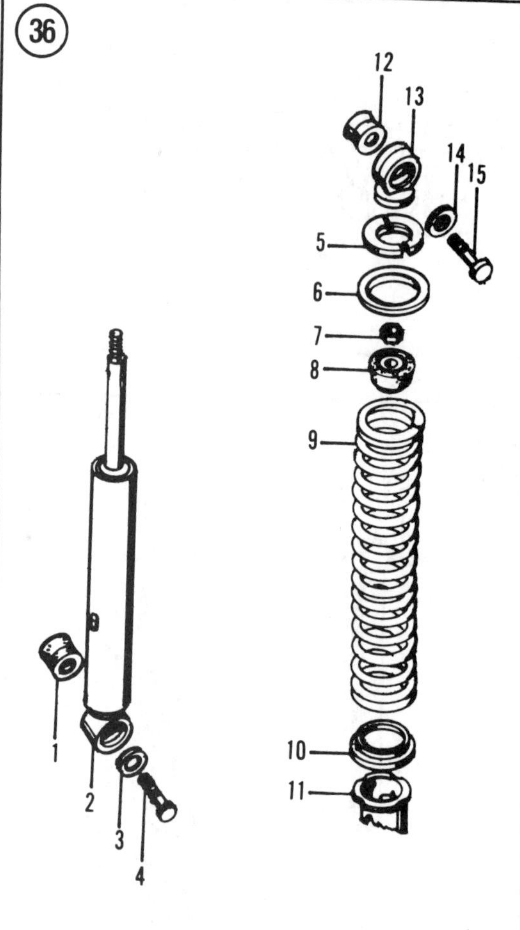

REAR SHOCK ABSORBER, TYPE III (CT125)

1. Rubber bushing
2. Damper unit
3. Washer
4. Bolt
5. Spring seat
6. Washer
7. Locknut
8. Rubber stopper
9. Spring
10. Spring seat
11. Spring adjuster
12. Rubber bushing
13. Upper joint
14. Washer
15. Bolt

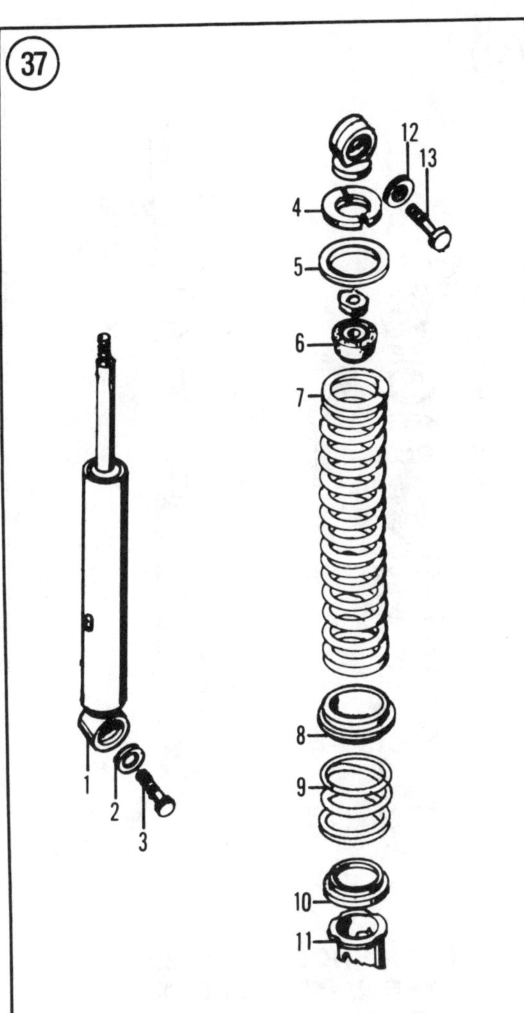

REAR SHOCK ABSORBER, TYPE III (XL175, XL250, XL250 K1-K2, XL350, XL350 K1)

1. Damper unit
2. Washer
3. Bolt
4. Spring seat
5. Washer
6. Rubber stopper
7. Upper long spring
8. Spring seat
9. Lower short spring
10. Spring seat
11. Spring adjuster
12. Washer
13. Bolt

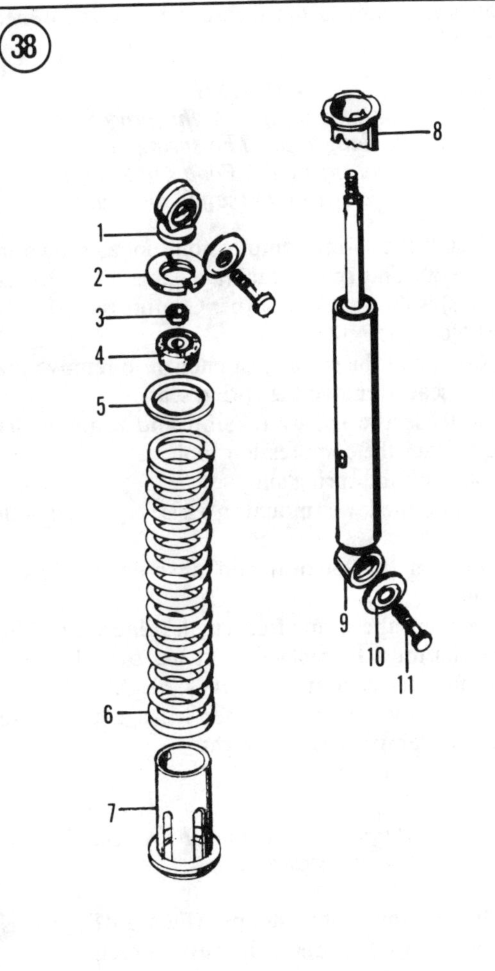

REAR SHOCK ABSORBER, TYPE III (TL250)

1. Upper joint
2. Spring seat
3. Locknut
4. Rubber stopper
5. Washer
6. Spring
7. Spring guide
8. Spring adjuster
9. Damper unit
10. Washer
11. Bolt

seats and guides to make sure they are positioned correctly.

WARNING
Without the proper tool, this procedure can be dangerous. The spring can fly loose, causing injury. For a small bench fee, a dealer can do the job for you.

1. Install the spring compression tool as shown in **Figure 40**. This special tool (available from Honda dealers) is the Shock Absorber Compressor (Honda part No. 07959-3290001).
2. Compress the spring just enough to remove the spring seat. Remove the spring seat.
3. Release the spring tension and remove the shock from the compression tool.
4. Slide off the spring(s).
5. Clamp the lower mount in a vise equipped with soft jaws.
6. Loosen the locknut and unscrew the lower mount.
7. Measure the spring free length (**Figure 32**). The spring(s) must be replaced if it has sagged to less than the service limit listed in **Table 2**.
8. Check the damper unit for leakage and make sure the damper rod is straight.

NOTE
The damper unit cannot be rebuilt; it must be replaced as a unit.

9. Inspect the rubber stopper (**Figure 41**). If it is damaged or deteriorated, it must be replaced.
10. On models so equipped, make sure the spring guide (**Figure 42**) is not cracked or damaged. Replace if necessary.
11. Assembly is the reverse of these disassembly steps, noting the following.
12. On models with 2 springs, be sure to install the short spring toward the bottom of the shock.
13. Install the locknut and screw it all the way on.
14. Apply Loctite Lock N' Seal to the threads prior to installing the lower joint. Screw on the lower joint until it stops.
15. Tighten the locknut securely.

SWING ARM

In time, the bushings or pivot collar will wear beyond the service limits and will have to be replaced. The condition of the bushings can greatly affect handling performance. If worn parts are not replaced they can produce erratic and dangerous handling. Common symptoms are wheel hop, pulling to one side during acceleration and pulling to the other side during braking.

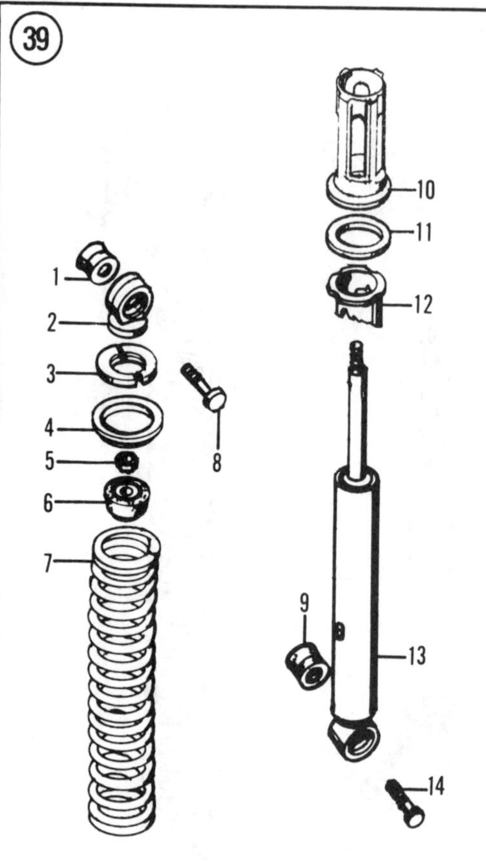

REAR SHOCK ABSORBER, TYPE III (1976 XL250, 1976-1978 XL350)

1. Rubber bushing
2. Upper joint
3. Spring seat
4. Washer
5. Locknut
6. Rubber stopper
7. Spring
8. Bolt
9. Rubber bushing
10. Spring guide
11. Spring seat
12. Spring adjuster
13. Damper unit
14. Bolt

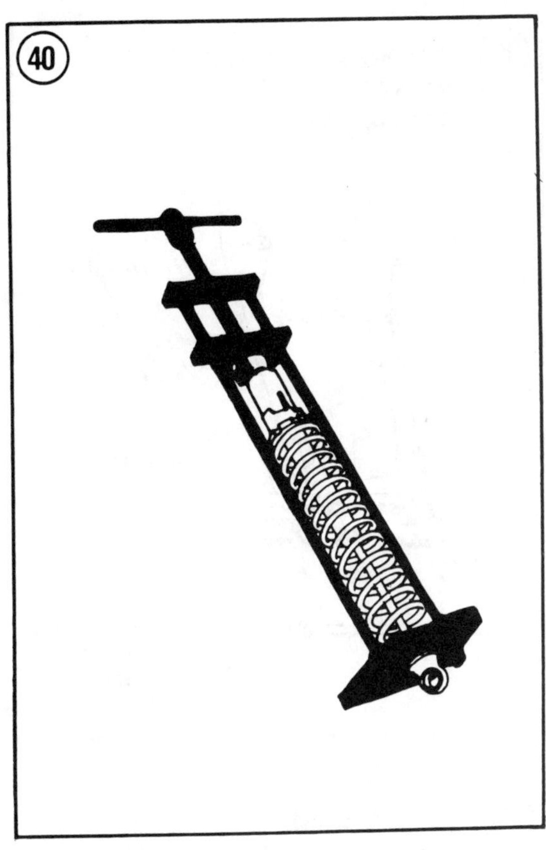

Removal

1. Place wood block(s) under the engine to support the bike securely with the rear wheel off of the ground.
2. Remove the rear wheel as described in this chapter.
3. Remove the drive chain guard (A, **Figure 43**).
4. Remove the chain guide on models so equipped.
5. Remove the lower mounting bolt or nut (B, **Figure 43**) on both shock absorbers. Pivot the shock absorbers up and out of the way.

NOTE
It is not necessary to completely remove the shock absorbers.

6. Grasp the rear end of the swing arm and try to move it from side to side in a horizontal arc. There should be no noticeable side play. If play is evident, and the pivot bolt is tightened correctly, the bushings or pivot collar should be replaced.

7A. On models so equipped, remove the cotter pin and the castellated nut.

7B. On models so equipped, remove the self-locking nut (**Figure 44**).

8A. Withdraw the pivot bolt from the left-hand side (C, **Figure 43**) on the following models:

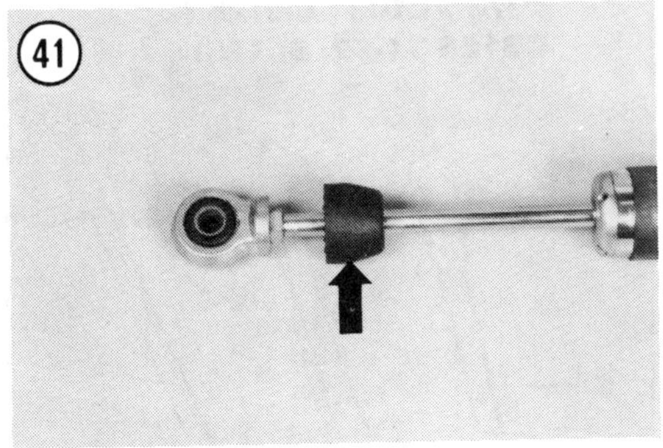

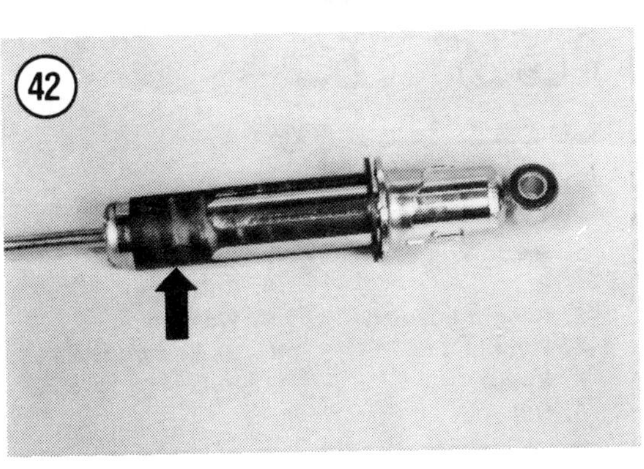

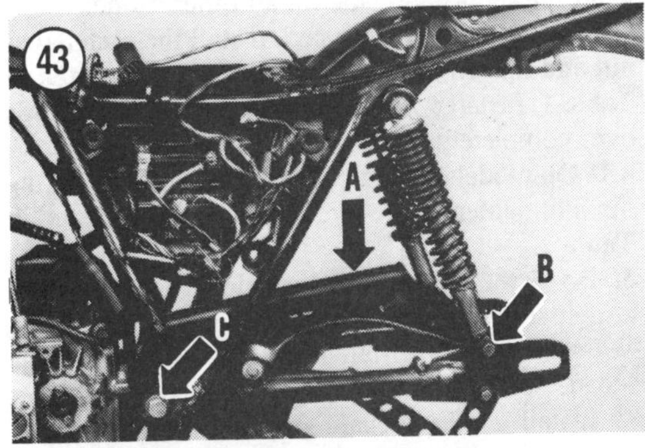

a. All CB100.
b. All CL100.
c. 1976-on CB125S.

8B. Withdraw the pivot bolt from the right-hand side on all other models.

9. Pull back on the swing arm, free it from the drive chain and remove the swing arm from the frame.

NOTE
On models so equipped, don't lose the dust seal caps on each side of the pivot points; they will usually fall off when the swing arm is removed.

Installation

1. Position the swing arm into the mounting area. Align the holes in the swing arm with the holes in the frame. To help align the holes, insert a drift in from the side opposite where the pivot bolt will be inserted.

2. Apply a light coat of multipurpose grease to the pivot bolt.

3A. After all holes are aligned insert the pivot bolt from the left-hand side on the following models:
a. All CB100.
b. All CL100.
c. 1976-on CB125S.

3B. After all holes are aligned, insert the pivot bolt from the right-hand side on all other models.

4A. On models so equipped, install the castellated nut and tighten to the torque specifications listed in **Table 1**. Install a new cotter pin and bend the ends over completely.

4B. On models so equipped, install the self-locking nut and tighten to the torque specifications listed in **Table 1**.

5. Pivot the shock absorbers down into position and install the shock absorber lower mounting bolts or nuts. Tighten the bolts or nuts to the torque specifications listed in **Table 1**.

6. Install the drive chain guard.

7. Install the rear wheel as described in this chapter.

Disassembly/Inspection/Assembly (100 and 125 cc Models)

Refer to the following exploded views during disassembly and assembly.
a. **Figure 45**—All CB100, all CL100, 1976-on CB125S.
b. **Figure 46**—All SL100, XL100, XL100 K1. 1976 XL100, CB125 S, CB125 S1-S2, all SL125.

(45) **SWING ARM ASSEMBLY (CL100, CB100, 1976-on CB125S)**

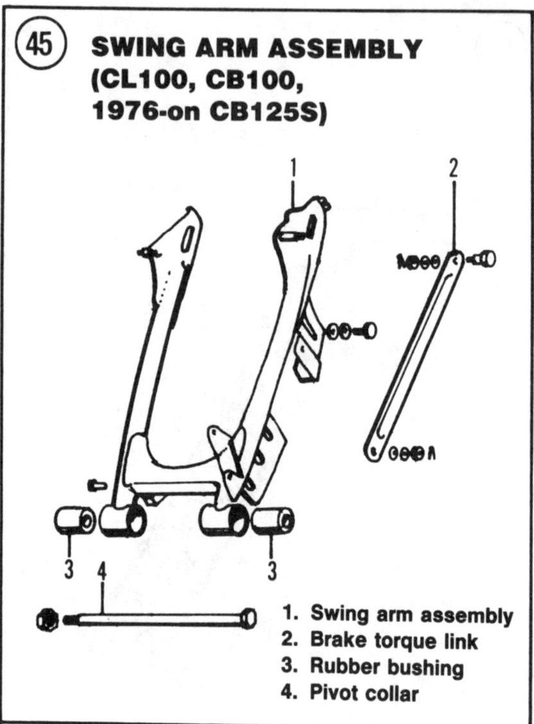

1. Swing arm assembly
2. Brake torque link
3. Rubber bushing
4. Pivot collar

(46) **SWING ARM ASSEMBLY (SL100, XL100, XL100 K1, 1976 XL100 , CB125 S, CB125 S1-S2, SL125)**

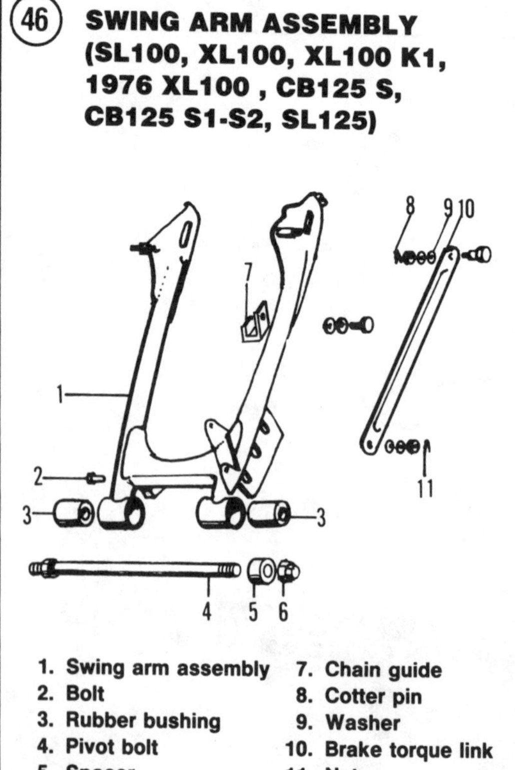

1. Swing arm assembly
2. Bolt
3. Rubber bushing
4. Pivot bolt
5. Spacer
6. Nut
7. Chain guide
8. Cotter pin
9. Washer
10. Brake torque link
11. Nut

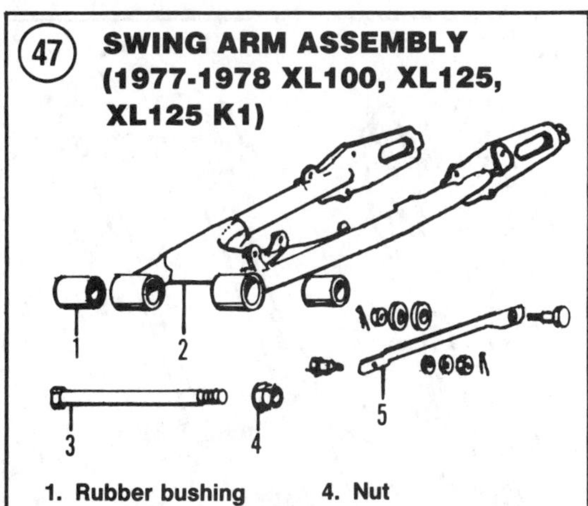

(47) SWING ARM ASSEMBLY (1977-1978 XL100, XL125, XL125 K1)

1. Rubber bushing
2. Swing arm assembly
3. Pivot bolt
4. Nut
5. Brake torque link

c. **Figure 47**—1977-1978 XL100, XL125, XL125 K1.
d. **Figure 48**—All TL125.
e. **Figure 49**—All CT125.

1. Remove the swing arm as described in this chapter.
2. Remove the rear brake torque link from the swing arm.
3. Remove the drive chain slider from the left-hand side of the swing arm.
4. Clean the pivot bolt in solvent and dry it.
5. Measure the outside diameter of the pivot bolt with a micrometer at both ends.
6. Wipe off any excess grease from the bushings at each end of the swing arm. Measure the inside diameter of both bushings.
7. Compare the dimensions taken in Step 5 and Step 6. If the difference is 0.5 mm (0.02 in.) or

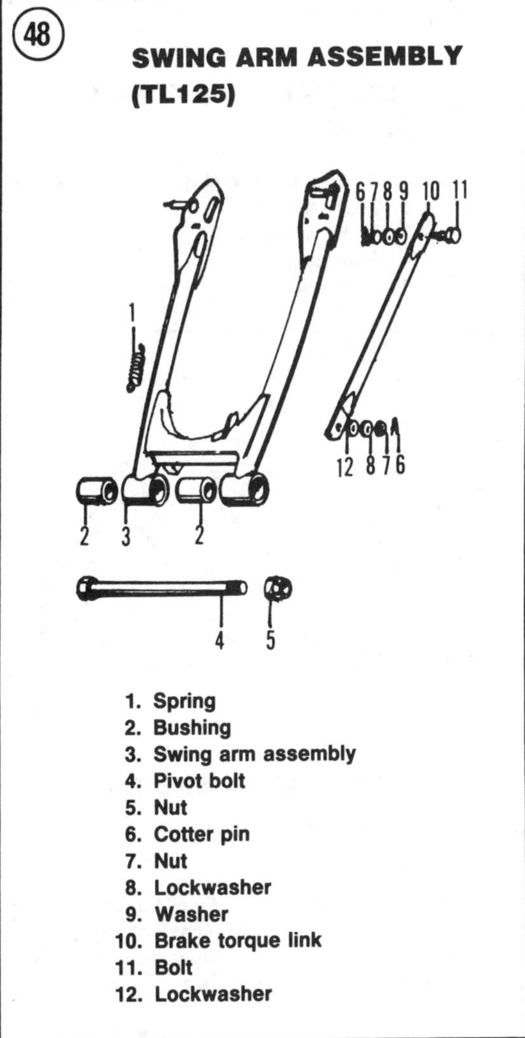

(48) SWING ARM ASSEMBLY (TL125)

1. Spring
2. Bushing
3. Swing arm assembly
4. Pivot bolt
5. Nut
6. Cotter pin
7. Nut
8. Lockwasher
9. Washer
10. Brake torque link
11. Bolt
12. Lockwasher

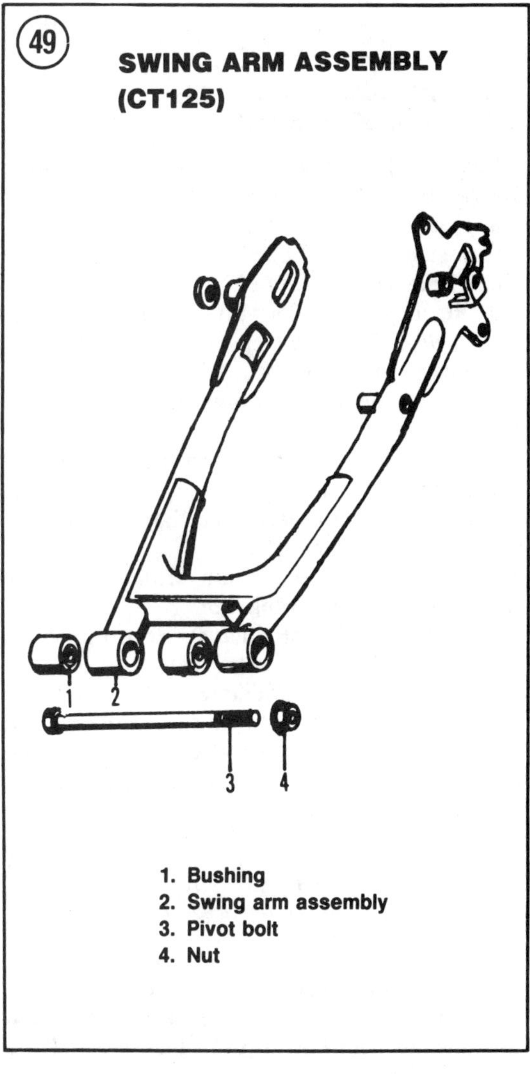

(49) SWING ARM ASSEMBLY (CT125)

1. Bushing
2. Swing arm assembly
3. Pivot bolt
4. Nut

greater either the pivot bolt or the bushings must be replaced.

NOTE
Honda does not provide specifications for either the pivot bolt or the bushings. Therefore, you must decide which part or parts are worn and require replacement.

NOTE
If the pivot collar is replaced, the bushings at each end must be replaced at the same time. Always replace both bushings even though only one may be worn.

8. If the bushings need replacement, refer to *Bushing Replacement* in this chapter.
9. Install the brake torque link arm and drive chain slider onto the swing arm.

Disassembly/Inspection/Assembly (175, 250 and 350 cc Models)

Refer to the following exploded views during disassembly and assembly:

a. **Figure 50**—All XL175.
b. **Figure 51**—All TL250.
c. **Figure 52**—1972 XL250.
d. **Figure 53**—XL250 K1-K2, 1976 XL250, 1976-1978 XL350.
e. **Figure 54**—XL350 K1.

1. Remove the swing arm as described in this chapter.
2. Remove the rear brake torque link from the swing arm.
3. Remove the dust seals if they have not already fallen off during removal.
4. Remove the drive chain slider from the left-hand side of the swing arm.
5. Withdraw the pivot collar(s), clean in solvent and dry completely.
6. Measure the outside diameter of the collar(s) with a micrometer at both ends (A, **Figure 55**). If the diameter is worn to less than the service limit listed in **Table 3**, the pivot collar(s) must be replaced.

NOTE
If the pivot collar(s) is replaced, all bushings must be replaced at the same time.

7. Wipe off any excess grease from the bushings at each end of the swing arm. Measure the inside diameter of both bushings (B, **Figure 55**). If the

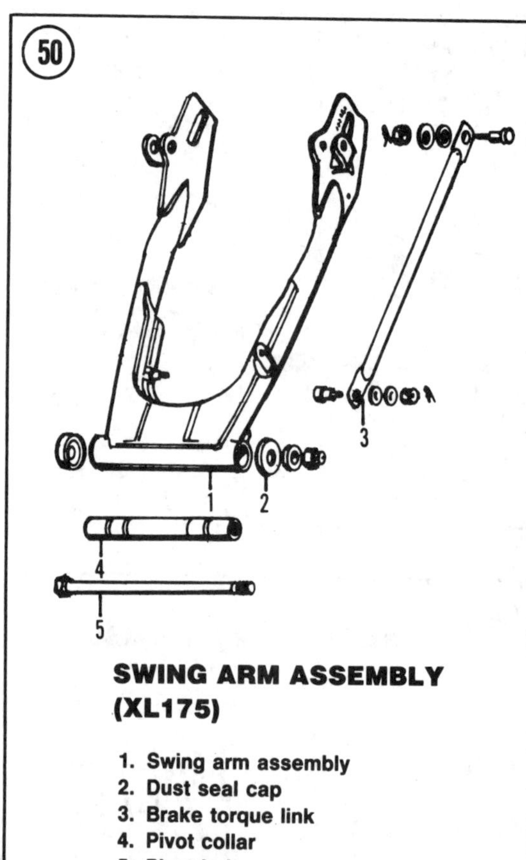

SWING ARM ASSEMBLY (XL175)

1. Swing arm assembly
2. Dust seal cap
3. Brake torque link
4. Pivot collar
5. Pivot bolt

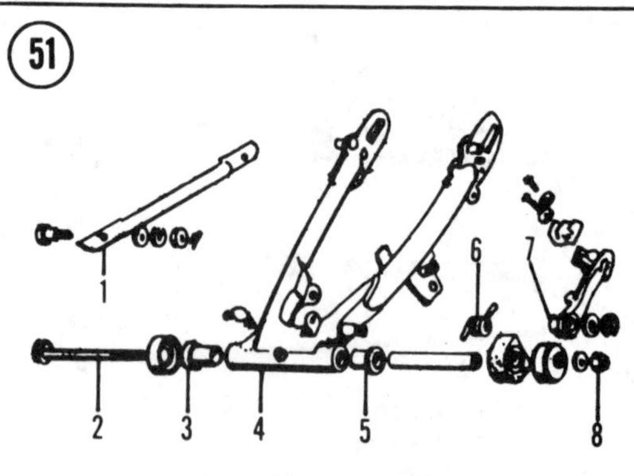

SWING ARM ASSEMBLY (TL250)

1. Brake torque link
2. Pivot bolt
3. Pivot bushing
4. Swing arm assembly
5. Pivot bushing
6. Tensioner spring
7. Drive chain tensioner
8. Nut

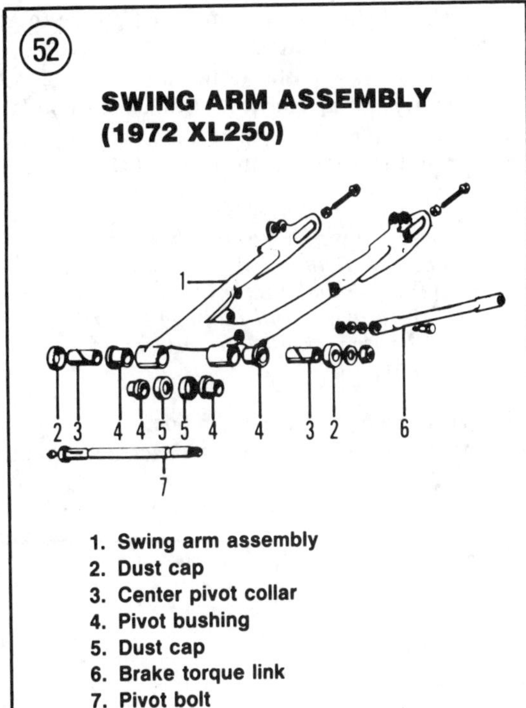

(52) **SWING ARM ASSEMBLY (1972 XL250)**

1. Swing arm assembly
2. Dust cap
3. Center pivot collar
4. Pivot bushing
5. Dust cap
6. Brake torque link
7. Pivot bolt

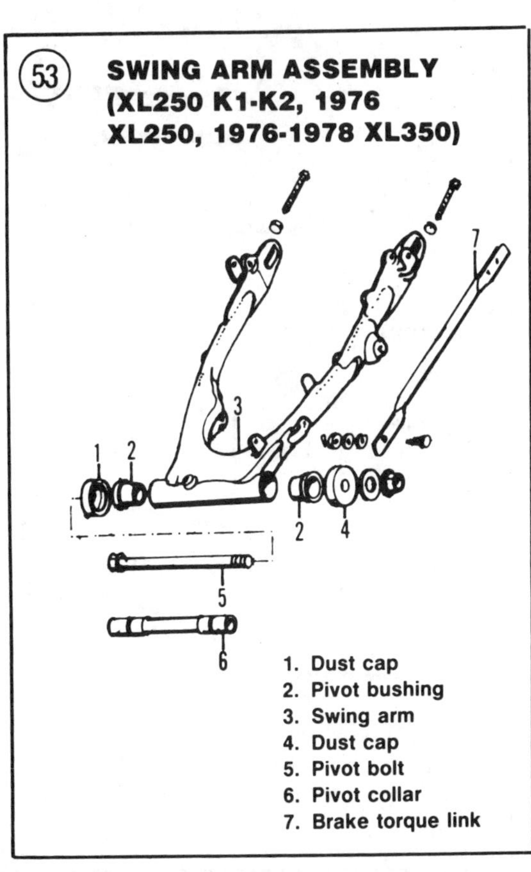

(53) **SWING ARM ASSEMBLY (XL250 K1-K2, 1976 XL250, 1976-1978 XL350)**

1. Dust cap
2. Pivot bushing
3. Swing arm
4. Dust cap
5. Pivot bolt
6. Pivot collar
7. Brake torque link

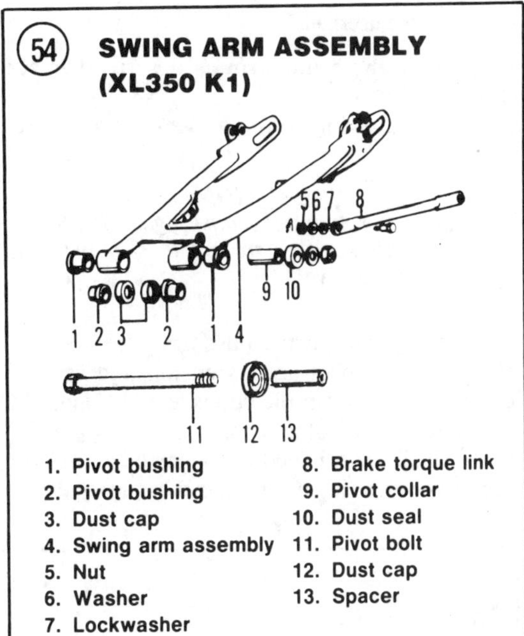

(54) **SWING ARM ASSEMBLY (XL350 K1)**

1. Pivot bushing
2. Pivot bushing
3. Dust cap
4. Swing arm assembly
5. Nut
6. Washer
7. Lockwasher
8. Brake torque link
9. Pivot collar
10. Dust seal
11. Pivot bolt
12. Dust cap
13. Spacer

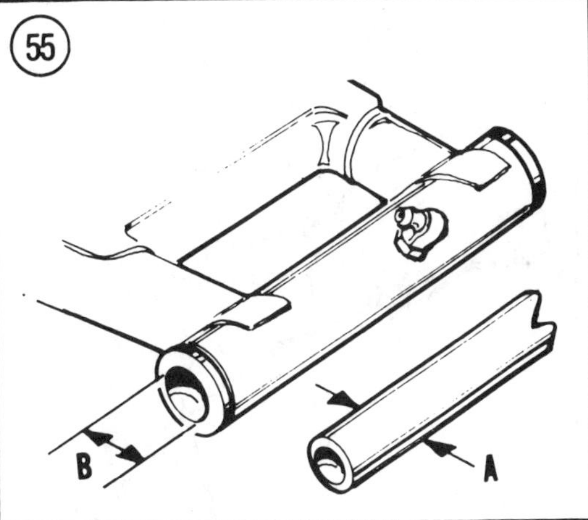

(55)

diameter is worn to less than the service limit listed in **Table 3**, the bushing must be replaced.

NOTE
Always replace all bushings even though only one may be worn.

8. If the bushings need replacement, refer to *Bushing Replacement* in this chapter.
9. Prior to installing the pivot collar, coat it throughly with multipurpose grease. Insert the pivot collar and install the drive chain slider on the left-hand side. Install both dust seal caps.
10. Install the brake torque link arm onto the swing arm.

Bushing Replacement

1. Remove the swing arm as described in this chapter.
2. Secure the swing arm in a vise with soft jaws.

CAUTION
Do not remove the bushings just for inspection as they are usually damaged during removal.

3. Carefully tap out the bushings. Use a suitable size drift or socket and extension and carefully drive them out from the opposite end (**Figure 56**).
4. Repeat for the other end.
5. Wash all parts, including the inside of the swing arm pivot area, in solvent and thoroughly dry.
6. Apply a light coat of waterproof grease to all parts prior to installation.
7. Install the new bushing. Tap new bushing into place slowly and squarely with a block of wood and hammer (**Figure 57**). Make sure that it is not cocked and that it is completely seated.

CAUTION
Never reinstall a bushing that has been removed. Removal slightly damages it so that it is no longer true to alignment. If installed, it will damage the pivot collar and create an unsafe riding condition.

8. Repeat Step 7 for the other side.
9. Install the swing arm as described in this chapter.

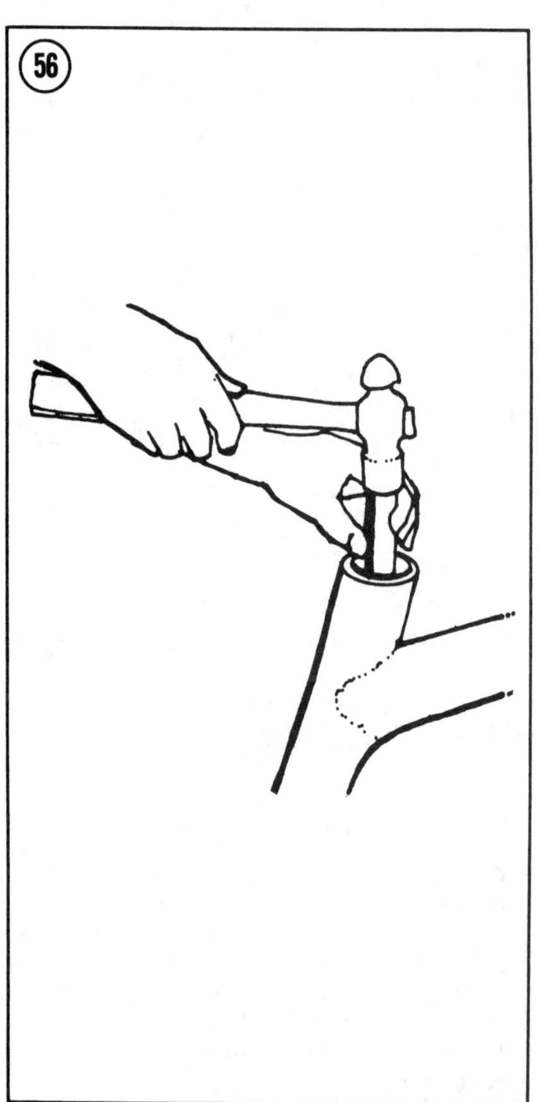

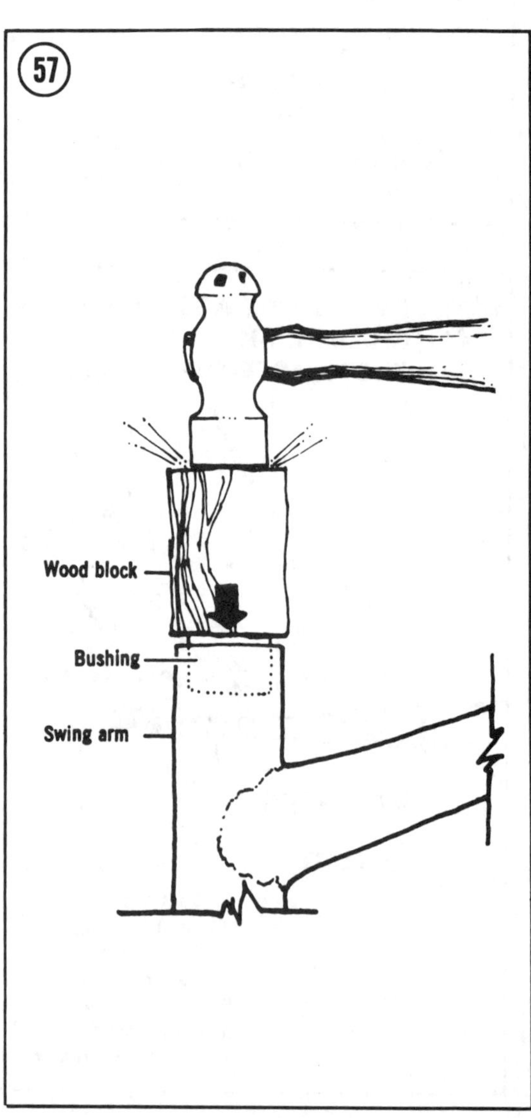

Table 1 REAR SUSPENSION TORQUE SPECIFICATIONS*

Item	N•m	ft.-lb.
Rear axle nut		
CB100, CL100, SL100, CB125S, SL125	40-50	29-36
XL100, XL125, CT125	40-60	29-43
TL125	N.A.	N.A.
XL175, TL250, XL250, XL350	60-80	43-58
Rear swing arm nut		
CB100, CL100, SL100, CB125S, SL125	30-40	22-29
XL100, XL125, CT125	35-50	25-36
TL125	N.A.	N.A.
XL175, TL250, XL250, XL350	55-70	40-51
Shock absorbers (upper and lower bolt and nut)		
TL125	N.A.	N.A.
TL250 (small screws)	7-10	5-8
All other models	30-40	22-29
Rear brake torque link bolt		
CB100, CL100, SL100, CB125S, SL125	20-25	14-18
XL100, XL125, CT125	10-20	7.3-14.5
TL125	N.A.	N.A.
XL175	8-12	5.9-8.7
TL250, XL250, XL350	18-25	13-18
Driven sprocket nuts		
CB100, CL100, SL100, CB125S, SL125, XL175	20-25	14-18
XL100, XL125	20-30	14.5-21.7
CT125	55-65	45-52
TL125	N.A.	N.A.
TL250	45-60	32-43
XL250, XL350	18-23	13-17

* Honda does not provide service information for all items nor all models. All available information is included in this table. "N.A." indicates that the information is not available.

Table 2 REAR SPRING FREE LENGTH*

Model	Standard Length	Service Limit
CB100, CL100, SL100, CB125S	180.9 mm (7.12 in.)	160 mm (6.30 in.)
SL125	190 mm (7.48 in.)	170 mm (6.69 in.)
XL100	213 mm (8.504 in.)	200 mm (7.874 in.)
TL125	N.A.	N.A.
XL125, CT125		
Spring A	180.5 mm (7.107 in.)	170 mm (6.693 in.)
Spring B	56.4 mm (2.221 in.)	52 mm (2.047 in.)
XL175		
Spring A	58.2 mm (2.291 in.)	54 mm (2.126 in.)
Spring B	178.6 mm (7.032 in.)	168 mm (6.614 in.)
TL250	237.5 mm (9.35 in.)	230 mm (9.06 in.)
1972-1975 XL250, XL350		
Spring "A" and "B" combined	236.4 mm (9.31 in.)	230 mm (9.06 in.)
1976-1978 XL250, XL350		
Standard	264.7 mm (10.42 in.)	262 mm (10.32 in.)
Optional	266.1 mm (10.51 in.)	260 mm (10.24 in.)

* Honda does not provide service information for all item nor all models. All available information is included in this table. "N.A." indicates that the information is not available.

Table 3 SWING ARM BUSHING AND COLLAR SERVICE LIMITS

Model	Pivot Bolt To Collar Clearance
CB100, CL100, SL100, CB125S, SL125	0.5 mm (0.019 in.)
XL100, XL125, CT125	0.8 mm (0.0315 in.)
TL125	N.A.

Model	Pivot Bushing ID	Collar OD
XL175	21.70 mm (0.8543 in.)	21.41 mm (0.8429 in.)
TL250	18.20 mm (0.7165 in.)	17.88 mm (0.7639 in.)
XL250, XL350	20.18 mm (0.7945 in.)	19.85 mm (0.7815 in.)

CHAPTER ELEVEN

BRAKES

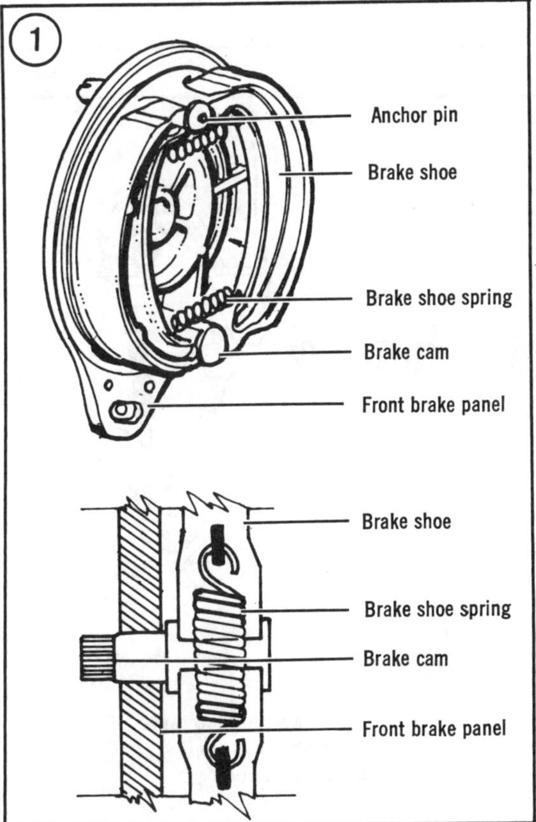

The front brake on the 1973-1978 CB125S is a mechanical type disc brake; the rear is a drum type. On all other models, both the front and the rear brake are drum type.

Figure 1 illustrates the major components of the drum brake assembly. Activating the brake hand lever or foot pedal pulls the cable or rod which in turn rotates the camshaft. This forces the brake shoes out into contact with the brake drum.

Lever and pedal free play must be maintained on both brakes to minimize brake drag and premature brake wear and maximize braking effectiveness. Refer to Chapter Three for complete adjustment procedures.

The front brake cable must be inspected and replaced periodically, as it will stretch with use until the cable can no longer be properly adjusted.

Table 1 and **Table 2** are at the end of this chapter.

DRUM BRAKES

The front and rear drum brake assemblies are almost identical and are covered in the same procedures.

Disassembly

Refer to **Figure 2** for the front brake and **Figure 3** for the rear brake.

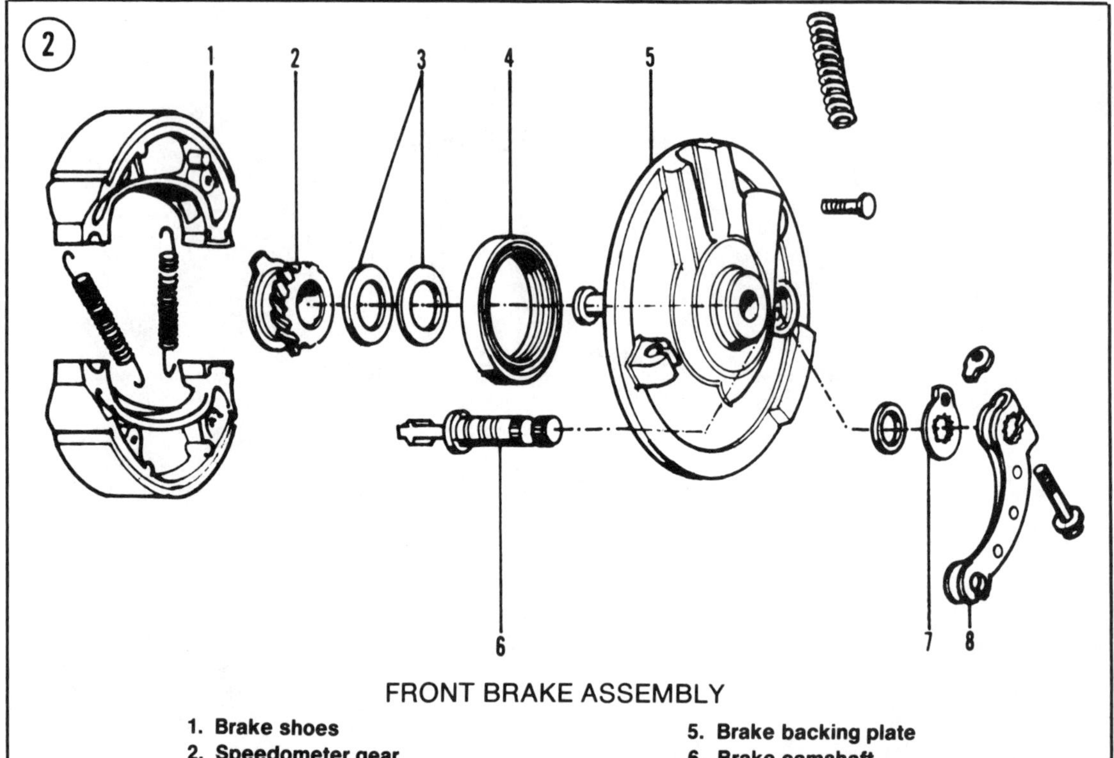

FRONT BRAKE ASSEMBLY

1. Brake shoes
2. Speedometer gear
3. Thrust washers
4. Dust seal
5. Brake backing plate
6. Brake camshaft
7. Brake lining wear indicator
8. Brake arm

3

REAR BRAKE ASSEMBLY

1. Brake arm
2. Brake lining wear indicator
3. Dust seal
4. Brake backing plate
5. Brake camshaft
6. Brake shoes

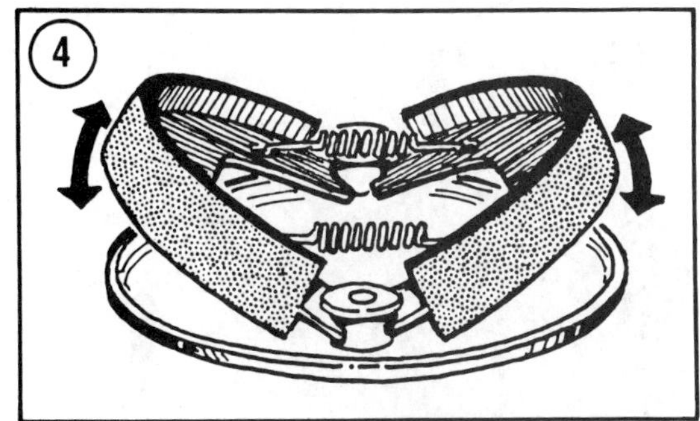

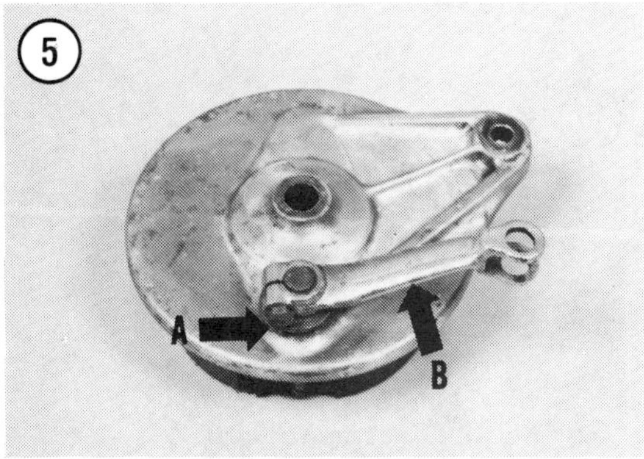

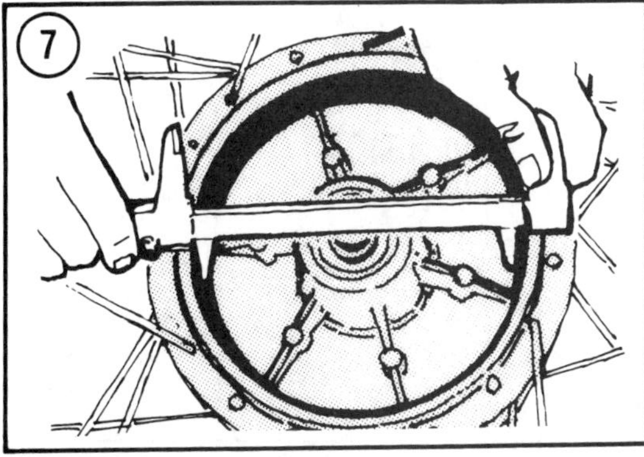

1. Remove the front or rear wheel as described in Chapter Nine or Chapter Ten.

NOTE
*Prior to removing the brake shoes from the backing plate, measure them as described under **Inspection** in this chapter.*

NOTE
Place a clean shop rag on the linings to protect them from oil and grease during removal.

2. Pull the brake assembly straight up and out of the brake drum.
3. Remove the brake shoes from the backing plate by firmly pulling up on the center of each shoe as shown in **Figure 4**.
4. Remove the return springs and separate the shoes.
5. Loosen the bolt (A, **Figure 5**) securing the brake lever to the cam. Remove the lever (B, **Figure 5**), the dust seal, the wear indicator and the camshaft.

Inspection

1. Thoroughly clean and dry all parts except the linings.
2. Check the contact surface of the drum (**Figure 6**) for scoring. If there are grooves deep enough to snag a fingernail, the drum should be reground and new shoes fitted. This type of wear can be avoided to a great extent if the brakes are disassembled and thoroughly cleaned after riding the bike in water, mud or deep sand.

NOTE
If oil or grease is on the drum surface, clean it off with a clean rag soaked in lacquer thinner—do not use any solvent that may leave an oil residue.

3. Use vernier calipers and check the inside diameter of the drum for out-of-round or excessive wear (**Figure 7**). Turn or replace the drum if it is worn to greater than service limit in **Table 1**.
4. If the drum is turned, the linings will have to be replaced and the new linings arced to conform to the new drum contour.
5. Inspect the linings for imbedded foreign material. Dirt can be removed with a stiff wire brush. Check for traces of oil or grease. If they are contaminated, they must be replaced.
6. Measure the brake linings with vernier calipers (**Figure 8**). They should be replaced if worn to less than the service limit (distance from the metal backing plate) listed in **Table 1**.

7. Inspect the cam lobe (A, **Figure 9**) and the pivot pin area (B, **Figure 9**) of the shaft for wear and corrosion. Minor roughness can be removed with fine emery cloth.
8. Inspect the camshaft bearing surface in the backing plate (C, **Figure 9**). If it is worn or damaged the backing plate must be replaced. The camshaft should also be replaced at the same time.
9. Inspect the brake shoe return springs (**Figure 10**) for wear. If they are stretched, they will not fully retract the brake shoes from the drum, resulting in a power-robbing drag on the drums and premature wear of the linings. Replace as necessary; always replace as a pair.

Assembly

1. Assemble the brake by reversing the disassembly steps, noting the following.
2. Grease the shaft, cam and pivot post with a light coat of molybdenum disulfide grease. Avoid getting any grease on the brake plate where the linings come in contact with it.
3. Install the cam into the backing plate from the backside. From the outside of the backing plate, install the dust seal. Align the wear indicator to the cam as shown in **Figure 11** and push it all the way down to the backing plate.
4. When installing the brake lever onto the brake camshaft, be sure to align the punch marks on the two parts (**Figure 12**).
5. Hold the brake shoes in a "V" formation with the return springs attached and snap them in place on the brake backing plate. Make sure they are firmly seated on it (**Figure 13**).

NOTE
*If new linings are being installed, file off the leading edge of each shoe a little (**Figure 14**) so that the brake will not grab when applied.*

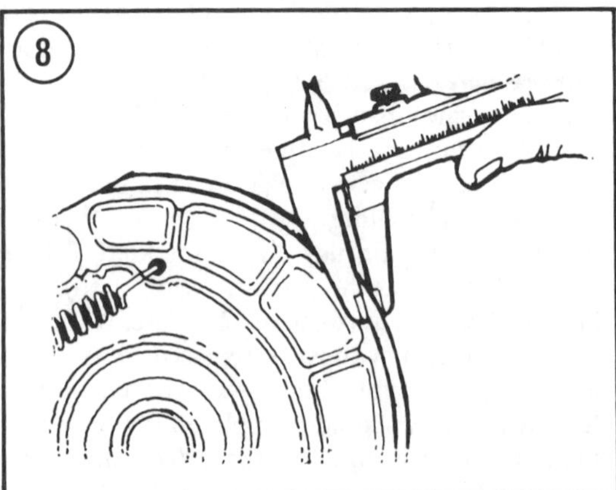

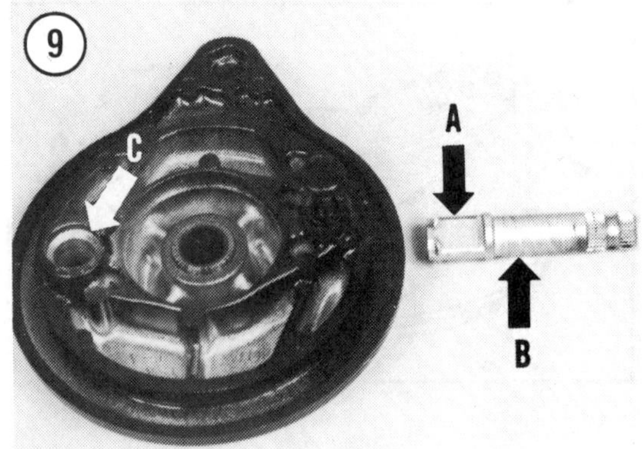

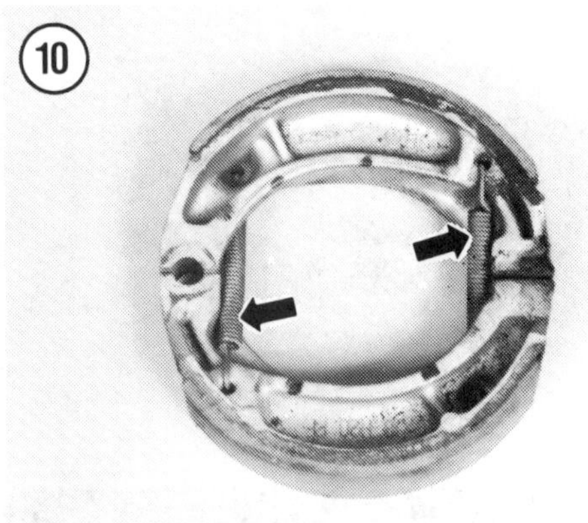

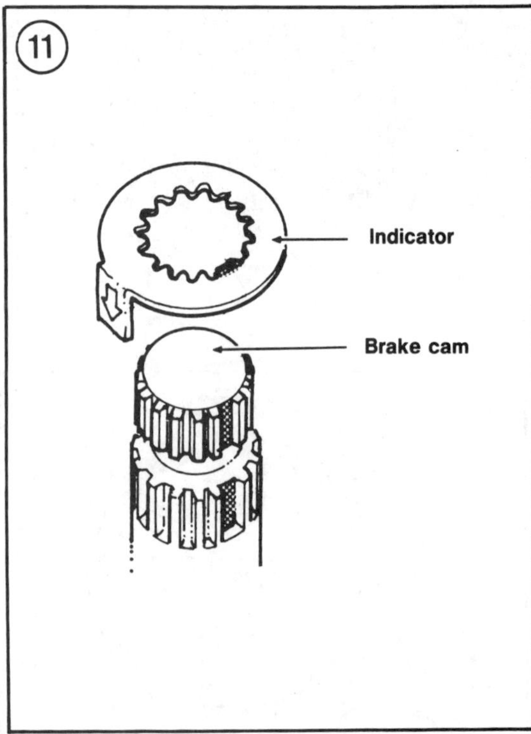

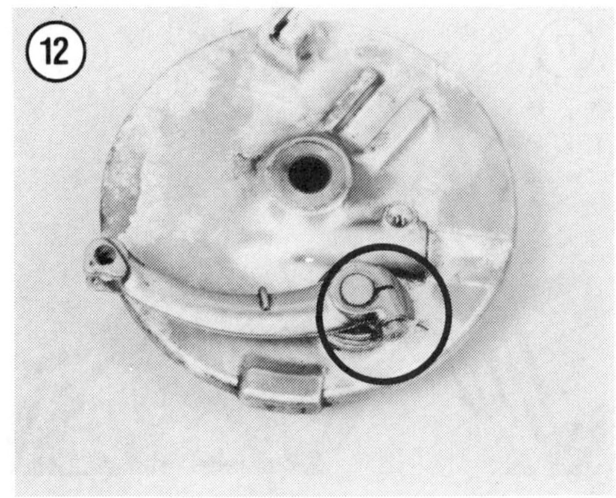

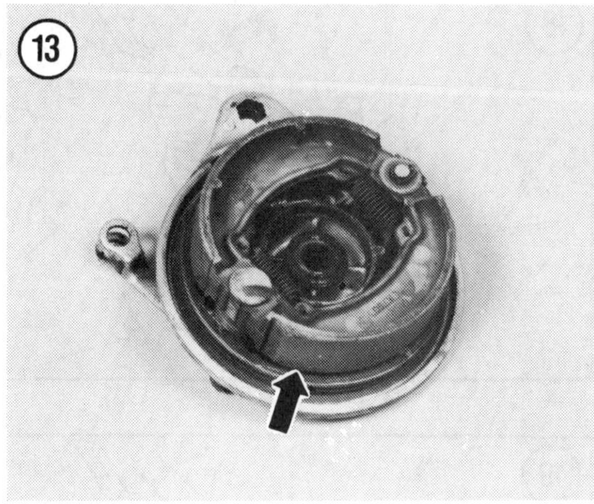

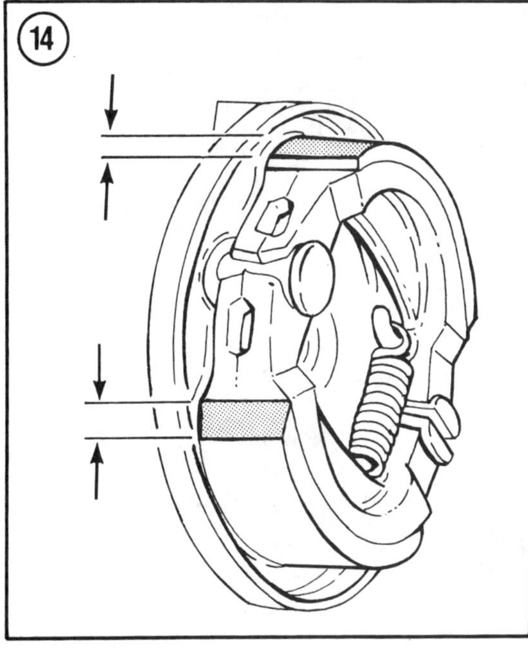

6. Install the brake panel assembly into the brake drum.
7. Install the front or rear wheel as described in Chapter Nine or Chapter Ten.

NOTE
When installing the front wheel, be sure that the locating slot in the brake panel is engaged with the boss on the front fork leg. This is necessary for proper brake operation.

8. Adjust the brakes as described in Chapter Three.

FRONT BRAKE CABLE

Front brake cable adjustment should be checked periodically as the cable stretches with use and increases brake lever free play. Free play is the distance that the brake lever travels between the released position and the point when the brake shoes come in contact with the drum or disc.

If the brake adjustment as described in Chapter Three can no longer be achieved, the cable must be replaced.

NOTE
This procedure represents a typical brake cable replacement procedure. Minor variations may exist among the various models in the area of the brake backing plate.

Replacement (Drum Brake)

1. At the hand lever, slide back the protective boot. Loosen the locknut and turn the adjusting barrel (**Figure 15**) all the way toward the cable sheath.

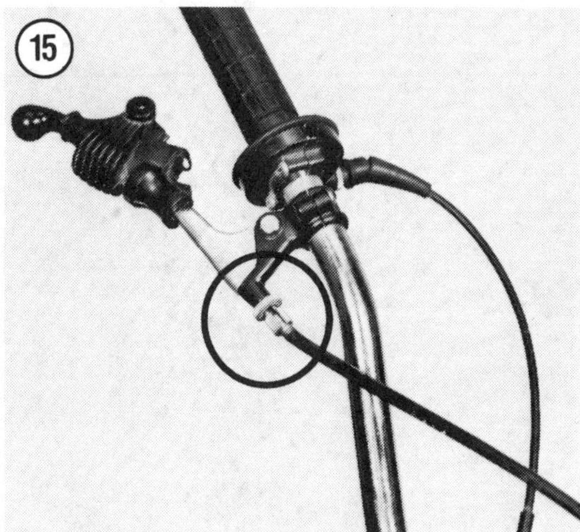

11

2. At the brake assembly, loosen the locknut (A, **Figure 16**) and screw it all the way toward the cable sheath. Unhook the cable end from the end of the brake lever (B, **Figure 16**) and disconnect the cable from the receptacle on the backing plate (C, **Figure 16**).
3. Pull the hand lever all the way to the grip, remove the cable nipple from the lever and remove the cable.

NOTE
Prior to removing the cable, make a drawing (or take a Polaroid picture) of the cable routing through the frame. It is very easy to forget once it has been removed. Replace it exactly as it was, avoiding any sharp turns.

4. Withdraw the cable from any holders (**Figure 17**) on the front fork.
5. Install by reversing these removal steps.
6. Adjust the brake as described.

Replacement (Disc Brake)

1. Place the bike on the centerstand and place wood block(s) under the engine so the front wheel is off the ground.
2. Turn the cable adjuster boot (**Figure 18**) inside-out to expose the adjuster.
3. At the caliper assembly, loosen the cable locknut and turn the cable adjuster bolt all the way in toward the caliper. This is to allow maximum brake cable slack.
4. Remove the bolts (**Figure 19**) securing the caliper cover and remove the caliper cover.
5. Disengage the brake cable end (A, **Figure 20**) from the brake arm assembly (B, **Figure 20**).

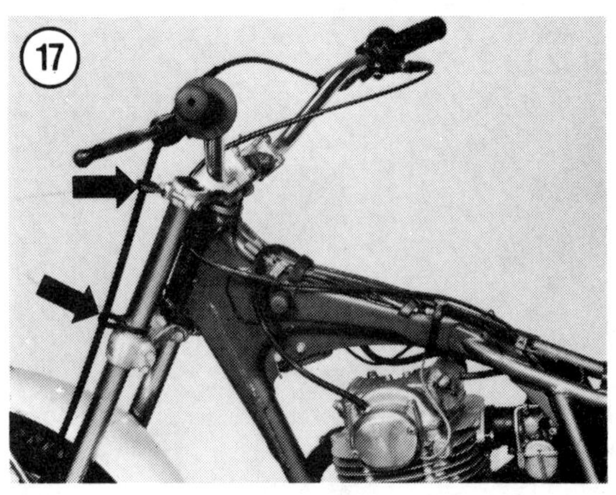

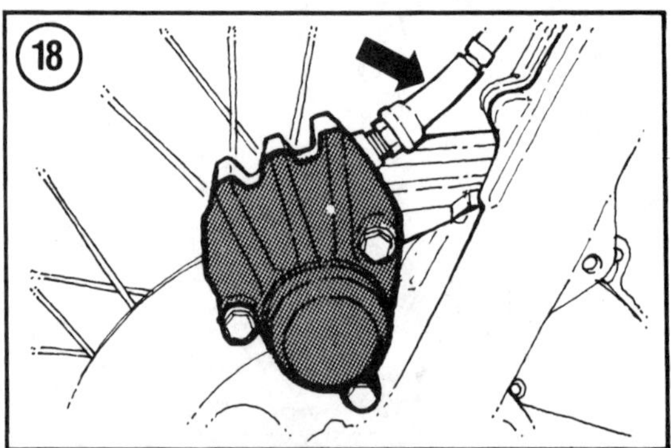

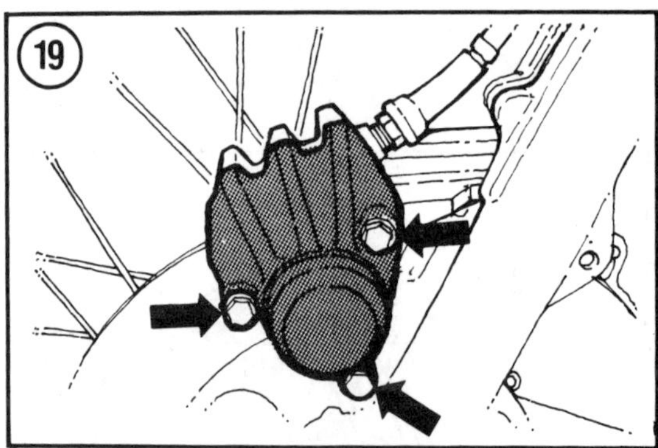

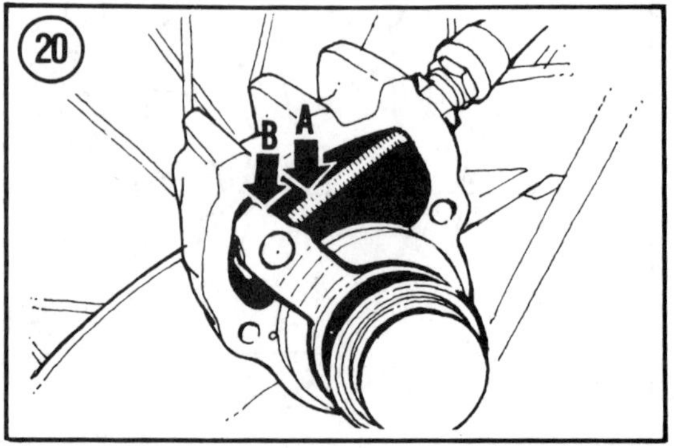

6. Slide the rubber boot back from the hand lever.
7. Pull the hand lever all the way to the grip, remove the cable nipple from the lever and remove the cable.

NOTE
Prior to removing the cable, make a drawing (or take a Polaroid picture) of the cable routing through the frame. It is very easy to forget once it has been removed. Replace it exactly as it was, avoiding any sharp turns.

8. Install by reversing these removal steps, noting the following.
9. Install a new caliper cover gasket.

FRONT DISC BRAKE

The mechanical front disc brake used on 1973-1978 CB125S models is cable actuated and is self-adjusting.

Refer to **Figure 21** for all service procedures on the disc brake.

BRAKE PAD REPLACEMENT

Removal

There is no recommended mileage interval for changing the friction pads in the disc brake. Pad wear depends greatly on riding habits and conditions. The pads should be checked for wear frequently and replaced when the red wear indicator line approaches the brake disc. To maintain an even brake pressure on the brake disc, always replace both brake pads at the same time.

CAUTION
Watch the pads more closely when the red wear indicator line approaches the disc. If pad wear happens to be uneven for some reason the backing plate may come in contact with the disc and cause damage.

1. Place the bike on the sidestand and place wood block(s) under the engine so the front wheel is off the ground.

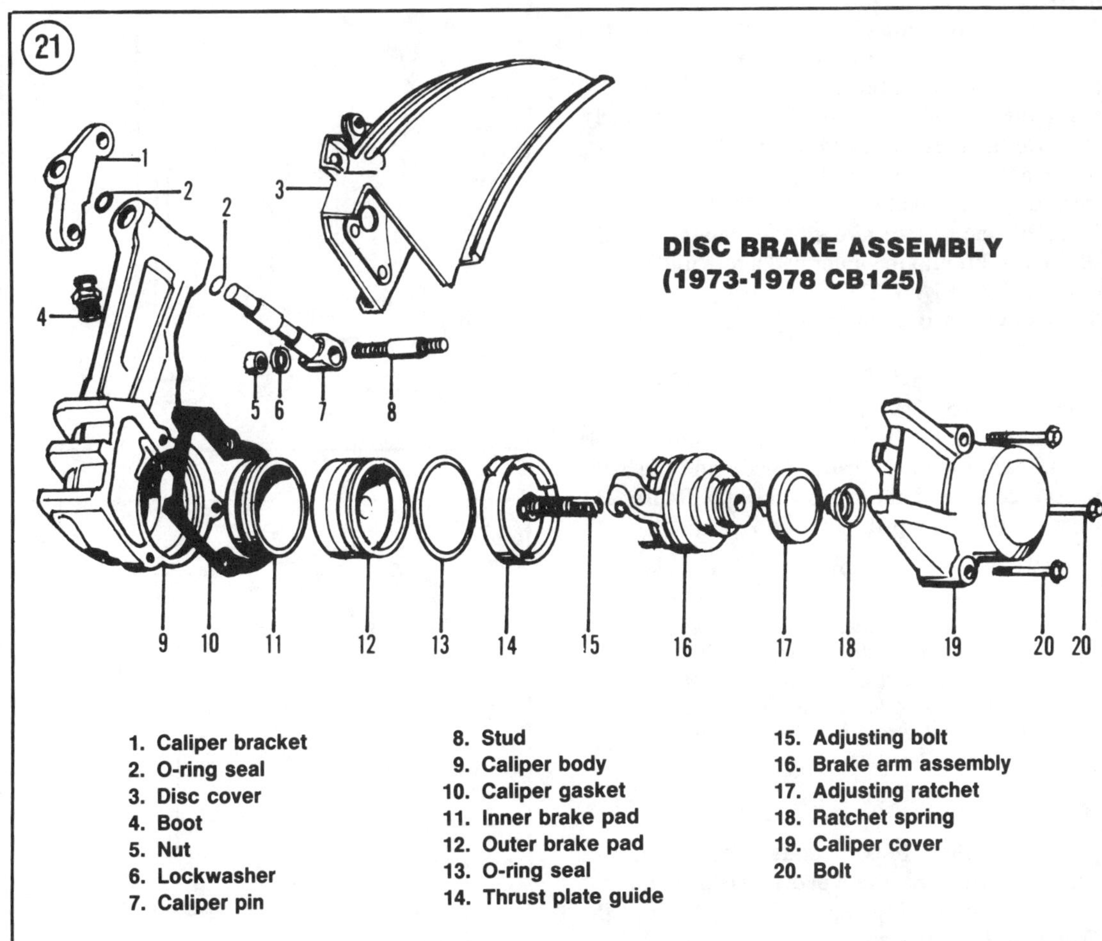

11

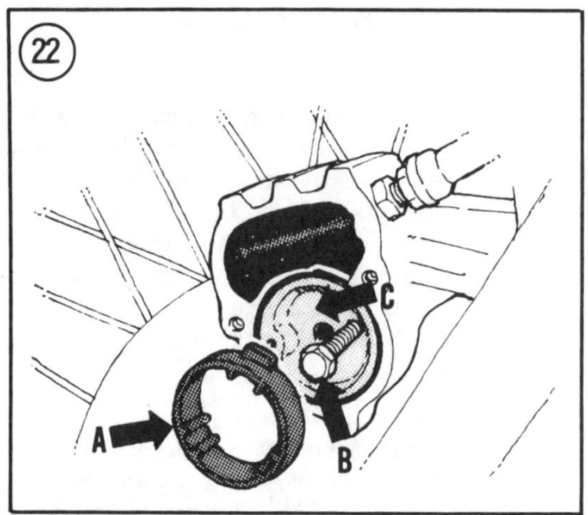

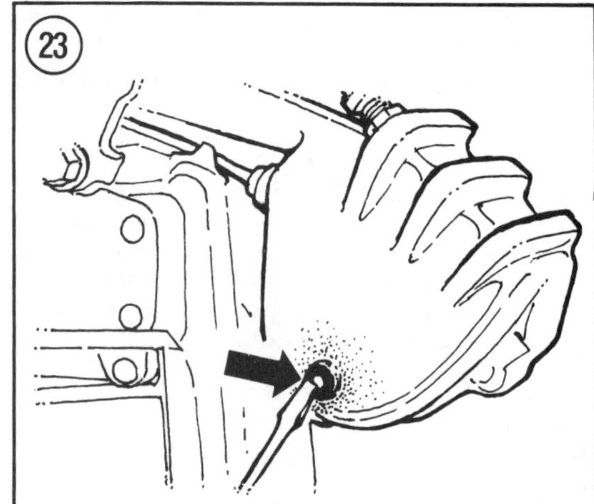

2. Turn the cable adjuster boot (**Figure 18**) inside-out to expose the adjuster.
3. At the caliper assembly, loosen the cable locknut and turn the cable adjuster bolt all the way in toward the caliper. This is to allow maximum brake cable slack.
4. Remove the bolts (**Figure 19**) securing the caliper cover and remove the caliper cover.
5. Disengage the brake cable end (A, **Figure 20**) from the brake arm assembly (B, **Figure 20**). Remove the brake arm assembly.
6. Remove the thrust plate guide (A, **Figure 22**) from the caliper body.
7. Screw one of the caliper cover mounting bolts (B, **Figure 22**) into the outer pad and withdraw the outer pad (C, **Figure 22**).
8. Remove the axle nut cotter pin and remove the axle nut.
9. Withdraw the axle from the right-hand side and remove the front wheel.
10. Insert a narrow-blade screwdriver into the hole in the backside of the caliper body and push the inner pad out of the caliper body (**Figure 23**). Remove the inner pad.

NOTE

*If the inner pad is worn to the wear line, the pad will fall out of the disc opening in the caliper body (**Figure 24**). If there is still sufficient pad material remaining, the pad will have to be pushed all the way out through the pad opening in the caliper body.*

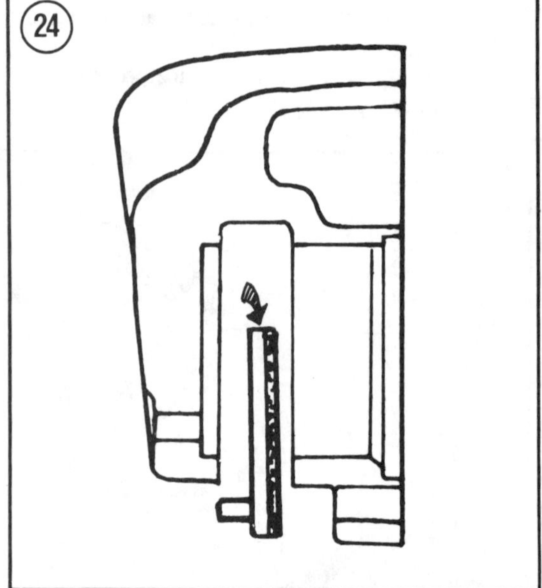

Inspection

1. Check the brake pads for wear or contamination. If either pad is worn to the red wear line (**Figure 25**), replace both pads and the O-ring on the outer pad.

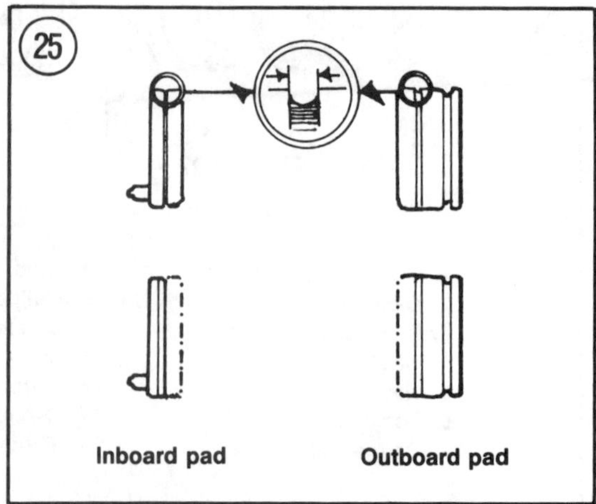

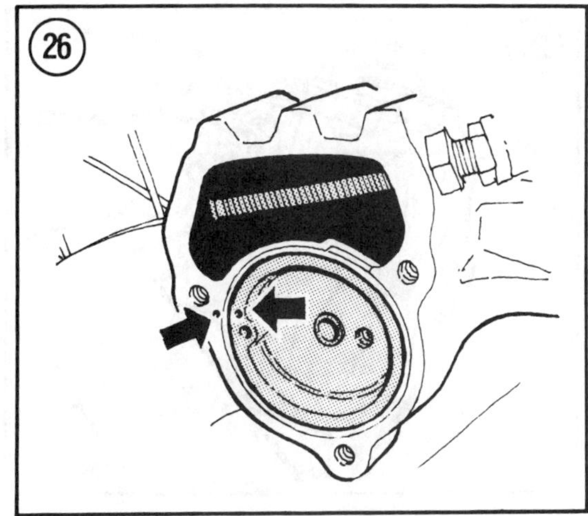

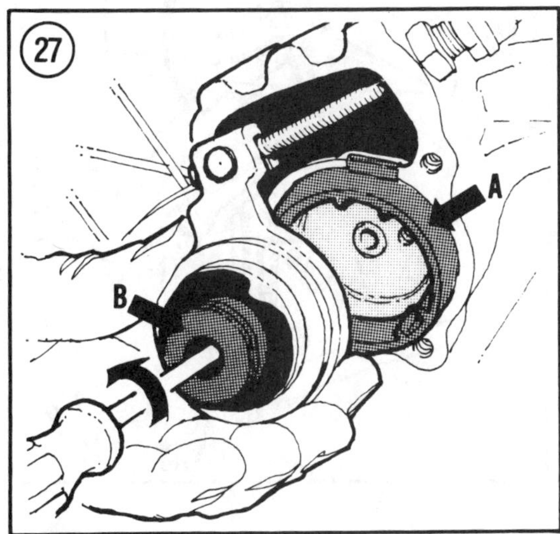

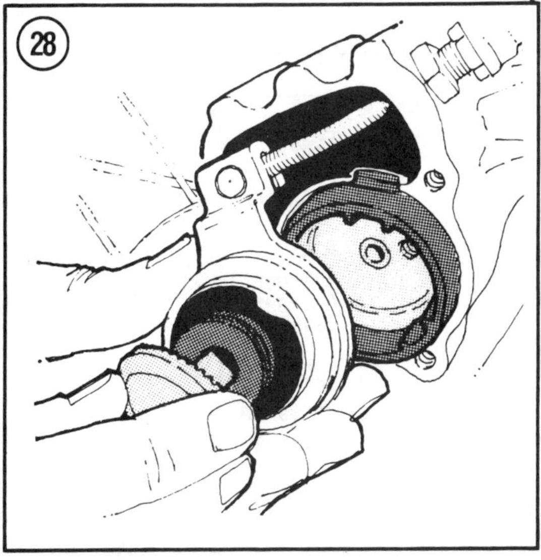

2. Clean the pad recess in the caliper body with a soft cloth. Do not use solvent, a wire brush or any hard tool which would cause damage to the caliper body where the pads ride.
3. Check with your dealer to make sure the friction compound of the new pads is compatible with the disc material. Remove any roughness from the backs of the new pads with a fine-cut file; blow them clean with compressed air.
4. Carefully remove any rust or corrosion from each side of the disc.

Installation

1. Lightly coat the back side of the inner brake pad (not the friction side) with disc brake lubricant (silicone grease). Install the inner brake pad into the caliper body.
2. Install the front wheel and insert the front axle from the right-hand side. Install the axle nut and tighten to the torque specifications listed in **Table 2**. Install a new cotter pin and bend the ends over completely.

CAUTION
Do allow the brake lubricant to get onto the friction surface of the brake pad or it will render the pad useless.

3. Install a new O-ring seal onto the outer pad. Apply brake lubricant (silicone grease) to the O-ring and to the outer circumference of the brake pad.
4. Align the index mark on the caliper body and the outer pad and install the outer pad (**Figure 26**).
5. Attach the brake cable to the brake arm assembly.
6. Install the thrust plate guide (A, **Figure 27**).
7. Remove the adjusting ratchet from the brake arm assembly.
8. Use a screwdriver to back off the adjusting bolt (B, **Figure 27**) as far as it will turn.
9. Install the adjusting ratchet (**Figure 28**) and make sure the pawl engages properly.
10. Install the brake arm assembly into the caliper body.
11. Install a new caliper gasket.
12. Install the caliper cover and the mounting bolts. Tighten the bolts securely.
13. To eliminate excessive clearance at the brake lever, loosen or turn the brake cable adjusting bolt away from the caliper body until the brake lever returns to its completely released position. Squeeze the brake lever and make sure the spring pressure within the caliper returns the brake lever to its completely released position. From this point turn the adjusting bolt an additional 2-3 full turns.

14. Operate the brake lever about 10-12 times. This will actuate the automatic adjuster. Then squeeze the brake lever and release it. The brake is now automatically adjusted to the specified of free play of 20-30 mm (3/4-1 1/8 in.).
15. Rotate the front wheel and make sure that the brake does not drag.

BRAKE CALIPER BODY

Removal/Installation

1. Remove the brake pads as described in this chapter.
2. Withdraw the brake cable from the caliper body (**Figure 29**).
3. Remove the bolt securing the disc cover and remove the disc cover.
4. Remove the bolts (A, **Figure 30**) securing the right-hand side of the front fender and the caliper bracket.
5. Remove the nut and lockwasher (B, **Figure 30**) securing the caliper body and caliper pin to the fork leg.
6. Remove the caliper body and the caliper pin.
7. Inspect the O-ring seals on the caliper pin; replace if necessary.
8. Install by reversing these removal steps, noting the following.
9. Be sure to install the caliper bracket between the fender bracket and the fork leg.
10. Tighten the bolts and nuts to the torque specifications listed in **Table 2**.

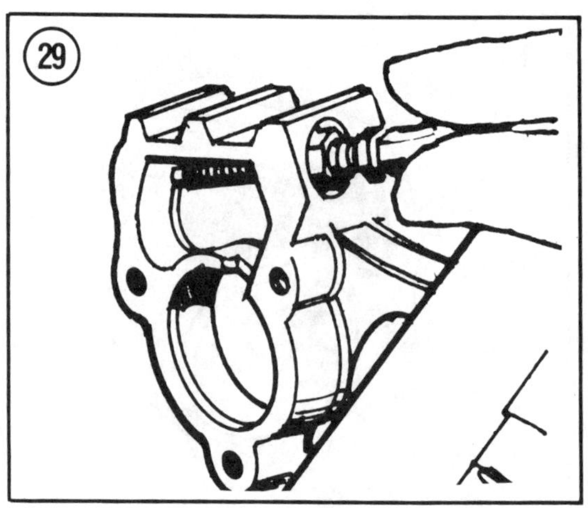

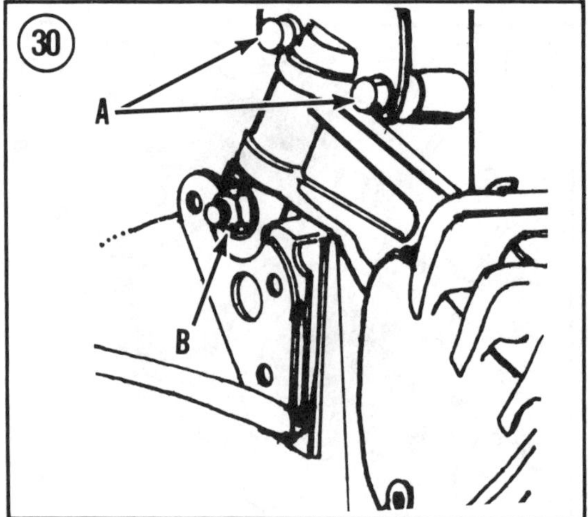

Table 1 BRAKE SPECIFICATIONS*

Item	Specifications	Wear Limit
Front brake drum ID		
CL100, CB100,	109.8-110.2 mm	112 mm
SL100, SL125,	(4.323-4.338 in.)	(4.409 in.)
1973-1978 CB125S		
1979-on CB125S	110.0-110.2 mm	111 mm (4.4 in.)
CT125	(4.33-4.34 in.)	
TL125	N.A.	N.A.
XL100, XL125,	109.8-110.2 mm	111 mm
TL250	(4.323-4.338 in.)	(4.370 in.)
XL175	140.0-140.3 mm	141 mm
	(5.512-5.524 in.)	(5.551 in.)
XL250, XL350	160.0-160.3 mm	161 mm
	(6.299-6.311 in.)	(6.339 in.)

(continued)

Table 1 BRAKE SPECIFICATIONS* (continued)

Item	Specifications	Wear Limit
Rear brake drum ID		
CL100, CB100,	109.8-110.2 mm	112 mm
1973-1978 CB125S	(4.323-4.338 in.)	(4.409 in.)
SL100, SL125	110.0-110.3 mm	112 mm
	(4.331 4.342 in.)	(4.409 in.)
1979-on CB125S	110.0-110.2 mm	111 mm (4.4 in.)
CT125, TL250	(4.33-4.34 in.)	
TL125	N.A.	N.A.
XL100, XL125	109.8-110.3 mm	111 mm
	(4.323-4.342 in.)	(4.370 in.)
XL175	130.0-130.3 mm	131 mm
	(5.118-5.129 in.)	(5.157 in.)
XL250, XL350	140.0-140.3 mm	141 mm
	(5.512-5.524 in.)	(5.551 in.)
Brake lining thickness front and rear		
CL100, CB100,	—	2.0 mm (0.08 in.)
SL100, XL125 CB125S,		
SL125, TL125		
XL125, CT125,	—	2.5 mm (0.098 in.)
XL175, TL250,		
XL250, XL350		
Front disc brake		
(1973-1978 CB125S)		
Brake disc axial		
and radial runout	0.5 mm (0.020 in.)	2.0 mm (0.079 in.)
Brake pad thickness	N.A.	Wear line

*Honda does not provide service information for all items nor all models. All available information is included in this table.

Table 2 BRAKE TORQUE SPECIFICATIONS*

	N•m	ft.-lb.
Rear brake torque link bolt		
CB100, CL100, SL100,	20-25	14-18
CB125S, SL125		
XL100, XL125, CT125	10-20	7.3-14.5
TL125	N.A.	N.A.
XL175	8-12	5.9-8.7
TL250, XL250, XL350	18-25	13-18
Disc brake		
Caliper joint	8-12	5.8-8.7
Caliper pin	15-25	11-18

*Honda does not provide service information for all items nor all models. All available information is included in this table.

INDEX

A

Air cleaner 190
Air filter element 34-35, 38
Alternator 228-237

B

Battery 13, 15-16
Brakes
  Caliper body 332
  Cam lubrication 23-24
  Drum 323-327
  Front brake cable 327-329
  Lining inspection 30
  Pad replacement 329-332
  Troubleshooting 12
Breaker point ignition 237-240

C

Camshaft .. 38-40, 55-58, 67, 91-93, 112-113, 136
Capacitor discharge ignition 240-243
Carburetor
  Adjustments 211-216
  Operation 190
  Service 190-211
Charging system 223-227
Clutch
  Adjustment 31-34
  Cable 158-159
  Drive sprocket 166-167
  External shift mechanism 159-166
  Inspection 157-158
  Operation 147
  100 and 125 engines 147-151
  175, 250 and 350 cc engines 151-157
Compression test 40-42
Contact breaker point 45
Crankcase and crankshaft 85-91, 131-136
Crankcase breather 36
Crankcase breather hose
  (1979-on U.S. models) 15
Cylinder 119-121
Cylinder head cover and camshaft 106-112, 113-115

D

Drive chain 22, 24-29, 304-306
Drive sprocket 166-167

E

Electrical system
  Alternator 228-237
  Breaker point ignition 237-240
  Capacitor discharge ignition 240-243
  Charging system 223-227
  Ignition advance mechanism 245-246
  Ignition coil 243-244
  Ignition pulse generator 244-245
  Lighting system 246-248
  Rectifier 227
  Switches 248-250
  Voltage regulator/rectifier 227-228
Engines, 100 and 125 cc
  Break-in procedure 97-98
  Camshaft (1969-1975) 55-58
  Camshaft chain 67
  Camshaft chain and tensioner 91-93
  Cooling 53
  Crankcase and crankshaft 85-91
  Cylinder 73-75
  Cylinder head 58-60, 68-69
  Cylinder head cover and camshaft 60-67
  Kickstarter 93-96
  Oil pump 80-85
  Piston, piston pin and piston rings 75-80
  Principles 53
  Removal/installation 53-55

12

Servicing in frame 53
Valves and valve components 69-73
Engines, 175, 250 and 350 cc
Break-in procedure 142
Camshaft chain 112-113
Camshaft chain and tensioner 136
Cooling 103
Crankcase and crankshaft 131-136
Cylinder 119-121
Cylinder head 113-115
Cylinder head cover and camshaft 106-112
Kickstarter 136-142
Oil pump 126-131
Piston, piston pin and piston rings 121-126
Principles 103
Removal/installation 103-105
Service in frame 103
Valves and valve components 116-119
Exhaust system 218-219

F

Fuel
Air cleaner 190
Carburetor 190-216
Fuel filter 217-218
Fuel tank 217
Throttle cable 216-217

G

General information 1-6

H

Hub and driven sprocket 255-259, 300-304

I

Idle mixture adjustment 48
Idle speed adjustment 48-49
Ignition
Coil 243-244
Advance mechanism 245-246
Pulse generator 244-245

K

Kickstarter 93-96, 136-142

L

Lighting system 246-248
Lubrication (see Maintenance)

M

Maintenance
Air filter element cleaning 34-35
Battery 13, 15-16
Brake cam lubrication 23-24
Brake lining inspection 30
Clutch adjustment 31-34
Control cables 22-23
Crankcase breather 36
Crankcase breather hose
(1979-on U.S. models) 15
Drive chain 22, 24-29
Engine oil change and
oil filter screen cleaning 17-21
Engine oil level 13, 16-17
Front brake lever adjustment 30
Front fork oil change 21-22
Front suspension check 36-37
Fuel shutoff valve and filter cleaning 35-36
General inspection 13
Lights, horn and kill switch 14
Meter cable lubrication 24
Miscellaneous lubrication points 24
Nuts, bolts and other fasteners 37-38
Rear brake pedal adjustment 31
Rear suspension check 37
Service intervals 14
Side stand rubber 38
Steering head adjustment check 36
Swing arm bushing lubrication 23
Throttle adjustment and operation 34
Tires and wheels 14-15
Wheel bearings 36
Wheel hubs, rim and spokes 36

O

Oil pump 80-85, 126-131

P

Piston, piston pin and piston rings 75-80, 121-126

R

Rectifier 227

S

Shock absorbers 306-314
Spark plugs 42-45
Static ignition timing adjustment 45-47
Steering, front
Fork 279-294
Steering head 266-279

Troubleshooting 12
Suspension, front
Handlebar 265-266
Hub 255-259
Tire changing 262-263
Tire repairs 263-265
Troubleshooting 12
Wheels 253-255, 259-262
Suspension, rear
Drive chain 304-306
Drive chain case 306
Hub and driven sprocket 300-304
Shock absorbers 306-314
Swing arm 314-320
Wheels 298-300
Swing arm 314-320
Switches 248-250

T

Throttle adjustment and operation 34
Throttle cable 216-217
Tires
Changing 262-263
Maintenance 14-15
Repairs 263-265
Transmission
Internal shift mechanism 167-174, 182-188
5-speed 174-182
Troubleshooting
Brake problems 12
Emergency 10
Engine noises 12
Engine starting 10-11
Engine performance 11-12
Excessive vibration 12
Front suspension and steering 12
Instruments 10
Operating requirements 9-10
Tune-up
Air filter element 38
Camshaft chain tensioner adjustment 38-40
Compression test 40-42
Contact breaker point 45
Dynamic ignition timing adjustment 47-48
Idle mixture adjustment 48
Idle speed adjustment 48-49
Spark plugs 42-45
Static ignition timing adjustment 45-47
Valve clearance adjustment 40

V

Valve clearance adjustment 40
Valves and valve components 116-119
Voltage regulator/rectifier 227-228

W

Wheel bearings 36
Wheel hubs, rim and spokes 36
Wheels 253-255, 259-262, 298-300

CB100, CB100K1 & K2

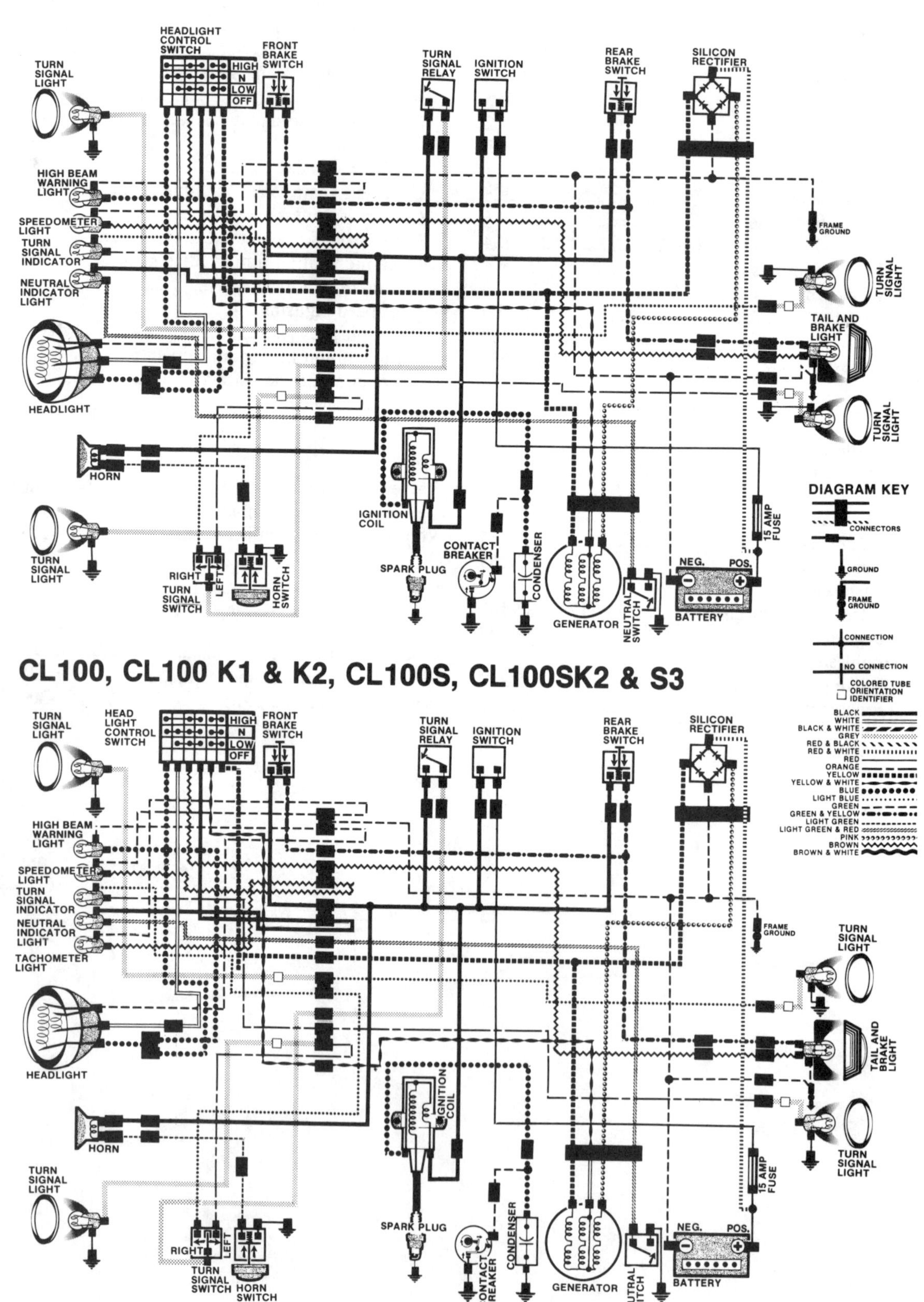

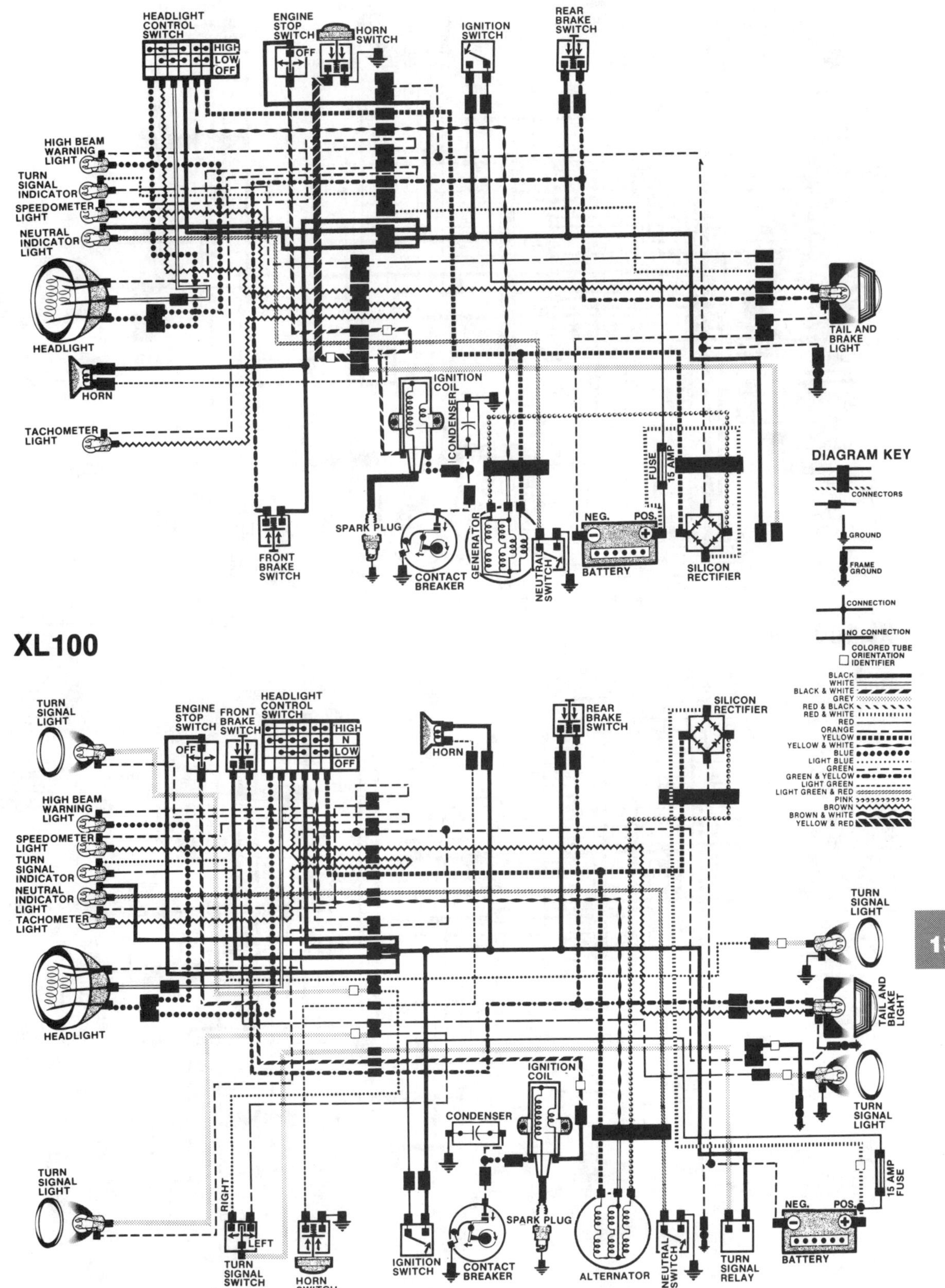
SL100, SL100K1-K3
HEADLIGHT CONTROL SWITCH
HIGH
LOW
OFF
ENGINE STOP SWITCH
OFF
HORN SWITCH
IGNITION SWITCH
REAR BRAKE SWITCH
HIGH BEAM WARNING LIGHT
TURN SIGNAL INDICATOR
SPEEDOMETER LIGHT
NEUTRAL INDICATOR LIGHT
HEADLIGHT
HORN
TACHOMETER LIGHT
TAIL AND BRAKE LIGHT
IGNITION COIL
CONDENSER
FUSE 15 AMP
SPARK PLUG
FRONT BRAKE SWITCH
CONTACT BREAKER
GENERATOR
NEUTRAL SWITCH
NEG.
POS.
BATTERY
SILICON RECTIFIER
DIAGRAM KEY
CONNECTORS
GROUND
FRAME GROUND
CONNECTION
NO CONNECTION
COLORED TUBE ORIENTATION IDENTIFIER
BLACK
WHITE
BLACK & WHITE
GREY
RED & BLACK
RED & WHITE
RED
ORANGE
YELLOW
YELLOW & WHITE
BLUE
LIGHT BLUE
GREEN
GREEN & YELLOW
LIGHT GREEN
LIGHT GREEN & RED
PINK
BROWN
BROWN & WHITE
YELLOW & RED
XL100
TURN SIGNAL LIGHT
ENGINE STOP SWITCH
OFF
FRONT BRAKE SWITCH
HEADLIGHT CONTROL SWITCH
HIGH
N
LOW
OFF
HORN
REAR BRAKE SWITCH
SILICON RECTIFIER
HIGH BEAM WARNING LIGHT
SPEEDOMETER LIGHT
TURN SIGNAL INDICATOR
NEUTRAL INDICATOR LIGHT
TACHOMETER LIGHT
TURN SIGNAL LIGHT
13
HEADLIGHT
TAIL AND BRAKE LIGHT
TURN SIGNAL LIGHT
IGNITION COIL
CONDENSER
15 AMP FUSE
TURN SIGNAL LIGHT
RIGHT
LEFT
TURN SIGNAL SWITCH
HORN SWITCH
IGNITION SWITCH
CONTACT BREAKER
SPARK PLUG
ALTERNATOR
NEUTRAL SWITCH
TURN SIGNAL RELAY
NEG.
POS.
BATTERY

XL100K1

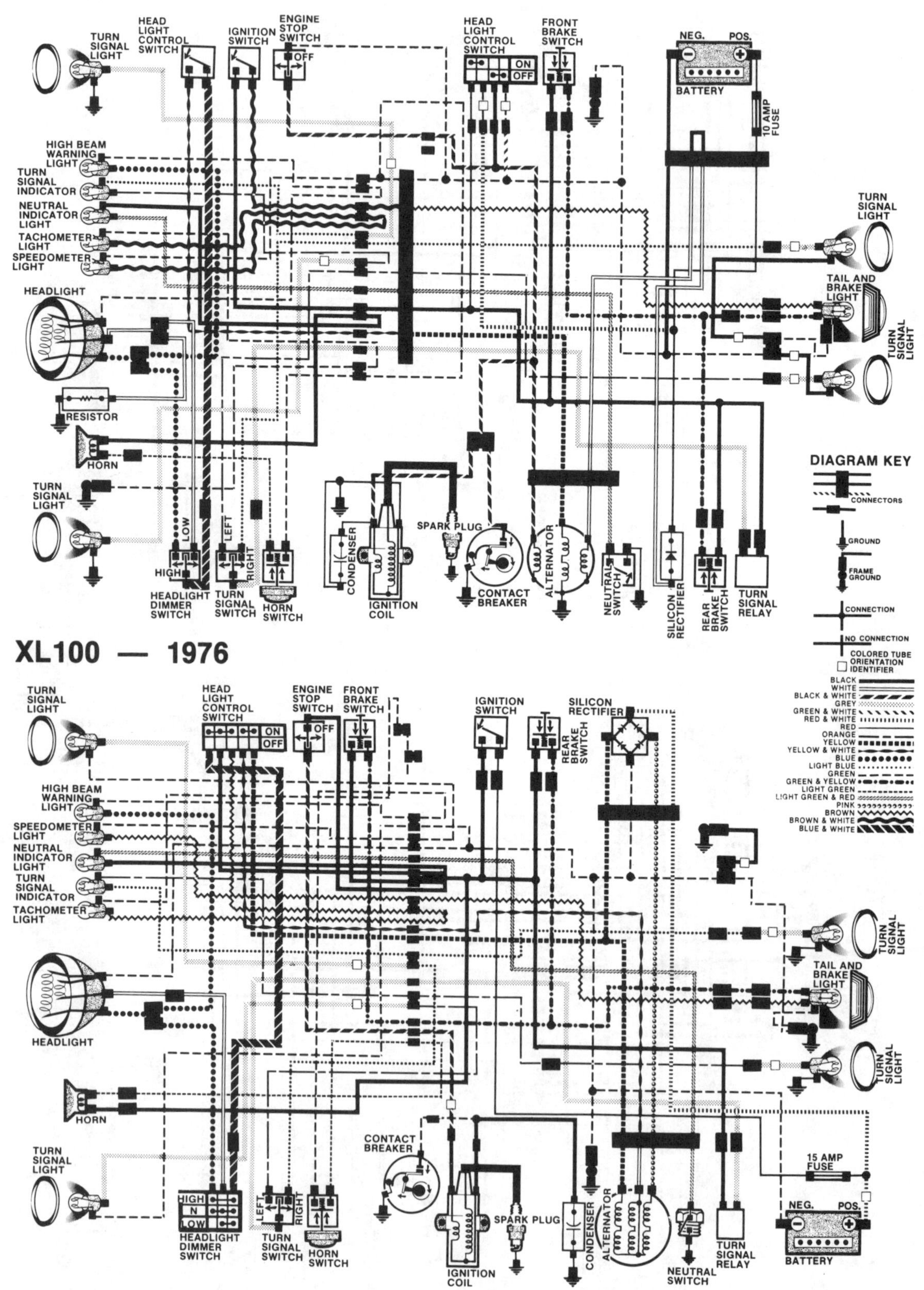
TURN SIGNAL LIGHT
HEAD LIGHT CONTROL SWITCH
IGNITION SWITCH
ENGINE STOP SWITCH
OFF
HEAD LIGHT CONTROL SWITCH
ON
OFF
FRONT BRAKE SWITCH
NEG.
POS.
BATTERY
10 AMP FUSE
HIGH BEAM WARNING LIGHT
TURN SIGNAL INDICATOR
NEUTRAL INDICATOR LIGHT
TACHOMETER LIGHT
SPEEDOMETER LIGHT
HEADLIGHT
RESISTOR
HORN
TURN SIGNAL LIGHT
TAIL AND BRAKE LIGHT
LOW
HIGH
LEFT
RIGHT
HEADLIGHT DIMMER SWITCH
TURN SIGNAL SWITCH
HORN SWITCH
CONDENSER
IGNITION COIL
SPARK PLUG
CONTACT BREAKER
ALTERNATOR
NEUTRAL SWITCH
SILICON RECTIFIER
REAR BRAKE SWITCH
TURN SIGNAL RELAY
DIAGRAM KEY
CONNECTORS
GROUND
FRAME GROUND
CONNECTION
NO CONNECTION
COLORED TUBE ORIENTATION IDENTIFIER
BLACK
WHITE
BLACK & WHITE
GREY
GREEN & WHITE
RED & WHITE
RED
ORANGE
YELLOW
YELLOW & WHITE
BLUE
LIGHT BLUE
GREEN
GREEN & YELLOW
LIGHT GREEN
LIGHT GREEN & RED
PINK
BROWN
BROWN & WHITE
BLUE & WHITE
XL100 — 1976
TURN SIGNAL LIGHT
HEAD LIGHT CONTROL SWITCH
ON
OFF
ENGINE STOP SWITCH
OFF
FRONT BRAKE SWITCH
IGNITION SWITCH
SILICON RECTIFIER
REAR BRAKE SWITCH
HIGH BEAM WARNING LIGHT
SPEEDOMETER LIGHT
NEUTRAL INDICATOR LIGHT
TURN SIGNAL INDICATOR
TACHOMETER LIGHT
HEADLIGHT
HORN
TURN SIGNAL LIGHT
TAIL AND BRAKE LIGHT
HIGH
N
LOW
HEADLIGHT DIMMER SWITCH
LEFT
RIGHT
TURN SIGNAL SWITCH
HORN SWITCH
CONTACT BREAKER
IGNITION COIL
SPARK PLUG
CONDENSER
ALTERNATOR
NEUTRAL SWITCH
TURN SIGNAL RELAY
15 AMP FUSE
NEG.
POS.
BATTERY

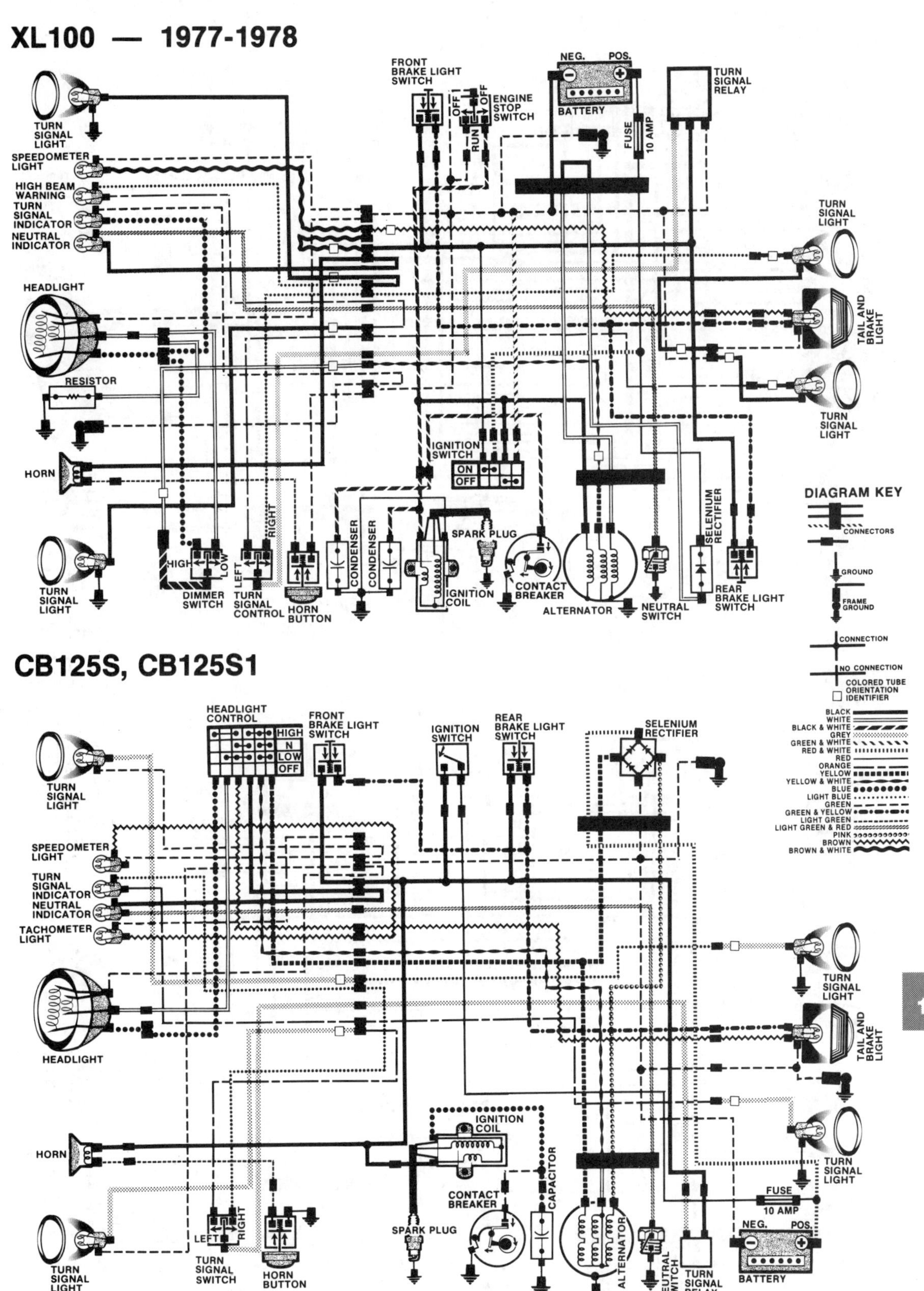
XL100 — 1977-1978
TURN SIGNAL LIGHT
SPEEDOMETER LIGHT
HIGH BEAM WARNING
TURN SIGNAL INDICATOR
NEUTRAL INDICATOR
HEADLIGHT
RESISTOR
HORN
FRONT BRAKE LIGHT SWITCH
ENGINE STOP SWITCH
OFF
RUN
BATTERY
NEG.
POS.
FUSE
10 AMP
TURN SIGNAL RELAY
TAIL AND BRAKE LIGHT
IGNITION SWITCH
ON
OFF
HIGH
LOW
DIMMER SWITCH
LEFT
RIGHT
TURN SIGNAL CONTROL
HORN BUTTON
CONDENSER
SPARK PLUG
IGNITION COIL
CONTACT BREAKER
ALTERNATOR
NEUTRAL SWITCH
SELENIUM RECTIFIER
REAR BRAKE LIGHT SWITCH
DIAGRAM KEY
CONNECTORS
GROUND
FRAME GROUND
CONNECTION
NO CONNECTION
COLORED TUBE ORIENTATION IDENTIFIER
BLACK
WHITE
BLACK & WHITE
GREY
GREEN & WHITE
RED & WHITE
RED
ORANGE
YELLOW
YELLOW & WHITE
BLUE
LIGHT BLUE
GREEN
GREEN & YELLOW
LIGHT GREEN
LIGHT GREEN & RED
PINK
BROWN
BROWN & WHITE
CB125S, CB125S1
HEADLIGHT CONTROL
HIGH
N
LOW
OFF
FRONT BRAKE LIGHT SWITCH
IGNITION SWITCH
REAR BRAKE LIGHT SWITCH
SELENIUM RECTIFIER
TURN SIGNAL LIGHT
SPEEDOMETER LIGHT
TURN SIGNAL INDICATOR
NEUTRAL INDICATOR
TACHOMETER LIGHT
HEADLIGHT
TAIL AND BRAKE LIGHT
HORN
IGNITION COIL
CAPACITOR
CONTACT BREAKER
SPARK PLUG
FUSE
10 AMP
NEG.
POS.
BATTERY
LEFT
RIGHT
TURN SIGNAL SWITCH
HORN BUTTON
ALTERNATOR
NEUTRAL SWITCH
TURN SIGNAL RELAY
13

CB125S2

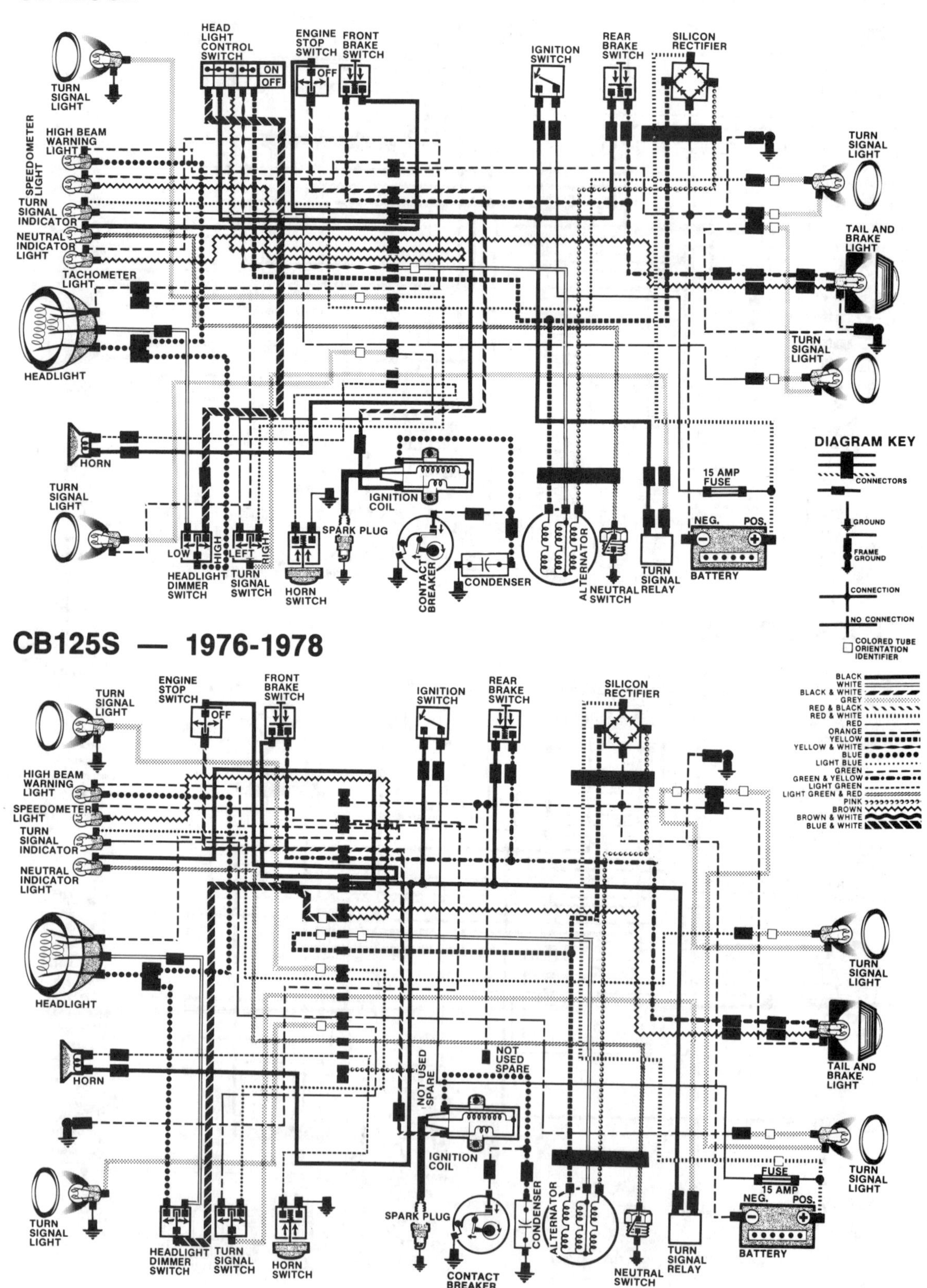
TURN SIGNAL LIGHT
HEAD LIGHT CONTROL SWITCH
ON
OFF
ENGINE STOP SWITCH
OFF
FRONT BRAKE SWITCH
IGNITION SWITCH
REAR BRAKE SWITCH
SILICON RECTIFIER
SPEEDOMETER LIGHT
HIGH BEAM WARNING LIGHT
TURN SIGNAL INDICATOR
NEUTRAL INDICATOR LIGHT
TACHOMETER LIGHT
HEADLIGHT
TAIL AND BRAKE LIGHT
HORN
IGNITION COIL
SPARK PLUG
15 AMP FUSE
NEG.
POS.
LOW
HIGH
LEFT
RIGHT
HEADLIGHT DIMMER SWITCH
TURN SIGNAL SWITCH
HORN SWITCH
CONTACT BREAKER
CONDENSER
ALTERNATOR
NEUTRAL SWITCH
TURN SIGNAL RELAY
BATTERY
DIAGRAM KEY
CONNECTORS
GROUND
FRAME GROUND
CONNECTION
NO CONNECTION
COLORED TUBE ORIENTATION IDENTIFIER
BLACK
WHITE
BLACK & WHITE
GREY
RED & BLACK
RED & WHITE
RED
ORANGE
YELLOW
YELLOW & WHITE
BLUE
LIGHT BLUE
GREEN
GREEN & YELLOW
LIGHT GREEN
LIGHT GREEN & RED
PINK
BROWN
BROWN & WHITE
BLUE & WHITE
CB125S — 1976-1978
ENGINE STOP SWITCH
OFF
FRONT BRAKE SWITCH
IGNITION SWITCH
REAR BRAKE SWITCH
SILICON RECTIFIER
TURN SIGNAL LIGHT
HIGH BEAM WARNING LIGHT
SPEEDOMETER LIGHT
TURN SIGNAL INDICATOR
NEUTRAL INDICATOR LIGHT
HEADLIGHT
HORN
NOT USED SPARE
NOT USED SPARE
IGNITION COIL
SPARK PLUG
CONTACT BREAKER
CONDENSER
ALTERNATOR
NEUTRAL SWITCH
TURN SIGNAL RELAY
FUSE
15 AMP
NEG.
POS.
BATTERY
TAIL AND BRAKE LIGHT
HEADLIGHT DIMMER SWITCH
TURN SIGNAL SWITCH
HORN SWITCH

CB125S — 1979-1980

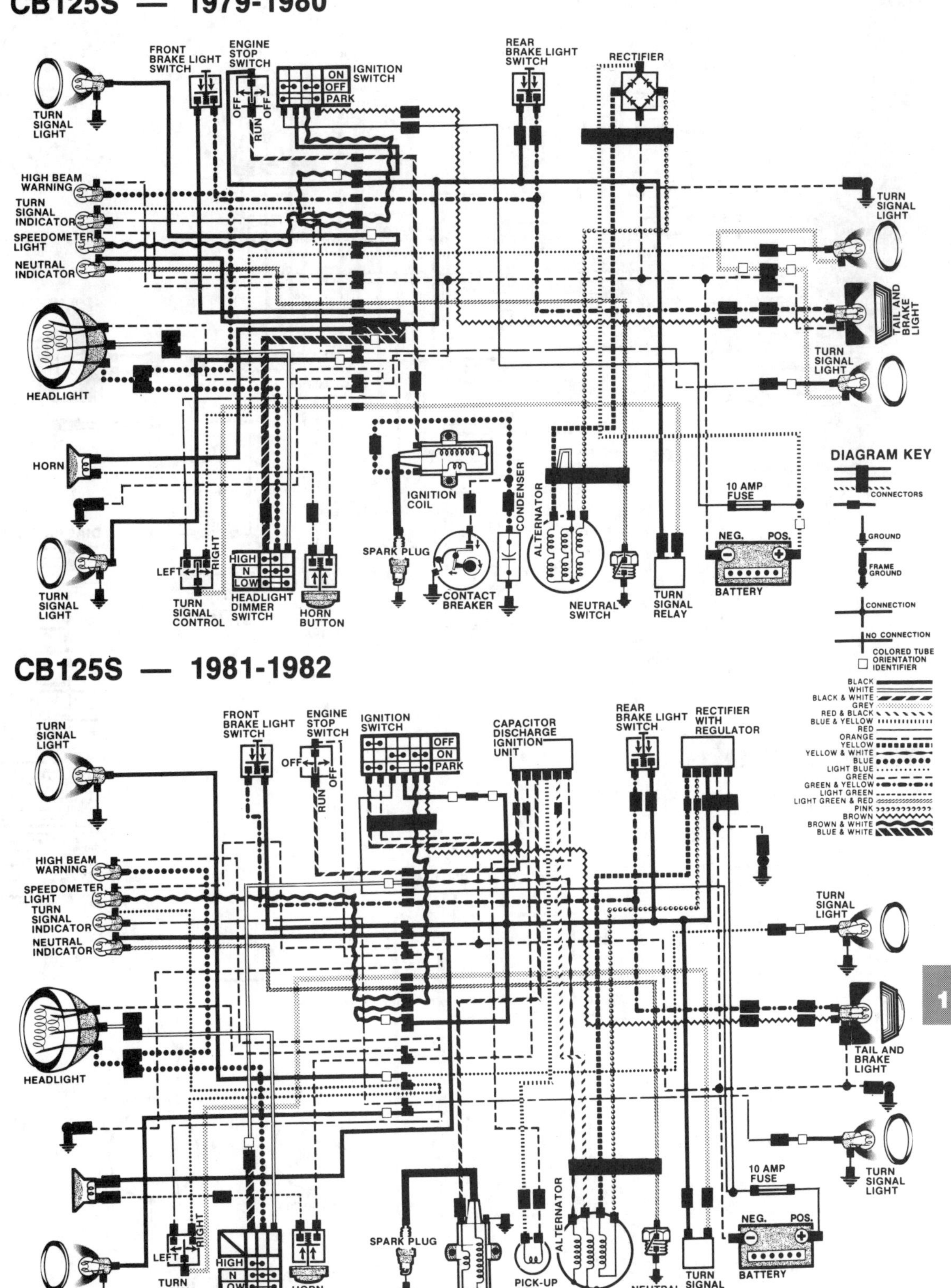

SL125, SL125K1 & K2

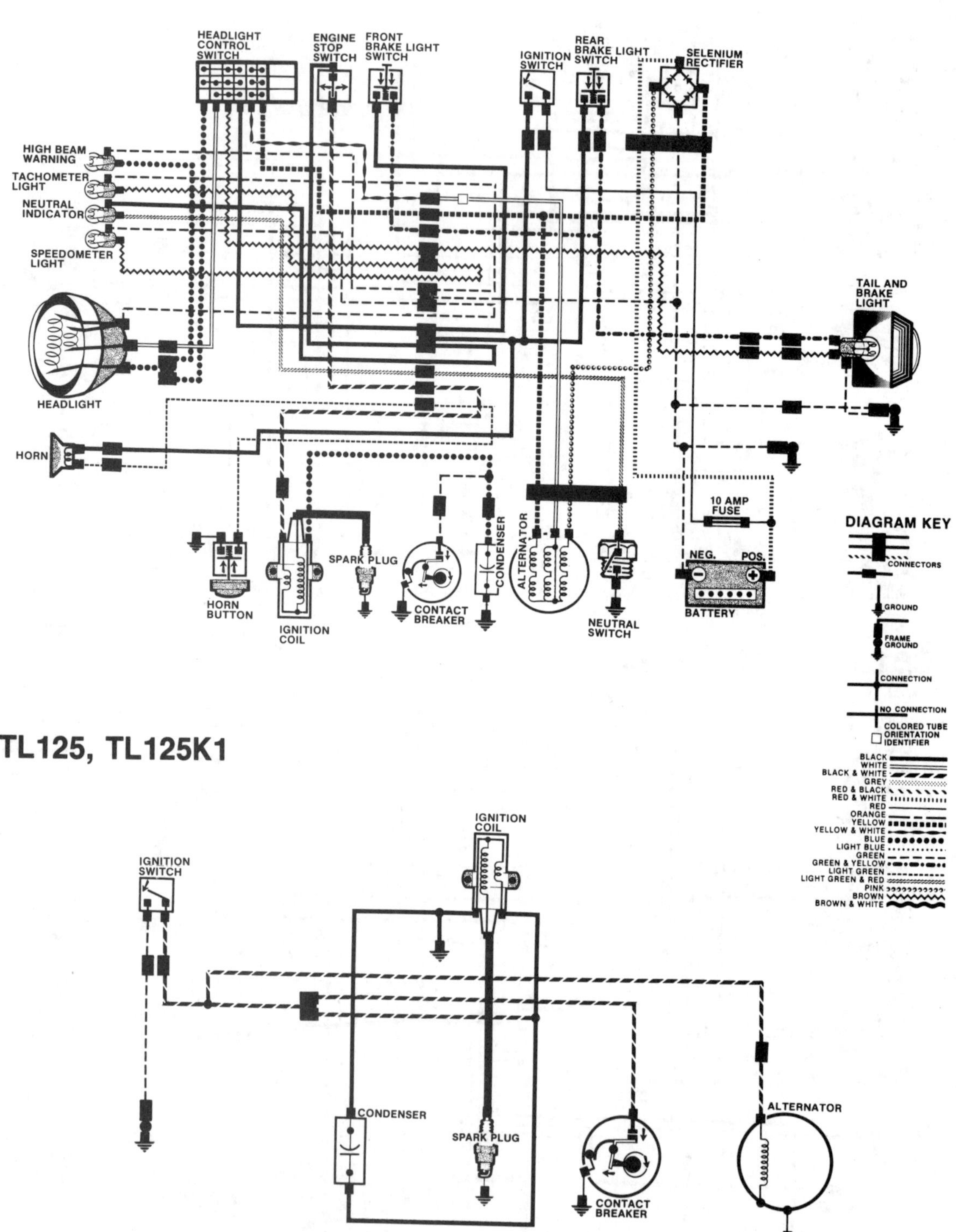

TL125, TL125K1

TL125K2

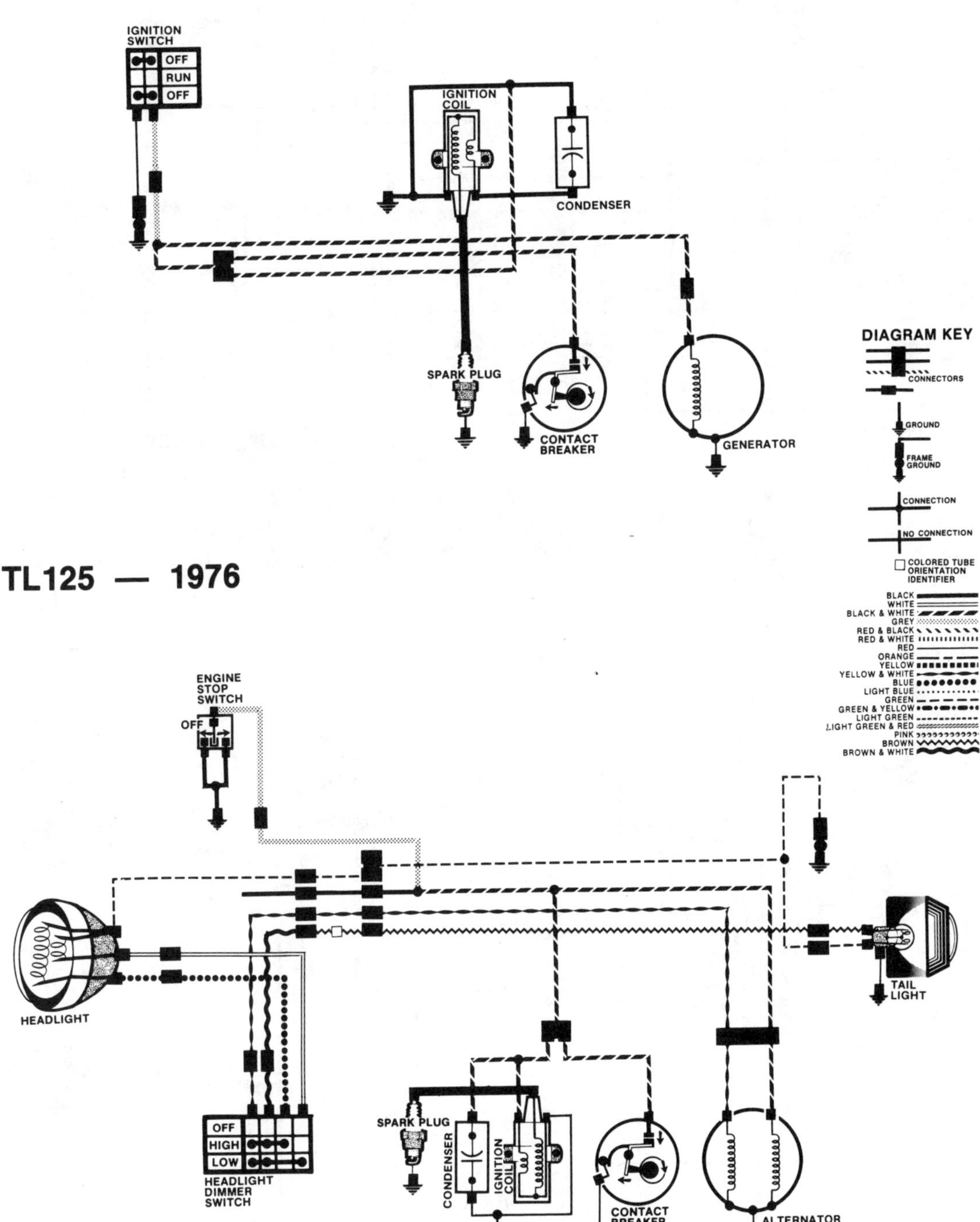
IGNITION SWITCH
OFF
RUN
OFF
IGNITION COIL
CONDENSER
SPARK PLUG
CONTACT BREAKER
GENERATOR
DIAGRAM KEY
CONNECTORS
GROUND
FRAME GROUND
CONNECTION
NO CONNECTION
COLORED TUBE ORIENTATION IDENTIFIER
BLACK
WHITE
BLACK & WHITE
GREY
RED & BLACK
RED & WHITE
RED
ORANGE
YELLOW
YELLOW & WHITE
BLUE
LIGHT BLUE
GREEN
GREEN & YELLOW
LIGHT GREEN
LIGHT GREEN & RED
PINK
BROWN
BROWN & WHITE
TL125 — 1976
ENGINE STOP SWITCH
OFF
HEADLIGHT
TAIL LIGHT
OFF
HIGH
LOW
HEADLIGHT DIMMER SWITCH
SPARK PLUG
CONDENSER
IGNITION COIL
CONTACT BREAKER
ALTERNATOR

13

XL125

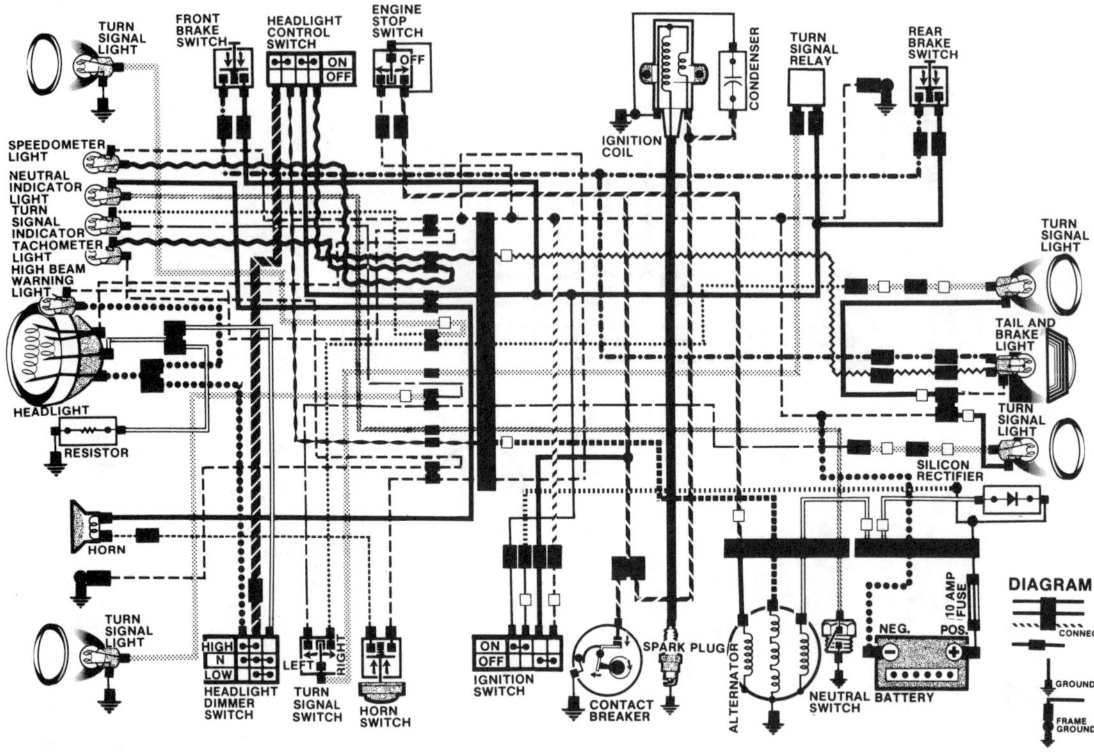

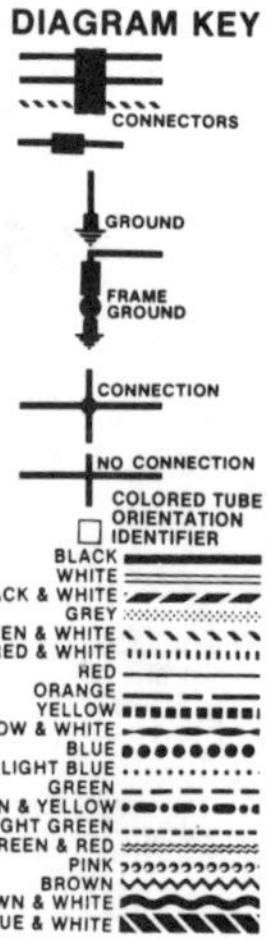

TURN SIGNAL LIGHT
FRONT BRAKE SWITCH
HEADLIGHT CONTROL SWITCH
ON
OFF
ENGINE STOP SWITCH
OFF
IGNITION COIL
CONDENSER
TURN SIGNAL RELAY
REAR BRAKE SWITCH
SPEEDOMETER LIGHT
NEUTRAL INDICATOR LIGHT
TURN SIGNAL INDICATOR
TACHOMETER LIGHT
HIGH BEAM WARNING LIGHT
TURN SIGNAL LIGHT
TAIL AND BRAKE LIGHT
TURN SIGNAL LIGHT
HEADLIGHT
RESISTOR
SILICON RECTIFIER
HORN
10 AMP FUSE
TURN SIGNAL LIGHT
HIGH
N
LOW
HEADLIGHT DIMMER SWITCH
LEFT
RIGHT
TURN SIGNAL SWITCH
HORN SWITCH
ON
OFF
IGNITION SWITCH
CONTACT BREAKER
SPARK PLUG
ALTERNATOR
NEUTRAL SWITCH
NEG.
POS.
BATTERY

DIAGRAM KEY

CONNECTORS
GROUND
FRAME GROUND
CONNECTION
NO CONNECTION
COLORED TUBE ORIENTATION IDENTIFIER
BLACK
WHITE
BLACK & WHITE
GREY
GREEN & WHITE
RED & WHITE
RED
ORANGE
YELLOW
YELLOW & WHITE
BLUE
LIGHT BLUE
GREEN
GREEN & YELLOW
LIGHT GREEN
LIGHT GREEN & RED
PINK
BROWN
BROWN & WHITE
BLUE & WHITE

XL125K1

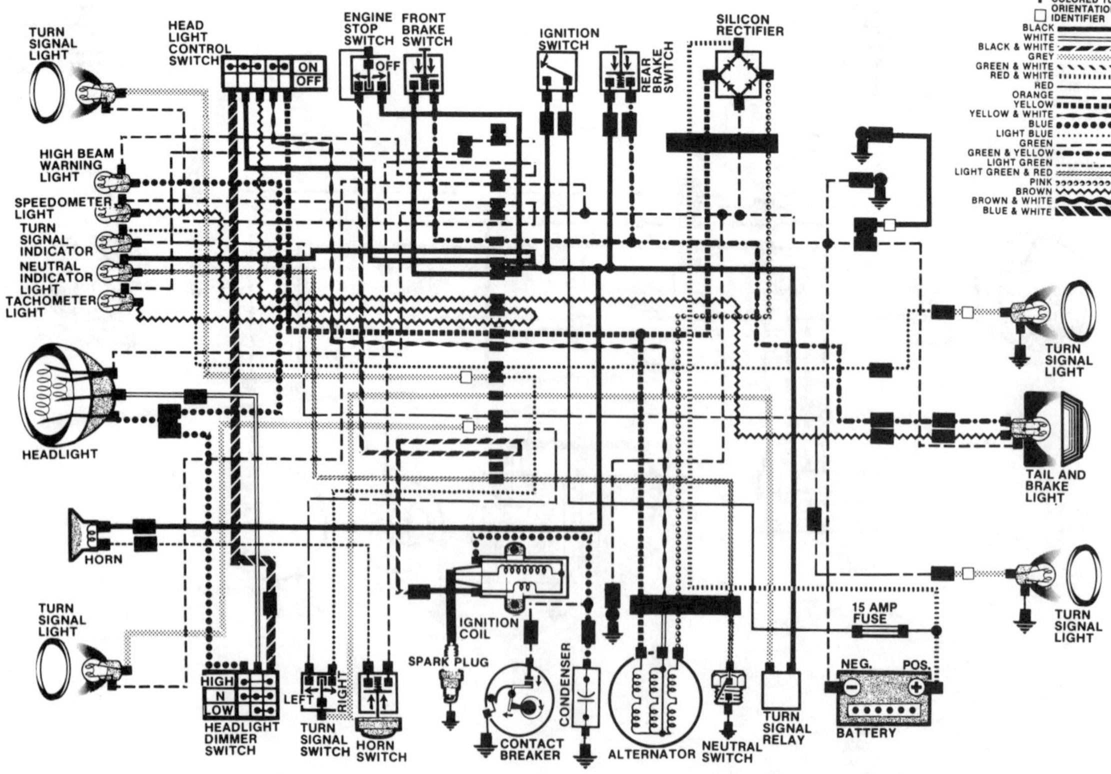

TURN SIGNAL LIGHT
HEAD LIGHT CONTROL SWITCH
ON
OFF
ENGINE STOP SWITCH
OFF
FRONT BRAKE SWITCH
IGNITION SWITCH
REAR BRAKE SWITCH
SILICON RECTIFIER
HIGH BEAM WARNING LIGHT
SPEEDOMETER LIGHT
TURN SIGNAL INDICATOR
NEUTRAL INDICATOR LIGHT
TACHOMETER LIGHT
TURN SIGNAL LIGHT
HEADLIGHT
TAIL AND BRAKE LIGHT
HORN
TURN SIGNAL LIGHT
IGNITION COIL
15 AMP FUSE
TURN SIGNAL LIGHT
SPARK PLUG
HIGH
N
LOW
HEADLIGHT DIMMER SWITCH
LEFT
RIGHT
TURN SIGNAL SWITCH
HORN SWITCH
CONTACT BREAKER
CONDENSER
ALTERNATOR
NEUTRAL SWITCH
TURN SIGNAL RELAY
NEG.
POS.
BATTERY

CT125 — 1977

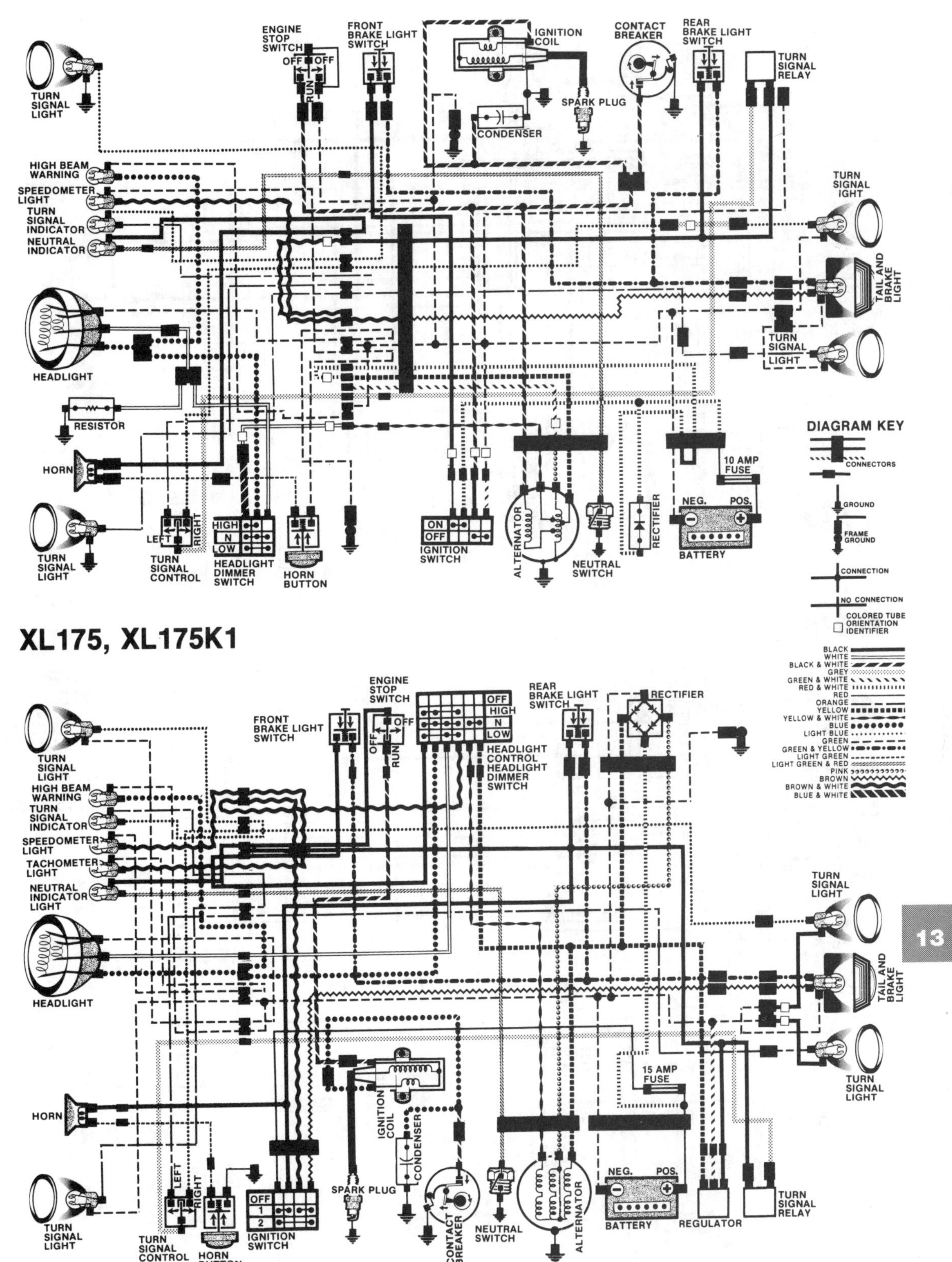
ENGINE STOP SWITCH
OFF RUN OFF
FRONT BRAKE LIGHT SWITCH
IGNITION COIL
CONTACT BREAKER
REAR BRAKE LIGHT SWITCH
TURN SIGNAL RELAY
TURN SIGNAL LIGHT
SPARK PLUG
CONDENSER
HIGH BEAM WARNING
SPEEDOMETER LIGHT
TURN SIGNAL INDICATOR
NEUTRAL INDICATOR
TURN SIGNAL IGHT
TAIL AND BRAKE LIGHT
HEADLIGHT
TURN SIGNAL LIGHT
RESISTOR
HORN
DIAGRAM KEY
10 AMP FUSE
NEG.
POS.
LEFT
RIGHT
HIGH
N
LOW
ON
OFF
RECTIFIER
ALTERNATOR
TURN SIGNAL LIGHT
TURN SIGNAL CONTROL
HEADLIGHT DIMMER SWITCH
HORN BUTTON
IGNITION SWITCH
NEUTRAL SWITCH
BATTERY
CONNECTORS
GROUND
FRAME GROUND
CONNECTION
NO CONNECTION
COLORED TUBE ORIENTATION IDENTIFIER
XL175, XL175K1
BLACK
WHITE
BLACK & WHITE
GREY
GREEN & WHITE
RED & WHITE
RED
ORANGE
YELLOW
YELLOW & WHITE
BLUE
LIGHT BLUE
GREEN
GREEN & YELLOW
LIGHT GREEN
LIGHT GREEN & RED
PINK
BROWN
BROWN & WHITE
BLUE & WHITE
ENGINE STOP SWITCH
FRONT BRAKE LIGHT SWITCH
OFF RUN OFF
OFF
HIGH
N
LOW
HEADLIGHT CONTROL
HEADLIGHT DIMMER SWITCH
REAR BRAKE LIGHT SWITCH
RECTIFIER
TURN SIGNAL LIGHT
HIGH BEAM WARNING
TURN SIGNAL INDICATOR
SPEEDOMETER LIGHT
TACHOMETER LIGHT
NEUTRAL INDICATOR LIGHT
TURN SIGNAL LIGHT
HEADLIGHT
TAIL AND BRAKE LIGHT
TURN SIGNAL LIGHT
15 AMP FUSE
HORN
IGNITION COIL
CONDENSER
LEFT
RIGHT
OFF
1
2
NEG.
POS.
SPARK PLUG
TURN SIGNAL LIGHT
TURN SIGNAL CONTROL UNIT
HORN BUTTON
IGNITION SWITCH
CONTACT BREAKER
NEUTRAL SWITCH
ALTERNATOR
BATTERY
REGULATOR
TURN SIGNAL RELAY

XL175K2

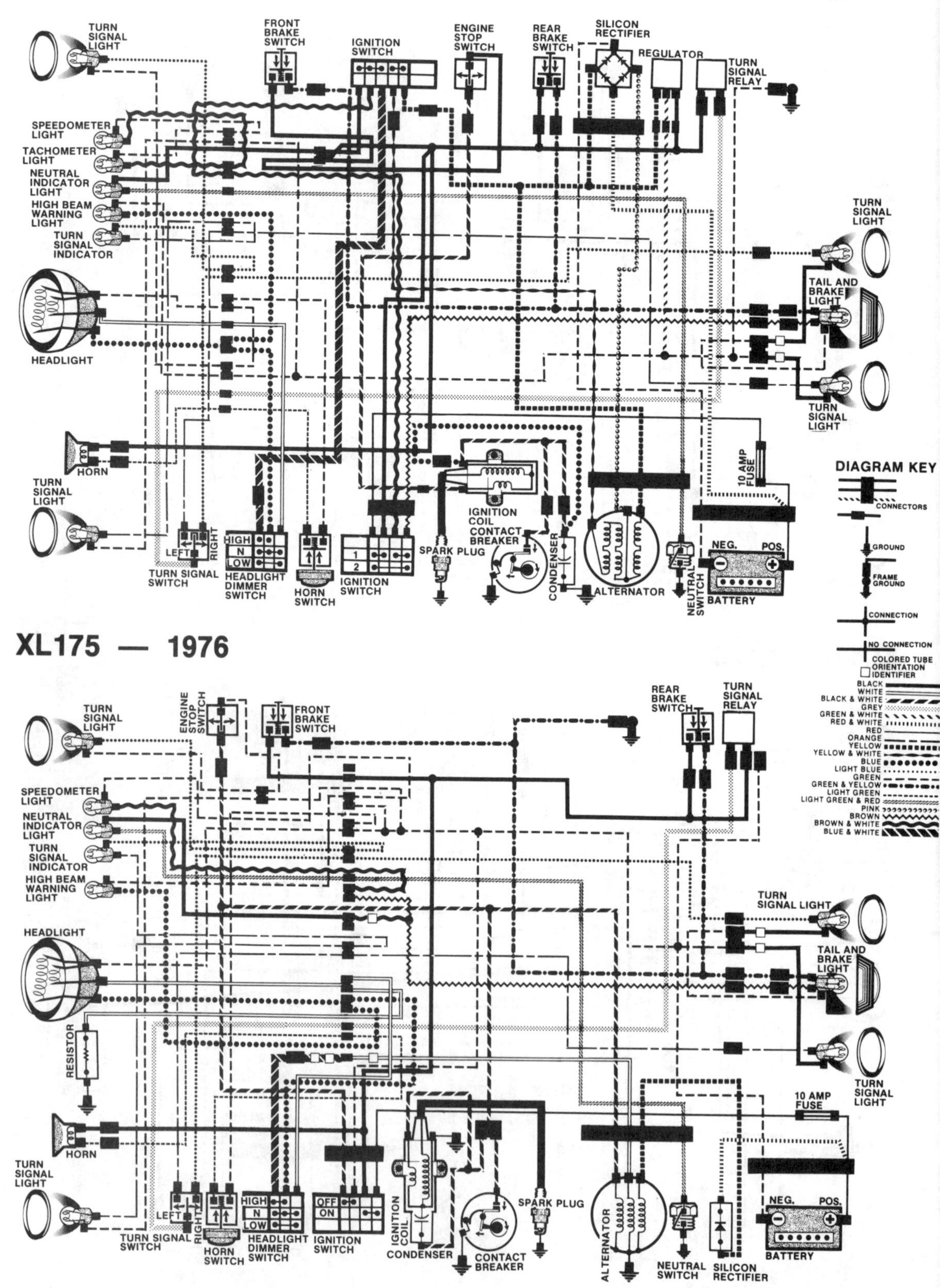
TURN SIGNAL LIGHT
FRONT BRAKE SWITCH
IGNITION SWITCH
ENGINE STOP SWITCH
REAR BRAKE SWITCH
SILICON RECTIFIER
REGULATOR
TURN SIGNAL RELAY
SPEEDOMETER LIGHT
TACHOMETER LIGHT
NEUTRAL INDICATOR LIGHT
HIGH BEAM WARNING LIGHT
TURN SIGNAL INDICATOR
TURN SIGNAL LIGHT
TAIL AND BRAKE LIGHT
HEADLIGHT
TURN SIGNAL LIGHT
HORN
10 AMP FUSE
TURN SIGNAL LIGHT
IGNITION COIL
CONTACT BREAKER
LEFT
RIGHT
HIGH
N
LOW
1
2
SPARK PLUG
CONDENSER
NEG.
POS.
TURN SIGNAL SWITCH
HEADLIGHT DIMMER SWITCH
HORN SWITCH
IGNITION SWITCH
ALTERNATOR
NEUTRAL SWITCH
BATTERY
DIAGRAM KEY
CONNECTORS
GROUND
FRAME GROUND
CONNECTION
NO CONNECTION
COLORED TUBE ORIENTATION IDENTIFIER
BLACK
WHITE
BLACK & WHITE
GREY
GREEN & WHITE
RED & WHITE
RED
ORANGE
YELLOW
YELLOW & WHITE
BLUE
LIGHT BLUE
GREEN
GREEN & YELLOW
LIGHT GREEN
LIGHT GREEN & RED
PINK
BROWN
BROWN & WHITE
BLUE & WHITE
XL175 — 1976
TURN SIGNAL LIGHT
ENGINE STOP SWITCH
FRONT BRAKE SWITCH
REAR BRAKE SWITCH
TURN SIGNAL RELAY
SPEEDOMETER LIGHT
NEUTRAL INDICATOR LIGHT
TURN SIGNAL INDICATOR
HIGH BEAM WARNING LIGHT
TURN SIGNAL LIGHT
HEADLIGHT
TAIL AND BRAKE LIGHT
RESISTOR
TURN SIGNAL LIGHT
10 AMP FUSE
HORN
TURN SIGNAL LIGHT
LEFT
RIGHT
HIGH
N
LOW
OFF
ON
IGNITION COIL
SPARK PLUG
ALTERNATOR
NEG.
POS.
TURN SIGNAL SWITCH
HORN SWITCH
HEADLIGHT DIMMER SWITCH
IGNITION SWITCH
CONDENSER
CONTACT BREAKER
NEUTRAL SWITCH
SILICON RECTIFIER
BATTERY

XL175 — 1977-1978

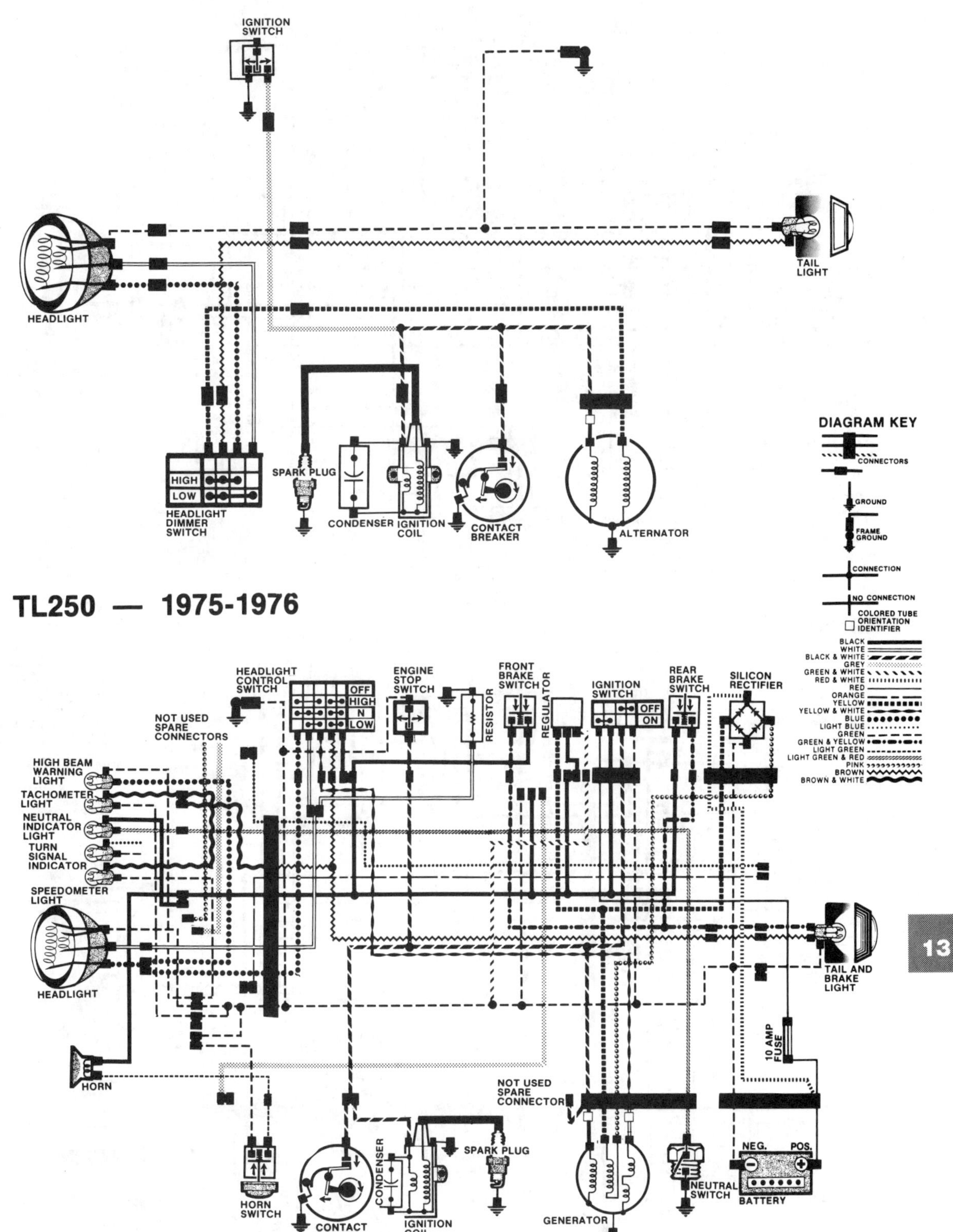

XL250K1

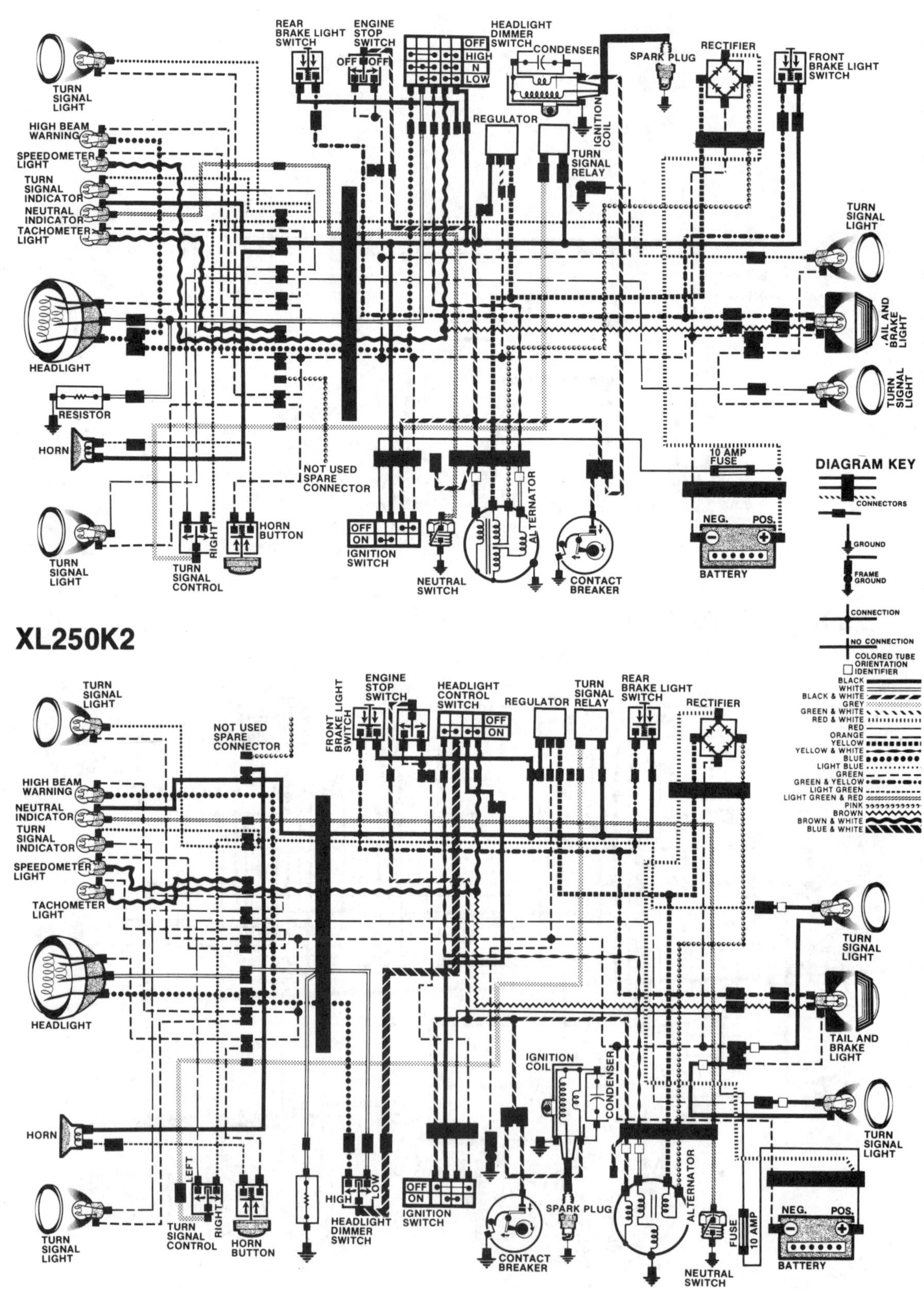
TURN SIGNAL LIGHT
HIGH BEAM WARNING
SPEEDOMETER LIGHT
TURN SIGNAL INDICATOR
NEUTRAL INDICATOR
TACHOMETER LIGHT
HEADLIGHT
RESISTOR
HORN
REAR BRAKE LIGHT SWITCH
ENGINE STOP SWITCH
OFF OFF
OFF HIGH N LOW
HEADLIGHT DIMMER SWITCH
CONDENSER
SPARK PLUG
RECTIFIER
FRONT BRAKE LIGHT SWITCH
REGULATOR
TURN SIGNAL RELAY
IGNITION COIL
TAIL AND BRAKE LIGHT
NOT USED SPARE CONNECTOR
RIGHT
HORN BUTTON
TURN SIGNAL CONTROL
OFF ON
IGNITION SWITCH
NEUTRAL SWITCH
ALTERNATOR
CONTACT BREAKER
10 AMP FUSE
NEG. POS.
BATTERY
DIAGRAM KEY
CONNECTORS
GROUND
FRAME GROUND
CONNECTION
NO CONNECTION
COLORED TUBE ORIENTATION IDENTIFIER
BLACK
WHITE
BLACK & WHITE
GREY
GREEN & WHITE
RED & WHITE
RED
ORANGE
YELLOW
YELLOW & WHITE
BLUE
LIGHT BLUE
GREEN
GREEN & YELLOW
LIGHT GREEN
LIGHT GREEN & RED
PINK
BROWN
BROWN & WHITE
BLUE & WHITE
XL250K2
HIGH BEAM WARNING
NEUTRAL INDICATOR
TURN SIGNAL INDICATOR
SPEEDOMETER LIGHT
TACHOMETER LIGHT
HEADLIGHT
HORN
LEFT
RIGHT
TURN SIGNAL CONTROL
HORN BUTTON
NOT USED SPARE CONNECTOR
FRONT BRAKE LIGHT SWITCH
ENGINE STOP SWITCH
HEADLIGHT CONTROL SWITCH
OFF ON
REGULATOR
TURN SIGNAL RELAY
REAR BRAKE LIGHT SWITCH
RECTIFIER
HIGH LOW
HEADLIGHT DIMMER SWITCH
IGNITION SWITCH
IGNITION COIL
CONDENSER
CONTACT BREAKER
SPARK PLUG
ALTERNATOR
NEUTRAL SWITCH
FUSE 10 AMP
NEG. POS.
BATTERY
TAIL AND BRAKE LIGHT

XL350

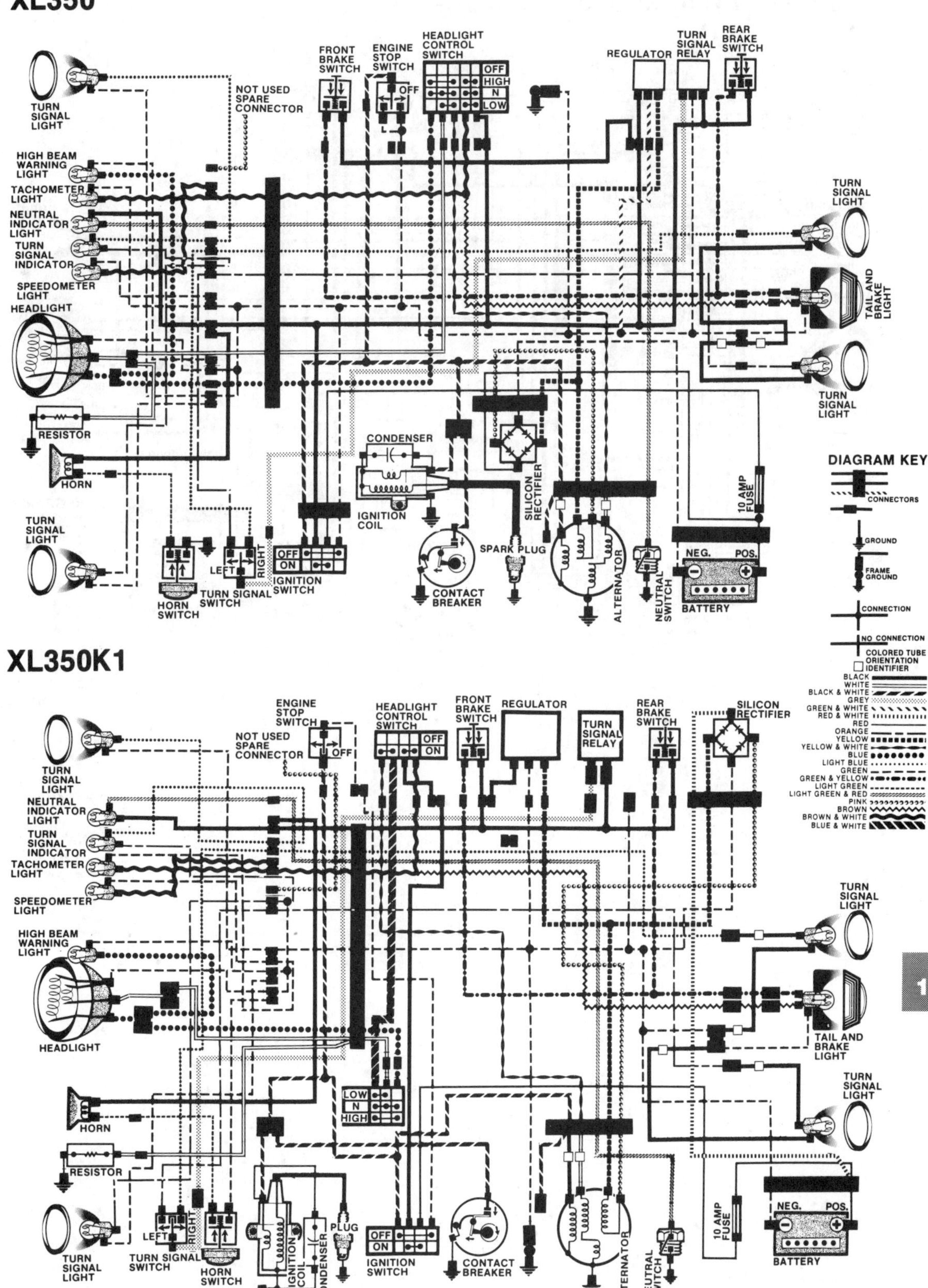
TURN SIGNAL LIGHT
NOT USED SPARE CONNECTOR
FRONT BRAKE SWITCH
ENGINE STOP SWITCH
OFF
HEADLIGHT CONTROL SWITCH
OFF
HIGH
N
LOW
REGULATOR
TURN SIGNAL RELAY
REAR BRAKE SWITCH
HIGH BEAM WARNING LIGHT
TACHOMETER LIGHT
NEUTRAL INDICATOR LIGHT
TURN SIGNAL INDICATOR
SPEEDOMETER LIGHT
HEADLIGHT
TURN SIGNAL LIGHT
TAIL AND BRAKE LIGHT
TURN SIGNAL LIGHT
RESISTOR
CONDENSER
HORN
IGNITION COIL
SILICON RECTIFIER
10 AMP FUSE
DIAGRAM KEY
CONNECTORS
GROUND
FRAME GROUND
CONNECTION
NO CONNECTION
COLORED TUBE ORIENTATION IDENTIFIER
BLACK
WHITE
BLACK & WHITE
GREY
GREEN & WHITE
RED & WHITE
RED
ORANGE
YELLOW
YELLOW & WHITE
BLUE
LIGHT BLUE
GREEN
GREEN & YELLOW
LIGHT GREEN
LIGHT GREEN & RED
PINK
BROWN
BROWN & WHITE
BLUE & WHITE
TURN SIGNAL LIGHT
OFF
ON
LEFT
RIGHT
IGNITION SWITCH
SPARK PLUG
CONTACT BREAKER
ALTERNATOR
NEUTRAL SWITCH
NEG.
POS.
BATTERY
HORN SWITCH
TURN SIGNAL SWITCH
XL350K1
ENGINE STOP SWITCH
OFF
HEADLIGHT CONTROL SWITCH
OFF
ON
FRONT BRAKE SWITCH
REGULATOR
TURN SIGNAL RELAY
REAR BRAKE SWITCH
SILICON RECTIFIER
TURN SIGNAL LIGHT
NOT USED SPARE CONNECTOR
NEUTRAL INDICATOR LIGHT
TURN SIGNAL INDICATOR
TACHOMETER LIGHT
SPEEDOMETER LIGHT
HIGH BEAM WARNING LIGHT
HEADLIGHT
TURN SIGNAL LIGHT
TAIL AND BRAKE LIGHT
TURN SIGNAL LIGHT
LOW
N
HIGH
HORN
RESISTOR
10 AMP FUSE
NEG.
POS.
BATTERY
TURN SIGNAL LIGHT
LEFT
RIGHT
TURN SIGNAL SWITCH
HORN SWITCH
IGNITION COIL
CONDENSER
PLUG
OFF
ON
IGNITION SWITCH
CONTACT BREAKER
ALTERNATOR
NEUTRAL SWITCH

13

XL250 — 1976, XL350 — 1976-1978

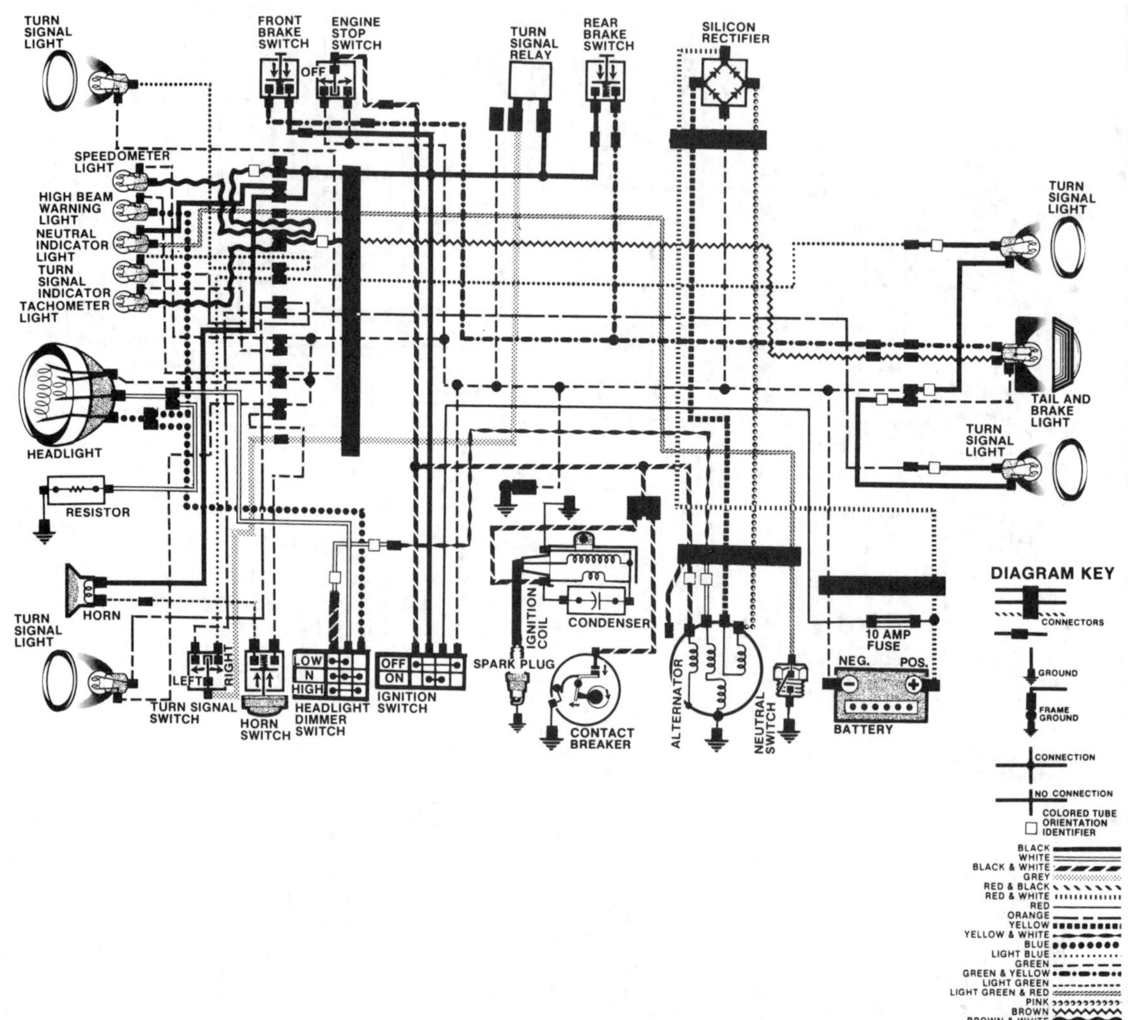

NOTES

NOTES

NOTES

NOTES

MAINTENANCE LOG

Date	Miles	Type of Service